Work after Globalization

Work after Globalization

Building Occupational Citizenship

Guy Standing

Professor of Economic Security, University of Bath, UK

Edward Elgar
Cheltenham, UK • Northampton, MA, USA

Published by
Edward Elgar Publishing Limited
The Lypiatts
15 Lansdown Road
Cheltenham
Glos GL50 2JA
UK

Edward Elgar Publishing, Inc.
William Pratt House
9 Dewey Court
Northampton
Massachusetts 01060
USA

A catalogue record for this book
is available from the British Library

Library of Congress Control Number: 2009930875

Mixed Sources
Product group from well-managed
forests and other controlled sources
www.fsc.org Cert no. SA-COC-1565
© 1996 Forest Stewardship Council
FSC

ISBN 978 1 84844 164 4 (cased)

Printed and bound by MPG Books Group, UK

Contents

Abbreviations

AARP	American Association of Retired Persons
AAUP	American Association of University Professors
ACAS	Advisory, Conciliation and Arbitration Service (UK)
ACFTU	All-China Federation of Trade Unions
AFL-CIO	American Federation of Labor/Congress of Industrial Organizations
AMA	American Medical Association
ANZCERTA	Australia-New Zealand Closer Economic Relations Trade Agreement
ASBO	Anti-Social Behaviour Order (UK)
ASEAN	Association of South-East Asian Nations
CAPPRT	Canadian Artists and Producers Professional Relations Tribunal
CARICOM	The Caribbean Community
CBT	Cognitive Behavioural Therapy
CCBE	Council of Bars and Law Societies of Europe
CCTV	Closed Circuit Television
CEO	Chief Executive Officer
CIPD	Chartered Institute of Personnel and Development (UK)
CKO	Chief Knowledge Officer
CLO	Chief Learning Officer
CME	Continuing Medical Education
CMI	Chartered Management Institute (UK)
CP	Community of Practice
CPD	Continuing Professional Development
CSI	Coalition of Service Industries (USA)
CSR	Corporate Social Responsibility
CV	Curriculum Vitae
EB	Enterprise Benefits
EBRD	European Bank for Reconstruction and Development
ECJ	European Court of Justice
EITC	Earned Income Tax Credit
EPZ	Export Processing Zone
EU	European Union
FB	Family Benefits
FEANI	European Federation of National Engineering Associations
FIP	International Pharmaceutical Federation
FSA	Financial Services Authority (UK)
GATS	General Agreement on Trade in Services
GATT	General Agreement on Tariffs and Trade
GDP	Gross Domestic Product
GMC	General Medical Council (UK)

GNP	Gross National Product
HRM	Human Resource Management
ICFTU	International Confederation of Free Trade Unions
IEK	Institution of Engineers of Kenya
IFA	Independent Financial Adviser (UK)
IFAC	International Federation of Accountants
ILO	International Labour Organization
IOD	Institute of Directors (UK)
IT	Information Technology
JIT	Just-In-Time
MBA	Master of Business Administration
MERCOSUR	Southern Cone Common Market
MEXA	MERCOSUR Experimental Mechanism for Career Accreditation
MRA	Mutual Recognition Agreement
NAFTA	North American Free Trade Agreement
NCL	National Commission on Labour (India)
NHS	National Health Service (UK)
NIC	Newly Industrializing Country
NLRB	National Labor Relations Board (USA)
OECD	Organisation for Economic Co-operation and Development
PB	Private Benefits (income from own savings/investments)
SAFTA	Singapore-Australia Free Trade Agreement
SB	State Benefits
SER	Standard Employment Relationship
SEWA	Self-Employed Women's Association (India)
SI	Social Income
SP	Self-Production
TQM	Total Quality Management
UIA	International Union of Architects
UN	United Nations
UNCTAD	United Nations Conference on Trade and Development
W	Wage (money/income received for work)
WFEO	World Federation of Engineering Organizations
WHO	World Health Organization
WHPA	World Health Professions Alliance
WPDR	Working Party on Domestic Regulation (WTO)
WTO	World Trade Organization

Note: In this book 'billion' means 1000 million and 'trillion' means 1000 billion.

Preface

It is a central claim of this book that twenty-first century 'modernization' should be defined in terms of the extent to which people can define themselves not by ethnicity, 'caste' or religion but by their sense of 'occupation'. Throughout history, many have done so, which is why surnames in many cultures refer to occupational titles originally held by long-forgotten ancestors. The names 'Smith' or 'Taylor' spring to mind in English. But many people have never had a chance to pursue an occupation; others have been obliged to pursue one that they would not have chosen themselves.

A second claim is that the era of 'industrial citizenship' – the 'embedded' phase of Polanyi's Great Transformation (Polanyi [1944] 2001) – has passed, although many of its institutional features are still struggling to survive. Now, in the aftermath of globalization – the 'disembedded' phase of the Global Transformation – we may see an era of 'occupational citizenship' taking shape. The key figures in the industrial citizenship era were the employer and employee. For much of the twentieth century social, economic and labour policy focused overwhelmingly on the employee, and his needs and aspirations. This served the interests of capitalism and the state very nicely. It was not appropriate then, and it is certainly not appropriate in the Global Transformation.

Most of us, consciously or latently, have a vision of the Good Life. It is usually a far cry from the life we actually live, or even pragmatically aspire to live, if only because our aspirations are constrained by the range of feasible options, our self-confidence and the way we expect the surrounding social institutions to evolve.

As social thinkers – and we all possess that talent, cowed or undeveloped as it usually is – we should encourage each other to contemplate what could be the Good Life in the future Good Society. In doing so, we should impose a 'veil of ignorance', recognizing that we do not know where we would be in the range of distributions of statuses in that Good Society. We should go further than that, and say that the desirable options to be considered should be based on a reduction in the inequalities in the world, so that we do not merely aspire to be among the tiny super-affluent elite who can do what they wish when they wish with no care for what happens beyond their elite circle and bundle of soft-toned privileges. And vitally, what is proposed must meet what is later called the Ecological Constraint Principle. The values of reproduction must be elevated to that end.

If we were to talk about how we would wish to live, and how we would wish our fellow citizens to live, we would soon come back to the great visionaries of human history. In the cultural sphere from which I come, that would lead to Thomas More with his *Utopia*, Tom Paine with *The Rights of Man*, William Morris with *News from Nowhere*, Karl Marx of the *Grundrisse*, Hannah Arendt with *The Human Condition*. Others would reach back to the great equivalents of their cultures.

If we could indulge in this mild utopianism, we would probably find a large number of social thinkers in broad agreement on an underlying vision of the Good Society. It would be egalitarian in some sense, and give a high priority to what Aristotle called civic friendship and conviviality. It would not be one in which the state set out to create mass happiness or constant euphoria. Work would consist largely of self-chosen activity, with individuals in control of their development, in a community of kindred spirits with enough checks and balances to limit exploitation and oppression of the vulnerable by the powerful, and to avoid stifling conformity. We would wonder how work should be organized, or rather how it could be both organized and not organized, achieving a fine balance between disciplined activity and creative freedom.

It is that mild utopianism that guides the book. The plan of it weaves three themes. After presenting basic concepts of labour, work and occupation in Chapter 1, Chapters 2 and 3 consider how fictitious labour decommodification was tried during Polanyi's Great Transformation and how labour recommodification occurred during globalization as a global labour market has emerged. Chapter 4 sketches how the global class structure has evolved under globalization. This introduces the two strata that will shape occupational citizenship, the precariat and proficians. Chapters 5 and 6 show how barriers to commodification have been weakened or dismantled, and Chapter 7 considers the powerful trend towards occupational licensing. Chapter 8, polemically, traces some of the social and labour consequences of the construction of the global market society. Chapter 9 sketches the sort of institutions and policies that could shape a future of occupational citizenship, and Chapter 10 suggests how basic income security would facilitate a richer working life.

By way of warning, I will indicate some conclusions. The first is that the labour decommodification pursued by social democrats during the twentieth century was mistaken. The second is that the 'libertarian paternalists', who came to prominence in the early years of the twenty-first century with some strong claims, are dangerous.

Issues of paternalism were addressed in an earlier book, *Beyond the New Paternalism* (Standing, 2002). Since then 'libertarian paternalism' has revealed itself as a child of globalization, a response to the bewilderment unleashed by a market society in which everything is commodified. Without giving a hint of realizing what they were doing, the two Chicago academics who have made their international name with this perspective, and who were advisers to Barack Obama in his presidential campaign, described their goal as the construction of an 'architecture of choice' (Thaler and Sunstein, 2008). It was Jeremy Bentham who in 1787 presented a societal model as an architecture of choice – for the design of prisons (Bentham [1787] 1995). His panopticon figures strongly in this book, recognizing how it was deployed in the work of Michel Foucault and his followers. The modern 'panopticonists' are almost as frightening as Bentham.

The third conclusion is that an 'emancipatory egalitarianism' is needed to create the basis of occupational citizenship. Any egalitarian at the end of globalization owes it to fellow progressives to offer a politics of paradise, in which freedom is married to equality. There is no going back to 'labourism'. Accordingly, the final two chapters sketch the sort of policies and institutions needed for occupational citizenship. It is essential that these enhance the occupational prospects of the growing number of people who are in the precariat, those without occupational profiles and without security, often living an almost nomadic existence, often unable to obtain regular employment or not actually wanting what used to be called 'a steady job'. I did wish to include reference to the precariat in the title of the book, until my publisher, Edward Elgar, and Commissioning Editor Felicity Plester sensibly persuaded me to drop it. However, the precariat and their more fortunate brethren, the proficians, are the future.

Chapter 9 makes much of the need to dismantle the trappings of labourism and turn instead to collaborative bargaining, occupational associations and work rights rather than 'labour rights'. This leads to the final theme, which has been dismissed by labourists for decades. I merely make a plea for those who believe in freedom, work and occupation to consider it as part of an egalitarian strategy and look at it afresh in the light of the evolving globalizing labour market.

For some years, I have argued for a basic income as a right of citizenship. Although some commentators still think this a strange idea it has had great and honourable advocates over the ages, including Thomas Paine, Bertrand Russell, several Nobel Prize-winning economists, and artists such as William Morris. As co-chair of BIEN (Basic Income Earth Network), I also argued that it would only become a mainstream policy once efforts at paternalism had been extended (and found wanting) and once it became part of an integrated progressive vision. Such a vision must combine equality *and* freedom.

The groups who were self-defined as progressives for much of the nineteenth and twentieth centuries typically emphasized equality while neglecting freedom. This left a vacuum, which was filled by the apostles of Friedrich Hayek, the Chicago School of law and economics and the libertarians. Social democracy was not against freedom, but it promoted what in this book is called 'labourism', which is unsustainable in the Global Transformation and which actually constrained liberty.

The writer of this book is inclined to call himself 'a peasant'. His family and friends regard this as an affectation, understandably given that he spends his life dealing with books, statistics, bureaucrats and electronic gadgets, in between drinking fine wine and enjoying the sight, sound, taste and touch of the fine things in life. Yet the peasant need not be the dull simpleton so beloved of caricature, a potato in a sack who mumbles uhs and ahs between the cowsheds. The peasant blends into the human and natural environment and takes in the senses of existence, uncontrolled by the dictates of consumerism or capital accumulation. This is not to idealize the peasant. That would be oafish sentimentality. What is good about the peasant is that life is varied and close to nature in its appreciation of time, space and the senses. Life is about working to reproduce and sustain the environment, and the peasant's *security* comes from the simplicities of human passions. That is certainly not enough. A modern peasant must have education, not schooling, and a sense of culture.

It is probably more accurate to think of oneself as an artisan, on a good day, and a journeyman on all days. One author said that all of us can be craftsmen, which he defined as being very good at doing one thing (Sennett, 2008). Perhaps that is placing the bar too high. Most of us cannot be great artists or craftsmen. Our best hope is to be reasonably good at several things. In that regard, we are in good company. That great artist, John Gielgud, said with impish false modesty, 'I am a journeyman; I try to make it a little better every night'. To be an artisan or a journeyman in today's world would not be a bad lot.

And so to my gratitude. All creative works are acts of plagiarism to some extent. One has argued with and learned from so many people that it is impossible to identify those to blame or thank for good or bad ideas. I have been extremely fortunate over the years to have interacted with some very fine people who have expertise on subjects covered by this book. I could not possibly give any order of precedence, and will merely thank them.

Among many others, I would like to mention, in alphabetical order, Miriam Abu-Sharkh, Richard Anker, Sam Butler, Ian Gough, Michael Hopkins, Renana Jhabvala, Claus Offe, Philippe van Parijs, Gerry Rodgers and Eduardo Suplicy. I would also like to thank Felicity Plester for her patience and advice. I should not mention the names of those from the ILO who gave me useful comments; however, I am grateful to them. I would also like to thank Kari Polanyi Levitt, Marguerite Mendell and Ayşe Buğra for having invited me to give a keynote address to the Karl Polanyi Conference in Istanbul in 2005. Kari's prodding over the years has been much appreciated, and I know much more about her father as a result.

A very special thanks goes to my son Graeme, on whom I have tested out a number of the ideas contained in the book. Another special one goes to Frances. I am still counting the ways, although will not risk the question mark this time. All I will say is that her help was real work.

Guy Standing
Ponte agli Stolli
November 2008

A NOTE ON GENDER

Although the author has used traditional and gender-specific occupational terms, such as 'craftsman', 'journeyman', 'middleman' and 'salaryman', throughout this book, these terms (and masculine pronouns) should be understood as referring to both men and women where appropriate. The same applies to feminine occupational terms, such as 'midwife', and feminine pronouns.

1.   Work and labour in Great Transformations

INTRODUCTION

In 1944 three documents were published at about the same time. One was a book by Karl Polanyi, who in 1943 left a disorganized manuscript in the hands of two German friends in Vermont, where he had spent part of the Second World War, in order to hurry back to the east end of London to support his family by teaching. That book was *The Great Transformation* (Polanyi [1944] 2001).

Although it had evident blemishes, the book had an early, respected life. But at the beginning of the twenty-first century it was to have a second life in the context of globalization. The book's main message was that in the nineteenth century a market society had been actively promoted, led by financial capital, in what Polanyi saw as a systematic attempt to strip the institutions that had constrained market forces. As he put it, 'Laissez-faire was planned'.

The Great Transformation is less profound than other works dealing with the development of capitalism. Polanyi lacked a sense of class struggle. Moreover, his analysis was about the emergence of 'welfare states' and the prior reactions to the excesses of a 'market society', namely fascism and communism. But his concepts of 'embeddedness', 'double movement' and 'commodification' have proved immensely valuable for analysing current global changes.

The second document was a book by Friedrich Hayek, *The Road to Serfdom* (Hayek, 1944). Like Polanyi, Hayek came from Vienna, but he saw freedom from a decidedly different perspective. Although widely rejected at the time, his book too was to have a second coming. In the 1940s, it was Polanyi who caught the political mood, in a world wearied by war and desirous to see stability and a rapid improvement in welfare for the working class that had suffered the Great Depression. He was one among many, including Keynes, Beveridge and other architects of post-war welfare states, notably the Swedish economists Gösta Rehn, Rudolf Meidner and Gunnar Myrdal who forged the 'Swedish model' that was to inspire several generations of social democrats across the world.

By contrast, Hayek was a voice of dissent at the time, seen by many as on the extreme of the ideological right, at least in terms of his economics. Vehemently against state planning to improve welfare, he wrote, 'There can be little doubt that it is largely a consequence of the striving for security by these means that unemployment and thus insecurity for large sections of the population has so much increased'. He believed in the supremacy of market forces.

In 1947, he set up the Mont Pelerin Society to work for a liberal market future. Thirty-six attended the first meeting in Montreux, Switzerland, among them a young Milton Friedman. The group of ideological soul mates never lost hope. If largely brushed aside at the time, Hayek's individualistic market perspective was to become hugely influential in the 1970s when Polanyi's Great Transformation broke down. Hayek had his revenge on his early critics when Ronald Reagan and Margaret Thatcher reverentially turned him into a guru of what has become known as neo-liberalism, ultimately helping him to a Nobel Prize in Economics. For conservatives, the prophet was honoured in his lifetime. He had the distinction of mentoring others who also became prophets; Milton Friedman also received the Nobel Prize, as did six other Mont Pelerin Society members, George Stigler, James Buchanan, Maurice Allais, Ronald Coase, Gary Becker and Vernon Smith.

In the background was a ghost whose ideas lay deep in the ideology of Hayek and his disciples, and who had helped set the nineteenth-century Great Transformation on its way. The ghost was that of Jeremy Bentham, the founding father of utilitarianism and, more ominously, inventor of a peculiar device known as the 'panopticon'. Whereas Hayek, following Bentham's contemporary Adam Smith, believed in the invisible hand, had little time for ethics of the marketplace and saw markets as creating the greatest happiness of the greatest number, Bentham had gone one stage further. Both Hayek and Bentham saw the need for coercion in pursuit of their vision of society. But Bentham wanted to put that into effect through invisible guards to back up the invisible hand. We will come back to Bentham's panopticon. At this stage, we will merely state that there is a direct line from Bentham through Hayek to the libertarian paternalists of the twenty-first century, whose writings were to sweep politics on both sides of the Atlantic and in many other parts of the world.

The third text of 1944, written a short distance away from where *The Great Transformation* was being put together, was to have a bright early life, although it was no academic treatise. It was the Philadelphia Declaration of the International Labour Organization (ILO), drafted by two men who were to go on to be ILO directors-general, crafted by committees of 'experts' and signed by ministers of labour, employer representatives and trade union leaders, anxious to build a world order based on social stability. The key statement was a one-line paragraph: 'Labour is not a commodity'.

Polanyi was meanwhile claiming that labour was a 'fictitious commodity'. We shall consider what this means shortly. But note that, in their demand that labour and employment should be made less subject to market forces, both Polanyi and the ILO delegates were following in the footsteps of the ILO's first director, Albert Thomas. In 1929 he had written in the preface of a book celebrating the ILO's first ten years that the laws of the market were not natural. As he put it, 'human intelligence must make every possible effort to organise the economic system and has in fact the power to do so. The social factor must take precedence over the economic factor; it must regulate and guide it in the highest cause of justice' (Thomas, 1931, p. 12).

Along with the economics of Keynes, extensively discussed in the ILO's journal, this was the mainstream reaction to the crises of what has been called the first era of globalization, the several decades before the First World War. Set up in 1919 in the wake of the Bolshevik revolution, the ILO was to become a pivotal body after 1945 in forging the labour and social policy institutions and regulations that comprised Polanyi's 'double movement', when the economy was re-embedded in society via welfare state and corporatist institutions. Based in its imposing headquarters built in 1923 overlooking Lake Geneva, its membership, budget and staff grew in the 1950s and 1960s, and in 1969 it received the Nobel Peace Prize. The timing was apt, since this was the apogee of Polanyi's Great Transformation.

Shortly after receiving that prize – perhaps reflecting the smugness of its position in a world seemingly committed to its standards – the ILO transferred to an even larger headquarters, a modernist building that resembled a stretched IBM computer card then used for mainframe computers. Its old headquarters were taken over by the General Agreement on Tariffs and Trade (GATT), later the World Trade Organization (WTO), which was to become the midwife of a new world order known as globalization. Symbolically, the new occupants hastily removed the paintings and boarded up the murals on the walls celebrating the nobility of labour. The labourist model forged by the ILO – based on industrial labour and collective bargaining between employers and trade unions – was being displaced by a global market model epitomized by the WTO.

Between 1919 and the 1960s, the ILO was an instrument in giving shape to the 'embedded' phase of Polanyi's Transformation, although one finds no recognition of that inside the ILO. Polanyi certainly recognized its significance. It helped shape the model of what we may call 'industrial citizenship', the essence of which was the extension of 'social rights' – entitlements and norms associated with industrial wage labour. As the designated standard-setter the ILO promulgated numerous conventions and recommendations for good labour practices. The values of labourism were elevated throughout most of the twentieth century and still attract rhetorical respect from public figures. Every year, presidents, prime ministers, ministers of labour and social welfare, employer bodies and trade unionists visit its headquarters, many to make speeches at its International Labour Conference in June, which is attended by about 4000 delegates.

Polanyi had written his book at an opportune time, which is perhaps why his perspective was rather teleological, having a whiff of 'end of history' about it. He spoke of new 'permanent institutions'. For him, and for those who followed in his intellectual footsteps, there was only one Great Transformation. It is a claim of this book that we are in the midst of another, a Global Transformation. To understand it, and to identify desirable responses, we must first see why Polanyi's Transformation was historically specific.

POLANYI'S GREAT TRANSFORMATION

Polanyi depicted the nineteenth century as an attempt to create a market society in which everything was turned into a commodity, driven by the rising power of financial capital. He thought it impossible to create a 'self-regulating market economy' because it would annihilate 'the human and natural substance of society'. This did not mean that powerful interests would cease to try to create such 'a stark utopia' (Polanyi [1944] 2001, p. 3).[1] But his claim was that when the state moved in that direction, there would be a re-action, or 'double movement', whereby the state would re-embed the economy in society by new forms of regulation, redistribution and social protection.

The early period was one of 'disembeddedness', in which financial and industrial capital broke down old systems of regulation, social protection and redistribution, as part of a strategy to create *national* markets, including a national labour market. They also broke down communities that were barriers to commodification. And there was extensive use of subsidies to facilitate the transition to a national labour market, epitomized by the Speenhamland system introduced in 1795 in Britain, which topped up poverty wages in the countryside. This held back excess workers in rural areas until needed by the factories and mines, when their exodus was accelerated by the Poor Law Reform of 1834 that more or less denied help to the able-bodied. The result was migration of pauperized workers to the mills and urban centres of mass production, some of which took the form of what is now called 'outsourcing'.

Recalling the suffering of that period, Polanyi understood that the insecurity generated by a market society would provoke extremist reactions. This he had seen in the emergence of fascism and Bolshevism. He omitted to mention anarchism, which spread in the early twentieth century. But he saw a total market society as conducive to what some in the twenty-first century would call 'terrorism'.

Polanyi was not a pessimist, however. Precisely because of the threat to humanity's survival he foresaw the 'double movement'. This took the form of 'industrial citizenship' through which social entitlements were linked to stable industrial labour. In that phase of embeddedness in Polanyi's Transformation, the key figures were the employer and employee. But as we shall see, these ideal types are problematical for analysing what is happening in the Global Transformation.

THE NOTION OF COMMODIFICATION

> This sums up the position under a system based on the postulate of the commodity character of labour. It is not for the commodity to decide where it should be offered for sale, to what purpose it should be used, at what price it should be allowed to change hands, and in what manner it should be consumed or destroyed.
>
> (GT, p. 185)

Polanyi gave a great deal of attention to commodification as the central aspect of a market society, and gave most attention to labour commodification. His analysis has puzzled social scientists ever since.

A commodity is a good or service that is bought and sold. It has 'exchange value', and may or may not have 'use value', although in most cases it does. For Polanyi, commodities were 'empirically defined as objects produced for sale on the market' and markets were 'empirically defined as actual contacts between buyers and sellers' (GT, p. 75). In Chapter 6 of his book, he also made the much-quoted distinction between 'fictitious' and 'real' commodities. For him, labour, as well as land and money, was a fictitious commodity because labour is 'not originally produced to be sold on a market'. He continued, 'Labour is simply the activity of human beings, land is subdivided nature, and the supply of money and credit in modern societies is necessarily shaped by government policies'.

On not being originally produced for the market, one could say the same of a lemon. One could even say that labour is more of a commodity, if a fictitious commodity is defined as something not originally produced for the market. Whereas a lemon grows regardless of whether it will be sold, labour only takes place *because* it is sold in the market. Indeed, it is one of the premises of this book that, contrary to the ILO's Philadelphia Declaration, labour *is* a commodity. To understand why, it is necessary to make two distinctions, between 'work' and 'labour' and between 'labour' and 'labour power'.

Not all languages have two words for work and labour. Many do. Russian has *trud* and *rabota*; German has *beruf* and *arbeit*. The English derivation of work is decidedly different from labour. In French, the nearest equivalent is between *travail* and *activité*. In Mandarin, the distinction is roughly between *laodong* (labour) and *gongzuo* (work).

Most commentators treat work and labour as synonymous. But not all work is labour, while not all labour is productive activity. By not making a distinction, one loses all sense of work that is not labour; it disappears. This is precisely what happened in twentieth-century labour statistics. The work done by more people for more time than any other, namely the work of caring for other people, became statistically, economically and politically invisible.

Polanyi was caught by the twentieth-century notion of labour. But he was far from alone. Ever since the ancient Greeks, each age has had its silliness when it comes to conceptualizing work. Ours is no different. At least the ancients gave precedence to reproductive work – the reproduction and extension of human relationships. In Greece this was the only work regarded as honourable. Reproductive activity, *praxis*, work done for its own sake, was a means of strengthening personal relationships, between relatives, friends and citizens, which was characterized by Aristotle as *philia*. Opposed to *praxis* was *poiesis* (and *techne*), activities done for the sake of the product. Productive labour was equated with non-citizenship; it was the activity done by slaves.

The enforced labour of one group was rationalized as necessary to liberate the time of citizens to indulge in deliberative public, political action. However strange the rationalization, the ancient Greeks made a distinction that we should recover. They had a concept of *schole*, which means more than the modern notion of leisure, and was separated from 'play', the relaxation needed for recuperation and reproduction.

In feudal society, labour was for the serfs, those tied to the land. The physiocrats and mercantilists saw only agricultural labour as productive work. Everything else was unproductive. Only with the emergence of industrial capitalism did productive labour become linked to citizenship. The capacity for 'free' productive labour became a badge of citizenship. This was a huge change.

We reach the ultimate silliness with Immanuel Kant and Adam Smith. Kant wished to deny full citizenship to those who merely served other people, reserving citizenship for those who produced objects. He singled out hair-cutters as not doing work worthy of citizenship. Adam Smith went even further, dismissing as 'unproductive labour' all occupations concerned with ethical reproductive activity, including 'churchmen, physicians, doctors, writers, dancers, menial servants and the buffoon' (Smith [1776] 1979, Book 2, p. 431). A surprising number of admirers of Adam Smith would have been dismissed by him as non-productive. For the father of modern economics, service providers did work that 'perishes in the very instance of its performance'. The treatment of work has paid a heavy price ever since.

The classical economists, including Karl Marx, also used the notion of productive and unproductive labour. By the nineteenth century, reproductive work had become 'unproductive', disappearing altogether from public view, excluded from censuses and emerging labour statistics. So work done by more people than any other became non-work. The twentieth century took this silliness to new heights. It became a fetish. The goal became to put as many people as possible into 'jobs' and out of reproductive work.

The distinction between productive and unproductive labour fed into the characterization of economic activity in terms of primary, secondary and tertiary sectors, or agricultural (extractive), manufacturing (industrial) and services sectors. In general, for early political economists and Marxists, services were unproductive. Ironically, long before the end of the twentieth century a majority of people in industrialized countries were doing 'service' jobs.

Because progressives have identified with workers, they have idealized labour. It should not have been romanticized. After all, *labour* is derived from the Latin *laborem*, implying toil, distress and trouble. *Laborare* meant to do heavy onerous work. Early medieval use of *labeur* was associated with hard agricultural work. The French *travailler* is derived from the Latin *tripaliare*, meaning torture with a nasty three-pronged instrument. The ancient Greek word for labour, *ponos*, signified pain and effort, and has a similar etymological root as the word for poverty, *penia*. So labour meant painful, onerous activity done in conditions of poverty. That is hardly something to be idealized.

Labour's function is to produce marketable output or services. Those who control labour usually want to take advantage of others, and often will oppress and exploit those performing labour, who in turn will want to shirk and avoid it as much as they can. Thus, to extract labour, controls must be considerable.

Labour is also associated with 'jobs' and the 'jobholder society' so memorably deplored in Hannah Arendt's *The Human Condition* (1958). In a job, a person performs 'labour'; some would call it alienated activity because it is instrumental and requires the person to carry out a predetermined set of tasks. This insight is one of Marx's enduring contributions. He described labour as 'active alienation, the alienation of activity, the activity of alienation' (Marx [1844] 1976, p. 274). The language of alienation has gone out of fashion, but for most people doing paid jobs it is real. Those who romanticize jobs should do a spell down a mine or sit at a checkout counter counting the minutes to the tea break or the end of the shift. Throughout history, large numbers of those in jobs have been in wretched degradation (Robinson, 2004).

The notion of job leads to the manipulated limitation of skill, because labour is instrumental. Performance of labour has disutility, captured in all economics textbooks. And since labour is a matter of supply and demand, employers and workers exit from the relationship if product demand or wages fall, or if contractual or moral obligations and expectations are not fulfilled.

As for employment, it means stabilized labour based on subordinated labour security. In the nineteenth century, the term 'in employment' was almost a badge of shame. Employment only became a fixation in the twentieth century, when social, labour market and economic policies were based on the simulated values of full-time labour that crystallized in the sexist notion of 'full employment' (which only envisaged 'full employment' for men) and in the welfare state based on the male 'breadwinner'.

The standard twentieth-century model of employment involved an implicit social compact (to call it a contract would be a misnomer, since much was not legally binding), in which employees received security, notably employment security, in return for accepting workplace controls that gave them a subordinated, disciplined role in the production process. Employment relationships emphasize loyalty to an employer, typically accompanied by a Voice role (collective bargaining capacities) within prescribed limits.

Both labour and employment are associated with several labour statuses combining controls and insecurities (Standing, 2000). One curious outcome of Polanyi's Transformation was the conflation of labour statuses into two categories, employer and employee, the latter treated as synonymous with worker. It is a theme of this book that in the Global Transformation a new perspective is required.

An error of twentieth-century progressives, in pursuing industrial citizenship, was to make labour and employment the focus of social protection, regulation and redistribution. If you laboured for wages, you built up entitlements to sick leave, unemployment benefits, maternity leave, disability benefits and a pension. If not, you picked up the crumbs. The performance of labour was placed on a pedestal, to be protected, idealized, remunerated, dignified. Plaintive voices such as Arendt's were ignored as the juggernaut of labourism swept forward. But it was a jobholder society that was built in this embedding part of the Great Transformation.

Now contrast 'labour' and 'jobs' with 'work'. The latter captures the positive side of productive, reproductive and creative activity, in which the conception and execution aspects are combined, in imagery made famous by Braverman (1974). In work, there is room and respect for inaction and contemplation. In labour, there is no respect for reproductive activity. When thinking of work in positive terms, we think of personal development, the utility of working, in which pressures come from within, in which we feel in control, so that space is given to the activity of stillness.

Labour and employment do not leave such space. The economic imperative rules. Labour is about maximizing efficiency and competitiveness. Modern technologies result in greater intensity of labour. Stress, burnout, loss of control over time are what characterize labour. Work, by contrast, gives a proper place to desirable inefficiencies. A focus on work should lead us to consider how to achieve liberating flexibility, enabling us to allocate time to a broad range of reproductive and productive activities.

Unlike labour, 'work' captures the activities of necessity, surviving and reproducing, *and* personal development. 'Work' conjures up a positive notion of rounded activity, combining the Promethean vision of the human being as creator and the Aristotelian vision of reproductive activity undertaken in *philia*, in civic friendship, involving community and a sense of occupation. In this spirit, caring is work – almost the best you can do.

In performing work a person has agency, a sense of self-determination. By contrast, a worker required to perform labour lacks agency. In this sense, work involves human rights and real freedom, defined in terms of what Isaiah Berlin ([1958] 1969) called negative liberty and positive liberty – the absence of controls not chosen or accepted willingly by the worker, and the opportunity to make choices, to pursue and to achieve a sense of fulfilment.

By contrast with labour, self-chosen work is done for its use value. And work done because a person wishes to do it, in the pursuit of self-chosen goals of development and social participation, is the essence of real decommodification. Tantalizingly, in the notes at the end of his book, Polanyi hinted at differences between work and labour, without making a distinction. But he cited his generation's anthropological sages to support his view on what motivated work in primitive societies – not profit or economic gain, but a mix of reciprocity, joy, competitiveness (for honour) and approbation.

Polanyi understood that to create a market society labour had to be separated from other activities (GT, p. 171). This involved 'the application of the principle of freedom of contract', which meant liquidation of 'non-contractual organisations of kinship, neighbourhood, profession, and creed'. Commodification – turning work into labour – thus entails the destruction of institutions of social protection as well as displacement of 'status' by 'contract'. Thus, the work one might do as a member of a network of professional scholarship becomes labour when done as a contractual relationship. But that is only a necessary condition of commodification, since there are many forms of contract and degrees of control.

Polanyi rejected Adam Smith's hypothesis that primitive man had a predilection for 'gainful occupation' and to 'truck and exchange' (GT, p. 46). Anthropologist at heart, he followed Rousseau in seeing labour as deliberately stimulated by society. In his image of a Melanesian community he delighted in 'the absence of the motive of gain; the absence of the principle of labouring for remuneration; the absence of the principle of least effort' (GT, p. 49). In such societies, production and distribution are ensured by principles of reciprocity and redistribution. People do a lot of work, but find the notion of labour alien.

Thus, Polanyi dismissed Smith's view that man has a predilection for labour, but did not deny that man has a predilection for work, which reflects a human desire to be creative, productive and regenerative, for the benefit of self, family and communities.

Now consider the distinction between 'labour' and 'labour power', first articulated, if ambiguously, by Marx (see the Appendix to this chapter). Polanyi sometimes did not make it. For instance, he asserted, 'But labour and land are no other than the human beings themselves of which every society consists and the natural surroundings in which it exists' (GT, p. 75). A few lines later, he asserted with equal fervour, 'Labour is only another name for a human activity which goes with life itself'. However, a human being is not an 'activity'. The statements are incompatible. Indeed, the second ploughs into further ambiguity in stating, 'which in its turn is not produced for sale but for entirely different reasons, nor can that activity be detached from the rest of life, be stored or mobilised'. Surely, labour *can* be detached from the rest of life; for most alienated workers, that is how they see it.

Just before that second assertion, Polanyi stated even more emphatically, 'But labour, land, and money are obviously *not* commodities; the postulate that anything that is bought and sold must have been produced for sale is emphatically untrue in regard to them'. The section ends with the famous point, 'The commodity description of labour, land, and money is entirely fictitious' (GT, p. 76). It remains puzzling why he went on to use the term 'commodity fiction'. Labour is not a fiction; its commodity status is real, however the activity comes about. To be a fiction is not to exist.

The issue is not to score semantic points. It is rather to claim that the essence of any transformation is a struggle between commodifying and decommodifying forces. To understand the dynamics one must distinguish between labour and labour power, because both can be bought and sold, to varying degrees.[2]

Labour power is the bundle of capacities one possesses. By the nature of life and society, nobody can develop or utilize all their capacities. But a decommodified person would be someone who felt able to develop those capacities and had the means of avoiding others' control. People may be commodified if market institutions, such as firms or state agencies acting on their behalf, determine what they can choose to do with the resources at their disposal. Thus, one could say that someone who could not interrupt employment, perhaps to take a sabbatical to replenish skills or energy, had been commodified as labour power. The same would hold for someone obliged to interrupt employment to take a training course as a condition for continued employment.

For Polanyi, 'wages are the price for the use of labour power and form the income of those who sell it' (GT, p. 72). Again, one must be careful about what is being 'used'. Normally, workers do not sell labour power; they sell labour. The distinction is important, because theoretically the labour *or* the labour power could be commodified. A slave is commodified labour power; a 'proletarian' is not, because he owns himself.[3] But not all workers are equally commodified or sell labour in equally commodified ways. In nineteenth-century Britain, for instance, workers sold their labour openly enough but many retained some independence, recognized by the likes of Carlyle and Ruskin who raged against its erosion.

Commodification is always a matter of degree. Whereas a migrant may be highly commodified, labouring for daily or hourly wages, without a contract or benefits, somebody in long-term employment would be far less so. But even then, a salaried 'company man', locked into quasi-permanent employment because the potential loss of pension and other entitlements makes it too expensive to leave his 'career' job, is partially commodified.

Labour is more commodified when people do it primarily for instrumental reasons and in economic insecurity, under somebody's control. In *White Collar*, a seminal book first published in 1951, Wright Mills made the distinction between the craft ethic and the instrumental ethic of labour and work. Labour is a commodity because the activity performed is done largely to receive a wage and benefits that make up the remuneration package. With market exchange, there are bargains and contracts. People labour so that they can exist, and their labour has to be sold and bought again and again.

Although never complete, commodification depends on a variety of pressures and circumstances, identification of which should enable us to discern whether the overall trend is towards more or less. A person can be subject to a wide range and types of control and forms of insecurity. The labour may be fully marketized or made less so by contracts or institutional safeguards. But it is still labour.

In some utopian paradise, full decommodification would mean that everybody could avoid labour; they would work to satisfy self-chosen needs, while morally recognizing the needs of society and the sense of balanced reciprocity that underpins it in the form of various communities to which they could choose to belong. One has to dream of the Good Society, if one wishes for policies and institutions to move in its direction.

SOCIAL INCOME

For assessing transformations, it is useful to introduce the concept of 'social income' to capture all sources of income. To survive, people must have some income, even if inadequate, and most have more than one type of income, the composition determining not just the level but also the security of the income.[4] For any individual in any society, social income may have up to six components defined as follows:

$$SI = SP + W + CB + EB + SB + PB$$

where SI is total social income, SP is self-production (whether self-consumed, bartered or sold), W is the money wage or income received from work, CB is the value of support provided by the family or the local community, EB is the amount of benefits provided by the enterprise in which the person might be working, SB is the value of state benefits (insurance benefits or other transfers, including subsidies paid directly to workers or through firms to them, and the value of social services) and PB represents private income benefits from investment including private social protection.[5]

The composition of social income indicates the degree to which an individual is subject to market forces. Thus, one can assess the degree to which a person's labour is commodified and the extent to which the person is commodified as labour power. To give the simplest example, if W is a large share of SI, commodification will be greater than if W is zero or relatively small. In an era of decommodification, W will shrink as a share of SI, whereas in an era of (re)commodification it will grow. Another expected result of commodification will be erosion of those elements of SI that are relatively secure, as a result of institutional interventions or legislation, and expansion of those elements that are insecure and conditional on the performance of labour.

If the state or enterprises try to remunerate 'labour power' by means other than the wage, one could surmise that they are 'decommodifying labour', but add that they are doing so 'fictitiously' because they are still expecting to acquire labour. If someone is paid US$100 a week in money wages for 40 hours of labour, is that labour more commodified than if the person is paid US$50 and given non-wage benefits with a market value of US$50?

If employees are remunerated via a high EB and a low W, this is a way of tying them to the firm, giving it leverage over what activities they can undertake. In sum, the structure of social income tells us much about the character of the labour market and the underlying model of society.

THE IDEA OF OCCUPATION

Work, rather than labour, conjures up the idea of occupation, a sense of a lifetime (or prolonged part of it) of creative and dignifying work around a self-chosen set of activities. It relates to a distinction made by one assessment of 'office work', as depicted in fictional literature, between 'way-of-life' and 'means-to-end' work (Ferris, 2007). A good occupation is a sphere of work where fascination meets intellectual challenge, where the mind and the hands are in balance according to a person's capabilities and aspirations. A 'happy' person is someone doing what he or she aspires to do. Few are so fortunate. It is nevertheless the thesis of this book that we should be moving towards giving everyone the opportunity to pursue 'occupation' and promoting 'occupational citizenship' conducive to building new forms of civic friendship and social solidarity in the Global Transformation.

Occupations have been historically forged social constructs. At some distant point, the plumber or mason did not exist. Once upon a time, people did a little plumbing or bricklaying, or whatever, while not doing various other tasks. The plumber came into existence when the technology became too complex for the untrained to handle well enough, or when the time taken by the 'amateur' became so long that it was affecting other work, or when the opportunity cost of doing such work became greater than the cost of paying someone else to do it. But even in ancient Rome, work and labour were organized in narrowly defined occupations (Maxey [1938] 1975; Treggiari, 1980).

The idea of occupation has a peculiar history. According to the *Oxford Dictionary of Word Histories* (Chantrell, 2004):

The word occupation is formed irregularly from Old French *occuper*, from Latin *occupare*, to seize. A now obsolete vulgar sense 'have sexual relations' seems to have led to the general avoidance of the word in the 17th century and most of the 18th century. Middle English occupation came via Old French from Latin *occupatio*(n), from the verb *occupare*. The sense 'fill the mind' dates from mid-16th century. Occupant dates from late 16th century in legal contexts as a term for a 'person who establishes a title'; this is from French, on from Latin *occupant*.

For our purposes, we may say that an occupation consists of an evolving set of related tasks based on traditions and accumulated knowledge, part of which is unique. An occupation involves some combination of forms of knowledge that go beyond conventional notions of skill – abstract, technical, inferential and procedural.

An occupation has a claimed jurisdiction, in which claimed 'rights' might include a monopoly of practice, a structure of public payments, a right to impose work procedures on its practitioners, an acquired capacity of self-discipline and regulation, and control over recruitment, training and licensing.

Another feature is non-homogeneity. Within any occupation, differentiation may be by task (specialization), subordination, type of client, type of workplace and forms of remuneration. These may be small or large, but once large will be a threat to the continuation of the occupation.

One should also see occupations in terms of conflict and at least moral competition. They are also inherently transient, not permanent constructs. They exist within wider societies and suffer from internal tensions and tensions with other economic and social interests. Indeed, to form an occupation, a group must be able to define itself in opposition to others or at minimum in contrast to another group. Prospective members must have a common identity – a perception of common interests, standards of practice and behaviour.

An occupation is never a purely productive activity. Members perform a social function, which may include imparting norms to recruits, monitoring standards of behaviour and expertise, and giving mutual support. An occupation embodies notions of social inclusion, entailing a sense of substantive belonging and continuity.

It also reflects the outcome of class and cultural forces as much as technology. Many find it hard or arbitrary to define themselves in occupational terms. Some of us even vary our 'occupational title' on visas and the forms we have to fill from time to time, depending on our mood and the purpose of the document! Yet an occupation still gives us an identity. It is also an 'institution', which alongside others, from the family to the state, helps in the civilizing functions essential for human development.

An occupation operates on the basis of purposive compacts, that is, formal and informal expectations as to outputs, goals and services to be provided. These are typically shared by fellow members of an occupation and by their clients. They operate with linguistic traditions that give their practitioners an edge on outsiders, through 'relational' compacts. Max Weber ([1922] 1978, Part II, Ch. 8) referred to a 'status contract' – ritual relationships based on kinship and generalized reciprocity. Later sociologists developed distinctions between 'status' and 'cognitive' communities. These are all ways of seeing how people, through their work and labour, bind together to function in society.

All occupations have both a hierarchical dimension, with divisions of labour and of status, and a network dimension, involving patterns of structured reciprocities and risk-averting, risk-spreading and risk-compensation mechanisms cemented by trust (non-altruistic) or mutual dependency.

Occupation is linked to the idea of vocation, a sense of calling, which has religious connotations. Thus, Martin Luther understood that whereas *arbeit* meant strenuous physical labour, work involved a 'calling' (*vocatio*) and 'station' (status) (Meireis, 2004). A vocation provides lasting meaning to people's lives and in doing so anchors their identity, for better or for worse. An occupation as a vocation sees a career as personal development through work. As such, 'career' should be differentiated from 'careerism', which is about climbing ladders of status, income and power.

Weber ([1922] 1978, Part II, Ch. 9) contrasted vocation and bureaucracy, the latter possessing a rigid organization of employment, in which written rules predominate. In a bureaucracy, motivation is engineered by grading and by the prospect of climbing internal ladders. In a vocation, motivation springs primarily from self-realization of capabilities. Whereas an occupation typically gives a place for ascriptive processes – rites of passage, traditions, collective restraints on opportunism and 'competitiveness' – these are given less weight in bureaucracies and in labour markets, where a drive for 'competitiveness' prevails.

Occupations can be embedded in society or disembedded, in that their functions can help reproduce social and economic relations of the wider community. An occupation driven purely by material self-interest, or by that combined with the interests of those controlling its activities, is alienating and open to commodification. An ideal occupation is one that allows for reflective activity, including the stillness that Cato so splendidly understood when he said, 2000 years ago, in describing man in action: 'Never is he more active than when he does nothing'.

An essential aspect of work as occupation is the integrated nature of productive and reproductive activity, rather than the conceptualization based on a distinction between 'productive work' (in the labour force) and whatever else we do. Traditionally, an occupation involved productive and reproductive aspects, binding practitioners together through a rough idea of civic friendship. But the productivist bias, fostered by the early political economists and utilitarians, created a breach between productive and reproductive work. The error of twentieth-century labourism was its bias in favour of the labour that produced goods or facilitated their production, while neglecting reproductive work and the social side of work.

The modern way of defining occupations is by reference to the obscure notion of 'skill'. Among labour statisticians, it is conventional to divide occupational titles on the basis of notions of skill, status and hierarchy, and by relations to people and things. An occupation may be defined in terms of breadth of skills, and be relatively static or relatively progressive.

A static occupation is similar to a job in that the practitioner's technique or status scarcely progress. Most occupations are not static, however, since those carrying out the work refine skills, extend jurisdiction (or have it curtailed) and are affected by changes in technology and the division of labour. An occupation will rarely be the same from start to finish of a person's career.

In popular use, skill refers to someone's technical capacity, usually measured by something like level of schooling. This is a feeble proxy. No country has an accurate measure of its population's 'skills'. At best, they have a picture of the distribution of jobs by some measure of skill, ignoring the obvious fact that many doing 'unskilled' jobs have unused skills. The picture is further complicated because skill has also been measured in terms of social and control status; an occupation is classified as skilled by culture or class, or position of authority, as much as by technical complexity.

If we could revise our image of skill, we could look at the development potential of any work activity in a less alienated way. In this regard, the idea of 'occupation' should be contrasted with the notion of a 'job'. Historically, the latter was a pejorative term, suggesting an ephemeral activity, menial, limited and limiting. People *do* jobs; people *are* occupations. A job is a teleological concept; its end is defined in its beginning. An occupation is ontological, constantly becoming and 'unbecoming'. An occupation suggests a career and a niche – occupying a space.

An occupation may be seen as a set of activities that blend into a career. Some are stepping-stone occupations – a person enters with one eye to a career in it, the other to moving into something else (for example, from law to politics, from engineering to management) – while others such as teaching are 'pool professions', which some people do while hoping for an opening in their profession of choice (musician, artist, writer, and so on).

Whereas an occupation is commonly defined by a career structure, a job has none. A career requires opportunity for development (or mobility), should an individual wish it. Yet career structures are also a means of enforcing hierarchy and controls, preventing certain intra-professional and inter-professional mobility. What Abbott (1988) called 'demographic rigidity' arises if an occupation's reproductive mechanisms – the controls exercised over its members – prevent it from expanding or contracting rapidly. This might arise from the fact that full practice requires long training, induction and status-based licence to operate, which comes from satisfying, prolonged experience – or what one might call internally controlled emancipation from occupational controls.

Career and niche have negative aspects as well as positive. A career suggests progression in terms of technique, status, income and security. It suggests entering and remaining in a single occupation, exiting only into retirement, surrounded by the trappings and rewards of the occupation. But it also suggests an elitist phenomenon, a situation reserved for a few privileged individuals, whereas most do humble jobs in repetitive drudgery. A niche suggests a comfort zone but also an image of static jobholding, trapped in yesterday's achievements or whatever allowed the niche to be gained.

Most concepts used in connection with work are riddled with such ambiguity. However, the historical or etymological roots tell us about the way work has evolved in successive social-economic revolutions, and warn us to appreciate that they are still evolving. Thus, occupation means both a process of obtaining and refining work-based knowledge and what was the etymologically earlier meaning of possessing territory (property).

OCCUPATION AS 'CIVIC FRIENDSHIP'

> When men are friends they have no need for justice, while when they are just they need friendship as well, and the truest form of justice is thought to be a friendly quality.
>
> (Aristotle, *Nicomachean Ethics*)

An integral part of any occupation is the 'reproductive' work done by its practitioners, which should be understood not just in terms of nurturing and caring, but also as involving acts of civic friendship that reproduce the community. Members of a thriving occupation value what Aristotle called *philia*, wishing well for the other, not for one's own sake but for theirs, and sharing their values and goals. In a labour market, there is no intrinsic place for friendship; each individual is encouraged to compete with others. If some are inclined to lower the wage at which they will do a task, others will lose or have to follow.

In a thriving occupation, by contrast, there is an embedded place for civic friendship. In an ideal occupational community, members admire each other's workmanship, share the craft ethic and value a shared identity. There is intrinsic psychic value in the work and the social relations in which it takes place. An occupation includes a place for social interaction, reproduction and reciprocities. It provides a mechanism for social solidarity. A labour market has none of these attributes.

For Aristotle, the perfect civic friendship was 'character friendship', a love for the goodness of the other person's whole character. This is why he regarded the reproductive activity of mothers so highly. This is also why an ideal occupation is one in which there is a place for the work of care, in which the objective should be to help a person become an independent mature equal capable of making ethical judgments and indulging in subtle reciprocities. Reproduction is the activity of 'bringing another person into being'. It gives a proper place to altruism, which stands in conflict with paternalism, the reproduction of another's norms and expectations, rather than the capacity to define one's own norms and expectations.

Civic friendship is essential for a just society. It makes us yield voluntarily to socially just relations. As such, a legislator's task, in Aristotle's view, was to strengthen a reproductive rather than a productive framework, an orientation to human excellence rather than to the excellence of property and wealth. Schwarzenbach (1996) makes the point that there is no reference to friendship between citizens in the founding doctrines of the USA. Yet Tom Paine's epoch-making pamphlet, 'Common Sense' ([1776] 2005), that was said to be in every cabin in North America, opens with a colourful depiction of deliberative democracy emerging from friendship. Civic friendship is about a richer idea of work and leisure than conventional theorizing allows. Work that is not labour includes political participation in forging and reproducing human capacities and ethical behaviour. It is about social interaction. If this form of work is crowded out by a drive for efficient labour there is a heavy price to be paid.

OCCUPATIONAL GUILDS

Ideas of civic friendship and citizenship overlap with the idea of community, derived from the ancient Greek implying 'a sharing'. Community was *koinonia*, from the verb 'to share'. A city community entailed a shared system of courts, a shared conception of justice and a shared scheme for cooperation or 'mode of life'. In a labour market, such sharing is not valued. In a community, citizens care what kind of character their fellow citizens have and develop. By contrast with a labour market, an occupational community binds individuality with community.

An occupation arises from a group doing similar work, a set of closely related tasks that require similar talents and interests. As those doing such work become aware of a common interest, they realize that competition with each other is dangerous to their income, status and existence. Appreciating that unity is strength, they are drawn together by shared ways of seeing the world to form a community. Some groups have been defeated in that endeavour, because they have lost out to another occupation offering something better, or because they are too weak to hold together against the forces of proletarianization and commodification. Yet many survive.

The classic occupational communities were the medieval guilds. Although flawed creations of their time, they comprised one of the greatest institutions of history and dominated economic and social life for several centuries. They were preceded by corporations of masons, metalworkers, potters and others in ancient Rome, groups bound together by worshipping a common deity and having common holidays and common responsibility for training apprentices.

In the Middle Ages, guilds shaped occupations in European towns and cities. They gave their members a community, status and identity. Their weaknesses, notably their tendency to rule themselves in their own interests, contributed to their marginalization from the sixteenth century onwards. However, their long survival owed a lot to the advantages they gave to their members and to society more generally. They were buffers against the emerging market society.

The word 'guild' stemmed from the Anglo-Saxon *geld*, meaning 'to pay or to contribute'; the noun *geld* means an association of persons contributing to a common set of purposes. It also derived from the term 'to sacrifice or to worship'. The guild had numerous synonyms in the Middle Ages, including fraternity. It conveyed a sense of Aristotle's *philia* and what the Roman historian Tacitus called *convivium,* in reference to the voluntary bodies known as *collegia* in the late Roman Empire. All of these words point to the social functions that accompanied the guilds' economic activities.

In medieval Europe, there were several types of guild – the merchant guild, the occupational guild and the religious or communal guild. Merchant guilds – whose modern-day near-equivalents are chambers of commerce – facilitated the growth of international trade for several hundred years and are most associated with the seaports of Genoa and Venice. They offered insurance, for their members and for those with whom they traded. They helped enforce contracts, even to the extent of being corporately liable for debts incurred by members. They did this because if a ruler where they traded seized their goods in retaliation for a bad debt by another member, they could sue for compensation on their return. If action was taken against one of their members abroad, they could impose a boycott, thereby deterring opportunistic behaviour by those with whom they did business.

However, it is the occupational guilds that are relevant for assessing occupational communities today. These usually operated with a hierarchy of master craftsmen, journeymen and apprentices, with today's apprentices expecting to be tomorrow's journeymen and, when openings occurred, future master craftsmen. Masters employed journeymen, usually on short-term contracts, and had their own equipment and premises. Journeymen usually worked while waiting to become masters, which depended not only on their own assets but on openings in the restricted community of master craftsmen. The guilds were self-governing, with state-granted entitlement to possess collective property and with legal privileges. While rarely democratic in the sense of every member having equal voting rights, they were relatively democratic in that decisions were usually made by majority vote from within the ranks of the master craftsmen.

In fourteenth-century Florence, the 21 guilds or *arti* – seven major, the rest minor

– provided members of the city's governing council or *Signoria* (Hibbert, 1974). The most prestigious guild was that of lawyers, the *Arte dei Giudici e Notai*, followed by the guilds of the wool, silk and cloth merchants. The bankers' guild grew in significance as its wealth grew, but was held back by the Catholic Church's condemnation of usury. Then came the guild of doctors, apothecaries, shopkeepers, merchants who sold spices, dyes and medicines, and some artists and craftsmen (including painters), and a guild for dealers and craftsmen in animal skins and furs. Members of the minor guilds – armourers, bakers, butchers, cooks, innkeepers, joiners, leatherworkers, smiths, stonemasons and vintners – were superior in status to ordinary workers, such as weavers and spinners, boatmen and labourers, who comprised about three-quarters of the city's population.

Ordinary workers were not allowed to form guilds, which caused occasional revolt over wages. When woollen workers were allowed to form guilds in 1378, resentment by others led to their hasty abolition, the result of a coalition of other guilds and their employers, using 'state' power. The city government was run by nine guild members aged over 30, six representing the major guilds, two representing the minor guilds and one chosen as the city's standard-bearer, all elected for two-month periods, during which they had to live away from their homes. The *Signoria* ruled Florence with several other elected and permanent officials. It was a form of occupational citizenship, however inegalitarian. The *Signoria* excluded both ordinary workers, the *minuto popolo*, and nobles, the *grandi*.

The Florentine guilds did not escape the problem that has dogged occupational communities throughout history, a tendency towards domination by the richest merchant families, who ensured their favourites were elected. This led to a form of plutocracy. To be rich was honourable, to be poor a disgrace. But those of highest esteem were those who had made their fortunes in honourable occupations, who were well married and who had held public office.

Between 1150 and 1400, guilds were the main way of organizing work in European cities and towns, based on associations of equals, a *universitas*, with self-government and power to levy duties and assess fines for breaking rules. Members were required to use guild courts to settle disputes. There was also nepotism and a second-class group of lifetime journeymen, who formed journeymen associations. As one student put it, 'In the craft guild, the "mystery" of craftsmanship is joined with the dynamic of the pressure group; skill and endurance, on which life and progress depend, are powered by a specific social bond' (Black, 1984, p. 7). Guilds embodied a model of Voice power, stemming from the base of society, confronting what one analyst has called descending power exerted by feudal rulers (Ullman, 1966).

Among the guilds' functions was control of work quality, with demands that their members provide minimally acceptable products and services. They thereby fostered expansion of transparent and anonymous exchange and raised the price of their outputs by the reputation of their guild, albeit at the 'cost' of managing labour relations and holding down wages of journeymen, apprentices and labourers. They also played an extensive role as providers of social protection, by extending credit to members, providing mutual insurance, aiding members in law cases, helping the children of members to afford apprenticeships and dowries, helping pay for funeral costs and marriages, and so on.

Guilds operated a system of incentives and sanctions. If members contravened their rules and expectations, perhaps by delivering poor service or by not paying off debts, the guilds imposed penalties that ranged from public reprobation to expulsion. It is relevant to modern debates that their rules could not supersede common law, so that the collective interest could not override the rights of individuals set by the legal system. They were not a state within a state.

It would be wrong to depict guilds simply as market manipulators and social protection bodies. They played a powerful religious role, helping to preserve the moral integration of society. At their peak, they were also the channel for the pursuit of salvation and eternal life. This played a role in societal management, acting to maintain social discipline, piety and functionally decent behaviour, with rituals that helped maintain sober dedication. They also helped limit labour, placing demands on their members to observe religious holidays and participate in bonding social ceremonies.

A critic might say they distorted the market and limited competition, thus impeding growth. This would be simplistic. The guilds helped reproduce society; it is no coincidence that they came into their own following the Black Death, when families were shattered and when the Church was impoverished. They fulfilled a fictive kinship role, helping to sustain families and individuals through periods of crisis. Those in fortunate circumstances were expected to help out those in trouble, based on the expectation that the donor at one time could be the one in need at another.

This explains the emphasis placed on righteous living and moderation. Social responsibility was required because fraternity was essential for survival of the community. There was protection based on social solidarity that was based on behavioural conditionality. This associational protection solidified in an era of state retreat; it induced everybody who could to bind themselves to guilds and encouraged a search for collective institutions as the means of protection. To disparage this function of occupational bodies is to reveal a prejudice against the reproductive character that people as citizens value.

The guilds were weakened by the Reformation and Protestantism, and were suppressed in England in the 1530s and 1540s, although some were allowed to continue on payment of large sums to the king. Merchant capitalism was incompatible with them, industrial capitalism even less so. In France they were banned during the Revolution in 1791 and Napoleon disbanded them in countries occupied by the French army. The Napoleonic Code abolished guild controls, setting up bourgeois rights to establish businesses and free trade across continental Europe. Napoleon's conquests thus established market rules.

The guilds stood against market capitalism and were marginalized as national markets emerged. Placing a premium on stability and consistent quality, they were ill-suited to the innovations that accompanied rapid technological and organizational change. They withered in Britain after the sixteenth century and their privileges were abolished in 1835 as the drive to a laissez-faire market society was accelerating. They were abolished in Austria, Germany and Italy in the nineteenth century and in Russia and China after revolutions in the twentieth century. In short, their abolition was part of the disembedded phase of Polanyi's Transformation. They were replaced by trade unions that emerged to give protection to wage employees.

THE NATURE OF OCCUPATIONAL COMMUNITIES

Nowadays, a standard way of looking at occupational communities is to depict them as groups who consider themselves engaged in the same sort of work, who share values,

norms and perspectives that extend beyond work-related matters and whose social relationships meld work and leisure (Van Maanen and Barley, 1984). They sustain relatively
unique cultures consisting of task rituals, standards for proper behaviour, work codes
surrounding routine practices and accounts attesting to the logic and value of these
rituals, standards and codes. The quest for self-control provides the motive for the development of occupational communities.

A good occupation has a cultural core, is non-economic in its structure and gives symbolic recognition to its sages and finest craftsmen that is often divorced from commercial
success. And as being in an occupation is a social activity, it cannot be understood outside
the idea of community. An occupation creates a sense of honour among its practitioners
and the honour of one's type helps to preserve solidarity.

A community sets rules and positivist laws that provide a framework within which we
can develop. These provide a social memory (to recall what Arendt wrote in her critique
of totalitarianism) to guide our actions and 'guarantee the existence of a common world,
the reality of a certain continuity which transcends the lifespan of one generation, which
absorbs all new beginnings and profits from them' (Arendt, 1951, p. 211). A community
based on an occupation provides memory, stability and opportunity within an evolving
work process. Without that framework, there can be no occupational security – men and
women would be commodified.

Occupational communities can combat commercial domination and religious, national
or supra-national ideologies. Perhaps John Stuart Mill was the first to capture the fear
that, in a capitalist economy, socially dominated men and women would be reduced
to wanting what society permitted them to want. He recognized that in capitalism a
worker is 'perpetually a child . . . the approved condition of the labouring classes'. But
an occupational community establishes mechanisms to combat conformist tendencies of
a dominant ideology. In our era, that is the set of dictates associated with globalization.
Belonging to an occupation is a way of preventing the paralysis of the will that commer-
cialism encourages. An occupation gives what some call 'agent freedom', which conjures
up the image of an individual able, through self-development, to act freely in spite of
conformist pressures.

A key aspect of any viable occupational community is security among its core
members. They must believe that they have access to a minimal level of 'property' and
income to retain a sense of community. At the same time, the structures of occupational
communities evolve to differentiate groups by status and set of tasks. Some create an elite
within their ranks, provided with rental income from the rest of their aspiring peers. The
elite may receive referrals only from their fellow professionals, as in medical practice (consultants) or the law (barristers). These status rules embody the disciplines of the whole
occupation, a reason for accepting the privileged niche of the elite. One may not approve,
but that is what they do.

Intra-occupation stratification can mean that the public image of an occupation devi-
ates from its reality. This may be matched with 'client differentiation' (Abbott, 1988, p.
122). Occupations that have complex career progression are most susceptible to internal
differentiation; they impose long training and qualification processes, as entry barriers and as a means of legitimizing the differentiation. If you have had to serve a long
'apprenticeship', you will be more inclined to defend insider privileges once safely inside,
with the qualification on the wall, on a badge or on a business card.

However, a crucial aspect of an occupational community is that there is space for systemic inefficiency, in that emphasis is placed on character. Occupational communities could even be said to be crucial for a good society because in emphasizing civic friendship they cultivate a sense of justice, of ethics. Occupations are a means of reconstructing imagined communities, combating individualization and the paternalistic tendencies of the family and state.

A strong occupation is one rooted in a strong community, in which the work of individuals is self-monitored and self-evaluated, where the self extends to one's self-chosen peers. Thus, as an economist, I accept the legitimacy of fellow economists, however much I may disagree with them. I implicitly confer that legitimacy on entering that community and can anticipate reciprocities intrinsic to any community of common interests and aspirations. A community maintains respect for standards, its development and its reproduction, and an occupational community stands in conflict with bureaucratic and other enterprise structures. To anticipate, it is regrettable that in the globalization period nobody stood up to defend occupational communities or to curb their faults while strengthening their virtues.

An occupational community embeds work in a context of association, with standards of self-discipline, civic friendship and character, in conflict with pressures for efficiency. There is a tension between the solidarity of an occupational community and that of a family structure. Just as the family can create subordination and stratification so can occupational communities. We thus need a set of overlapping communities to balance rent seeking, hierarchies and incestuous controls.

The downside of any occupational community includes a tendency to form cartels, a tendency to impede technological 'progress', a tendency to restrict services and a tendency for insiders to exploit peripheral outsiders. Its procedures may offend conventional rules of 'democracy' in a market society. But they usually have a rationale grounded in experience, which may or may not be defensible to outsiders.

Within occupational communities, the distinction between work and leisure is sometimes blurred, perhaps a defining aspect of work as 'decommodified' activity. Almost imperceptibly, chosen leisure pursuits are linked with work if one has a vocation and a sense of craftsmanship, a point brought out beautifully in an early study of a 'low' occupational community, the carnival, in which this blurring was evident (Bryant, 1972). This applies as much to cultural interests as to physical activities.

Occupational communities are a barrier to the market because they limit competition between their members. They have spread in periods of commodification as a form of resistance *and* as a means of taking advantage of market opportunities. Since for allocative efficiency a market economy requires competition 'undistorted' by such barriers, the state when trying to construct a market society can be expected to attack occupational communities. It will do so selectively, depending on the roles played by certain occupations. In most cases, limits will be placed on bodies representing occupational groups. In the absence of such bodies there will be more open competition, with forms of social dumping, as in the case of a service provider offering an initially lower and unsustainable price in order to obtain entry or loyalty from a client or to obtain reputational security.

Finally, occupational communities generally seek to establish Voice, the capacity to bargain collectively. The peculiar position of occupations is that they are faced by several groups with whom they have to bargain, and have several methods by which they do so. Besides direct bargaining, they may have Voice based on collective lobbying, internalization of information and collective practitioner control, perhaps through training, setting barriers to entry (such as exams), licences and ethics codes. To differentiate between what occupations do and standard collective bargaining we will describe their activities as 'collaborative bargaining'.

OCCUPATIONS AND COMMODIFICATION

An occupational community may be a barrier to commodification or a mechanism for labour, or both. If we can identify what it promotes that represent barriers to commodification and how it acts as an instrument for labour, we should be able to identify what type of occupational structure would be close to ideal.

An occupation that is an effective barrier to commodification creates and presents a cultural identity, allows individuals to develop their creative capacities, is a lobby for recognition and status, is a body of civic friendship legitimizing traditions of reproduction, guards the mysteries of the craft and sense of calling (vocation), prevents dilution of competence and promotes loyalty to the occupation over loyalty to individual employers.

As a mechanism for labour, an occupation may impose discipline on its members, provide a means for intensifying labour, excommunicate miscreants, limit as well as boost skill and create a bureaucracy, as in the case of splitting the occupation into job structures rather than allowing for a self-realizing process through a career. It may limit supply through controlling barriers to entry; it may impose initiation rules, giving older members advantages over newcomers; it may provide mechanisms for monitoring and evaluating performance; it can proletarianize lower echelons, and spin off or 'de-skill' subsidiary tasks; it can do that through standardizing abstract knowledge so that it can be easily packaged and reproduced; it can be a means of internal stratification.

Occupations usually have emotionally charged words that make traditions part of communal solidarity, continuity and creative development. In French winemaking, the notion of *terroir* conveys more than the land or its productive characteristics. It suggests a way of communicating between past, present and future generations, and between them, the earth and the activity of winemaking, as well as a call to those privileged to be attached to it to produce not just fine wine but to reproduce the traditions and the ecology that go with it. Winemaking is one of the sublime occupations, reflecting not just centuries of toil but also exquisite aesthetic values, as well as a pace of work that puts a limit to commodification.

More generally, one can say that occupational communities are more than can be expressed in market relationships. The social memory will limit opportunism, ecological irresponsibility and short-term profit maximization. If practices were set by shareholders in some distant place, they would not care for the ecology of, say, the village of Savigny-lès-Beaune or the sustainable rationale of many time-honoured practices.

Seen in this way, an ideal occupational community would be one that provided for social solidarity based around work, not labour, creating a structure of balanced reciprocities, where rental income would be shared and where governance would be by deliberative democracy, subject to rules blocking elite capture.

OCCUPATIONS AND CONTROL

All forms of labour involve control, by various people over various aspects. The standard 'textbook' presumes that the relationship involves an employer and employee bargaining over a deal, the one mighty, the other vulnerable, matching a wage for labour supplied. As it is presumed that the employer is more powerful, it has been deemed necessary to provide employees with protective regulations. This may have been a reasonable basis for legislation in the twentieth century. But it neglects too much for comfort.

Control in labour relationships may be exercised over eight aspects, and be exercised by an employer, a middleman, a fellow worker, a body to which the person belongs or a relative. Only in the idealized 'capitalist' labour market is an employer in control of all eight aspects. As this was not the norm for centuries, and is unlikely to be the norm in the future, it is worth recalling the eight aspects.

First, there is 'self-government', control over oneself. Clearly, a slave or a serf is controlled in a way that an employee is not. The freedom to negotiate a contract is the basis of a labour market. Having control over oneself means opportunity to be a rational agent, with agency, being able to make decisions about one's life.

Second, there is control over time and effort to be expended in the work or labour. For the person doing it, having control over time implies an ability to determine the pace of work, its intensity, the amount of time and effort in work, and so on.

Third, there is control over means of production, the equipment and space required for the work. It was this aspect that attracted most Marxian attention. It may be usual for an employer to have control over them but this is not always the case. Having control over means of production must mean, at least, having reasonably assured access to them. This may include control of certain settings of work and certain language to describe tasks and input, but also the work process.

Fourth, there is control over raw materials used in production. Many outworkers possess means of production but are controlled via access to raw materials. Control over raw materials includes having access to and use of the materials required for the work.

Fifth, there is control over the work content, including the division of labour between groups, and control over the way work is organized. From a worker's viewpoint, the ability to divide the work tasks within a work group and adjust to personal comparative advantage must count as critical in defining a desirable occupation. Who controls the content of work determines what constitutes skill, competence, status and much else.

Sixth, there is control over skill reproduction, the capacity of a person or group to develop technical competencies. For a worker, control in this sense should include the ability to acquire, maintain, enhance and use skill.

Seventh, there is the control over the actual output. Who determines what is produced, how it is produced and to whom it is sold or transferred? Having control over the output must include having the ability to determine the quality and quantity of output.

Finally, there is control over income, the proceeds of the output. Although income may be earned, this does not necessarily mean the worker will receive all or even any of it. This statement is likely to induce an image of an imbalance of power between employer and employee. But many workers lose control over at least part of their earnings to relatives, middlemen or agencies or to another third party, including a professional body.

In each of these aspects of labour, control may be exercised by one or more types of controller. It may be exercised by the individual worker, by an employer or representative manager, or by a middleman, such as a labour broker or employment agency. Such layers of control may also include some 'community' role, be it a family, neighbourhood or caste group, religious body or ethnic or migrant association. In addition, there is the control exercised by an occupation to which the worker belongs. And the state may intervene, to enforce or curtail the pattern of control.

For an occupation to emerge, success will depend on a group that is exercising similar tasks achieving collective security in which to develop, apply and refine the work that comprises an occupation. This will be determined by the ability of individual workers in the group to gain control over the eight aspects of work. A Good Occupation, on its own terms, would require reasonably strong control over most of those aspects.

To put it mildly, most workers in most occupations have less than this 'ideal'. However, just as not all forms of control are exercised by employers, there is also 'occupational control'. Rare is the economics textbook that recognizes its existence as a feature of labour markets. Yet it has existed at least since the guilds of the Roman Empire. It played a prominent role in the twentieth century as well, and in some form will continue to do so. Control over its own tasks is a defining characteristic of an entrenched occupation. It covers control of access (entry) to the occupation (including induction and training), control over what constitutes good or bad performance, work content, evaluation, social protection and subordination (ability to designate subordinate activities and determine the jobs of those in such 'occupations').

To some extent, occupations possess capacities to control what work is done and not done, and how it is done. Occupations seek to control their members, their clients, their competitors, their monitors and evaluators, and the state in its sphere of jurisdiction. To the extent they control their members, they may prevent the occupation from dividing, or they may do the opposite, delegating a range of tasks to a new occupation. As for performance, one key area is 'the power to define success'. Important is the incumbent power to define problems, to measure treatment and to avoid comparison with competitors. Another sphere is demand for professional confidentiality, as defined by the French Penal Code, for instance. An occupation may also impose control over its work through referral networks – perhaps entrenched by a club community, personal networks or clans. One group will refer some work to another group as a matter of convention.

Historically, a group performing what it considers similar tasks has emerged as an occupation and developed the capacity to enhance its interests, to determine who may perform the tasks under the occupational title, who may have access to the training and qualifications required in order to be allowed to perform the tasks, what should be covered by the occupation and what excluded, how performance should be evaluated, what penalties imposed if there is deemed to be a failing and what forms of protection should be provided to members. There is also countervailing action taken against employers through control exercised over labour supply by craft and industrial unions.

Numerous groups have achieved control in all these respects, from humble crafts such as blacksmiths to professions such as lawyers, engineers, accountants and architects. Occupational control has been pursued by bodies set up by members of the occupation itself, although sometimes a government takes the lead.

Medieval guilds assisted their members, protected the craft and regulated the level and standard of production, working conditions, training, Sunday work, night work and so on. Modern occupational associations have done much the same (Derber, 1982a; Simpson, 1985). Usually, they have tried to limit individual or group opportunism, maintain or raise the incomes, benefits and status of the occupation and preserve or enhance skills.

In some cases, control has grown so hegemonic that the occupation has been able to control the work of subordinate occupations, the members of which may be denied opportunity to enter the dominant occupation, or may be allowed to do so only at the discretion of the superior group. But sometimes controls can be too effective for their own good. Thus, in the UK, solicitors in the nineteenth century restricted the number of articled clerks to preserve income and status. When a sudden expansion of work occurred, the solicitors could not deal with it, resulting in loss of their control.

Occupational control probably reaches its peak when the state legitimizes the issuing of licences to individuals to allow them to practise. This restricts entry and raises the income of those inside the occupation (Pfeffer, 1974), leading in turn to the emergence of substitutes, or ways of avoiding the need for such workers, or actions by the state to restrict the occupational control. We will consider this in Chapter 7.

Internal controls include initiation rituals involving delegation of degrading tasks to recruits, which reinforces an ethic of hierarchy. Often the delegated work may be relatively 'skilled'. Thus, research may be delegated to 'juniors'. This may mean that the productivity of less well-paid juniors will exceed that of senior groups. If the gap becomes excessive, juniors will be deterred from entering or remaining in the occupation or will be inclined to split into a new occupation or take collective action within it. A puzzle is to identify when Exit, Voice or Disloyalty options would be most likely.

The more that technical skill is involved in an occupation, and the more that the 'jobs' people do are embedded in an occupation, the less managerial control can be exerted without involving high costs for enterprise administrations. The more that jobs belong to occupations, the greater the potential for those doing them to develop self-control and thus the more the work is likely to be motivated by incentives, including non-pecuniary incentives, rather than external pressure and direction. This has a bearing on the appropriate forms of remuneration and the forms of security to be promoted.

CRAFTS AND PROFESSIONS

Most occupations emerge from humble beginnings and their structure reflects a tension between old notions of craftsmanship based on artisan lifestyles and newer bourgeois notions of professionalism. All occupations are spheres of risk and uncertainty, since the division of labour may change, with some tasks being made subordinate, some the realm of an elite.

Occupations are usually divided into professions and crafts, the former being higher status, 'white collar' and associated with use of the brain rather than the hand, the latter being 'blue collar'. A profession is often defined as an occupation based on abstract knowledge whereas a craft involves the application of manual skills.[6] Professions emphasize theory rather than practice, using this to protect themselves against loss of legitimacy (Abbott, 1988). Marxists might argue that professions metamorphose expertise into property. Others have argued that professions constitute a form of decentralized regulatory power within nations (Dingwall and King, 1995).

Many analysts have differentiated on the basis of manual skills. Thus, a technician is someone who makes something to specification, on order. A professional is someone who brings to the work a sense of independent judgment about the end of the endeavour and the means by which it is pursued. A craftsman is someone who shapes with his hands. But all such distinctions break down. One might also make a distinction between 'dependent contractors', those delivering standardized services, and 'independent contractors', providing an individualized service.

In the end, the distinction between crafts and professions is socially constructed. Perhaps a property of a profession is possession of knowledge acquired outside the work, whereas the key property of the craftsman is derived through the work itself. But just as the famous dichotomy of 'conception' and 'execution' of work, linked to Taylorism, is a way of stratifying for control purposes – managers conceive, workers execute – so the dichotomy of professions and crafts may be little more than an artificial defence of privilege and occupational domination. The honourable origins of craft must be preserved. A craft is humble expertise, not a proud imposter based on symbols.

Professions make claims to a unique body of formally acquired knowledge, a freedom to set and administer controls over their work to preserve the quality and reliability of the service, a public interest that legitimizes their right to self-governance, a paternalistic norm of authority over clients and an occupational culture with clubs and associations (Trice, 1993). They create elaborate systems of instruction and training and enforce codes of ethics, as was recognized in a pioneering study of professions (Carr-Saunders and Wilson, 1933). Some have argued that they do not serve real social needs but impose their definition of needs as well as the manner of service (Johnson, 1972). And some professions try to guard their territory by subordinating some of their practitioners through a symbolic order – using formal qualifications, selective honours and uniforms, and instigating acts of exclusion (preventing access to their knowledge by workers outside the occupation) and acts of coercion (requiring others to perform certain tasks).

Two perspectives on professions have been influential. Theodore Caplow's (1954) narrative went as follows: professions emerge by establishing an association, then change their name to lose their past, claim a monopoly and give themselves a label capable of legislative restriction. They develop a code of ethics to assert their social utility, regulate the incompetent and reduce internal competition, and then agitate for political and legal recognition, professional title and criminalization of unlicensed work, ending up by establishing confidentiality rights. This highlights the pivotal control over output through setting standards. All the actions in this chain are functional, with the objectives of exclusion and an assertion of jurisdiction. However, the narrative leaves out the tensions and contradictions in the professionalization process.

Harold Wilensky (1964) saw professional development in terms of a sequence of emergence of full-time employment, which induces training, a transfer to schools, a consequent raising of standards and introduction of full-time teachers, leading to the formation of an association, exclusion of incompetents, delegation of work to para-professionals and a tendency for internal conflict to develop between generations (particularly between those formally trained and their elders who trained on the job). Meanwhile, state protection sets rules eliminating internal competition and charlatanry, and formalizing an ethics code. In this model, the emphasis is on control over skill, labour and output, plus use of external controls.

These perspectives may be too rigid for comfort. But they do establish a sense of occupational dynamics, showing how professions operate. Typically they build complex

organizations through activities (lobbying, disseminating information, setting up practitioner control groups); professional controls (schools for training practitioners, exams
for testing them, licences, ethics codes, determining methods of recruitment, induction,
numbers, standards and excommunication); and worksite controls (legitimizing sites for
practice, journals and research institutions that are accepted or required). A profession
may also use public opinion to establish and perpetuate its social and cultural power, and
to impose tasks on competing or subordinate professions. Governments in continental
Europe have tended to do that on behalf of dominant professions.

So, we could say that professions are complex and merit the distinction between them and
crafts. But it is unsatisfactory. Abbott (1988, p. 318) defined professions vaguely in the con-
cluding chapter of his book, stating, 'My loose definition – professions are somewhat exclu-
sive groups of individuals applying somewhat abstract knowledge to particular cases – works
well enough'. However, some professions do not deal with 'particular cases', while many
crafts do. Again, the vagueness makes one wary. The notion of a profession has been a means
of defending and institutionalizing inter-generational privilege, and the defining of skill,
which is a social construct, reflects how societies structure expertise and structure work.

The contrast of crafts and professions goes back a long way. But crafts have historical
primacy. In pre-industrial society, selected youth – sons of yeomen and burgers – entered
adulthood in a craft, through apprenticeship, fulfilling designated rites of passage, learning the mysteries of a trade and internalizing its morals. They also accepted its forms
of hierarchy, reciprocity, inequality and the socially determined standards of quality of
work. And they had a sense of what constituted legitimate information, on which to base
decisions with respect to their work. Professions have done much the same.

A final possible way of rescuing the contrast is to express it in terms of a dualistic
model of control. Where manual technique predominates, the occupation is a craft, in
which direct control is exercised by insiders. Where abstract knowledge predominates, the
occupation is a profession, in which control is indirect through information, concepts,
linguistic practices, processes, licensing, ethics codes and other mechanisms, including
delegation of technical work to subsidiary occupations. The more abstract the knowledge
base the more elitist the profession.

However, there is still something missing. The middle ground was always as interesting,
just as the yeoman was an under-appreciated category in agrarian pre-capitalist society.
The middle ground of industrial society was that of the artisan and journeyman. Both
had their roots in the Middle Ages. The artisan is less prestigious than the craftsman
and artist, and the image suggests a combination of practical skills and manual arts.
Christopher Marlowe marvelled: 'O what a world of profit and delight . . . Is promis'd to
the studious artisan' (*Doctor Faustus*, [1604] 2001, p. 6). Samuel Johnson ([1751] 2003, p.
239) was no less effusive: 'The meanest artisan . . . contributes more to the accommodation of life, than the profound scholar'. Both the artisan and journeyman learn as they go
along, practising and cultivating a way of working life, skills without pretensions, a box
of tools with small wisdoms. For the 'common man', it was a worthy sort of life.

Professionalism has produced a mix of statutory and Voice regulation, especially as
most professions have access to government officials and can affect legislation. Indeed,
the legal system helped in protecting professions, allowing monopoly of certain activities,
payments and types of workplace and even control over the language and concepts to
be used in professions, as in accounting. This has involved legislative struggles, since the

legislature may grant statutory rights to some groups, blocking entry to them or imped-ing the emergence of alternative divisions of labour.

Professionalism is unstable because technological, administrative and organizational changes generate sub-professions. Once physiotherapy was part of general medicine; now there are not just physiotherapists but specialists dealing with different parts of the body, with different traditions and 'proven' techniques. Other professions have split into those deemed to require tertiary education and those deemed to require apprenticeship or on-the-job training.

The existence of occupational control reflects a tendency for occupations to evolve, splinter or die, and for them to be in conflict with firms oriented to production and profit. How they evolve is often the cause and consequence of tensions between the occupation and re-divisions of labour. Because large organizations predominated in the twentieth century, many forms of occupational solidarity were undermined, resulting in dilution of work content, 'deskilling' and/or occupational splintering. However, even within large organizations some occupations managed to retain some autonomy.

Professions control by subordinating other workers. But this is an unstable form of control, since subordinated groups may become essential for successful practice of the profession and can have leverage over super-ordinates. Subordination requires use of symbolic order – honorifics, uniforms, other symbols of authority, acts of exclusion and acts of coercion. There are heavy supervisory costs and ample sources of tension.

Tight control of practitioners can be expected to induce forms of resistance and revolt. An oppressed group may withdraw cooperation or reduce effort, curbing the dominant group's own productivity. But one cannot assume that it is the most oppressed who will revolt. Nor can we be sure what forms revolt will take, or what reactions to revolt will be taken by the professions.

What we do know is that the social and economic security of a profession can be upset by 'a revolution from below', as was the case of barristers in the UK, whose powerful position in the nineteenth century was disrupted by the emergence of solicitors. Such disruption is likely if a dominant occupation or profession exercises monopolistic powers and acquires rental income, high social status and other elitist privileges. In reaction to a revolt, some professions may delegate lower-level work, extending jurisdiction in order to preserve their core activities.

Although civic friendship and altruism are features of occupational communities, their practices have created invasions of other territories or jurisdictional attack, as Abbott (1988) put it. Invasion can go either way. An occupation may expand or contract in scope. Or a new group may emerge or enter the system by a 'clientele settlement'; the occupa-tion may ignore a client group, which is then served by para-professionals, who form an occupation demanding jurisdiction. Invasion has only been one conflictual device. We will deal with the other three – oppression, suppression and splintering – in Chapter 6. All are features of occupational development.

OCCUPATIONS AND THE STATE

The state is where the system of occupations takes shape. Historically, dominant groups have co-opted state power to give their occupation privileges and erode those of competing occupations. The state has also been the arena of 'occupational capitalism'. The dominant model of capital breeds and nurtures its 'professions' that also make up its servants. Thus, global capitalism gives precedence and elite privileges (and hence above-market-clearing incomes) to lawyers, accountants, financiers, MBA-holders, and so on. National capitalism gave precedence to engineers. Both models have also required their personal-problem-solving and adjustment professions (paramedics, psychiatrists, psychologists, care workers, social workers, social police) to deal with the stragglers and the protesters (social and individual, destructive and self-destructive).

A dominant occupation can co-opt state power, to erode the position of others. The state can also deny flexibility to some groups and keep out others, legislating to impose or legitimate knowledge required for belonging to a profession. The courts can impose penalties for contravening occupational rules. Legislation and state administration can dismantle protections built up by occupations or prevent them from emerging. And courts and administration may be used to impose organizations on occupations or restrain their powers.

In some countries, the state has moulded the occupational structure to a greater extent than elsewhere. In France, for example, some professions were formalized by legislation, which permitted costs of entry, purchase of office and so on. Some states have been more inclined to create occupations than others. This may mean that an occupation has a different character in different countries.

However, a theme of this book is that the relationship between the state and occupations has been converging. Underlying that relationship has been one crucial issue. In his 1988 study, Abbott depicted professional associations as *offensive*, seeking to extend a jurisdiction. But some have emerged as *defensive* bodies, to preserve a way of life under threat. Often they turn inward, to orchestrate bargaining between factions or to structure it to the advantage of a group in it. In all respects, one must ask whether the bargaining is an exercise in collusion to create a monopoly or a legitimate way of advancing social interest. This poses a problem for the state. Are occupational bodies 'workers' bargaining with capital, in which case they come under labour law? Or are they service suppliers akin to a cartel, in which case they come under commercial law and are subject to anti-trust?

OCCUPATIONS AND CITIZENSHIP

Citizenship is defined in terms of rights and entitlements provided by the state. Rights are best seen as claim, republican or constitutional rights, that is, commitments made to individuals and groups to be realized progressively. Behind any right, there should be an apparatus to define and move towards its realization, and there should be mechanisms to deal with abuses. A citizen is someone who has entitlement to the proclaimed right, be it social, economic or cultural.

Most of us think of human rights as universal and indivisible, so that everybody in society has an equal claim to them. Yet historically, rights have been granted to some types of people and not others. We may say, provisionally, that rights guaranteed for one group in society and not others are less defensible than those granted to larger groups, which are in turn less acceptable than those given to all members of society.

Throughout history, occupations and citizenship have almost toyed with each other.

Historically, many occupations have been denied citizenship status and thus denied protection, security, social status, Voice and legitimation. As with concepts of work, this has always produced silliness – and, as with work, each age has had its silliness that subsequent generations see as stupid. We are no better.

For the ancient Greeks, productive labour was equated with non-citizenship, the activity performed by slaves; this continued with feudal society. The mercantilists saw only agricultural labour as deserving of citizenship. In the eighteenth century, Kant must have spoken for many when claiming that those in services should be denied full citizenship. But only with the emergence of industrial capitalism did all so-called labour become equated with citizenship. The capacity for labour became a badge of citizenship.

In the nineteenth century, industrialized countries began to spawn occupations and a new labour aristocracy. Abbott called this the era of 'associational professionalism'; occupations were practised mainly in small-scale workplaces. Intra-occupational and inter-occupational relations remained largely personal. These groups had common claim rights on the state, including protection in times of crisis and a right to participate in the public domain. But those who did not belong to the honoured crafts and professions were excluded from deliberative governance, protection and mechanisms of redistribution.

Thus, historically, certain occupations have been granted rights not given to others. From a justice point of view, this is unacceptable. A society of occupational citizenship would ensure that every occupation was treated equally and given the same rights, and that everybody could join the occupation of their choice, if they had the capabilities.

The twentieth century gave employees a citizenship right to bargain collectively and backed that up with a shaft of 'labour rights', privileging those in wage labour. The quest for the future is to define social, economic and cultural rights that apply to all occupations in all statuses. As we shall see, this requires a change in the way we think about occupation and work in general.

CONCLUDING REFLECTIONS

We must rescue work from labour and reposition it so that all types of work are treated equally. Concepts matter; they affect the way we think about a subject. If we think of labour, we think of the firm, the sector and then the state. If we think of work, images of care and voluntary work are likely to come to mind as well. If we think of craft work, we think next of the occupation, then the community and then society. Similarly, if we treat employment in isolation from other forms of work, we easily lose sight of its social context.

Thinking of work in terms of occupations sets off a different train of thought than thinking in terms of sectors or industries, or employers and employees, or firms and employees. Yet most economic analysis and data refer to these dualisms almost exclusively. Study textbooks on labour economics allocated to students at almost any university or college, and occupations are taken as technologically or socially determined classifiers; often, they are used almost synonymously with industries. This is misleading.

Work that is occupational in character allows for rational decision-making. To be rational, one has to be able to direct oneself. This is part of full freedom. In labour markets people respond to prices and controllers, whereas in a true occupation people are motivated by dignity and morality. Ethical *mores* emerge through long-established traditions and through sociability, the culture of a craft and of a craft community. That cannot be enforced by the state (Taylor, 1984). This is why Voice regulation should be the main form of regulation for a work-based society and 'occupational citizenship'.

Finally, we need to recall a distinction the ancient Greeks made between 'leisure' and 'play'. The former is a purpose of work, the latter a form of relaxation, to help a person to be able to work and to labour. Leisure is 'almost-work'. The Greek idea of *schole* may be defined as creative non-work demanding effort and use of time. In leisure, *schole*, we should include the undervalued sphere of contemplation, the ability to be still and to reflect. In a market society, such stillness has no value and may be regarded as time wasted. In general, there is a danger that leisure will be crowded out of the range of time uses. Yet leisure, as distinct from play, is necessary if we are to develop our capabilities as human beings. Too often, the popular notion of capabilities and the related notion of functionings are interpreted just in terms of a capacity to obtain and perform jobs and augment 'human capital' or earning power. This belittles the idea of human development and leisure. In short, even if all will persist, we need an agenda that respects work and leisure rather than labour and play.

NOTES

1. Henceforth, all references are to this edition, and are marked by GT, followed by the page number.
2. Some analysts use the terms in the opposite way (Offe, 1985). I prefer to see 'labour' as activity and 'labour power' as the bundle of competencies and potential capacities that make up an individual human being. In common parlance, 'labour' is also used to mean the collective body of workers.
3. On the concepts of ownership and control, see Standing (2000).
4. Some receive less income than they earn, not because of taxes but because intermediaries control access and deduct some of it. Women are often impoverished in this manner.
5. A further disaggregation has been made elsewhere (Standing, 2002).
6. In this regard, the oldest profession is better called a craft.

APPENDIX

The distinction between labour and labour power was made famously by Karl Marx, albeit in a tantalizingly confusing way. In *The Economic and Philosophic Manuscripts of 1844* ([1844] 1976), he defined labour as 'active alienation'. He thus saw it as essential to abolish labour and replace it by free activity. Later, he saw labour as necessary, but argued that the labouring day should be shortened to create the basis for freedom.

Marx saw labour power as a primary commodity. A person has a multi-dimensional capacity to labour. A sympathetic reading is that only in a market society (capitalism) is a person's capabilities conceived in terms of potential capacity to labour for exchange value (wages). We could extract the idea from its context by saying that a person has 'work power', that is, multiple capabilities, developed or undeveloped, to work in a range of activities. This would reconcile Marx's conception with his definition of labour power as 'the aggregate of those mental and physical capabilities existing in a human being, which he exercises whenever he produces a use-value of any description' (Marx [1867] 1967, p. 167).

One can extend this by asserting that human capabilities include more than what is regarded as 'skill' in the technical sense of that over-used word. They include emotional, attitudinal and personality traits that determine performance. This is crucial in service work, in which determining between good and bad may depend more on intangible characteristics than on physical or mental skills.

While labour power is the capacity to perform labour, the latter Marx called the 'living existence' of labour power and its 'temporary manifestation'. From a worker's bundle of capabilities the 'capitalist' demands some in the performance of labour. This will have an effect on labour power, in that non-performance, non-development or non-maintenance of other capacities will have a corrosive effect. If one is required to fill working time with labour, little energy will be available for other activities. In the same Marxisant spirit, one could add that capital needs labour power, a population prepared to labour in a disciplined way. Thus, Marx was correct in describing labour power – people with the double freedom, of being 'free' of the means of production and 'free' to supply labour – as a primary commodity. One may have capacity to work in any number of ways, but if one is not prepared to supply time for wages, to perform labour, one is scarcely a commodity. And even if one is prepared to work for wages, it is not labour power that is bought and sold. Some of our capacities are likely to have no exchange value, even if we regard them highly. This is consistent with Marx's statement that 'the activity of labour power' is 'labour'.

Some Marxists are confusing in arguing that workers sell their abilities, which may have been a reasonable way of looking at how workers existed in Marx's time, where most workers were reduced to ignorance and brute application of truncated capacities. Adding to that confusion, they have accepted the view that if labour power is left outside the labour process, it deteriorates. But human capacities may deteriorate precisely because one set of them is used intensively for a prolonged period. Being outside the labour market may give scope for development or recuperation of human capabilities. It may lead to a deterioration of some capacities and to a deterioration of discipline needed to be a reliable worker. But that is not the same, or necessarily true.

This leads us to the idea of potential that is integral to labour power. It has several meanings. Potential as latent is probably infinite, in what we could do. There is more than whimsy in the oft-expressed view of a child, 'What she could do if only . . .!' One could say that we are never what we could be. Then there is the potential that means capacities are developed, but the individual is undecided or unwilling to provide them, perhaps on the terms available. Another potential is that which cannot be realized or exercised because of other obligations or attractions. To some extent, actual activities are shaped by external forces. One could even say, impertinently to Descartes, 'I exist, therefore I am not'. We have to accept the social parameters confronting us, unless they can be changed through collective action, or unless we act to reject them at high personal cost.

In all these respects, labour power is potential capabilities. It is tempting to cut through the confusion by suggesting that the idea we are trying to express should be called 'capability power' or 'capability being', the latter implying an attempt to escape the aggressive, competitive connotation of power as force. The attraction of capability power lies in its implied assertion of independence.

Whether one uses the term labour power or capability power, neither is a synonym for 'human capital', a concept that emphasizes capabilities that have a marketable return and is profoundly alienating. Human capital is linked to a fourth notion of potential, the potential to labour effectively within a market society. This varies. A tribesman, nomad or peasant will react in dismay at a request to labour in a mine, factory or office. Someone liberated from years of doing such labour is likely to develop a barrier to any idea of returning to it. One is inclined to respect that lack of 'potential' as an expression of freedom. The chains are not for us!

At the other extreme, there are those habituated to the routines of labour activity or to the parameters to the point of feeling insecure at the prospect of losing the comforters. In a market society, the authorities try to induce enough people to develop this 'potential'. They do so in all sorts of ways. A proposal to extend compulsory schooling from age 16 to 18 invites us to imagine that this is about giving opportunity for more learning. How can the citizenry be sure it is not more about preparing the young for the fourth form of 'potential', rather than about developing other forms?

2. Fictitious decommodification: the failure of industrial citizenship

INTRODUCTION

Polanyi's Great Transformation was a story about the initial thrust of industrial capitalism, in which the spread of market mechanisms and the associated insecurities were followed by state reactions – a 'double movement' – that tried to prevent market forces becoming socially destructive. Roughly speaking, the disembedded phase lasted into the early twentieth century, whereas the embedded phase occurred in the three decades following the Second World War.

The essence of the Transformation was that mechanisms of protection, regulation and redistribution were used to embed the economy in society. It was a very specific form of embeddedness, in which the main policies and institutions focused on labour, not work or wider notions of living and citizenship. It deserves to be called a period of 'fictitious decommodification', since most of the social rights advanced were made dependent on performing labour or the demonstrated willingness to do so.

SOCIAL DEMOCRACY: LABOUR EMBEDDED

Polanyi's Transformation was about the creation of *national* markets, for capital and labour. He saw the destabilizing influence of finance as the primary problem, and had witnessed the hubris of financial markets in the 1920s. He foresaw a post-1945 world as consisting of national economic systems coexisting via managed inter-regional exchanges (Polanyi, 1945). This was based on 'relational capitalism', in which stability was preserved by long-term relationships between firms and banks. Potentially destabilizing capital mobility was restricted. There was control over holdings of foreign exchange, ceilings on interest rates, no interest paid on demand deposits and in the USA a separation of commercial and investment banking under the Glass-Steagall Act.

As for labour, national labour markets emerged in the nineteenth century, first in Britain and then elsewhere, intensifying inequality and insecurity, and culminating in the Great Depression. As an optimist, Polanyi believed that a coalition of interests would eventually redress the worst forms of inequality by developing appropriate national institutions and policies. This was his 'double movement'.

Although one can trace fictitious labour decommodification to the nineteenth century, with the UK Factory Acts, Bismarck's efforts to tie the middle class to the Prussian state and experiments in social insurance elsewhere, the main advance came between the 1940s and 1960s as variants of the welfare state were constructed.

The nineteenth century was the first period of proletarianization, as millions became industrial employees in full-time jobs. It also saw the emergence of professions, mostly resistant to proletarianization. The early twentieth century saw more generalized proletarianization. It also ushered in a period of partial decommodification, with a shift from money wages to enterprise benefits, particularly in the USA with its welfare paternalism and company towns but also in some other countries.

The period may have entrenched wage labour, but a feature was bureaucratic employment in large corporations. Polanyi did not dwell on the bureaucratic revolution; it reflected the norm of large-scale mass production and helped to embed it in society. But the growth of bureaucracy subjected more workers to subordinated employment, including many 'white-collar' clerical and technical workers.

It was after 1945 that industrial citizenship was cemented around the values of labour. This was epitomized by the view of one influential social thinker, T.H. Marshall; he saw citizenship as involving rights and duties, the 'essential duty' to work being one of them, along with the duty 'to put one's heart into one's job' (Marshall, 1950, p. 46). It was a prescription for subordination. Neither state socialism nor welfare states honoured the right to work as 'the right to follow the occupation of one's choice in the place of one's choice'. The labourist model and labour-based social security made sure of that.

The period in which welfare state capitalism flourished did involve partial decommodification of *male* labour and the advance of industrial citizenship, a system of entitlements based on the norm of industrial labour. But it was not decommodification of labour power, for workers were actually made *more* dependent on the performance of labour for their welfare and social status.

Gradually, welfare state paternalism evolved as state benefits rose as a share of social income. Labour-based citizenship 'rights' advanced, based on social insurance, family benefits and access to public social services. And there was what might be called corporate citizenship rights, epitomized by the 'standard employment relationship' and job-security unionism. The future of work, as labour, was assured. Or so it seemed.

THE GREAT TRANSFORMATION'S INTERNATIONAL MODEL

Polanyi's imagery was of industrial capitalism purged of its market excesses, within national borders. National capitalism needed rules for regulating the market, to curb free riders and opportunistic behaviour that would threaten its stability. The rogues of finance were to be held in check, and exploitation of workers had to be moderated.

An aspect of the evolution of industrial citizenship was the role played by the International Labour Organization (ILO), which advanced an agenda of social rights, not economic rights. These were in vogue when it was set up, having been first pronounced in the Constitutions of Mexico in 1917, Russia in 1918 and the Weimar Republic in 1919. The ILO was geared to labourism, with a model of industrial unions rather than craft unions or cooperatives in the forefront of its thinking.

Polanyi saw the ILO as one of the 'permanent institutions' of the Great Transformation. Its primary role was to set international standards, taking labour out of trade. But although it was committed to common standards, its norms were couched in terms that allowed national variations of interpretation. Governments could select standards they wished to ratify and ignore those that were inconvenient. Although the most egregious disregard for basic principles could be criticized, the Organization was not required to favour a particular form of state.

Polanyi recognized that the ILO was set up 'to equalise conditions of competition among the nations so that trade might be liberated without danger to standards of living' (GT, pp. 27–8). But in reality this only applied to countries competing in industrial goods and services, not between industrialized and underdeveloped countries. If countries that were potential competitors provided firms and workers with similar subsidies and regulations, this 'equalized competition' and was acceptable. But this deal hindered 'market entry' by the 'colonized' parts of the world. It was a means of locking in the international division of labour to the advantage of affluent capitalist countries.

A quarter of a century after it was set up, the ILO's leading members issued the Philadelphia Declaration, with its one-line paragraph: 'Labour is not a commodity'. It was a clarion call to take into the post-war era. By spreading labour standards around the world, entrenching 'tripartism' and helping 'backward' countries to introduce labour legislation along the lines developed in 'advanced' countries, it represented an institutional device to reduce the commodity character of labour. Twenty-five years later the ILO received the Nobel Peace Prize for its efforts. Remarkably, this accolade coincided with the zenith of labour decommodification around the world. Macroeconomic smugness was everywhere, the consensual view being that Keynesianism meant permanent 'full employment' and a steady reduction in labour-based inequalities.

The ILO's contribution to fictitious decommodification was impressive. By the end of the twentieth century, it had produced 188 conventions and 199 recommendations covering a wide range of labour matters. Almost every country joined. If a country ratified any convention it committed itself to binding obligations that could be investigated if a protest procedure was properly instigated by trades unions or employer organizations. The conventions and non-binding recommendations constituted a voluntary framework for national labour market regulation. Without saying it, the ILO stood for a model of national welfare capitalism, in which the standard employment relationship was the presumed norm. Employees were to be treated decently in return for accepting the employers' 'right to manage' and their 'right' to make and retain profits. Although all this made for a tense relationship with communist countries, above all the ILO stood for tripartism, espousing organized collective bargaining at national and sectoral levels between employers and employees mediated by government agencies.

From the outset the ILO largely limited itself to setting the parameters of employer–employee relationships. After 1945, its convention setting accelerated, and what was excluded was as significant as what was included. Its defining instruments were two conventions relating to collective bargaining and a particular form of 'freedom of association', that of employees in their bargaining with employers; a convention on social security (No. 102 of 1952), which will be considered later; a convention (No. 111 of 1958) on discrimination in employment; various conventions and recommendations on occupational health and safety; and late in the period of fictitious decommodification an Employment Policy Convention (No. 122 of 1964) by which ratifying countries committed themselves to 'full, productive and freely chosen employment'. In this last, the organization over-reached itself.

The ILO model hinged on labour-based collective bargaining between 'capital' and 'labour', oriented to large-scale workplaces. It favoured a particular form of freedom of association, based on labour. It fostered labour inspection, oriented to fixed workplaces, and labour law, which focused on disputes between employers and employees, centred on procedural justice. It encouraged conciliation, mediation and arbitration procedures and institutions concerned with employer–employee relations, mainly for unionized employees. It became a proponent of anti-discrimination measures, which focused on gender issues and employment equity, not equality. It supported labour-based social insurance and means-tested social assistance. And it promoted the collection of labour statistics that ignored work that was not labour. The ILO espoused a complete model of labourism.

Meanwhile, it gave no attention to occupations, little to migration and regarded non-regular labour as a throwback to be ended as soon as possible. As for work that was not labour, such as care, it was nowhere to be seen.

THE FIRM AND WORKPLACE UNDER INDUSTRIAL CITIZENSHIP

In the twentieth century, the organization of labour was dominated by three 'isms' – Fordism, Taylorism and Toyotism – although the last came right at the end of the period of industrial citizenship. They are all in disarray now, but for several decades each was eulogized or feared.

Fordism was about mass production and mass consumption. Taylorism was a management method suitable for a Ford motor company mass producing standardized commodities. Its defining feature was 'scientific management', suggesting that the techniques followed natural laws of time and motion. It was about direct control by supervisors over those performing labour, a particular form of control in which employees were expected to execute what management and engineers thought. This separation of concept from execution, memorably analysed by Braverman (1974), was coupled with a feature so crucial in the forging of the working class in Britain, namely control by the clock (Thompson, 1967, 1968). Labour was not only to be monotonous and repetitive but also to be performed in discrete blocks of time. Although there were attempts to 'humanize' the engineering model, such as the 'Hawthorne experiments', it was left to the Japanese to take labour control and organization to the next stage in what came to be called Toyotism.

Drawing on the corporate paternalism of *oyabunkobun* (roughly, simulated kinship), Toyotism took time control to a more sophisticated level, by such devices as the just-in-time inventory system (Dore, 1973; Littler, 1982). It was suited to a working class and salariat attuned to Confucian dictates of conformity and respect for elders and superiors, and to a society resigned to subordination following the traumatizing defeat in the Second World War. A feature that hinted at the Global Transformation that was to follow the breakdown of Polanyi's Transformation was that Toyotism suited a more volatile economy and could be adapted more easily to consumer demand. Its adoption by Japan and then by the newly industrializing countries (NICs) helped make their manufacturing goods competitive with those produced in the industrialized countries and precipitated stirrings of unease with the labourist model of those countries.

Whether as Taylorism or Toyotism, the disciplinary control system restricted the agency of workers. If one accepts that agency is a defining attribute of decommodification, then the production regime was profoundly commodifying. It was designed to take labour out of the market in the sense of taking workers into long-term, controlled labour relationships. Employees were expected to follow rules, and 'work to rule', which became a limited weapon used by unions in their dependency-induced collective bargaining.

The Fordist/Taylorist model acquired labour power for blocks of time, buying it for a fixed working day, for a fixed number of 'years of service'. 'Company man' was in a gilded cage, civil servants and lower-level professionals were fearful of causing offence to superiors, while the bulk of the labour force were cowed by their families who depended on them to stay in jobs. Employees embraced labour security in return for accepting subordination. The quest for dependable conformity was a feature of the era.

Besides the control over time and labour intensity, industrial citizenship was marked by its emphasis on a fixed workplace, albeit conceptualized at several levels – the 'factory floor', 'plant', 'office' or 'corporation'. The separation of the economic realm, the workplace, from the household, or family, was articulated early by Weber, who depicted the former as based on scientific and rational criteria and the latter on affective and personal criteria. This normative view coloured social and labour policy. Such was the desired separation that industrial home work was outlawed in the USA in the 1930s.

The idea of stable fixed workplaces facilitated a particular labour politics, in which freedom was neglected. The trade union did not want freedom for workers; it wanted them dependent on it for their well-being and labour security. The employer did not want freedom for workers either, wanting dependable and predictable labour; this meant granting employees labour security while they lobbied government for macroeconomic stability. Workers, as employees, wanted security, but in return had to give up claims to freedom. To idealize all this as labour decommodification is faintly ridiculous. For one thing, agency was not so much transformed into a representative set of institutions as surrendered in dependent labour.

The industrial labour model emphasized obedience, the clock, subordination and strict limits on acceptable behaviour in the workplace. It was associated with manufacturing and 'material production', even though the extent of service or tertiary labour, 'immaterial labour', was growing. With services, the industrial forms of disciplinary controls were harder to apply and had to be complemented by controls exercised from outside the workplace. This was scarcely seen at the time. Policy development and management practices were shaped by the industrial image and the challenge of bureaucracy. The clock and the calendar were perfect for the job. Or so it seemed.

THE MIXED ECONOMY – PUBLIC OWNERSHIP

Part of the fictitious decommodification came via public ownership of utilities, particularly those with network characteristics where national integration made economic as well as social sense – roads, railways, water, electricity, gas, and so on. Once nationalized, these became subsidized services, paid for from direct taxation. They favoured neo-corporatist governance, with collective bargaining, unionization and full-time jobs with strong employment security and other forms of labour security.

As the social democratic model also presumed that government would take responsibility for maintaining 'full employment', the public sector became employer of last resort. It also practised a particular form of labour security, committing governments to employment security and setting procedural standards for the rest of the economy. Consequently, the public sector share of total employment rose and its bureaucratic practices became increasingly rigid. This was to be a factor in the undoing of the model, since burgeoning public employment absorbed a rising share of public spending.

LABOUR SECURITY

During this whole period, the social democrats setting the political agenda advanced a model of labour-based security. Like most models, it contained structural inequalities, notably in its treatment of women and their work. Underlying it was an uneasy social compact in which, in return for bearing the risks, the owners of capital received a disproportionate share of the economic surplus and retained the right to manage, while workers were provided with labour-related securities. The era of welfare state capitalism – pre-globalization – saw the advance of seven forms of labour security linked to performance of labour or the willingness to perform it (Box 2.1).

Primacy was given to labour market security, particularly between 1945 and 1973,

---

BOX 2.1   THE SEVEN FORMS OF LABOUR SECURITY

Labour market security – adequate income-earning opportunities; at the macro-level, this is epitomized by a government commitment to 'full employment'

Employment security – protection against arbitrary dismissal, regulations on hiring and firing, imposition of costs on employers for failing to adhere to rules, and so on

Job security – ability and opportunity to retain a niche in employment, plus barriers to skill dilution, and opportunities for 'upward' mobility in terms of status and income

Work security – protection against accidents and illness at work, through, for example, safety and health regulations, and limits on working time, unsociable hours and night work for women, as well as compensation for mishaps

Skill reproduction security – opportunity to gain skills, through apprenticeships, employment training, and so on, as well as opportunity to make use of competencies

Income security – assurance of an adequate income, protected through, for example, minimum wage machinery, wage indexation, comprehensive social security, progressive taxation to reduce inequality and supplement low incomes

Representation security – possessing a collective voice in the labour market, through, for example, independent trade unions, with a right to strike

---

when Keynesianism was unquestioned by mainstream policymakers, and 'full employment' meant that most men between the ages of 16 and 65 were in employment and most women were outside the labour force, doing work not counted as work. It was presumed that most men would leave school as teenagers and remain in unionized full-time employment until they left to spend a short period of retirement, supported by a modest pension and transfers from their offspring.

Meanwhile, women would be family dependants, sporadically acting as secondary wage workers while doing 'housework'. Social security was designed primarily to provide compensation for contingency risks incurred in labouring. Governments, through acceptance of international standards, took labour out of international competition, which was essential to enable the gradual shift to state and enterprise benefits.

Part of the social arrangement was employment security, which applied mainly to men in industrial jobs. The process can be depicted as labour decommodification, but it was unreal. There was inegalitarian decasualization in that working-class *men* were provided with stable jobs. As female labour force participation rates rose, and as more women became attached to the labour market, they too obtained more employment security. But it remained a dualistic model, in which 'company men' and secondary women workers were regarded as norms.

Employment security involved a presumption that a man would stay a full-time employee in a firm for most of his adult life. It never worked out that way for many, but this was the norm. It almost amounted to an implicit 'social compact'. In some countries, notably the USA, it went to the point that companies laid off employees in a recession rather than make them redundant. Employees waited until business picked up and expected to return to their jobs. This concealed part of cyclical unemployment, while giving the appearance of employment security, and helped in the process of proletarianization.

Employees had reason to be loyal to their enterprise, being dependent on it for long-term employment and thereby entitled to a growing range of benefits, from the firm and the state. As unions played a role in this, it gave them a status as security providers. But the system was largely reserved for a privileged group, men in full-time jobs. Elderly male commentators who refer to the period with misty eyes as a 'Golden Age' should be reminded of that.

THE 'RIGHT TO WORK' UNDER LABOURISM

For two centuries, there has been earnest debate about the existence of a right to work. It has blended with concerns over what constitutes citizenship and the notion of a right to practise what work one pleases. Attempts to define it have fallen into confusion; thus, Marshall (1950), when he set out in the late 1940s to define social rights, ended up saying that citizens had a duty to labour.

The 'right to work' has always been coloured by paternalism, which is why it has been so promoted by Catholics. Most famously, Pope Leo XIII, a progressive paternalist, pushed it in his *Rerum Novarum* (The Condition of Labour) of 1891, although this saw work ideally as embedded in medieval guilds. Subsequently, the right to work was interpreted as a right to employment, as epitomized in the ILO's Employment Policy Convention of 1964. At that point, labourism had moved from the dominant cry of progressives for the 'rights of labour' to a comfort zone where they were claiming the right to labour, the right to have a job. It was a peculiar sort of right, to ask to be put in a subordinated position and to have one's work dictated by another. But it was better than being unemployed and impoverished, as was the case for millions in the 1930s.

Debate around the right to work took a different course in the USA. In the country's founding period, the ideal citizen was a landholding head of household. Other household members, including servants and slaves, were disqualified from citizenship by their dependency on 'the master'. Wage earners were also non-citizens (Forbath, 1985). In the nineteenth century, republican Americans likened wage labour to slavery and extolled 'free labour' in terms of self-ownership and the right to make contracts to sell one's labour. Early radical workers realized that, without ownership of productive property, the act of supplying labour could not be free. But after abolition of slavery, with adoption of the Fourteenth Amendment, the notion of free labour lost its attachment to property ownership, becoming defined by 'liberty of contract' – the right to sell one's labour and to buy the labour of others, determined by the market, free from state interference. This set the tone for future debate. Under the 'due process' clauses of the Fifth and Fourteenth Amendments, the Supreme Court could rule that interference with liberty of contract was to deprive both employers and employees of liberty without due process, unless it meant protecting public health and safety (Forbath, 1985; Estlund, 2002).

The development of US law created the basis of labour commodification. It was to be reiterated in the famous case of *Lochner* v. *New York* of 1905. This struck down a state law establishing maximum hours for wage-earning bakers on the grounds that it violated liberty of contract. The ruling ushered in the Lochner era, which lasted from 1905 until 1937, during which state and federal courts invalidated all efforts by unions and progressive politicians to protect workers – laws on minimum wages, maximum hours, legitimizing union activity, prohibiting the discharge of workers on grounds of union activity, and so on. All were dismissed as unlawful interference with the rights of employers and employees to buy and sell labour, their right to work. This was as close to labour commodification as imaginable in a modern society.

The Lochner era ended with the New Deal, when a progressive majority on the Supreme Court repudiated the Constitutional liberty of contract and enabled the legislature to set laws relating to economic matters without deference to the Constitution. The major legislative outcomes were the National Labor Relations Act (NLRA), which protected union representation, and the Fair Labor Standards Act, which established minimum wages and maximum hours in most of the private labour market, thereby protecting employees.

Freedom of association was found to be protected under the First Amendment to the Constitution in Supreme Court cases in 1939 and 1940. But juridical action declined after that. In 1947, the Taft-Hartley amendments to the NLRA banned some labour activities, and thereafter Congress set labour regulations as part of economic activity, beyond constitutional scrutiny. With unions and employers still powerful enough to influence Congress, further labour law reform was ruled out.

Other countries paid lip service to the right to work by claiming they were preserving 'full employment', which was a sham because many women were excluded. But there were efforts to formalize a commitment (Standing, 2002). Suffice it to give one example. Steered by its US occupiers after 1945, Japan introduced a right to choose an occupation in Article 22 of its new Constitution. This actually guaranteed no more than a right to choose an employer and an employer's right to do business. The right to work was an obligation to take employment. Article 27, para.1, of Japan's Constitution states: 'All people shall have the right to work and the obligation to work'. This led to a slew of labour legislation – the Employment Security Law (1947), the Unemployment Insurance Law (1947), the Disabled Persons' Employment Promotion Law (1960), the Employment Measures Law (1966), the Human Resources Development Promotion Law (1969), the Law Concerning Stabilization of Employment of Older Persons (1971) and the Employment Insurance Law (1974). In addition, Japan's unfair labour practices system was modelled on the US Wagner Act of 1935. Thus, Japan epitomized labourism. Neither there nor anywhere else was the right to work interpreted in terms of doing *any* form of work or the right to practise an *occupation*.

The era of fictitious labour decommodification coincided with the evolution of an international discourse on human rights. The Universal Declaration of Human Rights in 1948 came after the ILO's Philadelphia Declaration, and was followed by regional human rights declarations and by the 1966 International Covenant on Economic, Social and Cultural Rights. This gave most attention to work and deserves to be cited. Article 6 of the Covenant states:

> The States parties to the Covenant recognize the right to work, which includes the right of everyone to the opportunity to gain his living by work, which he freely chooses or accepts, and will take appropriate steps to safeguard his rights.

There is much one could say about this declamation, mostly critical. But its historical timing is significant, coming late in the era of fictitious decommodification, just after the ILO adopted its Employment Policy Convention. The ILO itself did not come to grips with the contradictions in the convention. In their reviews of reports on employment and unemployment by countries that had ratified it, ILO staff focused on what was happening to official unemployment rates. In the late 1960s rates were mostly low, so this was an easy job, given the way the convention was interpreted and the narrow and sexist way that unemployment was measured. In any case, ILO conventions were guidelines for national labour systems. Work was interpreted as synonymous with employment, and workers as synonymous with employees. This omitted many working on their own account and left out care work altogether. The notion of 'freely chosen' was interpreted as condemnation of pre-capitalist forms of labour, notably slavery, bonded labour, forced labour and 'child labour'. Later, the focus shifted to combating 'discrimination' in employment. But at all times the idea of 'freely chosen' was narrowly interpreted to mean absence of physical coercion. The lack of debate on what constituted 'freely chosen' activity allowed the quiet growth of fiscal incentives and sanctions to push people into subordinated employment. The right to work as a freedom right was simply not considered.

THE GENDERED NATURE OF INDUSTRIAL CITIZENSHIP

The most striking feature of the embedded phase of the Great Transformation was the way policymakers treated women, and then how social democratic analysts later mythified it as a 'Golden Age of full employment'.

The rot started early. Statistical measurement of unemployment began in 1878 in

Massachusetts. Carroll Wright, who went on to become the first director of the US Bureau of Labor Statistics and to set statistical standards for the world, decided to measure unemployment by counting only men who 'really wanted employment'. This approach was then used for censuses and labour force surveys everywhere. Although the technique has been refined over the years, and although women were later included, there has always been a tendency to omit 'discouraged workers'. The unemployment rate became an artefact to be manipulated. But the outstanding feature was the concealment of women as working citizens.

Women were also excluded from the inner circles of trade unions, if not excluded as members altogether. In employment, they were commonly excluded from competitions for promotion and from training schemes. The paternalistic protection afforded women through restrictions on night work and working time was used to discriminate against them. And the family benefits some received for being outside the labour force acted as a poverty trap, given the low wages they could expect if they took jobs. If women became unemployed they rarely obtained unemployment benefits because they had not accumulated enough contributions. In the USA, most states excluded pregnant women, mothers with young children and those obliged to move to keep their families together. With conventional notions of 'fairness', men and women had different kinds of social 'rights'.

Industrial citizenship left women as secondary labourers, mostly not entitled to social security benefits. Many were decommodified by economic marginalization, leaving them subject to male domination. While men were paid a 'family wage', designed to cover the basic needs of their immediate family, women were expected to become wives and mothers who had to be protected and thus restricted in the activities they could do. Above all, the care work women mainly did was excluded from economic respect.

Highlighting the sexism of the period, women's share of the professions was extremely low. In some cases it regressed, as in medicine in the USA, where the number of female students fell (Walsh, 1977). In the French legal profession, women were largely excluded in the post-war period (Krause, 1996, p. 151). In West Germany, women made up a tiny share of the legal profession between the 1930s and 1970s, and in 1972 comprised only 5 per cent of the total (Blankenberg and Schultz, 1988). And everywhere women in the professions were disproportionately in wage employment, leading a process of proletarianization.

So, industrial citizenship was about sexual inequality, with 'social rights' granted to some men, those in stable wage labour, and very few women. It was an odd sort of citizenship.

INDUSTRIAL CITIZENSHIP AND SOCIAL INCOME

As governments and the ILO were shaping national labour markets, industrial citizenship evolved. Because the Transformation was about national markets, variants of the model of fictitious decommodification could be accommodated. The factors influencing these variants are mostly beyond our concern; they include 'legal origins', class structure and sectoral patterns of production and employment. The point is that, with labour costs taken out of international trade, variants of capitalism and welfare states could coexist without pressure to converge because the international division of labour and the trading system did not pit one against another.

Even so the relevant interests had to abide by common rules. Once developing countries, with their lower wage and non-wage labour costs, began to be major export-ers of manufactured goods and magnets for foreign direct investment, the cosy model of national capitalism, in its embedded welfare state mould, could not survive. This was to come about in the 1970s.

Prior to that, industrial citizenship based on the standard employment relationship proceeded smoothly. Symptomatic was the way labour contracts were moulded. For instance, by the 1950s, US firms were locking employees into long-term employment through COLA (Cost of Living Adjustment) contracts that also tied pay increases to productivity growth, implying that unions accepted the distribution of surplus. COLA contracts led to a decline in union pressure for state benefits, which helps to explain why US welfare capitalism involved a rise in enterprise benefits relative to state benefits and wages, whereas in Europe state benefits rose relative to wages and to enterprise benefits (Lichtenstein, 1989).

The decommodification was fictitious because what appeared to be social rights were actually only entitlements, conditional on a certain range of experience and behaviour. If an employee laboured well, he would have 'cradle-to-grave' or 'womb-to-tomb' benefits and access to social services. If not, trouble. The Swedes were the first to develop the 'workfare' state; social democrats have turned a blind eye to that.

The fictitious decommodification was global, although in industrializing countries commodification occurred at the same time. While millions became migrant labourers, a few, mostly civil servants, were provided with a social income package that was a copy of the norm for comparable employees in rich countries. The defining feature was that the state and capital weakened the link between the performance of labour and the money wage. It is scarcely an exaggeration to state that, to receive a salary or wage, a person had to turn up to a workplace (or have an acceptable excuse for not doing even that). Whether he then worked above or below the norm made only a small difference to his social income.

This was an attempt to make labour something it could never be, a fictitious commod-ity. It was 'bought', but the price, the wage, was not a reflection of the service provided, or of the cost to the employer, let alone the income of the employee. Demonetization weakened the incentive to labour and distorted the market mechanisms needed for effi-cient resource allocation. But the labour-based welfare state, paradoxically, commodified labour power by making more people dependent for their welfare on being in a labour status.

If decommodification is defined as non-reliance on market mechanisms, then in both welfare state capitalism and state socialism there were moves in that direction, with a 'withering of the wage' and a shift to enterprise and state benefits and services. But labour decommodification should be defined more broadly than Esping-Andersen did in his much-quoted book. He defined it as 'the degree to which individuals, or families, can uphold a socially acceptable standard of living independently of market participation' (Esping-Andersen, 1990, p. 37). He said there had been widespread decommodification. But the fact is that participation in the labour market was increasingly required to obtain a socially acceptable standard of living.

Whether under state socialism or welfare state capitalism there was still proletarianiza-tion, with more and more people locked into full-time wage labour. It was partly because labour decommodification went furthest in the Soviet Union that the system ground to a halt in the 1980s, when workers joked, 'They pretend to pay us, we pretend to work'. The state decommodifies labour at its peril.

The message to workers qua employees everywhere was clear. If you were committed and loyal to the employing enterprise and to your trade union, you would receive labour entitlements, including a defined-benefit pension, medical leave and labour reproduction benefits (paid maternity leave, child benefits, and so on). It was a sort of decommodification but it was not freedom.

The main changes in the distributional pattern during this period were clear (Standing, 2002). In terms of social income, as defined in Chapter 1, wages shrank as a share of the total and, in most societies, state benefits and enterprise benefits rose. So, labour was partially decommodified while labour power was commodified. Workers had to adhere to the standard employment relationship, which was made into decent labour. It was better than what had gone beforehand but it was not truly decommodifying.

The regulatory structure also shaped the fictitious decommodification. In the middle decades of the century statutory regulations put a downward limit to forms of exploitation and oppression and strengthened neo-corporatist institutions that helped raise living standards of employees and their families. Welfare state analysts such as Korpi (1983) and Stephens (1979) have emphasized the role of 'organized labour', arguing that the more workers (employees) were in unions, the greater the tendency for the welfare state to be 'universalistic' and oriented to 'social solidarity'. But these terms were not as all-embracing as they seemed.

'Universalistic' meant covering the needs of formal employees. The needs of other workers were not given anything like the same priority. Much the same could be said about 'social solidarity'. It was primarily a matter of solidaristic reciprocities between employees in the 'standard employment relationship', not between them and other workers or within occupational communities. There was also a tendency for the benefit system to favour the middle class (Goodwin and Le Grand, 1987).

Nevertheless, this was the main way by which market mechanisms were curbed, performing a role the guilds had played in the mercantilist system (GT, pp. 73–4). Industrial unions had their moment and, given their history, it was scarcely surprising that they missed their chance to be in the vanguard of a progressive agenda for freedom for workers pursuing occupations.

In terms of social protection, the dominant image was 'social insurance' – ex post compensation for contingency risks such as sickness or unemployment. With social insurance, contributions are paid into a pool from which those in sudden need are compensated, while others cross-subsidize their fellow citizens. The principle is familiar enough and for a while it seemed to be the future.

Unemployment insurance was expected to spread across the world to cover a growing proportion of the unemployed. Pay-as-you-go pensions were seen as decommodifying, because they were based on inter-generational employee solidarity, each generation paying for the pensions of the preceding one. Even company pension plans could be construed as decommodifying in that they constituted part of the social income (enterprise benefits) but not part of the wage. But by locking employees into a dependent relationship, inducing pliability and job commitment, they were a mechanism of control.

State benefits had system-locking qualities, rewarding labour attachment and discouraging other forms of work. Employees and their families were protected from income insecurity by subsidies on wage goods and by state benefits paid from employment-based contributions and taxes. Progressive income tax on employment income and other direct taxes limited the income of high earners.

In brief, socioeconomic security was developed for those who performed labour and their 'dependants'. It was a system of redistribution based on fiscal policy, unionization and centralized collective bargaining to keep wage differentials in check, and a system of social protection based on contributions from employment. Echoing Polanyi's use of the term, it was a Fool's Paradise. As the process went from one twist of fictitious decommodification to the next, monetary incentives to labour dried up, markets became distorted, subsidies grew, a growing share of jobs were in the public sector, more women stopped being secondary workers (making the fiction of 'full employment' less credible), labour market rigidities multiplied, social tensions became chronic. It could not last.

Meanwhile, fiscal policy was expected to reduce inequality, which was essential to embed the economy in society. The appropriate way in closed industrial economies was direct taxation, with taxes used to pay for the extension of social services and entitlements. Under labourism, redistribution could not come from the system of social protection, although employees gained relative to those outside employment. The main motors for reducing income inequality were capital taxation, income tax and subsidies on goods and services consumed by workers and low-income communities.

However, it became steadily harder for fiscal policy to reduce inequality. Reliance on progressive income taxes pushed marginal tax rates higher and higher. They became a disincentive to labour or to invest. Subsidies encouraged inefficient use of goods and services being subsidized. And the absorption of more of the potentially unemployed in public employment meant an increasingly onerous tax burden. All this could be sustained in a closed system of national mixed market economies. But it could not last if the market economy became global.

THE LIMITS OF LABOUR REGULATION

Labour law became a pillar of the fictitious decommodification. It proceeded on the presumption that workers exist as employees, needing protection against exploitation and oppression by their 'masters', the employers, while being expected to internalize a position of subordination. The terminology often gave the game away. Entitlement to pensions and other benefits depended on what were called 'years of service'. This is a term of subordination, not freedom. Similarly, 'fairness' had to be legislated and upheld by labour courts, or their equivalents such as labour tribunals and arbitration and conciliation agencies.

Labour law hinged on the notions of employee and employer. As it sought to protect the employee, it had to define this category quite carefully, which was usually done in a precise and dualistic way. For example, the Canadian Labour Code, a model of its kind, defines an employee as 'any person employed by an employer and includes a dependent contractor and a private constable, but does not include a person who performs management functions or is employed in a confidential capacity in matters relating to industrial relations'.

This combines a notion of employment status with one of class – an employee is not someone who is in control. In the Canadian case, as in others, employee status is also determined by legal tests – a business integration or organization test, an economic realities test, a test to determine whether the individual controls the performance of his labour, a test of whether he owns his tools, a test of whether he has a possibility of receiving profit and a test of whether he has a risk of loss (Fudge and Vosko, 2001). The key in the Code is thus subordination, being under control by another at a specific worksite. This complex definition means that if a person is in subordinated labour he can receive protection. If not he is largely excluded from it.

Labour law has varied across the world and there are several taxonomies of national models, notably those based on the 'varieties of capitalism' and 'legal origins' frameworks. Often the result is history without history, classifying countries at a point of arrested movement. One approach has been to differentiate between countries having a 'civil law origin' and those having a 'common law origin' (Djankov et al., 2003; Botero et al., 2004; Pistor, 2005; Deakin and Ahlering, 2006). Close inspection points to more similarities than differences, with tendencies towards convergence rather than divergence. Even so, the civil law tradition seems to have resulted in a more paternalistic stance towards employees, while the common law tradition gave more protection to commercial interests (La Porta et al., 1998). This is related to a dualism of the 'relational/insider' and 'market/outsider' systems (Gospel and Pendleton, 2004), or the 'coordinated market' and 'liberal market' varieties of capitalism (Hall and Soskice, 2001).

In this period, the relational/insider model had a stronger influence, holding in check those countries with a stronger tradition of market liberalism. The social democratic ethos curbed a tendency to treat employees as factors of production, giving employees protection but not agency. Part of the deal was acceptance of subordination. Employees were seen as 'vulnerable', in need of protection by laws specifying unfair labour practices and laws legitimizing employee Voice mechanisms. For instance, German labour legislation ensured employee representation on company boards and 'rights' of 'consultation' over corporate restructuring.

In general, labour law promoted collective bargaining and freedom of association for employees. In continental Europe, it was intended to advance the status and rights of those subject to domination of private power in the economic sphere (Hepple, 1986, p. 19). They were integrated as citizens through factory inspectors and institutional mechanisms such as 'mixed' labour courts, the first being the French *conseils des prud'hommes*.

In the UK, more was left to collective bargaining and unions were protected from common law courts by trade dispute immunities. Legally non-binding procedural agreements, mostly sectoral, were central to the system. From 1896 until the 1970s, a government-based conciliation, mediation and arbitration service supported voluntary collective bargaining (Hawes, 2000). But the system privileged a particular form of labour, which was to become awkward as services became the main economic activity.

The regulatory regime required monitoring by labour inspectorates. Their initial objective was to curb sweatshops and free riders, but they became a means of reinforcing the norms of the standard employment relationship (SER). They offered protection almost exclusively to those in stable jobs in identifiable workplaces, barely touching those in more autonomous work relationships. They exposed malodorous practices and helped generate work security, but they widened the gulf in social 'rights' between those in the SER and those outside it, reinforced labourism and were ill-suited to what emerged when national systems crumbled as flexible labour relations spread in the 1980s. What had been unappreciated was that bureaucratic inspectors and labour law generated a care-less-ness, an adherence to procedures rather than a search for innovative ways of working. That apart, one should not see labour law as protective of workers; it was protective of subordinated employees.

VOICE OF LABOUR

It may seem paradoxical that trade unions were agents of fictitious decommodification. But what emerged was a deal involving a trade-off in which employees were provided with dependent security in return for accepting the managerial 'right to manage' and the 'right to acquire and retain profits'.

All the major unions represented employees. They sought to enforce social compacts by which they could maximize the number of employees in jobs and increase entitlements associated with subordinated employment. They fought mainly for employment security, job security, work security and labour market security, to the lasting detriment of universal income security and universal Voice security. Priority was given to full-time employees, 'our members', not independent workers, let alone all those doing unpaid care work in their homes or communities. Unions subscribed to the disciplinary dictates of formal employment, accepting the managerial right to manage as long as managers adhered to 'fair' employment practices. Those outside employment were to be pitied and returned to jobs as soon as possible (the unemployed) or dismissed as 'not our concern' (the economically inactive, such as the much patronized 'housewives').

Trade unions were to pay a heavy price for this position; in helping to legitimize labourism they became perceived as an obstacle to the liberation of work, unable to represent those who did not wish for a life of constant labour in a constant job. In effect, returning to a Polanyian theme, workers lacked an emancipating agency because the unions stood for subordinated labour, more 'bread' or invitations to Downing Street, or its equivalent elsewhere. A worker required to perform labour necessarily surrenders agency. He must do as he is told.

The key aspects of regulation were reliance on labour law and on sectoral or industrial trade unionism for one form of action, collective bargaining. This was roughly suited to industrial capitalism in which manufacturing and Tayloristic management practices predominated, and in which the norm consisted of SER employees expected to perform 'jobs'. It was not a model for occupational complexity.

Unions became identified as a body of employees, and that is how labour law defined them, when for the first time in history workers were defined as those in employment. Under the labourist model, protection of freedom of association was based on subordination. Thus, in most countries only employees could form unions. The self-employed, contract workers, part-time workers and independent contractors were rarely covered. Non-employees who formed a 'combination' were liable to prosecution for being a 'conspiracy in restraint of trade', as in Canada under its Competition Act.

The trap was there, and unions and their political representatives, backed by the ILO model, allowed it to grow at a time when they could have done something to avoid it. The unions were the symbol of a labourist view of work. The belief that they were the voice of labour was their hubris.

By contrast with a union, an occupational association is a body for members of a self-defined profession or craft. If a person is an independent 'service' provider, he is likely to be classified as an entrepreneur or independent contractor. A market economy is regulated by rules designed to prevent anti-competitive collusion. Since a body of independent contractors could be construed as limiting or interfering with competition, independent workers are likely to be denied Voice. Under the labourist model, a worker had to prove he was a subordinated employee to have Voice.

Labour unions also played a role in cementing job structures and shaping the occupational system. Basically, they acted as a corporate group, trying to maximize income and the job security of members by increasing their jurisdiction. This was the explicit objective of the American Federation of Labor (AFL), which aimed to preserve its members' jurisdictions and distribute labour among the occupations they covered (Bok and Dunlop, 1970). But short-term job security built up long-term problems.

The craft union model that had flourished in the nineteenth century, with its intermediary role as labour controller, was geared to occupational and job security coupled with modest employment security. High rates of labour mobility were presumed, with young workers expected to become independent. Craft unions performed a wide range of welfare functions, partly because many of their members worked for several employers during the year.

This model withered as labour was decasualized in the early twentieth century. The unions pushed at an open door of employment security and then fought for job security. As labour unions became established, they and their political allies managed to transfer welfare functions to the state. This helped in the development of national labour processes but in the longer run it was to reduce employees' perceived need for unions. Improvements in employment and labour market security ended up eroding labour representation security, which weakened employees' ability to defend income and employment security in the first phase of the Global Transformation.

THE INEQUITIES OF SOCIAL SECURITY

While labour law, unions and collective bargaining were building industrial citizenship, a matching system of social protection was constructed. Though rarely acknowledged by social democrats who have defended their legacy, the two founding fathers of 'social security' were robust paternalists, not radical egalitarians. Otto von Bismarck was interested primarily in binding civil servants to the Prussian state when he introduced a partial social insurance system. He also wished to maintain an adequate standard of living for craftsmen protected by their guilds, and used social insurance in his struggle against the socialists, to bind workers to the state. William Beveridge was a liberal, in a patrician nineteenth-century mould, who railed against 'idleness' and wanted to support the deserving victims of industrial capitalism. Both wanted to preserve the structures they found around them, not overthrow them. Those who followed in their wake wanted to laud their reforms and 'extend' them, building on their models, not establishing an egalitarian alternative.

Under industrial citizenship, the mainstream labourist model of social security was succinctly summarized by the ILO's primary convention on the subject, Convention No. 102 of 1952. In a few pages, it captured the assumptions of the time, being vividly sexist and labourist, and explicitly for national labour markets. It recommended 'standards' for contingency benefits covering sickness, unemployment, old age, employment injury, maternity, invalidity and being a 'survivor'. It used the term 'breadwinner', depicting the standard beneficiary as 'a man with wife and two children'. It sanctioned a divide between those doing 'gainful activity' and the retired, suggesting that full pensions should be paid if employees had 30 years of contributions (Art. 29), with a reduced amount if they had been in contributory employment for between 15 and 30 years. The pension should be suspended or reduced if the person was doing any gainful activity (Art. 26(3)).

In Article 1(c) the convention stated that 'the term "wife" means a wife who is maintained by her husband'; there is no definition of a 'husband'. It added, 'the term "widow" means a woman who was maintained by her husband at the time of his death'; widowers did not figure. In recommending 'survivors' benefits', it made clear these were for widows. A condition was that the widow should not be 'earning from employment', ignoring the implied poverty trap. Entitlement to 'invalidity benefits' was to be determined by 'inability to engage in any gainful activity' (Art. 54). The convention guided countries to have a qualifying period for entitlement of 15 years of employment (Art. 57). The recommendations on unemployment benefits were labourist; they should not be paid if the worker was dismissed for 'wilful misconduct' or had 'failed to make use of the employment services', or had 'lost his employment as a direct result of a stoppage of work due to a trade dispute'.

The convention established 'maternity benefits' (not paternity) for women who were employees (Art. 48(a)) or wives of employees (Art. 48(b)) if in enterprises of 20 employees or more. Again, the benefit was not universal; those without a labour record would not qualify. The convention even specified there should be a qualifying period of employment 'to preclude abuse' (Art. 51). 'Family benefits' were to be based on contributions from employment; the prescribed value was '3% of the wage of the ordinary male labourer' multiplied by the number of persons protected (Art. 44(a)). In sum, the recommended benefits were linked to employment and were not universal.

Of course, the convention left it open for governments to build a social security system that differed in detail. But the essence, that of compensating employees for contingency risks, was incorporated in all welfare states. This was not decommodification. It was helping to lock workers into employment and families into sexual dualism. Over the years, its proponents tried to 'extend' entitlements to those excluded by its labourist core. But as that happened, the paternalism of arbitrary distinctions became more clearly matters of inequity and inefficiency. The system could not survive if the myth of 'full employment' collapsed and if more of the jobs at the lower end of the labour market were neither full time nor well paid.

BUREAUCRATIZATION

One feature of the Great Transformation was the growth of mass bureaucracies and the bureaucratization of labour more generally. It was no coincidence that the great sociologists Max Weber and Emile Durkheim cut their teeth on what this implied. Bureaucratization comes with salaried employment of professionals, creating multi-professional environments in which occupations lose their distinctive characteristics. Employment security was a primary means of strengthening the cage of bureaucratic organizations. In bureaucracies, paternalism and 'team' work dilute occupational development and remove the autonomy of practitioners, leading usually to 'management' domination of specialist occupations.

As bureaucracies took hold, most occupations within large-scale enterprises and organizations came under strain. When job-demarcating jurisdictions had to be negotiated in a bureaucracy, the ability of practitioners to preserve occupational standards was lost. Both open labour markets and bureaucracies wrest control of work and skill reproduction from the occupation.

Bureaucracies usually opted for job training rather than broader vocational education, destroying a feature of occupational communities, with their specific ethics, standards, career norms, and so on. As job training gathered momentum, members of occupations lost touch with the abstract expertise and linkages that defined their occupation; losing control of that expertise is an aspect of proletarianization.

In a bureaucracy, most occupations are subsumed under administrative managers. This may extend to the imposition of quality control, efficiency audits, targets and intermediary and strategic objectives, all of which lead to a loss of control over the content of the work. Much of this was to come later but the establishment of great bureaucracies in the early decades of the twentieth century was scarcely decommodifying.

Bureaucracies generated a large new 'community', middle managers. Most had a professional or occupational qualification, often with an engineering background. But in becoming managers they usually gave up hopes of advancing in occupational terms. They had a peculiar 'class' position too, making up a central part of what we call in Chapter 4 the 'salariat'. In effect, they formed a community without a home, and were to experience considerable stress as the Great Transformation unravelled.

OCCUPATIONS AND PROFESSIONS UNDER INDUSTRIAL CITIZENSHIP

In this period, the professions experienced fictitious decommodification in two ways. Some remained independent, protected from market forces, allowed to regulate their work, labour and leisure and to operate monopoly practices. But swathes of most professions were proletarianized as they were incorporated into large firms or bureaucracies.

The nineteenth century was characterized by what Abbott (1988) called 'associational professionalism'. Professionals practised in small groups, so negotiations on jurisdiction were public and transparent. The twentieth century ushered in the 'era of organizational professionalism', in which more were sucked into bureaucratic organizations while craft unions lost power to control their occupations. Thus, the AFL craft unions in the USA lost strength after practising 'job control unionism' based on controlling entry to crafts and systems of apprenticeship. In bureaucratic workplaces, the power of professional associations was eroded, preparing the way for proletarianization.

The professions had emphasized relations of trust, between themselves and clients and between practitioners and management. This reliance meant they were susceptible to incorporation, as was understood by early students of professionalism, such as Carr-Saunders and Wilson (1933) and Marshall (1950). Talcott Parsons (1951) attempted to merge this perspective with Weber's thesis of a rational-legal social order, producing what subsequent observers have criticized as an excessively functionalist perspective (Dingwall and Lewis, 1983). But large numbers of professional employees were subject to organizational control. The emphasis on 'discretion' over their work was curtailed.

Trust is no more part of labour than loyalty. Back in the eighteenth century, the emergence of the first 'manufactories' was put down to a lack of trust between entrepreneurs and the outworkers and craftsmen on whom they relied. In the twentieth century, professions were initially 'trusted', but as they were absorbed into bureaucracies, the trust relationship between professionals and their employers ('clients') dissipated.

The mainstream to which state policies were oriented was industrial citizenship. The standard employee was to be encouraged and rewarded for fulfilling regular labour. An employee was expected to show loyalty to his enterprise of employment. The culture of large-scale factories, offices and corporations was paternalistic, and the state policies that evolved were correspondingly paternalistic, as were unions, which became mainly labour security unions. The outcome was a special form of dependency. If you performed labour in industrial enterprises, you could build up labour-based entitlements, strengthened by the state through its social security and labour market policies.

A worker's career was marked by progression through the organizational ranks – the internal labour market. The informal outsiders were seen as a reserve army, a disciplinary threat to insiders, and as a source of reproduction, as well as a sink to receive failures, rejects and rebels. This is a reason why it is wrong to see this as a Golden Age, since the responses to Taylorism were restrictive, providing job security that blocked occupational development.

The professions resisted commodification by an array of defensive tactics, but were gradually drawn into bureaucratic salaried employment. The 'white-collar' class was growing. At the height of the fictitious decommodification, Wilensky (1964) published his influential article in which he predicted the professionalization of everyone. It caught the mood of the time, a sense that in industrialized countries almost everybody would find themselves in professions with all the trappings of status, access to enterprise benefits, employment security and the cushion of state benefits in the unlikely event of needing them. The image was of steady decommodification.

As noted in Chapter 1, Wilensky thought all adults would be in full-time employment, and that this would lead to higher standards, full-time trainers and professional associations that would exclude incompetents. To offset conflict between the generations inside and outside professions, there would be state protection, with rules eliminating internal competition and charlatanry. While he gave insufficient emphasis to the role of employers and state policy in determining what professions emerged and how they would be treated, he captured the period's normative expectations.

In reality, the enterprise-oriented employment structure transformed notions of career, distorting work from where it would have gone if occupational structures had been dominant. The idea of career, which figured strongly in the influential Chicago School of sociology, has been taken to mean a sequence of life events, centred on labour. In the industrial citizenship era, a career was defined in terms of labour done outside the household and family. While there is no reason to restrict a career to what is done in jobs, this notion coloured perspectives for much of the century.

In an occupational community, personal progress is measured in terms of competence and respect within one's peer group. In an enterprise community, career is measured by capacity to climb a ladder in an internal labour market, which is dependent in part on what may be generously described as political skill. Development of occupational skill may even be a disadvantage.

The period's organization model was scarcely decommodifying. Careerism became not just a derogatory description of what went on in large organizations, it generated stress. Employee behaviour became – and was encouraged to become – personally competitive and driven by a commercial logic. A person's income became dependent on his ability to climb a careerist ladder, not on demonstrating increasing skill in an occupational field. In a sense, craftsmanship did not pay.

Self-control, or autonomy, is greater inside an occupational community than in an organizational one driven by a division of labour oriented to profit-making. Indeed, some occupational groups inside an enterprise could gain financially from deskilling, if maintaining a range of skills ceased to correspond to the enterprise's needs. The principle of social solidarity, when applied to an enterprise, means an occupational group might have to sacrifice its integrity in the interest of a commercial whole.

From an organizational perspective, deviance was identified as behaviour contrary to managerial expectations, which had to be curbed. Yet this deviance was often behaviour that would have been regarded as normal within an occupational community. Similarly, with the enterprise, corporation or organization being the presumed zone of a working life, expectations were generated about behaviour outside the workplace as well. The 'company man' was expected to vote in the interests of the company, save in its interests and live a lifestyle consistent with the organizational community, taking fellow employees as his reference group rather than fellow occupational members outside the company.

This even made interaction with those in the same occupation working for other organizations a matter of suspicion, if not criticism for implicit collusion. 'Company secrets' could be used as a rationalization for keeping members of the same occupation apart. To the extent that a person's work depended on belonging to a vibrant occupational community, absorption into an enterprise and a localized workplace was stultifying.

Within an enterprise, managers and administrators know that control and monitoring of 'performance' are best served by codifying knowledge. It can then be measured by outsiders, uninterested in the intricacies of an occupational community and wanting identifiable criteria by which to assess employee performance. An internal labour market based on a deal to preserve employment security required employee adherence to rules of engagement, including rules of performance evaluation.[1]

Whereas occupational communities provide something close to a craft ethic and reinforce values of work rather than labour, the pressures of organizational structures are commodifying. Large organizations require a hierarchical division of labour, which conflicts with personal autonomy. Directive control permeates the whole system. In short, the central tendencies were pressures to belong to bureaucratic enterprises, accept job direction and accept a structure of social income in which the money wage was a diminishing part. This set up untenable trends, since there was a loss of professional control and a loss of incentive to labour.

As that tension evolved, labour controls were tightened and occupational communities were weakened. The unions played a part in this decline, epitomized by the AFL versus Congress of Industrial Organizations (CIO) struggle in the USA. Typically, unions required employee members to obey the collective will of their enterprises as part of their deal with management and employers. And by insisting on narrowly defined job security through demarcation agreements, they froze job structures as far as they could, impeding technological change and stunting the character of work in crafts. There were many concession bargains, with benefits traded for autonomy. In the USA, the AFL did deals with employers by which member unions gained the splendid 'right' to control job demarcation. This was to rigidify job structures while artificially breaking down occupations, adding strength to 'scientific management' techniques. The system of 'job security' was widely admired and emulated.

If occupational work is what lends work its creativity, against the pressure of market forces, then this control by management, labour unions and the state with its pro-labour regulations and social security system was surely commodifying. It is notable that many who have claimed the welfare state was decommodifying were adherents of state socialism, in which values of creativity and autonomy were derided as remnants of romanticism.

Confronted by tension between organizational management and diffuse occupational controls by professions and crafts, social democrats, union leaders, employer bodies and state enterprises all knew which side they wished to take. They also had another tension to resolve, between administrative managers and 'experts', each having a distinctive logic. Expertise had to be harnessed in the interest of those organizations. A Faustian bargain was to impose an organizational logic on occupations, as far as they could.

However, not all occupations were sucked into a proletarianized existence. The social character of occupational development can be illustrated by the differentiating tendencies in the social division of labour. During the crisis preceding the Great Transformation, two types of occupation crystallized, one dealing with financial management of national capitalism, one dealing with the strains among those required to adapt to its pressures, the latter being what might be called 'adjustment professions'. The first included lawyers of various kinds, solicitors and accountants. The second included psychiatrists and various paramedical professions.

These groups were treated as service providers outside the labour law regime; largely, they were allowed to operate outside the market society. They were enabled to rule themselves as professions and could create anti-competition mechanisms protecting their incomes, status and authority. They could not do that with absolute impunity, because if they acted too opportunistically they might have prompted the emergence of competitor professions or changes in the law. It was conditional decommodification, largely sanctioned by the state that passed laws to allow self-governance, self-licensing rules, certification and subsidies for favoured professions.

Meanwhile, occupations that figured directly in capitalist production were more subject to bureaucratic control. As large-scale enterprises generated higher incomes, surrender of occupational control often went without protest. Often practitioners scarcely noticed. There was some resistance. But there were means of dealing with that, through legislation or by more subtle interventions via collective bargaining.

In sum, large enterprises proletarianized occupations. Bureaucratization went with a multi-professional environment, which provided opportunities for conflict between occupations. The era of large enterprises produced occupational struggles within workplaces, which ultimately left many once-strong professions open to attack.

PROFESSIONALIZATION

The phenomenon of 'professionalism' emerged in the nineteenth century as a means of protecting middle-class occupations from the insecurities of capitalist employment. Those entering an occupation would spend years learning their trade and did not want to face obsolescence in 'mid-career'. For that and other reasons, occupations set up barriers to entry, and resisted 'skill dilution' and duplication by others.

Early observers depicted professionalism as helping to civilize social systems. Thus Tawney, the great socialist historian, noted, 'In what are described *par excellence* as "the services" it has always been recognized that *esprit de corps* is the foundation of efficiency, and all means, some wise and some mischievous, are used to encourage it' (Tawney, 1921, p. 148).

One interpretation is that professionalism was a middle-class attempt to differentiate higher-earning groups from working-class occupations as well as from employers, managers and administrative controls. Professionalism embeds some occupations in the economic system to their material and status advantage, generating and guarding privileges, status, income and representation security, while marginalizing others.

In the USA, from the Jacksonian era in the 1840s until the end of the nineteenth century, states required no certification by those practising law or medicine. Almost anybody could practise medicine and many did. 'Professionalization' only started in the late 1880s and the 'culture of professionalism' became a feature of the middle class in the late nineteenth century (Bledstein, 1976; Krause, 1996). This coincided with the emergence of state licensing for medicine and law between 1880 and 1920. Professional associations continued to grow up to the early 1960s but so too did the role of federal regulatory agencies. They were part of the embedded phase of the Great Transformation, regulating for standards.

Throughout the period, professions and some old crafts struggled in structures imposing administrative-managerial control. A celebrated case at the end of the Great Transformation was the assimilation of printers to bureaucratic control, culminating in Rupert Murdoch's dramatic decision in 1986 to move *The Times* of London to new premises overnight, locking out the printers' union that had obstructed the changeover to computerization from page setting in lead type. The demise of the printers highlighted the tendency for bureaucratic control to lead to 'deskilling' or 'deprofessionalization' (Rothman, 1984). In some cases, deskilling was more about the status and control aspects of skill than the technique sense. One aspect was routinization, requiring employees to perform a limited range of tasks on a continuing basis. The other was skill dilution, demanding employees to respond to administrative obligations outside their sphere of professional competence, which included more time spent on selling, chasing clients, attending meetings, seeking funders and networking. Both represented management strategies, eroding professionalism and building up an ethos of subordination.

However, even as administrative control triumphed, the continued existence of occupations made supervision a two-edged tool. Many workers could adjust the effort bargain and quality of output, so attempts to tighten managerial control could result in lower effort and quality (Steiger and Form, 1991). Unappreciated at the time was that fictitious decommodification had eroded the capacity of the labour market to act as a market. Since the wage share of remuneration had shrunk, the main mechanisms for inducing labour performance had to be disciplinary controls and the carrot of climbing the corporate ladder. Job grading became increasingly complex and contrived.

Writing after the First World War, Tawney also witnessed the growth of what he called 'an intellectual proletariat'. He thought it would be allied with wage earners, although he was unsure 'in what direction it will throw its weight', seeing that 'the salaried brain workers appear to be undergoing the same gradual conversion to a cautious and doctrine-less trade unionism, as took place among the manual workers' (Tawney, 1921, p. 161). He went on to preach industrial democracy, in which salaried professionals would be treated with respect as colleagues by wage workers. He also depicted a wonderful concept of 'clerkocracy'. But not long before, Upton Sinclair, in his 1919 novel *The Brass Check*, had described white-collar workers as 'petty underlings of the business world'. Skilled manual workers looked down on office-based employees. The proletarianization of professionals helped to erode class solidarity.

This highlights a dualism that characterized many professions. While there was extensive 'proletarianization' (Derber, 1982a; McKinlay, 1982), some professions were privileged by the state. Most evolved with an elite serving the dominant class and middle-class needs. This was the case with US lawyers even in the nineteenth century (Krause, 1996, p. 51). It characterized Italian law, and was also the case in British law, with an elite of solicitors doing corporate work, while the mass served the middle class. In health, the story was similar. When Britain's National Health Service was set up in 1948, Nye Bevan, the Minister of Health, offered general practitioners salaried positions to buy their acquiescence. The majority were offered the pre-war insurance model with all patients covered and each doctor contracted by the NHS to treat a panel of patients. But specialized hospital consultants could continue to treat patients privately in addition to their NHS commitments. In France, the dualism in the educational system has been distinctive, consisting of an elite linked to the *grandes écoles* closely related to the state, and a mass of lower-status academics in universities.

Dualism was often assisted by unions, as in the case of French medical reforms in the late 1950s when most doctors were proletarianized. Subsequently, the incomes and status of general practitioners lagged behind those of the medical elite, with rural doctors earning a quarter of what specialists earned and often less than local factory workers (Bezat, 1987).

Professionalism was a source of ambivalence among social democrats who shaped the Great Transformation. It represented a barrier to commodification and proletarianization, but it gave privileged independence to groups who were likely to favour a market society and an inegalitarian social structure, and who were prone to subject groups within their occupations to a proletarianized existence. Just as tertiary employment was becoming the norm, Raymond Williams (1961, p. 312) claimed that the reforming bourgeois modification of individualism was 'the idea of service'. A service mentality is opposed to the ethic of solidarity and is a form of paternalism. Occupations involve a continuing tension between solidarity and individualism. Professionalism as it stood could not resolve that tension.

So, the post-1945 period was one of proletarianization, as more people shifted into wage and salary employment, with the obligations and entitlements that came with it. Briefly, by moving into a 'profession', there was escape from the routinized existence that came with bureaucratic administrative controls. But that was solace for a privileged minority.

CONCLUSIONS

In the Great Transformation, advances in all forms of labour security came at the price of producing a false paradise of labourism, in which regulations, social protection and redistribution were based on the norm of full-time labour by a man ('the breadwinner') supporting a dependent wife ('the caregiver'). Behavioural norms were promoted that were ultimately stultifying. It was a prescription for dumbing down, for 'jobholders'. It also produced labour rigidities and thus rising labour costs. That was sustainable in a world of closed economies, in which trade took place primarily between countries with similar levels of labour security and cost structures, and an international division of labour based on 'underdeveloped' countries producing primary goods while 'developed' countries produced manufactured goods and services. Once the world began to shift towards an open economy, there was no way the labourist model could be sustained.

If the intention was to decommodify labour, through shifting from wages and community benefits to enterprise benefits and state benefits, the result was an erosion of incentives to labour and labour mobility, an incapacity to respond to globalization and the disappearance of community networks, leaving people increasingly vulnerable to shocks and hazards. The state had usurped those networks and, when state and enterprise benefits were rolled back, there were no community benefits to replace them.

One outcome of the fictitious decommodification was the triumph of the labouring ethic. In the late nineteenth century, prominent artists and social critics lauded crafts as humanizing, opposed to the alienating anonymity of industrial capitalism that was sweeping away craft production. Among the most passionate defenders of a passing way of life were John Ruskin, Thomas Carlyle and William Morris in Britain, Adolf Loos, the Viennese architect, and German architect Walter Gropius. It is commonly argued that the era of crafts died with the First World War, leaving them to languish as eccentric backwaters of 'arts-and-crafts', with residual splendours such as the violin-making community of Cremona in Italy. While one must be careful not to sentimentalize crafts and the way of living around them, what Wright Mills (1956) called the craft ethic was a casualty of the period of industrial citizenship.

The Great Transformation was about the triumph of labourism, and involved numerous ironies. There is a well-known story that the first batch of 30 Labour members of the British parliament, after their election in 1906, were asked by an enterprising journalist which book had most influenced them and led them to enter politics. He probably expected most to answer Karl Marx or another great socialist thinker. In fact, most cited John Ruskin's *Unto the Last*, in which he had raged against the erosion of the freedoms of the working man as he was dragooned into wage labour. The irony was that the world's labour parties were to become the architects of disciplined labour and were to forge a fictitious decommodification that could not be sustained as the system of national labour markets collapsed under the impact of globalization.

NOTE

1. The ILO took this to extreme levels. Providing technical assistance to governments, employer organizations, unions and companies, it produced a manual for on-the-job training in 'modules of employable skill', breaking down jobs into tiny segments or bundles of tasks, so as to help the new occupational group of human resource managers operationalize 'manpower planning'. This symbolized an ethos of commodification, albeit dressed up as employment enhancement.

3. Labour recommodification in the Global Transformation

In Rome, everything is for sale.

(Prince Jugurtha, in Sallust's *Bellum Jugurthinum*, c. 30 BC)[1]

HAYEK'S TRIUMPH: THE ASCENDANCY OF 'NEO-LIBERALISM'

In the 1970s, Polanyi's Transformation unravelled, sending industrial citizenship into retreat. What had been perceived as permanent institutions were swept aside, and assumptions of the recent past became bitterly contested terrain. The result was the dis-embedded phase of the Global Transformation.

There is little point in looking for a smoking gun – Margaret Thatcher and Ronald Reagan, information technology, the oil crises, the emergence of Japan as an industrial power or the newly industrializing countries (NICs) eroding the ability of welfare states to compete in terms of costs and speed of change. The fact is that industrial citizenship crumbled, aided by policies that crystallized in the 1980s as the Washington Consensus. By the end of the century, the dictates of competitiveness had become the yardstick for assessing all institutions, policies and reforms.

The changes were reflected in the intellectual and political ascendancy of the Chicago School of law and economics forged in the 1970s. Although its roots lay in the eighteenth century, notably in the writings of Adam Smith, it drew its inspiration from Hayek, Milton Friedman and his colleagues. It put regulations in a new perspective, stating that they could be justified only if they did not distort the market and promoted economic growth. Whereas protective and pro-collective regulations were previously part of social policy, helping to redistribute income, now regulations were to promote competition and support individuals against collective action. In the name of 'rolling back the state', state regulations were extended in the clever guise of 'deregulation'.

The resultant doctrine has come to be known as 'neo-liberalism'. Contrary to classic liberalism, which put emphasis on the market as exchange relations, neo-liberalism focuses on the need for firms, individuals and nations to become more competitive, by comparison with their present and past and relative to others. One can never be competitive enough, never drop one's guard. It is a prescription for permanent anxiety. Whereas exchange conjures up images of fairness and equality, of handshakes, compe-tition conjures up images of deviousness, opportunism and inequality, of winners and losers.

Neo-liberalism came into ascendancy at the same time as a technological revolution, surely the most rapid and far-reaching in history, surpassing the less internationally transformative breakthrough that precipitated Britain's Industrial Revolution. Informatics accelerated the demise of the closed economy model that underpinned welfare states and Keynesian policy. Once liberalization was in full flow, there was unremitting pressure to cut labour costs as country after country accepted that competitiveness was crucial. In industrialized countries, where non-wage labour costs had risen to a high level in the Great Transformation, governments and firms were led to take drastic action to curb enterprise benefits.

Under pressure from interests eager to make a profit from spheres previously denied them, policymakers rolled back the state through liberalization, commercialization and privatization. Policies and institutional arrangements had to pass the test of competition policy, and social policy was turned over to judges and legal criteria. Property rights became de facto fundamental rights.

Hayekian views underpinned the Washington Consensus, which permeated thinking in the international financial agencies, notably the IMF and World Bank, and in US universities and among their international students, who produced a generation of bureaucrats, politicians and teachers armed with a new way of thinking. If Pinochet's Chile was a depraved caricature of their policies, so too was the 'shock therapy' in the ex-Soviet Union, vigorously promoted by young brash US economists, some of whom ended up in criminal quagmires brought on by their conceit and the wealth showered upon them.

Globally, the main political struggle has been about restructuring systems of regulation, redistribution and social protection. Many terms have been used to describe the era, including 'electronics capitalism', 'turbo capitalism' and 'supercapitalism' (Reich, 2007). Whatever it is called, it has been the disembedding phase of a Global Transformation, which has produced unsustainable inequalities and insecurities.

This period has been the first time in history when all parts of the world were urged to adopt the same economic model. In the embedded phase of the Great Transformation, capital took the risks and was rewarded by above-average income, while workers were offered labour security. In the neo-liberal model, capital has been protected, while risks and uncertainties have been shifted onto workers, who have had to tolerate more economic and social insecurity as well as lower incomes.

For 30 years after 1945, Keynesian macroeconomics was hegemonic. Then the global economy ran into a stagflationary crisis. There followed 30 years of Chicagoism, leading to the financial crisis of 2008, when the independence of central banks and the requirement that they should concentrate on inflation came under strain. Fears of a global recession, along with a collapse of financial markets, had central banks rushing to loosen liquidity and pump spending power into the economy. Counter-cyclical monetary and fiscal policy was back.

To maintain the global market system, governments concluded that the insecurity of the world's financial elite had to be overcome. The moral underpinning of the market model was exposed. To save it from meltdown, the very rich had to be given more subsidies. They had risked, and had to be compensated for their failure. The invisible hand was very visible indeed. That ended the globalization era. But by then the global market society had taken shape.

THE ARCHITECTURE OF THE GLOBAL MARKET SOCIETY

Just as Polanyi saw financial capital as central to the emergence of a national market society, international finance was crucial to the early phase of the Global Transformation (Helleiner, 2000). By 2005 the value of global financial assets had risen to 316 per cent of the world's annual output (McKinsey Global Institute, 2005). And the financial system had become global, with Europe and Asia accounting for a growing proportion of world-wide assets, the USA a declining share.

Returns to short-term portfolio investment long exceeded profits from productive investment, stimulating the financialization of corporations and a transfer of income to financial asset holders. The share of US corporate profits accounted for by financial services rose from 10 per cent in 1980 to 40 per cent in 2007. Capital markets came to perform functions that banks used to do, and became international and more speculative, shifting funds quickly to where prospective rates of return were highest and inventing ever more sophisticated financial instruments.[2] This created new occupational communities, such as the International Swaps and Derivatives Association. At the end of 2007, the notional value of outstanding swaps and derivatives contracts reached 11 times the value of world output.

Major financial institutions emerged. By 2008, 10 000 hedge funds were managing US$2 trillion of assets, and sovereign wealth funds (state-owned investment funds) US$5 trillion. In 2007, private equity funds raised US$500 billion and accounted for a quarter of the record US$1800 billion in foreign direct investment (UNCTAD, 2008). In the UK, private equity-owned firms employed one in five private sector employees (Teather and Treanor, 2007).

Private equity funds bought up shares of public companies, replaced their management, cut jobs while restructuring and then sold them off.[3] Once called asset stripping, this intensified corporate insecurity, made career planning riskier and encouraged managers to make only short-term commitments. Household-name enterprises could be bought up at short notice, and radically restructured. A roll-call of corporations taken over by private equity in the UK included the AA, Travelodge, John Laing and Associated British Ports.

The money lent to private equity funds to buy companies came from rich individuals and financial institutions such as pension funds. By the turn of the century, pension fund assets were equivalent to 46 per cent of the world's income, up from 30 per cent seven years earlier, with over half of those assets held by US firms. As of 2006, private pension funds had assets greater than the value of national income in countries such as Iceland, the Netherlands and Switzerland and over 50 per cent in Australia, the UK, the USA, Chile, Singapore and Canada.

Pension funds had become a form of regulation, able to shift assets from firms and countries that did not perform in ways they wanted, destabilizing economies, companies and communities. They pushed corporations to focus on short-term profits – 'maximizing shareholder value' – at the cost of employee security. And by tying pensions to market performance, their volatility increased the income insecurity of older employees and pensioners.

As the high return to equities led corporations to divert resources to financial speculation, moral and immoral hazards multiplied.[4] The name Enron became a metaphor for the age. Just after being lauded as one of the ten best US companies to work for, regarded by credit rating agencies as exemplary in terms of corporate social responsibility, the company imploded, revealing a pattern of abuse that ruined the lives of most of its employees. The market had been allowed to operate without protective regulation; the result was disastrous.[5]

The affair demonstrated the inadequacy of relying on market forces. It showed managers acting illegally, while accounting professionals were compromised. Bank analysts had not raised the alarm, nor had ratings agencies, Enron's board or the company's auditors, who received lucrative consultancy contracts from Enron as well as auditing fees. There was no responsible monitoring by the professionals, and no regulations to protect employees from the consequence of wrongdoing by managers or their advisers. Enron was not alone. Other corporations were caught in similar circumstances, including WorldCom in the USA, Ahold in the Netherlands and Parmalat in Italy. In this global market society, the individual as worker could not look to a corporate employer as a haven of security and lifetime protection.

Underlying financialization has been international political integration, including abandonment of the so-called Westphalian system, which granted states jurisdiction over their own territories and laws. This has been replaced by 'the new liberal cosmopolitanism': national sovereignty has been curbed by global institutions set up and reshaped to serve economic liberalization based ostensibly on common legal norms, free trade and mobility of capital, labour power and technology (Taylor, 1999). The UN has been shifted in that direction, as have the international financial agencies.

The midwife of globalization was the World Trade Organization (WTO). Whereas its predecessor, the General Agreement on Tariffs and Trade (GATT), had concerned itself mainly with tariffs and manufacturing, since 1995 WTO rules have been extended to cover issues long considered the sovereign territory of governments, including industrial policy, farm subsidies, regulation of services and intellectual property rights. WTO rules prohibiting selective industrial policy and local content requirements for foreign investment have been devices for opening developing country markets to foreign investment, while the General Agreement on Trade in Services (GATS) gives capital security by protecting foreign firms from eviction and differential treatment.

Alongside the WTO, the market agenda has been advanced by regional blocs – the now 27-member European Union, the Association of South-East Asian Nations (ASEAN), the Southern Cone Common Market (MERCOSUR), the North American Free Trade Agreement (NAFTA) and so on – and by over 200 bilateral and regional trade agreements. These have mostly set stronger pro-liberalization rules than the WTO, which in 2008 was struggling to conclude the latest round of global trade talks, dubbed the Doha Development Agenda.

One harbinger of the Global Transformation was the decision by the creators of the European Economic Community in 1957 to exclude social policy from its founding treaties, on the grounds that it was unnecessary to have a European social policy because economic integration would lead automatically to harmonization. Article 118 of the Treaty of Rome merely encouraged the European Commission to promote cross-national cooperation on social policy. The main task was to create institutions and mechanisms for a common market, with free movement of capital, workers, investment and trade. The scope for social dumping, and use of social policy to gain competitive advantage, was not appreciated at the time. But the treaties set Europe on the path to a market society.

By the 1970s, those constructing the common market realized that the sanguine view of social policy was not working, and that there was a need to develop a response to rising unemployment and poverty. The European Community issued directives on social policies, but ran into a blockage after the election of the UK's Thatcher government. This ruled out the development of European-level social policy, depending as it did on unanimous decision-making. Thatcher vehemently opposed the idea of a European Community social policy. Matters came to a head in 1989 when the British refused to sign the Community Charter of Fundamental Social Rights of Workers, and then opted out of the Maastricht Social Protocol, thereby showing that social policy had not been a fundamental part of the European project.

The EU has instead been a vehicle for spreading the market society, and not just within its expanding borders. It has done so through its directives, through the European Court of Justice (ECJ), which has advanced neo-liberal competition policy, through subsidies and development aid. EU directives have set benchmarks for other regional bodies and for trade agreements generally. The most pivotal is the Services Directive, which established rules to facilitate private provision of services in EU countries. The original proposal (the Bolkestein draft) would have allowed companies to operate according to country-of-origin regulations rather than those in force in the country of operation. This could have led to regulatory dumping, with countries lowering standards to attract foreign investment. In the end, the country-of-origin principle was held back.

Meanwhile, the IMF, the World Bank (including its International Finance Corporation, mandated to boost capitalism in developing countries), the European Bank for Reconstruction and Development (EBRD) and other regional development banks have ratcheted up conditions behind their loans and grants. Initially these were concerned with macroeconomic policy; then conditions were added to shape microeconomic policy, and then others were added to ensure social reforms conformed to the global market model. This ratcheting of conditionality leveraged market society across the globe.

Reregulation in support of the global market society was accompanied by the creeping privatization of regulation, by which financial market pressure was placed on governments and corporations to alter policies to accord with what were deemed to be internationally acceptable norms. Among the agents of this privatization were the credit rating agencies, led by three US-based firms – Moody's, Standard & Poor's and Fitch – whose ratings of sovereign and corporate debt have had the power to de-legitimize governments and companies. They have passed judgment, from a US perspective, as when telling European governments to cut social spending if they wished to avoid being relegated to second-rank borrowers.

The global capitalism model thereby denies legitimacy to collective and universalistic institutions. Multinationals have also manipulated national politics, commodifying politics by buying votes and legislators' actions through lobbying, making political contributions and using the media to serve the ends of multinational corporations and the elite. This has been a global trend. The moral bankruptcy of mainstream political parties is a feature of globalization, not just an incidental aspect of post-modernism. Everybody as well as everything seems for sale.

The global market society has also been built through globalized teaching, which groomed an elite of economists to implement its policies. Displacing Keynesianism, the Chicago School became hegemonic in academia and policymaking circles. Its apostles would claim this was because of its intellectual rightness and rigour. But they would have to admit that it owed much to the fact that it accorded with the ideology and economic power of the USA. The economics profession was captured by a pro-market elite, which was showered with funds from sympathetic governments. Its members took over the main economics journals and powerful committees awarding research funds. It is a measure of their dominance that between 1980 and 2008 no fewer than 17 of the Nobel Prizes in Economics went to former or current Chicago economists.

There could scarcely be a better testament to the hegemony than a boast made by Arnold Harberger, one of the Chicago School's influential members and an adviser to Augusto Pinochet, who said regally in an interview in 1999: 'I think my number of ministers is now crossing 25, and I know my number of central bank presidents has already crossed a dozen. Right now the central bank presidents of Chile, Argentina and Israel were my students, and the immediate former central bank presidents in Argentina, Chile and Costa Rica were also my students' (Fourcade, 2006, p. 181).

Global capitalism had fallen into the hands of a tiny number of institutions and individuals. Portraying the economy as a hive of individuals in dogged competition would be misleading. Hayek may have triumphed, but his imagery was far from what the global market economy had become.

ECONOMIC OUTCOMES AND THE DISMANTLING OF LABOURISM

The primary claim for globalization was that it would boost economic growth. Even before 2008, the evidence was mixed. The emerging giants of China and India grew rapidly; a few other countries, mostly in Asia, were drawn along in their wake. But many countries grew only slowly, while the volatility of growth increased, with more instances of sharp GDP contractions and financial market crashes. Although trade liberalization increased the advantages for 'winners', notably those with low production costs, capital account liberalization allowed markets to punish those seen as inefficient. Greater capital mobility – and potential mobility – increased economic insecurity (ILO, 2004, ch. 3). Liberalization tied more people's well-being to financial markets, yet globalization has been marked by more financial crises than ever – including the Asian crisis, the Long-Term Capital Management debacle, the dot-com crash, the sub-prime crisis and the crisis of securitization of 2007–08.

Historically, transformations shift the centre of economic leadership. Although the USA was hegemonic in the early phase of the Global Transformation, it soon paid the price. It indulged in profligate consumerism, made possible only because the dollar was the main international currency. By contrast with the equivalent phase of the Great Transformation, when the UK mostly exported its capital in long-term bond-financed investment, the USA splurged on consumption by importing capital, including from low-income countries such as China. It was living on borrowed time.

The Emergence of 'Chindia'

While the USA was drifting into chronic budget and trade deficits, with consumers living beyond their means, the world's most populous countries, China and India, emerged as the industrial workshops of the world. These countries (and several others, including Vietnam) helped to leverage a global labour market, primarily by providing a global labour surplus. The fact that firms could relocate to 'Chindia', or transfer labour there, eroded workers' bargaining power everywhere.

The size of 'Chindia' and its combination of low incomes and low labour costs meant that supply-side effects were greater than demand-side effects. The entry of an economy trading with others in the system boosts the demand for goods and services as well as supply. The threat to club members is greater if the addition to supply exceeds the extra demand. So, the dislocation effect will depend on whether the country entering the global market is mainly complementary or competitive (Sayers, 1965; Singh, 1977). Given the pace of export-led production of competitive goods (from China) and goods and services (from India), the supply-side effects of 'Chindia' will be substantial for a long time.

Richard Freeman (2005) has argued that in 1985 the global open economy – defined as countries linked by something like free trade and capital mobility – had about 1 billion workers competing with each other. By 2000, the labour force of those countries had increased to 1.5 billion. But the ex-Soviet bloc, China and India had joined the global economy, adding a further 1.5 billion. Although Freeman (1995) had earlier argued the opposite, he made the point that these new sources came with little 'capital' and thus sharply altered the world's capital–labour ratio, raising the returns to capital and lowering those to labour, as shown by the growth of functional income inequality.

The difficulty with studies trying to separate the effects of aspects of globalization – labour supply, trade, technological change and so on – is that the behavioural effects are hard to capture and there has been adaptive policy accommodation. But there is anecdotal evidence that fear of this global labour market has induced politicians in industrialized countries to make policy adjustments, employers to make demands for change and workers to make concessions to retain jobs. One way in which Asian countries exerted downward pressure on labour conditions in OECD countries was via the discipline induced by centuries of Confucian traditions, in which deference to a superior is fundamental. Recommodification has been advanced by Confucian-based pressure.

The IMF, a leading institutional advocate of globalization, also concluded that the main impact was psychological. As its chief economist put it in 2006, 'In my view, however, the true impact of globalization has been in contributing to wage and price restraint at a time when central bankers were establishing their inflation-fighting credibility' (Rajan, 2006).

As the Global Transformation proceeds, China is shifting from being the world's main factory to being among its biggest customers. But the effects on the global labour market will continue. The Chinese economy grew by 12 per cent in 2007, and growth is expected to hover around 8 per cent in the years ahead, with below that regarded as a recession. Its labour surplus is still vast. China needs to add 10 million jobs a year merely to keep pace with the labour force, whereas each one percentage point of GDP growth generates only 850 000 additional jobs (Batson, 2008).[6] The economy must therefore grow by over 11 per cent a year merely to keep unemployment constant, unless the employment elasticity can be increased. This would mean slowing productivity growth, which is more likely to increase.

The rise of 'Chindia' continues a process that began in the 1970s when Japan and the NICs became exporters of manufactured goods, based on a low-cost labour supply. Perceiving a threat to living standards, rich countries accommodated the Japan-led industrial revolution by boosting aggregate demand and drifting into trade deficits, dein-dustrialization and rising inflation. The fictitious 'Golden Age' was preserved for a while. But the price of the accommodation was later paid through a period of deflation, until inflationary expectations were squeezed from the economic system. This led to years of high unemployment in Europe and stagnant real wages in the USA. Less noticed was a global change in labour market institutions and a global shift of social protection systems that dismantled the old labourist regime.

Trade and Deindustrialization

In the Great Transformation, trade was not an integral part of production. It was a way of increasing profits or acquiring inputs for production, but was rarely used to shape the nature of the firm or labour relations. Today, trade and labour flexibility are inter-related. As the share of trade in world output rose from 36 per cent in 1980 to 55 per cent in 2007, relative labour costs became a significant driver of competitive success. Workers have become risk bearers and many have become, in all but name, dependent or independent contractors rather than stable employees. This has implications not only for labour law and collective bargaining, as we will see, but also for the capacity to develop occupational careers.

Contributing to this is the changing character of trade. Unlike in the pre-1914 period, intra-product rather than inter-product trade has been growing, intra-firm trade is vastly greater and trade is dominated by transnational companies. One outcome of this 'deep integration' is that much of the risk has been transferred from major corporations to sub-contractors and nominally self-employed suppliers in global production chains. This has accelerated the re-division of labour, giving corporations enhanced power in bargaining over the level and structure of payments.

The spread of global supply chains has coincided with global deindustrialization. The share of industry in GDP has plunged across the industrialized world since the 1970s. In Germany, it shrank from over one-third to under 20 per cent in a decade, and in the UK it fell from nearly a quarter in 1990 to below 15 per cent in 2005. Deindustrialization in terms of employment is global. As China and India became economic powers, manufac-turing jobs in both countries stagnated while service jobs increased. In India, services have been the leading source of employment growth for several decades (Mazumdar and Sarkar, 2006).

Capital Outsourcing, Tax Dumping and Fiscal Regulation

Central to globalization has been capital outsourcing, often to avoid or evade corporate tax. Numerous companies have moved their headquarters and subsidiaries to tax havens, from where they can indulge in transfer pricing to disguise profits. Capital mobility has led to the convenient claim that capital cannot be taxed heavily because this will accelerate the outsourcing of capital and jobs. In response, governments have indulged in beggar-my-neighbour tax dumping, producing a situation in which not only have taxes on capital fallen, while taxes on labour have risen (relatively, at least), but also one in which subsidies to capital have risen (to attract foreign investment) while subsidies to workers have fallen. Neo-liberals have argued against subsidies for workers on the grounds that they are market distorting; they have been rather quiet on those for capital.

Tax competition has become endemic. In the OECD, corporate tax rates were cut from an average of 45 per cent in the 1980s to below 29 per cent in 2005; between 2000 and 2005, 24 of the 30 OECD countries cut their rates. The argument that this was necessary to attract or retain investment is disingenuous. Although 6 per cent of all multinationals claimed to have relocated between 1997 and 2007 partly for tax reasons (Houlder, 2008), there is little evidence that lowering taxes on capital draws it from elsewhere (Weise, 2007). Rather, the rate-cutting reflected the power of capital and a desire of politicians to appease backers and critics. And besides being expected to pay less corporate tax on profits, multinationals have found 'creative' ways of avoiding or evading taxes they are expected to pay. Before the global economic crisis broke in 2008, some were predicting that corporate tax would virtually disappear, with the tax burden passed onto workers (Houlder, 2007).

Oddly enough, the tax share of national income has tended to rise, even though many countries have cut direct tax and made their tax systems regressive to attract and retain capital. Fiscal policy has also been used for regulatory purposes. Governments of all political hues have used taxes, subsidies and benefit schemes to guide behaviour, penalize certain activities and reward others. Tax credits have become part of economic and social policy. Fiscal policy has ceased to be an instrument of decommodification and progressive redistribution. It has become part of social engineering, with earned-income tax credits and 'in-work' benefits designed to oblige the unemployed to take and stay in low-wage jobs.

Privatization and Social Dumping

The privatization of economic activities that started in the 1980s has been followed by the global privatization of social policies and services, with implications for patterns of labour use and income distribution. Privatization has rolled back the protective character of the public economy, making more activities subject to market forces and commercial ventures. Utilities and social services have been commercialized, liberalized and privatized, ostensibly to increase efficiency. In Europe, the process has been accelerated by EU liberalization directives, part of the construction of a single European market. Often changing their names to something more glamorous, corporations forged from the privatization of utilities – such as France Telecom, Vivendi and Telefónos de Mexico – have become global capitalists. Contracting to numerous small firms and generating huge investment, some have gone into financial services, as in the case of postal services.

All this has generated social policy dumping, a tendency for one country to cut social policy on the grounds that another has done so, and if it does not follow, competitiveness will be lost. Claims that this is leading to a race to the bottom are too strong. But there is a race to some market-favouring convergence, involving less social protection and pro-collective regulation than had been achieved in welfare states. Meanwhile, the public sector has ceased to be the labour standard setter or employer of last resort.

Globalized Insecurity

International financial capitalism has created systemic economic insecurity, which is shaping the global labour market and defining the context in which progressive strategies must be considered. While the elite have made fortunes, there has been a disregard for the economic security of those lower down the social scale.

A feature of the global market society model is that competitiveness is meant to go with generalized insecurity. By comparison with the embedded phase of the Great Transformation, risk, uncertainty and insecurity have shifted from holders of capital to those providing labour. The trend towards more frequent shocks, coupled with economic and financial interdependence, has exposed more of the world and most people to a higher probability of an adverse outcome.

The globalizing economy has also transformed the character of economic security, since it has destroyed the foundations of labourism. This will be considered later. Suffice it to note that there has been a shift from idiosyncratic and contingency risks, which are relatively insurable and amenable to systems of social solidarity, to systemic risks involved in economic and social shocks, which are less insurable or suited to the social security schemes developed in the period of fictitious decommodification.

THE FIRM IN TRANSITION

Industrial citizenship was based on manufacturing and mining, with a public sector providing services, all oriented to fixed workplaces where workers were under a common roof. Policies and institutions, as well as public consciousness, were shaped by those images. But by the 1980s, most employment was in services.[7] The notion of a post-industrial society is inadequate, since it was a service economy still framed by policies and institutions of an industrial society. If path dependency means anything it is that institutions take time to adjust, and their slow adjustment resulted in distress, unemployment and economic insecurity.

Linked to the expansion of services was the information technology (IT) revolution. Transforming many aspects of labour, it altered the character of the firm and the workplace. The old model consisted of an integrated enterprise, belonging to an industrial sector, employing a mass of employees administered by a management bureaucracy. Much was based on the concept of 'the workplace' and the 'public company'.

'Public companies' have long been written off (Jensen, 1989). Although this was an exaggeration, financialization weakened the public company model. Private equity funds were only the latest financial wolves, ready to move in if firms were not maximizing profits. By listing shares on a stock market, corporations left themselves open to attack, to which they responded with share buybacks and the raising of funds through profits and debt-related instruments rather than equity issues. As stock markets became riskier, the practice of issuing stocks to favoured employees (share options) also shrank. The shift back to wages affected even senior employees. Meanwhile, a larger role for debt relative to equity, encouraged by favourable tax treatment (involving subsidies), increased the risk of macroeconomic volatility and weakened employment security by making companies more sensitive to interest rate changes.

Simultaneously, more corporations were converted into unlisted private companies, enabling them to conceal earnings, perks and working arrangements from scrutiny by shareholders and pressure groups, including those monitoring codes of conduct. While household-name corporations faced regulatory pressure, and while neo-liberals made claims in favour of soft regulation, those managing private firms could escape scrutiny.

Thus, quite apart from the direct impact of the economic crisis that began in 2008, the firm as a locus of labour security has become more fragile. Building a career based on employment in a corporation has become riskier. Even the biggest firms are vulnerable to takeover, with a slew of mega-mergers one reason for a quadrupling of the global value of mergers and acquisitions from 1995 to 2006 (Wolf, 2007a). Owners and managers change more often, and long-term financial, employment and customer relationships are declining. This fluidity represents a triumph for financial capital, for the globalized speculator over managers and owners. You build, you own, you are taken over, you retire early or start again, take your pick. That could be a motto in the business community.

The firm itself has become a major tradable commodity. The demise of relational contracts has led to more foreign owners and managers, who have no obligations to the host country or its citizens. In this sense, global financial capital erodes national forms of social solidarity. Those able to benefit from the global market gain multiple sources of income and develop multiple loyalties, while those unable to do so risk neglect by the winners.

A related aspect is commodification of managers. They must focus exclusively on maximizing efficiency and subject themselves to market-driven discipline. This limits their sense of agency and subjects them to more stress and uncertainty, inducing them to inflict more insecurity on employees. The mutual loyalty supposed to characterize the relationship between manager and employee is made even more tenuous.

GLOBAL LABOUR FLEXIBILITY

While policymakers proceeded to liberalize the economy, a global labour market was taking shape. Although capital mobility may have grown faster, production and labour mobility have surged, transforming the international division of labour with new forms of production and divisions of tasks that are changing ways of thinking about trade. Labour and labour costs have become a central part of trade.

The following does not review the labour changes in detail, but recalls them so as to consider the implications for occupational work. In summary form, whereas in the previous era there was more proletarianization than commodification, the first phase of the Global Transformation has involved recommodification. Proletarianization implies a shift to labouring in a full-time job for years on end, as an employee, whereas the emerging model requires workers to be mobile, available to sell their labour in flexible ways.

Labour Churning

Since the 1970s, new technologies and working patterns have raised labour turnover, or at least turnover desired by firms. Manufacturing jobs have shrunk, leading to global deindustrialization. There has been a decline in demand for mechanical skills and an increase in demand for problem-solving skills and for capacities to be adaptive and resourceful, meaning that more people are expected to change their type of labour every few years. Older workers find skills becoming obsolete, while more workers find that once they lose a job their job prospects involve lower earnings and loss of 'career'. This has contributed to stagnant real wages, partly because seniority-rated pay has been declining.

Labour churning has also weakened mutual solidarity between enterprises and employees. This does not mean necessarily that many more employees have short-term employment, but it does mean that more are at risk of losing their jobs. The mutual commitment has become conjectural rather than moral and normal. Again, as in the USA, the old labourist practice of lay-off during downturns has been fading. More are expected to change jobs from time to time.

Labour Migration

In the crisis before Polanyi's Transformation, labour-related migration rose, mainly reflecting movement of Europeans to the 'New World'. Migrants as a share of the US population peaked at 15 per cent in 1913. Most was settler migration, supplying emerging capitalist economies with the nucleus of national working classes, and undermining resistance to industrial disciplines by providing immigrants resigned to hard labour.

In the corresponding phase of the Global Transformation, migration is more heterogeneous. There are plenty of settler migrants. But much of the rise in mobility has been circular or temporary, while more has been illegal, unauthorized, undocumented and 'without nationality'. Guest-worker systems have featured in several countries, such as Germany and the USA. Students, real and bogus, comprise another mobile group, along with professionals and managerial employees transferred within multinationals. More odiously, millions are in bonded labour or contract labour, many in debt that threatens loss of the land or homes they left. Millions more are migrants in shanty towns and Export Processing Zones (EPZs), where production depends on subsidies, low labour costs and denial of labour standards.

Migration is growing. In 2005, according to UN estimates, there were 191 million migrants living outside their country of citizenship, including those migrating for employment, dependants, refugees and asylum seekers (UN Population Division, 2006). This was more than double the number in 1970. And they have been increasingly concentrated in the developed world, which accounts for nearly two-thirds of all migrants. One in every three lives in a developed country and comes from a developing country; another one in three is in a developing country and comes from a developing country; the remainder have migrated within the industrialized world.

By 2000, migrants accounted for more than 10 per cent of the population in 70 countries, compared with 48 in 1970 (Global Commission on International Migration, 2005). In 2007, one in every ten people in the UK was a migrant; in the USA it was one in eight. The USA has allowed in more than a million legal migrants each year since 2000, and it is estimated that a further 500 000 a year go there illegally.

Migrants to rich countries take a large proportion of newly created jobs. Perhaps half of all jobs created in the UK between 1997 and 2006 were taken by foreigners.[8] Migrants are the light infantry of global capitalism. Unattached to local customs of solidarity and class identity, they weaken the effect of protective regulations and the bargaining power of local groups, particularly when the migration is temporary or illegal. And it is because using illegal immigrant labour is so profitable that it has grown. Governments have targeted illegal migrants and traffickers rather than the firms that employ migrants (Naim, 2005).

In the USA, illegal immigrants have been employed not just by marginal firms but also by state enterprises and major companies (Johnson, 2006). Their role is systemic, not peripheral. According to one analysis, in 2005 the US government issued just two visas to Mexican labourers, when the number of undocumented Mexican immigrants was 500 000 (Preston, 2006). The presence of this army of unprotected workers surely did not reflect an inefficient surveillance system. Had the authorities wished to change the situation, they could have done so.

Migration in the Global Transformation is more migratory in the old sense of the term, being almost nomadic and 'homeless', rather than about reconstructing home. Homelessness is akin to precariousness. The main migration in the Great Transformation was about building a new home, setting down roots and accepting the norms and values of the host society. Migrants who do not expect to stay where they are labouring, whose goal is to send money 'home', or who do not have a legal right to stay, cannot easily enter an indigenous community. Nor, unless it is internationalized, can they easily join an occupational community.

As shown later, entry barriers for numerous occupations are contrived. But, while many migrants with qualifications – such as lawyers, engineers and dentists – cannot work legally in their spheres of competence, their departure deprives their home country of skills. In small low-income countries, the brain drain enfeebles occupational communities. In 2005, only 50 of the 600 doctors trained in Zambia since the country gained independence were practising there; more Malawian doctors were working in Manchester than in Malawi (Global Commission on International Migration, 2005). This global labour process involves not just a brain drain but brain waste, in that educated people move to take jobs that do not utilize their occupational skills.

Professional migration is being facilitated by the GATS, Mutual Recognition Agreements and bilateral arrangements, often within an international market for specific occupations. The temporary movement of qualified employees and consultants alleviates constraints imposed by a shortage of specialist workers in the host countries. Although direct labour costs may be higher, firms do not have to bear the costs of training and longer-term enterprise benefits.

Rich countries are also using controls to select migrants with desired occupations. In the USA, employer-sponsored H-1B visas enable firms to recruit professionals from developing countries, though corporate America has complained that the number is insufficient. The quota is limited to 65 000 a year, but in 2007 that was filled in a single day (Vara, 2008). With India, the process has been institutionalized by ties between Indian IT companies and firms such as Microsoft and Dell, which have set up offices in Indian cities.

Though security concerns have led the USA to restrict immigration, other countries have devised subtle schemes for attracting educated immigrants. Canada and Australia, copied by others, award 'points' for educational qualifications; the UK gives graduates of the world's top 50 business schools an automatic work visa for up to a year, and is constructing a points system that would allow people in if they fulfil a list of credentials. The EU is introducing a 'Blue Card' scheme to attract 'skilled' migrants, which will couple two-year work permits with financial and housing benefits for professionals having at least a one-year employment contract earning at least three times the minimum wage.

By such means, countries have been competing to obtain commodified talent, a unique feature of the Global Transformation. This is commodified labour power. It is a form of mercantilism, not free trade or free labour mobility. Migration is a defining feature of the Global Transformation. It will continue to grow. Migrants themselves may be demonized by populist politicians. But they are leveraging the global labour process, and inducing changes in labour relations that will have far-reaching ramifications for what is feasible and desirable in the twenty-first century.

Casualization

Even though more people have written contracts than at any time in history, globalization and labour market flexibility are associated with more informal and casual labour relations.

Informalization takes three forms. The first, found mostly in developing countries, consists of petty production in slums. The second consists of firms informalizing employment by using subcontractors and outworkers. The third involves use of illegal forms of labour, to avoid tax and social contributions and to evade regulatory safeguards. All three have spread to industrialized countries and became the norm in Eastern Europe after 1989. Black economy labour is increasing. Often, the employer and worker split the difference, with a higher wage being paid because the employer is saving by not paying contributions or taxes.

Casualization refers to a shift from quasi-permanent to short-term employment. Although there has been explicit casualization involving a shift from regular to casual statuses, probably more pervasive has been implicit casualization, a weakening of conditions such that regular employment takes on the character of casual in all but name. One must beware of using figures on employment tenure to identify casualization. A shift from regular to casual status does not necessarily mean the average duration of employment will decline. It means that more people have insecure tenure.

Even so, the number in casual statuses has jumped. For example, in Australia the share of the casual labour force has been rising for several decades (Campbell and Brosnan, 2005). In Germany, there has been a shift from primary employment, for which social insurance contributions are compulsory, to 'mini-jobs' and Z*eitarbeit* (temporary work), accompanied by a growth of temporary employment agencies. In Japan, temporaries now account for more than a third of all jobs, up from 23 per cent in 1997, and are paid about two-thirds of what full-timers receive (Hayashi, 2008).

One factor boosting casualization is the privatization of public utilities. Many privatized companies have emulated the labour relations of private corporations. Thus, Spain's Telefónica promptly replaced employees through an early retirement scheme and turned to 16 000 outsourced workers (European Industrial Relations Observatory, 1998). Almost everywhere, postal services have resorted to non-regular contracts, temporary employment agencies and outsourcing.

While some countries have a definition of 'casual', it takes many forms, including 'casual-casuals, regular-casuals and permanent-casuals', as in New Zealand (Whatman et al., 1999). At the extreme are those with no employment contract and no security at all. Next are those who have a temporary contract, perhaps as short as a day or as long as six months. Sometimes a temporary contract may be renewable and continue for years. More often, to ensure workers do not qualify for benefits, they are required to have a break in employment after a few months, a practice widespread even in civil services and UN agencies.

Some workers are classified as casual by virtue of the limited number of hours they are contracted to provide. They may be called 'part-time' and not classified as casual, but that is what they are. Some may be contracted for a limited number of hours, but be required to work longer when needed. Another group not described as casual are workers on probation, paid lower wages and denied entitlements, including protection against arbitrary dismissal. Unless hindered by legislation or collective agreements, employers can alter the terms and conditions of probationary employment at will. Lengthening probationary periods is casualization by stealth.

Another casual status consists of 'temps' hired out by employment agencies, probably the most rapidly growing form of employment. In effect, firms are contracting out their employment. Workers may be put in a casual status, but be employed by the agency on a longer-term contract. More often they are casually hired by an agency and then hired out to a firm, perhaps with a holding contract with the agency.

Casualization has also meant more subcontracting, outsourcing, use of illegal migrants, use of illegal labour to evade taxes, and use of prison labour, the most casual form of all, in that the worker has no rights, cannot bargain and can be made to do as much labour as somebody sees fit. Not all these jobs are casual in every sense of the term. However, their casual nature stems from lack of the various forms of security mentioned earlier. And they are subject to more diverse forms of control than others, a reflection of their subordination and commodification.

There is also casual work that is not labour. Foremost is care work, which is casual in that there are no labour securities. This might also be said of a rising form of casual work, civil society activity. Not all is casual, in that sometimes employment contracts are involved. But much voluntary, community and NGO work is casual, even if more people are gaining contracts.

Governments have assisted in the spread of casual labour all over the world. For instance, Peru passed a law to allow temporary contracts to continue for up to five years without requiring employers to pay severance pay; Argentina after its economic crisis established temporary contracts exempt from severance pay and social security benefits. In Italy and in Japan, changes in the law have been designed to boost the use of casual labour. China has moved in the same direction.

The UK has pushed for casualization particularly assiduously. In 2008 it opposed efforts by other EU countries to require employers to provide 'temps' with full pay and standard working conditions after six weeks in their jobs. When the UK government found itself isolated, it sought to apply the directive flexibly, so that the law would not apply if there were collective agreements and a 'forum' for unions and employers.

Casualization is part of the armoury of global flexibilization. The benefits for employers are well known. Casual workers usually receive lower wages, although in Australia and New Zealand there has been casual loading pay of up to 20 per cent extra. Firms can also avoid linking pay to experience and providing various enterprise benefits. This extends to the ability to lay off employees without cost whenever there is a downturn in demand. Indeed, employers can avoid most non-wage labour costs, in the form of paid leave, sick leave, healthcare compensation and so on. As these costs mounted, using casual status workers became a way to avoid enterprise benefits.

An indirect benefit for employers comes from the threat casual workers represent to regular workers. Not only do they put up with wage cuts, loss of benefits, variations in working time and arbitrary penalties for errors, real or imagined. They may also make others more resigned to such treatment themselves. Employers, particularly small-scale businesses, may also derive ideological comfort from their greater managerial control. The employer can feel satisfaction in the reflection: 'I am the boss. If they [the workers] do not do what I tell them, or as I expect, then I can get rid of the blighters'. This may even dominate the economic rationale for using casual workers (Smith and Ewer, 1999).

There are potential downsides of casualization for employers. Casualized workers may lack commitment, have lower productivity, be careless of equipment and raw materials and be less likely to acquire skills. This argument has been given spice by management 'scientists' who urge service companies to place a high priority on 'emotional' skill, which is apparently best harnessed to the needs of companies by employment that engenders feelings of loyalty and commitment.

For workers, there is bad and good news in casualization. We will consider the upsides later. Besides the psychic cost of feeling unwanted on a long-term basis, the downsides include employment insecurity, which may translate into lower status as consumer and citizen. Try obtaining a loan or mortgage when you have only a casual job. But casual workers experience all the forms of labour insecurity outlined earlier. Their income insecurity flows not only from having lower wages but also no entitlement to most enterprise benefits and no chance to obtain seniority and/or experience-rated pay.

Casual workers also have a lower probability of entitlement to employment-related state benefits. Disentitlement has grown, often subtly, as when governments lengthen required contribution periods. And casual workers risk losing access to family-based benefits (FB). Giving support to relatives and friends is usually based on an implicit reciprocity, an understanding that the recipient will in turn extend help if the donor is in need. The nature of the class re-stratification outlined in the next chapter makes such reciprocity less likely; those who could be donors will be more reluctant to help those in casual jobs because there is no assurance of reciprocity.

Casual workers have less access to training, more often have to pay for it and have less reason to go on training courses because they cannot expect to receive a return on their investment, especially if the skills are firm-specific. Casual workers are also more exposed to various forms of harassment. Women in casual jobs are more susceptible to sexual harassment, since they are more subject to pressure in return for a promise of employment renewal.

Still, while current forms have adverse effects for many workers, casualization could induce a greater sense of personal responsibility for forging a working life. As argued later, one can imagine freedom-enhancing measures that would enable people, if they wished, to choose casual jobs that did not tie them to a company, workplace or specific hours, without the exploitative pressures now associated with casualization.

Outsourcing and Offshoring

Outsourcing has caught popular attention. It is a metaphor, one manifestation of the fear that characterizes the globalization of labour market flexibility. It goes with businessman and presidential candidate Ross Perot's infamous imagery of 'the great sucking sound' of Mexico (Perot, 1992). Historically, outsourcing grows at times of economic restructuring. It reflects resistance by workers to loss of established entitlements. It is also a means of accelerating change by inducing concessions from workers. But now it is contributing to the global re-division of labour. It involves several levels: the highly paid, educated IT specialist; the clerical 'call centre' or book-keeping type; and the 'unskilled' worker, usually a woman, required to do assembly labour, often located in an Export Processing Zone. Each form of outsourcing imparts both insecurity and some advantages for those doing the work.

A distinction should be made here between outsourcing (the acquisition of inputs or services from an unaffiliated firm, at home or abroad) and offshoring (the sourcing of inputs from abroad via foreign affiliates or non-affiliates through arm's-length contracts) (WTO, 2008, p. 99). The popular image of outsourcing actually relates to offshoring, that of corporations in rich countries transferring jobs to poorer ones. This can take the form of 'insourcing offshoring', whereby multinationals shift employment to their subsidiaries, and 'outsourcing offshoring', whereby firms transfer employment to quasi-independent suppliers.

In 2006, John Sweeney, AFL-CIO President, claimed that as many as 52 million US jobs were at risk of being offshored (Sweeney, 2006, attributed to Blinder, 2005). Such claims should remind economists of similar claims about technological unemployment and the 'lump-of-labour fallacy'[9]. What is happening is an international re-division of labour. There is no reason to presume the number of jobs is fixed or that there is a limited amount of work to be done.

That said, services offshoring has been rising rapidly, notably by US and UK companies (Amiti and Wei, 2005). In 2006, three-quarters of financial institutions had offshore activities, compared with 10 per cent in 2001 (Deloitte Touche Tohmatsu, 2007). Up to 20 per cent of financial service jobs in rich countries could be moved to countries such as India and the Philippines by 2010 (Croft, 2005).

Several studies have divided types of work by whether they are 'offshorable' or 'non-offshorable'. One estimated that 20 per cent of US jobs were offshorable (Van Welsum and Vickery, 2005); another gave a range of 22–29 per cent (Blinder, 2007). The OECD (2006) concluded that 20 per cent of employment in the EU-15, the USA, Canada and Australia could 'potentially be affected' by offshoring.

Economists differ in their opinion of the impact of offshoring. Stephen Roach, then Morgan Stanley's chief economist, argued that low job growth and stagnant wages in the USA were due to 'powerful cross-border labour arbitrage' (Wighton, 2006). However, Diana Farrell, director of the McKinsey Global Institute (MGI), said such fears were overblown because a third of US workers were in companies with fewer than 100 employees, too small to justify offshoring. She estimated that no more than 'several hundred thousand jobs per year will be lost to offshoring' (Wighton, 2006). Since this was tiny relative to the size of the labour force, the impact on wages would also be negligible. According to an MGI survey (2005), about 4.6 million Americans start a new employment every month, and while this churning means many face a period of concern, labour turnover dwarfs the number of jobs being offshored. The WTO has taken the same view, stating that, 'The impact of offshoring services jobs is far stronger in the popular perception than on actual production, employment and trade patterns' (WTO, 2005). In 2005, offshored IT services accounted for less than 10 per cent of world exports of business services.

Nevertheless, popular perceptions matter in an information-driven market system. The perception is that offshoring is growing. The WTO (2008) recognized that it has been growing rapidly, especially in financial services. Moreover, as with capital mobility, it is *potential* outsourcing that has the most powerful effect, by inducing concessions that chip away at labour security and entitlement to enterprise and state benefits. Some unions have given up the fight against offshoring and have tried to gain some advantage from it. For example, in 2005, Computer Sciences Corporation, one of the world's largest IT service providers, agreed with Amicus, a UK union, to plough some of its savings from moving tasks offshore into retraining those whose jobs were threatened. That has not been the only such deal.

As for the actual effects, one study found that outsourcing had affected the skill structure of demand in the UK and hit the prospects of 'unskilled' workers (Hijzen et al., 2004). Another suggested that it had lowered demand for 'unskilled' labour within the EU, while increasing the demand for skilled labour (Dumont, 2006).

Outsourcing and offshoring will continue as long as they produce savings for firms. Deloitte found that financial companies that had moved operations offshore typically reported a cost saving of 20 per cent; some saved 40–50 per cent. These gains are huge, even if many encounter a drop-off in savings (Croft, 2005). Though some companies have been shifting services (not necessarily jobs) back again, this is unlikely to be the main trend.

There may be short-term constraints on the growth of offshoring. MGI (2005) estimated that the demand for engineers from the UK and USA alone would use up the suitable supply in China, India and the Philippines by 2011. India's IT industry, whose offshore business has been growing by 30 per cent annually, has also suffered bottlenecks. According to one report, the industry faced a shortfall of 500 000 professionals by 2010 (Johnson and Merchant, 2005). But these are teething pains. And offshoring is becoming globalized, in that firms in developing countries are outsourcing jobs to others as well as being a location themselves (Giridharadas, 2007).

In sum, offshoring and outsourcing are growing. The actual number of jobs involved is only part of the challenge. It is the *anticipation* of job losses that leads to fear among workers, driving them and their representatives, including government agencies, to give up enterprise and state benefits, or to give up employment security and accept more flexible labour relations and payment systems. Making people fearful is a device for inducing them to accept a lower social income.

Given the difference in labour costs, even net of productivity differences, between the USA and the world's new industrial workshops, one should rather wonder why offshoring has been so modest. Given the changes in labour policies taking place in those countries, one can predict a rapid increase. In China, in terms of the restructuring of social income, the shift from enterprise benefits to state benefits will profoundly affect the global labour market, since recent reforms have cut labour costs and made it easier to create flexible jobs desired by rapidly innovating multinationals.

In effect, social policy dumping in industrialized countries is being matched by regula-tory reform in the energized workshop countries. It is wrong to have an image of a 'race to the bottom', in which wages and benefits will fall to those currently received by workers in India or China. But there is a slow convergence, implying moves from what have been 'best practice' employment relations in affluent countries towards a situation of much less labour security. This is the future.

The old development model assumed that developing countries would grow by taking low-skilled jobs in which they had a comparative advantage. A transfer of lower-skilled jobs and production to developing countries would enable developed countries to benefit from a rising share of high-productivity production while developing countries would also gain because industrial low-skilled jobs have higher productivity than agricultural jobs. This model needs revision. The greater gains for capital come from transferring high-productivity, high-income tasks, not low-productivity, low-wage jobs.

The international re-division of labour, enabled by IT, is fragmenting production processes and redistributing tasks. It started with call centres and back-office processing. But many complex services can be handled by teams, the members of which are located in several places. US tax returns are partly handled by a Bangalore-based company that coordinates workers utilizing document management software (Roberts, 2004). A contact lens company, Bausch & Lomb, brings together product designers from around the world in a virtual 'e-room'. Companies are hiving off human resource functions, such as management of pensions, health benefits and payrolls, inventory administration and procurement services, such as travel and printing. Digitization enables complex processes to be broken into discrete parts, and so-called knowledge workers exist everywhere.

Public services are being outsourced too, including health and education. Thus, health insurance companies in the USA are beginning to cover health benefits when someone goes oversees for treatment; some have contracts with foreign hospitals. This makes finan-cial sense – a heart bypass operation cost US$130 000 in the USA in 2008, 13 times more than in India or Thailand (Einhorn and Arnst, 2008). But it will surely put pressure on the medical professions in rich countries.

Each recession in industrialized countries will lead to a jump in offshoring, especially in the upturn after jobs have been shed. And recession in a major economy may have a greater impact on employment elsewhere. The effects of offshoring may not be measur-able in terms of jobs in any one country. Together they form a pressure package making workers in the global labour market ever more insecure.

Labour 'Triangulation': Temporary Employment Agencies

Temporary employment agencies have become major multinationals. Swiss-based Adecco, with 700 000 on its books, is one of the world's biggest private employers. Pasona, a Japanese temporary-staffing agency set up in the late 1970s, was sending a quarter of a million workers out to firms every day by 2007. From being a peripheral component of Japan's labour force, part-time and temporary agency employees now account for a third of it. Pasona's founder says the flexibility is beneficial for both com-panies and workers and dismisses the old norm of long-term employment as sentimental: 'Be a regular worker – and exploited for the rest of your life' (Economist, 2007d). Like big employment agencies in Europe and North America, Pasona has established dozens of subsidiaries dealing with outsourcing projects and operations in Asian countries and the USA.

The significance of triangulation is considerable. It was symptomatic of the crumbling of the ILO's labourist model that in 1997 it abandoned its long opposition to private employment agencies and passed the Private Employment Agencies Convention. The standard employment relationship and industrial citizenship were based on direct employment, ideally sealed by a collective agreement between employers and unions at national or sectoral level. This left no room for third parties. Allowance was grudgingly made for the eventuality that besides a collective agreement there might be an individual contract, but this too was presumed to be a labour deal between two parties.

The model regarded employment exchanges as government agencies acting as conduits. But the global market society has transformed them into vehicles of social policy while employment services have been commodified. The agencies have become employers or what look like employers. The challenges thrown up by the marketization of their services are huge. Their emergence as major capitalist ventures raises questions of governance, accountability, transparency and equity. For instance, if an agency supplies workers to firms, to whom will it have more commitment? If it draws up a contract with a firm to provide temporary labour, and then supplies someone registered with the agency, the identity of the employer becomes moot. If the agency is the employer, the firm can avoid responsibility for what happens to the worker. There are all sorts of gradations between agencies that are merely conduits, receiving a fee for putting workers in touch with employers, and those that are really employers who rent out workers. The scope for workers to become purely commodified is considerable.

The point here is that triangulation has become an integral part of the global labour process. Trying to hold the several parties to specific responsibilities is an unresolved aspect. But this form of flexible labour relationship is creating an institutional framework with enormous implications for the construction of occupational careers.

Contractualization

There is also a trend to what we can call 'contractualization'; more people are entering into written contracts covering ever more numerous aspects of life, particularly in employment and the provision of services. All encourage and reflect the growth of individualization. They have helped dissolve forms of collective identity and social solidarity, and are pushing society towards a legalism that gives greater scope for surveillance, social auditing and control.

Contractualization refers to the global trend towards individualized labour contracts. It reflects the decline in collective contracts, the proletarianization of professions and the shift to services in general. Contracts are a means of strengthening control, especially when the labour required is more individualized and when direct supervision is harder. The employment relationship is always an incomplete contract, since employees can adjust their effort bargain as an employment relationship unfolds. But individualized contracts attempt to tighten employment conditions to minimize uncertainty for the employer, backed by the threat of penalties for abrogation of the terms of the agreement. To some extent, they derive from the existence of complex labour law, which leads firms to try to protect themselves by limiting obligations via written contracts. As shown later, this process has been assisted by labour law reforms and judicial interpretations.

To open the way for contractualization, governments and employers have whittled away at collectively bargained contracts, where the strength of bargaining power is relatively equal. As collective bargaining has been abandoned, or narrowed, the scope for individualized contracts has increased. This may lead to an illusion. The shrinkage of collective agreements will mean that even though there is a shift to individualized contracts globally, greatly accelerated by China's Labour Law of 1994, fewer workers will have formal contractual employment, for a while.

The picture is growing even more complicated, because one can envisage more situations in which workers will have several contracts. They could have one individual contract with their direct employer, one with an agency or personal agent, one via a collective bargain and one with their professional organization stipulating what practices are acceptable or not. While it is most unlikely that anybody would have all types of contract, the complexity may require a stronger legal framework to sort out priorities and acceptable terms.

Finally, a form of labour contractualization is reaching the unemployed, and has begun to receive attention from labour lawyers (Sol and Westerveld, 2005). The imposition of contracts on the unemployed, renamed 'clients' as befits the modern therapeutic culture, is part of the restructuring of the welfare state, extending labourism in a way scarcely envisaged by early generations of social democrats.

Tertiarization

The twenty-first century will be dominated by services and the tertiarization of societies and economies. The implications for social and economic policy have yet to be fully appreciated. There is still manual labour. But the norm for social and other policy is the service worker.

Informalization, casualization, triangulation and contractualization come together in the concept of tertiarization. This is not just about a shift from manufacturing to services. It is also about a restructuring of systems of control, bringing a more exploitative treatment of time. An influential Italian school of thought, drawing on Marxism and Foucault (1977), depicts this restructuring as creating 'the social factory', in which the production regime treats society as an extension of the workplace (Hardt and Negri, 2000, 2004).

The factory image is not quite right. Factory work involved sharply defined time blocks, mass production and direct control in a fixed workplace. All of this has been displaced to some extent by a more flexible system in which more work-for-labour, often away from the workplace, complements on-the-job labour and in which direct supervision has been replaced by sophisticated technological control, through surveillance, auditing, performance assessment and a restructuring of social income so that remuneration is tied more to performance than to workplace attendance and observed time on the job. Workers are also turned into permanent competitors rather than colleagues banded in integrated labour.

The process could produce not the 'virtuoso worker', as the Italian school portrays it, but the dilettante labourer. The 'precariat' outlined in the next chapter loses control not only over time but also over the reproduction of 'skill' and sense of personal occupation.

Thus, for precarious workers it would be irrational to learn a deep body of techniques if faced by a constantly changing production system in which the division of labour is not slowly and predictably changing but is subject to radical uncertainty. The 'flexibility' implies more risk to labour learning. This has not been adequately incorporated in assessments of labour markets and inequality. If there is an increased probability of having to learn new skills to maintain a decent income, the rate of return to any job training is reduced. To compound the problem, by the nature of human physiology, it is harder with age to learn new skills. This must impart insecurity, since everybody ages.

A good example is the academic community. The current generation of students will be armed with techniques that surpass those of their teachers and, disconcertingly for the latter, much of what they learned decades earlier is now relegated to dust-covered books on unused shelves. The stress on teachers will be reproduced through the need to be permanent students, if they are to stay up-to-date. There is a Chinese aphorism, 'When a teacher meets his student, he meets his master'. This is not only truer than it used to be, but the student will also realize that mastery is an ephemeral, fleeting achievement.

This set of images applies to numerous spheres of work and labour. There is a diminishing sense of personal control over the knowledge and technology built up by past labour and work. This reflects tertiarization.

RESTRUCTURING SOCIAL INCOME

The global market economy is inducing a restructuring of social income everywhere. This does not mean that all countries will have the same structure or that one country's social income structure will prevail. However, more countries are under pressure to move towards a similar model. It is not the US model of the 1990s, the European 'social model' or the Chinese model of recent decades. But it does seem to be one suited to open economies and rapid economic and technological change. It is one in which enterprise benefits are shrinking, state benefits are being curbed via means-testing and behaviour-testing, and money wages are rising.

The presumption is that unless firms and national economies can treat labour as a commodity, their competitive position will be threatened. Labour recommodification has been accelerated by the restructuring of social income, which has made it harder to trace the full extent of the growth of inequality. To see what has happened, consider the main trends.

Wages

Fundamental to recommodification has been the shift back to money wages (W in the social income identity outlined in Chapter 1) relative to enterprise non-wage benefits and services (EB) and state benefits and services (SB) provided to employees to cover employment-related contingencies. The shift has made it difficult to interpret wage statistics as measures of living standards or income inequality, but it means that any given money wage is associated with fewer benefits, on average.

In fact, despite a shift back to money wages in the social income structure, real wages in the rich countries have stagnated. In the USA, median wages (for the middle fifth of wage earners) declined by 3.8 per cent between 1998 and 2006, when the economy grew by over 25 per cent. In Germany, real wages have fallen, tacitly accepted in collective agreements. Since 2000, the wage share of national income has fallen from 60 per cent to 55 per cent. In Japan real wages fell by 10 per cent between 1997 and 2007.

Economists quibble over the exact causes of stagnant real wages in rich countries; trade, technology, bargaining power are all cited. The major factor is 'Chindia'. The effective global supply of labour power quadrupled in the globalization period, most of that coming after 1990 and most of that from low-wage, labour surplus countries (IMF, 2007, ch. 5). This is even more than implied by Freeman's estimates cited earlier.

Though the bargaining position of workers in the emerging economies may strengthen as labour markets tighten, the gap between wages in the rich countries and those in major developing countries is so huge that the downward pressure will remain for many years. In 2004, the average hourly labour cost in manufacturing in the USA was US$23. Taking that as an index of 100, the equivalent in China and India was 3, in Mexico 12, in Brazil 15. The Japanese equivalent was over 90 and the EU average was nearly 120.

Because of the pressure to make wages more 'flexible', there has also been a shift from fixed wages, or the notion of a 'monthly salary', to productivity-based and 'performance-based' schemes, bonuses and the like. This has imparted more variability and income insecurity. It has also facilitated the growth of wage differentials that are a feature of the global market economy.

A reaction to wage flexibilization has been a political revival of the minimum wage. Without a floor, a flexible labour system would drive the wages of too many workers below a tolerable level. Thus, the UK and 19 other EU countries have economy-wide minimum wages. But a minimum wage is a blunt instrument for rectifying income insecurity, rarely reaching the really desperate (Standing, 2002). It is a barrier to employment for some who might have low productivity or would be prepared to work for little, for whatever reason. Surveys show that only a small proportion of those receiving low wages are in poor households, while many of those unable to find a minimum-wage job could survive in dignity if they could obtain a lower-earning job, simply because they have some income support from other sources. Above all, minimum wages do not protect many people in lowly occupations who are outside the standard employment relationship.

Enterprise Benefits

Enterprise benefits have been shrinking almost everywhere. In Japan, the scaling back of company benefits for the famed 'salaryman' began in the 1980s, facilitated by the increased use of short-term and part-time contracts. Companies in the USA, UK and other European countries have followed suit, winding up occupational pension plans or closing them to new members and, in the USA, reducing or ceasing to provide health cover for employees.

The legacy of labourism was that enterprise benefits had come to constitute a high share of labour costs and a source of rigidity in the face of competitive challenges posed by globalization and technological change. If employees have entitlement to healthcare, prospective redundancy benefits and occupational pensions, but little in terms of wages, the incentive to be efficient is reduced. Moreover, large companies that had built up a system of expensive benefits found themselves landed with hefty 'legacy costs' in the form of obligations to former employees, so that simply cutting employment was not an effective means of raising measured productivity or reducing unit labour costs.

Pay-as-you-go pensions only work if employment is stable and if the number of retirees does not rise dramatically. In the globalization period, the great US carmakers found they had more retirees than active employees.[10] Healthcare expenses ballooned, since these were paid to current and ex-employees and their dependants. Pensions and healthcare together were costing them about US$1000 per vehicle sold, compared with a fifth of that for their Japanese competitors.

Legacy costs, or 'post-employment benefits', threaten the future of GM and Ford, once flagships of the US economy, and have dragged down the steel industry and US airlines. In response to such pressure, firms have turned to desperate and ruthless tactics. One ruse in the USA is the infamous 'Chapter 11' device. This allows companies to declare bankruptcy as a way of offloading pension and health insurance costs, and forcing workforces to accept wage cuts. As one observer put it, 'Chapter 11 has become a device for reasserting management fiat over workers with the backing of bankers' (Gapper, 2005).

Other companies have adopted less drastic measures, but with similar effect. Pensions have been hardest hit. One consequence of the financialization of companies, reflected in the decline in reliance on shares and the rise in holding of debt, is that company pension schemes are made less secure by the increased risk of bankruptcy or takeover. Many quoted-company schemes have been closed to new members, or converted from defined-benefit to defined-contribution schemes that substantially reduce enterprise obligations.

In the USA, and elsewhere, the other major benefit being eroded has been healthcare. Traditionally, medical benefits were a mechanism to raise employee efficiency, morale and commitment to the company. As healthcare costs rose, their share of labour costs soared. Firms responded by changing from wholly employer-funded schemes to systems that split the premium between employer and employee or loaded most of the contributions on to the employee. But this failed to arrest the escalating cost, because people are living longer than the actuaries anticipated and medical treatment is becoming ever more expensive.

By 2007, 47 million Americans were not covered by health insurance, and only 60 per cent of firms were offering employees healthcare compared with 69 per cent in 2000. In scaling back health plans, firms obliged employees to pay a higher share of treatment costs and refused to cover family members, which means enterprise benefits (EB) have shrunk by more than it appears. Those required to pay their own health insurance have found the cost rising faster than wages.

In the USA, the shrinkage of EB has been greater than that of state benefits, because the latter were never extensive. As a result, workers there have felt more insecure. Employment insecurity has fed into this, because losing a job loses health insurance as well as the wage. Those with a pre-existing medical condition can be plunged into financial ruin. The problem has been compounded because firms were encouraged to rely on this model by vast tax subsidies, which went to employers for operating health insurance and not to employees.

Newer firms have simply taken steps to offload EB or have avoided making such commitments, or have turned to external labour arrangements where the workers have no entitlement to such benefits. EB have also become more dualistic, with employees in high-tech, high-profit enterprises receiving them and most in smaller firms and out-workers losing them. This dualism is regressive, since EB have been rising for higher-earning employees and shrinking for the rest.

In some economies, EB are more nominal than real. China's 2008 Labour Contract Law required employers to pay medical insurance for their employees, but many migrants are recruited off the books. More than half the population still has no medical insurance. China and India are among the countries that are setting the new remuneration system, in which EB will only be given to privileged insiders. That is perhaps the biggest source of inequality of all.

State Benefits

Meanwhile, state benefits (SB) have been shrinking and have been transformed. Although national differences remain, the trends point towards international convergence as a globalized labour market takes shape. It is hard to exaggerate the extent to which social protection has been 'reformed' in the interest of recommodification. The roll-back has been greatest in Europe where labour-based entitlements went farthest. Since the 1970s governments everywhere have chipped away at the welfare state. In some countries it is realistic to call the outcome the 'workfare state', and in others social policy dumping is moving that way, as governments rationalize making access to SB more difficult and lowering their value.

Contributing to recommodification are efforts to make 'social protection a productive factor'. This public relations term gained popularity inside the European Community in the 1990s as a way of defending social spending by giving it market appeal. But it has not done much to arrest the trend. Basically, powerful interests have wanted to use social policy to increase competitiveness, by lowering labour costs and fostering a more flexible labour market.

Within SB, universal or rights-based benefits have been cut and potential recipients are increasingly categorized as deserving or undeserving poor. Most countries have increased child support, ostensibly to reduce child poverty, but the motivation has also been to produce more 'human capital' and induce mothers to spend more time in wage labour. Germany is a case in point, where child benefits have been raised, crèches have been subsidized and the number of places increased. But state paternalism has also increased, making access dependent on behaviour and reserving the right to intervene to control what schooling should be provided.

Insurance-based benefits are also in decline as the European 'social model' crumbles. In 2005 the EU's Commissioner for Employment, Social Protection and Equal Opportunities wrote that social insurance remained its hallmark (Spidla, 2005). But in reality, social insurance is withering and becoming more fictitious. Means testing and behaviour testing have been displacing contribution-based schemes.

SB have fallen in monetary value as well as coverage. They have become less universal in character, making them less like social rights. They are limited entitlements, which have to be earned by means of contributions, increasingly by personal contributions, or by virtue of demonstrated and proven need.

As with EB, what is happening to SB has accentuated inequalities in ways rarely picked up in economic analysis. Pension reforms have led the way, so much so that we may be witnessing the slow death of occupational pensions. The average level of pension has declined in most rich countries, and the level received by low-income workers has declined even more (OECD, 2007a). One reason is the shift from public to private pensions, with the associated shift from defined-benefit to defined-contribution schemes. Risk, or responsibility for insurance, has been transferred to individuals, away from the state and employers. The number of years of contributions to obtain a full or even partial pension has increased, and the age of entitlement has gone up steadily.

Unemployment benefits have been chipped away too, to the point where one can predict that old-style unemployment insurance benefits will disappear before long. One-third of all OECD countries cut unemployment benefits between 2002 and 2007, and the average income replacement rate fell in many of them. The US reform to place 'time limits' on benefits was a clever way of driving the unemployed to take jobs they did not like, and to discourage employees who did not like their jobs from leaving them. In early 2008, the UK's Conservative Party announced it wished to do the same. Similar changes have been made elsewhere.

However, the main story about SB is the shift from both 'universal' or citizenship-based benefits and 'social insurance' benefits to means-tested social assistance and 'behaviour-tested' benefits. This has been a global trend, not restricted to countries perceived as having a 'residual welfare state'. A common trend has been a decline in the share of workers covered by rights-based benefits. In Germany, for instance, the number of employees covered by social insurance, and thus SB, has fallen sharply, particularly since 2000. Contrary to a stubborn image, the growth of means testing and behaviour testing has been fastest in countries long depicted as exemplary welfare states, steeped in traditions of labourism, or where fictitious decommodification was most pronounced.

Means tests produce notorious poverty and unemployment traps, where loss of benefit income in going from low-earning labour or from unemployment is greater than, or nearly as great as, the gain in earned income. Governments have tried to deal with this by lowering benefits, introducing in-work benefits and coercing the unemployed and those on incapacity benefits into jobs, rationalized in paternalistic terms. Such moves erode individual freedom and have other undesirable effects, including indirect effects on others at the lower end of the labour market.

Means testing is also socially divisive, since unlike social insurance it offers help to those who fall into a state of need instead of being paid as an entitlement built up as an acquired right. In Europe, means testing is causing anti-immigrant attitudes among working-class whites, because transfers are given on the basis of recorded need rather than on what people have contributed (Dench et al., 2006). This is eroding support for social democracy and playing into the hands of political populists. For instance, in the UK, the 1968 Housing (Local Government) Act made homelessness the key to housing entitlement, which moved newcomers such as migrants up the public housing queue at the expense of children of long-time residents. Council housing was pushed away from 'the respectable poor' to 'the rough', reviving the notion of welfare as charity and eroding notions of reciprocity.

Besides direct state transfers, privatization and commercialization of public services have contributed to labour recommodification. It is not just that citizens have to obtain services from private providers; they also have to satisfy market criteria in searching for them, choosing providers on the basis of price or quality of service that they may be in no position to assess. This applies not only to public utilities such as electricity and water but to core public services such as health where the rhetoric of choice disguises growing inequalities.

Fiscal Policy for Recommodification

Part of the restructuring of social income is attributable to the restructuring of fiscal policy. Taxation has become regressive, with cuts in income tax and taxes on profits. This has been compounded by the shift of subsidies from labour to capital; subsidies relevant to consumption of lower-income groups have been cut while those for corporations and rich investors have increased. The non-earned share of income has risen and, for more groups, financial income came to dominate their earnings from labour.

While state benefits drifted into social assistance, the neo-liberal state erected a complex system of fiscal benefits that resemble the Speenhamland system that so preoccupied Polanyi. The parallels are remarkable. The Speenhamland Law of 1795 introduced a wage subsidy for rural labourers based on the cost of bread, intended to provide subsistence irrespective of earnings. Although it slowed the emergence of a competitive labour market, it lowered tensions associated with the disruption of the Industrial Revolution. Hungry stomachs with hope of a little help produce passive, scared workers; hungry stomachs without hope produce angry people with little to lose. The subsidy kept the rural poor grumbling but not revolting.

Unfortunately for the ruling classes, the scheme also produced inefficient labour. In chronic surplus conditions, labourers earned the same whatever the amount of labour they performed. The 'allowance system' lowered productivity and fostered 'boon-doggling' (the pretence of labouring). According to Polanyi, 'the result was ghastly'. Abolished in 1834 by the Poor Law reform, it marked the floundering of paternalistic landlordism. As Polanyi concluded, 'The attempt to create a capitalistic order without a labour market had failed disastrously'. For many, what followed was even worse. As Polanyi ruefully commented, 'Never perhaps in all modern history has a more ruthless act of social reform been perpetrated; it crushed multitudes of lives while merely pretending to provide a criterion of genuine destitution in the workhouse test' (GT, p. 84).

Whereas the 1834 Poor Law rushed to commodify labour, the 'aid-in-wages' of Speenhamland was partially decommodifying. Actually a subsidy to employers, while keeping wages down, it is relevant to what is happening now. The subsidy was coupled with measures to curb workers' bargaining. The Anti-Combination Laws, retained for much longer than Speenhamland, prevented workers from taking union action. The subsidy gave 'subsistence' but labourers were blocked from gaining more than that. When the Poor Law reform moved to commodify labour more fully, making labourers dependent on money wages, it led to such suffering that it induced the state to act for 'the self-protection of society' (GT, p. 87), through protective factory acts and social legislation, and political acceptance of unions and reformist movements.

So, fiscal subsidies were used initially as a lever, in combination with anti-collective action and then the workhouse, first to pacify workers and then to commodify them. The modern parallel is the system of tax credits, comprising variants of the US Earned Income Tax Credit (EITC), which by the end of the twentieth century had become the world's largest income transfer scheme. It is a negative income tax, whereby incomes of low-wage employees are topped up to a nominal minimum wage level. The EITC allows firms to pay sub-subsistence wages and is a subsidy to capital. To the extent that it subsidizes low-skilled employment, it is an implicit trade barrier, deterring imports from low-cost producers and making exports cheaper. It also deters productivity-enhancing technological change and tends to lock firms into systems where jobs are unskilled and low-paid, even inducing a substitution of low-paid jobs for others. It has large deadweight and substitution effects and is conducive to petty fraud, including deals between employees and employers to share the subsidy while part of the actual wage is paid under the table.

Fiscal subsidies thus contribute to inefficiency, by firms that need not value employees at a decent money wage and by workers who do not have incentive to raise their wages because they would lose their tax credit. Were the tax credits minor, all of this would not matter much. The fact is that they comprise one of the biggest distortions to market economies ever constructed.

Like Speenhamland, they have allowed the old system of social protection and redistribution to be dismantled by limiting the pain, and they have slowed the pace of transition to a global labour market in which a large proportion of workers in rich countries cannot obtain an adequate income solely from money wages.

Community Transfers and Private Benefits

In the Great Transformation, the main beneficiaries of the shift from W to SB and EB were regular employees and the civil services that administered the benefits. Those with entitlements tended to weaken their links with those outside employment, because the reciprocity that is the essence of social solidarity was no longer there.

One consequence was that informal systems of protection declined as the state and enterprises took over risk-covering functions. In developing countries, informal community and kinship arrangements were stretched as urbanization and population mobility accelerated. In other words, the Great Transformation weakened informal systems of social protection. When state and enterprise benefits were cut under the impact of globalization, people found they did not have those community support systems to rely on.

The shift in social income to money wages has been accompanied by a rise in the share of private benefits. The state is encouraging and subsidizing employees and others to rely more on their savings and private insurance benefits, which is only possible if earnings are sufficient. The main development has been individualized savings accounts, for pensions, healthcare and other contingencies. Starting with pensions in Chile, this has spread globally. We need not review the emergence of multi-pillar pension systems. Usually, governments and employers make contributions to what are mainly employee-contribution schemes. However, many workers, particularly in developing countries but also wherever flexible labour relations are spreading, are not covered by contributory schemes. So governments have tried to 'extend' protection to informal workers by setting up modest non-contributory schemes for the poor. This has merely encouraged more informalization; if workers can gain access to non-contributory schemes only by being outside regular employment, it becomes advantageous for both workers and employers to move them from low-wage employment to informal statuses. This is what is happening globally.

The fact is that private individualized pension schemes are spreading, pushed by financial interests, including credit rating agencies and the international financial agencies.

Healthcare and other contingency benefits have moved in the same direction, including employment savings accounts and even wage insurance schemes. All these schemes are, however, based on regular labour; there is no strengthening of citizenship-based social rights. Risks from labour are being marketized, which benefits those in stable well-paid employment, not those in precarious situations. Any notion of social solidarity is lost.

In sum, recommodification has occurred through a globalized restructuring of social income that has put more onus on money wages to remunerate labour. Labour has been partially commodified, albeit held back by wage subsidies and residual benefits. We shall argue later that in some respects the restructuring has not gone far enough, but at present, the restructuring of social income has simply made labour and work more insecure.

RESTRUCTURING LABOUR REGULATION

> In every case the core of the free market that has been constructed is a deregulated labour market . . . the outcome has been an approximation to a free market in which labour is traded freely as a commodity just like any other.
>
> (Gray, 1998, p. 11)

The period of disembeddedness of the Global Transformation has been one of labour market reregulation, not deregulation. Probably more labour regulations have been introduced since the 1970s than at any time in history. A difficulty lies in understanding what constitutes regulation. Thus, a modern form of regulation is what Michel Foucault ([1976] 1998) called 'biopower', which he defined as the management of people for ends that are not theirs, or not of their own choosing. In this, a largely untold story has been about the restructuring of labour law.

Labour Law Restructuring

In the middle decades of the twentieth century, labour law was a means of reducing inequality between capital (employers) and workers (employees) by providing social rights (entitlements). But the assumptions of labour law have not applied in the Global Transformation. Labour law was designed to protect those in standard employment in national labour markets, not the growing number whose activity lies outside its mandate, including those working informally or doing care work, voluntary community work or freelance or 'distance work'. Outsourcing accelerates that trend. Labour law is in disarray, because more workers are not covered by the concept of employee and because companies can operate outside national labour law systems. Multinationals can move from where labour law is relatively comprehensive (Hepple, 2002). As if to help, all OECD countries except Belgium place restrictions on international solidarity action.

Consider what is happening in major economies. In the USA, labour law is being reinterpreted by the Supreme Court and the National Labor Relations Board (NLRB). Notions of employer and employee are becoming anachronistic. Many corporate headquarters are delegating their employment function to subsidiaries, which outsource to suppliers, which subcontract to agencies, intermediaries and contract workers. This makes it hard to determine who is responsible for working conditions and remuneration. US labour law is being adjusted to suit the desires of capital, in that 'contingent workers' are being denied legal rights gained for those in standard employment. The Supreme Court and NLRB have ruled that more categories are not to be counted as employees since they do not pass the common 'agency' and 'master–servant' test, or the 'right-to-control' test. For example, outsourcing has led to more people being classified as independent contractors. Falling outside the legal definition of employee, they lose entitlement to so-called labour rights. And those in standard employment will continue to make concessions to management to limit outsourcing and use of other non-standard labour.

Labour law reform in the world's emerging industrial workshops is setting the pattern. In India, a report in 2002 by the second National Commission on Labour (NCL) proposed an overhaul of labour law that would convert it into an instrument of national competitiveness and flexibility rather than employee protection. Implementing its recommendations would accelerate the offshoring of jobs from the USA and Europe. The NCL proposed a narrowing of the definition of a worker covered by labour law protection, which, crucially for its implication for offshoring, would exclude those earning more than a certain amount. Another thrust of the proposed reform is to reassert the duty to labour, with renewed emphasis on worker 'responsibilities'.

In China, labour law reform has been geared to the creation of a flexible labour market, a far cry from the *danwei*, the workplace-based system known as the 'iron rice bowl' that meant a very high EB relative to W. The Labour Law of 1994 formalized individual contracts and promoted labour administration institutions to regulate labour markets, including compulsory arbitration and mediation. This was followed by reforms increasing the emphasis on workers' duties and responsibilities. While labour law may reduce the incidence of extreme abuses, it is being constructed as an instrument of proletarianization. And, contrary to public posturing by US industry, the reform that came into effect in 2008 made it more attractive for multinationals to shift production and employment to China, since it created a more predictable, regulated labour market.

China's 2008 Labour Contract Law symbolized the transition to a capitalistic labour market, requiring employers to provide written contracts, putting restrictions on employment terminations, limiting the repeat use of temporary and probationary contracts, outlawing discrimination against migrants and requiring contracts to comply with minimum wage and safety regulations. The law also legitimized employee Voice by stipulating that employers must bargain with company-based branches of the state-run union on salaries, benefits, training and labour duties. It did so with typical state control, since workers are still not allowed to form independent unions. And although it was interpreted as a landmark, giving legal protection to the vast majority of workers who had no way to protect their rights under the old system, as one Chinese lawyer put it (cited in Kahn and Barboza, 2007), labour law in China is implemented selectively and irregularly.

The reforms have been forging a disciplined, low-cost labour supply. The law strengthened employment security, locking employees into labourism. Employees with over ten years of service with a firm were to have 'open-ended' or 'permanent' contracts, and employers were required to inform the union before firing any employee. These appear to be advances for workers' bargaining position, but the union is part of management, a means of labour control. And employers easily avoid having to grant permanent contracts by obliging medium-term employees to resign and compete for new short-term jobs.

Although the law was a boost for the government-controlled All-China Federation of

Trade Unions (ACFTU), which had been losing power with the collapse of state enterprises, few expect the ACFTU to emerge as a powerful independent Voice. There is no right to strike, abolished in 1982, and the government has seen the ACFTU as a means of limiting growing employee unrest. Meanwhile, the new law does nothing to improve the conditions of migrant workers or of others being made insecure.

Nowhere does the law of unintended consequences figure more strongly than in the labour market. Such employee protection as is now offered in China can be expected to lead to the same outcome as elsewhere. It will foster new forms of dualism, even if the law were enforced more effectively than its predecessors in China's rush to establish a national labour market. The state and the union can be expected to put national interest ahead of the interests of workers. The law is really a measure to foster a more orderly labour process in the interest of longer-term development of labour productivity. It is a productivist measure.

The law is also not as radical as some have claimed, since contractualization has been growing in China for many years. But it did entrench fixed-term and open-term contracts, banning employers from putting employees on more than two short-term contracts and requiring them to provide enterprise benefits to all those on open-term contracts. One can predict that this will boost 'triangulation', as it has done elsewhere. Major corporations will contract out part of their employment function and the 'precariat' working for agents and brokers will expand.

The legal and institutional difficulties of deciding who is responsible for employee protection will follow. Is the company using agency workers the employer or a 'client' receiving a 'service'? Is the broker (temporary employment agency) an 'intermediary' or an employer? The next stage will be a concerted effort to define an employee more comprehensively for purposes of labour law protection, a process that leads to an intellectual and legislative mess. In South Africa, which has tried to move in that direction, the definition of an employee hinges on no fewer than seven 'tests' of control or subordination that can be read into any specific labour relationship.

For the moment, China is trying to install a system of industrial citizenship. But a reason for believing this will be only a transitional phase is that multinational capital is externalizing the employment function, which is easier in services than in manufacturing or primary sectors. China comprises one-quarter of the world's population and, along with India, will shape the world's labour market. What happens there will determine what is feasible elsewhere in the global economy.

Globally, labour law has become more dualistic – protecting relatively privileged employees vis-à-vis direct employers. In trying to redefine 'employees' to cover more statuses, labour law has offered weaker protection and is losing its special status, being assimilated into common law. When advocates wish to 'extend' labour law to 'informal workers', they are pushing for a policy that would strengthen that long-term trend.

In Latin America, Piore and Schrank (2006) have claimed that recent labour law reform has expanded worker protection and that governments have 'rededicated themselves to labour law enforcement'. But they paint a picture of weakness. Instead of a compliance system in which violations are punished, 'the inspector operates more as an advisor or consultant than as a policeman'. Describing a visit to a garment factory with inspectors, they reveal a cosy relationship in which inspectors use 'their discretion', which apparently gives the system 'considerable flexibility over the business cycle', enabling inspectors to vary standards according to the unemployment level. This is scarcely indicative of a stronger system of labour law. It puts an onus on the inspectors ('advisors') rather than the law.

In Europe, labour law is struggling to retain independence. The European Court of Justice (ECJ) has made clear that competition law has precedence over labour law. As Wedderburn concluded, 'Again and again analysis of EC [European Community] law has followed through this theme, that competition law and the law that promotes integration of the market dominate labour relations in the EC legal order' (2002, p. 46). ECJ decisions support the competition and commercial freedom articles of the EU Treaty. The reality is that the EU is a market society in the making, and labour law is a messy obstacle. The rhetoric about Europe's 'social model' is belied by the fact that it is being dismantled by stealth, epitomized by the exclusion of freedom of association from the EU Charter.

The weakening of labour law is a mixed blessing for workers. As long as it seemed to offer a route to protection for a majority, it satisfied utilitarian objectives, even though it left many unprotected. Now that it does not offer much protection to the majority, there is more interest in building a framework for work rights, rather than so-called labour rights.

During the twenty-first century, commercial contracts will spread for most forms of labour. There will be more independent contractors, men and women who supply skills, time and energy to firms, to households and even to some employees. A distinction has been drawn between independent and dependent contractors, the dividing line being that the latter works for just one client. Some labour lawyers have suggested that the dependent contractor is a disguised employee, and needs the protection accorded to the standard employee. This implies a search to legitimize an extension of paternalistic protection. There is no need for that. The labour process will continue to evolve in ways that blur the boundaries between employee, independent contractor, dependent contractor and own-account worker. The power of any individual will vary. This is the reality that social policy will have to deal with.

The Withering of Collective Bargaining

The centrepiece of labourism was collective bargaining, usually within a tripartite system. This regime has been shrivelling. Sectoral bargaining has become harder to maintain, unions have been shedding members, employer organizations have become little more than rent-a-quote lobbying bodies, and tripartite institutions have been reduced to little more than gestures.

Even in Germany, a bastion of neo-corporatism, collective bargaining is withering. While unionization has declined (with membership halved since 1990), employers' associations are losing members even faster, particularly in engineering. Fewer firms are bound by wage bargains and in 2004, in a change symbolizing the Global Transformation, firms were allowed to deviate from sectoral agreements. As a result, unions came to accept company agreements even though they diverged from sectoral agreements. Called Alliances for Employment, these imparted wage flexibility in spite of the appearance of centralized bargaining. Meanwhile, union solidarity has crumbled with the unravelling of umbrella labour contracts, opposed by companies on the grounds that they threaten competitiveness.

In the UK, between 1896 and the late 1970s, voluntary collective bargaining predominated. In 1980, two-thirds of all firms recognized unions. By 1998, this was down to two-fifths and it has continued to decline. In 1984, wages were determined by collective bargaining in 60 per cent of firms; by 1998 it was less than half that. By 2000, industrial agreements had virtually disappeared and the scope of collective bargains had narrowed. Industrial action – mainly strikes – had become rarer than at any time since records were started in 1897.

The doctrine of 'enterprise confinement', that collective bargaining has to occur within an enterprise, has constrained bargaining for social rights. Thus, secondary picketing is no longer protected from common law liability. The spread of individual 'rights' coincided with stricter controls on collective bargaining, such 'rights' being enforced not by bargaining but by means of tripartite employment (formerly industrial) tribunals, with many cases being settled by the government's Advisory, Conciliation and Arbitration Service (ACAS). By 2005, tribunals were receiving 130 000 registered claims a year, which led the government to deter claims. One ruse was to require workers to pay a higher deposit to obtain a hearing; another was to strike out cases deemed to have no prospect of success; another was to allow tribunals to impose costs on claimants of up to £10 000, instead of £500 as had been the case (Hepple, 2002). Stricter time limits for claims were also introduced. These changes were inegalitarian, making it more costly for low-income workers to make claims. It also indicates how legislative barriers to agency are being constructed, a feature of recommodification.

Also indicative was the inducement to shift from public law to private commercial practice via the introduction in 2001 of an 'arbitration alternative' to employment tribunals, echoing a US trend. This is part of the privatization of labour regulation. It requires a worker to waive statutory rights in accepting that any dispute will be referred to private arbitration. The US Supreme Court has confirmed the legality of pre-dispute waivers, called the new 'Yellow Dog Contract' (Stone, 1996). In the UK, private arbitration is allowed only when there is a dispute. Its proponents claim that it speeds up the process and makes it cheaper, while creating an 'investigative' approach (Lewis and Clark, 1993). But the fact is that the employee, perhaps without realizing, waives a right to a public hearing, a right to cross-examine witnesses, a right to compel witnesses to attend a hearing and a right to a published and reasoned decision. And both parties waive their right to have the dispute resolved in accordance with the law (Hepple, 2002, p. 249).

There has been an erosion of personal agency. Lower-income workers cannot be expected to have the resources to proceed, while a lack of transparency increases the potential for unfairness. And private arbitrators are given unfettered discretionary power. They are allowed to apply 'good industrial relations practice', likely to be defined by employers, rather than rely on employment law applied by tribunals. So, as in the USA, the arbitrator can become what Katherine Stone (1981) called a 'labour relations physician' or 'labour relations psychiatrist' rather than a neutral adjudicator.

In the USA, curtailment of collective bargaining has led to use of mandatory arbitration in discrimination cases plus federal determination of minimum standards, with variation delegated to state level. This has set a framework for the rest of the world. In considering the demise of collective bargaining, Piore and Safford (2006) depicted its replacement by an 'employment rights regime', in which workplace rules are imposed by law, judicial opinions and administrative rulings. They claimed this was not a market regime, and that it involved 'a shift in the axes of social mobilization from mobilization around economic identities associated with class, industry, occupation and enterprise to mobilization around identities rooted outside the workplace: sex, race, ethnicity, age, disability, and sexual orientation' (Piore and Safford, 2006, p. 300). Perhaps it should be better interpreted as an employment management regime, linked to labour contractualization and standardization of personnel policy as 'human resource management' (Dobbin and Sutton, 1998). With individualized contracts has come the spread of private arbitration. These are all consistent with a market society.

Erosion of collective bargaining has coincided with construction of a human resource management system in which psychological manipulation is central, deploying controls based on a mix of incentives, pressures and penalties emphasizing employment equity, meritocracy and a rhetoric of equality of opportunity. Instead of focusing on distributions between capital and labour, or between managers and employees, the emphasis is on reducing gender-based, race-based and age-based inequality. But most inequalities are linked to occupations and positions in the productive process, not to demographic aspects, although social groups may be channelled into privileged or disadvantaged positions.

The USA has moved towards mandatory arbitration in discrimination cases as a substitute for judicial resolution of claims, so favouring employers (Estlund, 2002, p. 204). A landmark decision in *Circuit City Stores* v. *Adams* (2001) upheld employers' right to demand, as a condition for employment, that employees waive their right to bring a discrimination claim or any employment claim to court and instead accept private arbitration. It has been strengthened by a Supreme Court ruling that mandatory arbitration is acceptable. The use of private arbitration, in response to the rising cost of employment litigation, is part of the privatization of labour relations. Along similar lines, in the UK and South Africa arbitration alternatives to statutory tribunals are being developed. The discretion of arbitrators is displacing legal protection, a trend that further disadvantages those outside regular employment.

The shift in labour relations towards private mediation and arbitration is a threat to social rights. With commercialized services, quality depends on the ability to pay. A corporation can afford to pay and drag out legal processes; workers usually cannot.

A related reregulation is intrusion by private commercial agents. Credit rating agencies have influenced government and company pension and healthcare schemes; for example, Standard & Poor's downgraded the shares of several German companies to 'junk status' by applying US standards to their pension fund arrangements.

Finally, labour law and collective bargaining are being overruled by competition law, with the European Court of Justice being a primary engine. A landmark ruling came in 2007, when it ruled that Swedish unions were acting contrary to competition policy by blocking a Latvian construction firm that had brought in foreign workers to undercut local wages. This case created such nervousness that no fewer than 17 EU countries exercised their right to make representations to the ECJ, without success. The case showed not only the role being played by the courts in shaping labour matters, but also that national systems are being reformed by supra-national legal interventions. The immediate problem was that Sweden had no statutory minimum wage, so the unions did not have a right to force a foreign firm to adhere to locally bargained minimum wages. The outcome was a chip off the famed 'Swedish model', in which negotiated wage flexibility was a part, and a shift to a system based on statutory minima. That will be part of the global convergence to a market system overseen by juridical mechanisms.

THE DEMISE OF THE ILO MODEL AND THE RISE OF 'SOFT LAW'

The roll-back of collective bargaining and labour law, arbitration and inspection amounts to a roll-back of the ILO model of labourism. As national regulated labour markets of Polanyi's Transformation unravelled, so his 'permanent institutions', which included the ILO, lost their legitimacy and charm.

Labour standard setting and attempts to update conventions and the system of labour regulation drifted, as the ILO's modest efforts to oblige countries to adhere to conventions they had ratified ran into criticism by governments keen to reconstruct labour systems to strengthen competitiveness. Japan set the pattern in the 1960s, with an objection to an ILO report questioning its respect for freedom of association. Then there was Chile, where Pinochet's coup in 1973 resulted in suppression of unions, collective bargaining and much else. But the hiatus for the ILO came with the USA.

Just after the ILO received the Nobel Prize in 1969, the USA stopped paying its dues and then suspended membership – with Henry Kissinger sending a strident letter drafted by John Dunlop, doyen of US industrial relations. The reasons given for withdrawal were political, but the bigger reason was the ideological shift in the USA. It coincided with the supply-side economics revolution, which cast regulations as market distortions. The ILO was a symbol of a discredited way of thinking (Standing, 2008). Although the USA eventually returned, it did so only after securing concessions and an enlarged role for US staff.

The US withdrawal hastened the partial commercialization of the ILO itself. The major industrialized countries, which paid the bulk of its regular budget, insisted on a zero-growth budget or close to it. The ILO reacted with a clumsy mixture of restrictions on standard-setting activities, moving more into technical assistance and trying to raise more 'soft money' for projects. This resulted in a loss of focus and a failure to develop a response to the neo-liberal agenda that was transparently hostile to its raison d'être.

The World Bank moved into social policy, even though it had no business to be there. The IMF ratcheted up its conditionality with loans to include elements of social policy. The bank's structural adjustment programmes and the Washington Consensus were also designed to jettison the labourist model. The ILO was traumatized, by its budgetary crisis, its eagerness to regain favour with the USA and its desire to attract funds from the World Bank, among other things. No defence of labourism was attempted and no alternative was developed.

The subsequent unravelling of the labourist model can be summarized by what happened to some of the ILO's defining conventions. One of the first to run into difficulty was the Employment Policy Convention of 1964, by which governments committed themselves to 'full, productive and freely chosen employment'. By the 1980s scarcely any industrialized country could realistically claim to be honouring that Keynesian convention. Meanwhile, the Social Security Convention No. 102 of 1952, described in Chapter 2, became blatantly out of date as state benefits started to shrink and change character.

There was no ILO consensus on what to do about it, or even a desire to do anything. Governments were still encouraged to ratify it. In 2001 the ILO declared that it was one of the 'up-to-date' conventions, even though in the 50 years since it was passed the social security model it had laid out, with its emphasis on standard breadwinners and dependent wives, had been emasculated.

Underscoring its drift to the sidelines, the ILO quietly ceased to be a body concerned with redressing structural inequality, and focused on promoting employment equity. Earlier, building up social rights meant a transfer of income from capital to employees, since the former was expected to pay for benefits through insurance contributions and direct taxation. This was feasible in a closed national economy. But the assumptions did not apply in the Global Transformation. A growing majority did not have the type of employment that yielded such entitlements, and had to bear more of the costs of social protection. The ILO was unable to recommend alternative mechanisms.

In line with what was happening in member countries, it focused increasingly on horizontal rather than vertical redistribution, on matters such as gender equity. The main instruments were the Discrimination (Employment and Occupation) Convention No. 111 of 1958 and the Equal Remuneration Convention No. 100 of 1951. The 1958 convention, addressing discrimination based on gender, age and other personal characteristics, is one of the most ratified of all ILO conventions, by 158 countries. It promotes 'equality as consistency', 'equality of opportunity' and 'equality of the sharing of common humanity', none of which is about material equality. They relate to procedural justice, not economic rights. The convention could be used to justify 'affirmative action' in favour of a group that had faced discrimination, but not to criticize legislation strengthening the advantages of managers or high-income employees.

In the 1990s, the ILO failed to respond to the labour market flexibility debate. But it did try to adapt its standard setting in response to the increasing difficulty of identifying and defining employers and employees and the increasing attack on statutory protective regulations in general. Unless employees and employers can be identified clearly, labour law and regulation become hard to apply. As flexibility meant a growing fuzziness in this respect, ILO conventions began to look inapplicable for a lot of labour statuses. One reaction was the Home Work Convention No. 177, eventually passed in 1996 after vehement opposition from the employers on the ILO governing body, which tried to extend protection to workers labouring at home to the order of somebody else. As of 2008, that convention had been ratified by only four small European countries. It is effectively a dead letter. And it failed to address the general issue of care work.

Another significant change, in tune with the privatization agenda of supply-side economics, was the Private Employment Agencies Convention No. 181 of 1997. By this the ILO conceded the legitimacy of private employment exchanges, having previously held that this function was a government responsibility. The convention was recognition of the increasingly indirect nature of labour relations.

The ILO tried to confront another challenge to its model, the distinction between employment and commercial contracts, by trying to produce a Convention on Contract Labour. It was a sorry affair. This was an effort to bring contract workers under the umbrella of labour law by redefining them as quasi-employees. The ruse was to focus on situations of what the drafters called 'disguised employment'.[11] The employers' group resolutely resisted this ruse and succeeded in killing the draft convention, the first occasion in the ILO's 80 years when the standard-setting machinery failed. It marked the end of the road of employment regulation.

The main outcome of criticism of regulations embodied in ILO conventions was the 1998 Declaration on Fundamental Principles and Rights at Work. This was the creation of the ILO's then Director-General, Michel Hansenne. His self-perceived mission was to rescue labour standards, which for him meant that conventions needed prioritizing. Accordingly, he devised a Declaration by which all member countries, and their employer and union bodies, were constitutionally required to commit to eight conventions covering freedom of association, the right to collective bargaining, the elimination of forced and compulsory labour, the abolition of the worst forms of child labour and elimination of discrimination in the workplace.

The Declaration was unanimously accepted. But is it a floor of labour principles or a ceiling? At a time when developing countries were worrying about a social clause being included in trade deals, it took the heat out of the debate on standards. Because it gave the impression of being a charter against 'sweatshops' and 'free riders', it was welcomed by multinational capital, which found such 'fundamental' principles easy to apply, and by civil society groups who saw the Declaration in isolation. But it corresponded with a neo-liberal economic view, which has not been understood by many who ritually declare support for it while opposing neo-liberalism. The core standards in the Declaration are 'negative rights' that lie outside the sphere of social or work rights. Banning 'the worst forms of child labour', banning forced labour, campaigning against gender discrimination and defending freedom of association are matters of civil law. They do not constitute a progressive agenda.

It is doubtful whether the Declaration has had any effect, other than to bring in millions of dollars to the ILO from the US administration to support it. Governments are obliged to make a commitment to the relevant conventions, but application has not been enforced. Indeed, it is not enforceable. It weakened the ILO by making even the core 'standards' subject only to monitoring by means that were 'strictly promotional'. This is what the employers and the US administration had wanted. The latter hailed the Declaration as 'a big step forward' and the AFL-CIO President described it as 'an historic breakthrough'. Another interpretation is that it was a small step for those wishing to see a global market society without adherence to a web of protective regulations. Instead of a 'social clause' in the WTO, which would have been subject to binding arbitration, the Declaration explicitly ruled out trade sanctions for breach of the rights specified in it. Soft law was replacing binding law.

The Declaration's selection of a few standards as 'fundamental' was inconsistent with the principle established by the 1948 Universal Declaration of Human Rights that rights are indivisible and interdependent. By focusing on civil rights, it contributed to the neglect of economic rights, such as income security, work safety and health, maternity provision, pensions and disability benefits (DiMatteo et al., 2003; Alston and Heenan, 2004). Through its body of conventions and recommendations the ILO had built a model of social justice that had not prioritized aspects based on perceived political convenience. The various 'social rights' were an interdependent whole. The Declaration removed the transformative character of international labour standards.

Emphasis on a few standards left more space for 'self-regulation', in the form of voluntary codes of conduct and corporate social responsibility (CSR) initiatives by firms, topped by the UN's Global Compact. The ILO was little involved in developing these codes, but slipped into endorsing them by association. Scarcely noted, they do not commit employers to abide by ILO conventions ratified in countries in which they operate, and few make reference to them, a further instance of how the ILO regime has been marginalized.

The codes are part of the drift to soft law, consisting of non-binding recommendations, codes of practice and corporate guidelines, all replacing binding 'hard law'. Soft law opens the doors to further labour commodification. At the global level, this was reflected not only by the 1998 Declaration but by the ILO's Tripartite Declaration of Principles Concerning Multinational Enterprises and Social Policy of 1977, which followed the OECD's Guidelines for Multinational Enterprises in 1976. The distinguished labour lawyer Bob Hepple described the Tripartite Declaration as 'disappointing'. It is legally unenforceable and cannot be invoked in courts or tribunals. As for the Declaration of 1998, it involves no sanctions, and many governments submit their required reports without consultation with employers or unions.

The drift was reproduced at regional level. By 2008, there were over 200 regional and bilateral trade agreements in force. Many made no reference to worker 'rights' and did not cite ILO conventions. Although the North American Free Trade Agreement (NAFTA) mentioned a need to respect national labour standards and stipulated that parties should ensure enforcement of collective agreements, it excluded rights of association and bargaining from its enforcement mechanism.

In 1991, complementing the Single European Act of 1986, the European employer and union bureaucracies signed an Agreement on Social Policy, later incorporated into the *acquis communautaire* through the Treaties of Maastricht and Amsterdam. This entitled the 'social partners' to be consulted on social policy, to reach collective agreements and to be consulted on European regulations. The privileged position given to these increasingly unrepresentative bureaucracies gave labour 'rights' a diminished role by default. Social dialogue was all rather soft.

EU social policy has been moving towards soft law in other ways. Unlike earlier efforts, the Medium-Term Action Programmes of 1995–97 and 1998–2000, as well as the Strategic Objectives 2000–05 and the EC (European Community) Employment Title, relied largely on soft law measures, designed to be persuasive rather than legally binding. There has been a shift from directives to codes and guidelines. This is held to accord with the principle of subsidiarity, as enshrined in Article 5 of the EC Treaty, which has been interpreted as meaning that recourse to binding measures should only be a last resort (Hepple, 2002, p. 242). It also reflects the difficulty of obtaining political agreement, connected to the growing number of member states and diversity of traditions. And the drift has been facilitated by the trend towards flexibility in EU standards in allowing opt-outs or options for implementation. The EU Charter of Fundamental Rights of 2000 had no independent legal status and created no new rights.

In building the market society, European initiatives have moved towards soft regulation, giving the appearance of involving workers but allowing employers discretionary power. Formally, they have adhered to the labourist framework, trying to preserve industrial citizenship. The euphemism is social dialogue, a term favoured by employers (Gold et al., 2007). Defined as consultation between 'the social partners', it has been restricted to representatives of employers and employees. Consider the list of approved 'social partners' in sectoral dialogue processes: the European Trade Union Confederation; EUROCADRES (Council of European Professional and Managerial Staff); the European Confederation of Executives and Managerial Staff; the Confederation of European Business; the European Centre of Enterprises with Public Participation and of Enterprises of General Economic Interest; and the European Association of Craft, Small and Medium-Sized Enterprises.[12] A feature is the absence of professional associations and representatives of workers outside formal employment. Moreover, the EU has focused on sectoral dialogue, even though bargaining decentralization has been the trend (Keller and Platzer, 2003).

The drift to soft law has been coupled with an undemocratically determined international decision to give supremacy to competition law. The European Court of Justice, which has consistently ruled that competition law has precedence over labour law, has conspicuously avoided taking account of the ILO Constitution, including the article that labour is not a commodity, or the Declaration of 1998. The omission further highlights the marginalization of the global body for setting labour standards.

SOCIAL RIGHTS AND RECOMMODIFICATION

It has been said that fundamental rights are those beyond the sphere of legislative revision. Not much in the labour and work sphere has proved to be fundamental. Estlund (2002) refers to four categories of labour rights. The first are collective, notably the right to workplace representation. Here the scope and forms of representation have been curbed. Second, there are equal status rights, the right not to be subject to discrimination and harassment. Third are individual employee rights, such as the right to privacy and protection against unfair dismissal. Fourth, there are minimum terms of employment, such as minimum wages, maximum hours, job safety and mandated leave. All four have been weakened and are more dualistic in the protection they offer even if enforced. Possessing an effective right depends on the strength of the means of pursuing it and on being in a labour status that is covered.

Social rights were traditionally advanced through neo-corporatism and social solidarity institutions. As labourism was dismantled, so was the capacity to define, implement and enforce social rights. The UK has been particularly affected. In the 1960s there were no legally enforced social rights. Unions had confidence in collective bargaining and 'wanted nothing more of the law than it should leave them alone' (Wedderburn, 1965, p. 1). Social rights were seen as political values, not determined by law. But the 'right to associate' depended on fragile negative immunities, granted by Parliament, against common law liabilities.[13] When these were taken away by the Thatcher government and its successors, there were insufficient institutional safeguards to preserve social rights. Faced by the neo-liberal dictate that regulation should serve the purpose of 'competitiveness', what Wedderburn (2002) has called 'extravagant individualism' left workers unprotected.

In Europe generally, social rights have been circumscribed by the Treaty of the European Union and the EC Treaty. Article 28 of the EU's Charter of Fundamental Rights promotes the rights to negotiate and take collective action, but Article 137(6) of the EC Treaty denies the Community the legislative competence to enforce this. And, according to Hare (2002), the European Court of Human Rights has not upheld any positive social rights.

What is happening to 'labour rights' in the USA is intriguing, partly because what happens there tends to spill over into the global system. The US Constitution makes no reference to social provision: rights remain in essence eighteenth-century freedoms (Henkin, 1994). The Supreme Court has repeatedly held that government programmes are lawful as long as they possess a rational basis. There has been a proliferation of individual employment rights, such as privacy rights. But as there is no national right of protection against unjust discharge, employers have power over most aspects of employment, including privacy.

Finally, there is the famous right to work. Here the debate is at a delicate stage. It will be recalled that for over 30 years in the USA, the notion of the right to work was used to deny unions and progressive politicians the right to develop protective labour laws and regulations. Although the Lochner era ended in 1937, the spirit of Lochner has never died (see Chapter 2). It could not gain ascendancy while the generation of public figures scarred by the Great Depression held sway, but by the 1970s that began to change. Libertarians, particularly lawyers amongst them, reverted to the claim behind the Lochner judgment – that state interference in labour matters constitutes denial of a citizen's right to work as he or she chooses. This has led to an onslaught on forms of regulation, notably in the sphere of occupations, which will be considered later.

CONCLUDING POINTS

As the global labour process evolves, labour recommodification has been advanced by a dismantling of the institutions, policies and procedures that had given labour security. Companies and workplaces are less stable, social income has been restructured to make it more insecure, and the drift of labour law and collective bargaining has weakened the Voice of employees. Beyond all that is the tertiarization of economic activity in which services and insecure forms of labour status have taken over from manufacturing and stable standard employment.

The utilitarians in the Chicago School, following Hayek, understood that to move to a market society from one with collective institutions and protective regulations, the state would need to steer people to behave consistently as market participants. This meant dismantling institutional barriers and laws and imposing new institutions and laws to help those unable or unwilling to adapt to do so.

Just as Polanyi saw that laissez-faire was planned, so the global market society has not come about spontaneously. There is the nucleus of a global labour market, and the spread of precarious labour relationships has posed new challenges. What was long unappreciated is that the apparatus for planning the global market society comes from the same source, the ghost of Jeremy Bentham, whose fertile mind had not only formulated the utilitarian mantra of 'the greatest happiness of the greatest number' but also the means of encouraging the remainder to behave in the interests of the majority. We shall come to that. Suffice it to end this chapter by noting that, as the neo-liberal state unwound the labourist model of the Great Transformation, it was obliged to turn to paternalistic ways of reshaping behaviour, nowhere more so than in the labour market.

NOTES

1. Sallustius Crispus, writing during the collapse of Rome.
2. Before the 2008 market meltdown, Warren Buffett, who became one of the world's richest men on the back of 'financialization', presciently called derivatives 'financial weapons of mass destruction'.
3. Typically, private equity and hedge funds have borrowed shares from pension and mutual funds, driven the share price down by selling them short, and then bought a chunk of the company at a fire-sale price.
4. Moral hazards arise when people are induced to act in different or more risky ways because they are (or feel) insulated from the consequences, Immoral hazards arise when people are induced to act dishonestly.
5. One way in which managers ramped up the firm's share price, and their pay, was to oblige employees to invest pension contributions in its shares. When Enron collapsed, workers lost both job and pension.
6. The Chinese Prime Minister, Wen Jiabao, said in April 2008 that China needed to generate 10 million jobs a year between 2008 and 2013.
7. In the USA, services account for 80 per cent of private employment and 81 per cent of private GDP, according to the Coalition of Service Industries (CSI).
8. Free labour mobility in the face of huge wage differentials would fan social tensions. Those who advocate globalization and open markets become inconsistent when discussing migration (Wolf, 2007b). There is a delicate argument over mobility of 'factors of production'. Proponents of a global market economy favour free capital mobility on the grounds that it will flow to where returns are highest, boosting overall income. By that argument, they should favour free labour mobility. Many do not, on the expedient grounds that a country is a 'home' and the residents should be free to choose whom they want to join them.
9. According to *The Economist*, the erroneous notion that there is a fixed amount of work to be done, so dividing it among more or fewer people creates more or fewer jobs, was first described as 'the lump of labour fallacy' in 1891 (*The Economist*, 2009).
10. In 2008 GM and Chrysler employed 145 000 people in the USA and 600 000 retirees (and their families) depended on the companies for healthcare and pensions (McCracken and Stoll, 2008).
11. In the recommendation linked to the draft convention, this was defined as 'when the employer treats an individual as other than an employee in a manner that hides his or her true legal status'. This was distinguished from 'objectively ambiguous' employment, where services are provided amid doubt about the nature of the relationship, and the 'triangular employment relationship', where an agency or broker is an intermediary. The distinction between 'disguised' and 'ambiguous' was to depend on the employer's 'intention'. Determining that would be a legal quagmire.
12. For the evolution of employer organizations, see Bouwen (2006).
13. Kahn-Freund (1968) described the UK system in the 1960s as 'collective laissez-faire', a system of permissive collective bargaining.

4. Inequality, class and the 'precariat'

INTRODUCTION

Any market society generates patterns of inequality, which can be displayed in class terms and tensions that offer the avenue for a reaction or 'double movement'. Halperin (2004) rightly argued that Polanyi underplayed the role of class conflict and the forces from below, rather than from the top. He associated the strength of financial capital with war and civil repression, and argued that class conflict only characterized the final fall of the market economy (GT, p. 219). He cannot have meant that literally because class conflict characterized the whole period of disembeddedness. But the collapse of the last period of market society surely reflected a breakdown in the class compromises and rejection of dominance by a financial elite. Although the old political parties of progress had acceded to that dominance, new groups emerged to oppose it. Something similar is likely in the second decade of the twenty-first century. The old social democratic and labour parties have surrendered their legitimacy as representatives of progress and egalitarianism. In and out of office, throughout the era of globalization, they rushed to embrace the elite and financial capital.

In the mid-twentieth century, the main class compromise was based on negotiation between representatives of productive capital and the employed working class, in which financial capital was marginalized. This was historically specific. The puzzle before us is what form of class alliance will emerge next.

In the industrial citizenship era, the working class was misled into thinking that employment security was emancipatory while industrial capital welcomed the stability of the standard employment relationship. It is still widely believed that workers triumphed by acquiring employment security. But it was industrial capital that first fought to lock employees into long-term, inflexible contracts. In the UK, early examples of employer tactics included the 'yearly bond' for coalminers and efforts to make employees legally liable to adhere to their jobs via the contract law of 1823. Right through into the 1960s, the working and middle classes were presented with a distributional model in which they had the promise of employment security in return for accepting income inequality.

The Global Transformation has not destroyed the class structure but it has helped transform it. In the industrial citizenship era, the notion of the 'working class' shaped intellectual thinking, collective action and state policy. That industrial class structure has fragmented into what can be called the 'globalization class structure'. We cannot analyse the changing sphere of work and labour without coming to terms with the new classes and forms of social and economic stratification. Although the subject is more complex than can be painted here, we need to identify groups with distinctive sets of entitlements and patterns of security, since each will have distinctive attitudes to forms of social protection and commodification.

A feature of the class fragmentation is that growing numbers of people are detaching themselves, or being detached, from national regulatory and protective systems. The fragmentation is accentuating seven distinctive strata, which can be presented in descending order of average social income: a global elite, a 'salariat', 'proficians', the 'core' working class, a 'precariat', the unemployed and the detached.

Before turning to how this structure has evolved, we should take stock of the changing pattern of inequality. Undoubtedly income and wealth have become more unequally distributed under globalization. Earnings inequality has been growing since the 1970s and may have accelerated more recently (Burniaux and Padrini, 2006). It has widened sharply in the USA where the richest 5 per cent experienced a 60 per cent rise in income between the late 1980s and 2006 and the richest 20 per cent (quintile) a 36 per cent rise. By contrast, income of the middle quintile rose by 13 per cent and that of the poorest quintile by 11 per cent; between 1998 and 2004, the income of the bottom 20 per cent fell by 2.5 per cent (Pimlott, 2008).

Although inequality has risen in most countries, the USA has set the trend. Much of the increased inequality there has been shaped by policy changes. Thus, in spite of historically high functional (capital–labour) inequality, in 2003 the US administration cut capital gains and dividend taxes at a time when stagnant real wages and declining health insurance coverage had left wage earners facing more income insecurity. The real income of the richest 0.1 per cent of the US population rose by 51 per cent between 2003 and 2005, and corporate profits rose by three-quarters between 2003 and 2007.

In 2007 the OECD (2007b) found it 'remarkable' that the share of wages in national income had fallen in most of its member countries. The wage share had fallen by about a quarter in Japan in the previous three decades, by 13 per cent on average in the 15 wealthiest EU countries and by 7 per cent in the USA. In Italy and France labour's share had dropped from 80 per cent to 60 per cent and in Germany from 70 per cent to 55 per cent. Given that wage earners are paying a larger share of total taxation as well, income inequality in net terms has grown even more. Meanwhile, wage dispersion has risen in most countries, although apparently not in Japan.

By 2005, inequality in the USA was as great as when it last peaked in the 1920s, just before the crisis of the Great Transformation. According to the Internal Revenue Service, the wealthiest 1 per cent of Americans received 21.2 per cent of income. Much of it came in capital gains. Meanwhile, the bottom 50 per cent received 12.8 per cent of total income. The trend in inequality had lasted for three decades, and showed no sign of reversal.

Scarcely anybody questioned the stylized facts. Yet the reaction was muted. There was a tendency to promote minimum standards, including minimum wages and tax credits for low-income earners, rather than constrain incomes at the top end. Growing inequality was treated as largely inevitable and, for neo-liberals, even desirable as an incentive for effort and risk-taking.[1] Indeed, there were tax cuts for higher-income earners. The average tax rate for the richest 1 per cent of Americans dropped to 23 per cent in 2005 from 27.5 per cent in 2000 (Ip, 2007).

Increased inequality is attributable to a mix of globalization, technological change (including advances in telecommunications that facilitate 'superstar' and 'winner-takes-all' tendencies), higher returns to schooling, weaker collective bargaining, labour market flexibilization, increasing returns to financial capital and fiscal policy. Globalization has also widened inequality through more foreign direct investment. FDI results in a decline in the relative wages of lower-skilled workers in the rich countries of capital outflow and benefits higher-skilled workers in the poorer host countries, raising wage inequality in both types of economy.

Some, including Ben Bernanke, Chairman of the US Federal Reserve, have largely attributed rising inequality to technology, arguing that the internet has increased the productivity of the highly skilled compared with the less skilled (*Financial Times*, 2007). However, the inequality that has grown most is not between groups of workers but between recipients of capital income and recipients of labour income. While it is understandable that Bernanke would choose to direct attention to technology and divert public gaze from the increased income share going to finance, he could not honestly believe that growing inequality reflected the internet.

Above all, growing inequality reflects the existence of a global labour market based on a labour surplus in 'Chindia', which is weakening workers' bargaining position everywhere. And globalization has reduced the relative price of labour-intensive goods, partly because of the opening up of China and India with their hundreds of millions of low-paid workers.

While inequality has increased, income instability has increased even more. According to one estimate for the USA, volatility trebled between the mid-1970s and the mid-2000s (Hacker, 2006). On average, an American family had a 17 per cent chance of a drop in income of more than half from one year to the next. Reflecting the hubris of the time, this was dismissed by *The Economist*, which argued that most people can cope with temporary income volatility. It added:

> For a start, rising instability of incomes is not necessarily a bad thing. A dynamic, mobile society is one in which people's income varies a lot. . . Short-term fluctuations could be smoothed out by borrowing and saving. The fact that household saving rates have plunged in the past three decades does not suggest Americans are terrified by the spectre of more variable incomes. More likely, the increased sophistication of credit markets, particularly the ability to extract equity from housing, has made temporary income instability easier to cope with.
>
> (*Economist*, 2007a)

Some US bankers also claimed that inequality was less than it seemed, arguing that although the richest quintile was receiving a larger share of total income and the lowest quintile a smaller share, lower-income families had access to sources of spending money that did not count as income. They argued that consumption was a better guide to inequality, pointing out the numerous household goods that are the norm in the USA (Cox and Alm, 2008). This extraordinary argument suggests how the financial community suspended economics in the run-up to the crash of 2008, accumulating liabilities based on mortgage lending to poor people who could not repay their loans.[2]

In late 2007 *The Economist*, referring to a 'new improved gilded age', went so far as to declare that 'America is experiencing a period of unprecedented material equality' (Economist, 2007i). It cited a study suggesting that consumption inequality had scarcely changed since the 1980s (Krueger and Perri, 2006), added the claim made by 'happiness researchers' that inequality in self-reported life satisfaction had shrunk in rich market societies, and pointed out that the cost of consumer durables and food distribution had fallen, making them more accessible to low-income earners. What it failed to do was recognize that for those on low incomes this consumption had resulted in negative savings and thus exposure to economic insecurity on an 'unprecedented' scale. The poor had been encouraged to live beyond their means. Sooner or later there had to be a reckoning.

If inequality is linked to globalization, it is partly through raising economic insecurity. The globalization model seeks flexible markets, so that competitive forces can prevail with minimal 'distortions'. It is a model of generalized risk-taking and thus generalized insecurity. Neo-liberals argued that this would boost growth and that the rising water would lift all ships. Jim O'Neill, chief economist at Goldman Sachs, claimed that globalization was producing 'an explosion of the world's middle class', such that by 2030 'an astonishing 2 billion people will have joined the ranks' (O'Neill, 2008). It was appropriate that the person making this argument represented the pinnacle of global finance capital. Although one could quibble with his figures, and find his definition of the middle class generously broad, let us presume that the numbers are correct. There remain five flaws in the argument.

First, it is not the income received that matters but what one needs to spend. If I have free healthcare and free schooling for my children, I could 'get by' on much less than if I had to pay the full cost of those social needs. Chapter 3 argued that there has been a shift from enterprise and state benefits towards money incomes, giving a false picture of improvement.

Second, the neo-liberal model has transformed the character of economic risk, from a predominance of idiosyncratic, contingency risks that hit individuals, the basis of labourist social security, to systemic risks and a heady mix of shocks, hazards, uncertainty and risk. The value of any level of income is less if there is a higher probability of exposure to a shock. For most people in most societies this is what has happened. For instance, one in every six Americans has no health insurance and a further one in six is underinsured, meaning that if they have a serious illness they will be bankrupted. This is a lifetime hazard. Many of the underinsured would fit into O'Neill's definition of the middle class. Yet many would probably be prepared to take a pay cut to below 'middle class' levels if they were provided with the assurance of free adequate healthcare if they fell ill.

Third, the idea of *the* middle class is outdated. It is not a solid body of people. There are the Jim O'Neills who, even after the financial crash, can sleep soundly knowing their wealth insulates them from disaster. But many more people are middle class on sufferance, waking at four o'clock in the morning wondering what they would do if they or a member of their family fell seriously ill or lost their job. They face a high probability of falling painfully out of the middle class.

Fourth, in a flexible liberalized economy incomes fluctuate more. Today's income is a less good predictor of tomorrow's than used to be the case, at least for many outside salaried jobs, which is the rising category of people. Psychologists have shown that rises and falls in income do not have matching effects. If income rises by US$1000 the euphoria is short-lived, whereas if it falls by US$1000 the effect is long-lasting. The scar effect is greater than the grin effect. One reason is that people plan on the basis of current and expected income, so a sudden drop causes adjustment problems.

Fifth, economists, psychologists and sociologists are united in recognizing that relative incomes matter. One might be reasonably sanguine if more people simply moved into 'the middle class', and nothing happened to the incomes of those above and below. But that is not what has happened. Many forms of relative deprivation seem to have worsened. While those in the elite, surely including O'Neill, leapt ahead, those below them saw the elite's lifestyle out of reach, however hard they worked. There is also a relative deprivation associated with the declining probability of social mobility, which has been most striking in the USA. And there is a relative deprivation that comes from realizing that your own personal income is unlikely to go up as you grow older, linked to the slow demise of seniority pay systems and on-the-job promotion schemes.

Space has been given to O'Neill's claims because they represented a common way of thinking in the globalization era. But the inequality story should be seen as an indictment of a finance-driven market society and the prolonged acquiescence to it. There are three stylized facts that should be borne in mind for the narrative of this book. The inequality has been more class-driven; the wealthy have received much more income because they have gained from capital, even if part of that gain is classified as 'earned income'. There has been a spread of winner-takes-all markets; this explains why, in many occupational groups as well as more generally, the highest income earners have gained most (Atkinson, 2007). And governments gave up on progressive income redistribution; they allowed the new global class structure to strengthen, which will affect the labour process and social policy for decades. The remainder of this chapter sketches the nature of that structure, beginning at the top.

THE GLOBAL ELITE

At the zenith of the globalizing economy is a tiny minority of absurdly rich and high-earning people, whose political power and impact are out of all proportion to their number. On one calculation, shortly before the market meltdown in 2008, the assets of the world's 1100 richest people were almost twice those of the poorest 2.5 billion (Rothkopf, 2008b). Billionaires earned more in an hour, any hour of the day or night, than most earn in a year in industrialized countries and a lifetime in some parts of the world. Some reached the stage of seeing their incomes rising almost exponentially. They are global citizens.[3]

Expanding the stratum down to multi-millionaires, all are detached from national regulatory and social security systems, not needing or contributing to them, neither psychologically – feeling committed to their maintenance – nor politically. The very rich have strong income security, and whatever they need in other forms of security. Their biggest danger is hubris, and being caught in criminality.

By the twenty-first century, a US elite comprising less than 0.01 per cent of income earners was receiving 5 per cent of total national income, each receiving US$10 million or more each year. Adjusted for inflation and the changing value of money, the pattern of extreme inequality was back to where it was just before the stock market crash of 1929. The size of the elite could be 1 per cent of a rich country's adult population, if multi-millionaires are included. But whatever the exact definition, the number has been growing. In 2004 there were about 110 000 households in the USA with wealth of more than US$25 million, more than double the number in 1995.[4]

The global elite is not confined to a few rich countries. In 2007, the world's second richest man, according to Forbes, was Mexican Carlos Slim, who built a business empire on the foundations of a privatized telecoms monopoly (Clifton et al., 2007). In Mexico, 20 individuals received 6 per cent of GNP. Unlike the situation in the early twentieth century, today's elite includes a sizable number in low-income countries, multi-millionaires and billionaires who have mostly acquired their wealth by their links to international finance.

Various names have emerged to describe the new super-rich, including the 'superclass' (Rothkopf, 2008a) and the New Olympians (Elliott and Atkinson, 2008). We may just call them the elite. Some work hard, some do not. But most of their income comes from sources other than wages or salaries. A high percentage came from financial markets; hedge fund managers between them made at least US$3 billion in 2007. In the USA, one study concluded that increasing returns to financial capital was the main factor explaining the rise of the super-rich and that the rising share going to top earners was largely 'a Wall Street, financial industry-based story' (Ip, 2007).

This elite has presided over an incredible concentration of financial power, in which the top 50 financial institutions controlled about US$50 trillion in assets, a third of the world's total. Whenever there is an economic crisis, behind the scenes politicians have turned to these institutions and the individuals running them to ask for support. Ironically, when the crisis of 2007–08 hit the financial community, the elite asked the authorities for support and received it.

Part of the elite consists of corporate executives. Their pay may seem unextraordinary. In the early twenty-first century, the chief executive of a large US company was paid about US$1 million a year. This would not put him into the elite class. However, with bonuses, total remuneration was about US$5 million, and perks were worth a lot more.

A factor behind the shift to financialization of manufacturing companies has been the increased tendency to pay executives performance-related bonuses based on short-term profits, the yardstick of 'meritocracy' in the world's company boardrooms. An example was Porsche. Nearly bankrupt in 1993, its new chief executive turned it into the world's most profitable car company, earning himself US$67 million in 2007 alone while producing higher share prices and bonuses for the remaining employees. But this largely reflected a shift from production of cars to derivatives trading (Thornhill et al., 2008).

Although apologists claimed that executive pay was performance-related, implying risk-sharing with shareholders, pay continued to grow through good and bad times. Whereas in the early 1990s, US executives were receiving 140 times the earnings of the average worker, by 2007 they were receiving over 500 times as much (ILO, 2008, p. 18). Although not to the same extent, the disconnect grew in Europe and elsewhere as well.

One trick was a practice of leaving bad debts aside when calculating performance-based bonuses, a practice likened to removing strike-outs in calculating a baseball player's average (or ducks in calculating a cricketer's batting average). According to Equilar, a compensation research firm, the chiefs of the ten largest financial service firms in its 2007 survey received US$320 million in the year, even though their firms reported mortgage-related losses of US$55 billion and wiped US$200 billion off shareholder value (Deutsch, 2008). The billions of dollars in losses run up by Merrill Lynch led to the departure of its chief executive, but his replacement did not do too badly, earning, with a sign-on bonus, an annual compensation package of US$84 million (Deutsch, 2008).

Corporate executives dismissed or induced to resign when companies have done poorly have also received huge 'golden parachutes'. These have been peculiarly justified on the grounds that they encourage executives to reveal rather than conceal mistakes, to the benefit of shareholders, and ease the replacement of executives by making them more willing to leave (Thornhill et al., 2008). While workers are penalized for inadequacies, the rich are rewarded for theirs.

A growing part of the income of the elite has been in the form of enterprise benefits, EB in the structure of social income, which are lightly taxed and not linked to labour performance. An egregious example came to light in 2008 when it was revealed that many US executives were being promised huge 'posthumous benefits', large sums, often described as salaries, for years after they died (Maremont, 2008). These have been called 'golden coffin' payments. Senior managers of major corporations were being paid 'non-compete' benefits for promising not to compete with the company after they left, payments that continued to their estate if they died. In one case, the company agreed to pay its former chief executive his salary until he reached age 99. Sadly for him, he died when he was 92; fortunately for his heirs, the company continued to pay for another seven years. It is not known if he honoured his non-compete clause.

While the elite is immunized against the risks of the market society, we are being encouraged to feel sorry for them. In 2008, the *Wall Street Journal* revealed that Bill Gates was donating US$400 000 to fund a study by Boston College's Center on Wealth and Philanthropy called 'The Joys and Dilemmas of Wealth'. The Center's Director said, 'We'll be looking at the moral compass and journey of wealth holders, including their aspirations, prospects and dilemmas'. He said of the study, 'It will explore the hearts and minds of the wealthy, not just their financial plans' (cited in Frank, 2007b). The researchers' grovelling is scarcely surprising. The esteemed Director stated, 'We will let the respondents guide the outcomes'. He let it be known that many of the super-rich were not happy.

They apparently also suffer from insecurity, partly to do with the fear of slipping out of the elite, coupled with an insatiable greed (Frank, 2007a). The compulsion to accumulate ever more money is pervasive. Some claim it becomes a pleasureless treadmill (Wachtel, 2003). There is also the alleged angst of 'affluenza', the guilt about being super-rich and way above others in society.

In Polanyi's Transformation, an elite of fabulously rich also emerged, concentrated in the USA, in a gilded age that lasted into the 1920s. From then until the 1970s no group of financial barons strode the world stage. The new elite emerged solely due to financial liberalization. Their wealth was policy induced, not the result of sudden brilliance.

One exemplar is Sanford Weill, who turned Citigroup into a powerful institution. His success was based on the repeal in 1999 of the Glass-Steagall Act that since the New Deal had prohibited combinations of commercial and investment banking, insurance and stockbroking operations. Weill was disingenuous when he told the media in 2007 that he and others with the sort of wealth he had accumulated had prospered solely through their own efforts. 'We didn't rely on somebody else to build what we built', he asserted (cited in Uchitelle, 2007). There is no evidence that Weill was a better builder than his predecessors. Tax breaks, accounting rules and other policies introduced or condoned by governments all contributed to the enrichment of the elite.

In the USA the Bush administration and many Republicans claimed high incomes and benefits for the super-rich were a reflection of entrepreneurialism. Governments and policy advisers there and elsewhere claimed to believe that the rewards to the elite were beyond their control, fearing that action to reduce their income and wealth would induce them to move assets and investment elsewhere.

Instead, the elite became entangled in a web of money and politics. The heads of the world's largest financial firms are on the boards of numerous other firms (Rothkopf, 2008a). They have unique access to governments, and politicians move easily into their arena on leaving office. At the top is Goldman Sachs, the investment bank, whose alumni have been Secretaries of the US Treasury (Hank Paulson and Robert Rubin), heads of the US National Economic Council (Rubin and Stephen Friedman), President of the World Bank (Robert Zoellick) or in US politics (Joe Corzine, Governor of New Jersey). The UK Prime Minister, Gordon Brown, was relying on former employees of Goldman Sachs and Morgan Stanley, and Tony Blair's chief of staff went from Downing Street to work for Morgan Stanley. The occupation of politician is increasingly linked to finance.

The elite is also shaping social policy around the world, taking up the space left by shrinking state spending by indulging in selective philanthropy. The super-rich are also selectively funding research in universities, international agencies and corporations, for better or for worse distorting the choices and results. For instance, WHO officials have complained that the dominance in malaria research of the Gates Foundation is encouraging researchers to focus on certain lines of enquiry the foundation wants to finance, to the neglect of others (McNeil, 2008).

To sum up, there are five reasons for being disturbed by the elite's income and power. First, as the repercussions of the 2007–08 financial crisis have made only too clear, their greed and opportunism sucks money out of companies at the expense of employees, shareholders and productive investment. Second, practices such as posthumous pay reflect the tone of the global market society. If the elite can indulge in such wheezes with impunity, why should others abide by moral and legal rules? Third, the elite can and do use their money to influence political developments for their benefit. Increasingly, politicians and political parties depend on private donations, many from the elite. Fourth, none of the income is linked to society; the elite are able to shift their money around the world without any sense of community involvement. Finally, wealth accumulated by the elite is being used as discretionary funding for selective social policy around the world.

THE SALARIAT

Beneath the elite is a privileged category of high-income earners in stable, full-time employment. The salariat consists of employees paid on a monthly basis, in civil services, corporations, parastatals and other bureaucracies. Of all those doing labour, they are the least subject to commodification. They have employment security, but probably suffer from job and skill reproduction insecurity because they may be moved around and/or gain promotion only by leaving technical skills behind.

Because of their high incomes and a tendency to identify with management, with employers, members of the salariat typically feel detached from the state social protection system, seeing their security in terms of private insurance benefits and earnings from judicious investment. The salariat benefited most from the era of fictitious decommodification, receiving high enterprise benefits and money wages with access to state benefits if they ever needed them. However, many sank into unhappy middle age, trapped in a gilded cage of long-term employment and frustrated with a stale lifestyle.

In modern times, bureaucratic proletarianization has been the fate of the salariat, including professionals such as academics. Target-based labour relations and a culture of processing people and cases erode a sense of purpose in work, leading to psychological withdrawal. Managerial employees in large organizations are among the least likely to find meaning in their jobs (Holbeche and Springett, 2004).

There has been a trend, even in places like India, to remove the salariat from protection by labour law entirely on the grounds that it constitutes management. The salariat is seen as privileged and over-protected, which in relative terms it is. But its numbers may be shrinking. Paradoxically, the reduced labour law protection (for example, on unfair dismissal) serves the interests of the more privileged of the salariat, since they can negotiate individualized contracts with insurance benefits and untaxed perks.

There is an ideological dimension in this. Dividing the salariat from other workers facilitates a process by which managers and owners of firms can give favoured individuals non-wage benefits and privileges not given to others. And differentiating at the upper end of the income spectrum makes it easier to differentiate at the lower end.

A complementary tendency in labour law reform is to differentiate by status. Those deemed part of management are not supposed to have the same 'rights' as other employees. This weakens the identification of high-income employees with core workers and the precariat, and puts many in the salariat in a weaker bargaining position. Its members are increasingly obliged to bargain with employers for an individual contract without the collective strength that comes from being part of a coherent group.

Labour law reform is curbing employee 'rights' in general. These are being converted into the remuneration system and contractual obligations, but usually only for those whose labour is valued over the long term. In the UK, for example, much of the middle class – in its British sense – has become 'the coping class', financially squeezed in the attempt to maintain a standard of living that enterprise and state benefits once helped assure. As it is losing employment security, it seeks more income and savings to compensate. Thus, middle-class dissatisfaction grew even though real median disposable income rose between 1997 and 2006 by about 20 per cent (Guthrie, 2008).

Measures of disposable income fail to take into account the erosion of current or prospective benefits. Estimating the value of the trade-off would be subjective and reflect a balance of probabilities and values. For instance, would an income of £50 000 without the prospect of a pension be worth more than an income of £25 000 and the promise of a pension worth 50 per cent of income? It is difficult to determine which groups have done better than others based on disposable money income. On the basis of standard statistics, the losers from recent trends may appear to include the salariat. In reality, their loss may be cushioned by enterprise benefits or, for many, deepened by the loss of them. While some of the salariat may aspire to join the elite, the top 5 per cent of earners have been drawing away, which is conducive to more dissatisfaction among the 'well-off-but-not-rich' category.

The salariat is being partially globalized; a growing proportion is subject to a standardized set of experiences, creating what one review has depicted as a new organizational archetype (Hassard et al., 2007). It also appears that in a multinational corporate context there are fewer opportunities for 'white-collar' community building and solidarity in salaried employment than in old industrial corporations (Casey, 1995).

Part of the salariat is being converted into something close to proficians, expected to spend time working away from home, either commuting abroad or taking up postings in another country while their families stay behind (Mayerhofer et al., 2004). This weakens family ties and the middle-management community. It is one means by which the notion of a fixed workplace is giving way to ideas of multiple workplaces, undermining a sense of place (Peltonen, 2006). This is producing feelings of distress, fear of being laid off and confusion over disruption to career and the loss of collegial solidarity (Casey, 1995).

The salariat often aspire to achieve independence. An international Borderless Workforce Survey conducted by Manpower, the recruitment agency, showed that employers were worried that talented employees would migrate. More than a third of employees claimed they would be prepared to go anywhere for employment if the wage were attractive. Whether they would do so in reality is moot. What is more relevant is that they are detached from the mainstream regulatory and social income structures. They are unlikely to struggle to preserve them.

THE PROFICIANS

Proficians are an emerging social category, perhaps the modern equivalent of the yeomen before the agrarian revolution that created agricultural capitalism. They offer a model with a resonance with the past (enviable skills, independence, self-control), and an attractive alternative to standard employment. Perversely, they thrived on the inequalities generated by globalization, but risk falling into a lower socioeconomic stratum.

They choose to be independent contractors or 'consultants'. To some extent, they fit what Handy (1995, 2001) characterized as 'portfolio workers' and 'the fleas' (or flea elite, to be precise). If one wished to be optimistic, they could be depicted as the craftsmen of the global flexible economy. As the proposed name implies, they are a mix of professional and technician, mostly working on short-term contracts. Many operate in a climate of insecurity, but are well compensated. Perhaps their main form of insecurity is work insecurity, epitomized by the frenzied pace of their erratic schedules, stress and burnout.

Their ranks are growing. In 2007 there were about 200 000 solo practitioner consultants incorporated in the USA, more than twice as many as in the 1970s, according to the Society for Advancement of Consulting (Chura, 2007). People were changing from giving their own name to designating themselves by fancy titles.

Often able to evade or avoid personal taxation, proficians are partially detached by choice from state-based social protection and regulatory systems. Many are commodified in that they sell themselves with bravado. They glorify market society, until they burn out. Proficians comprise one group of 'casual' workers. They are detached from labour law protection, easily categorized as providing entrepreneurial services, not labour.

Proficians earn high money incomes, and while they are unlikely to receive much in the way of enterprise benefits they may receive what could be described as 'guild benefits' or occupational benefits. These might include retraining subsidies from a levy within the occupation, guild-like benefit funds, low-cost loans, and access to free information services. There may also be a work-sharing agency role, enabling practitioners to 'recommend' others on a reciprocity basis.

Proficians may also benefit from universal state transfers, and from private income benefits (portable income insurance) as well as profit shares, as in the case of lawyers. Some may also be members of cooperatives, although perhaps not named as such. Mostly they do not identify with state benefits, protective regulations or labour law. Among those doing particularly well are technically qualified individuals who can bargain for themselves or use an agent or lawyer to do so, such as sports stars, executives and others identified as having 'talent' in their field. More will find 'triangulation' rather attractive.

Proficians, in the guise of professionals working on contract, have attracted interest from ethnographers (Barley and Kunda, 2004, 2006). And there has also been some class activism, with talk in the USA of a 'free agent' movement in which technically qualified people spurn corporate career paths. Some might call the proficians the 'professions of spectacle', a term used by several Italian analysts of immaterial labour. Another popular term is 'nomad'. A café called the Nomad Café was opened in Oakland, California in 2003 to cater for what the owner called 'techno-Bedouins'. There is even a book devoted to the 'digital nomad' (Makimoto and Manners, 1997).

The sad term 'knowledge worker' has also crept into popular usage. It is used to imply possession of qualifications and a capacity to use information technology. But knowledge workers do not belong to definable professions. Those in an occupation are expected to have a similar education and range of skills and career trajectory, in terms of past and expected experience. Knowledge workers are so general that they are unlikely to feel part of an occupational community. To avoid being proletarianized – made subject to market forces without security – they would need a sufficiently common identity to coalesce, set standards and bargain collectively, at least to the extent of setting minimal working conditions and constraints to exploitation and self-exploitation. Self-exploitation, manifested by stress and burnout, is something knowledge workers share with care workers. They need an occupational identity to provide a route to representation security.

A modern example is investment banking. There are many specialists in this privileged sector of globalization – traders, brokers, market analysts, corporate finance experts and the like (Winroth, 2003). Their education varies widely, as does their work experience. They collaborate out of necessity, and form mechanisms of short-term reciprocities. This is roughly what is meant by the term 'community of practice' (Wenger, 1998). But that is not the same as an occupational community, in which long-term reciprocities and a similar structure of social income predominate. In such a community, the elders or those who have risen through an occupation set the tone and limits for acceptable practice.

Another group belonging to the proficians are professionals who retire from salaried employment and then, pensioned, return to their old or similar jobs on short-term contracts. In ageing societies this has become common, altering the nature of the labour force. In the USA, teachers retire, start receiving a pension and then register with an employment agency that hires them out on contract. One agency is SmartSchoolsPlus, which contracts ex-teachers back into their jobs or into others for which they are qualified, enabling them to receive a salary and a pension. This double-dipping weakens the bargaining position of younger teachers. And the existence of contracting agencies has helped other pensioned professionals to bypass regulations stipulating that they cannot return to their jobs. They have been welcomed by public authorities because they can be laid off, gaining retirement income, and be rehired at lower cost because they do not have seniority pay. Double-dipping has become a way for the salariat to move genteelly into the profician class.

Undoubtedly, the proficians are here to stay. Their existence holds out great potential for building a new kind of 'career' and working life. However, as we shall argue, there is much to be done to overcome the drawbacks of their existence.

THE CORE: A WITHERING WORKING CLASS

Below the salariat and proficians, in terms of income and status, are core workers who comprise what those with long memories used to call the working class, typically men in manual jobs, stably employed, paid relatively high wages and inclined to belong to unions. They also include some people working in services, in regular jobs, many of whom are women. Many in the core would define themselves by an occupational title such as carpenter, electrician or secretary, even if they did so with hesitation.

Welfare states were created to serve their needs. Before globalization, it was presumed that they represented the norm and that most workers would eventually belong to this stratum. The larger the proportion of workers belonging to the core, the more people would be in a position to benefit from an insurance-based social protection system and the mainstream regulatory system.

Although the formation and legitimacy of welfare states depended on them, core workers actually never comprised a majority in most countries. Since the 1970s their numbers have been shrinking, a reflection of 'deindustrialization', the dispersion of manufacturing labour around the world and the pursuit of labour market flexibility. Core workers had most forms of labour security, but as the wage system has become more flexible a growing share of their income has been insecure. They also suffer from increasing job and employment insecurity, while their unions have been enfeebled.

With numbers dwindling, their old labourist agenda lacks legitimacy. They have experienced more recommodification than any other group and more casualization. Worst of all, they have lost access to both social security and protective regulations, in the process suffering an erosion of both enterprise benefits and state benefits (EB and SB). The industrial working class is in disarray.

In some countries, the core has clung tenaciously to some welfare benefits even as the agents of these benefits, the unions, have shrunk. By 2008 only 5 per cent of private sector employees in France were in unions. And yet an illusion of relevance persists, partly due to the continued tripartite governance of certain institutions (a system known as *paritisme*), which manage unemployment benefits, health insurance and pensions. However, under the Sarkozy government the system is being challenged by the employer body, MEDEF, and may not survive.

In Sweden, little noticed at the time, one of the first acts of the new 'bourgeois' government was to give notice that unions would no longer be responsible for implementing certain state benefits. In Northern Europe that linkage had been one powerful way of holding up the unionization rate. The forward march of the working class had been led and shaped by the trade unions, and the severing of that benefit link was indicative of the collapse of the old labourist model.

THE PRECARIAT

Recycle – The route of my life.

(Slogan on Italian T-shirt)

Below the core are the new legions of the precariat, flitting between jobs, unsure of their occupational title, with little labour security, few enterprise benefits and tenuous access to state benefits. They include the more fortunate of the vast informal economy, the remainder being further down in the spectrum. The precariat is the group that has grown most, and its role in the recommodification process is pivotal, since its existence pressures those above to make concessions to make themselves more marketable.

Throughout history, a high proportion of those doing labour have been in insecure, low-paid, low-status jobs. Their numbers were expected to decline under industrial citizenship. No longer. The new precariat (or 'flexiworkers') comprises a disparate group in non-regular statuses, including casual workers, outworkers and agency workers. Their common characteristic is labour insecurity in all the seven forms outlined earlier (Chapter 2, Box 2.1). They appear to be the future. Not only have the numbers trapped in petty activities in rural and peri-urban areas grown in developing countries, but flexible labour processes have boosted informalization everywhere. Growing proportions of labour forces lack entitlement to mainstream statutory protection and are disentitled to social transfers.

The precariat may also be defined in terms of its relationship to other socioeconomic groups, or in terms of what it means to live and work precariously. But let us focus on images, since these are essential for guiding us in thinking of the future of work and labour. Part of the precariat is from the so-called 'Generation Y' (those born after 1980). As one commentator said, they do not 'do slow'. E-mails are laborious, meetings are time-consuming; instant messaging, texting and dynamic social networking via Facebook, MySpace and other means provide a milieu of multi-tasking. The precariat seems to be comprised largely of younger workers. Partly this reflects a youthful partial engagement in labour force activity; partly it reflects the recent growth of this type of labour relation, affecting newcomers to the labour market. However, precariat membership in prime-age and older age groups has been growing too. In Japan, 26 per cent of those aged 25 to 34 were in temporary jobs in 2007.

Those in the precariat lack employment security, being in jobs usually regarded by employers as short-term or casual, and seen that way by those doing the work. Often, they have no employment contract, or if they do it is casual. They are thus denied labour law protection by virtue of status (not classified as employees) and by precariousness. They are also disadvantaged by having no control over skill development, at least not in the jobs they are doing. And they lack Voice – representation security – because they are denied the opportunity to join unions or because they are either 'in service', subordinated in precarious labour, or 'providing services', where associational bargaining is constrained. In short, they have no occupational security.

The precariat is a global phenomenon, and its growth is central to labour recommodification. Remuneration consists largely of money wages, and though these are usually lower than those received by employees in 'permanent' jobs, wages make up a higher percentage of social income. The precariat has few if any enterprise benefits, which is why many corporations have shifted to the use of contingent and temporary workers of diverse descriptions. Most lack access to state benefits as well, particularly those based on social insurance, since neither they nor their occasional employers pay the necessary contributions.

The precariat has several guises. It includes what in New York are called 'permalancers', young workers employed on long-term freelance contracts. Though many in the precariat are or call themselves freelancers, most are really disguised employees, without enterprise benefits. However, some value the opportunity to flourish independently rather than opt for employment security.

The precariat is not just expanding in 'freelance' work. For example, among US workers without college schooling the proportion in precarious, low-paid service jobs increased from 13 per cent in 1980 to 20 per cent in 2005. The precariat has also been boosted by manufacturing firms. In 2007–08, Ford persuaded thousands of its employees to leave to set up as self-employed. The objective was to cut core employees and replace them with those from the precariat, prepared to work for half the wage and without employment security. General Motors did the same, offering 'buyouts' to all its 74 000 hourly employees in the USA. One objective was to offload legacy costs. Thus, at Ford, although departing workers received a lump sum, they lost healthcare benefits after six months.

Although it has grown everywhere, the precariat has mushroomed in the USA. Most fit into the 'near poor', those living just above the official poverty line, about 60 million people in 2008. Although not poor by world standards, they lack sources of income security that modern society has come to presume as the norm for decency – affordable healthcare and the prospect of an adequate pension. They see wages stagnating and the capacity to save for contingency risks diminishing. Any shock could plunge them into crisis, without the means to cope or recover. Observers of the US economic scene have long lamented the years of low savings and the general slide into a lifestyle of indebtedness. It is the precariat that bears the brunt of the systemic insecurity.

The problems have grown elsewhere too. In Germany the number of employees covered by social insurance has been falling sharply. Millions more are in temporary labour (*Zeitarbeit*) and in so-called mini-jobs, lacking access to social security benefits, which have been made harder to obtain or retain. Many people are being employed through private employment agencies, such as Switzerland's Adecco, the USA's Manpower and Randstad of the Netherlands. And firms acting as labour brokers are growing. Just-in-time practices are spreading for social services, with hospitals, for instance, cutting permanent staff, carrying no reserves on their books and then using temporary agencies to cover for the fluctuating need for labour.

The Japanese precariat has grown particularly rapidly, partly explaining why average wages have fallen, along with consumption and savings by so-called working families (Hayashi, 2008). There has been talk of the end of seniority pay, which would have been unthinkable in the labourism era. The trend to temporary employment has been attributed to the greater reliance on exports and the resultant increased vulnerability of the Japanese economy. But changes in labour law have played a part. For instance, until 1999 temporary labour contracts were forbidden, but since then temporary agencies have been allowed to provide workers for many more jobs than before, including, since 2004, in manufacturing companies. Those restrictions that still exist can be bypassed. One rule says that if a temporary employee has been in a job for three years the job must be classified as permanent. So, firms change job descriptions slightly from time to time, restarting the three-year clock.

Japan is now home to a group of young workers known as 'freeters' – a combination of 'free' and *Arbeiter*, German for worker – who have come to accept a work style of casual labour. While temporary employment agencies such as Pasona have encouraged 'freeters' to save in individual retirement-savings accounts, this does not come near matching the benefits enjoyed by 'salarymen'. One agency called Mobiato.com sends workers on its books e-mails on their mobile phones telling them of short-term jobs, often for the same day or the following morning. This just-in-time labour on call implies that the workers must be ready at very short notice, with obvious implications for their other commitments.

These changes have helped increase income inequality in the labour market. Status-based changes have been more important than technology or a rise in the relative demand for skilled labour. As elsewhere, those in temporary or part-time jobs have difficulty in moving to full-time regular jobs, and rarely have access to training, which puts them in a precariat trap. Legitimized as normal, the conditions of the Japanese precariat have suffered, with lost access to transport expenses, attendance bonuses and rest breaks. And the average duration of contract has been falling. These losses have been partly offset by increases in hourly rates of pay, reflecting the shift of social income and the process of commodification. But it is a radically different labour process.

In the UK the precariat is also substantial. A 2008 report by the Commission on Vulnerable Employment set up by the Trades Union Congress claimed that some 2 million people were 'trapped in a continual round of low-paid and insecure work where mistreatment is the norm' (p. 7), with problems at work particularly common in care homes, cleaning, hotels and restaurants, hairdressing and beauty, construction and security (p. 11). These were solidly in the precariat. But more are nearly in it, and appear to suffer from identity confusion. In surveys of class identification, a majority describe themselves as working class, but in spite of predictions that the middle class would decline – made famous by George Orwell's forecast in 1937 (1962, p. 202) that it would 'sink without further struggles into the working class' – the share identifying themselves as middle class has stayed constant for decades. The younger the respondent, the more likely they are to consider themselves as working class. Nearly two-thirds of those aged 25–34 do so, compared with less than half of those aged 55–64, which suggests members of the same family see themselves as belonging to different classes.

It may be because many in the younger generation are in precarious jobs that they see themselves as working class. A corroborating indicator is that in a 2007 poll, a third of those in 'professions' (categories A and B in the official socioeconomic classification scheme) saw themselves as working class. One long-time researcher on class attitudes tried to interpret this:

> Fifty years ago there was almost an official and agreed class ranking, and everyone knew where they were located. . .. That has completely gone now. So that whereas once it would have been just straightforwardly objectively wrong for somebody in a middle class profession to think of themselves as working class, that's not necessarily true that it is objectively wrong any more, because these aren't terms that have any agreed meaning any more.
>
> (Roger Whitmore of polling company MORI, cited in Aitkenhead, 2007)

Quite. Another indicator of confusion is that a majority of 18- to 24-year-olds see their parents as middle class, even though a majority of that age see themselves as working class. This suggests downward social mobility. But it may also reflect the fact that a large number work in the precariat and feel a sense of detachment from the labourist model.

The key trait of the precariat is not being in control of one's life, or having the capacity to sustain a work narrative and develop a coherent 'work history' that one could describe proudly to children or friends. The precariousness comes not from employment insecurity but from lacking an occupational identity. Thus, a spreading phenomenon in Japan is a new type of homeless working poor made up of youths who sleep in internet cafés (Hayashi, 2008).

Although statistics are scarce, anecdotal evidence suggests that for the most part the labour done by the precariat is instrumental, to earn income. It is obviously rational to treat precarious jobs as instrumental, since it would be costly and risky to regard them as 'occupational' when they could end at any time. The prospect of failure is too high to justify investment in skills or a psychological commitment.[5] This produces a sense of both alienation and anomie, which pushes those in the precariat to a lifestyle of passive, fetishistic consumerism, and the phenomenon of privatism.

The precariat typically earns lower wages and suffers more from poverty than higher classes. In the EU, poverty is twice as high among workers with fixed-term contracts as among those with long-term contracts, and twice as high for those in part-time jobs as for those in full-time jobs. A similar situation is likely to prevail in other parts of the world.

Many of the precariat have jobs classified as part-time, but this can be misleading. In the USA, for instance, there has been a sustained growth in the number with multiple part-time jobs; a majority are women. Retail trade has led the way, where the just-in-time labour system has spread from manufacturing. Computerized scheduling systems, aimed at raising service efficiency and reducing labour costs, match staffing levels to customer traffic, hour by hour. By this means, more workers can be put on part-time status, even if their labour time may be full-time in any particular week. Some are called full-time but find that they actually only receive a part-time allocation.

The reverse can also be true. Often jobs are full-time in reality but are classified as part-time so the employer can avoid paying health benefits. As one woman told the *Wall Street Journal*, 'I have part-time status with full-time hours' (Maher, 2008). Even if a person is required to work 40 or more hours a week, US law does not oblige the employer to classify the job as 'full-time' or to pay the corresponding benefits. Usually, those on part-time status receive lower hourly wage rates and have no benefits or employment security. And those doing two part-time jobs may find they have to pay unemployment insurance twice, even though they could, at best, receive only one benefit.

Although the precariat has been growing everywhere, in some places it has become socially defining. In Italy, temporary workers are already known as *precari*, and their predicaments have begun to influence and be represented in art. A play called *Tutto Precario* (All Precarious) by Noemi Serracini was a big success in Rome, and the film *Tutta la Vita Davanti* (All Your Life Ahead of You) gripped the Italian public in 2008. It has been estimated that 20 per cent of the Italian labour force are in temporary jobs, and in some other European countries, such as Spain, the share is already over one-third.

The Italian precariat was enlarged by the Treu law of 1997 that introduced temporary labour contracts and the 2003 Biagi law that allowed private recruitment agencies. However, most Italians still rely on personal contacts to obtain jobs. *Mal di Merito* (Merit Sickness), a widely-read book by Giovanni Floris (2007), traced the use of influence in achieving job placements and promotions, a practice that exists in all countries but has reached epidemic proportions in Italy. It implies that labour force participants are dependent on someone who is powerful; talk of meritocracy in the face of this reality is dishonest. The casualization behind the growth of the precariat suggests that job opportunities will continue to be distributed in this way.

Being insecure, it is scarcely surprising that many turn on immigrants as the alleged source of their insecurity, which has helped populist politicians to electoral success. In April 2008, a coalition of the elite and the precariat voted Silvio Berlusconi back as Italy's prime minister. He immediately pledged to defeat 'the army of evil', which is how he characterized illegal immigrants, with a policy of 'expulsion of those who break the law' or deemed to be acting anti-socially. This spelled the end of equality before the law and acted almost as a licence to provocative gangsterism towards migrants.

Some, including Lazaratto (2006), depict the precariat as a floating population subject to what Foucault called 'security' techniques. Instead of controlling workers through disciplinary devices in the workplace, social and economic policy is reconstructing them as autonomous risk-takers, 'entrepreneurs', possessors of human capital. If citizens are induced to behave and think as mini-capitalists, they will focus on balancing costs and profits of various actions and investments. One could say the agenda is to reconstruct the worker as someone with a perception of autonomy who is actually being disciplined and shaped by social policy.

Related to the precariat is the 'cybertariat', defined as those forced to live a double shift existence, as in the case of women doing care work and wage labour (Huws, 2003). Dividing groups by their relation to the economic system, by class, should not ignore the way people are obliged to combine labour with reproductive, recuperative and regenerative activities. To the extent that these functions are done by women, labour feminization implies not only precariousness alongside integration into labour activity, but also that those affected must do multiple forms of labour and work, in the process losing more control over their time.

Reflecting the growth of the precariat, in the early twenty-first century, while the US unemployment rate hovered around 5 per cent, the lowest level since the 1960s, the percentage of men aged 25–54 classified as 'not working' and not unemployed was higher than at any time since the Second World War – 13 per cent compared with 6 per cent in 1968 at the end of the Great Transformation. The situation for prime-age women was even more striking; 27 per cent were 'not working' in 2008, up from 25 per cent in 2000. Part of the reason is the way unemployment is measured – being without any job, having actively searched for one in the past four weeks and being available for a job. Theoretically, more men and women could have been opting for play and living off savings or loans. More likely, they were surviving by casual labour interspersed with spells of unemployment or non-labour work.

Contrary to long-held expectations, the precariat has also grown in developing countries, adding to rather than diminishing the already large proportion working in informal ways. In South Korea, by early in the twenty-first century 60 per cent of all workers (and 70 per cent of women) were in insecure casual jobs, many in the high-tech sectors (Neary, 2002). In South Africa, over a quarter of the employed could be classified as in the precariat (Standing, 2007a). In India, where over 80 per cent of the total labour force is outside 'formal' employment, it is hard to know just how large the precariat has become. But being a member of the precariat is the likely fate of many millions everywhere.

THE UNEMPLOYED

In Polanyi's Transformation, the image of streets of unemployed men shaped social policy. Most people felt they or a close relative could be plunged into a period of unemployment.

That image has changed. In the Global Transformation, the unemployed are more typically depicted as a category with particular traits and responsibilities, less victims of industrial restructuring than victims of character defects. For this reason, although there are obviously still many who lose jobs during cyclical downturns, the unemployed can be seen as a distinctive social category to a greater extent.

In the UK, for instance, in mid-2008 400 000 people were classified as long-term unemployed. Many had been unemployed for so long that to classify them in some other social class related to their previous employment would be misleading. After a time, being unemployed surely becomes an identity.

The long-term unemployed cross traditional class boundaries. Many have never had any formal employment. Globally, the number of openly unemployed has risen in this era, although the geographical distribution of the unemployed – and their class background – have shifted. Probably a lot more are unmeasured in official statistics.

In general, the unemployed suffer from labour market and income insecurity. Unemployment benefits have been cut, duration of entitlement to benefits has been shortened and conditions for entitlement have been tightened, while a form of contractualization (discussed later) is turning their status into something close to labour-in-unemployment.

THE DETACHED

Finally, at the bottom of society there is a growing category cut off from mainstream state benefits, lingering in chronic poverty, anomic and, more by their presence than by their actions, threatening those above them in the income spectrum. Politicians have been inclined to treat these victims of economic liberalization as needing 'reintegration'. They linger in the streets, in bus and train stations, in city parks. They make those above them in the social order feel uncomfortable or smug, depending on where they fit. The detached represent fear. And it is fear that induces concessions from the near poor, an ultimate tool of inequality and casualization. The term that earlier generations of social observers would have used is a *lumpenproletariat*. Nobody wants them as neighbours.

CONCLUSIONS

As the global market society has taken shape, class groupings have evolved. Roughly speaking, the top three classes are detaching themselves from state-based social protection, the bottom three are being detached by disentitlement to state benefits and services. Although a different way of presenting the stratification could be chosen, the analytical device may help to picture the growing *inequality* of social income, the deterioration of economic security and the loss of a unifying sense of social solidarity.

The class restructuring is related to changing attitudes towards inequality and the direction of social policy. The affluent – the elite, salariat and proficians – opt out of public institutions rather than lobby and vote for their improvement. This contributes to their erosion and more inequality in access to dignifying social services. The core clings to labourism, but lacks the political strength to reconstruct it. The precariat suffers from weakness-of-will due to their detachment, and could if ignored become the dangerous class. The proficians seem to enjoy themselves – until the tank runs dry.

Meanwhile, inequality has gone unaddressed. For those advocating or supporting the global market society, it was not seen as a system failure, a problem waiting to be solved. It was regarded as essential. But citizens were worried. In 2008, an opinion poll showed that three-quarters of all Germans feared old-age poverty and were concerned about rising income inequality. No doubt half of them were in the 'middle class' or in the salariat.

While greater inequality has been tolerated without mass action, there is no democratic support for the gross inequality that has characterized the global market society. A majority of people in all the countries where surveys have been conducted think inequality is too great, that the wealthy should be taxed more and that inequality will widen further. This is even the case in the USA, a country inclined to tolerate if not welcome inequality. In 2008 78 per cent thought the income gap was too wide and over 60 per cent supported higher taxes on the wealthy.

Yet the class fragmentation may explain some oddities. While inequality in the UK has grown since the 1980s, there has been a decline in sympathy for the poor, with polls suggesting that people think they are lazy and coddled, rather than unfortunate (*Economist*, 2008c). Similarly, lack of solidarity is reflected in widening gaps in living standards between those employed in public services and those in the private economy, between the salariat and the elite, and between them and the precariat. This has extended to lifestyle options. Thus, prices for services that used to be affordable for most of the salariat, notably education, have risen sharply, leading to a dent in their self-esteem and resentment of yacht owners.

It was more than symbolic of a dying breed of labourism that in early 2008, in a situation of greater inequality and economic stagnation, the UK government still thought it necessary to say that it would be cutting taxes on capital even more than it had done already. In May 2008, in the wake of devastating local election losses, attributed in part to a hastily withdrawn proposal to raise taxes for the poor, the Prime Minister told the Institute of Directors: 'Our aim, I tell you, is to reduce corporation tax even further when we can afford to do so' (cited in Eaglesham, 2008).

The government's reluctance to tackle inequality was further shown by its climbdown over taxation of 'non-doms', rich non-domiciled residents who receive relatively favourable tax treatment. When it was proposed that they should pay more tax, representatives of the rich argued that 'non-doms' would move abroad, depriving the government of tax revenue and the country of the benefits of their spending. The measures were watered down accordingly. But the logic of the argument is that taxes should be cut for wealthy citizens, because they could all go overseas, taking their money with them. One could even argue (and some have) that they should be given subsidies to discourage them from moving. Shortly afterwards, the UK Treasury Minister told a banking conference that pay and bonuses were not matters for government but for company boards and shareholders.

The financial crash of 2008, accompanied by a political backlash against the elite, has changed the rhetoric of governments. However, it is not clear what form of class alliance will emerge to influence political strategy. One fraught with danger is between the elite and precariat, following the Italian model, with the elite willing to divert attention from its own opulence and opportunism by depicting outsiders as the threat and cause of insecurity. A more progressive agenda could come from an alliance of the proficians and the precariat, since each has an interest in achieving income security without compromising their freedom to pursue broad ideas of occupation. We will come back to what this might mean in the final two chapters.

NOTES

1. According to Margaret Thatcher, 'It is our job to glory in inequality and see that talents and abilities are given vent and expression for the benefit of us all' (cited in George, 1997).
2. Cox and Alm were economists at the Federal Reserve Bank of Dallas.
3. According to Forbes, the number of billionaires doubled between 2003 and 2008, when the youngest was aged 23, the founder of Facebook.
4. Globally, the 'high net worth' group with more than US$1 million of investable assets excluding their primary dwelling rose to 8 million in 2007 (Thomas, 2008).
5. Lacking the company trappings and the sense of obligation that went with them, the Japanese precariat has become a source of whistleblowers drawing attention to bad practices of firms that employ them. The old corporate loyalty derived from the feudal system of *bushido*, which governed a samurai's allegiance to his overlord and a master's duty of care towards his inferiors, has gone.

5. Crumbling barriers to decommodification

INTRODUCTION

In the light of the emergent class structure and changing forms of inequality, let us return to the Global Transformation and consider how barriers to labour recommodification have been crumbling. Institutions that had limited commodification have been eroded, leaving people with weaker agency and under more pressure to labour in ways required by the global labour process and tertiarization. By no means have all the changes been negative in terms of freedom. Some have cleared the space for new institutions that could restructure work and labour in positive ways. But the changes have left people more exposed to market forces and pressure to be competitive, conforming to the central feature of neo-liberalism.

This chapter considers four institutional barriers to commodification – the family, the educational system and the unemployment and disability systems. In each case, old institutional forms involved relationships that limited the power of market forces.

THE FAMILY

Although some depict the family as an enduring feature constituting a solid base of society, it has in reality been one of the most fluid institutions in human history. It is a locus of a wide range of activities that defy easy categorization as work, play or leisure, which is why there was such a protracted debate on 'reproductive labour' some years ago. Work done in a family is part gift, part a component of a chain of culturally shaped reciprocities binding the family together, part a reflection of oppression and patriarchy. Recreation or play blurs into learning, care blurs into preparing for labour or recovering from labour, teaching blurs into discipline for labour, so making future workers more efficient. To treat all those activities solely as labour or work or 'leisure' would be arbitrary, since many combine elements of all three.

Sociologists such as Talcott Parsons and William Goode painted the family as transformed by modernization, moving from non-market centres of socialization to nuclear units focusing on procreation. This idealized the changes. In the nineteenth century and early twentieth century, the working-class family had little capacity to perform these socialization functions, even though Peter Laslett and colleagues have suggested that the English family showed the required flexibility by adapting to the changing needs of industrial capital (see, for example, Laslett, 1972). In higher classes, the employment of servants and retainers meant many domestic functions, including childcare, had already been turned into market relationships, often as a mark of social differentiation. Lest we think that modern outsourcing of domestic functions is new, recall that in Europe at that time it was usual for aristocratic women to outsource breastfeeding of their babies to paid surrogates.

Nevertheless, however imperfectly, the family as a social institution fostered a sense of community and encouraged behaviour and attitudes resistant to external pressures to be efficient and instrumental. But buffeted by modern market and global forces, it has lost that capacity in several ways. As a result, we may be witnessing a gradual 'defamiliarization' of human life. Family size has been shrinking, with the gradual disappearance of the three-generational family household. The old family, at least as a social norm, was relatively immobile and consisted of a mix of balanced reciprocities. Nowadays, in both rich and industrializing societies, the two-earner nuclear household is regarded as the norm and even this is under pressure.

The End of Patriarchy?

Historically, patriarchy has been a means of social control and oppression, and its decline during the twentieth century was a progressive achievement (Therborn, 2004). However, this has also lowered a bulwark against the forces of commercialization.

Patriarchy was strengthened in early industrialization, because the middle class saw it as a way of anchoring moral stability. Later, that was more than offset by industrial citizenship, because the workplace was separated from the home, proletarianization meant male workers had no property to transmit, and fathers and husbands were dependent on enterprises and the state for benefits for themselves and their families. To some extent patriarchy was sustained by the 'breadwinner model' on which much of the welfare state was based. But this model collapsed as globalization took off, since neither family wages nor full-time male 'full employment' could be maintained. The normative basis of the working-class family faded further as means-tested social assistance displaced social insurance and other mechanisms of labourist social solidarity.

Patriarchy had provided a system of control. Without it, the family as an institution was left to the mercy of external forces. Family members could begin to express themselves and respond to external incentives to be more individualistic, more opportunistic and more self-centred. As Polanyi put it, the market society depends on self-interest. The decline of patriarchy was liberating, but it unleashed more self-interest.

The New Demographic Transition

The demographic transition corresponding to globalization has some common trends, although one could cite exceptions. The average age of first marriage has risen, the rate of divorce and separation has risen along with the rate of remarriage, the age of first childbearing has risen, the number of births per woman has fallen and there are more common-law relationships and single-person households. Internationally, there has been convergence in that the average number of children born within an average family has fallen to two or three. Fertility in the world has fallen from 4.8 children per woman two decades ago to 2.6. Globalization has been associated with a shift to 'replacement fertility'.

Labour recommodification has meant high female labour force participation and what Therborn (2004) and others have called the post-industrial model of delayed childbearing. In Europe, the fertility rate has fallen below the net reproduction rate, so that countries such as Germany and Italy have shrinking populations and are ageing rapidly. Apocalyptic predictions have been made; French historian Pierre Chaunu has called it the 'White Plague' (*La Peste Blanche*), comparable in its effects to the Black Death (Chaunu and Suffert, 1976). On the assumption that low fertility reflects a desire among women for a career coupled with a high cost of child-raising, the mainstream political response has been to try to reduce the cost of interruption of employment and to facilitate childbearing without a break in employment. Neither of these policies may be sufficient to raise fertility, especially if they are being introduced when career opportunities are shrinking and as the precariat spreads. As they have no career to build, women in the precariat may have children early but have few of them because they cannot afford them. The middle-class young aspiring to join the salariat or proficians may merely postpone childbearing. These are speculations. But it is surely commercial pressures that are influencing these personal and family decisions.

Meanwhile, in most societies, longevity has meant not just more people living to old age but a decline in infant and child mortality that has reduced the average amount of time women spend in childbearing and childcare. People are expected to live longer and to live healthier active lives for longer, giving them a new perspective on work and lifestyles.

In the context of these changes, the family as an institution could hardly be expected to remain unchanged. The claim here is that not only has it become more fragile, but it has been unable to offer resistance to market forces or to pressure to labour efficiently and intensively.

In the industrial citizenship era, the nuclear family was idealized. With labour still set by reference to the clock and calendar, coupled with norms for years of schooling and retirement, it was easy to characterize the situation as the working-class 'housewife' helping in the reproduction of labour power of her 'breadwinner' husband and future-worker children. In the upper and middle classes, married women fulfilled the role of vicarious consumer, as Veblen ([1899] 1967) described it, and gradually moved into a labour role, as lower-level professionals or secretaries, albeit mostly with no 'career' ambitions or expectations from their men-folk or employers.

That society has gone, and good riddance. But it produced the highest rate of formal marriage in history. In 1960 nearly three-quarters of women in the USA aged 20–24 were married. As labour and consumption patterns changed, so did the propensity to marry; by 2000 fewer than one in four American women of that age were married.

Illegitimacy spread in Europe in the late nineteenth century. More than half the births in some cities, Polanyi's Vienna among them, were out of wedlock. Although the phenomenon is different today, in affluent societies extra-marital births have risen from less than 1 in 20 to 1 in 4, with 1 in 2 in a few countries such as Norway. This reflects a revolution in social and personal behaviour (Hobsbawm, 2005, p. 9). Among related changes, adoption has become a growing business, while cohabitation has become almost a commercial arrangement, with contracts to protect incomes, assets and savings.

The two-earner household is a form of private social protection, in which each partner supports the other in case of need. This may weaken attachment to more social forms of solidarity, such as trades unions. But it is fragile, often couched in behavioural conditionality. If, for example, one partner loses a job and cannot quickly obtain another, the relationship may soon come under strain.

Marriage and Contractualization of the Body

Longevity and better health have made for radical changes in the way the family is perceived. In a colourful analysis, Hervé Juvin (2005) has characterized this as a modern cult of the body. His claim is that, along with a redistribution of wealth from workers to the retired in affluent societies, longevity and better health are making a mockery of conventional values. With a hint of hyperbole, he argued: 'For someone who has a life expectancy of a century ahead of him, everything that has been built, thought or legislated in the context of a short life is erroneous. Everything – family, marriage, cultural heritage, savings, morality – has to be re-examined in the light of long life'.

Thus, the institutions of marriage and the family are less marketable because the price of monogamy has risen steeply, from about 20 years of commitment to about 40 years. Marriage is a matter of contract as well as sentiment and convenience. Its opportunity cost has risen, due to birth control and Viagra. People are encouraged to live for corporeal pleasures, which become matters of heavy investment. The body becomes capital, or at least people think of it as a matter of personal investment, which has contributed to expansion of the new service economy selling tourism, fitness, food and sex. Juvin concludes by asserting that modern society has replaced the traditional trinity of liberty, equality and fraternity with a new trinity of health, security and pleasure. In this scenario, marriage becomes part of a contractualization of society.

Payment for sex has always been common. But Therborn (2004) sees 'pimps' as a continuation of patriarchy, with increased power in certain societies. Pimping is hardly a new occupation, but with more fragile marital and extra-marital relationships, it may have expanded, in part to meet demand for sexual services among migrants and the precariat. From this perspective, the existence of pimps would seem to reflect the weakness of the family as a social institution and a commodification of sexual services. For the most part, pimps are degraded exploiters, or employment agents, with neither security nor rights. Their span of control is likely to be short and risky. And they may actually be in a weaker position than those providing the sexual services.

More recent developments associated with extension of the market are the sperm bank and artificial insemination, two peculiar expressions of commodified existence. Suffice it to note that they are linked to the fragile family form and the commercialization of our human functions. And the capacity to manipulate the genetics of our species opens up ugly possibilities of producing more efficient humans in the future.

While these are worrying aspects, others could be more positive. The sexual revolution of the 1970s that accompanied feminism and the contraceptive pill led to fewer 'shotgun' marriages and more sexual freedom, especially for women. The average number of partners over a lifetime has risen and serial relationships have become the norm in most Western societies, although the USA remains an outlier, albeit with twice as many births to teenagers as any Western European country.

The New 'Extended Family'

The growth of geographically divided families has been a feature of globalization, with global household chains and remittances flowing in several directions. This has accompanied global labour circulation, surrogate parenting and semi-commercialized care work.

The Western marriage system has become globalized in one respect; an increasing proportion of marriages involve establishment of new households. This in itself weakens the provision of informal family benefits (FB in the social income structure). Migration and increased longevity have pushed in the same direction.

Nowhere is this stretching of family more evident than in China, where the twin trends towards small families and ageing, accelerated by the one-child policy, have strained the Confucian tradition of depending on families for welfare support (Dixon, 1992). The combination has also put downward pressure on wages, since migrants must accept whatever job they can find.

In India, the extended family is shrinking fast. In just two decades, the size of the average household has dropped from six to four (Prasad, 2007). This reflects urbanization, ageing, consumerism and women's rising labour force participation, particularly among middle-class married women. With only 4 per cent of the 80 million Indians aged over 60 receiving a pension, the government has introduced a law to fine or imprison those who fail to care for elderly parents. It also plans to introduce fast-track tribunals where people aged over 60 can bring cases of neglect against their own children.

The globalized family is creating new forms of community or expanding forms that were previously little more than historical curiosities. Among these are home-based associations of migrants. Obviously, the geographically extended family network is much looser than the single-household model, accelerating the demise of strong inter-generational reciprocities.

Commodifying Care

The family has always been the primary institution of care, in which relatives look after each other. However done, care has three complementary aspects – reproductive, recuperative and regenerative. Since it is central to our working lives, it deserves more attention than it usually receives.

The difficulty starts with linguistic ambiguity. 'To care for someone' has meanings that blur into one another. 'I care for Jane' may mean no more than I care *about* her, or it may mean I want to be her lover, or I take responsibility for her well-being, or that I tend to her needs. This multitude of meanings has contributed to its neglect. Another factor is its universality. Most of us have done what we would call care work, and think we could do it, if we wished. This perception of near-universal capacity contributes to its under-valuation. It is nothing special. The image is unfortunate, since the skills are as great as in most other forms of work, and the capacity to perform care well is acquired by experience and training just as in other 'skilled' work.

Another cause of neglect is the variable intensity of care. It may mean no more than being a presence, available in case of an untoward event. Or it may mean constant attention to a bed-ridden invalid. This variability of intensity makes it hard for policymakers and statisticians to measure care work.

The neglect of care work was nevertheless a shameful failure of labourism. Feminists demanded it should be taken seriously, as did Marxists in debating productive and unproductive labour. But even now, a labour economist is likely to say (or think) it is a subject for sociologists or the 'welfare community'. For decades, policymakers were inclined to ignore care, because of how growth was measured and because jobs were regarded as the objective. People doing unpaid care reduced growth and the number in jobs.

Throughout the twentieth century the big issues were: who should receive care? What sort of care was appropriate? How should care work be compensated? And, lingering in the background, how should those providing and receiving care be protected, from others and from abusing themselves?

The answer to the first question long seemed obvious – children, the sick, the disabled and the few elderly. Societies have favoured different forms of care for each of these, making infants and the elderly primarily a family responsibility while supporting paid forms of care for the sick and disabled, who were seen as victims of risk contingencies requiring a redistributive response. But the classification of family care needs reflected changing social norms. For example, in industrialized societies there was a drop in the age to which infants were deemed to *require* childcare by their mothers, linked to the fact that more women wished to take jobs or were under pressure to do so. Conversely, for a while there was a widening of the definition of sick and disabled considered to merit care, and recognition that the elderly could receive care outside families. Later, there was a tendency to narrow definitions of care need categories, which accompanied the shift in favour of cutting social spending and the belief that state support induced moral hazards.

The main issue was how care done within a family should be compensated. In the labourist era, there was sanctimonious rationalization of non-payment, on the grounds that care was a gift relationship, not a market one. Care was not work because it was done for love, charity, duty or societal recognition. As the motive was not to make money, bringing in the 'cash nexus' belittled it. This reasoning should have been regarded with disdain. While identifying motives for providing care is hard, pure altruism is rare. Oppressive pressure and self-exploitation have also been involved. The gift perspective smacked of middle-class complacency, even as it paid respect to the sublime nature of the gift of care. For these reasons, it was a poor guide for policymaking.

There was also a rationalization that care in a family should not be regarded as work on the grounds that it reflected a 'reciprocity relationship', provided on the expectation that it would be reciprocated later, by the person or by somebody else. While anticipated reciprocity may have been an incentive to do care, it has similar dangers to the gift relationship, in that family members are scarcely equals in terms of bargaining strength or social status.

In any case, the idea of gift and the assumptions of reciprocity became less convincing as more women entered the labour market, as family structures changed and as the market society offered more services. The reciprocity relationship in particular broke down, intensified by mobility and fragility of households and families. More people found they were not receiving the care they thought they had earned from providing it earlier, or were not prepared to provide it because they could not anticipate receiving some later. Put bluntly, younger generations found the opportunity cost of their time was too high for them to bother.

As the care deficit became clearer, with pressure to provide care for groups previously regarded as not needing care or not being large enough to merit attention, the state recognized that care had to be financed. The perceived options were to pay family members providing care, provide a public service or provide the means for people to purchase a service.

The public service relationship was expected to become the norm in welfare states. For the recipient, public provision was seen as offering a greater sense of trust than a commercial relationship, because of the public service motive and the presumption that standards of care would be more assured. These claims are less accepted than they were. If paid for out of taxation, a lack of budgetary responsibility by care recipients and carers was added to the drawbacks of impersonal relationships and bureaucratic rules, breeding variable care quality.

A consequence was greater faith in commercial relationships, in which the person requiring care, or a surrogate, hired care for cash. Commodification had arrived as a general practice. The purchaser could require a standard of service and receive compensation or other redress if the service was poor or erratically supplied. Neo-liberals and libertarians could support this because purchased services widen choice and encourage efficiency. Others welcomed it because they saw it as empowering (Morris, 1993). But the paid carer can act opportunistically or withdraw at short notice. The carer is also vulnerable, since the cost of error could be high, leading to acrimonious charges of misconduct or negligence, which have led to some sad court cases. Often the terms of contract are vague, and conditions may change after an agreement has been reached. Great onus is put on trust.

Difficulties have also mounted in relation to paying for the commodified care. Who should be paid, how should payment be made and what should be paid? Here, as the family has crumbled, a pattern has taken shape. The state has turned to social insurance, social assistance and subsidies to encourage voluntary work. None of these have done well by any egalitarian principle one could name.

Early in the twentieth century, there was a struggle to enable women to undertake care work, through 'breadwinner' or family wages, pensions for widows and single mothers and maternity leave. That made women dependent on husbands, even if there was selective 'liberation' from labour. By mid-century, there was a two-track system, with family benefits paid to husbands and a professional care system. Then, with labour recommodification, state-based entitlements to care were cut, leading to more reliance on social assistance for single mothers, maternity leave for women in jobs and residential and home care for the elderly (Jamieson, 1991). By the end of the century new forms of care were being legitimized, with parental leave and subsidized privatized care.

The welfare state prepared the ground for commodification of care, which became a more clearly defined set of activities, separated from labour. Child and family benefits recognized its role with regard to childcare and the socialization of children as future workers. And middle-class parents were encouraged to turn childcare into a commercial arrangement. This is being taken to new levels of convenience; one trend is the use of video links to nurseries and nannies.

In the post-1945 welfare state there was some decommodifying of domestic work. Universal and family benefits, coupled with free or subsidized public services, helped working-class families support women's domestic work. However, this forced women into what Ruth Lister (1994) described as the modern variant of Wollstonecraft's dilemma. Women at home lacked a role in the public sphere. But in the labour force they were treated as secondary workers, largely confined to low-paid low-status jobs. Over time, however, women's participation in the labour market rose and the nature of that participation changed, becoming more like that of men. In turn, men found their participation becoming more like women's in the past, that is, precarious. Old patterns of family care could not survive.

For much of the twentieth century, even in rich countries, the working class had little capacity to perform high-productivity care. Nevertheless, welfare state policies did allow some enrichment of family life, providing time and a little income for a widening range of domestic work and support activities. That space for enrichment has since been whittled away amid encroachment by the market into the domestic sphere. As state benefits and social services have stagnated, working hours have lengthened and two-earner households have become the norm. Commercial companies are selling packaged paid services for all sorts of activity that formerly the idealized family was expected to provide. Thus, coming in your direction is the easily caricatured 'rent-a-mum' service, the 'care-for-dad' provider, the service to provide birthday parties for children, a dinner party service and a host of others. There is a tendency to standardization (albeit packaged as variants from which the consumer can choose), and more social pressure on people to do more labour for money to pay for the services.

Activities that used to be part of domestic and reproductive work are being supplied by commercial 'emotional' labour. Care work, for children, the elderly and the sick and disabled, has been taken over by commercial providers. Though vulnerable to 'self-exploitation', the suppliers of emotional labour, in caring occupations, profess relatively high job satisfaction, which may reflect the nature of the work or low expectations. But they are usually poorly paid, in precarious positions. The division of labour is evolving, so that the same tendencies as in other commodified spheres of work emerge, including differentiation, standardization, intensification, auditing and instrumentality.

Elder Care and Commercialization

With global ageing, elder care has come to public prominence. Although people are active and reasonably healthy for longer, the number of frail elderly is also increasing rapidly. The over-80s is expanding faster than any other age group. A scenario is taking shape where one or two children will find themselves with responsibility for two parents and a grandparent, as well as their own children. Continuing in jobs will be one response, since savings rates will fall. Final-salary pension schemes (where they still exist) will be converted into 'career average income' schemes, enabling people to take less senior jobs as they age. They may also alter the distribution of their labour, taking time out to accord with their family situations.

Meanwhile, the generations are being geographically divided in ways that weaken inter-generational reciprocity. Symptomatically, by 2008 there were 67 'retirement communities' or 'villages' in the UK, the largest being on the site of a former holiday camp (Blackhurst, 2008). All consisted of elderly residents, with infrastructure and services for their needs, matching the retirement enclaves in the sunshine states of the USA. In essence, the elderly – or their children – buy a package of elder services including a dwelling to make it possible.

The welfare state involved an inter-generational compact. Instead of family and local community support for the elderly and infirm, it was based on the premise that today's employees paid for the pensions of yesterday's, their parents. This worked reasonably well when most in the labour force were in full-time jobs with 'family wages' and when the number of pensioners was small. After a while, the inter-generational compact included expenditure and contributions for healthcare for current and past workers. Contribution rates rose steadily. But, while incomes of the elderly were protected, under the impact of globalization not only did contributions go up for younger workers but wages stagnated. The inter-generational compact simply could not survive.

The growth of the precariat also put family relationships and reciprocities under strain. In the USA, as middle-aged men and women lost secure full-time jobs and had to accept part-time or casual labour, some also lost their homes and became obliged to live with elderly parents or other relatives. The model of middle-aged children taking in their impoverished parents has been reversed (Eckholm, 2008).

As a barrier to commodification the family has been weakened by the breakdown in the inter-generational social compact, the system of reciprocity that underpinned pre-industrial and industrial society. The norm used to be that parents provided care and school-ing from birth to age 16 or thereabouts. In return they could expect about the same number of years of care in retirement if they were fortunate. Now, the situation has become more onerous at both ends of the age spectrum, and has intensified a double source of insecurity. Parents can expect to have to support their children for at least 20 years and children can expect to find their aged parents living in retirement for 20 years or more.

The psychological burden or cost may be even more daunting. Parents may wonder whether there is a contract to assure any 'return' on 'investment' in their children, espe-cially in a world of growing geographical mobility. Family bonds are weaker when people move far from where their parents live, or when parents move themselves. And the off-spring have the prospect of having to care for, or pay for the care of, elderly parents whose fading memories make for a relationship of diminishing value. For many, the psychologi-cal, time and financial burden will be borne with no prospect of a subsequent return, in this world at least, other than a clearer conscience.

This situation is ripe for opportunistic behaviour. When parents give a child years of care and a high share of their income, then years of positive interaction lie ahead. The psychological cost of the 'sacrifice' is usually borne lightly. Most parents would be dis-mayed if their actions were not depicted as primarily 'altruistic' and 'natural', rather than self-centred and commercial.

The elder-care issue is more fraught, particularly if the offspring have childcare commitments. Their priority will be their children, partly because the time and money invested in childcare would have an expected rate of return, whereas care given to an elderly frail relative would have little or none. Indeed, although it is depressing to think about it, 'good' care of an elderly frail person with diminished capacity to interact would have a negative rate of return, to the extent that it would extend that person's life and thus involve more time and expenditure from the carer. This is a quintessentially twenty-first century dilemma.

Globally, the number providing unpaid elder care is growing. According to a 2007 survey by the US National Alliance for Caregiving and the AARP (the US pensioners' organization), one in five Americans was providing unpaid care for an elderly person (Gibson and Houser, 2007). This is a 'gift' relationship under pressure. But it should be seen in the context of the new demographic transition, since the 'baby boom' generation in industrialized countries is reaching retirement. Social policymakers should be trying to pre-empt the coming crisis of care work.

The strain that pension systems are facing reflects the beginning of the end of pensions as a way of dealing with the elderly. Governments have introduced reforms to encourage people to delay taking their pension, to encourage early retirement, to facilitate partial retirement and to dissolve pensions into multiple 'pillars' – a bit of a state pension, a bit of a social insurance pension, a bit of an occupational pension, and so on. The reality is that pensions were for an industrial age in which family life fell into three neat phases – short childhood, fixed and long labouring life and short retirement. Family life is no longer like that.

Emotional Labour

As the family became less resolute, new forms of commercial activity emerged, including what is called 'emotional labour'.[1] The family is a zone of emotions, demonstrated by behaviour, attitudes and the way time is allocated. Now the market is identifying emotional needs, even to the point of creating norms for what good parents should do. Instead of a carefree birthday gathering, which you may do 'badly', there must be a proper party organized by experts offering a menu of choice (Cowboys-and-Indians, and so on). Dinner parties can be pre-packaged, including 'conversation animators'. 'Rent-a-mum' services fill maternal care deficits. Dads are worse. They never spend enough time with their 'kids'. They never did. Now, the market offers solutions. Firms in the USA are providing training to their employees on making time for family life.

One can foresee a bright future for emotional labour. It is supposed to help family members handle pressures and family life more efficiently. The market is converting domestic work into emotional labour and is generating *more* labour activities, since in the past much of the work portrayed as the desirable norm was not actually done. An idealized commercialized norm is being created, whereas only an imagined one existed in the past.

To the extent that emotional labour is part of a widening array of commercialized services, sold through advertising and social pressure, it is displacing domestic work activities, so narrowing the sphere of work while extending that of labour. The commodification of reproductive and regenerative work erodes the capacity of the family to be a barrier to commodification more generally. Inter-generational reciprocities are made more fragile. And if domestic activities are geared more to efficiency, there is less scope for them to be an antidote to the pressures of labour, giving a balancing perspective on lifestyle. Being focused on labour, people are more likely to suffer from burnout and other disorders, after bringing 'work-to-home' and 'home-to-work'.

The growth of emotional labour has been accompanied by use of commercial criteria for assessing domestic work. In the USA, companies have started to provide executives and other employees with training and guidelines on how to manage family life efficiently, so as to fit family activities with the demands of employment; the evaluation of the person's performance as parent and spouse is based on workplace programmes (Tough, 2002). This is a commercialized service – family management, to free up time for better labour.

The outsourcing of domestic functions is part of personal commodification. One should not idealize 'traditional family values'. Yet outsourcing of tasks disrupts the family's capacity to reproduce itself. Although commodification may 'free' women from domestic chores and weaken patriarchal structures, it generates other forms of tyranny.

The restructuring of the family, partly due to the spread of commercialized services, has weakened men's role as guardians of social morality and as a disciplinary force over labour. This is healthy. But dealing with the anomic behaviour of young men without role models has been left increasingly to the state. In the UK this has led to the disturbing Anti-Social Behaviour Orders (ASBOs), popular with the modal voter, but which may criminalize young people who have not committed any crime. Between 2000, when ASBOs were launched, and 2008, more than 1000 teenagers were sent to jail simply for breaching the terms of their ASBOs, such as breaking curfews or visiting places ruled off-limits (Morris and Russell, 2008). The link between recommodification and rationalization of social control of the non-conforming is easily ignored.

In sum, the family is under strain. More people are 'bowling alone', or adjusting family commitments to what is economically rational. Elderly relations are a 'burden'; our duty extends to making sure their old-age care in a nursing home is financed. Children are investment goods, a drain on resources. Grandparents are to be humoured. Other relatives have quaint names, rarely heard of, even more rarely seen.

In his scholarly if social democratic assessment of the family, Therborn (2004) postulated three regimes – patriarchy (who rules), marriage (how people link up) and fertility. Globalization seems to be producing a gradual convergence here too, around more fragile conditional quasi-commercial relationships. Sociologists have been slow to devise a 'separation regime' or one for morbidity and mortality (how people deal with long-term illness and frailty). But how and when people separate, and how couples and families deal with morbidity, are all subject to commercialization through the market rationalization for self-interest. Market considerations make altruism and intra-family reciprocities more tenuous and brittle. It is no surprise that divorce rates among the wealthy go up in recessions. Spouses of rich earners get out while the going is good.

As Habermas (1984) recognized, for all its stifling effects, the bourgeois family fostered personality traits that could sustain a sense of social solidarity required for effective social movements. But commercialization has made the family a source of privatism and separation from wider communities just as it is fading as a social force.

There is a link here to the notion of 'connectivity' (Granovetter, 1973), which is said to bring close family members closer, while reducing attentiveness to 'strangers'. It weakens 'weak ties', so reducing civility and civic friendship. More connectivity could have the effect of narrowing the family to an inner circle while weakening ties beyond the immediate household. The cousin or grandparent who cannot help in consumption, labour, work or play is unlikely to figure in the circle of strong ties or contacts. In short, the family as an engine of social solidarity is enfeebled by a culture of markets and modern connectivity.

THE EDUCATIONAL SYSTEM

Throughout history, education has stood as a barrier to commodification. Although in the nineteenth century, schools evolved as places of discipline for the industrial proletariat, inculcating respect for the clock and labour rules, the upper echelons of society regarded schools and universities as embodiments of the Enlightenment. Education was seen as fostering independent, creative and subversive thinking and expressions of diversity of opinion.[2] In the globalization era, that has changed.

Human Capital Versus Education

It is appropriate that the term 'human capital' stemmed from the ranks of Hayek's disciples at the University of Chicago. Traditionally, schooling had a double meaning. Public schooling has always had a dialectical character, in that it is a means of discipline and a means of liberation. And historically, state schooling has been an arena in which citizenship has been advanced, setting standards of competence, criteria for social inclusion and reinforcing identity.

Changes in educational systems are now helping in the recommodification of labour power. If the state provides free public schooling and subsidized college and university, young people emerge as embryonic citizens. Once education becomes little more than commercialized preparation for the job market, they emerge as partially commodified youths, with designated 'human capital' value, and probably with a debt from student loans that will act as a powerful disciplinary device for years.

Hegel captured the noble role of education when he commented, 'The final purpose of education therefore is liberation and the struggle for higher liberation still' ([1820] 1952, §187). For him, education was 'the art of making men ethical' (§151). Marx was more aware of realities, and saw education as 'producing' labour power, for better or for worse (see, for example, Marx [1867] 1967, p. 172). Then in the twentieth century, T.H. Marshall (1950), claiming that skill was at the heart of citizenship, argued that education must be socialized learning, with social recognition and continuity built into it. All these comments go back to Rousseau and the Enlightenment spirit of education, though they recognize that external criteria can defeat its potential.

This is roughly what has happened. Education is imagined as a liberating experience. We revere the Renaissance spirit, the sense of curiosity, learning and culture. Yet mass education, far from spreading this spirit, has been accompanied by increased instrumentalism and scepticism about the desirability of knowledge for its own sake or in the search for wisdom. Increasingly, knowledge is perceived not as the search for truth but as the search for *relevance*.

Schooling is seen in functional terms, as preparing people for the market economy as jobseekers and jobholders. The desire to shape labour power through educational institutions is vastly greater than it was in the period of industrial citizenship. Politicians and commercial interests argue that schools must be designed and judged by whether they produce skills wanted in the labour market, including the emotional and behavioural skills required for a flexible competitive labour market. Schooling is seen as the means of enhancing national competitiveness and producing, or failing to produce, disciplined labour (Cole, 1998; Banfield, 2000; Rikowski, 2001; Rosskam, 2006). This is not so much about raising the quality of labour power as altering its character in order to raise individual and collective labour productivity. In a competitive environment, with no known maximum level of productivity, the emphasis leads towards constant pressure for improvement in human capital. This is surely unhealthy.

The role of schooling in the battle for competitiveness has led to a competition to produce more efficient citizens, aided by more spending and selection of potential 'winners'. In OECD countries, spending on primary and secondary schooling on average rose by 40 per cent in real terms between 1995 and 2004. Yet this and early selection procedures did not seem too successful. Average attainment was unchanged. Early 'tracking' by allocating pupils to different sorts of school and programme appeared to hurt weaker students without benefiting the others. It seems that streaming is a mechanism of inequality, without a positive effect on overall levels. Countries either do well by all types of student or fail all of them. But this has not stopped the more inegalitarian character of school systems.

A few examples highlight some of the trends. In 2005, the UK government urged the Financial Services Authority to advise on how to 'embed an entrepreneurial culture' in schools. Is that what schools are for? Silvio Berlusconi, Italy's Prime Minister, was even more blatant, in 2001 saying all that students needed to learn were the 'three i's' – *inglese, internet, impresa* (English, internet, enterprise) (Herbert, 2001). In France a 2008 report commissioned by President Nicolas Sarkozy (Attali, 2008) argued that schooling should focus on employability and that economics should be taught in all primary schools. Here was a shameless shift from learning about culture and identity to learning how to be an efficient consumer and worker. One wonders what subjects would be displaced and what type of economics would be taught to those young pupils.[3]

Yet it is in the universities that the market society is most advanced. The contrast with the past could not be sharper. The change has been recent. In the social democratic era, education was seen as opening the door to social mobility. In the globalization era, it has been depicted as the avenue to competitiveness and higher incomes.

At the time of Polanyi's Transformation, higher education still had its liberating functions. It was understood that universities had a social role that stood apart from the market economy. This continued the ethos established in the nineteenth century, captured so beautifully by John Stuart Mill, whose defence of liberal education in his speech on being installed as Rector of St Andrews University in 1867 still resonates:

> At least there is tolerably general agreement about what an [sic] University is not. It is not a place of professional education. Universities are not intended to teach the knowledge required to fit men for some special mode of gaining their livelihood. Their object is not to make skilful lawyers, or physicians or engineers, but capable and cultivated human beings. . . Men are men before they are lawyers, or physicians, or merchants, or manufacturers; and if you make them capable and sensible men, they will make themselves capable and sensible lawyers or physicians (Mill, 1867).

Then and for a century afterwards, universities were expected to promote character. They stood apart from the messy business of commercial activity. But gradually they became the primary agency for higher-status professions. Bledstein (1976) saw the university as the institution that promoted a culture of professionalism, enabling the bourgeois to defeat the gentry. Universities legitimized professions and became spheres of inter-occupational competition, as well as advancing abstract knowledge and training recruits for the rising number of professions. Professions' affiliation with universities first emerged in the USA and at the University of London, gradually 'making the university a holding company for largely autonomous faculties, usually closer to their professional associations than to a particular university' (Abbott, 1988, p. 208).

The tension between academic learning and professionalism simmered in the early phase of globalization, but by the 1990s the market had turned universities into commercial institutions with market objectives, including the making of profits. Students became products to be processed, commodities to be prepared and sold, with university success rates measured in numbers of students, pass rates and subsequent employment rates. Universities became centres of commercial activity. Mill and Hegel would have been bemused. Polanyi would have been aghast, while Hayek would have approved, as did his disciples.

The state also altered its governing institutions. In the UK, a telling decision was when polytechnics were merged with universities. But the reconstruction of 'higher education' as a commodifying service was more vividly epitomized by the creation by the British government of an almost Orwellian Department for Innovation, Universities and Skills. It went with the 46-country 'Bologna Process', a coordinated strategy to create a European Higher Education Area to orient universities to human capital development. The bias of the Department (one is tempted to call it by that over-used prescript 'postmodernist') makes one wonder how a progressive ministry would have looked. Perhaps a Department for Education, Culture and the Arts would have tilted the balance towards liberal learning and development of human potential. There is a need for an agency to promote the values of human capability, and leisure as participatory, political action. Universities and the state system set up to support them should be geared to refinement of intelligent citizens and to research on how to improve the human condition. Instead, the market is dominant and human capital is the desired commodity.

The Commodification of Schooling

Labourism and social democracy contributed to it, but nothing so ill becomes the globalization era as the commodification of 'learning'. Rather than being a barrier to commodification, the educational system has become a means of furthering it through a shift to the values and methods of human capital.

Everywhere schooling is being privatized, often by stealth in that parents and students have to pay more of the accessory expenses. And private schooling has become expensive; parents drift into debt without an easy option of escape once they have put their children on the private path. Rationally, parents may not be 'investing' wisely because the expected net returns are minimal, if only because with more stretched and fragile family reciprocities the offspring are unlikely to give an income flow to the parents that corresponds to a rate of return they could have obtained by investing in other assets. In the UK, this realization may account for the fact that more middle-class parents have been taking what could be called the work route, sending their children to state schools and involving themselves by participating in school activities and enhancing performance with tutoring at home.

Commercialization and privatization have been encouraged by capital and international financial agencies. In 1998, the World Bank published *The Financing and Management of Higher Education: A Status Report on Worldwide Reforms* (Johnstone et al., 1998), whose rhetoric is an example of dominant thinking. It asserted that decision-making:

> will shift not only from government, but from higher education institutions – and especially from faculty – [and from] inappropriate curricula unrelated to the needs of the emerging economies. Performance budgeting will undoubtedly [be tied] to acceptance of principles of rational actors who respond to incentives. . . Entrepreneurship on the part of institutions, departments and individual faculty is already growing almost everywhere – adding revenue to institutions and benefit to society.

The certainty with which those statements were made reflects the hegemony of the human capital approach. But commercialization and privatization are making education a misnomer for what is being offered. One of the features is the stepping-stone approach to privatization where the state subsidizes commercial provision or forms partnerships with commercial interests. For instance, state schools have been lured into 'school–business partnerships'. In the London Borough of Tower Hamlets, a well-established state secondary school linked up with an American bank to run the school. This is a means of spreading an ideology. The bank had 'invested' about £500 000 over a decade of involvement, its executives chaired the school's governing body and bank staff helped in classes. Apparently pupils talked about the bank 'as though they were a department at the end of the corridor' (Skapinker, 2007). The headmistress claimed that for a school–business partnership to work it was necessary to have a 'shared culture'.

An educationalist or philosopher might ask whether a school should share the culture of a US investment bank. Is this what the local community wanted or had been asked to have as their local school? At the very least, there was a democratic deficit, since no democratic process had taken place. The market was running the show. The fact was that the school had been turned into an instrument of commerce. It was good to know that with money from the bank the headmistress had been able to take a group of pupils to Beijing and another to New York.[4]

Of course, a bank is likely to instil market values in pupils, and no doubt the smart suits helped. This type of partnership is just one way by which state educational systems are being restructured as commercial enterprises promoting an ideology rather than critical social thinking. For the record, the bank providing the role model was none other than Lehman Brothers, which went spectacularly bankrupt in 2008 after gambling recklessly with the money of millions of people.

Another trend is the rhetoric of 'choice', a euphemism for commercialization and selectivity. Here we run into the revival of religion and 'faith schools', all geared to the promotion of values that run against ideas of universality and social solidarity. Some religions have enormous wealth and a proselytizing objective that transcends all else. Meanwhile, a growing number of parents are taking their children out of school altogether and giving them home-based education. The UK Department for Education and Science suggested that up to 35 000 children were being educated at home in 2007 (Hill, 2007).

A key development is the commercial supply of educational services. Schooling, especially in English-speaking countries, is becoming a huge industry. Fees for British, US and other schools have risen to £20 000 a year. Harrow, a well-known English fee-paying school, limits the number of foreign students to about 12 per cent so as not to spoil the market because parents want their children immersed in a British environment (Turner, 2008a).

A way of commodifying international schooling has been through academies linked to foreign schools, usually arranged by a franchise. Thus, there is a Harrow International Bangkok and a Harrow International Beijing, the latter owned by a Chinese businessman. New Zealand openly sells its schooling too, the government claiming that education is 'one of New Zealand's top five export industries' (Turner, 2008b). As befits a globalized market, demand for the product fluctuates according to the volatile New Zealand dollar. Ironically, testifying to the commodification trend, the biggest source of students is South Korea, even though Korean schools rank among the world's best.

The globalizing labour market is being assisted by the international market in schooling, led by the USA. The US National Science Foundation, in a 2006 report, described the USA as 'educator of the world'. Foreign graduate enrolment there has been rising. Foreign students account for over a third of all US doctorates in science and engineering, and 17 per cent in other fields, with students from India in the lead, followed by China and South Korea. Most international students rely on their families and personal resources, so the process is selective in class terms.

At every level, private commercial services are spreading, mainly through e-learning. Multinational corporations are packaging courses and setting up facilities all over the world. Many are US-based, although other English-speaking countries have entered the global educational services market. Some developing countries have joined the suppliers while still being purchasers of foreign services. One Indian company, nattily named TutorVista, offers tutoring services to students who hope to go abroad. Its founder and CEO commented in 2008, 'India can become the education capital of the world and our plans to foray into test prep, vocational education, formal education are all in sync with this trend' (Biswas, 2008). Another Indian company, Educomp, has been expanding at an extraordinary rate and by 2008 was supplying 6000 schools with learning laboratories, virtual classrooms and digital libraries. The Indian government has also invested heavily in e-learning through public–private partnerships. Companies with names like Career Launcher and Educomp Solutions have raised large sums on the Indian stock exchange and provided their investors with high returns. Private equity has also become involved. There have even been fears of an educational sector bubble, which could leave a lot of educational establishments, teachers and students in dire straits.

As educational services have become part of the global market, they are being reformed to focus on preparing youth for jobs. The search for profit is leading to cuts in courses that do not yield a high rate of return. For many people, this is what they want, an efficiently acquired qualification that can be used to obtain a job. But the commodification of eucation is a threat to a progressive vision based on occupational identity and development.

Learning and pupils become products to be processed efficiently to provide conventional measures of success. This has been taken to extremes at university and college level, where universities are now judged by their ability to attract funds and foreign fee-paying students. Globalization has produced the global university, driven by commercial companies with huge networks. The largest US university of all is the for-profit University of Phoenix, with over 280 000 students in 239 campuses and offshoots in other countries. Others are expanding fast. Alongside them are thousands of 'corporate universities' run by multinationals such as McDonalds and Microsoft. These institutions are changing the character of learning, now being led by market forces. They are set on trying to empty universities of political, critical thinking. In developing countries, as well as elsewhere, for-profit universities openly discourage political thinking in favour of securing income-raising credentials (*Economist*, 2005). Choice architects blithely ignore these realities.

The commodifying trend is linked to the way 'higher education' is being funded, by fees levied on students and their families. A growing proportion of students come from upper-income and middle-class backgrounds, resulting in lower social mobility and more inequality. But the effect is complicated because of the increased use of means testing, by the state or by the universities themselves. In practice, means testing is inequitable and inefficient. It is also inegalitarian: while a few students from low-income families may gain upward mobility, those just above the income cut-off face an income squeeze, tipping them into a state of income insecurity and debt.

Commodifying Academics

The work of intellectuals is becoming intellectual labour. Universities and colleges have become centres of 'professional academics', most little more than workers labouring to produce a product, eager to go forth as good members of the salariat.

As with every commodifying trend, academic commodification will not become complete. But the countervailing trend is weak at the moment. The philistines are at the gate. Academics have become remarkably commodified. In the UK, and increasingly elsewhere, they are assessed by measurable, standardized targets and lured to compete individually and collectively via league tables of inter-faculty and inter-university performance indicators. They are losing control over their work to non-academic administrators who let loose on them an army of monitors, auditors and assessors. As Frank Furedi (2004) and others have argued, post-modernist reasoning is used as a tool of instrumentalism. If there is no such thing as truth, everything is relative and can be judged on its appeal to the emotions, artificial targets and the whims of fashion, prejudice and commercial funding. The response by academics may be cynicism and manipulation to create false outputs. But this is passive resistance; it is not a means of recapturing relative freedom or a decommodifying strategy.

In the main, academics have shown the required Pavlovian tendencies their new masters want. They compete to sell research proposals to funders, seeking the most appealing buzzwords. Those who commodify themselves best receive tenure and promotion – classic tools of commodification – and are rewarded financially and in status, becoming a labour meritocracy. Those who dissent or who refuse to play by the new rules of academia are likely to disappear from the scene, labelled as 'misfits' or dismissed as not 'team players'. Being critical – the essence of creative and scientific work throughout history – is often regarded as endangering 'the project' or 'the centre'. This is resulting in a Warholism of intellectual life. It seems many young academics hope for a 15-minute moment of popular acclaim, resulting in a 15-year leap in financial reward.

The commodification is epitomized by the way academics are being graded by number of publications and type of journal in which they have published. Certain journals are graded much higher than others, and in many subjects these are US-based. Mainstream journals are being converted into control mechanisms, for to publish in them the academic must use standard models, techniques, language and, underneath, standard ideologies. For example, a Marxist economist would find it hard to publish anything in a class A economics journal; since tenure and survival depend on publishing in such journals, a young academic would be penalized for trying to publish elsewhere.

Globally, commercialization and liberalization of tertiary 'education' have increased the control exercised by outsiders over the scientific and cultural communities, reducing their autonomy and increasing the emphasis on market rewards (Hartmann et al., 2006). The poor academic is a failure, the rich one an object of adulation, cited reverentially, feted with awards, invited to speak at numerous venues for suitably large fees and granted consultancy contracts by fancy institutions. The celebrity academic is a creature of our time. He or she is a parody of the agonized intellectual characteristic of the Enlightenment eras.

It is unnecessary to romanticize the intellectual, because the commodifying tendency has long been there. But it is necessary to understand the depth of the crisis in order to consider what is required to alter the trend. Polanyi would have treated the 'fictitious' commodification of intellectuals as one of the horrors of the triumph of financial capitalism.

From Vocational Training to Job Training

Another feature of globalization is the shift outside the school system from vocational education to job training. Bureaucracies and the state that serves their interests have opted for job training rather than the broader idea of occupational education. This breaks the association of work with an occupational community, with its specific ethics, standards and career norms. Members of the occupation lose touch with the expertise and linkages that define their occupation, and losing control of that is the essence of proletarianization.

If skill is part of citizenship, as T.H. Marshall (1950) argued, then among the threats to citizenship are short-term employment and training contracts. These have spread with the transfer of responsibility for training to companies, leaving the state to play a passive facilitating or legitimating role. Employers, not workers, become the training market's central consumers. Transferring training to commercial providers results in the commodification of training and skill formation, removing a worker's control over skills that is the essence of artisanship and occupational citizenship.

Lifelong Learning

Adult education has become almost compulsory for those with secondary or tertiary education and hope of professional careers. The vogue term is 'continuing professional development' (CPD). This is a far cry from the sort of adult teaching Polanyi did for the Workers' Educational Association in London's East End in the 1940s. CPD is geared to the market economy with rigorous efficiency. People need to 'update' constantly and be more up-to-date than their potential competitors. The wisdom of yesterday is the smirk on somebody's face today. As the 'adviser on learning' at the UK's Chartered Institute of Personnel and Development (CIPD) put it, 'A certificate on the wall can no longer be accepted as a guarantee of competence'. One could say it never was, but one might add that, if this way of thinking is extended, such a certificate could become a disadvantage, drawing attention to the fact that the practitioner acquired his credentials some time ago; perhaps special banners should be taped on them, 'Updated'.

Human resources specialists – a modern profession with dubious motives – debate whether companies should seek to develop talent or buy it. Some argue that if companies train their employees they will demand higher salaries and promotions, or leave; others claim that training induces loyalty and commitment. The externalizing of CPD is probably winning, with advertising by providers increasing the perceived need.

According to the UK's Chartered Management Institute (CMI), 'The days of the paternalistic organization that looks after the career development of its employees are over. Average managers today will have nine moves in their working lives'. The worker may be an employee, but he must remodel and market himself, by turning to professional bodies rather than to employers for development of his labour power. This is a change from the presumption of industrial citizenship.

The CIPD and CMI have launched CPD schemes for individual members, while the General Medical Council has developed a 'revalidation programme', using evidence of CPD and appraisals, for renewing doctors' licences. Most professional associations in the UK now have CPD programmes; some have moved from voluntary to compulsory schemes, claiming that professionals have a duty to maintain and update their skills and competences. This may seem laudable, but it opens up awkward dilemmas. Many breakthroughs and refinements that spring from personal practice could be frozen by professional correctness. The discretionary space is being curbed.

We consider the issue of the right to practise in Chapter 7. But it is hard to deny that the individual is being retooled. Predictably, insurance companies are also moving the goalposts. Firms and professionals increasingly must demonstrate to professional indemnity insurers that they are regularly updating their skills and practices if they want to be insured against malpractice claims or accidents. No doubt, knowledge of 'professional ethics' will be next. The knot is tightening.

The situation is complicated further by the fact that in a service-oriented society, training takes on a new meaning, with emphasis more on personality traits than on just technical competence. 'Leadership', 'team playing', 'learning to listen', 'challenging ingrained expectations' and 'overcoming self-limiting beliefs' are catchphrases but must be defined as skills so as to be taught. Unlike the industrial proletariat, the tertiary worker is being subjected to proletarianization of the mind.

The litigation culture is contributing. Spreading from its US base, it is constraining the age-old notion of professional discretion. Those professions that cannot avoid being charged with professional incompetence will suffer from malpractice suits and the prospect of them. Thus, professional associations are requiring members to acquire training from named suppliers of training to safeguard against claims of negligence.

Administrative control is overcoming occupational control at all levels. The UK's Institute of Directors (IOD) requires its members to undertake at least 30 hours of CPD training each year if they wish to retain the IOD's Chartered Director qualification; at least 20 of those hours must be in 'formal' CPD. This is an example of obligatory rather than compulsory training; a person could still practice as a director without completing the training, but would lack the vital stamp of approval. Of the three models of training – obligatory, voluntary and compulsory – the obligatory route is consistent with the accreditation system discussed in the next chapter, whereas the compulsory route is consistent with licensing. The way the market and litigation culture are moving, one can predict that compulsion will triumph, unless political action is taken in favour of alternatives. Unless validated by law, the voluntary route will leave professionals open to lawsuits. Compulsion is also a means by which a profession can enforce a monopoly, particularly if it can raise the costs of practice by near-equivalent occupations or suppress them altogether.

The UK government 'revalidates' doctors' licences through annual, and more complex five-yearly, appraisals of their skills. Doctors are required to show they provide good clinical care, maintain a good practice, and demonstrate good relationships with patients.

This amounts to behavioural control, the essence of proletarianization. They have to satisfy bureaucratically defined criteria in order to retain the right to practise. In such circumstances, one is bound to ask what rights exist for the practitioner and how governance should be developed in order to ensure that their interests are taken into account and honoured?

In the USA, doctors are required to go for regular continuing medical education (CME) for a stipulated number of hours each year, often in the form of 'retreats'. Increasingly, these are funded and organized by drug companies and medical education firms dependent on drug companies. By 2002, 40 per cent of funding for CME came from commercial sponsors. Although government guidelines forbid manufacturers from controlling CME courses, these are not strongly enforced. The dividing line between 'questionable influence' and bribery is blurred, even though there is an Accreditation Council for CME, a non-profit body with a board from medical associations and hospital groups. Capital is controlling the process and commodifying the profession through CME training.

Financial advisory services constitute a profession spawned by globalization and the market society. In the UK, the professional is an Independent Financial Adviser (IFA), who must pass the Financial Planning Certificate (FPC) mandated by the Financial Services Authority (FSA). It is an adjustment profession suited to the Global Transformation. But it promptly defined a monopolistic space for itself, while subjecting its members to rites of passage. In order to maintain professional status as an IFA, advisers must maintain a log of their annual CPD and show they have undertaken between 20 and 60 hours of training in the past year. This is work-for-labour.

The legal profession has also been dragged into CPD. The UK's Law Society requires solicitors to complete 16 hours of CPD-accredited work and training in the three years after qualification, which is a form of apprenticeship. But obligations continue, for they must fulfil 48 hours of CPD training every three years. Barristers have their own CPD requirements. The world's largest law firm has turned all this into a specialized zone, setting up the Clifford Chance Academy, with a central database on CPD participation and a 'warning' system for idle practitioners. The International Federation of Accountants has also made it compulsory for accountants to have regular CPD. This is modern-day proletarianization.

Traditionally, a university degree was based on the presumption that professional knowledge lasted a working lifetime. As skill obsolescence has accelerated, that is now only a start. Corporations, or specialist suppliers, have taken up a growing proportion of skill training. And the commercialization of all levels of schooling has made people feel in need of regular training. It is no coincidence that corporations and consortia of corporations have created degree-granting programmes, setting up systems that compete for clients with universities and colleges.

Could universities become corporate extensions? Corporations have been directing them towards commercial interests and attacking traditional liberal education. Abbott (1988, p. 211) predicted that this would divide the professions:

> Those dependent directly on corporate employment – engineering, management, to some extent science and accounting, and perhaps even law – will find themselves seriously torn between the universities that are now the chief supports of their independence and the employers who, although themselves divided, can control them. Professions less dependent on corporate employment – the professoriate, medicine, librarianship, social work, dentistry – will not face

the same problem. Although the impact of these forces on particular inter-professional contests is hard to predict, they may well change the nature of competition itself, in particular by attenuating even further the professions' power to directly control their own work and careers.

The first part of that prognosis has proved correct, except that the force has been with the commercial corporations. The second part has proved too sanguine, in that none of the professions has avoided the problem. Commercial control of skill formation has proved powerful; it should be weakened.

The Paternalistic Intrusion

The enrolment of schooling in constructing a global market society has been accompanied by other intrusions into the educational system, especially by medicine and psychology. There is also a possibility of a global 'religification' of education.

Psychology and medicine go together. The fashionable diagnosis for slow-learning or disruptive children is Attention Deficit Hyperactivity Disorder. Apparently, this has either been undiagnosed in the past or has grown sharply. Many millions have ADHD. Children suffering from it can disrupt classes and fail to learn as efficiently as desired or necessary in a culture that overwhelmingly emphasizes exam passes, grade-point averages, rote learning and other quantifiable measures. These are devices for sorting and measuring discipline, not imagination. Techniques to teach students how to succeed by these criteria are part of a functional approach alien to education's finer purposes. It is designed to produce a product and to make it more standardized.

Non-conformity risks failure. As labour markets are based on the sorting system, the consequences could be long-lasting. Great education courts failure; it tests depth of understanding, not the easily grasped capacity to play a game rated by affirmations of simple success. It is no surprise, therefore, that a vogue expression for exam failure is 'deferred success'.

A feature of a commercialized system driven by processing products, a finely tuned grading process and diagnosis and treatment of norm-deficient pupils is that teenagers emerge with a conformist mentality, attuned to adapt to the market society and self-centred as they pursue the next round of scores and tot up a life of notches, a classic feature of bourgeois existence. Those images may appear exaggerated, but it is hard to dismiss the feeling that they sum up the general direction. To reverse the trend would require a radical de-commercialization of education. That is not currently on the horizon.

THE UNEMPLOYED: FROM SUBJECT TO OBJECT

The next barrier to commodification was the unemployment regime. Since the demise of industrial citizenship, that has been transformed. Unemployment benefit schemes have been marginalized and changed in character. Here Polanyi was prescient. In analysing the nineteenth century, he noted the collapse of local unemployment relief (GT, p. 92). Local systems were jettisoned because the economic system required a national labour market; rural–urban migration of young workers into the mills and mines was needed to replenish the worn out, threaten the discontented and add to the pool of surplus workers.

The twenty-first century analogue is the supra-national labour market required by the globalized economic system. This has contributed to the decline in national unemployment benefit systems. They are hard to maintain if there is a flow of claimants from outside national borders who have not had contributions paid for them (or paid them themselves), or if companies can avoid paying contributions by flexibilizing employment or transferring production to where there are no benefits.

Insurance-based unemployment benefits are in terminal decline. In industrialized countries, a shrinking minority of the unemployed now receive them. Many countries have shifted to unemployment assistance, that is, means-tested transfers. But they have also done nothing less than commodify the unemployed.

For the early social democrats, unemployment insurance benefits, and public employment exchanges that helped reduce job search costs, enabled those losing jobs to retain dignity and search for alternative jobs in modest comfort. As an insurance benefit, they were paid to those hit by misfortune, corresponding to contributions made over years, providing a predictable transfer.

The presumption was that people who were unemployed wanted jobs and would not wish to stay unemployed. Unemployment benefits enabled them to avoid behaving like a commodity, because they did not have to take any job at any price. Although this was always a fraudulent image, in that the benefits only protected those whose employers had paid the contributions for long enough, it was reasonably accurate. And as long as there was a high level of full-time employment and only a small number in open registered unemployment, the cost of having a few who did not accord with the behavioural presumption was minor. The regime gave the impression of social solidarity, since unemployment was a contingency risk.

That is not how most schemes work these days. They have become instruments of social engineering. Someone making a contribution today cannot predict how much he or she would receive if hit by unemployment later or for how long a benefit would be paid. No government seems immune to the desire to tinker with the rules, almost always in ways that make it harder for the unemployed to receive benefits or lower the amount they can receive, or make receipt more dependent on some behavioural conditionality.

Basically, as unemployment rose in the 1980s, the dominant presumption came to be that many of the unemployed were 'voluntarily' choosing to remain unemployed. For various reasons, the benefit regime has been transformed, and its decommodifying character has gone.

The spread of flexible labour and the growth of the precariat with a weak or no record of insurance contributions meant that the cost of the system rose, requiring a growing contribution from general taxation at a time when neo-liberal governments were intent on cutting taxes and non-wage labour costs in the pursuit of competitiveness. This gave a rationale for cutting unemployment benefits and for presenting the unemployed as scroungers rather than victims.

The response by the state was to cut benefits by trying to cut the income replacement rate, to encourage the unemployed to take jobs. The trouble was that as the labour market was flexibilizing, fewer unemployed could expect to find jobs paying a wage as high as their former jobs. So the income replacement rate remained close to what they could expect to earn, implying an unemployment trap. Many of the unemployed would pay, in effect, a marginal tax rate of nearly 100 per cent if they took an available job. So the state shortened the duration of earnings-related benefits and tightened conditions for entitlement, demanding proof of job search, demanding acceptance of job offers, stipulating that those who quit a job had to wait longer before receiving a benefit or, as in the USA, denying them benefit for the whole period of unemployment. Gradually, the earnings-related character of unemployment benefit declined, reducing the unemployed to a commodity with a standard price in a buyer's market. Meanwhile, to try to lower unemployment, governments shifted more out of the jobless pool into early retirement or disability, modern concepts and categories that have come back to haunt them.

Unemployment insurance schemes became essentially a deception. What sort of insurance is it where, after you have paid your contributions based on clear expectations, the rules for entitlement are changed? Yet all those changes failed to solve the perceived problem. Fewer unemployed were gaining unemployment benefits, and more of them were being shifted onto means-tested unemployment assistance. But the changes deepened poverty and unemployment traps, multiplying moral and immoral hazards. This led to a demonization of the unemployed, further cuts in income replacement rates and greater use of 'in-work benefits', subsidies intended to make labour pay, which as noted earlier were a subsidy to capital.

This was still not enough. Active labour market policy was reinvented. The state obliged the unemployed to seek, train for and take jobs at lower wages than in their previous jobs; it then forced them to take any job. This was inconsistent with governments' ratification of the ILO's Employment Policy Convention No. 122 where they committed themselves to promoting 'freely chosen' employment. Symptomatically, the ILO remained silent through all the changes. By this point, the unemployed as a group was stigmatized as consisting largely of lazy welfare cheats, dependency prone and unworthy of being citizens. Unemployed migrants were soon being threatened by deportation.

The character of 'unemployment benefits' has changed. They have ceased to be a labour-based entitlement and an insurance benefit, and have ceased to have any claim to be decommodifying. The new regime severs the pursuit of career, because it directs people to take any job as quickly as possible. In the UK, the benefit was renamed the 'Jobseeker's Allowance', making it clear that it was a conditional measure of state benevolence rather than a right of citizenship. It is only paid if the person can convince the local Jobcentre that he or she is actively seeking a job, and the weekly allowance (£59.15 as of mid-2008) becomes means-tested after six months.

'Claimants' have become 'customers' or 'clients', implying that they are buying a service rather than obtaining a right or entitlement. If the customers do not do as they are told or do not do it well enough, they may be 'advised' (instructed) to change their behaviour or lose benefits for not doing so. 'Active labour market policy' trips off the tongue of bureaucrats, suggesting a macho image, when it means the state is active, the 'customer' merely passive, being told to take a selected job or 'training' place. This is recommodifying, reducing the freedom with which people can pursue their working lives and making them more flexible as suppliers of labour.

Clever use of the image of social exclusion was a further step. Enter the state, via the Third Way and the language and instruments of social inclusion. Instead of seeing the unemployed as surplus workers between jobs, they are portrayed as defective, in need of restructuring to make them more marketable. They need to be retooled, socially integrated.

Since the 1980s, the state has moved to commodify the unemployed by increasingly sophisticated social engineering. Besides using tax credits to reward certain behaviour, governments set the tone for how they expect their agents (employment service workers, case managers, and so on) to achieve social inclusion by manipulating the attitudes and behaviour of those at the bottom of the labour process, the precariat, the unemployed and social 'misfits'. The modern state governs at a distance, giving authority to agents made responsible for moulding the behaviour of those it wishes to see socially included (Rose, 1999). The new commodifiers are kindly souls. They are expected to treat the unemployed as deficient, socially excluded by their failures and failings, to be aided through case management. As epitomized by developments in Australia (McDonald and Marston, 2005), they must be taught how to present themselves for job interviews, how to fill in job questionnaires, how to market themselves, how to adhere to time schedules, and so on. They have to be taught to be 'active citizens'.

So-called activation policies are a mix of psychological pressure and financial penalties, so that it is realistic to think of the trend as putting the unemployed into a state of 'unemployed-in-labour'. They are being tailored to act as a trained threat to those in jobs who might be recalcitrant or resist labour intensification. This is the modern form of the reserve army function. The case managers of employment services are drill sergeants of recommodification. But they must battle with their own demons, for it is psychologically costly to manipulate, cajole, penalize and encourage their fellows.

There have been substantial increases in expenditure on active labour market policy, intended to raise employment and labour force participation, particularly of youth. This has occurred not only in 'social democratic' welfare states, contrary to Esping-Andersen's claim (1990), but in all types. And in all welfare states, not just so-called conservative regimes, more of the care burden has been transferred onto the family and local communities. And all types of welfare state, not just 'liberal' regimes, have seen reregulation (not deregulation) of labour markets, privatization of social services and marketization of risks. The pace may differ, but the direction is the same.

Active labour market policy merges into 'workfare', a commodifying mechanism now entrenched in many countries, including the USA, the UK, Australia, Austria, the Netherlands and Denmark (Handler, 2005). In France and elsewhere, the *revenu minimum d'insertion* and similar schemes were intended to activate the unemployed, but created a new form of dependency (Standing, 2003). Germany's 'Hartz IV' reform increased commodification in one of the few countries that had resisted the trend. Activation is central to recommodification all over the world.

Paternalists and neo-liberals attempt to manipulate the public with phrases intended to convey a benign image while actually promoting social control. Activation policies are dressed up as an extension of the notion of contract, enshrining individualization and social responsibility. There is also a trend to playing up 'the positive'. Those who are restructuring welfare states are seeking, at vast cost, to alter the public sense of morality on what is and is not correct behaviour.[5] At present, countervailing pressures are weak. That is unlikely to last.

Meanwhile, the neo-liberal state is busy turning unemployment into an arena of commercial services and profits – the welfare-to-work industry, which has spawned a host of professions. Following similar developments in Australia and the USA, in 2007 the UK government backed private 'welfare-to-work' services following advice from a merchant banker they had appointed. It will award contracts to firms to shift lone parents and people on incapacity benefits into jobs, with the firms paid from the resultant benefit savings. The Prime Minister linked the policy to the growth of China and the apparent need to 'win the skills race' if the UK was to 'remain competitive'. He set out a plan to expand apprenticeships to cover one in every five young workers.

As the employment and welfare-to-work services industry has grown, it has taken on the forms of other marketed services. Many of the unemployed are provided with contracts by private employment services, although they are renamed clients as befits the therapeutic culture that guides social policy. Giving them contracts is part of the redefinition of the welfare state, extending labourism in a way scarcely envisaged by earlier social democrats. These are instruments of recommodification, to increase efficiency and reintegration, not to provide temporary liberation from market forces. Unlike social insurance, there is no pretence of compensation for labour market risks.

Does this contractualization lead to more dependency on the state? Reformers claim the objective is to reduce dependency. But anybody studying what social workers do would be impressed by the paternalism, turning the unemployed from citizens needing compensation into clients who are objects for restructuring and improvement, objects with obligations. Neither the contracts nor the subsequent actions can be interpreted as freely chosen. The unemployed are more vulnerable than employees, and yet they are not covered by labour law, protective regulations, collective bargaining or freedom of association.

What is lost is respect for the agency of those targeted. These services are becoming a surveillance instrument, through use of contracts and case workers whose remit is to maximize placement rates and maintain awkward cases in jobs, using probationary status and stigmatizing practices, penalties and incentives. There is a danger that some services could become modern workhouses, holding citizens in dependent labour arrangements where the agency is the employer and supervisor, a far cry from the idea of a free public service aiding citizens to develop a career in freedom. A commercial service will suffer from moral and immoral hazards, since its objectives are not the same as those of clients. While the service is given powers over those it handles, there is no Voice on behalf of the citizens it processes.

Finally, the privatization and commercialization of the business of unemployment is linked to the shift from national systems to a global system in which multinational agencies are emerging to supply labour globally. This is part of the Global Transformation, and multinational employment services corporations will grow. Unless a powerful Voice on behalf of those seeking to perform labour can be constructed, the commodification process will create an unsavoury situation in which personal capability development will be given very low priority.

THE 'INCAPACITATED' AND 'LONE PARENTS' AS NEW LABOUR

In commodifying the unemployed, governments have gradually extended the groups targeted for similar treatment, to draw them into labour. Two groups have stood out, lone parents and those with disabilities.

With the restructuring of the unemployment regime, more people have found themselves officially designated as incapacitated or 'disabled'. Human beings have always been prone to physical and mental impairments; all of us suffer from something that makes us less than perfect. But the categorizing of citizens by medically and socially decreed ailments is a modern phenomenon. In the labourist system, it became a way of identifying those not expected to labour who were entitled to incapacity benefit paid from the contributions of those deemed able-bodied and in labour. But as the treatment of the unemployed became more restrictive, more people drifted into an incapacity benefit trap. In a competitive labour market, the unemployed consist largely of those less competitive because of some impairment. But when is impairment a disability and a barrier to labour?

The neo-liberal state inherited a predicament. Under late labourism, the reaction to rising unemployment and the tendency of flexible labour markets to marginalize those with competitive disadvantages led to more people being shifted into the modern category of 'the disabled'. Political expediency was not far away. Lowering unemployment was useful.

However, the disabled had to be compensated, and it was hard to draw the line on what constituted a labour-excusing disability. For a time, this was treated laxly. In the USA 6 per cent of the working-age population are receiving invalidity benefits, in the UK 8 per cent. However, as the recommodification drive gathered strength, paring the number of disabled became a policy objective. Definitions can be changed. A momentous decision was a US court ruling that, instead of being classified as disabled by whether a person could do labour force work, henceforth it would be determined by whether they could do at least three hours of domestic work.

The disability regime derived from labourism had put the disabled in a category entitling them to disability or incapacity benefits. Belonging to that category was medically determined by doctors whose self-interest made them more inclined to sign sick notes, at no cost to themselves, than to refuse. Basically a sick note was a bread ticket, and without bread a patient might become a bigger problem. And in a competitive market economy, failure to do well is almost a signal of impairment. If you are failing, it is likely to be due to a personal defect.

The number on incapacity benefits has boomed across the industrialized world, at a time of improving health. The predictable sequence of social policy thinking has led to a situation where the disabled are under threat of being branded idle and welfare cheats. Governments have begun to monitor and steer the disabled into jobs.

In the UK in 2008, 2.8 million people were receiving this form of income support, three times as many as were counted as unemployed. That number had crept up from three quarters of a million in 1979, when the incidence of ill-health was probably greater. Several explanations have been offered. Consider the motivation that such benefits encourage and reward. There is a poverty trap: moving from benefits into the sort of job most could obtain could mean a bigger loss than gained from earnings, especially as inca-pacity benefits have also been a passport to other benefits, such as housing benefit and free prescriptions, dentistry and eye tests. So taking a job becomes a major risk because the right to such benefits would be lost.

In fact, the number of disability claimants has risen because fewer people leave the roster, not because more are entering it. This is not due just to moral hazard and the poverty trap. Employers in a flexible globalizing labour market can choose and change more easily. They are less likely to recruit someone on incapacity benefit, who may be seen as risky and prone to cause problems. Moreover, knowing that incapacity benefits exist, an employer obliged to cut employment might reason that a disabled person would at least receive an income. Such moral hazards on the demand side also arise with respect to long-term employees who in the days of full-time employment and company stabil-ity would have been retained until retirement even if their productivity did not justify it. With competitiveness and labour costs so paramount, they are likely to be asked to leave. Once out of a job, they may be reclassified as disabled until they qualify for a pension.

Governments have tried to ban discrimination against the disabled, but the labour market dynamics increase their disadvantage. Migrants and women replace older men and those with health problems. Yet, policymakers want to push the disabled into jobs and so have tightened up tests of disability and obliged claimants to be interviewed more often and intrusively, to put them under pressure to take whatever jobs are on offer. And since mental problems are seen as a rising cause of disability, psychological and medical specialists are being used to make them more employable.

For the person with an illness or impairment, it pays to remain sick and not to develop skills that might gain the sort of job on offer. Compared with an 'able-bodied' person, the expected return to skill investment will be less. That suggests that a better policy would be one that equalized the expected rate of return, perhaps through a subsidy for training. But the poverty trap is huge.

Then there is the psychological side. In the UK, many incapacity claimants were suf-fering from ailments such as tiredness and eating disorders, and 100 000 were suffering from alcoholism or drug addiction. The biggest group, half a million, were reportedly suffering from depression. Armed with labourist images and a desire to appeal to middle-class prejudices, the government attributed the high number of incapacitated to idleness and fraud. It introduced a tougher 'fitness-to-work' test, aimed at driving claimants into jobs.

The official response reflected the paternalistic instincts of Lord (Richard) Layard, an economist and New Labour adviser. In his view, depression is a reflection of social exclusion; sufferers must be rescued, and the way to do that is through jobs. But why are all these people depressed? Perhaps many have turned a normal human condition into a means of survival, doing so because the social space in front of them is so alienating. To become depressed in the face of a precariat existence is scarcely a crime.

In 2008, the UK government decided to change the 'sick-note', which since the era of industrial citizenship had been the means of obtaining medical leave from jobs and from the requirement to seek employment in case of unemployment, into a 'well-note'. In justifying this, the Secretary of State for Health claimed that 'work is generally good for people's health'. He said doctors should indicate in well-notes what tasks the person could be expected to do, after conducting a test to determine what they could do rather than what they could not. The state was converting medical specialists into social policy practitioners, into a modern adjustment profession.

The UK government set a ten-year target of removing 1 million from the 2.8 million receiving disability benefits. Evidence showed that two-thirds of recipients returned to jobs within two years; pilot schemes had suggested that more could do so if aided by personal advisers, job coaches, occupational health specialists and finance and debt counsellors. This was the objective of the new scheme that became fully operational in 2008. Given claimants' reluctance to take jobs for fear of losing benefits, pilot 'pathways-to-work' schemes allowed them to take £40 of their benefit into a job with a guarantee that they could return to full benefit if the job did not work out. The scheme treated a social group as a target, but their members lacked agency. They were being processed, and the primary objective was to raise the job rate.

Lone parents have also been targeted. In 2007, the UK government announced plans to oblige single mothers of school-age children over the age of 11 to show they were looking for jobs or face benefit sanctions. Single parents previously had the right to stay at home until their children reached 16. The same week the government announced it was privatizing the welfare-to-work programme. Private employment companies were to be given bonuses if they kept claimants, whether lone parents or others, in a job for at least three years. The Work and Pensions Secretary rationalized compulsion by claiming that three-quarters of lone parents of older children were in jobs. The National Council for One Parent Families said the rest might have good reason for staying at home, such as being unable to afford childcare. The plan to use compulsion came from an official review by a banker commissioned to look at welfare reform as part of Tony Blair's 'legacy'. Drawing on Australian and US models, he proposed that private employment agencies and charities should be invited to work with 'repeat clients' and be paid a share of the benefits that would otherwise go to claimants.

In sum, the unemployed and those on the margins of the labour force were being pushed into labour, by commercial services. The groups being commodified did not have a Voice to contest decisions supposedly taken in their interest. The private firms paid to deal with them had a commercial interest in making profits and, in a market society, this would always triumph over more social and altruistic motives.

CONCLUDING REFLECTIONS

Commodification takes place when something is bought and sold without agency. Imperfectly, the family and the education system had provided mechanisms of social solidarity that gave groups the means of developing agency and a distance from market forces. Their capacity to do so and to reinforce values of solidarity and structured reciprocities has been eroded. This is not inevitable. Similarly, the unemployment regime has the potential of reducing the commodity character of the labour market and the potential to accentuate it. It has moved to the latter. These trends point to a need for countervailing mechanisms by which citizens, particularly those in the precariat and on the edges of society, can offset market pressures.

There are other institutions that could be barriers to commodification. One might be religious communities. During the Great Transformation, religion seemed a fading force, overcome by secularism. It had been used in the early phase of capitalist development, as Weber and others showed. Then, religious movements had emerged to give succour to the victims of industrialism and urban impoverishment. But as welfare states took shape, religion faded. It is clear that in the crisis of economic insecurity in the early phase of the Global Transformation, religion has revived and is once again playing a double role, extending the market society and providing solace for its victims.

The winning forms of religion in this disembedded phase are those brands wishing to extend the market society. Religious services have become a mighty industry, involving competitive brand selling, billions of dollars, huge advertising expenditure and manipulation of the state. They have also been privatized, with a shift to non-established religious bodies prepared to market their wares and services. As befits a market society without much time for reflection and doubt, it is the strands that sell certainty that have been growing.

Faith was a barrier to change but, as put by a report in *The Economist* (2007f), faith has become 'a lifestyle coach'. The early market economists, notably Adam Smith, understood the connection between religion and free markets. Peter Drucker, the management expert, hailed modern 'pastor-preneurs' for their marketing expertise. They certainly sell themselves and earn high incomes in various ways, living lives of luxurious consumption that set visible and vicarious examples to their multitude of followers.

Religion has blended easily with the surveillance state. Most religions have a long record of dealing intolerantly with deviants. And the growing Christian movements have usually backed politicians and parties favouring the market society. This is particularly the case in the dominant economy of the USA and in countries such as South Korea and Brazil. Religion has also become a mechanism for dismantling the secular welfare state system; religious philanthropy and religion-backed development services have been spreading around the world.

Thus, religion, especially in its Christian forms, does not appear to offer a barrier to human commodification. The minority of opponents to the market society have been hushed by the mega-churches and television evangelism. The capacity of the churches to counter market forces is minimal. Like the family and the education system, they have been converted. It remains to consider one other institutional barrier, that of occupational communities.

NOTES

1. Unsurprisingly, this is generating a new sphere of academic interest. A new publication is aptly named the *International Journal of Work Organisation and Emotion*.
2. In the eighteenth century, some of the pioneers of the Industrial Revolution took their children out of school, so as to further their education. For a delightful description of the reasoning, see Uglow (2002).
3. The emphasis on speed and exam passes has also resulted in a loss of educational discipline. Tolerance of poor spelling and grammar has produced what some have called 'linguistic whatever'. The focus on speed displaces time to reflect, inducing an intellectual torpor and a tendency to think in snippets, impulsively and driven by conventional attitudes. Student essays rely on hasty searches of websites and rote answers rather than reflective consideration of their own thoughts. This starts early and continues into university.
4. At a school reception, the *Financial Times* correspondent was so moved that he broke down in tears, or so he claimed.
5. Elsewhere (Standing, 2004) I have referred to the moral crisis as one of eight 'crises' of social protection. I endorse Vivien Schmidt's point (Schmidt, 2000, p. 231): 'No major and initially unpopular welfare-state reform could succeed in the medium term if it did not also succeed in changing the underlying definition of moral appropriateness'.

6. Occupational dismantling and commodification

INTRODUCTION

In the Global Transformation, one sub-plot has scarcely been noticed. Initially, the neo-liberals targeted regulations protecting employees through labour law, unions and collective bargaining. They successfully demonized unions as interfering with flexible labour markets. But once collective bargaining had shrivelled, progressives did not wake up to the new target, perhaps because those being attacked hardly counted as proletarians or 'one of us'. The neo-liberals went after the professions, demanding they dismantle non-market practices and their communities and privileges.

One barrier to labour commodification was the system of occupations. They can control the pace and intensity of work, set standards of efficiency and quality, codes of conduct and patterns of social responsibility towards clients, colleagues and friends. In the course of a transformation, once proud crafts or occupations lose status and autonomy while others emerge. But the dictates of a market society jeopardize occupational work in general.

No occupational community has had an ideal structure consisting of equals indulging in deliberative democratic decision-making, with openly shared knowledge and an ability to monitor and limit opportunism, internal oppression and hierarchy. All tend towards oppressive inequalities that have to be combated from inside and outside their community. But they have acted to resist commodification.

In their own way, occupations build up an ethos of dignified behaviour that places social values above opportunistic money-making. They build an ethical code, usually over generations. It involves a sense of trust, with 'gentlemanly', convivial values that place the occupation's long-term interests high on the set of priorities. Short-term opportunism is undignifying and understood as a threat to the occupation and its status.

Commodification occurs as a craft or profession loses control of its ability to reproduce itself (setting standards of practice, levels of acceptable qualification, training methods and so on), or loses the capacity to operate its own association (the way it runs itself), or loses control of its work, the ability to determine what quality is acceptable, the ability to control the timing and extent of work to be performed, what goes on in the workplace, the market for its services and its relation with the state. When these are determined by external bodies, commodification is well advanced. Loss of autonomy has usually come via attack from state bureaucrats, the courts, corporate tactics or divisions within the occupation. The capacity to control one's work and define a career in terms of non-market criteria is whittled away. Some occupations just fade because they no longer serve a social or productive purpose. More often they evolve or splinter into something else.

The disruptive phase of the Global Transformation has resulted in commodification of occupations, eroding their capacity to provide a balanced way of working and living. The pressure to become more attuned to the market has meant loss of control. This is not being atavistic, looking back to some Golden Age of professionalism and craftsmanship. The point is to identify features worth taking into a future of occupational citizenship. The chapter considers how occupations are being subject to commercial, state and international control, with practitioners obliged to earn wages set by others and with dwindling agency or associational Voice.

The focus is on services, particularly professions, even though much of what follows applies to most occupations. The fact is that in all industrialized countries most people are now providing services, those activities so disparaged by Adam Smith. And the tertiary sector is also the expanding one in all rapidly growing developing countries.

Lurches towards a market society are marked by 'advances' in the technical and social division of labour. On this, Polanyi is of limited use since he displayed little grasp of class and occupational struggle. He did appreciate how guilds put a brake on commodification, recognizing that they embedded productive activities in society. They made custom-and-guild rules unifying forces and prevented workers 'from becoming the objects of commerce', assisted in Britain by legislation such as the Statute of Artificers (1563) and the Poor Law of 1601. Although he should have given more attention to the repeal of the Statute of Artificers in 1813–14, he highlighted the 1834 Poor Law Reform in accelerating commodification.

Polanyi understood that, for commodification, 'non-contractual organizations have to be liquidated' (GT, p. 171). Presumably, these included craft guilds, which had their closed communities, codes, rules of entry, qualifications, behavioural norms, ethics and so on. Good or bad, they stood against the market. But they became a locus of struggle, with efforts to weaken their defensive capabilities and turn them into managerial instruments for setting standards and enforcing labour discipline. The fact that their organizations were transformed from within raises a point that is just as relevant in the Global Transformation. The continued existence of a professional body is not necessarily evidence of its continuing independence or decommodifying capacity.

Compared with Polanyi's Transformation, what distinguishes the Global Transformation is that class fragmentation is coupled with a proletarianization and splintering of occupations. Professions are generating specialisms, which are setting up associations and standards, societies and procedures of their own. And, as befits the global restructuring, standards are being harmonized by new supra-national bodies and agreements.

Throughout history, great professions and crafts have risen and fallen. As they have fallen, their members have suffered insecurity, crises of identity, loss of status and loss of control over their lives. In recent decades, numerous groups, such as printers, have struggled in vain to retain hard-won privileges and the mechanisms by which they had secured rental income and their niche in society.

The occupational fragmentation relates to standardization and internal differentiation. There are more occupational titles than ever. There is a trend towards international standardization of what constitutes particular occupations or professions and what should entitle someone to membership. And differences are growing between elites and the remainder within specific occupations.

In each era, some professions are favoured because they serve the dominant interests and forms of production. In the industrial citizenship era, engineers were among those receiving rental income, although their treatment varied. Now they have been displaced by accountants, lawyers, financial experts and auditors, among others. But it is only a minority who have benefited. In general, while those who are privileged owe that largely to their strategic functions, capitalism disregards occupational reputations, often emptying of content crafts praised for their virtues for ages. Many have suffered from 'deskilling' in technical capacity, social status and position of control.

The state's treatment of occupations has never been egalitarian. Thus, successive UK governments, in pursuing labour flexibility, condemned protective restrictive practices for workers. When it came to middle-class professions they were more selective. This was epitomized by the attitude to 'silks', an elite club of lawyers allowed to practise in the highest courts. There was to be no flexibility there, at least not until other battles had been won.

The neo-liberal state's initial onslaught on professions chipped away at associational strength, the capacity to act collectively in their interest. This took some time in coming. Hayek's principal apostle, Milton Friedman, cut his intellectual teeth in 1945 with a study of the US medical profession (Friedman and Kuznets, 1945), which he attacked as a monopolistic organization distorting the market economy. It took several decades for the state to move decisively to dismantle its agency freedom.

One point must be emphasized to avoid misunderstanding. There are arguments for and against occupations having control over aspects of their work and labour. All we are seeking to show here is how occupational controls have been weakened or removed. The implications are considered later. We will indicate the type of changes with examples drawn from professions that have been among the most carefully studied by others.

CONTROL OVER THE MARKET

Traditionally, occupations have been able to determine what and how they sold to contractors or consumers. In building the global market society, one objective of state policy has been to remove professional control over relations with consumers. Financial interests have helped. Thus, insurance companies have created cartels to bargain with professions ostensibly in the name of the client population, insisting on certain practices and blocking others.

The state has curbed professional jurisdiction by insisting that market interests must prevail. For instance, in the UK in 2007, the Legal Services Act set up an Office for Legal Complaints, which removed the handling of consumer complaints from lawyers, established an ombudsman as a single entity for complaints and introduced an independent oversight regulator, the Legal Services Board, to be chaired by a non-lawyer. The Act also gave consumers more choice among legal services and made business practices more flexible, allowing lawyers and non-lawyers to set up businesses together for the first time, with up to 25 per cent non-lawyer partners in any law firm. The government depicted this as boosting competitiveness and improving services. In celebrating the Act's passage, the Legal Services Minister made the intention plain: 'These reforms are all about fairness to consumers'.

Another example is the medical profession, long preserved from market pressures. But once medicine became an arena of profitable commerce and a source of high non-wage labour costs (EB) to capitalist firms, the neo-liberal state changed its position. A lesson was that any profession would be subject to commercial pressure as its economic importance grew. Privileged occupations were only autonomous on sufferance. Ironically, as medical benefits became part of labour costs in the era of fictitious decommodification, so the ground was prepared for the state to assert regulatory control in the era of 'deregulation'.

In the USA, since the early 1970s, professions have had their 'guild' power taken away by firms and the state. Much of their work has been redefined by regulatory agencies, notably the Federal Trade Commission, in favour of commercial practices, rescinding the exemption of professions from anti-trust rules (Kissam, 1983). Most revealingly, the Supreme Court weakened the medical profession through ruling on restraint of trade, and the Federal Trade Commission nullified rules on professional advertising in the late 1970s. Here was reregulation for commodification, not deregulation.

In the UK, the New Labour government privatized healthcare services by stealth, mainly by inducing NHS hospitals to contract out services to corporations. Tony Blair's adviser on the NHS and the architect of health reforms, Simon Stevens, left his Downing Street job in 2004 to become an executive in UnitedHealth, the USA's largest health insurer, which has 70 million Americans on its books and employs 400000 doctors in 4000 hospitals. UnitedHealth soon started general medical practices in the UK and in 2008 bid to take contracts from the primary care trusts that run NHS hospitals. By then, there were plans to enable US insurance companies to manage NHS patients' healthcare plans (Revill, 2007). Privatizing lucrative parts of a public service is a global trend, as is the technique of doing it in steps to allow multinationals to build a market without exciting too much political debate. In the case of healthcare plans and insurance, it is easy for private firms to raise the price for high-risk patients or deny them cover altogether, as vividly shown in Michael Moore's film, *Sicko*. Once privatized and liberalized, a service will be subject to market principles, and firms will be protected by international rules under the WTO's General Agreement on Trade in Services (GATS).

This drive to commercialize was rationalized as a way of introducing competition into the NHS, breaking the surgeons' hold on the number and pace of operations and lowering hospital waiting lists. But the move eroded occupational control, transferring it to administrators and external commercial interests.

Another tactic has been disruption to inter-occupational collaboration that had split up markets for their respective expertise. In the USA, the Supreme Court and the Federal Trade Commission have blocked this in the name of combating restraint of trade. The professions could no longer set the rules, and even lawyers came to sell their services in a buyer's market (Spangler, 1986). Occupations denied the right to define their spheres of expertise would argue that this reduces the return to prolonged investment, so raising the income needed to induce people to enter the occupation, and that blocking collaboration puts at risk the expertise of each occupation. A neo-liberal would dismiss such claims as specious.

As the state curbed occupational control, corporations began reorganizing professions to turn them into sources of profit. By the twenty-first century, most occupations were facing control by commercial interests. In some, the producers of goods and technology used in the services were gaining a bigger share of the income. Often buying one product puts practitioners in a position of dependency. Once an occupation is obliged to rely on externally chosen equipment and procedures its capacity to shape its market is gone.

In the UK and elsewhere, medical services are among occupations losing control over their work through dependency on equipment owned by corporations or the state. Public–private partnerships have enabled private firms to set the agenda and induce doctors to use costly products they sell to them and to focus on goods-intensive illnesses rather than on service-intensive or low-cost treatments. The use of expensive means of production and raw materials raises costs for consumers and lowers doctors' net income.

One way of influencing doctors is through commercial sponsoring of training courses, such as Continuing Medical Education (CME). By subsidizing these courses, companies can determine their content and the medicines and products recommended, and make it cheaper for doctors to attend them rather than independent CME. Not surprisingly, doctors have come to regard CME classes as 'infomercials'.

Another way of inducing professions to become more responsive to market forces and to commercialize activities is by funding or subsidizing research. Governments long provided financial help without forcing researchers to commercialize. But as the state became more market-oriented, it used the fact that occupational bodies, research institutions and research-oriented firms had come to depend on state funds to demand changes. Commercial companies (and their foundations) are also playing a more active role in research funding. Grant dependency has exerted incredible control over academics' behaviour, attitudes and mobility. Medical, engineering, science and other specialist schools have also succumbed to pressure.

While the state and corporations have sapped the capacity of occupations to dominate their markets, the financial sector has also contributed. It gained from the higher profits earned by corporate capital and its capacity to secure more of the income generated by professional work. Financial institutions have also weakened occupational self-control by insisting on changes as conditions for insurance or loans.

Intriguingly, banking itself has never been professionalized, which Abbott (1988, p. 147) attributed to high turnover of bank personnel and an unwillingness of capital to allow an autonomous group to govern flows of capital through 'scientific' knowledge of their own. Perhaps that interpretation is too functionalist. But clearly banking is an arm of the market, without a coherent sense of occupational community. In a period of marketization bankers' loyalty and pecuniary interest have been with the market builders, not the occupation preservers. There has been no professional association to preserve and impose an ethical code, to limit profiteering. Society pays for the absence of communities. Individual self-interest is not reined in by collective interest and the ethos that goes with it. A lesson of the financial debacle of 2008 was that there had been no professional ethic in the financial occupations. They were purely controlled by market instincts.

CONTROL OVER 'LABOUR POWER'

Throughout history, occupations have tried to control the supply of labour power by restricting the number able and allowed to practise their trade. Pro-market theorists presume the objective is to raise incomes by limiting supply. No doubt that has often been a reason. But it may not be the only one. It may be to retain the reputation of the occupation or to preserve control over the mysteries of a craft when misuse or excessive use could jeopardize its future.

Restricting numbers requires mechanisms and a will and capacity to use them. The usual methods have been an association, with rules for qualifications, coupled with control over routes to entry, mainly meaning training institutions, and control over means of exit. In controlling entry, occupations have wanted to control the curricula, the numbers offered training and the level of expertise required, which they can alter depending on supply conditions. In controlling exit, occupations have operated devices for suspending, expelling or downgrading practitioners, rules they can also alter depending on demand and supply.

In controlling entry and exit, the professions achieved their greatest success in the early twentieth century. Professional control in the USA reached its peak between 1930 and 1960 (Krause, 1996). It declined after the 1970s as the neo-liberal state launched a regulatory counter-attack. Indeed, perhaps the major aspect of recommodification has been loss of control by occupations over their numbers, the supply of people able to practise the occupation. Adam Smith's libertarian descendants were recreating their version of the 'right to practise'.

They were aided by the commodification of the educational system, which transferred powers from representatives of occupations to administrators and commercial interests. Direct interventions, subsidies and grants were used to leverage reforms. But the collapse of professional control over labour power came with a rush as globalization took off, opening the floodgates to an international supply of qualified practitioners in many occupations, from lawyers and doctors to plumbers and carpenters. The fight over licensing is considered in Chapter 7. But in most cases it meant both an influx of practitioners to countries where supply had been restricted and an outsourcing to where there were potential practitioners. It also meant an increased ability of corporations and consumers to turn to alternatives. Splits in occupations created a precariat resigned to supplying lower-level services while leaving specialist work to a smaller, higher-income group in the profession. The end result was loss of control over supply.

By chipping away at associational power, mainly by using anti-trust arguments to obtain legislative or regulatory reforms, the state has made practitioners less inclined to join or participate in their own profession's associations. This has led to a vicious circle of declining control.

Again, the medical profession is a good example. In the USA, it lost control over its numbers in the 1970s. From a peak of 73 per cent in 1963, by 1971 only 61 per cent of doctors belonged to the American Medical Association (AMA) and by 1990 the proportion was under 50 per cent. This reflected the AMA's lost ability to limit the number of doctors. The ratio of doctors to population doubled between 1970 and 1990. Government research grants to medical schools were used to demand that more students be admitted. The same happened in law, where the ratio of lawyers to population doubled between 1960 and 1984 (Abel, 1989, p. 109).

While the UK equivalent held out for longer, similar developments were taking place in Europe. In France, for generations the number of medical students was limited by a numerus clausus arrangement; this was repealed in 1968. In law, a lengthy education process and apprenticeship were ways by which the French Bar limited supply and blocked working-class students from entry. In engineering, an increased supply of graduates weakened the profession, although it had been weak anyhow as unionization had been blocked by the profession's class position.

In Germany, engineers lost control over supply in the 1980s following a huge expansion in the number attending technical universities, which were swamped beyond capacity (Kirk, 1989). Lawyers fared no better, losing bargaining strength in the 1970s and 1980s, when their numbers rapidly expanded. Whereas the number doubled between 1950 and 1975, it doubled again in the next ten years (Blankenberg and Schultz, 1988).

In the UK, class traditionally held down numbers in the professions. For instance, it was only after 1945 that lawyers formed a central Bar Council to control entry. For generations, access to the barrister community was determined simply by social class, with written statements on family position being a standard requirement, along with two references from serving barristers. Very low initial earnings were a way of blocking working-class access. Then there were barriers to obtaining work by young barristers, who were obliged to take jobs only from a barrister's clerk in chambers. Youthful radicalism was checked by the fear that critics would have promotion prospects blocked at the discretion of seniors. All this came unstuck as liberalization proceeded.

There are many other examples. One aspect of the struggle for control over labour power is that where there has been little occupational control, there has been little professionalization either. For instance, banking and the civil service have been controlled by the state or by dominant classes. The civil service should be considered as a distinctive occupational community. It indicates how one person may belong to two or more communities, one covering his or her professional life, another other functions. The US civil service has never been fully professionalized, because governments appoint temporary outsiders to most senior positions, stunting the bureaucracy. In the UK and France, the civil service has been class-driven, with a screening system long preserving class control. By contrast, although class has played a role in Germany and Italy, the civil service has been dominated by the legal profession, making legal training almost essential for senior positions.

All have operated a screening system that helped the upper class retain a high share of employment, and controlled the number and type of person able and allowed to practise. What happened in the globalization period is that the state turned on its civil service, making it less class-driven and splintering it into a privileged salariat, a more proletarianized group with limited opportunities for occupational careers, and a growing precariat with no labour security. The onslaught was taken to extremes in developing countries, many of which were subject to the World Bank's structural adjustment strategy, which demanded cuts in and 'deregulation' of civil services. The result, predictably, was inefficiency and corruption as underpaid civil servants struggled to survive.

In general, one is led back to the educational system. One unsung way by which professions have been commodified is state co-option of academics in their area of expertise to undermine their independence. For instance, in the USA, it was academics in medicine and law who opted to increase the supply of qualified people, eroding the incomes of professional practitioners (Krause, 1996, p. 54). Occupational solidarity was overridden by pecuniary considerations. The state succeeded by divide-and-rule tactics.

Increasing the number with credentials has been a way of reducing the power of occupations, by increasing supply and inducing re-divisions of labour within occupations that reduce the solidarity needed for effective bargaining. Professions had power in the era of labourism because their numbers were small. The expansion of 'education' in the 1960s and 1970s assisted capital in cheapening professional labour power, by loosening their associational power. Although the increased numbers played a big part, the erosion of occupational control was facilitated as much by the changing character of education. Many more labour force entrants had credentials that enabled them to practise at the lower end of occupations, and this encouraged the occupational splintering considered later.

There is one general point though. When the number of practitioners is controlled by the profession itself, both its elite and its lower ranks tend to gain, since the elite can dominate relations with the state and market, while the remainder have sufficient income and security to be inclined to accept the status quo. Once such control is lost, the structured solidarity is destroyed, while the bargaining strength of both the occupational elite and the mass is jeopardized.

Ultimately, globalization is driving the loss of control over labour power and limiting the occupational capacity to control entry to professions. Open occupations are a way of increasing global labour mobility, which is what capital wants and needs.

CONTROL OVER INCOME

A feature of being decommodified is being able to bargain and determine one's income. Control is greater when the practitioner can negotiate with the purchaser directly, or when the practitioner is working on own-account or as an independent contractor, or when an occupational association can set pay scales unilaterally or through collective bargaining. The last possibility was weak in the industrial citizenship era because collective bargaining was limited to employees bargaining with employers, and was denied to independent providers of services. When the state woke up to the fact, hitherto tolerated largely for class reasons, that professions were setting procedures that took income determination out of the market, governments began reforms that have transformed the situation.

The trend had begun earlier. For instance, French doctors lost control slowly between the 1950s and 1980s, going from a mainly fee-for-service system to one where about two-thirds of doctors were salaried. By then, many scarcely belonged to the salariat, being poorly paid and insecure, with minimal voice on social security boards dominated by employers, union bosses and state bureaucrats (Krause, 1996, p. 139). By the twenty-first century they probably belonged to the second tier of the salariat rather than the core proletariat; their status, education and professional identity put them in the salariat, their income and security put them below it.

In the UK, the Thatcher government changed the payment system for doctors and rolled back their autonomy, so that subsequent governments could make changes to the medical professions without consulting them or obtaining their consent. Similar developments occurred in other countries.

In some professions, external control has become more influential in determining occupational income. Most conspicuously, medicine has been increasingly dominated by the insurance industry and pharmaceutical corporations, eager to ensure that their products and processes are prescribed. In the USA, health insurance companies have imposed price controls that limit income. Tighter regulations have required doctors to take out insurance against malpractice claims, inducing them to take more costly precautions that cut their net income. And the state has begun to stipulate what tests doctors must do to avoid lawsuits.

Another way by which external interests have come to shape occupational incomes is conglomeration, an integral part of globalization, which has put occupational income schemes under strain. Law firms provide good examples. In 2000 Clifford Chance acquired a New York firm, making it the world's biggest law firm. Unhappiness on the US side arose because Clifford Chance operated an English 'lockstep' remuneration system by which profits are shared among partners according to a sliding scale based on seniority. This limits commercial pressure on individuals. In the US firm, pay was higher, since it operated what is known delightfully as an 'eat-what-you-kill' system, by which profits are shared according to the amount of business brought in by each partner. A sense of social solidarity (let alone probity) is hardly consistent with this mentality. Discontent led to a compromise whereby star lawyers in the US arm of the firm were paid above the top 'lockstep rate'. However, this meant they 'only' earned just below US$1 million a year, compared with over US$3 million paid to top 'rain-makers' in some US firms. Some partners left while UK-based lawyers resented the better pay deal at the US branch.

The lesson of these developments is that commercial criteria come to dominate occupational restraint, allowing more opportunistic self-interested practices in order to maximize individual income. The state, in dismantling and pursuing occupational commodification, was creating a nasty market. Those New York lawyers were not joking.

CONTROL OVER LABOUR: PROLETARIANIZATION

Traditionally, most crafts and professions were able to control the ways they worked, how much they worked and what they did when they worked. They lose that ability when outside bodies take charge. That can happen if a government steps in to stipulate how work is to be done, or if one segment of the occupation takes charge, or if another occupation invades or dominates it, or if its practitioners are absorbed into salaried employment. This is the essence of proletarianization.

Even in the era of fictitious decommodification, some occupations were being sucked into dependent employment, ceding control over work practices to administrative management and bureaucratic procedures. But in the globalization era the state has aided managements in making their control much more effective and complete.

In some countries, certain professions have been largely proletarianized for a long time. In Italy, engineers and architects were partly bureaucratized by the state in the 1700s. In both Italy and France, professional independence was sharply curtailed by the Napoleonic Code. The Italian case is intriguing. Its occupations have been shaped by a politicized environment, called *partitocrazia*, rule by parties. The state has regulated professions through *ordini*, bodies instigated by Napoleon. They spread to the legal profession in the 1870s and doctors in 1910. Mussolini dismantled them, creating a unified professional confederation, but when they were restored every doctor had to belong to a regional *ordine*, which defined the division of labour in healthcare. Meanwhile, thousands of private healthcare insurers had emerged, for unions, professions, farmers, craftsmen and civil servants. By 1980 they covered nearly all the population. But the restoration of the *ordini* also meant that by the 1960s, health professionals were in control of health services, which led to an escalation of medical costs and an increase in the average time patients spent in hospitals. This bankrupted private insurers and led to a political alliance that established the Italian National Health Service (SSN), with responsibility for capping costs through global budgeting. Although general practitioners formed an association in 1982, after they were allowed to form bargaining units, henceforth the medical profession was largely proletarianized. It could not control work or incomes.

The Italian case is typical of how the state took power away. If occupational control is the ability of practitioners to set their own goals, then by the 1970s most professionals were proletarianized. As one authoritative study concluded:

> Unlike their self-employed 'free' ancestors, modern salaried professionals . . . must ultimately serve their employers' goals and clients. Such loss of control was experienced by other workers in the earliest stages of capitalism. It now threatens the professional's soul, creating a type of worker whose integrity is threatened by the expropriation of his values or sense of purpose. It reduces the domain of freedom and creativity to problems of technique; it creates workers, no matter how skilled, who act as technicians or functionaries.
>
> (Derber et al., 1990, p. 136)

Proletarianization, almost definitionally, implies a weakening of Voice. Once a majority of an occupation is in stable wage or salaried employment, its capacity for collective expression of identity and collective action is debilitated, often by threats that promotion will be jeopardized by any show of independence or occupational pride. In this respect, the experience of engineers has been instructive.

Engineers have been treated differently in different countries, usually unable to act in their own interests. In most countries, they have been used to assist in the commodification of others, even though an elite of the profession has been privileged and affluent. Throughout the twentieth century, they were a 'profession without community' (Perucci and Gerstl, 1969). When some tried to start an association in the USA at the end of the nineteenth century, firms made clear that those joining it would automatically lose any prospect of promotion. The strategy worked.

In the UK, most engineers have come from working-class backgrounds, rare for a 'profession'. Most have not belonged to any collective body, and the main association has been mainly an employers' body. In France, engineers were in the upper-middle class, allied to management. While the state resisted their attempts to have a licensing system, employers were able to decide who could be called an engineer at the workplace, highlighting the profession's lack of control over work and job title.

In Italy, the loss of independence of engineers in salaried jobs went so far that they were openly used to control working-class employees. As one analyst put it, 'Engineering was used to expropriate the ability of the working class to organize itself, primarily through the manipulative techniques of "scientific management"' (Sapelli, 1981, p. 694).

In the UK, France and the USA, engineers have long been 'trusted employees' (Whalley, 1985). Like many in the salariat, they have lacked a professional tradition, a class-for-itself identity, and usually have been loyal to their enterprises, showing low inter-enterprise mobility. But loss of occupational control is demonstrated by managerial tactics. In France and the USA after 1945, it became normal for employers to screen potential employee engineers through psychological testing for loyalty, dependability and conformity, which became a hallmark of industrial management.

In Germany, engineering was split on the basis of training, with the mass being secondary school graduates integrated into firms. After 1945, the state and corporations made sure engineers did not develop a strong union or professional association. This was not decommodification but two-tier labour control. A related feature was the larger role played by engineers in management and on boards of directors. There was no occupational solidarity; the mass was left to fend for itself.

Engineers may have been particularly prone to loss of independent identity and thus loss of control over their work. But many other occupations have lost that as they have been put into stable wage labour. It has been an occupational Faustian bargain – labour security in return for loss of future identity. Yet once identity and the means of asserting it are lost, the labour security can be taken away as well.

Globalization has intensified proletarianization. Not only have more people in various occupations been in subordinated labour but they have been increasingly concentrated in multinationals that can sweep away occupational traditions with disdain. Control passes from the occupation to the corporation.

Globalization leads to conglomeration of services because multinationals need global services. This is epitomized by the legal profession, in which a global elite of law firms serves the world's economic elite. As of 2008, Clifford Chance had about 3000 lawyers, 2000 working abroad, and was globalizing by hiring foreign lawyers who knew the system and needs of companies from their countries. Linklaters, another London-based firm, was doing the same, hiring a group of Japanese lawyers. Soon, a majority of lawyers will be salaried employees of a few large law firms; others will be in supermarkets, as we shall see.

With proletarianization accelerating, mechanisms to deprive occupations of control over their labour time were stepped up. Some professions held out for longer than others. Having written a book 16 years earlier documenting the dominance of professionals in the workplace, one reviewer of their position in the USA in 1986 concluded that, although partly proletarianized by being salaried, they remained dominant (Freidson, 1970, 1986). If so, pressures were building up. Already in the late 1970s, analysts were noting how professionals were being subject to control by non-professionals, with a trend towards speed-up (Larson, 1980). Administrative control even occurred in US law firms, with more lawyers being in salaried employment inside corporations.

Proletarianization has turned the notion of professionalism against professionals. Since the 1970s the aura of autonomy that had preserved a sense of ethics has been undermined. The early criticisms were that professionalism was a disguise for ideology, allowing market closure and monopolistic control of spheres of work (Johnson, 1972; Larson, 1977; Larkin, 1983). Some pleaded that the professions' practices were in the public interest (Saks, 1995). And one could claim that many imbued with a spirit of professionalism were relatively inclined to 'self-exploit' and risk burnout from a stressful sense of professional responsibility. But the main change was that appeals to salaried employees to show professionalism could be depicted as a disciplinary device (Fournier, 1999).

'Human resource management' gave discipline a boost. Whereas professions had exercised 'professionalism from within' (controlling their practices and market relations), in the globalization era 'professionalism from above' took over, that is, domination by market forces and capital (McClelland, 1990; Evetts, 2003). Professionalism contains the seeds of both discretionary control over labour by practitioners themselves and organizational control by users of their labour. In a market society, the latter gains ground. Professionalism can be used to inculcate traits desired by administrative management.

What Evetts (2005), following Abbott (1988), called 'organizational professionalism' amounts to proletarianization. This has crystallized, with more being subject to standardized procedures, supervision, surveillance, externally imposed accountability, administrative management rather than self-management by the occupation, target setting, performance review and auditing, all designed to control performance and reduce discretion by the professional group. The ethical space disappears too, making opportunistic behaviour more likely.

The medical profession has lost self-regulatory power more than most, partly reflecting its former lofty position. In the UK, loss of independence was shown by a new obligation on its practitioners to submit to periodic reappraisals and revalidation, and loss of the right to decide whether doctors' alleged misconduct makes them unfit to practise. In both aspects, the government decreed changes, in what observers called the biggest shake-up of medical regulation for a century. According to a White Paper issued by the Department of Health in 2007, the General Medical Council (GMC) would be allowed to continue to set standards and investigate allegations of serious misconduct by its member doctors. But the right to adjudicate on allegations would pass to a new independent body, with legal and lay members as well as medical representatives.

The government also envisaged a smaller GMC with equal numbers of non-medical and medical members, appointed by an Appointments Commission, ostensibly 'to dispel the perception that councils are overly sympathetic to the professionals they regulate'. More contentiously, the White Paper weakened the occupation by making fitness-to-practise cases subject not to the criminal standard of proof beyond reasonable doubt but to a lower civil standard of 'balance of probability'. Thus, the external adjudicators could disbar doctors they *thought* were unfit. One might say this is justifiable given the nature of the work, but it represents loss of power by the profession. The White Paper softened the blow by introducing a classic bureaucratic device, a sliding scale, with tougher standards of proof required in serious cases where a doctor's livelihood is threatened. But once the principle is accepted, that too could be moderated quite easily.

Here was the state imposing lower standards of justice on an occupation than would be applied in society. The practitioners' civil rights were threatened. As the 'medico-legal adviser' to the Medical Defence Union commented: 'When a doctor's whole career and livelihood is at stake, the allegations should be tested against the highest standard of proof'. The Chairman of the British Medical Association pointed out that, by exposing doctors to the risk of allegations being accepted without proof, the reforms 'could lead to a climate of defensive medicine in which doctors are forever looking over their shoulders instead of concentrating on working in the best interest of their patients'. Allowing for self-interest, the point about defensiveness is surely valid.

A feature of every occupation is a tendency for its special knowledge to become 'common knowledge', packaged or standardized in some way. Elliott and Atkinson (2008), arguing that the British middle class was suffering, railed against loss of professional status, exemplified by a new competitor confronting lawyers in the form of 'Tesco law'. This followed the announcement by the Tesco supermarket chain that it would launch a low-cost computerized property-conveyancing service in its stores. The government went further by liberalizing legal advisory services, to be completed by 2011, which may henceforth be dispensed from booths in supermarkets.

The process is similar to the City of London's 'Big Bang', which converted stockbrokers from professional 'partners' to employees of investment banks. In the case of the legal profession, its historical community was to be shattered to create a more efficient commodity, 'legal services', supplied by para-legal employees. On offer was the promise of a lower-cost, lower-priced, transparent service. But new inequalities will emerge. More lawyers and solicitors will be submerged in the salariat, denied the prospect of becoming partners with a share of the income of a professional partnership. The majority will be reduced to offering a standardized, commodified service. It is no stretch of imagination to see a future in which the citizen as consumer of such services will be expected to undertake much stressful unpaid work, filling in electronic forms and going through questionnaires to identify their problem and the package of knowledge and type of service required, along with an estimate of the time for each task and an estimate of the cost of the selected menu. Where will the data go? Suppose one makes a mistake? Such questions will be daunting. The citizen may be the loser, even if it seems cheaper.

Commercialization is depersonalizing what was a personal advisory relationship, based on a sense of trust, confidentiality and a little bit of civic friendship that may have long-lasting social benefits. What is being erected is a commodity relationship, creating a new type of dependency, since it will be in the commercial interest of the law market to generate new and repeat demand for products it wants to sell. Where personal deliberation once prevailed, citizens as consumers will be encouraged to purchase a legal product to remedy or avoid a problem. Turning to the 'legal industry' will be a consumerist response to perceived risk and uncertainty. It will be part of the trend to contractualization.

To the extent that it remains a community, the profession will become more fragmented, with many steered into a salariat expected to provide standardized products, while an elite and a few proficians will earn higher incomes and deal with high-status clients and types of case. This tendency, always there, will become much greater. And as inequality within the legal profession grows, the money wage will rise as a share of lawyers' social income, a characteristic of labour commodification.

The deconstruction of a crusty old profession, while accelerating legalization of social and economic life, will erode the legal community itself. To the extent that the profession has been a source of monopoly rent and privilege, one could say this will be socially beneficial. But the positive aspects of a professional community should not be overlooked, including the internal pressure to foster ethical codes based on personal and collective integrity, respect for ethical and technical standards, and the transmission of traditions of learning and peer respect. With commercialization there may be a disregard for reputational risk, encouraging the opportunistic sale of legal products. As with commercialized insurance schemes, high-risk cases will be identified, using statistical discrimination screening devices, and be excluded from coverage or charged higher fees. The need for regulation by an external body will grow. But a danger is that such regulation will be driven by market principles and the 'consumer interest', to the neglect of the interest of the profession. In the process, the art of law could be sacrificed.

Relationships *between* legal practitioners are becoming more competitive and so more likely to induce opportunism. Knowledge, contacts and networks will become sources of commercial advantage to be guarded, whereas a community based, however imperfectly, on principles of civic friendship favours knowledge sharing and respect for principles that safeguard the traditions and status of the profession. If the system is mainly about making more money than others offering a similar commodity, those who advance are likely to be those who eschew such ethical proprieties. There is a more pointed way of putting this. Within an occupational community it is unedifying to 'eat-what-you-kill'. It is unbecoming to be greedy. The respect of one's peers is not acquired that way.

Meanwhile, occupational control over the workplace has been chipped away, with few exceptions. Krause (1996, p. 138) concluded that French doctors still had retained control in the early 1980s. But medical audit procedures have spread as much there as elsewhere. In US medicine, control has been transferred to administrators as a result of rationalization. Most medical students can expect to start and remain on salary. As one study concluded, 'Displaced by administrators, doctors have slipped down to the position of middle management where their prerogatives are also challenged or encroached upon by other health workers' (McKinlay and Stoekle, 1988). They have been pushed into the salariat, with a minority joining the profician class. Doctors have lost autonomy and control.

Some professions, such as engineers, have never had much control over their workplaces. But even they have lost much of what they did have. In the 1980s, computer-assisted design and computer-assisted manufacturing processes resulted in labour intensification and technological control, which also reduced scope for collaboration.

For reasons spelt out in Chapter 5, the education system, including academia, has been proletarianized, having its Voice taken away and being subject to administrative controls. The decline has been abject, notably in the USA. In 1915, the American Association of University Professors (AAUP) was established by elite university professors, alongside pre-existing single discipline associations such as the American Economic Association and the American Sociological Association. Salaried employees used their academic Voice to secure tenure and oversee probationary procedures. But tenure was bought at the price of adhering to freedom-constraining rules. Employment security, the bane of labourism, always has a price. They were soon obliged to accede to administrators' decisions on tenure, had only advisory roles in university administration and accepted they could be dismissed for embarrassing the university through controversial public speeches, political bias and moral turpitude (Krause, 1996, p. 70). Even the AAUP has always had only minority membership, and has given in regularly to political pressure, as in the McCarthy period.

In the 1970s, as the supply of academics increased, US universities reduced tenure-track positions, encouraged by their growing dependency on external funding (Bowen and Schuster, 1986). A precariat emerged on campuses, alongside a barely more secure academic proletariat, with neither Voice nor security. Members of this group move from university to university for years, like nomads, hoping to find a home. Meanwhile, teaching loads have grown and expectations on publications have risen. Academics have further lost control over working conditions as financial stringency has cut maintenance, travel and secretaries. They have been losing control over the type of research they can do, through a shift from academically controlled research funds to direct funding from corporations and foundations. Companies often stipulate that research findings must be kept confidential, a denial of the original function of an academic community. Those who reject this route are deprived of resources and forced into competing with a mass of job applicants, all fearful of being marginalized. Departments that receive corporate funding grow more powerful inside the university, exerting a politically conservative influence. This facilitates the process by which administrators justify expanding departments that bring in the resources.

Revealingly, labour law has been used to block faculty association in private universities. In 1980, the Supreme Court upheld a decision of the National Labor Relations Board that private university faculty did not have the right to unionize because they were part of management. This applied even though they were marginalized inside the administrative system of private universities. Labour law was supposed to protect workers, including their freedom to associate and to bargain, and yet in the twilight of the labourist period it was being used against a body of workers in an occupation.

In the UK, academic proletarianization has also been extensive. For generations, higher education stood against the market, extolling an ethos of cultural learning, with a pedagogical ideal of personalized relationships based on tutorials and a shared communal life in a college environment, with separate roles for teachers and examiners. Democratic self-government prevailed, with administrative staff being supportive. The Robbins plan of the early 1960s envisaged an expansion of that model to the 'redbrick' universities, with a ratio of one faculty member to eight students, a short schooling year to allow time for research, a short probation of three years before tenure, and a set of research councils to fund individual researchers. Although the process led to more external governance, this was the nearest it could go to decommodification.

Since then, independence has withered. British academia has gone from being a profession to 'a harassed mass' (Krause, 1996, p. 116). It has been professionalized, then unionized and then atomized, the dismantling of tenure confirming proletarianization. Donnish dominion has gone (Halsey, 1992). For generations, much of the teaching of undergraduates was done by graduates. Now senior academics are expected to do much of that.

Margaret Thatcher wanted to weaken the academic system's independence, and set about it with customary gusto. In the late 1980s the government abolished tenure at state-funded universities for those who had not already achieved it. Universities developed a more hierarchical structure and operational budgets were cut, making them more dependent on commercial funds. Finance for Oxford and Cambridge was reduced and government funds were shifted to polytechnics and universities geared to the needs of industry. The later shift to a culture of performance targeting was merely the next step in the process of commodification.

Commercialization of academia was slower in other EU countries, but it came. In West Germany, the professoriate lost control of universities in the 1960s and after 1968 there was democratization of university administration. Perversely, this boosted state control. University democracy fell into confusion while the state retained control over financial matters, which it used to allow entry of international commercial interests in the 1990s. It then introduced quantitative teaching obligations, downgrading research (Mommsen, 1987). While older universities had pursued knowledge for its own sake the modern university is driven by commerce. Academic involvement in shaping German society has shrunk. Careerism has taken over.

What has happened to academic professions is similar to what has been happening to civil services. The salariat has tried to shield itself from commercial pressure by abandoning lower ranks to casualization, allowing more to join the precariat. This has left a smaller and divided labour force without a coherent sense of solidarity to defend the ethics of their community. Civil services have thus lost control of their work.

In most occupations, dismantling has gone with the changing character of the workplace, and a shift in the direction of 'project' and 'team' labour organization. Companies increasingly want short-duration arrangements and 'supply chains' rather than integrated employment (Kunda et al., 2002). As this happens, occupations will be broken into groups with provisional identities and made more reliant on labour market intermediaries (Houseman et al., 2003), who will shift people from job to job, affecting both proficians and the precariat. Flexibilization disrupts occupational careers.

The 'choice' agenda is another way by which occupations have lost control over their work. The leading examples are schooling and medicine. Until 1974, a feature of medical dualism in the UK was the independence of teaching hospitals, dominated by consultants. This was ended when they were integrated into the administrative NHS structure. Later, Thatcher weakened the NHS by encouraging private and for-profit medicine, notably through private insurance, reducing occupational control. The NHS found itself unable to afford new technology that the private sector was obtaining. Citizens were encouraged to go private, while salaried professionals were losing control of their working practices.

In effect, Thatcher put doctors on their way to being expert employees on the model of engineers, pushing them into the salariat and subjecting them to administrative control. The payment system was reformed to make wages a function of actual services provided, while the NHS was reformed to allow greater administrative regulation of diagnosis and treatment. The rhetoric of choice was used to whittle away at professional control.

In 2005 the government extended 'choice' for patients of up to four hospitals. The President of the Royal College of Surgeons said the arrangements would destroy professionalism in the NHS, which was being undermined by a target-led culture and a choice agenda. Delegation of decision-making to patients meant that general practitioners (GPs) could not send patients to the consultants they thought most able to help them. The profession was losing control of an aspect of its work. The change also weakened GPs' sense of moral responsibility, and the link between them and consultant specialists. The choice agenda went further in 2006, when patients were allowed to choose between NHS and private hospitals, extending a 'choose-and-book' computerized approach introduced in 2004.

Choice in legal services has also grown, starting in 1990 when the government rearranged the boundaries between state and professional control of practice (Johnson, 1990). Barriers between barristers and solicitors were lowered, and barristers were obliged to give up practices deemed restrictive, including curbs on advertising and limits on opening new chambers. Then, in 1992, UK lawyers came under European Community market rules, the start of growing international control. The New Labour government continued in the vein of opening up the profession and removing its control over the way it arranged its work. The 'Tesco law' was the culmination. Proletarianization is a lever for commodification, and what has happened in law, medicine and education will be replicated in many other occupations.

CONTROL OVER TIME

A defining feature of being proletarianized is loss of control of time. A modern way is through computers that provide ways of disseminating information at a dizzying speed and with a lack of predictability that means occupational members do not know whether clients know what they know.

In terms of working time, the professions have been under direct attack. Again the most conspicuous case is law. The prime symbol of its proletarianization is 'the billable hour'. Since maximizing revenue is a law of the market, US legal firms have devised a mechanism to achieve that by monitoring labour with Tayloristic precision. The idea is simple. Both 'partners' and 'associates' – as lawyers in law firms are still called – are required to bill (charge) clients for the hours they put into their service and to maximize the number of hours they bill. Lawyers are expected to attain a high number of billable hours; incentives and sanctions are used to ensure they do. Predictably, this leads to pressure to spend less time on the reflective and reproductive aspects of lawyering, including the study of jurisprudence as it develops.

It also leads lawyers to claim as many billable hours as they can. What would once have been a working discussion becomes a frenzied consultation, with the client watching the ticking clock. Informal consideration is pushed aside in the interest of efficiency. And there is an in-built bias in favour of those who can pay more, and against taking cases where non-billable work could be anticipated. For the lawyer there is a corrosion of character, a dimming of the imagination that could fire the zeal to take complex cases that require diligence, reflection and scholarly risk-taking.

US lawyers used to charge for specific services, with the expectation that bonuses would be added by satisfied clients. Minimum fees were established in the 1930s, and the Bar took disciplinary action against lawyers for undercharging, the ethical code stipulating that they should not 'undervalue' their services. The increasing complexity and unpredictability of legal work led to disillusion with set fees, and in 1975 the Supreme Court killed them, declaring that they were 'a classic illustration of price fixing' that violated anti-trust laws.

Since the 1970s the profession has been proletarianized by means of the clock, just as industrial labourers were in the nineteenth century. There was even a national campaign by the American Bar Association to 'preach the gospel that the lawyer who keeps time records makes more money'. The billable hour is coupled with profit targets and monthly financial reports. Corporatization of law has made billable hours an easy way of imposing labour discipline, especially when these can be compared with the 'realization rate', the fees gained for the hours worked. It has been estimated that for each billable hour the lawyer must do an extra half an hour, in meetings, reading e-mails, and so on. Often, lawyers must bill at least a certain number of hours annually, with targets enforced through incentives or penalties. They must work 12-hour days to achieve the eight hours of target billable hours. The loss of control over time is remarkable, with billable hours being broken into six-minute elements. This has led to the marginalization of informal services that the profession traditionally provided, such as general advice to clients. The labour of lawyering pushes out the service of justice. Efficiency and profits are what matter. As the President of the American Bar Association lamented, 'The billable hour is fundamentally about quantity over quality, repetition over creativity' (Hirshon, 2002).

The time-control scheme invites and rewards sharp practice, since the client is rarely able to determine how much time is put into the work and the output cannot be easily related to the time. Even if a lawyer is scrupulously honest about the time devoted to a case, the client will still feel suspicious. It turns a service into a tense transaction. As the size of the potential market and the size of law firm grow, so will the scope for opportunistic behaviour.

The imposition of the industrial model on a professional service has costs. These include loss of collegiality, less free or subsidized work for low-income clients (another source of inequality) and less work for social causes. Non-billable time is squeezed between going on courses, spending time with family, participating in the governance of the profession and serving on committees dealing with pro bono cases. Cheating on billable hours drifts from exaggeration to fraud. Many well-known lawyers and law firms have been caught and disbarred or forced to resign. Commercial practices lead to fraudulent practices. It was ever so. One US law professor, who resigned from practising because of the pressure, tells his law students they are entering a profession that is 'one of the most unhappy and unhealthy on the face of the earth – and, in the view of many, one of the most unethical' (cited in Kuckes, 2007).

Medical professions have also lost control of time. Their proletarianization is linked to pressure to be answerable to market forces. In the UK, the government pushed for extended hours for GPs' surgeries, raising fears among medical experts that this was a step towards establishment of 'polyclinics' run by commercial companies, notably the US firm UnitedHealth. In the process, doctors would lose even more control over their time, with detrimental consequences for care and expertise.

In general, professions have a pace that derives from their culture, usually for reasons connected with the reproductive needs of the occupation and practitioners. Commercial capital has taken control of some occupations in such a way that the practitioners have become degraded, losing all control over their work. An example comes from the labourist state of Sweden. In 1994 the government allowed private schools to take children at the state's expense, a generous form of privatization. By 2008 over 10 per cent of children were in private schools. Much of the growth has been in one chain, *Kunskapsskolan* ('Knowledge Schools'), which profitably operates 30 schools with 10 000 pupils. Characteristic of the market service economy, the chain makes the pupils do much of the work around the learning; they are required to use Knowledge Portal, a website containing the syllabus, and to study mainly on their own, spending just 15 minutes a week with a tutor. Each subject is divided into 35 steps, and pupils must reach step 25 to pass, with step 30 earning a merit, 35 a distinction. Facilities are sparse, with outsourcing of specialist subjects. Teachers are expected to update the website during school holidays and have seven weeks off annually, about the same as office workers. The schools use electronic performance monitoring to track the efficiency of teachers, offering bonuses for the most successful. The company boss told *The Economist* (2008), 'We don't want teachers preparing lessons during term time. Instead, we steal that preparation time, and use it so they can spend more time with students'. Even more revealingly, he added, 'We do not mind being compared to McDonald's. If we're religious about anything, it's standardization. We tell our teachers it is more important to do things the same way than to do them well'. Once the system was refined, the firm set out to export its do-it-yourself schooling. In 2008, it was named preferred bidder to operate two London 'academies', state-funded schools largely run by private bodies.

Finally, proletarianization and loss of control over work have been associated with a rise in the share of women in occupations. Thus, as salaried employment of US legal services grew in the 1970s, women's share of the profession grew. The same happened in France in the 1970s and 1980s, and, from a very low level, in West Germany in the 1980s. Some see this as evidence of marginalization of the profession in a sexist society. It is about the occupation's de-professionalization.

Internal degradation of an occupation has also been associated with ethnic and migrant-status differentiation. A strategy of labour flexibility may accentuate gender and ethnic segregation, since opening up internal labour markets may lead to a flooding of the lower end of an occupation's structure and cause a reaction by insiders higher up the hierarchy to create sub-occupational boundaries. The ultimate loss of control by an occupation is reflected in the ability of outsiders to divide labour along lines they choose. At this point, proletarianization is almost complete.

CONTROL OVER KNOWLEDGE

Having control over knowledge is crucial to any occupation. To feel one knows what is needed and to learn in ways that have predictable outcomes are essential aspects of freedom. This is more than is conveyed in conventional notions of 'freedom of choice of occupation'. Controlling knowledge is a lifetime matter, lasting long after an occupation has been chosen.

Once its knowledge can be packaged or simplified, an occupation becomes vulnerable to being split into less defendable fragments. The educational and training system, for instance, is being restructured to make this happen. An example is the largest global university, the 'for-profit' University of Phoenix, where administrators have taken control of the curriculum and package courses as they see fit.

Occupational control over knowledge is eroded by lack of associational solidarity, proletarianization and the commodification of knowledge. The state has weakened associational strength; labour unions have scarcely helped. With proletarianization, corporate and bureaucratic managements have the means of deciding on divisions of labour and forms of training. Globalization has given corporations stronger bargaining power over occupations trying to retain control of their knowledge and the mysteries of their craft or profession. Technological change has made it easier to commodify knowledge.

The crucial change is when knowledge can be standardized. This removes professional expertise, leaving it vulnerable to attack in other respects. It leaves practitioners prone to absorption into a bureaucratic labour process in which they are sent for modular job training, refresher courses or other administratively guided training. Many occupations have lost control over their knowledge in this way. As Abbott (1988, p. 149) concluded, 'Commodification steadily absorbs expertise, and thereby work, from professions'. It results in deskilling.

Technological and organizational change may accelerate commodification of knowledge, particularly when it can be packaged in do-it-yourself manuals or in products, or can be delegated to sub-professionals, or incorporated into 'forms'. Commodification can come at the diagnostic and treatment stages. Computer software has made this almost the norm.

The packaging tends to commodify professions by removing an occupational niche and their command over abstract knowledge. It also strengthens proletarianization, since practitioners are more easily absorbed into a bureaucracy where administrative job structures can de-professionalize them. Many persist in using an occupational title long after they have ceased to perform the tasks of their occupation or even remember how to do so. Obsolescence comes from lack of practice of the occupation.

Commodified knowledge can also allow corporations to use flexible labour drawn from the precariat, brought in as and when needed. Through loss of control of knowledge, dominating occupations soon become subordinate ones. Once knowledge is incorporated into products that can be bought by clients or para-professionals, the occupation is in trouble.

A related feature is loss of control over occupational education. Bureaucracies and the state opt for job training, rather than vocational education, and take administrative control of skill formation. This breaks the association of work with an occupational community, with its culture, identity, ethics, standards and career norms. Members of the occupation lose touch with the expertise and linkages that define their occupation, a feature of proletarianization.

Where occupational knowledge is retained and distilled within a community, passed from one cohort to another through teaching and practice, those who rule it can set its standards, procedures and culture. But once the core knowledge is packaged, control passes from the profession to outside administrators.

The way knowledge is passed on leads back to the idea of an occupational career. There are various ways by which this is being disrupted. For instance, trade liberalization has indirectly undermined occupations. Trade in tasks means fragmenting production, which makes it harder for workers to build conventional careers. Outsourcing makes it hard to predict where jobs will be located and whether there will be an opportunity to take them.

More rapid technological change also threatens occupational control by making the duration of a career exceed the duration of specialist knowledge. To retain the notion of career, the heart of an occupation, some professions have opted for continuing education. But this is fraught with problems, as we have seen.

To some extent, occupational knowledge reflects the mystery of a craft and the social memory of an occupation, with bits gleaned from the wisdom of generations. Loss of social memory goes with proletarianization. An occupation has its heroes, folk who provide ethical anchors, models for emulation and even dynastic control. Once the heroes are put aside, risk of commodification is intensified. Take economics. Once, to be an economist was to be a political economist. Looking back to the founders of the profession – Smith, Ricardo, Marx, Marshall, Keynes, Joan Robinson and others – they were reflective thinkers with few 'outputs'. Those they did produce were meant to count. Compare them with modern economists, whose formulaic outputs tumble from word processors (and those of their research assistants), with dazzling mathematical games aimed at securing rapid publication in journals run by like-minded colleagues, each output generating a predictable increase in lifetime income, but little else. Meanwhile, stratification advances. The profession institutionalizes hierarchy and exploitation based on the proletarianization of subsidiary workers, designated as research or teaching assistants.

Nowadays, bureaucratization is the fate of most who qualify as economists. And specialization means that few have command of economics as perceived by the dominant group. A microeconomist is likely to look foolish if he indulges in a debate with a specialist on macroeconomics, and vice versa. Specialisms multiply, so that titles become hyphenated – monetary economist, labour economist, trade economist, and so on. Then, sub-titles become sub-sub-titles. The reason looks obvious: one cannot be a world expert in a broad area because knowledge is expanding so fast. It is not that simple. One reason is that subdivisions are rarely self-chosen. In some cases, people may not realize they have become or want to become a particular type of specialist. The market will often play a role, as will the hierarchy. The mass of any profession lose control over their sphere of knowledge, becoming amateurs and relegated to a niche of partial understanding.

Control of knowledge relates to the famous ideas of Thomas Kuhn ([1970] 1996) on the existence of intellectual paradigms. A dominant paradigm will determine what outputs are accepted as legitimate. As a profession loses autonomy and internal structure, it loses its paradigm-setting capacity. Intellectual property generated within an occupation can be expropriated by other occupations, or by an elite that breaks away as a new profession and downgrades, or consigns to irrelevance, segments of the old occupation. For example, a modern economist is likely to dismiss development economics as non-scientific, not legitimate. And loss of control of knowledge by a united community will invite invasion. To continue with the example, economics was briefly dominated by engineering, with several engineers switching to leadership roles in economics. Now it is being invaded by psychology and neuroscience.

The colonization of occupations may not result in a change of nomenclature, so that an economist may have the same title as someone a generation older, except that they may barely be able to talk the same language or share conceptual interpretations. This technological progress may be common. However, a danger is that older generations are pushed out as role models or as preservers of customs, etiquette, solidarity and reflection. This is not to argue against change, but that in a period of occupational splintering, alternative methods to preserve valuable aspects of occupational communities are needed.

The threats to occupational knowledge generate forms of occupational risk that are almost uninsurable. Knowledge may be made obsolescent by technical change, by radical advances in knowledge or by workplace changes in which practitioners are steered in directions that erode their occupational skills. It is easy for neo-liberals to cite meritocracy, but if the reality is uninsurable risk and uncertainty, individuals cannot control their situation. At the extreme, choosing an occupation may be a bad choice.

CONTROL OVER OTHERS' LABOUR POWER

Since occupations are not independent, technologically determined and fixed entities, there is wide scope for the state and capitalism to cooperate with professions or crafts in dominating others or to intervene to disrupt them. Three types of situation have occurred – oppression, suppression and splintering.

Occupational Oppression

In any occupational regime, some groups have been permitted to have control over others. A feature of being decommodified in a market economy is not being controlled by competing occupations. However, oppression of one group by another has been common and tolerated if not openly promoted. It arises when one occupation asserts primacy, usually based on a notion of higher skills or control over resources or reputation, such that it obliges another occupation to perform tasks only on approved terms. Typically, the dominant profession restricts the work of another so as to improve its income, while claiming it does so to improve the quality of the service. Studies of clinical laboratories have shown this can be misleading (Healey, 1973).

Oppression of a group within an occupation can lead to differences in public exposure and loss of status and career potential. Internal differentiation may generate front-line professionals, with those dealing with clients often the lowest-status groups inside an occupation; their time and skills are less specialized. Stratification allows the publicly typical to become the intra-professionally atypical. Some tasks are ghettoized, while elites enmesh themselves in a referral network, as in medicine and law. In general, oppression grows as specialization grows.

Some professions oppress others through their governance arrangements. But these weaken as the market invades the occupation. Once, US doctors had extensive power over other occupations, but this crumbled when the AMA lost its places on licensing and accrediting boards of other healthcare professions. Similarly, psychiatry no longer controls a pyramid of mental health occupations, which can now collect payments from the Blue Cross/Blue Shield health insurance network. In these cases, oppression has declined, which is mostly beneficial, except for the fact that an occupational structure creates a barrier to the commodification of all parts of an occupational community. By itself, this may not matter. But it adds to a broader picture.

In the modern market society, occupations can be oppressed through private insurance practices. Insurance increases the demand for services for which there is insurance, as Arrow (1963) showed in a classic article. This raises the price of the service and the premium for insurance, which hit groups who do not have the right to practise under insurance policy rules.

Again the medical occupations have led the way. Generally speaking, health insurers do not reimburse if the service is not performed by those mandated to do it. In the case of Medicaid in some US states, reimbursement is made at a much lower rate if the service is carried out by a certified nurse rather than a doctor (Jackson et al., 2003). By this means, the superior occupation reduces the income of the subordinated one, thereby increasing one form of inequality.

Oppression may be muted. An old arrangement was inter-occupational collaboration, with informal reciprocal arrangements that limited opportunism and poaching of territory or clients. Now, professions are set against each other, depicted as competing for fixed resources. As Krause (1996, p. 48) observed in the USA, 'What remains of medical group solidarity is evaporating as the state acts to set one group of doctors against the other, and as each group lobbies to get a larger share of federal funds at the expense of the others'.

Oppression can come from unexpected directions. Part of commodification is the setting of performance targets in public services. The UK has gone down this road, erecting a regime of league tables, inspection and auditing in evermore wondrous ways. In 2008, the government launched a 'compassion index', put on an official website, to show which hospitals were being kindest to their patients. Such actions remove a feature of being a professional, the discretion to use independent judgment. Once bureaucratization of performance is established, the next step is for professions subject to auditing to be split into an administrative-managerial group and a performance-monitored group, whose functions are turned over to subordinated workers, given narrower training and jobs. This has applied to support workers in hospitals, classroom assistants in schools and community support officers in the police, all of whom are subject to administrative control. Many are pushed into the precariat. One law of unintended consequences is that targets generate a need for more targets, as each one leaves loopholes. And targets lead to surveillance, whether by webcam or some other device, to check compliance.

Oppression has been most common in medical services, most notably in the USA, where medicine has long suffered from the antics of the AMA, the doctors' own body. In the 1930s, the AMA opposed Roosevelt's plans for a universal health insurance system, pushing instead for a voluntary health insurance scheme, consistent with fee-for-service practices and under the control of doctors. It ignored the needs of low-income groups. The unions also opposed a national system, showing how labourist unions opposed universalism. So, Roosevelt gave up on national health insurance. The AMA also long opposed expansion of medical schooling, and tried to create a pyramid of occupations within its domain, helping subsidiary occupations – nurses, X-ray technologists, physical therapists, occupational therapists – obtain state licensing laws with the proviso that they should submit to supervision by licensed physicians. At that time, hospitals were run mainly by privately practising physicians, not administrators, who were hired by the doctors.

Speciality medicine grew, contributing to intra-occupational inequality. By 1970, three-quarters of doctors called themselves specialists. Then, rising healthcare costs led industrial corporations to side with the state to control costs, with support from salaried doctors in schools of medicine and public health. This alliance, dubbed 'corporate rationalizers' (Alford, 1975), was a reaction to the profession's monopolistic control. Expensive healthcare had pushed up non-wage costs and taxes, while the fee-for-service system was a spur to medical providers to supply more healthcare than was justified. So, excessive control brought the occupation loss of control.

In supporting one element of an occupation, the usual practice has been to oppress the remainder by subjecting them to commodifying pressures. In the Great Transformation, the tendency was to proletarianize large parts of professions – those requiring technical training and at least secondary schooling. There are many examples. Le Bianic (2003) showed how in France between 1945 and 1960 the state took the lead in employing psychologists and subjecting them to bureaucratic procedures. There and elsewhere, professionals found their intellectual labour being commodified while they helped the state fashion social behaviour (Johnson, 1982; Larkin, 1983). But in the globalization period the oppression went further. Many who were proletarianized found their labour securities taken away as they were pushed into the precariat, unsure of whether they would remain in the occupation at all.

The lesson of the history of occupational oppression is that it has been an unappreciated form of societal inequality but one that can become self-destructive. Oppression points to a need for what we will later call collaborative bargaining.

Occupational Suppression

Historically, dominant professions or interests have also suppressed other occupations, preventing those skilled in its tasks from practising altogether. This could be by denying a group with a claim to a skill the right to practise, or by making it impossible for them to do so profitably. This has been the case with alternative medicine, and was long the case with midwifery in the USA, where emerging professions, such as chiropractors and osteopaths, were also suppressed. Mostly, it is a matter of the state agreeing with a dominant profession that a set of practices is unsafe or legally or socially reprehensible. We scientists disapprove of those witchcrafts; we professionals know those amateurs are charlatans.

Suppression can also occur via occupational invasion. Abbott (1988, pp. 98–100) noted how some occupations extend control over other activities by rhetorics justifying jurisdictional attack. He differentiated between rhetorics of reduction, metaphor and treatment. Reduction replaces one occupation's diagnosis of a problem by its own. Thus, child misbehaviour is reduced to the disease of hyperactivity, suitable for medical treatment. A feature of reduction is linguistic manipulation (my phrase, not Abbott's) or 'the global professional metaphor', notably medical, legal or efficiency. Metaphor extends one profession's model of inference to others. Finally, treatment claims refer to the assertion that its treatments are the best.

Suppression may occur as an occupation expands into another's territory. Or a new group may emerge via a 'clientele settlement'. In this case, a client group may be served by new para-professionals, which form an occupation demanding formal jurisdiction. Another way is by enclosure, where a group claims jurisdiction over a task previously common to a number of professions.

In general, outright suppression has probably been less common than scheming suppression. Deals can be made between representatives of a dominant profession to prevent a potential rival from practising, or to impose such costs on potential users that it becomes in their interest to accede to the suppression. Associational rights to combat such practices have rarely been considered.

Occupational Splintering

Occupational splintering occurs when a homogeneous occupation splits or is split into groups. It is not the same as oppression, although there is often some of that. It may be a way of weakening the old occupation. Most commonly, professions split into small elites of specialists and a mass of the 'specialized'. Splintering can be engineered from within the occupation or by corporations, or by governments, by creating subsidiary categories to take over functions hitherto done by a major profession. Often professionals are replaced by para-professionals or untrained staff without corresponding changes of function; within bureaucracies the division of labour may change to accommodate organizational imperatives.

By way of example, within the UK's NHS, tasks long performed by doctors have been delegated to a new grade of medical care practitioners, a large group equivalent to physician assistants in the USA. They do not need professional qualifications, cannot progress to become doctors, are subject to tight supervision, and are paid about half the salary of doctors. Their legitimation was preceded by use of insecure healthcare support workers, which induced the fragmentation of the hospital occupational structure. The legal profession is another where the emergence of a few multinational firms employing thousands of lawyers has accentuated the profession's differentiation.

Splintering is linked to aspects of commodification discussed earlier. For instance, UK law firms have been moving from hourly billing, but have pressured employees to meet revenue targets, leading junior lawyers to try to raise their billable hours. While they are being proletarianized by labour intensification, an outcome will be a more fragmented service and workforce. Even the *Financial Times* (2008) called for basic legal services to be 'commoditized', to be routinized and charged as a product. That will accentuate the splintering of the legal profession.

Occupations historically have resisted market forces by creating closed communities and bounded cultures. However, markets divide. Consider law again, a profession that has typified aloofness from commercial pressure. Although its commodification is partial, it exhibits a tendency of an occupation under pressure to split into an elite protected from market forces and a majority subject to them. For generations, the profession was a byword for a fraternity, which resisted corporate pressures successfully as long as it was serving civil society and affluent interests. But as it became an integral part of global capitalism and as law infiltrated economics and commerce, the number of lawyers multiplied, inviting a splintering.

Legal firms take advantage of their capacity to compete for the huge demand for legal work by packaging standardized services for low-income activities while competing for niche markets. As the divide between the mundane and the profitable has sharpened, the profession has reserved the professional ethos for the higher end of the market, for clients able to pay for high-value credence services. But it is what has been happening to the lower end that is so characteristic of the era. Those there are finding their life close to that of the precariat, as they struggle with stress and labour intensification.

* * *

In general, suppression, oppression and splintering come about because an alliance of interests wants it. It may be an alliance between the state and part of an occupation, or between corporations and elements of an occupation. There are also tripartite alliances. All are likely to create a Faustian bargain, in which short-term pecuniary or status gains are exchanged for a future of insecurity for the whole occupational community. Such bargains have proliferated with globalization.

Several tendencies flow from oppression, suppression and splintering. Intra-occupational inequality grows and is a source of stress, since for those near the bottom the expanding economic distance between them and those at the top of their occupation creates powerful status frustration effects.

The inequality is only partially captured by images of winner-takes-all markets, since it is largely due to institutional mechanisms. It derives from very different levels of employment, job and skill security. Those near the bottom of an occupation may be pushed into the precariat, without tenure, contracts or employment protection. These count as lost components of their social income. They may be affected by organizational and technical change more than those further up the occupational ladder, making it harder to build career profiles. And they may be obliged to learn new bundles of tricks – skills – at regular intervals. An auxiliary knows what this feels like and what it adds up to, a lower social income. Possession of secure skills is valuable because acquiring new skills is costly. In addition to these forms of labour insecurity, oppressed groups are least likely to have representation security, or Voice, and may see their occupational association as operating merely as the mouthpiece of insiders rather than themselves.

OCCUPATIONAL COMPETITION

One aspect of commodification is the strategy of pitching occupations against each other in competition for resources. This has gone with the desire to make individuals more competitive towards others in their occupation.

Relationships *between* practitioners become more competitive. The market triumphs over the occupational community. Guarding knowledge, contacts and networks become sources of commercial advantage, whereas communities based on principles of civic friendship tend towards knowledge-sharing and respect for the occupation's traditions.

If the system is primarily about making more money than others offering a similar commodity, and if one advances only on the basis of money-making skills, why abide by practices of chivalry and 'greatness'? The 'old boy' becomes depicted as a time-using impediment to efficiency, rather than a sage to be respected as a matter of civility and reciprocity. In short, competition intensifies the market deconstruction of occupational communities. Collaborative bargaining within occupations, as proposed later, could restrict that.

A profession's commercialization may turn situations of individual risk into systemic risk, resulting in a wider threat. This happened with the commercialization of the financial professions, which produced 'rogue traders', loners without a sense of professional ethics built through a community. Isolated in their pursuit of profitable earnings, there was no professional control. Competition may have productive potential, but it must be reined in for the benefit of those involved as well as for society.

SOCIAL ADJUSTMENT PROFESSIONS

In each transformation, occupations emerge to deal with the tensions and restructuring needs of the emerging economic system and with the traumas of those hit by the upheavals. Some occupations are privileged because of their strategic importance, for forging the economic and production system or for dealing with the adjustment problems. Some arise out of control functions desired by dominant interests, as in the case of psychiatry in the late nineteenth century and social workers in the globalization era. Initially, such professions are depicted as social curers; later they become custodial or societal administrators. They break down into occupations with a primary function of increasing efficiency and occupations dealing with adjustment problems of society.

In the crisis preceding the establishment of industrial citizenship, five types of occupation vied for adjustment and efficiency roles: management-efficiency, disciplinary-and-policing, financial-adjustment, social-recovery and religious or Salvationist occupations.

All reflected some occupational dismantling and restructuring. Until legitimized, they were para-medical, para-legal or para-financial occupations, in which practitioners had basic training in one accepted discipline but were not seen as constituting a recognizable occupation.

All five types overlapped and competed for legitimacy before the Great Transformation. The scientific managers, with their engineering background, spawned working-class labour managers, including foremen, shop stewards and clerical employees with cost-accounting functions. Their disciplinary actions extended outside the factories, farms, mines and bureaucracies. Some penalized misfits and those who had failed and drifted into social illnesses. The psychiatrists and psychological guidance professions helped with therapies but blurred into the policing community, as they offered treatments to calm nerves and sedate the ill-tempered, trying to curb the self-destructive or rebellious behaviour of economic victims. The financial adjustment occupations, such as accountants and solicitors, tried to help employees manage their incomes more prudently.

Secular social recovery occupations mainly tried to rescue the remnants of dying cultures. Looking back, one can appreciate Polanyi's preoccupation with workers' education, echoed by a generation of spirited intellectuals. And one can see the attempt to rescue crafts by artists such as William Morris. They were the ecologists of their day, focusing on preservation and reproduction. They offered a secular recovery. But they struggled with their Salvationist brethren. The crisis witnessed a flourishing of religious groups selling competing messages, with new forms of religious activism reaching into the street, home and workplace. They included temperance societies and mainly working-class organizations such as the Methodists and Presbyterians, offering workers salvation and relief from the unfairness of their lot.

All para-occupational communities helped in forging industrial citizenship. They became part of a new order in which insecurities had to be managed in a market society. But there was a time of competition between religious groups and the emerging 'scientific' occupations, notably psychiatry. On their better days, they were shaped by a desire to help people adjust to an insecure and stressful environment. On their worse, they were concerned just with making the new economic system more efficient and stable. The secular romantics were pushed aside, many to become the subject of evocative biographies and films later in the twentieth century.

The equivalent para-occupations in the Global Transformation are worryingly different. The scale of the challenge, and the technological and financial capacities available to those in tune with the global market society, are greater relative to those trying to resist or adjust to them. One big difference is that the service-oriented system has created more diffused workplaces, a blurring of the social space and the labour space, in which labour activities are not amenable to direct disciplinary devices, or not only such devices. Bentham's panopticon has arrived. But, as Foucault understood, the watchtower has to be everywhere. For this, the adjustment para-occupations have to be combined in a new cocktail of complementary functions.

At one level, adjustment occupations are combining breakthroughs in behavioural sciences with breakthroughs in surveillance techniques to increase market and productive efficiency. Management and administration are now depicted as sciences. New professions have emerged to improve efficiency, intent on manipulating service workers and adjusting their competences, attitudes and behaviour. Thus, there are CLOs (Chief Learning

Officers) and CKOs (Chief Knowledge Officers) in multinational corporations. CLOs often double up their training functions with heading 'corporate universities', among the worst contradictions in terms ever invented (Earl and Scott, 1999; Foote et al., 2001).

Middle managers comprise an organizational group verging on being an occupational group. Having grown in the late stages of labourism, the para-occupation is suffering from waves of restructuring in global corporations and public organizations (Hecksher, 1995; Grey, 1999). As part of the salariat, they are in an awkward class position, between executives and employees (Jackall, 1988). They suffer from the ills of proletarianization, lacking an independent Voice to help them gain control of their work and development. But they are busy in the adjustment process. They lack a sense of fraternity, which means a lack of ethics that comes from being a community. Some Marxists would call them the most alienated of all. That would make them dangerous, liable to become guards in the modern panopticon. There are attempts to incorporate the surveillance system associated with policing into administration and supervision of the production system. Management occupations have incorporated lessons of psychology and surveillance, and have to operate practices they would reject as citizens, such as devising methods that invade the privacy of their charges.

Outside the sphere of labour, policing and surveillance occupations are spreading at a phenomenal rate. An expanded set of occupations consists of those dealing with crime and its aftermath, including probationary services. In 2006, the UK government announced that it would put the probation service out to private tender, under which £9 billion worth of services in prison and probation work – a quarter of the total – was to be offered to civil-society organizations and private security companies. Helen Edwards, Chief Executive of the National Offender Management Service, told *The Guardian*, 'There has been talk of this being all about privatisation. That is not right. This is as much about letting the third sector play more of a role in all this' (Travis, 2006). This sector was becoming part of the new management of social services.

Less noticed has been the growth of occupations geared to helping workers adjust to an increasingly financial life and insecure labour existence. These include tax consultants, which have formed partnerships, as in Germany, offering comprehensive business services, including drafting of contracts. Lawyers lost much of this work because they had concentrated on areas where they had a monopoly.

Adjustment occupations have played several roles. The blurring of efficiency and welfare criteria is a problem. For instance, an emerging profession is the employment agent, equivalent to an estate agent who deals with the transfer of property. Predictably, there have been claims that only those licensed should be allowed to do this job. They deal with the precariat for much of the time, but have also become significant for proficians and the salariat. The state wants them to be the occupation dealing with the detached, the unemployed and those needing social integration. Certainly, commercialization and the privatization of employment services will boost the occupation, which involves a heady mixture of social psychology and social policy with knowledge of benefit systems, social work, training, community health, counselling, para-legal services and personnel practice. It is unclear whose interests the occupation will represent. At present, it is more oriented to the market than to anything else.

There are commercial and political pressures pushing employment agents to become paternalistic controllers, as part of the 'workfare' agenda. But there is also a countervailing public service function, to provide a service to clients. The clients most likely to influence their behaviour are employers, particularly if they are paying. To complicate the incentive structure, government fiscal authorities may push them to maximize placement and job retention rates, and offer subsidies and grants to encourage that. The unemployed and workers cannot compete with those inducements. Their interests could be relegated to third place, after those of companies and middle-class voters wanting them off the streets and off their tax bills.

Employment agents may be assimilated into the labour control system, even though many will want to provide a neutral public service. The market pressures are just too unbalanced. The way to counter this is for public authorities to ensure Voice regulation of employment services by those who use the services and their representative organizations. Only then could the paternalistic tendency and the opportunistic treatment of vulnerable clients be combated.

Another emerging adjustment profession is the para-legal citizenship adviser, who can help proficians avoid the pitfalls of their high-income existence and help the precariat recover from periodic crises. Advisers will have to steer a fine line between being part of the surveillance society, drawing up tighter employment contracts for firms and so on, and helping citizens to adjust to the demands of the market society. Some have gone over the edge of their old profession's code. Thus, employers have been using labour lawyers, supposedly protectors of labour rights, as 'union avoidance consultants', to deter union efforts to organize employees and the precariat. In the USA, even when a union manages to win a vote for unionization, the employer, aided by labour lawyers, now can simply postpone negotiations for years.

Other lawyers have become social adjusters, trying to combat the excesses of corporations and the state, typically combining legal and political work. The strains must be considerable, since this puts them on the edge of two occupational communities. It is unfair to expect them to resolve the conflicting pressures. Lawyers have rarely been in the vanguard of a progressive transformation. Their role has been to make a system work consistently, not overthrow it.

There are other emerging occupations, para-financial, para-medical and para-legal, most with conflicting functions. However, it is the adjustment role being played by religious occupations that is most striking. God is watching. The global religious revival, so symptomatic of a pre-transformation era, draws strength from its message of hope in the future in exchange for putting up with a frenzy of insecure consumption now. The neo-liberal state welcomes this religiosity. It is more than compatible with a global market society; its practitioners celebrate the dictates of competition, money-making and opulent consumption while preaching family values of privatism, rather than a progressive secular emancipation. The new fundamentalist religious practitioners and their mass of auxiliary workers are in tune with financial capital, which has spawned a burst of religious philanthropy on a global scale. The religiosity has blended with the medicalization of social ills, through faith-based welfare organizations, who can feel good as they do good, helping people to put up with the outcomes of yawning inequalities and insecurities. Medicines are offered with behavioural conditionality.

This portrait of religious adjustment occupations may seem to be a description of the USA. But, while displayed to the world through predominantly US images, via TV, films, advertising and other media, the tendencies are global. The largest fundamentalist churches are in South Korea; the *favelas* of Brazil are spawning fundamentalist welfare societies that share control with criminal gangs. Religious bodies are becoming more competitive in the global market.

While religious practices are refashioned for a market society, another influence on adjustment occupations is the almost hegemonic discipline of psychology, made up of mind-readers and mind-writers. Along with law, psychology is on the march, as it was in the last Transformation. Psychologists are in the middle of social life. No corporation or bureaucracy can do without them. Religion toys with their insights and tools. They have invaded economics. Politicians look to them for guidance, the police employ them in droves. For workers with fragmented careers, they offer pragmatic ways of coping. For corporate management they offer the means of selecting employees and more refined surveillance. Psychological testing is a 'personal problem' occupational activity, but it is also a control mechanism. It limits entry of the 'wrong' people to jobs and prepares or adjusts people for organizations. Social work is also involved, as are law enforcement occupations, which have expanded dramatically.

Para-psychologists are in a contradictory position, and may be at the forefront of occupational restructuring. That is potentially positive. But the most exciting sphere of adjustment is that of social recovery occupations, since they are a response to the crisis of globalization. As just before the Great Transformation, some are trying to rescue arts and crafts; they are trying to prevent art being commercialized and 'dumbed down', in order to restore it to its historical mission of being emancipatory. Part is about rescuing civic friendship; these NGOs are capable of being social recovery bodies. But the most vital social recovery occupations are those responding to the ecological crisis. New 'green' occupations are taking shape, responding to the externalities of the market society. They promise to provide new occupational profiles. They must make their global footprint.

GLOBALIZING OCCUPATIONS

The dismantling of national occupational communities has helped to create space for the global construction of occupations. As befitting globalization, the supra-state has begun to reshape them. As Krause (1996, p. 273) pointed out, 'Professions remain primarily national creations, international conferences notwithstanding. But capitalism, international to some extent by 1960 and to a much greater extent by 1990, began to view professions as obstacles to economic progress'.

Once that happened, not only did the state move to dismantle them but neo-liberals sought to build market-oriented global institutions to restructure them in the interests of the global market. Transnational bureaucracies increasingly control an occupation or professional practice, as in the case of auditors, lawyers and doctors. They do so by establishing best practices, codes of conduct and standardized criteria for entry and recognition, globalized norms for a profession.

Global occupations require common standards. Corporations dealing in professional services are eager to take advantage of a global market. There has been a rush to outsource legal services, notably by US and UK firms to India. As one observer (cited in Bellman, 2005) noted, 'The people to whom you are outsourcing are well educated and can work at an hourly rate that is 10 per cent of what large-firm lawyers charge'. And

Indian lawyers have not demanded perks such as large offices and personal assistants, which increases their competitive advantage and puts pressure on suppliers in rich countries to cut enterprise benefits there. The effect varies from occupation to occupation, but it is not restricted to lower-level, low-paying occupations. Over 200 000 Indians graduate from law schools each year, and they are trained in English common law. This will be a factor in the global convergence to the common law model.

Offshoring is affecting occupational restructuring because it is the standardized functions that can be converted into tradable service jobs, such as accounting or legal services. Globalization has accelerated proletarianization and occupational splintering by generating sharper geographical divisions of labour and reducing solidarity within professions. As noted in Chapter 3, trade in tasks is growing particularly fast. This disrupts occupational careers, meaning that a person may have to move in order to advance a career or that upward progression is simply blocked.

Occupational trade has boomed. The global market in professional services is worth over US$1 trillion and exports have grown to account for a quarter of world exports of commercial services (UNCTAD, 2005). The multinationalization of professional services is a feature of the Global Transformation, concentrated in a few corporations. For instance, the top 100 law firms, all located in the UK and the USA, account for 60 per cent of all revenue generated by legal work. Management consultancy, a rapidly growing service, is also concentrated in a few large firms. In accounting, big firms account for most of the revenue, and a few big agencies dominate advertising.

The state has boosted trade in occupational services. In rich countries this has been mainly through subsidies to higher-level educational and training institutions, research and development subsidies designed to promote investment in professional services and regulations designed to give them protection and rental incomes. Developing countries have faced trade barriers not so much from regulations, the focus of negotiations in the WTO and elsewhere, but from subsidies given to selected professions and institutions employing them.

Under pressure of globalizing labour markets, professions in developing countries are becoming more commercial. The Indian legal profession is an example. Under the 1961 Indian Advocates Act, foreign firms were blocked from practising. As the market society deepened, foreign law firms saw India as a potential goldmine, as *The Economist* put it (2008i). India had 15 000 corporate lawyers, but law firms were not allowed to have more than 20 partners, could not advertise via websites and could not even give out business cards unless requested. Indian lawyers could set up in other countries, but nationals of those countries could not do so in India. This resulted in subterfuge, with British and US firms setting up virtual Indian practices in London or Dubai and forging 'best friend' alliances with firms in India.

While Indian lawyers were persuading their government to block foreign law firms, the South Koreans and others were moving to open their markets. It seemed only a matter of time before liberalization became universal, or near enough so. An international convergence in practices is taking place.

This is a controversial claim but, amidst the dismantling of occupations, national differences are declining as a global model takes shape. We know that the idea of profession varies in different cultures (Szreter, 1993). Some believe that what counts depends on the role of the state; in continental European countries the state creates professional jurisdictions. The French state has been depicted as among the most interventionist, in contrast with the Anglo-Saxon tradition, based on licensing, credentials and permitted monopoly of practice. The variable role of the state has, predictably, led sociologists to develop typologies of country by degree of 'stateness' ranging from those that create, regulate and employ professionals to those that merely create conditions for self-government (Heidenheimer, 1989; Freidson, 2001).

Although such typologies can be overstretched, if this roughly describes regimes in the Great Transformation, based as it was on national labour markets, then one may anticipate a convergence as the global labour market evolves. This will happen by several means, from reducing state employment of professionals to weakening profession-preserving regulations. In between, an age-old tendency will persist, of the state aligning with elite elements of a profession, whose interests and aspirations may differ sharply from the whole of it.

One suggestion is that professions create 'status communities' and 'cognitive communities', the former reflecting a profession's proximity to the state, the latter being constructed around a technical legitimacy and common educational background. Globalization may lead occupations in different countries to become more alike as cognitive communities, while distinctive status communities may be preserved for longer. Status communities may hamper globalization of an occupation if state agencies and insiders block intrusion of foreign standards and international regulation. Economic liberalization erodes status communities and strengthens cognitive communities, and one can predict that something close to the so-called Anglo-Saxon market model will emerge.

An example of a status community being defended was the decision by the Indian government in 2008 not to liberalize its legal profession, following heavy lobbying by Indian lawyers. A counter-example was the action taken by the South Korean government to liberalize its legal services, committing to full liberalization by 2013. It was acknowledging US and global pressure to turn professional services into global commodities. The South Korean action is more likely to be in tune with globalization.

CONCLUDING CONCERNS: OCCUPATIONAL SADNESS

The ultimate expression of commodification is loss of non-capitalist values within an occupation. Loss of control of work results in the erosion of three features of what a good occupational community is thought to promote – civic friendship or fraternity, social solidarity or reciprocity, and reproductive respect, the healthy regard for etiquette, tolerance of diversity and the ethics of civility and altruism. Perhaps the worst aspect of commodification is when practitioners become complicit, pressurizing colleagues to conform to new controls and forms of expected behaviour, to adapt in the way they have adapted. If not careful, collective misery will come from collective pressure.

One could say that when an occupation is in control of itself it emphasizes behavioural traits connected with civic friendship and the reproduction of its community. When it loses control, those values are marginalized. A market society emphasizes technique over character and solidarity. Character was the basis of Victorian professional legitimacy, giving high value to 'gentlemanliness', altruism, disinterest, probity, rectitude and social responsibility. This has largely gone, as public legitimacy has come to rest on competitive efficiency.

In the period of fictitious decommodification there was a drift from character to technique, accompanied by a restructuring of professions to accord with scientific modes of practice, with professionalization via standardized exams and licensing. The emphasis on efficiency led to the displacement of output criteria by more easily measured procedural criteria. This has gone further during the Global Transformation; market imperatives imperil etiquette and ethics.

As the neo-liberal state and corporations dismantle occupational communities, occupational life is jeopardized. No two generations enter the same occupation. Far from anchoring life and work, occupational life has become a zone of insecurity. When trainees graduate, they should be told, 'You may not be what you are for long'. Occupational risk should be added to the other risks of the risk society.

Ironically, the period described as one of decommodification involved erosion of professional autonomy, via proletarianization, whereas in the 'deregulation' era the state stepped up its regulation of professional activity. Occupational freedom has been eroded by extension of management jurisdiction and intervention by financial capital. Among the first casualties is the right of an occupation to police itself.

In the Great Transformation, some occupations, mostly professions, were able to erect barriers to commodification, creating circles of privilege. The neo-liberal state has forced them to respond to market forces and to comply with the needs of commercial capital. The old situation may have been unsatisfactory, but the dismantling has done much to jeopardize occupational citizenship. However, before we consider the consequences and the remedy, Chapter 7 reviews one area of acrimonious debate.

7. Occupational regulation

INTRODUCTION

Occupational regulation can be traced to the Code of Hammurabi of ancient Babylon, and was extensive in ancient Rome and, via the guilds, through the Middle Ages. Occupations have always been subject to regulation, with the state role varying from minimal to almost complete. The picture is complicated because regulation takes several forms and because there are layers of internal and external regulation. In many cases an occupation has used the state to strengthen *self-regulation*, so the appearance of the state role may be deceptive. However, we may start by contrasting self-regulation with state regulation. Some occupations have formed associations to 'self-regulate' their activities; others have persuaded the state to regulate for their benefit. Usually, those that have turned the regulatory system to their advantage have been small and specialized.

With any system, tension exists between practitioner and consumer interests, each pressing governments to regulate in their favour. A third party is the public interest, commonly though incorrectly equated with the consumer interest. In a transformation period, the tendency has been to regulate in favour of market forces, except in the case of professions in the vanguard of the new production system. Although state regulation has been ostensibly concerned with consumer protection whereas self-regulation has been concerned with protection of those inside an occupation, this can be over-stressed.

In the debate over labour flexibility little attention has been given to the impact of occupational regulation. Yet barriers to entry to occupations and the right to practise, and the resultant price effects, may have more impact on employment than most of the factors cited as causing labour market rigidities.

There is an extensive literature on forms of occupational regulation, one of the most comprehensive and widely cited reviews being by Cox and Foster (1990). Those favouring a market society have opposed state regulation and forms of self-regulation that involve collective associations. Libertarians draw their inspiration from Adam Smith, who depicted regulatory interventions as limiting the right to work. His rationale for opposing apprenticeship in *The Wealth of Nations* deserves to be recaptured:

> The patrimony of a poor man lies in the strength and dexterity of his hands; and to hinder him from employing this strength and dexterity in what manner he thinks proper without injury to his neighbour, is a plain violation of this most sacred property. It is a manifest encroachment upon the just liberty both of the workman, and of those who might be disposed to employ him. As it hinders the one from working at what he thinks proper, so it hinders the others from employing whom they think proper. To judge whether he is fit to be employed, may surely be trusted to the discretion of the employers whose interest it so much concerns. The affected anxiety of the law-giver lest they should employ an improper person, is evidently as impertinent as it is oppressive. The institution of long apprenticeships can give no security that insufficient workmanship shall not frequently be exposed to public sale.
>
> (Smith [1776] 1979, Book 1, Chapter 10, Part II, p. 225)

Smith was writing when knowledge embodied in most occupations was transparent. Most crafts could be learned by practice guided by experienced workers. Long apprenticeships had other objectives. Even then, though, there were grounds to challenge his robust assertions. As for his general attitude to regulation, modern and ancient legislators around the world have not agreed.

By contrast, Polanyi understood that state regulation and self-regulation provided barriers to commodification. As noted earlier, he appreciated how guilds put a brake on market pressures, recognizing that they embedded productive activities in society and prevented workers 'from becoming the objects of commerce'. Self-regulation was under threat. In the Global Transformation, it is again.

This chapter assesses the arguments for and against self-regulation and state regulation. To start, recall the conventional arguments for regulating occupations:

1. There is a need to limit market power and prevent monopolistic practices that would raise prices of the goods or services.
2. There is a need to counteract asymmetries of information, in that buyers do not have as much or as reliable information as sellers.
3. There is a need to counteract negative externalities; many transactions have consequences for third parties that may not be taken into account by sellers and buyers.
4. There are social objectives that lie outside the occupation, requiring differential pricing or some practice that would not otherwise occur.

Occupational regulation is about control. And any regulation involves four questions – for whom, by whom, over what and by what means? First, for whose interest is the regulation intended? The following are possibilities, with a combination being most likely: all members of the occupation; seniors in it; juniors in it; competitors with the occupation; consumers of its services or products; client enterprises using the occupation; potential consumers who are not consumers at present; citizens in general.

Second, by whom is the control being exercised? Possible situations are: 'occupational control', with full regulation by a professional body or combined with a state agency; 'statutory control' by a state agency, with membership drawn from the occupation who are not employed in it or with members who are neither qualified nor employed in it; 'client control', as in the case of hospitals setting rules for auxiliaries; and 'supra-national control' via international agencies.

Third, over what is the control or regulation exercised? For most occupations the range of issues is wide, reflecting the diverse means of entering and moving within them. Fourth, by what means are the regulatory controls being carried out? Again, potential incentives and sanctions are considerable, and vary according to the form of regulation.

SELF-REGULATION

Self-regulation actually covers two forms of regulation, by the individual as a practitioner or 'professional' and by associations that represent an occupation. The term has usually been used to refer to the latter, a practice continued here.

Throughout history, groups identifying themselves as an occupation have sought to legitimize their position through self-regulation and to have that institutionalized by the state. But self-regulation has also developed as part of the modern regulatory state, becoming a feature of modern capitalism. An occupation sets rules for its members, which may range from conditions for entry to rules for expulsion. Usually, self-regulatory bodies are more comprehensive than state bodies, making rules, monitoring conduct and punishing bad practice (Scott, 2002). Full self-regulation exists, but usually it has been mixed with statutory regulation. For example, a survey of the accountancy profession in 38 countries that had member bodies of the International Federation of Accountants found that 8 per cent were regulated entirely by government, 74 per cent by a combination of government and their professional association and just 18 per cent had complete self-regulation (Heeter, 1995).

Five types of occupational self-regulation have been identified:

1. mandated, in which a collective body is required or designated by the state to formulate and enforce norms, standards and practices within a framework laid out by the state;
2. sanctioned, in which the collective association formulates its own rules, which are then approved by the state;
3. coerced, in which the collective formulates and imposes regulations under threat of statutory regulation;
4. voluntary, where there is no state involvement;
5. quasi-regulation, which refers to situations where indirect, non-coercive pressure leads to self-regulation by several bodies.

Most lay observers would regard (4) as encapsulating self-regulation. But it has been relatively rare. Coerced self-regulation has been more common. A government may put pressure on an occupational body by taking statutory powers to impose regulation if necessary, leading to action aptly described as 'regulation in the shadow of the law', or 'co-regulation' (Black, 2003). In general, categories (1) and (2) have been the norms.

The extent of self-regulation may vary simply because in some occupations, practitioners must belong to their professional body to be able to practise legally, while in others membership is voluntary, so that practitioners can continue to practise even if they do not choose to belong. Part of the explanation may reflect the variable capacity of occupations to appeal to the political authorities.

Often, several associations purport to represent an occupation. Mostly a government recognizes one as having the regulatory powers, if regulation is delegated to the occupation. There is a continuum, from occupations with no bodies in a position to regulate to those with several bodies that share regulation. Often, a professional association is delegated to regulate by government, even though this may not apply to all occupations. Thus, in India as of 2008, professional associations covering legal services, accountancy, architecture and medical and dental services had authority delegated by the federal government.

The main claim made in favour of self-regulation is that it is a flexible means by which competence and behavioural standards, or probity, can be maintained and strengthened. The achievement of a reputation is seen to enhance the demand for and legitimacy of the work, and the status of those performing it.

Ensuring competence is the usual claim by any occupation setting up a self-regulatory body, and has been the main rationale for licensing and certification. Self-regulatory bodies usually try to block and attack unqualified persons. Their actions may be said to encourage potential practitioners to invest more in skills. Not all agree, as we shall see. But many occupational associations have recognized that often competence cannot be determined at the outset, and have accordingly allowed for probationary membership.

To achieve competence objectives, self-regulatory bodies have used numerous measures, including service standards, qualifications and experience requirements, rules requiring regular testing, continuous training, annual reporting, required use of indemnity insurance, provision of information for practitioners and consumers, limits on prepayment and up-front fees that professionals can charge and auditing requirements.

Probity has been another goal of self-regulation. The intention is to prohibit or penalize undesirable conduct and exclude those deemed likely to engage in undesirable conduct. Probity-enhancing measures have included prohibition of certain conduct, character requirements, restrictions on use of titles, trust fund requirements and use of written contracts. Measures to deal with probity failure include establishment of funds to compensate those who suffer from misconduct or poor service, disciplinary procedures for members charged with breaching rules or failure to provide adequate service, penalties if they are found guilty, publications of action on a register, suspension of the right to practise and use of liability insurance.

Besides competence and probity, self-regulation may represent an attempt to deal with what economists call 'bounded rationality', according to which people make (and often prefer to make) choices from a limited set of options rather than from the universe of all possible options. An occupational community embodies a bounded culture, comprising a group with similar work identities that transcend those embodied in a particular enterprise of employment (Lawrence, 1998). The group organizes to limit the range of decision-making by individual workers, setting parameters so as to reduce uncertainty and stipulating the information that has to be sought in order to make decisions rationally and according to the occupation's ethical norms. This is a principled argument for self-regulation. It recognizes the reality of bounded rationality and institutionalizes a mechanism to provide security.

Self-regulation has also been used to preserve the jurisdiction of professions, their legitimacy. All professions over the ages have claimed that trust must be forged between professional and client, as well as between fellow professionals, partly because there is an asymmetry of expertise and information. This has been recognized as the rationale for elaborate systems of instruction and training and codes of behaviour, a theme of the pioneering study by Carr-Saunders and Wilson (1933). Adam Smith's point on apprenticeships ignores their several objectives, including inculcation of values and ways of behaving towards colleagues and outsiders, and the formation of attitudes in a more political sense.

However, self-regulation has been subject to a barrage of criticisms. The primary one is regulatory capture, the view that a self-regulating occupation turns into a quasi-monopoly, acquiring rental surplus for its members. Another claim is that it is prone to regulatory drift, a tendency for a regulation to persist after it has ceased to be appropriate due to technological or social change. And it is claimed it is prone to regulatory failure, a tendency for regulation to fail to achieve its aims even when the motivation and desirable objectives correspond.

Regulatory capture has been the subject of a large literature. It was, predictably, the first issue raised in a paper prepared by the Australian Treasury as part of the National Competition Policy Reform process in the 1990s (Parker et al., 1997). Almost always, the critics claim that self-regulation gives occupations market power by which they can limit entry and push up the price of their services. In their classic study, Milton Friedman and Simon Kuznets (1945) interpreted their findings as showing how US doctors in the 1940s forced up their earnings by restricting entry to medical schools, whereas dentists did not restrict entry and found their earnings lagging behind those of doctors.[1] The dentists soon adopted similar practices and their average earnings rose above those of doctors.

The legal profession has been the most assiduous in self-regulating. It developed a restrictive entry system in order to raise and sustain earning power, and manipulated the controls flexibly to its own advantage. Thus, in the USA there have been many instances in which the profession lowered the pass rate when the number of applicants rose, reducing the percentage of students passing the bar exam. It has also restricted accreditation of law schools so as to limit the supply of lawyers (Shepherd, 2000).

The legal profession is not alone. Many self-regulatory bodies have set minimum quality standards excessively high to restrict entry, force up prices or exclude lower-cost alternatives that could be delivered by less qualified persons. In some cases, the body itself enforces regulations that raise the costs for those offering lower-cost alternatives. And the greater the occupational control, the more likely the price of their services is to rise, as shown in optometry (Haas-Wilson, 1992).

Critics have also complained that self-regulation does not necessarily lead to higher competence. Self-appointed associations can 'sit on their laurels', becoming complacent, while erecting barriers to entry that deter people from improving skills by stages and learning-by-doing. Not even probationary membership schemes may overcome that, since these may be used to limit numbers or turn junior practitioners into a source of low-cost labour.

The most common form of self-regulation has been to erect entry barriers, with the avowed objective of preventing substandard service. Although this is usually one motive, there is something in Mancur Olson's terse comment directed at the medical profession about the fact that examinations have usually been imposed only on entrants: 'If the limits were mainly motivated by the interest of patients, older physicians would also be required to pass periodic qualifying examinations to demonstrate that they have kept their medical knowledge up to date' (Olson, 1982, p. 66). This is a fair point. But one cannot conclude that the competence rationale is not valid, merely that there are other motives as well.

It has long been understood that if professional bodies control their profession, they will limit the number entering it to below what it would be otherwise, and to below what the public would wish (Shaked and Sutton, 1981). As this may be taken for granted, it is worth noting that a UK assessment did not find this was happening (Office of Fair Trading, 2001, p. 6). But there is plenty of evidence that such restrictions have been widespread.

Self-regulatory bodies have raised barriers to entry not only by imposing numerical restrictions and excessive qualification requirements but also by setting conditions not relevant to performance of the work. This has been a means of discrimination, as in the case of residency and citizenship requirements. Many associations have excluded persons with criminal records, even though their offences may have no relevance to the work.

Excluding people from a self-regulatory association is a powerful means of blocking them from having a right to practise. The association might claim that allowing them to practise would harm the profession's reputation. But there are other ways of defending reputation without excluding people from practising.

Another criticism is that self-regulatory bodies increase practitioners' own costs as a subtle means of raising barriers to entry. They do this by imposing restrictions on their own behaviour (Office of Fair Trading, 2001, p. 50). Measures include restricting advertising and marketing, restricting types of business, prohibiting negotiations on fees and banning contingency fees. By constraining some types of competition, occupational insiders can focus more on forms in which they have a comparative advantage, such as playing on established reputation. Restricting advertising can raise search costs for consumers and lead them to opt for established 'names' rather than find lower-cost, less well-known alternatives. This can be interpreted as making the demand curve more inelastic by making it more costly for consumers to find a cheaper option. Established practitioners can thus retain market share and their income. Thus, restrictions on advertising and fee competition have raised professional incomes in Canada (Muzondo and Pazderka, 1980). This constitutes regulatory failure since it increases prices and blocks off dissemination of transparent information.

For cost-raising tactics to be successful for insiders, they must possess strong market power (that is, the service itself must face an inelastic demand curve). If they do not have such power, consumers will be able to substitute lower-cost alternatives (or forego the service). Such power comes from having control over market entry and the right to practise, or by having a surrogate agency exercise control on behalf of the occupation. High costs of switching providers also increase market power, presuming those costs are enforceable and there are no easily available substitutes. Langenfeld and Silvia (1993), who analysed 81 anti-competition cases in the USA, found that raising own costs was a more common tactic than collusion or raising costs for competitors. The main mechanism was advertising restrictions.

A question for policymakers is whether such restrictive practices are unacceptable in principle or unacceptable only if they adversely affect the quality or price of the service. If they do not raise prices or lower quality, it does not follow that they are unnecessary, a conclusion drawn in the report by the UK's Office of Fair Trading on professional practices (Office of Fair Trading, 2001, p. 54). That conclusion stems from taking a purely market perspective. Certain practices deemed restrictive may have an intended consequence of strengthening the ethos of an occupational community or the status of some of its practitioners, without that having an impact on the service or its price.

Another criticism is that collective bodies interfere with the right to practise. Most attention has been paid to entry barriers but regulation does not stop there. It extends to the right to continue practising and the right to (upward) mobility. In many occupations, the self-regulatory body (or the licensing system run by it) stipulates a recency-of-practise test, whereby people are allowed to practise only if they have done so within a recent prescribed period. The test can vary, even within the same country. For instance, the Australian states have different recency-of-practice requirements in their respective Physiotherapy Acts.

Critics also argue that self-regulatory bodies are too self-interested to enforce proper regulation. Thus, being bodies that represent their members, they will be reluctant to impose disciplinary procedures or sanctions on indiscretions by them (Young, 1993; Summers, 2007). This may be true but the criticism is one-sided, since the collective also has an interest in preserving its reputation, and may wish to show it does not tolerate those who contravene its ethical standards.

Another criticism of self-regulation is 'grandfathering'; a clause is inserted in the rules, or in a licensing law devised by the profession, whereby older practitioners are exempted from regulations imposed on entrants. These are common in newly established licensing systems, where they protect those who learned their trade before knowing what the established norms would be. They are also used as standards are raised. The elders, threatened by skill obsolescence and advancing techniques, shield themselves. Whether explicit in rules or operated implicitly, grandfathering is a form of protection that may jeopardize consumer welfare and the occupation's reputation.

Such practices are related to the tendency to put a brake on innovation. Self-regulatory bodies are seen as a source of occupational inertia and even decay. This can be overstated; some resistance to rapid change can be beneficial, particularly where new practices bring unforeseen risks and uncertainty. But there are many examples of self-regulation becoming too tradition-bound for an occupation's own good.

Some observers depict self-regulation as a modern version of the guilds. Self-regulatory bodies achieved most success in the embedded era of the Great Transformation, between the 1940s and the 1970s. We saw earlier how US doctors used the AMA to regulate for their advantage. Through its state associations, it controlled entry to the profession, dominated other occupations in its cluster and ensured that the ratio of doctors to population stayed constant. Most doctors remained in control of their work, through having their own practices or operating in hospitals controlled by doctors. They successfully opposed efforts to introduce universal health insurance, which would have threatened their capacity to determine their fees. The doctors lost power as the AMA lost membership; by the 1990s, restrictions on entry to the profession had been eroded, the ratio of doctors to the population had doubled and more than half the doctors had entered the salariat.

This story of defeat for self-regulation is incomplete. Another narrative is that the occupational community was restructured in a period of recommodification when the pattern of self-regulation shifted. Internal differentiation was intensified as the occupation expanded and commanded more resources and technology, while pressures for democratic control (and more equitable distribution of the rental income) were pitted against the desire by powerful groups within the profession to retain most of the rental income.

A vast edifice of medical services was created, run by an administrative group of managers who knew about balance sheets but not much about medicine or surgery. Doctors lost their ability to control subsidiary occupations, and could not resist the introduction of federal subsidy schemes for patients, Medicaid and Medicare. These were welcomed by administrators and financiers because they channelled resources into the client community.

As the number of doctors grew, as more resources went into medicine and as technological innovation accelerated (aided by a profession keen to sell its elixirs), commercial interests attracted to the sector found barriers to profit-making. An association that represented doctors' interests was not only a threat to consumers, which might have been acceptable, but it was an obstacle for the financiers.

Salaried employment became the norm for most doctors. Specialists detached themselves by forming their own bodies, unconcerned about new insurance-type schemes for the poor and elderly, while doctors were becoming part of a subordinated salariat. The occupational elites were serving a wealthier clientele. Identification with their proletarianized brethren would have threatened their elevated status and magnificent earnings.

The dynamics of US medical services highlight a point about occupational regulation in general and self-regulation in particular. Just as specific occupations should be seen as belonging to clusters of complementary and potentially competing occupations, any regulation is part of a system in which different forms of regulation are in constant tension. In sum, although self-regulation has withstood the test of time, and been a barrier to commodification, its self-serving tendency is too strong for comfort.

STATE REGULATION: LICENSING AND REGULATORY CAPTURE

While the extent of self-regulation has ebbed and flowed, state regulation has spread. It has done so in the period characterized by many as one of systematic deregulation. Never has there been a greater misnomer.

Although state regulation has been justified on several grounds, largely it has been designed for and by special interests, usually the profession being regulated. But in the globalization era state regulation has been restructured to serve consumer interests more and competition principles most of all.

Over the centuries, the main reasons for state regulation have been the need to combat the professions' market power and to protect consumers from low-quality or dangerous practices. The standard arguments are that, without state intervention, occupations will collude to raise prices and take advantage of consumers' ignorance. Regulation, according to this view, prevents collusion, overcomes informational asymmetry and deals with adverse externalities likely to arise if the public interest is not taken into account in private transactions.

Collusion or tacit agreement is most likely in occupations that have few members or in which there is a high degree of specialization (Olson, 1965). Collusion is likely to lead to mechanisms limiting entry to the occupation, price rises and lower quality. In such circumstances, it has been argued that by limiting opportunistic competitive behaviour and by limiting entry by 'unqualified' persons, the state can ensure quality control. The perceived challenge has been to increase the contestability of occupational markets while ensuring quality services. This has been used to justify occupational licensing and other statutory measures including state control of self-regulatory occupational associations.

In most government reports, protecting consumers has been the main reason given for state regulation. Thus, a paper by Australia's National Competition Council declared, 'The primary objective of this regulation of the professions is to protect the welfare of consumers of professional services and to protect the wider public' (Deighton-Smith et al., 2001). This opens up all sorts of ambiguity designed to set the pulses of lawyers racing. If consumer protection is the 'primary objective', what weight should be given to 'secondary objectives', including that of protecting members of the profession against such threats as erosion of professional status and exploitation and oppression within the profession or by outsiders?

Besides assuring quality standards, state regulation has been justified as protecting consumers from the consequences of ignorance. Information asymmetry is considerable in most services. For instance, consumers of doctors' services may not know whether a prescription is appropriate, and if they are prescribed the wrong treatment or are operated on by an incompetent surgeon, the personal consequences could be severe, even fatal.

The usual information asymmetry argument is that one party, the producer, has more information than the other, the customer. But this is an over-simplification. Three types of problem arise: information deficiency, where both parties lack information needed to make an optimal decision; information bias, where one or both parties have flawed information, including incorrect risk perceptions, or where they process information differently; and information misalignment, where the parties' interests differ but where the relevance of particular information cannot be discerned before a problem arises (Maks and Philipsen, 2005).

Lack of information is a barrier to the purchase of professional services, including financial services (Financial Services Authority, 2000, pp. 27–8). Without the information needed to make rational judgments, consumers will tend to opt for the lower-cost, lower-quality alternative or avoid buying the service at all. Thus, according to this view, regulation is needed to correct for information failure.

However, for many goods and services the quality of service is unobservable, ex ante and/or ex post. In this regard, commodities can be divided into 'search goods', where quality can be seen in advance, 'experience goods', where a consumer can learn about quality through experience, and 'credence goods', where quality is unknown until long afterwards, if at all (Darby and Karni, 1973). Many services are seen as 'credence goods' or 'trust goods', and thus candidates for government regulation. Consumers do not know beforehand, or cannot know, whether the person providing the service is expert, competent or incompetent. Often they cannot judge competence even after the service has been rendered, since other factors may explain an adverse (or favourable) outcome. For instance, a person may lose a legal case due to a poor lawyer or because the case was poor. And typically there is no 'repeat purchase' to allow for a learning function.

The standard economic argument is that credence goods require regulation to improve consumer welfare, by shifting the quality-adjusted demand curve rightward (Leland, 1979; Shapiro, 1986). Without state regulation, the risk of buying a 'lemon' lowers the value of the required expenditure and acts as a deterrent to purchase. As this will lower the price, higher-quality, higher-cost producers may simply not provide the service (Akerlof, 1970). Put another way, if consumers can only decide on the basis of price because they cannot determine quality differences, professionals will have no incentive to offer more expensive, higher-quality services.

In the case of occupational services, the standard market-based mechanisms to deal with informational asymmetry include reliance on reputation, contractual guarantees of performance quality, performance bonds, quality-rating schemes, third-party accreditation and civil liability rules. Reputation works least well when ex-ante and ex-post observation of quality of service is not feasible, when competition is weak, when purchase or need for the service is rare and when assigning responsibility for an outcome is hard. And reputation and all market-based mechanisms are particularly risky when the consequences of poor service are irreversible (Contreras, 2003, p. 2). These are all arguments for state regulation. Auditors are a case in point. Consumers cannot easily determine the quality of the work because audit failure is rare, customers hardly ever see auditors doing their work and those who hire them are usually those being audited (Sunder, 2005).

Another argument for state regulation is the need to deal with the 'free rider' problem. In some cases, the state may allow a profession to hold up prices in return for agreeing to provide a subsidized, or lower-cost, service for designated groups such as those on low incomes. If the state then allowed free entry by professionals from outside its jurisdiction, the latter could have an unfair advantage and undercut local providers, since they would not normally have to fulfil any social role. Clearly, the authorities could counter that by imposing similar obligations on 'foreign' providers.

Finally, a frequent justification for state regulation of services is that the adverse consequences of poor decisions are high. But what does 'high' mean? Standard theories of risk and uncertainty have been enriched by the concept of 'outrage' (Sandman, 1997). This has been applied to environmental and safety issues, but its use could be extended to various occupations. The idea is that the case for regulation depends not only on the public's perception of the risks and hazards (measured scientifically) but also the degree of social outrage associated with the risk. Although outrage is a peculiarly pliable notion, it will be higher if some or all of the following aspects of risk apply:

- taking the risk is coerced rather than voluntary;
- the risk is taken in the course of required work;
- the risk relates to a rare or unfamiliar type of event;
- it relates to something dreaded by many people;
- it relates to a catastrophe (shock), not something that is continuous or chronic;
- it relates to something that is 'knowable';
- it relates to an event or activity controlled by someone else, not the individual;
- the outcome is deemed unfair;
- there is a situation of trust;
- the issue is morally relevant, rather than irrelevant.

Before coming to specific forms of state regulation, note that by no means all analysts believe that information asymmetries – and the three forms of information problem identified earlier – justify a regulatory response. For instance, the fact that personal reasoning may not accord with actual information would not justify regulation to remove all risk or uncertainty, because individuals should be allowed the freedom to take risks, subject to certain well-known constraints.

Similarly, critics would argue that externalities do not necessarily justify state regulation, which could be replaced by litigation, better targeting of taxes and subsidies, or the creation of new property rights. As for regulation being used to promote social objectives, they could claim that regulation of occupations would not be the appropriate route and, more generally, that the state has no right to determine such policy.

In spite of these and other criticisms, three forms of state regulation have predominated. Whatever the arguments for and against each of them, in practice the political economy of regulation has played a dominant role in restructuring occupations.

Occupational Licensing

In the globalization era, the most prevalent form of state regulation has been occupational licensing. This includes 'quantity licensing', where an occupation simply limits the number of practitioners or alters qualification standards in order to do so, and 'quality licensing' that allows any number of practitioners provided they meet required standards. Globally, both types have grown, though quality licensing may be growing more rapidly.

By the 1980s, over 800 occupations in the USA required a licence to practice; by 2005 it may have been over 1000 (Rottenberg, 1980; Kleiner, 2006). Whereas in the 1960s less than 5 per cent of workers were covered by licensing, by 2000 it was 20 per cent. The percentage covered by licences rose to exceed the share of the workforce in unions by 1990, and the gap has continued to widen. One careful study showed how the growth in the number subject to licensing in the state of Minnesota accelerated after the 1970s (Office of the Legislative Auditor, 1999).

Historically, licensing developed first in the medical occupations. After the Second World War a spate of other occupations in the USA approached state legislatures to have licensing schemes. The presumption was that the regulation yielded better information for consumers and raised the quality of professional services.

In many other countries the trend has been similarly upward. In Canada, official estimates also put the number in regulated occupations at about 20 per cent. In the UK, the number has risen sharply as well. In Australia, state governments have received many requests for licences to operate as a group from, besides the well known professions, travel agents, opticians, amusement parlour operators, martial arts promoters, refrigeration mechanics, electrical contractors, automotive mechanics, beauticians and life insurance agents, among others (Moore and Tarr, 1989).

Why has licensing grown? Factors include the spread of paternalistic state policy, the increasing complexity of many occupations, the difficulty of comprehending information required to make rational choices, the litigious nature of modern society, with risk of error having insurance implications, and consumerism, with mass markets exposing more people to more risks.

There is a belief that there are more instances of asymmetrical information, and thus more vulnerability among consumers. But pressure for licensing has also come from occupations fearing reputational damage by rogue or incompetent practitioners, whose activities could lower the price of the service and prompt a search for alternatives. Licensing is also desired as protection against the threat of obsolescence, including intergenerational obsolescence, as well as the threat from emerging occupations and threats to the occupation's social and political status.

One reason for the spread of licensing is political consensus. Insiders see their interests strengthened by licensing, which reduces labour supply; administrators of occupational bodies see financial and other returns; and state agencies that operate licensing schemes benefit from the fees and the kudos from being seen to protect consumer interests. For governments, the costs of not having a regulation if something goes wrong exceed the costs of having a regulation when nothing goes wrong. Even if licensing did have the negative effects claimed by critics, including higher costs, slower innovation and fewer jobs, these could not easily be traced to the regulatory system.

Thus, licensing presents a problem of political asymmetry.[2] Members of an occupation benefit from licensing, and can be expected to lobby for it and for its retention. Politicians can anticipate voter support and donations from members of an occupation if they support licensing, and could anticipate losing both if they opposed it. There is no countervailing force with anything like the same political weight. Citizens would not gain nearly as much from the removal of licensing of any occupation that was only required or 'consumed' by a minority and that had only a marginal effect on their costs of living. They would be most unlikely to change their voting intentions if occupation X were suddenly not covered by licensing.

The nature of licensing varies. In some cases, a person can become licensed simply by having the requisite qualifications specified by the state or other licensing body. In many others, this is only a necessary condition, others being citizenship, residency in the state for a predetermined period, good moral character, recommendations from members of the occupation and recency of practice.

Licences may involve application fees, registration fees, examination fees and renewal fees. Applicants may also have to go to designated accredited colleges, where fees are based on a monopolistic position, and they may have to undergo an apprenticeship or lower-level period of employment, providing the service at a below-market price and giving an employer or occupational senior a rental income.

Often incomers to an area have to subject themselves to retesting. And the area may establish its own pass rate or exam score deemed as a pass, which it may raise or lower depending on perceived shortages or surpluses of practitioners, as done in some US states. In some cases, the applicant must work for or with a licensed practitioner for a period before obtaining a licence. Many of these conditions can be rationalized as safeguarding consumers and the reputation and status of the occupation. Many can also be depicted as simple barriers to entry and thus, particularly when seen from an international perspective, as a barrier to trade in services.

Arguments for and against licensing have been well-rehearsed. There are many reasons given. For instance, a report commissioned by the government of the Australian state of Victoria declared that among its objectives for licensing were probity, competence, making markets work, consumer redress, informed consumer choice and equity (Allen Consulting Group, 2007).

Licences reduce consumer uncertainty about service quality (Arrow, 1971). That may increase demand for the service, since fewer potential consumers will be put off using it. Licensing reduces the downside risk, which is valued more than the equivalent upside 'risk' of a beneficial outcome. But the belief that licensing raises service quality has not been supported by empirical research. The UK's Office of Fair Trading reviewed studies, mostly referring to the USA in the 1980s, and reported that, although the findings should be interpreted with caution, in most cases there had been no overall benefit (Office of Fair Trading, 2001).

A more subtle argument is that licensing is a way of responding to the bounded rationality of consumers, the tendency for people to process only part of the available information simply because the cost of searching for more exceeds the expected benefit. Libertarians mostly steer clear of this issue. If licensing is a way of signalling to consumers, it could be said to reduce the cost of searching. Just as associational regulation reduces the range of decisions that have to be taken by practitioners, so licensing is an aid to rational decision-making by consumers. No sensible defender of licensing would claim that it is infallible, but it helps.

Another economic argument for licensing is that it actually increases the supply of practitioners. By giving potential entrants to an occupation greater assurance that they will obtain a high return on their investment in the specific vocational education and training, more people will go into the occupation because they will be less fearful of having to face lower-quality substitutes (Akerlof, 1970; Shapiro, 1986). Critics have complained there is no evidence that licensing has this supply-inducing effect, and have argued that, even if there were those effects, certification would have the same benefits at lower cost. However, the latter claim is unconvincing because certification schemes permit unqualified people to practise alongside, or in competition with, qualified persons.

Licensing is also seen as a response to wider social and economic concerns. To give an extreme example, if a doctor misdiagnoses a patient's infectious illness, it could result in an epidemic. This is not a risk that citizens or governments would wish to run. Thus, licensing is seen as a form of soft paternalism, not only truncating the risk at the bottom (preventing the worst of bad treatment, for example) but of protecting society against the worst types of risk of wrong decisions. A safer justification would be that the licensing confers protection against economic externalities.

A question this might prompt is whether there should be a fixed licence, implying a threshold of acceptable standard, or a graduated system that recognizes increased competency needed for more complex service requirements. Some would argue that this should depend on the extent of externalities that a particular service involves. An architect designing high-rise buildings needs to be licensed to a greater extent than one who designs bungalows. A doctor who deals with physical injuries may need less scrutiny than one dealing with infectious diseases.

Although licensing is claimed to protect consumers from incompetent or unreliable service, critics contend that it makes no difference to quality standards. The professions of optometry and dentistry have been the focus of US researchers, with mixed conclusions (Carroll and Gaston, 1981; Haas-Wilson, 1986). One study found that licensing regulations had a positive effect on quality of service, measured by thoroughness of eye examinations (Feldman and Begun, 1985). But it concluded that the improvement was not valued by consumers at its marginal cost.

Some complain that licensing rules are arbitrary. The diversity of rules seems to support this, an implication being that principles cannot be applied scientifically or objectively. Some examples would be farcical were they not affecting people's working lives and standards of living. Rules on the work of optometrists in the USA are illustrative. The stated objective is to protect those with eye problems. So, not anybody should be allowed to practise as an optometrist, optician or ophthalmologist. But the different rules across the US states and cities suggest questionable motivation for licensing as well as bureaucratic confusion. And studies suggest that tighter licensing restrictions, as opposed to the decision to have licensing or not, have had no effect on the quality of service, even though they have put up the price.

An example picked up by *The Economist* (2007e) concerned the delightful occupation of 'horse-tooth floating', a time-honoured occupation in Texas. Horses in the wild eat coarse grass, which wears down their teeth. In captivity they do not eat tough grass so their teeth grow and threaten to cut their cheeks. Teeth must be filed, a process known as floating, which requires delicate handling. There are not many with those skills, or the desire to put their hands in horses' mouths. Yet the few who do are threatened with being blocked from their work on the grounds that they are not registered veterinarians, the only people entitled to file horses' teeth, according to the Texas Board of Veterinarian Medical Examiners. The Board said those wishing to be 'floaters' would have to earn their licence by taking long fee-paying courses. This is a case where licensing forces up costs and acts as a barrier to people practising work at which they have demonstrated more than adequate competence.

There are many less bizarre examples. Licensing boards have tended to raise the training required to practise. Some argue that this is not motivated by a desire to raise standards but to restrict price and quality competition and limit the number of practitioners. Thus, the Oregon Board of Cosmetology increased the number of hours of training required to practise, not because of consumer discontent but at the urging of beauty schools that obtained more customers (students) as well as higher prices for their courses (Hood, 1992). Another example concerned the rules for funeral services in some US states, where funeral directors, to obtain a licence, must be trained in body embalming even though they actually make burial caskets and do no embalming (Neily, 2005).

As for reducing informational asymmetry – the expert confronting the ill-informed consumer – critics claim that licensing results in less generation and dissemination of information for consumers, who use the existence of licensing as a shortcut and thus take less care than they otherwise would. Meanwhile, the lower incentive to search for information means a lower return for information providers, giving them less incentive to generate and distribute relevant information. So licensing can provide a false sense of security, leading consumers to make 'Type II' errors, accepting a service as good when it is not (Nelson, 1974). Additionally, usually there is no penalty for the regulator if somebody is given a licence to practise who should not have been, so careful scrutiny of applicants cannot be presumed.

Even if licensing raises the quality of the service, by raising the price some low-income consumers will be deterred from using it. The higher price may also cause more to use riskier or dangerous alternatives or turn to informal illegal services that give them no legal or insurance protection in case of mishap. So, licensing induces a mix of moral and immoral hazards.

Higher prices may also result in less incentive or pressure on the occupation to innovate or invest in research to improve the quality of service or lower its cost. Critics also claim licensing blocks people's right to work. As one put it bluntly, 'By erecting artificial and arbitrary barriers, licensing regulations prevent people from working in the job of their choosing' (Summers, 2007, p. ii).

The effects of licensing on the occupations themselves are hard to gauge, although many researchers believe the benefits for practitioners outweigh those for consumers. Some have concluded that licensing has a positive effect on the practitioners of an occupation but a negative effect on consumers (Rottenberg, 1980; Kleiner, 2006). How does licensing benefit the occupations being regulated by it?

First, it seems to raise earnings. Although some studies have not found an independent effect (for example, Pashigian, 1980, for medical occupations; White, 1983, for nursing), there is evidence that licensed occupations experience a higher growth of wages, and that this has increased inequality in the USA (Kleiner, 2006). Being in an occupation has an independent effect on relative wage growth (Eckstein and Nagypál, 2004). And licensing rules that enable one occupation to limit the work of competitors also raise earnings

(Anderson et al., 2000). So, barriers to entry may indeed boost the earnings of those in an occupation. Although the evidence is not overwhelming, some occupations such as dentistry appear to use licensing to practise price discrimination and raise prices in general (Shepard, 1978; Boulier, 1980).

Licensing creates a greater barrier to entry for some occupations than for others. Some observers claim it acts as a greater deterrent for low-skill, low-income occupations because the fixed cost of licensing is relatively high (Summers, 2007, p. 2). This is not self-evident since the cost of the licence is likely to be lower than for higher-income occupations. Lawyers have been conspicuously successful at controlling entry, and they are scarcely among the lower-paid. In the USA, their power and wealth have enabled them to use licensing as a barrier, and to weaken regulations that would lower their incomes (Howard, 1998).

Finally, licensing may deter migration, particularly where migrants would have to retake tests or exams they had passed years earlier somewhere else. There is evidence that this has been an impediment to mobility between US states. But one study found that the effect of entry restrictions for foreign graduates in the US medical occupations, significant for many years, had almost disappeared by the 1980s (Noether, 1986).

For workers in a licensed occupation, the perceived benefits may be compared with those from joining a trade union. A difference is that licensing strengthens job security more than employment security, whereas union membership has the reverse effect. Another difference is that whereas an enterprise may become de-unionized or an individual may move from a unionized to a non-unionized firm, the risk of being 'de-licensed' is less. In the USA, there have been hundreds of decertification elections in firms, removing union representation rights. But there has been scarcely any removal of licensing (Fossum, 2002). Kleiner (2006) could find only one case of an occupation being de-licensed, that of watchmakers in Minnesota, after the number of registered watchmakers dropped below the required 100.

The protection afforded by licensing may nevertheless diminish. Doctors in the USA were long protected by rules safeguarding them from malpractice or negligence suits. Patients making complaints were not allowed to bring in expert witnesses from outside the locale of the doctor, and the medical bodies made it hard for members to testify against fellow members. That rule has been overhauled, leaving doctors more exposed. Malpractice cases have escalated, and the success rate for clients has risen sharply. The nature of licensing has changed.

Another claim is that licensing blocks labour market re-entry for welfare recipients (Hazlett and Fearing, 1998). The argument is that, by limiting entry to certain occupations, licensing crowds more people into low-skilled jobs, lowering wages in them and weakening the incentive to labour. Again, this focuses on those outside the occupations in question and presumes that barriers to entry are improper. One retort is that facilitating entry to low-skilled occupations would merely drag down their wages relative to other jobs. This would widen wage inequality and could depress those wages to below the poverty level, particularly if the 'welfare' workers received a subsidy enabling them to take lower wages, as is increasingly the case. The fact that this is how welfare policy has been redesigned does not mean that it is justifiable.

Nevertheless, there are too many unresolved drawbacks to be impressed by the global spread of licensing. The biggest challenge is to ensure that the legitimate interests of all parties are identified and respected, while the drawbacks are eradicated.

Negative Licensing

Alongside licensing is negative occupational licensing, which is common in many countries. Whereas with licensing, people have to qualify to earn a right to practise, here they can be disqualified by contravening some rule or standard of competence.

Considered from a rights perspective, one should ask what behaviour could justify someone being locked out of his chosen work. One needs to consider whether there should be rules for suspension of the right to practise, or if there should be penalties short of excommunication. And then there is the awkward issue of determining who should have the right to throw someone out of their occupation.

Many regulatory bodies use disciplinary actions to control behaviour and to limit membership. The techniques include suspension of licence, for a fixed period or until such time as a condition has been met; revocation of licence; prosecution for practising without approval; denial of licence renewal until specified conditions are met; restriction or limitation of the right to practise; a requirement to participate in an investigation; requirement to provide information to the agency; requirement to undertake remedial action; public censure or reprimand; placement on probation; and payment of a fine.

In all respects, licensing has been used as a means of discrimination. The imposition of some requirement may result in excluding all or most members of a particular group, such as women or a racial minority. Historically, often there is evidence that the rules were deliberately designed to have that effect. The difficulty has been to prove it.

As the global labour market takes shape, one can confidently predict that negative licensing will gradually be revealed as very extensive and often an unwarranted barrier to occupational practice.

Accreditation

Besides licensing, there is occupational accreditation (certification). This has been less criticized by libertarians, since it does not involve a ban on the right to practise. Basically, a person may become an accredited practitioner, but others may practise as unaccredited practitioners. Customers can then decide whether the risk of opting for the 'unqualified' is worth taking. They are particularly likely to take the risk if they have limited resources, if the cost differential is large, if the increased risk is small or if the possible consequences of the risk are expected to be small.

With certification, or accreditation, the normal rule is that people can use a title only if they pass designated exams and satisfy other conditions. Certified practitioners are usually expected to belong to an association and to abide by a code of ethics and practice set by that association. Examples are certified accountants and certified management accountants, as in Canada.

Certification provides information to consumers about the training standards of practitioners. But it has been argued that it is only superior to licensing if training is a good indicator of the quality of the service, whereas under certain assumptions it may be inferior to licensing (Shapiro, 1986, pp. 855–6).

Some analysts have proposed that private certification agencies should replace licensing. But while certification may allow more choice for consumers, the problems of regulatory capture associated with forms of self-regulation could still arise. Quite simply, many decisions on service acquisition do not relate only to individual welfare, but involve forms of externality that private bodies concerned with efficiency and market transactions would not necessarily take into account.

Private certification agencies are liked by neo-liberals because they allow for competition between agencies. Some have even argued for a graduated rating system, with notions of Class A and Class B practitioners, depending on test scores (Summers, 2007, p. 35). The idea is that this would give consumers the information they need to make quality and price comparisons. But it would open up some unattractive moral hazard issues regarding quality control, especially if ratings went further by taking experience into account. Thinking along these lines provides an instrumental reason for strong freedom-of-information guarantees, so that consumers can obtain information on people's qualifications and experience. What would be wrong is if such information were to be disseminated widely or used for other purposes.

It is strange – in that proposals along these lines have come from libertarians – that the graduated rating system is designed to steer choice by enlarging the definitions of acceptable norms. It also makes a presumption that a private rating agency is more capable than a public one of determining what information and rating standards are appropriate.

MARKET REGULATION

In the initial phase of the Global Transformation, in the extension of market forces, there has been a concerted attack on the right of occupations to police themselves. Correspondingly, there has been a systematic shift to regulation by competition law.

It is a global trend. In Belgium and the Netherlands, for example, professionals have been made subject to supervision by the competition authorities (Maks and Philipsen, 2005). In Australia, since 1996 all occupations have come under the Australian Competition and Consumer Commission, and are subject to competition law, the Trade Practices Act. In the USA, a major change occurred in 1975 when the Supreme Court ruled (in *Goldfarb* v. *Virginia*) that the association fee of Virginia's legal Bar violated the federal prohibition on monopolies in restraint of trade (the Sherman Act).

Both the timing and nature of that decision were significant because it heralded a decisive shift towards making market competition the primary test in determining whether occupational protection was legitimate. Thereafter, occupations were more systematically depicted as profit-making entities subject to anti-trust scrutiny. They were not social bodies providing services to society that stood apart from market considerations. The providers were supplying commodities. The prominence given to competition principles has undermined the independence of occupations, even though many governments have chosen to leave some forms of self-regulation untouched.

New personal services tend to be regulated by voluntary codes of practice (or conduct) that leave consumers exposed to more risks. This is aptly demonstrated by the occupation of cosmetic surgery. In the UK the number of women resorting to this service has risen sharply. In 2001 there were 202 000 treatments; in 2006 there were 700 000, involving a market of £500 million. The industry is regulated by the Good Medical Practice in Cosmetic Surgery Code of Conduct, drawn up by its Independent Healthcare Advisory Services. Investigations show the code is breached with impunity (Campbell, 2007).

Characteristic of the commercial practices of many services, the voluntary rules broken included prohibitions on cut-price offers, advertising and use of legally banned substances, an agreement not to use misleading terminology and an agreement not to indulge in pressure selling.

Such cases highlight a problem with voluntary regulation – soft bark, no bite. The impression is given that standards are set to give consumers protection. But there is little desire by the industry to enforce them, largely because the code is really a means of increasing demand for the services. This self-regulation is the least defensible of all. Furthermore, the service combines opportunities for dangerous practice and a range of treatment options, some of which are expensive, decided by practitioners.

REGULATING OCCUPATIONAL OPPRESSION AND SUPPRESSION

All types of occupational regulation affect the distribution of income and welfare in some way and all are subject to what might be called 'distributional failure', raising the income of some at the expense of others, usually unjustifiably and in an inegalitarian way.

The most basic distributional failure arises from the tendency for self-regulatory bodies to take on a life of their own, such that the interests of those who administer them diverge from those of members and outsiders. The association's agents may base their pay on contributions from members, from dues and from fees for training and exams. And they may benefit from extending their status and influence through political lobbying.

While self-regulation gives some groups an opportunity to acquire rental surplus at the expense of clients and other occupations, it also gives the occupation as a collective the chance to redistribute that surplus within the occupational community, and to oppress certain groups within it and perhaps within other occupations. These tendencies mean one should be careful about accepting the claim that occupations seek to regulate their activities for the benefit of their members.

Although aggressive occupations have always featured in labour markets and shaped labour relations, economists and policymakers have ignored these features of competitiveness, which have been prominent in periods of transformation when market forces have been encouraged. Occupations, or their representatives, compete for advantage, and have used regulatory devices as well as other techniques such as promotional and negative advertising, lobbying and normative research.

The impact of licensing on occupational structures is under-researched. Although it may boost earnings and opportunities for insiders, it also gives them a means of limiting the provision of services by unlicensed persons offering similar services and those offering substitute services. We saw in Chapter 6 that they can do this by suppression, oppression (forcing another occupation to provide services on terms dictated by them) or splintering (hiving off part of the occupational community to provide lower-level tasks hitherto deemed to be part of the occupation). Oppression has been a particularly common outcome of self-regulation.

A common tactic of professions has been to commandeer the language and routines of a service, shutting out others from performing all or part of the activities. The challenge for regulation is to determine when this is contrived and what corrections can be made to reduce arbitrary and unwarranted control. There is little evidence that this has been done.

Doctors have been among the most prone to using regulatory devices to oppress other groups, dictating to the nursing profession among others. In many US states nurses are banned from prescribing medication independently and have to take formal instruction from doctors. In effect, the nurses lack control over some of the raw materials or inputs used to carry out their work. One can see a legitimate rationale for such a rule, and equally one can see how it could be abused and manipulated.

As mentioned in Chapter 6, one ruse over the years has been to use insurance to oppress lower occupational groups, and this is often done through licensing. In some cases, there can be a multi-tier pattern of occupational oppression. For instance, licensed dentists in the USA have demanded licences to prevent dental hygienists from practising without the supervision of a dentist. In turn, hygienists have sought to restrain the tasks and autonomy of dental assistants.

This pattern of oppression corresponds to the growth of 'proficians', who have autonomy and control of their work, and the 'precariat', who are at the whim of others, denied control over their work and made precarious and dependent on the success of others. In class terms, occupational oppression results in people moving from the profician stratum to the precariat. One can trace a form of structured inequality that has rarely received any attention from economists.

Occupational oppression is rarely stable for long, and there have been cases of occupational revolt. Indeed, restricting entry through licensure has tended to generate new disciplines, as was the case with osteopathy and chiropractice. Doctors lost the capacity to control nurses and auxiliary occupations as they lost their autonomy in the restructuring of the US medical scene. One should nevertheless be careful about interpreting this as a sign of nurses' liberation. A plausible interpretation is that both doctors and nurses found themselves under increasing control by a new occupational group, professional administrators. It is the junior doctors and those crowded out of the upper echelons of the doctoring fraternity who have found themselves proletarianized, with less sense of agency and loss of status and control over subordinated occupations. The oppression of nurses had turned elsewhere.

Occupational suppression is also achieved via formal and informal regulation. A classic case was the treatment in the USA in the early twentieth century of one of the world's oldest professions, namely midwifery. It was suppressed so successfully that until the 1970s midwives delivered 1 per cent of all babies in the country. Midwifery was revived only because of feminist campaigns and the escalating cost of childbirth services provided by obstetricians and hospitals (Butter and Kay, 1988). By 2000, the share of babies delivered by midwives was back to 6 per cent. This still compared poorly with the level of up to 75 per cent in Europe where infant and maternal mortality rates have been much lower (Jackson et al., 2003).

Another example was the suppression of alternative medicine. In US states where alternative medicine was restricted, conventional doctors earned much higher incomes (Anderson et al., 2000). And yet there is evidence that alternative medicine can be effective for a range of physical and psychosomatic ailments (Bivins, 2007). The legal profession has also long suppressed lower-cost alternatives. In some US states and in many countries, non-lawyers are banned from doing such routine tasks as writing wills.

As with oppression, suppression is rarely stable. Thus, in the USA it has been challenged as contrary to the Fourteenth Amendment of the Constitution. A case concerned the provision of eyeglasses by optometrists, who were judged by the boards of optometry to be in breach of a rule restricting the practice of the occupation on the premises of a commercial company (Haas-Wilson, 1992). The specifics of the case need not detain us, but the underlying issue is of general interest. The legal argument was that the rule was not only a restraint of trade but a conspiracy to monopolize, conducted by a board on which each member had a financial interest by virtue of being in an occupation benefiting from denial of the right to practise on commercial premises.

OCCUPATIONAL MARGINALIZATION

The regulatory system may also accentuate some forms of social and labour market marginalization. Licensing is a legal way of excluding some workers from entering or remaining in spheres of work that they might wish to do. Thus, migrants may not have their qualifications recognized, or may have difficulty in producing the required proof. They may also not understand the procedures or have the communication skills required to navigate their way into an occupational community.

People with criminal records are another group marginalized by occupational barriers. They may be refused a licence to enter a specific occupation, and thus face a barrier to labour market entry that deters them from working or pushes them into precarious jobs. A result of such barriers to good occupations is that certain groups are crowded into a market for low-level jobs, which drives down the wages and incomes in those activities, which may lead to behavioural reactions that further marginalize those workers. Those qualified for higher-paying occupations, forced into jobs with low income and status, are entitled to feel frustrated. They may offer a low effort bargain or resist taking these jobs, perhaps in fear that they may be forced to continue doing such labour while losing the skills of the higher occupation.

An aspect of modern services is that more groups can and do establish themselves as occupations and then set up their own regulatory body. In many respects, this is to be welcomed; more workers are covered by occupational bodies and more are in small groups that make state regulation harder. However, the smaller and more specialized the group, the greater the scope for rent seeking (Olson, 1965). And part of that is achieved by excluding people on contrived criteria.

Other ways in which some are marginalized by the occupational regulation system are probably more pervasive. All raise questions about the denial of a 'right to practise'. For instance, people can be shut out of occupations by excessive training requirements. In Vancouver, Canada, women wishing to be waitresses must attend lengthy training courses, while one US state requires completion of a two-year course before being allowed to practise as a wigmaker. Then there is the marginalization associated with being in oppressed or suppressed occupations. Members of these often largely female occupations, such as nursing auxiliaries, midwives and sex service workers, invariably face restricted opportunities.

The mechanisms for restricting the right to practise are often discriminatory in that certain groups are more likely to fail them than others. The recency-of-practice test is a mechanism that discriminates against women who withdraw from the labour force to have children, as well as ex-prisoners, migrants and the long-term unemployed. And rules limiting the right to practise of those with qualifications acquired elsewhere discriminate against migrants.

Workers can be marginalized by being relegated to helper status or by being allowed to practise only under the supervision of delegated superiors or by being forbidden to have control over raw materials, means of production or final services. These little rules may have enormous implications for those ensnared by them. Finally, some groups may be marginalized within occupational associations, and be denied Voice rights. This is particularly likely if supposedly democratic practices result in a tyranny of the majority, in which a majority sets rules that suit the majority but effectively discriminate against minorities.

In sum, the regulatory apparatus provides ample scope for structuring the labour force in frankly inegalitarian and socially unjustifiable ways.

GLOBALIZATION OF OCCUPATIONAL REGULATION

While the struggle over regulations has intensified in market societies, an even bigger development has been the gradual emergence of an international regulatory regime. As part of globalization, countries are under increasing pressure to have similar policies on domestic occupational regulation. There is pressure to converge around a specific regulatory structure. This may come to be steered through the rule setting in the WTO's General Agreement on Trade in Services (GATS). But the GATS may turn out to be just one mechanism for developing regulatory frameworks, while more specific regulations will be translated into binding form through the growing number of Mutual Recognition Agreements (MRAs) between groups of countries.

At national level, libertarians have lamented that 'it is becoming harder and harder to work freely without having to traverse burdensome government regulations' (Summers, 2007, p. 4). The irony is not just that these regulations are pushing towards market-conforming practices but that the international trend is towards regulation in favour of competition to comply with the perceived rules of market forces and standardizing procedures. Regulatory instruments are being judged primarily by whether they interfere with competition and the market. For instance, the UK's Office of Fair Trading recommended that the Competition Act of 1998 should be extended to cover all professions; it advocated a case-by-case approach to determine whether specific practices contravened competition principles to the extent that the cost to consumers exceeded the benefit to them, whether they were indispensable to overcome some market failure, or whether they did not eliminate competition excessively (Office of Fair Trading, 2001, p. 31, para. 94). This recommendation accorded with EU competition law and reflected the powerful trend towards legalization of labour market relations.

An aspect of the Global Transformation is the growing pressure to synchronize occupational regulations. However, even within some countries there is no synchronization, as in federal states such as Australia, Canada and the USA. The observed consequences in those countries can be considered predictive of what will happen at the international level.

The difficulty in securing convergence starts with agreeing on what is included in a specific occupation. One peculiarity of occupational regulation is that occupational boundaries are rarely predetermined or permanent. As a result, national or subnational rules for particular occupations have varied sharply. For instance, in some countries accountants are licensed to provide tax advice and management consultancy; in others these activities are reserved for separate professions. In some countries engineers are allowed to provide design services; in others they are banned from doing so, that being the preserve of architects. Just as the reasons for such differences are largely historical and cultural, so it is likely that institutional factors have played a large part in shaping the extent and nature of state systems of regulation. But the emerging global labour system is likely to reduce both national and occupational differences.

The problem starts within countries, where forging coherent national systems is incomplete. In Australia, for instance, licensing and MRAs curtail the right to practise. The Commonwealth (federal) government does not have constitutional power to regulate occupations, which is the responsibility of state governments. They have drawn up MRAs with each other. Two issues have dominated policy debates. Some states do not have similar or comprehensive MRAs with each other. And some classify occupations in ways that are quite different from how they are classified in others. Builders in Tasmania do not need a licence in order to work there. But they do need a licence if they want to work in Victoria just over the water. As of 2007, an osteopath in New South Wales could not practise as a chiropractor in Victoria. But an osteopath in Queensland *could* practise as a chiropractor in Victoria. So an osteopath in New South Wales should move to Queensland before applying to practise as a chiropractor in Victoria. This is due to the MRAs, and to the fact that in Queensland the two occupations are treated as one while elsewhere they are separate (Council of Australian Governments, 2005).

As a result of the liberalization and globalization of services, inter-country MRAs are spreading and becoming regional or multi-country in character. An early version was the North American Free Trade Agreement (NAFTA) between Canada, Mexico and the USA, which includes an annex to the chapter on trade in services setting out procedures for standard setting and recommendations for professional bodies. Another path-breaking MRA was the one on nursing signed by ten Asian countries in 2006.

A difficulty with assessing MRAs is that there are several types. The popular image is an agreement reached by two or more governments. But many are negotiated directly by professional associations with little or no government involvement. They include several MRAs for architects via the International Union of Architects and the Commonwealth Association of Architects, MRAs for engineers via the Washington Accord of nine professional bodies and the European Federation of National Engineering Associations, and MRAs for nurses via the International Council of Nurses. Only where the bodies have legal status in their own countries, usually with delegated legal authority at state or national level, can the resultant MRA have legal authority. But this model seems destined to spread across more occupations and more countries.

Bilateral agreements between self-regulating professions do not create binding commitments for governments in the WTO, but do create the basis for more formal MRAs. For example, in 2006 the US and Indian law associations launched a working group to explore ways of 'deregulating' (really, harmonizing) and in 2007 Britain's Law Society and the Society of Indian Law Firms reached a deal on cooperation. Foreign lawyers have been virtually banned from India since the late 1990s, when a court ruled that they could neither appear in court nor offer legal services. So the new agreement was regarded as a significant development by the major law firms, which are all based in London (Peel, 2007). A few months later, the Indian government circulated a 'discussion paper' on liberalizing legal services, with a view to giving permission for consulting services in corporate and international law, although not for practising domestic law in Indian courts. The primary motive was clear. The paper gave an estimate of the global market in legal services of about US$20 billion annually, and argued that Indian lawyers could capitalize on the growth in legal service business.

The debate on opening up India's legal sector to foreign firms encapsulates many of the problems ahead. The profession there has opposed liberalization allowing entry of foreign firms for fear this would cut their share of what are hugely profitable activities. Speaking in October 2007, the President of the Delhi High Court Bar Association, said:

> Abroad law is a business, not a profession and lawyers are allowed to have websites. Before you open up the legal profession, there is need to introduce advance-level legal courses in the country. We have enough talent in the country to beat anyone in the world. We just need safeguards and training. If their lawyers are allowed in, it may raise some jobs hopes, but on the whole it will lead to exploitation of our legal services. (Quoted in *Financial Express*, 2007)

In fact, by 2007 thousands of Indian lawyers were working for foreign law firms, supplying services via outsourced means to foreign markets. The Indian lawyers wanted to continue to exclude foreign lawyers from Indian courts and restrict them to advisory services, but Indian law schools took a more welcoming approach, seeing foreign firms as potential recruiters of their graduates and as a means of raising legal standards. Indeed, one prominent lawyer pointed out that junior lawyers and interns would benefit, since they had long been forced to work for very little in Indian firms. It seems unlikely that the profession will hold out indefinitely against the liberalization trend.

Meanwhile, MRAs are covering single occupations and groups of occupations. Thus, there are bilateral agreements between the USA and Chile, and between the USA and Singapore, under which the governments have committed themselves to encourage their respective occupational bodies to develop mutually acceptable standards and licensing criteria. There is an agreement between Australia and New Zealand, ANZCERTA (Australia-New Zealand Closer Economic Relations Trade Agreement), by which professionals, with the exception of medical practitioners, can practise their occupation in both countries. An agreement between Australia and Singapore, SAFTA (Singapore-Australia Free Trade Agreement), eased residence requirements for professionals wishing to practise in the other country, and the two countries launched negotiations on mutual recognition.

Regional bodies, led by the EU, are moving in the same direction. CARICOM (the Caribbean Community) has progressively allowed mobility for professionals, giving precedence to those with university degrees. The Andean Community has facilitated movement of professionals between member countries, focusing on intra-corporate transfers. ASEAN (Association of South-East Asian Nations) has instituted a dual-track liberalization scheme, in which some countries have moved at a faster pace than the others, with the long-term objective of a free flow of 'skilled labour and talents'.

What comes across from all these initiatives is that mobility is being facilitated more for relatively privileged occupations, with their higher incomes, education and social status. This is a form of inequality. Another possible source of inequality linked to the spread of MRAs is that some countries and some occupations are being left out. Negotiating MRAs properly depends on the existence of a fairly sophisticated regulatory framework, without which comparisons and standard setting become very hard.

Alongside right-to-practise MRAs, there is a parallel trend towards mutual recognition of professional qualifications, allowing those qualifying in one country to be recognized in the other. Thus, MERCOSUR (Southern Cone Common Market) moved to have mutual recognition of degrees and curricula in its member countries, with an initial list of baseline Quality MERCOSUR Standards for agronomy, engineering and medicine. This was followed by the MERCOSUR Experimental Mechanism for Career Accreditation (MEXA) for recognition of accredited curricula in the selected professions. It is expected that the model will be extended to other occupations in a gradual liberalization process.

The convergence of regulations is hindered by weak capacity to regulate in many countries. Since a global labour market is being forged around notions of flexibility and mobility, one can expect regulatory convergence or at least efforts to achieve that. For those pushing for a global market, reform must reduce differences between national and regional regulatory frameworks. But in many developing countries self-regulating bodies simply do not exist. For instance, in 2006 only 21 of 53 African countries had professional bodies belonging to the International Federation of Accountants. In many cases, the professional association that does exist is voluntary, without regulatory powers, as in the case of medical services in Kenya (Ikiara, 2000). Kenya did, however, have a mandatory body for the legal profession, while the Architectural Association and the Institution of Engineers (IEK) had comprehensive delegated powers.

In many developing countries, tension between what are perceived to be public and private interests led to reduced tolerance for self-regulation. A result has been a growth of statutory regulation by supposedly independent bodies. Often, the country lacks the professionalism to be able to operate adequate procedures.

In terms of the Global Transformation, developments in the WTO's GATS will be crucial. In progress since 1995, the GATS negotiations have focused almost exclusively on top-earning professional services, notably accountancy, followed by legal services and architectural services. Thus far, with the exception of accountancy, the negotiations have been protracted and inconclusive. Even in the case of accountancy, prominent representatives of the profession have expressed disappointment with the nature of the international agreement that was reached.

The purpose is to liberalize trade in professional services by moving towards a mix of international standards and common regulatory frameworks at national level. Much has been made of the four modes of trade in services, a suggestion being that different regulations are needed for each mode – cross-border trade, consumption abroad, commercial presence and movement of natural persons. The exhortation has been that domestic regulations should be 'no more burdensome than necessary' to ensure service quality, that licensing should be restricted to requirements that are 'relevant' to the provision of the service and are not in themselves a restriction on supply of the service, and that the regulations are 'objective and transparent'.

All of these requirements have been considered in a context of deciding what is acceptable as 'national policy' to justify overriding or limiting their applicability. The preamble to the GATS states that WTO members can regulate services within their countries 'to meet national policy objectives'. But all the principles in the GATS have proved controversial. For example, if licensing fees are to be restricted to the cost of administering the scheme, a government would be prevented from using dedicated revenues to offset social costs that might be incurred as a result of the licensed activity (for example, habitat restoration needed as a result of tourism). Another example is where a government sets a standard of education for qualification above what is strictly necessary to do the work, but does so as a way of establishing credentials for entry.

Issues that have exercised WTO negotiators include the ability to establish and practise in another member's jurisdiction, limitations on the business form of the practice, restrictions on the use of company names, limitations on the temporary entry of professionals, licensure restrictions that 'unreasonably restrict the right to assist a client', restrictions on international payments and limitations on the use of foreign capital.

The negotiations have been conducted within the WTO's Working Party on Domestic Regulation (WPDR), which in 1999 took over from the disbanded Working Party on Professional Services. Unfortunately, the GATS does not provide a definition of 'domestic regulation' and definitional problems have persisted. The WPDR seems to have in mind all forms of state intervention involving targeted authoritative rules, usually involving a regulatory body or agency. So the GATS process appears to be aiming for movement towards a universal regulatory framework for each occupation.

From the professions' side, there has been talk about the 'three freedoms' – the right to establish, the right to associate in a form of their own choosing and the right to practise. The legal profession has given high priority to these freedoms. It has argued for less restrictive citizenship requirements to obtain a licence to practise as a lawyer, fewer restrictions on establishing partnerships with local lawyers, and removal of restrictions on hiring or working for local lawyers.

An issue that has assumed high priority is the freedom to practise one country's law while residing in another country, primarily on a consultancy basis. With the internet, one presumes this will become a spur to the globalization of occupational practice. Sixteen US states have adopted a foreign legal consulting policy. However, this is not an issue only for the legal profession, and would be relevant to accountancy, auditing, other financial services and medical services.

Many civil society groups have depicted the GATS provisions on domestic regulation as a threat to democratic decision-making. Article VI.4 calls on WTO members to have regulations that 'do not constitute unnecessary barriers to trade' and, under WTO rules, once a country has signed up it is subject to scrutiny by WTO panels if challenged. The notion of necessity has been interpreted by the main negotiators as necessary 'to ensure the quality of the services'. But others have insisted on stretching it to include consumer protection, professional competence, professional integrity and social objectives. Controversy has persisted.

The implied objectives are to reduce the regulatory authority of all levels of government, and to limit the range of legitimate objectives of regulation to ensuring quality of a service to consumers. It would give no weight to objectives conveyed by the sense of occupational community. The objective is to make the market work better and to open up a service sector to equal participation by citizens of WTO member countries.

There is some way to go. There are many areas where different regulations prevail in individual occupations. This was brought out in the GATS negotiations on accountancy. The survey by the International Federation of Accountants (IFAC) found there were hardly any areas that had similar regulations in all countries. In 40 per cent of countries, accountants were not allowed to practise combinations of services for the same client; in the majority, they were allowed to do so.[3] In some countries accountants were allowed to work with other licensed professions, but in 79 per cent they were restricted from doing so, often in the specific case of working with lawyers. There were also many ways by which auditors were required to be independent – with variable measures on rotation of firms, rotation of engagement partners, fixed terms for auditors, scope-of-practice restrictions and limitations on fees from any one client (Heeter, 1995, p. 7).

As the accountants' case has demonstrated, reaching global agreement on regulatory principles is complicated by virtue of the range of issues covered by domestic regulations and the different levels of requirement such as level of education and extent of experience. This is why US and other negotiators have placed primary emphasis on achieving transparency. Any idea of harmonization is a long way off.

WTO members have made proposals on many aspects of professional services, including removal of market access limitations such as ceilings on numbers of service providers, foreign equity limits and legal entity requirements; standardizing registration requirements and local training requirements; and standardizing prior professional employment requirements and descriptions of 'economic needs tests'. There has also been debate on whether to have a commitment of 'prior comment', by which WTO members planning a regulatory reform would notify others, solicit comments from them and take these into account in finalizing the reform. This is a prospect that has alarmed small low-income countries, which fear that foreign firms and governments might exert pressure on domestic legislators.

The plethora of issues highlights how difficult it will be to reach consensus. Yet there has been progress on aspects of the process, which has moved away from an approach designed to cover all services for all countries towards looking at issues on a case-by-case basis. The Guidelines on the Accountancy Sector set a model; they are voluntary and non-binding, aimed at facilitating negotiations of MRAs on procedures and substance of regulations. They could steer countries that do not have the capacity to develop or apply their own regulatory framework to adopt regulations from abroad.

While the GATS has been a struggle, the EU has moved ahead. The European Parliament voted in 2005 to establish common minimum professional standards, with EU-wide cards indicating a person's career qualifications and work experience. The main instrument to emerge was the Services Directive, designed to promote free movement of service providers within the European internal market.

Although the French and German governments opposed the original directive in 2005, focusing on the 'country-of-origin' principle, which allows those licensed in their home country to practise that work in another member country, the Services Directive was agreed in 2006, coming into full effect in December 2009.[4] It should be seen in combination with the Directive on the recognition of professional qualifications that came into effect in October 2007, guaranteeing mutual recognition of qualifications, and setting rules for harmonization of training requirements, notably in the health sector, and recognition of professional experience.

The Services Directive is far from inclusive in terms of what services are covered.

Excluded under Article 2 are financial services, electronic communications, transport, temporary employment agencies, healthcare, audiovisual services, gambling, private security services, notary and bailiff work, taxation and social services relating to social housing, childcare and family support for those in need.

In the negotiations, the Commission made one major concession to its critics, by inserting a clause stating that countries could continue their own rules on employment conditions and industrial relations, as long as they were 'non-discriminatory, necessary and proportionate'. Had that concession not been granted, the directive would not have been passed. Trade unions across Europe were alarmed by the prospect of more social dumping, with foreign firms bringing lower-level working conditions into their labour markets. Under the final directive, member states could impose their labour laws on foreign providers. But the European Court of Justice was to interpret the directive as opening up markets to a greater degree than promised. The ECJ was to be a Trojan horse.

The Services Directive also stipulates a wide range of information that service providers must supply to recipients. This is a move to reduce the information asymmetry problem, though it does not remove it altogether. It includes the need to provide information on activities that would involve a conflict of interest and information on the available means of dispute settlement (Article 22 (3c)). The directive also states that member states should set up codes of conduct for occupations covered by it, drawn up by professional bodies at Community level (Article 37). The codes are expected to specify rules for commercial communication and rules of ethics and conduct, setting minimum EU-wide standards.

In effect, the EU has set the pace in creating an international market-conforming regulatory system. Bilateral and regional trade agreements can be expected to continue to move in the same direction. Gradually a global labour market is being constructed.

THE IMPASSE

Occupational regulation is in turmoil. Under globalization, regulatory changes have increased labour recommodification, although both state regulation and self-regulation have been used to defend the interests of some strategic professions. Gradually, at all levels, the ability of occupations to resist commodification has been worn down. In the process, there was no attempt to find a balance. The immediate needs of consumers and commerce triumphed over the perceived needs of occupational groups. A painful lesson of the financial debacle of 2008 was that self-regulation had not been strong enough in financial occupations, allowing rogue profiteers to practise in their short-term market interests. It was not just the absence of state regulation that was to blame for their recklessness; it was the absence of an ethical self-regulation by people inside their community who could understand what they were doing and the dangers inherent in it.

Historically, the professions have used self-regulation to shield themselves from market forces, decommodifying themselves while seeking to commodify oppressed occupations. With labour market flexibility and the global shift to services, more occupations have tried to use licensing and self-regulation to protect themselves. But regulatory reforms are recommodifying more of them. Licensing and state regulations have increased their exposure to market forces.

The scene is an unresolved tension between the state and occupations. The state is depicting self-regulation as the source of market distortions. But in doing so, old claims in favour of collective self-regulation have not been refuted. For instance, professional bodies establish practices intended to increase the sense of trust, between themselves and clients, and between professionals. Trust is valuable for all concerned, and results in a subtle, continuing negotiation, ill-served by either competition anti-trust law or labour law. Members of occupations are not protected by labour law in their dealings with each other, and members may be prohibited from collective action on the grounds that they would be avoiding competition between themselves.

Among other outcomes of self-regulation and licensing is that, as occupations have been commodified, many workers have been pushed into the precariat by regulatory mechanisms. Members of the precariat are shut out of an occupation or become marginal members of it. Being marginalized reflects a lack of belonging to an occupational community and to any viable community providing solidarity and civic friendship.

Meanwhile, the more privileged professions, with their members mostly in the salariat and among the proficians, help to proletarianize a mass of lower occupations, subjecting them to market regulation. Even the most prestigious occupations are becoming subject to commodification – academics, teachers, doctors, nurses and even lawyers. While some occupations have resisted, they have lost a great deal of strength, even if some remain bastions of privilege and a mechanism of inequality. There has been a lessening of civic friendship inside occupations and a loss of the craft ethic, derived from shifting from a self-regulating system to an external, market-driven one.

There is also a trend towards legalization, involving tighter contractualization of occupational practices. Service and employment contracts are becoming more detailed, and case law to adjudicate on the propriety of practices is being built up to limit the range of what is acceptable. This too raises unresolved questions about the respective capacity of people to negotiate or enforce such occupational contracts.

At international level, the pressure to produce common standards and to harmonize occupational rules, notably for licensing and mutual recognition, may give advantages to occupational groups in rich countries. Suppose a licensing board sets a standard of entry for an occupation as 12 years of schooling. This could be no more than a convenient screening device or credentialist recruitment practice. For a developing country, that would be hard to apply and be little more than an aspirational qualification.

The trend to standardization and harmonization of international 'disciplines' (rules) fostered by the WTO will benefit market leaders, and thus be inegalitarian, at least initially. For example, US architects have been eager to draft disciplines on domestic regulation of architectural services. For them, the standards likely to emerge are relatively low, by comparison with those normal in a rich country. Already, there is a global standard recognized by more than 90 countries, drawn up by the International Union of Architects, known as the UIA Accord on Recommended International Standards of Professionalism in Architectural Practice. It will be a boon for US architects.

National and international regulatory reforms are strengthening market behaviour, increasing competition and eroding the capacity of occupational communities to self-regulate in the interest of their own practitioners. The trend has been from regulation *for* occupations to the regulation *of* occupations, from a primary concern for national practitioners and quality of services to a primary concern for cost control and competitive markets. At international level, painfully and slowly, there is a trend towards regulatory convergence, fostered by MRAs, bilateral and regional trade agreements and the EU Services Directive. The GATS may be central, but actually the lead is being taken at bilateral and regional level rather than at global level.

The global trend is for more people in more occupations to be subjected to occupational regulations. And a growing number of working people are being regulated by internationally-agreed standards and frameworks. What is distinctive about the general trends is that members of more occupations are being required to conform to market principles.

NOTES

1. They estimated the expected rate of return to the education required and attributed the difference between that and the actual return to regulatory practices. Subsequent studies, correcting for hours worked, have shown the early estimates were exaggerated. One by Leffler also questioned the return by taking account of progressive tax and an increase in mortality among doctors (Lindsay, 1973; Leffler, 1978).
2. A similar problem arises with trade liberalization. Those losing from trade form powerful lobbies for protection, but because consumers individually gain little there is no countervailing lobby for liberalization.
3. Ironically, Arthur Anderson, which was responsible for the IFAC survey, spectacularly fell foul of errors associated with just this awkward practice, and ultimately went bankrupt.
4. Article 4 of the final Services Directive defines 'service' as 'any self-employed economic activity provided for remuneration, as referred to in Article 50 of the Treaty'. In the text preceding the directive in the EU's *Official Journal* (European Union, 2006), paragraph 87 on 'false self-employed persons' reminds readers that 'the essential characteristic of an employment relationship within the meaning of Article 39 of the Treaty should be the fact that for a certain period of time a person provides services for and under the direction of another person in return for which he receives remuneration. Any activity which a person performs outside a relationship of subordination must be classified as an activity pursued in a self-employed capacity for the purposes of Articles 43 and 49 of the Treaty'.

8.   The horror

The dark forces rise like a flood.
> (Sir Michael Tippett, from the alto solo in the oratorio *A Child of Our Time*, 1939–41)

INTRODUCTION

Globalization has created a global market society. The disembeddedness is complete, the economy is out of sync with society. So, we must ask what strains could prompt an effective double movement. Polanyi saw what prompted it last time, in identifying the effects of robbing people of 'the protective covering of cultural institutions', leaving them as 'victims of acute social dislocation' (GT, p. 76). That could not go on.

The period of recommodification has not been a great time for the advance of human freedom and equality. Ecologically, it is terrifying. Culturally, it is unedifying, characterized by a philistine tendency that is creating a modern version of a 'bread-and-circuses' existence for the masses. Educationally, it is marked by an intellectual 'dumbing down'. In terms of work, it is marked by labour intensification, job-related stress, loss of control over labour time and dissatisfaction with jobholding.

The statistical evidence of the malaise tumbles at us like a cascade. Increased wealth is not associated with more 'happiness', nor with more economic security. Drawing on the most detailed international data set ever constructed, the ILO's Socio-Economic Security Programme found that conventional measures of national happiness are inversely related to inequality and positively related to economic security (ILO, 2004, ch. 11). In the 1950s over half British adults said they were very happy; in 2007 only one-third did, although national income had tripled in the interval (Ben-Shahar, 2007). In the USA, even before the financial turmoil of 2007–08, the incidence of depression was ten times higher than in the 1960s, and the average age at the onset of depression was 14.5 years compared with 29.5 in the 1960s.

Even the rich have retreated to 'gated communities', spending vast amounts on protecting themselves as they try to enjoy their smugly protected (albeit dented) fortunes. Millions of people are reduced to a quasi-nomadic existence, moving around without roots or even the prospect of a final destination. 'Illegal' migration means their numbers are greater than shown by official statistics. Inequalities multiply, even though disguised by conventional statistics that ignore the several dimensions of social income.

Spokespersons for this post-modern nirvana proclaim the virtues of meritocracy, claiming that those who become rich do so because of their superior merit; those who are poor are there because they lack merit. Inequality is not bad per se, because the wealthy generate the wealth for the 'nation' to share, while the poor must learn to be more merit-worthy. The state will help the deserving poor, by assisting them to be more 'employable' and 'socially integrated'.

Neo-liberals flaunt the virtues of self-interest, individualism and the market's alleged ability to reward merit. A person's merit is measured by their capacity defined in terms of human capital. Given this rhetoric, it is well to recall Polanyi's claim that the 'true criticism of market society' is that its economy is 'based on self-interest' (GT, p. 257). Drawing on anthropological research, Polanyi surmised that man 'does not act so as to safeguard his individual interest in the possession of material goods; he acts so as to safeguard his social standing, his social claims, his social assets. He values material goods only in so far as they serve this end' (GT, p. 48). He was not idealizing human motivation. He merely thought that in an appropriate framework, motivation for social goals would curb pecuniary ambitions and the urges that markets unfurl.

The neo-liberal agenda has been to displace any such motivation and to make social status dependent on the possession of material goods and on consumption. Some years ago social scientists announced the end of 'Fordism'. It would be more accurate to think of globalization of the Fordist model. Shopping malls loom larger. This era requires the masses to consume tirelessly. 'I shop, therefore I am' could be the motto of those rushing to be commodified. They need more money to conform to this undignified life. Some critics have depicted it as unrestrained consumerist debauchery and castigated the excesses. Thus, Barber (2007) argued that modern capitalism produces vices that strengthen consumerism and undermine democracy and civic involvement. Democracy thrives on deliberation, on leisure. But you cannot allocate time for deliberation if it is all taken up in making and spending money. 'Sorry, no time!' has become an eerily common aphorism of the age.

The relentless pressure of market freedom leads to what has been called 'unbounded rationality', in which the consumer has too many options from which to choose. We as consumers overspend on gadgets we may not understand, let alone want or intend to use. Think of those complex cameras and the capacities of one's computer or in-car electronics. People also develop, or try to develop, too many 'skills'. We labour and work harder than necessary, often just in case it might yield a return later or as a form of insurance (Ariely, 2008). We need checks on individualistic behaviour to give ourselves more rational control. This is what occupational communities could do, even though they could also exacerbate the problem if wrongly conceived. They could be the means of rationally binding our range of rational choices. But as we saw in Chapter 6, those building the neo-liberal state have rushed to dismantle such communities.

A dominant theme in late globalization was what George W. Bush trumpeted as 'the empowerment of the individual' through 'the ownership society', with 'people taking responsibility for their own needs'. This ideology sells well. But a person cannot take responsibility without security and access to resources. In a market society, those who out-compete others gain, and their advantages multiply; winner-takes-all leads to losers-lose-all. Once-moderate inequalities become chasms of disadvantage. One horror is that, to counter chronic inequalities and mass marginalization, the establishment waxes lyrical over the need to combat social exclusion. No EU, OECD or UN report is complete unless devotion to this is pledged. No politician misses an opportunity to express their concern. The message is that the poor have become dysfunctional and socially weak. The state must reintegrate them. There were comparable cries in the nineteenth century. The modern variant is more subtle, perhaps. Put them into jobs, and if they do not appreciate their good fortune, oblige them to take the jobs we choose for them, or take away their benefits as punishment for their ingratitude.

The avowed concern over exclusion helps to rationalize coercion and mass therapy.

Besides using social policy to make people malleable jobholders – including 'house calls' to see they are doing the right thing – the UK government has instructed subsidized cultural institutions such as museums and art galleries to boost social inclusion. As noted by Frank Furedi (2004), this forms part of an agenda of 'dumbing down' what people are offered, while making them feel 'successful'.

An outcome of commodification is that, as Habermas (1984, p. 356) put it, 'privatized hopes for self-actualization and self-determination' are located in 'the roles of consumer and client', which leads to civic privatism. This makes people apolitical, shown by how the media empty the space for critical evaluation. There is no news vacuum, but rather a shock-and-horror sentimentality that deprives individuals and groups of the capacity to act. Subversive leisure is crowded out. Habermas argued that people were prevented from gaining competencies needed to generate communicative power. These can arise and be sustained only in communities that provide barriers to market forces. In a market society, they are torn down, as we saw in Chapters 5 and 6. Modern civil society organizations may reflect a rebellion against civic privatism, but it is moot whether they are real barriers to commodification. They seem, so far, to be safety valves, salving the conscience of activists while helping to check the worst excesses of profit seeking and economic greed. We must hope for more, but not presume it.

Civic disengagement, reflected in loss of popular energy opposed to commodifying trends, has gone with loss of control over *time*. The market society wants a mass culture of intensified time use. The pores of the day must be closed, by multi-tasking, taking work to home and home to work, relearning while labouring, consuming with frenzy, multiplying the number of goods we possess so that we use each less and less.[1] The anxiety of the long-distance consumer, never having enough, is a learned disability of modern-day teenagers. It can be permanent.

Meanwhile the citizen as worker should be uncomfortable. Reflect on the 'unhappiness' of commodities. Being bought and sold, they must impress their charms on potential purchasers. This is alienation. To be a good commodity, a worker must be competitive, to the extent of reducing or disparaging the competitiveness of others. This behaviour sets up existential stress, which may result in a frenzy of activity but engenders passivity as a social citizen. Ironically, workers treated as commodities, being insecure, have been shown to be less productive than those who are not.

In a chillingly brilliant set of essays, Jack Hirschleifer (2001) depicts the pure market economy as akin to anarchy. Neo-liberalism would, if its central claim were taken literally, be a prescription for legalized anarchy, circumscribed only by contract and criminal law. A pure market economy is inefficient and corrosive of ecological assets and civil assets, such as trust and altruism, because it permits several forms of anarchic competition, notably what biologists such as Wilson (1975) have called scramble competition (as with fish in the sea that move about without seeking territorial dominance) and interference (resource defence) competition. Globalization has given fresh licence to both. Multinationals are literally given a licence to kill, in that they receive generous subsidies to exhaust the resources they scramble to obtain. But it does not stop there. In an anarchic world, competitors divide their resources, including their time, between 'productive' and 'fighting' effort. Competition is partly destructive. Without countervailing mechanisms, it will become largely so. In a large enterprise, human behaviour may become almost entirely devoted to fighting effort.

Another horror is that We do not see Ourselves in other people. There is a breakdown in reciprocity that is the essence of civilization. The rich do not expect to become poor, and most on low incomes do not expect to become rich, unless they win the lottery. This weakens social solidarity and reciprocity. So, calls for the restoration of social insurance, founded on assumptions of solidarity and reciprocity, are unrealistic. They are also wrong, since more people are subject to systemic risk (affecting whole groups, not just unlucky individuals), rather than idiosyncratic contingency risk of the sort social insurance was intended to remedy.

The social protection system in a market society, being unconcerned with egalitarian social solidarity, is prey to moralistic capture. Paternalism and its new improved version, 'libertarian paternalism', has crept up alongside religious zeal. We live in a moralistic era, when people are told they must behave in certain ways for their own good and for the good of their 'community'. While preaching freedom and democracy, those designing social and economic policy use a moralistic tone. The 'religification' accompanying the moralizing produces sanctimonious babbling. The moralizing verges on social engineering. It is designed to make us marketable workers and wise consumers, consuming to excess but only those goods and services regarded as sensible.

As market forces intensify inequalities and insecurities, the state turns to more constraints on freedom. Cries of 'order' predominate over those of 'liberty'. In one form, they result in 'ending welfare as we know it', 'workfare' and behaviour-conditional state benefits. In a more malign form, they include suspension of habeas corpus, imprisonment without trial, Anti-Social Behaviour Orders (ASBOs) and 'homeland security' measures, all chipping away at hard-won freedoms.

An aspect of intensification yet to attract policy angst is the social cost. If people are treated as commodities, they will behave as such. In adopting an instrumental ethic of 'jobholding', they become passive, opportunistic and less productive than they could be, if they wished. In response, employers rely on contrived incentives and coercion, with standards, targets and auditing. These are costly. And as administrative, monitoring and auditing costs rise, so do the costs associated with anxiety and stress, for workers and their families, for firms and governments.

If people are expected to be flexible and mobile, they tend to lose any sense of identity. The horror of mass recommodification can be appreciated by reflecting on Polanyi's recall of Robert Owen's description of the early nineteenth century: 'For the most obvious effect of the new institutional system was the destruction of the traditional character of settled populations and their transmutation into a new type of people, migratory, nomadic, lacking in self-respect and discipline – crude, callous beings of whom both capital and labour were an example' (GT, p. 134). Well, 1817 does not seem so far away when one reads that.

THE NEMESIS OF FINANCE

> Unregulated competition will self-destruct.
>
> (Etzioni, 1988, p. 256)

However, it was 1929 that came to most people's minds in 2008. Globalization as we had known it ended in 2008. It did so with the implosion of Wall Street and the disappearance or effacement of financial institutions that had epitomized globalization, such as Merrill

Lynch and Lehman Brothers. Perhaps it was the end of Wall Street when the remaining investment banks were converted into deposit banks, bringing them under capital account regulations. It was a bit late; the horses had bolted, with billions in their saddles. Wells Fargo picked up some of the debris.

The neo-liberal model was founded on economic and financial market liberalization. Backed by a system of tax cuts, low interest rates, easy access credit and high rates of return to financial investment, it was a recipe for high levels of inequality and consumer spending. Add stagnant real wages due to globalization and the outcome was bound to be a financial elite losing touch with material reality and a citizenry mired in debt without the means or hope of paying it off. Three points of horror relate to the proposals in the following two chapters.

Systemic Indebtedness

The first is systemic indebtedness, which is not accidental. Debt is a disciplinary component of the neo-liberal model. Those in debt might grumble about their feelings of insecurity and about the inequality that before globalization would have led to street riots. But they did not protest too vociferously. Debt and exposure to risks were enough to rationalize docility and induce a drift into self-exploitative hard labour.

Ordinary citizens were plunged into unprecedented debt. In the USA, median family income stagnated, but the debt-to-income ratio rose from 0.45 in 1983 to 1.19 in 2008. Americans splurged on housing; whereas in the 1970s they paid about twice their family income for their home, by 2005 they were paying five times. This was 'ownership without equity'. Middle-class homeowners in 2007–08 were tapping into their retirement funds to maintain mortgage payments. Those with 401(k) or defined contribution plans were allowed to withdraw even more funds. Homeowner stress fed into old-age income insecurity. Britons as well as Americans were encouraged to live beyond their means. In early 2008, according to the Money Advice Trust, a debt charity, the average person had only enough money to survive for 52 days if the earned income was lost; a third would be out of money in 14 days. Financial anxiety was rife even before the markets collapsed.

Of course, debt as a way of living has behavioural and attitudinal consequences. It deprives citizens of a sense of economic security that is conducive to altruism, social solidarity and capability development. Debt makes people self-centred and conformist, avoiding developmental or occupational risk taking for fear of the consequences of a slight setback. Debt is a social controller.

The outstanding question is: why was the financial system allowed to play on the citizen's weakness of will and not apply prudential market principles?

Asymmetrical Injustice

While debt created fearful behaviour, the nemesis of financial markets exposed the systemic functional injustice underpinning globalization. This too was no accidental feature. The neo-liberal state had rationalized underwriting the risk to capital while its supporters preached to the rest of us the virtues of a risk-taking society.

When the financial markets crashed, threatening a contagion effect on the global economy, it was ironic that a billionaire financier, who had enriched himself as chief executive of Goldman Sachs, was left to clear up the mess as US Treasury Secretary.

Hank Paulson promptly pleaded to Congress for a US$700 billion dollar handout to his old fraternity, whose profligate behaviour over the previous decade had been the cause of the debacle. The CEO of Merrill Lynch, which had to be rescued by a takeover, was the top-paid executive in the USA in 2007, pocketing over US$80 million. The CEO of bankrupt Lehman Brothers had earned US$480 million since taking over the firm in 2000. These were not blemishes on the system; they were the system.

Neo-liberals had preached that success should be rewarded, that the hand of the state should stay out of markets, and that citizens should not be cushioned by 'generous' income transfers because that induced 'dependency', 'sloth' and 'market distortions'. Yet here the highest earners were the biggest failures and the state stepped into the market in a big way with a largely unconditional bailout of the financial system. Henceforth, 'deregulationists' could only be called charlatans.

The practice of underwriting risks to capital but not to others extends to government insurance. In bilateral and regional trade agreements, multinationals are given protection against changes in government regulations or policies that affect their investment. Corporations can challenge government measures in court, or go to the arbitration facility set up by the World Bank. Governments that may have subsidized or facilitated an investment do not have an equivalent right if the multinational subsequently decides to pull out. One could argue for equal protection or that neither should be protected, but an asymmetrical model is hard to defend. The asymmetry operates domestically as well; workers are not insured against changes in policies affecting them.

The most relevant question is: if high finance and the financial elite were given income security, why should Jo and Jane not be given it?

Inequality's Inequalities

Market-induced inequality has adverse societal effects that make policies that promote and celebrate inequality indefensible. To many, this hardly amounts to a revelation. But each time there is a disembedded phase of a transformation, the lesson has had to be relearned, while on each occasion inequality has taken new forms.

The fact is that income inequality feeds through into other forms of inequality. For instance, life expectancy has been declining in those parts of the USA where incomes have stagnated, but while overall health has deteriorated the inequality of mortality has increased. In 1980 the rich lived 2.8 years longer than the poor; by 2008 they were living 4.5 years longer (Caldwell, 2008b). Another indicator is that as income inequality grows so does the difference in height between rich and poor. In spite of rapid economic growth in 'Chindia', growing inequality there seems to have increased gender inequality in stature; the rise in height of Indian men is three times that of Indian women.

Inequality makes people unhealthy in more subtle ways. Lower-income groups suffer from the stress of disrespect and lack of self esteem (Wilkinson, 2005). Low status, reflecting relative deprivation, and lack of control over one's life are destroyers of health and happiness.

Modern inequality, in a context of new class structures, a decline in upward social and economic mobility and loss of institutional anchors, has been associated with a rise in stress. In 2006 a British Medical Association study found that mental disorders had increased among children aged 5 to 16; one in ten suffered from severe malfunctioning and more than 1 million required specialist services. Although partly due to poor diet, mental health problems were linked to greater pressure in school and loss of family cohesion, even though incomes had risen. Monbiot (2006) described this as the 'Willy Loman syndrome' after Arthur Miller's character in *Death of a Salesman*, who is afflicted by a gulf between expectations (promise of fame and fortune) and reality. In the USA, UK and elsewhere, upward social mobility has been low and declining since the 1970s. But public belief in economic mobility has grown, fed by the media, advertising and 'celebrity' culture. A system driven by dissatisfaction with what we have and what we are is bound to produce mental dysfunction and anxiety.

Inequality feeds through social income inequality into greater insecurity, the costs of which are higher for lower-income groups, particularly those living a precariat existence. Those on lower incomes face a bigger threat from shocks and hazards, and have more difficulty in coping and in recovering from them. With respect to the conventional contingency risks covered by old-style social security, they are more likely to become unemployed, fall ill or have accidents. But now they are less likely to be able to meet the costs associated with those mishaps and less likely to be able to recover from them or the consequences.

Similarly, lower-income groups are more likely to suffer from socioeconomic shocks hitting whole communities or regions. These may take the form of 'natural' disasters such as floods, drought or epidemics, or economic shocks such as the 2008 surge in food prices. When they are hit the costs are likely to represent a far higher proportion of their income or wealth than would be the case for the more affluent. And, of course, globalization and global warming have brought about a greatly increased incidence of such shocks.

Relative costs will also be higher for those on lower incomes confronting hazards – lifetime events or crises, whether desired (a wedding or birth of a child) or unwanted (a death in the family). Sometimes the obligatory costs may be just enough to tip them into a spiral of impoverishment. And they will face more uncertainty, making it harder to plan and use time productively.

In addition, lower-income groups are disproportionately affected by two other forms of risk that have grown under globalization. Occupational risk (the risk of skill and occupational obsolescence, mentioned in Chapter 6) will be relatively high and may even act as a barrier to entering or staying in an occupation. The same applies to company risk; with an increased probability that the employing company will dissolve or downsize, it becomes risky for a worker to make a commitment to a particular firm.

Thus, while most people have been affected by an overall increase in economic insecurity, and a shift from contingency risk to systemic risks, shocks and uncertainty, those on lower incomes have experienced a worse deterioration.

The question is: how can progressives justify their failure to offer a way of redistributing income in the globalization period? They certainly did not do so.

THE PANOPTICON OF LABOURISM

One cannot appreciate the nature and depth of the challenge of the Global Transformation without appreciating its roots in utilitarianism and a piece of the neo-liberal model that dare not speak its name.

The ghost in the background of the Hayekian counter-revolution, who has also influenced the libertarian paternalists who have emerged in reaction to it, was Jeremy Bentham, an eighteenth-century social reformer with legal, architectural and philosophical skills and pretensions. He came to embody a form of paternalism dressed up in utilitarianism, dedicated to the promotion of the greatest happiness of the greatest number. Bentham designed and patented a prison building called the 'panopticon', which he initially sketched in 1787 and promoted over many years.

The panopticon, from the Greek 'all-seeing', consisted of a large circular watchtower surrounded by a peripheral ring of cells from which one window faced outwards and one faced the tower. A guard in the central watchtower could observe all the prisoners in their cells, without them knowing whether they were being watched, creating a 'sentiment of an invisible omniscience'. Under pressure to labour, prisoners will want to escape or reduce effort. The inspector in the watchtower seeks to minimize shirking by seeing without being seen, making the inspected believe they are being watched at the same time as they are exercising 'free' choice. This belief gives the sense of omnipresence.

Not content with seeing his creation as a model prison, Bentham saw it as suitable for factories, workhouses, hospitals, asylums and schools. Describing the 'inspection house' as 'a new mode of obtaining power of mind over mind' and a way of 'punishing the incorrigible, guarding the insane, reforming the vicious, confining the suspected, employing the idle, maintaining the helpless, curing the sick, instructing the willing in any branch of industry, or training the rising race in the path of education', he modestly claimed it would achieve a remarkable amount: 'Morals reformed – health preserved – industry invigorated – instruction diffused – public burthens lightened – Economy seated, as it were, upon a rock – the Gordian knot of the poor law not cut, but untied – all by a simple idea in Architecture' (Bentham [1787] 1995).

Bentham's panopticon famously inspired Michel Foucault's concept of 'biopolitics'. But it is also linked to Hayek's atomistic market society and modern paternalists. For neo-liberals, following Bentham, government means a 'ministry of police' more than a 'ministry of welfare'. Like Bentham, they have faith in a mechanism, the market, but they back that up with a willingness to coerce people in the interest of building and maintaining the market society. Hayek (1944, p. 27) was quite open about that; his disciples could not pretend otherwise. Thus, most of 'the Chicago boys' backed Pinochet and advised him after his bloody coup.

Hayek saw the market as coordinating individual plans, so that tacit knowledge resulted in coordination. For him, the market was beyond ethics. His vision of free choice within a constructed market society was not far from the panopticon, because Bentham too put prisoners in a position where they felt they were exercising choice for which they could reap a reward. However, if a prisoner did not make the right choice, to work, he would languish on 'bad bread and drink his water, without a soul to speak to'.

For both Bentham and Hayek, the coordinating power is invisible, for one the watchtower and inspector-guard, for the other the diffused power of money and the market. Beneath the construction of choice is also a confinement. Physical barriers prevent escape in the case of the panopticon, which also isolates the inspected from each other so as to prevent them from having a 'concert among minds' (Bentham [1787] 1995, p. 32). For Hayek, property rights restrain social mobility and the market acts as a coordinating mechanism of private actions so that individuals do not realize the constraints under which they make choices.

Hayek and his disciples, including Milton Friedman, espoused a constructivist strategy for creating a market utopia, even though Hayek spoke huffily of Bentham's utilitarianism as 'constructivism'. They had more in common than he wished to acknowledge. Hayek was explicit in stating that the triumph of the market required coercion and state intervention. Bentham's utilitarianism was not about rights but the creation of happiness for the greatest number, while the minority was not so much to be ignored as made abject and miserable. Bentham saw a need to harness technology, architecture and surveillance to control the unhappy minority and to discourage others from deviance. This streak, sometimes linked to religious self-righteousness and 'market Leninism' (a belief in the inevitability of markets), has come through into the twenty-first century.

Every transformation has involved storms in which the state has been brought in to clear up the mess through paternalistic authoritarianism. The losers from that transformation must be cajoled, watched and socially reintegrated, made like the rest of us living in 'the community'. For neo-liberals the community is an abstract notion, without collective institutions of solidarity and mutual dependency. They want to tear down such institutions, just as they have done with professional bodies in the latest round of globalization and just as they did earlier with the trade unions.

The main followers of Hayek were Friedman, Arnold Harberger and, at a distance, Jeffrey Sachs, whose 'shock therapy' for countries in Latin America and Eastern Europe wilfully depicted social institutions as obstacles to economic success. Sachs failed to see the need for social institutions to be established as a precondition for economic growth and security. A pure market system, without institutions and rules, leads inevitably to kleptocracy and societal stress, as the Russian experience has shown. There is no excuse for mock horror at its occurrence.

What links Bentham, Hayek, Friedman and Sachs is a crude Darwinism, based on the belief that competition results in the survival of the fittest, those able to adjust to 'natural' laws of supply and demand. The unfit must be given the chance to become fit or be taken out of society in case they infect the remainder or act to cause the majority discomfort, whether by acts of retribution or by civil disobedience that discourages foreign investment and international 'confidence' in the economy. Free market societies have not hesitated to imprison and stigmatize their discontented. Bentham would have approved. He would have approved of the paternalistic pacification even more.

For Bentham's panopticon leads to the libertarian paternalism of *Nudge*, a book produced by two advisers to Barack Obama's presidential campaign and hugely influential in political circles in 2008 (Thaler and Sunstein, 2008). They refer to building an 'architecture of choice', recalling Bentham's architecture, except that they give no inkling of knowing it. They want to make people make better choices while not feeling their choices are being constrained. Recognizing the power of inertia and fear of the unknown, they advocate policies that require people to make opt-out rather than opt-in decisions. For instance, because it takes a conscious decision to choose to invest in a pension scheme, they would alter the rules to ensure that everyone is automatically enrolled in such schemes unless they opt out, which involves an administrative process. This is manipulation. The practices are not equivalent, since the opt-out rule imposes costs in terms of time and stress on the individual. In the same paternalistic vein, it has been proposed that couples should be required to have a mandatory pre-marriage waiting period, to help them avoid rushing into something they may regret. Where would they stop?

In the early twentieth century, industrial citizenship advanced on the back of tighter controls in labour relations, with 'scientific management', Fordism and mechanisms to enforce respect for the clock and calendar. The shift from manufacturing and the fixed workplace and working space made those wanting disciplined labour and efficient consumers search for techniques of surveillance, monitoring and evaluation. They have been aided by developments in information technology that have allowed a strengthening of the surveillance society, rationalized by reference to the need to respond to competitive pressure from elsewhere. There are more than echoes of Bentham's panopticon in what is happening in the city of Shenzhen, where an opening of Chinese society to easier external gaze has revealed the extent of its sinister social and labour experiment.

Shenzhen, China's first 'special economic zone', has grown rapidly to over 12 million inhabitants and become the world's largest supplier of manufactured goods. It is the closest the world has yet come to a 'social factory'. Over 200 000 surveillance cameras have been installed across the city and by 2011 there will be 2 million, which compares with half a million in London, a worrying trendsetter itself. The cameras are part of a hi-tech surveillance and censorship system in Shenzhen known as the Golden Shield Project designed to create a zone of behavioural control. This is not just a creature of the Chinese Communist Party; much of the technology used in people tracking has been supplied by US multinationals such as General Electric, Honeywell and IBM. As Naomi Klein caustically put it: 'Remember how we've always been told that free markets and free people go hand in hand? That was a lie. It turns out that the most efficient delivery system for capitalism is actually a communist-style police state, fortressed with American "homeland security" technologies' (Klein, 2008, p. 6).

One can anticipate that 'Shenzhenism' will be replicated and evolve into a more sophisticated version of Bentham's panopticon society. Indeed, factories in Shenzhen are making surveillance cameras for export all over the world. One spinoff is the Chinese project known as SafeCities, which requires all internet cafés, restaurants and other 'entertainment' venues to have video cameras with feeds to local police stations. Mobile phone conversations and e-mails are monitored, and when Golden Shield is complete, a database will exist on every person in China. Facial recognition software is being refined, purchased from a US defence contractor that produces passports and biometric security systems for the US government.

What is happening in China is not far removed from what is happening almost everywhere. Drawing on Foucault's conception of power/knowledge in his *Discipline and Punish* (1977), some have argued that surveillance mechanisms are used in just-in-time (JIT) and total-quality-management (TQM) production systems to improve on factory regimes by instilling discipline and enhancing control (Sewell and Wilkinson, 1992). While responsibility for labour is delegated, strategic control is centralized. The JIT/TQM approach is aided by two disciplinary forces. The first derives from scrutiny of one's peers in a manufacturing cell or quality circle, a process supported by the organizational structure. The second derives from the use of management information systems that provide shop-floor surveillance, a controlling mechanism. The surveillance system is designed so that labour discipline is established efficiently and minute control is possible with a minimal number of supervisors. The desired effect of harnessing these dual forces is to minimize negative divergence from expected behaviour and management-defined norms while identifying positive divergence and maximizing creative potential.

The growth of electronic surveillance in the workplace is a reflection of recommodification. There is erosion of the right to privacy (Simitis, 1987a). Some neo-liberal law-and-economics theorists even question the right to privacy (Posner, 1978). Privacy-destroying technologies have grown (Froomkin, 2000). 'Dataveillance' is the latest phase, with carefully collected data creating the capacity for profiling and monitoring. Employers make more systemic use of references, automated decision-taking and CV scanning, aptitude and psychometric tests, automated performance monitoring, health records and practices including HIV/AIDS information, alcohol and drugs testing, genetic testing, criminal records, fraud monitoring, e-mail interception, 'intelligent' CCTV surveillance and international data transfers (Wedderburn, 2002, pp. 38–9). Italian and German laws forbid certain surveillance techniques in the workplace, but surveillance is spreading. It introduces a spectre of statistical discrimination that makes conventional forms look outdated.

In workplaces traditional disciplinary techniques may be allied with surveillance of the most intrusive kind. In 2007 Walmart, the biggest private employer in the USA, set up a team drawn from former officials of the Central Intelligence Agency, Federal Bureau of Investigation and other policing agencies to monitor the behaviour of its 1.8 million employees. The company claimed this was to enforce ethical practices but such monitoring can be used as a discretionary tool of control and sanction, and even to fabricate evidence or to cajole employees to testify against or report on their colleagues. A female Walmart advertising executive, fired for allegedly fraternizing with a male subordinate, said the use of anonymous witnesses and selected e-mails amounted to 'Big Brother tactics' (McWilliams, 2007).

The panopticon society does not rely just on surveillance via cameras in the workplace and 'dataveillance'. It is creating more sophisticated behavioural control mechanisms and new occupations and therapies to put them into effect. The boundary between the workplace and home is being blurred, while legal changes are eroding the sphere of legalized privacy (Gladstone, 2006). As that happens, the scope for monitoring and controlling behaviour is extended. Cognitive behavioural therapy is on the march.

However, monitoring and control are done mainly by tightening discipline. In 2008, the British government introduced one monitoring and control scheme that makes parody superfluous. Promptly nicknamed the 'nappy curriculum', all 25 000 state and private nursery schools, child minders and playgroups in England were to be compelled to assess the progress of children in their charge from the age of two according to 69 'early learning goals' set out in a monitoring programme called EYFS (Early Years Foundation Stage). Each primary school teacher, already subject to Ofsted (Office for Standards in Education) inspections, would have to comply with a standard routine sketched in a 150-page manual and produce an EYFS profile every few months, with achievements recorded on 13 assessment scales, each containing nine points. All this information will not only be used to monitor the teacher but will be fed into a new children's database, ContactPoint. Although opting out is possible, as befits the choice architects, the procedure for doing so has been made extremely cumbersome and time consuming.

Governments are also steadily extending their surveillance of the precariat. In 2007 the new neo-liberal Swedish government created a fraud squad, the Delegation Against Benefit Fraud and Errors, to chase fraudulent claimants, and made it easier to prosecute benefit fraud. The Confederation of Swedish Enterprises claimed that up to 95 per cent of Swedes had abused the welfare system. The government said it intended to cut benefit payments and use the savings to lower taxes, including company taxes. Apparently, one fraud arises when people who cohabit claim they live alone. A predictable result of the fraud drive will be that fewer people will live together. Other problems will emerge. For instance, Swedish parents may claim about 80 per cent of salary if they have to stay at home to look after a sick child. The fraud squad welcomed anonymous tip-offs of cheating on this. The surveillance state was being strengthened.

In most countries, 'dataveillance' is advancing unchecked. Sophisticated data banks are being assembled, without any citizenship oversight. And behavioural obligations are being extended. In June 2008 the UK's Home Secretary announced plans to identify children as young as five *at risk* of becoming criminals, the idea being to oblige parents to sign legally binding contracts to control their children. Earlier, the government had launched what it called the Transformational Government project, which will merge all official databases into one giant surveillance system. France has moved in the same direction.

Such refinements to the surveillance society have been accompanied by the conversion of fiscal policy to fiscal paternalism, or so-called soft paternalism. The trouble is that once the rationale for steering people's choices is accepted by policymakers and corporations, a utilitarian rationalization for moving to harder forms of surveillance, discipline and punishment is not difficult. This is what has happened with 'workfare' and the officially-sanctioned snooping on potential 'welfare cheats', which only succeeds in turning citizens into stigmatized types. The next stage is criminalization, which lowers the person's life-time capability potential.

Above all, paternalism and panopticon techniques are part of a strategy for 'dealing with' the precariat and those worse off in the social stratification, who are deemed incapable of making rational and socially desirable decisions. They are treated as problems, an awkward minority prone to 'antisocial behaviour'. Ironically, social democrats have led the way in pushing soft paternalism, even though it penalizes the vulnerable more than others. Social democrats have failed to show empathy with the precariat, which is not an underclass but a growing body of people without a sense of career or occupational lifestyle.

The utilitarians have reacted as moralistic majoritarians. The liberty and the rights of the precariat and the detached can be ignored via a democratic rationalization. Thus, Tony Blair revealed himself as a true utilitarian when he wrote in *The Observer* newspaper in 2006:

> I don't destroy liberties, I protect them . . . I believe in live and let live, except where your behaviour harms the freedom of others. A society with rules but without prejudices is how I might sum it up. But the rules are becoming harder to enforce. Antisocial behaviour isn't susceptible to normal court process. Modern organised crime is really ugly, with groups, often from overseas, frequently prepared to use horrific violence . . . If we fail to tackle antisocial behaviour because the court system is inadequate, other people's liberties suffer.

Punishing people before finding them guilty by due process is the closest one can get to 'prejudice'. In a few sentences, he had equated unruly behaviour of the precariat with organized violence carried out by aliens, and rationalized extra-legal methods of tackling the deviants in the name of the majority, for their happiness. Bentham's vote would have been in the post, along with Hayek's. But Blair was only being honest. He was giving vent to a paternalism that regards law as just one of a range of tools for steering behaviour.

COMMODIFYING THE MIND: THE FETISH OF HAPPINESS

The utilitarian paternalists have been helped by the fact that the neo-liberal model turns everything into a commodity and goes one stage further by inventing things to be commodified including a strange 'good', happiness itself. According to the new hedonists, to be happy is having what you want. This can be identified as possession of a set of commodities. Social scientists can then identify the levers that have to be switched to increase societal happiness and to maximize the number of people who feel happy. We have not yet reached the stage where all the levers are identified, but social scientists are working on them. Predictably, a new school of social science has taken shape. There is a veritable industry consisting of well-funded research programmes, publications, self-help manuals, prizes, celebrities, celebrity shows, agony aunts dispensing worldly advice and lifestyle coaches selling their wares and services so that people can become happier.

The fetish of happiness has been extended through a market in unreality. If citizens do not like their situation, if it does not make them happy, there is no need to confront the causes; they can buy a substitute unreality. Electronic simulation can be purchased to ease the pain and fill a void. The market threatens people's sense of reality by spreading virtual reality, not only through TV shows that are sad spectacles of humanity, but through isolating virtual worlds such as 'Second Life', which in 2007 had more than nine million members creating online 'avatars', or alternative selves. These second identities live lives manipulated by their creators, but their lives are shaped online by companies that participate in order to sell products and lifestyles. A result could only be loss of a sense of responsibility and the self-discipline that develops through making real mistakes with real consequences, for the individual and whatever real community the person inhabits. The avatars and their kind are part of the modern opium of the masses. There is a feverish alienation, a gap between what is manufactured online and reality (Caldwell, 2007). The online world also creates a scene for subtle advertising, with everybody subject to repetitions of the same messages. Happiness and unreality go together, sold in standard packages. Just do it, because you're worth it!

Of course, the unreality and contrived happiness merely intensify the urgency for real communities to give structure in reality to the development of human capabilities and civic friendship. As we shall see, some of the ingredients for that are taking shape, but the commodification of happiness has yet to be challenged.

We discuss later how time is being commodified. Loss of control over time is matched by loss of control over quality space. The commons, public space, is shrinking, partly because it is being turned into property rather than being an integral part of all forms of community. While the private space of the home is being invaded by the dictates of production and consumption, it is the wider ecological space that is most at risk; once lost or eroded, restoring it will be enormously difficult.

Even privacy is not immune from market penetration. It is not just that techniques for invading and eroding privacy are evolving. Ominously, neo-liberals and libertarians are questioning the very right to privacy and the citizenry, lured by market enticements, is contributing to the erosion. Privacy used to be a precious right covering many aspects of living and working, matters of intimacy. But it is a 'good'. All goods can be commodified in a market society, and privacy is no exception. Privacy is defined by reference to societal norms. If norms change, the right to privacy changes too. This is how legal cases have been interpreted. So, if something that was traditionally private becomes more generally public, the right to privacy is modified.[2] Privacy has been commodified because people can make profit from selling and buying it. Thus, people sell stories of their intimate experiences or those of others. If you sleep with a celebrity, you sleep with a future commodity, 'the story'. Once someone has sold theirs, others enter the market, until a supply comes onto TV reality shows, at which point the sphere ceases to have any claim to being one of privacy. If virtually nothing is private, panopticon powers can be extended into private lives, with the implicit threat that what is revealed will be used to exercise power over the person.

The one remaining defence might be that what goes on in the home is protected. But that is no longer true. If privacy is being commodified, it ceases to be a right anywhere. Surveillance and 'dataveillance' are rationalized legally in the workplace. But if people are expected to take their jobs into their home, how can privacy be defended? An alarming development was a US legal ruling in 2001 that use of a thermal imaging device to identify drug taking in someone's home was only a violation of the right to privacy because the defendant had no expectation such a surveillance technique might be used. It follows that if the technique became common it would not be considered a violation of privacy.

Another development is the commodification of feelings of insecurity. Surely, that is stretching the framework. Well, consider it. Every decision we take and every role we seek to play in life exposes us to some risk. That creates a need for a product, broadly described as insurance. A market society tends to commodify all lifetime risks. So, increasingly, people demand compensation for personal injuries. One critic has called this a 'culture of gratuitous compensation' (Harkins, 2007). We want money, the market reward, for outcomes that we have not, in our minds, deserved. This applies to victims of reputational damage, rape, false detention as a crime suspect and many other issues, as well as to class actions for ecological damage and claims against employers for numerous failings. This way of thinking accords with the market ethos – convert all aspects of life into something that can be valued by money. But valuing everything in monetary terms accentuates 'commodity fetishism'. Activities that cannot be measured in monetary terms become valueless. Work that is not labour or not related to labour, such as leisure as we have defined it, is regarded as a luxury that we cannot afford.

The final sphere of commodification is the wounded mind, or the mind that is made wounded by the utilitarian nature of market society in which minorities suffer from being different from the majority or from uninsured risks or adverse outcomes of a risky lifestyle. Commodification has extended inwards. Citizens are encouraged to see themselves as imperfect and fortunate to have access to tools for achieving something closer to perfectibility. A standardized ideal is depicted, and imperfections are assessed by deviance from it. In a global market society, citizens with money can buy goods and services that will move them towards physical perfection. A little flesh on here, a little flesh off there, that tooth moved, and so on. It is not just the physical self that is being commodified. Our personalities and minds are also zones of commercialization. A life coach can be acquired to teach people to handle everything from shyness to ambition, at a price. And the soul can be made perfect, through paying for religious services. For most, there is no excuse for imperfection. Moreover, the media and advertising indicate what counts as perfection. The adjunct to the global market is cognitive behavioural therapy. This modern form of panopticon 'science' basically says that a disorder is defined by visible or behavioural symptoms. The symptoms are what must be controlled.

THE EPIDEMIC OF STRESS

The defining malaise of the global market society is encapsulated in the word *stress*. Constant competition and pursuit of efficiency are stressful enough, but if one adds the greater inequality and economic insecurity there are grounds for a societal crisis.

Stress comes from inequality across the spectrum. If you are doing better than others, you worry about losing the edge; if you have been doing worse even though you are still above average, you worry about your ability to keep up; if you are doing average, you worry about both continuing and falling below average; if you are doing below average, you just worry. By contrast with modern inequality, a society of moderate differences that institutions are expected to reduce sets up fewer stress costs.

Stress is linked to labour intensification. In opinion polls in the European Union, 41 per cent of employees claimed their jobs were too stressful, and 48 per cent said they were being required to make a bigger effort (Gallie, 2002; Burchell, 2006). In the UK, 70 per cent of organizations – 86 per cent in the public sector – reported that workplace stress is rife (Cave, 2008). In 2007 10 million days were lost to stress-related health problems at a cost of £26 billion. Wealth, it appears, is part of the problem, since the higher the income the more likely a person was to report being stressed (Goodin et al., 2008). Perhaps this partly reflected the high opportunity cost of time, making the affluent feel they could not afford leisure!

However, the main factors behind the epidemic of stress appear to be the bewildering range of choices people have, a perceived lack of control over time and a sense of meaninglessness and powerlessness in jobs. The Whitehall Study, conducted among British civil servants since 1967, has shown a strong correlation between feelings of powerlessness and stress, with those regulated by others more likely to die of heart attack or stroke (Marmot et al., 1991).

Studies have shown that even managers feel their employment lacks personal meaning. As a result many withdraw psychologically, to the point of permanently looking to change or talking of changing their jobs (Holbeche and Springett, 2004). Disenchantment is linked to internal competition between employees, a lack of personal loyalty and a decline in autonomy linked to the 'target' culture that has supplanted individual conscientiousness.

Part of the growth of job-related stress reflects a tendency of control systems to eat into other aspects of life. In 2000 Aon Corporation, a holding company of insurance firms, found that only 9 per cent of UK employees felt their employers adequately recognized the need for work–life balance and 54 per cent said they felt 'burnt out'. A majority did not feel committed to their firms and wished to change jobs if they could.

Stress-related absenteeism from jobs has been rising in the UK. The trouble is that stress is subjective and hard to define. *The Economist* (2004) dismissed long hours as the cause of the rise, on the grounds that recorded working hours had fallen since the nineteenth century. That is scarcely convincing, since intensity of labour could have increased and more people could have been induced to work more hours outside the workplace. Indeed, the President of the London Chamber of Commerce and Industry was quoted as saying that 'stress and sickness have undoubtedly increased as the internet and mobile phones have quickened the pace of life in the workplace'.

The Economist cited a Dr George Beard as identifying neurotic disorders in the 1870s caused, he felt, by the pressures of advanced civilization and a speed up of life due to the railways, telephone and the press. Because it had been said before, *The Economist* dismissed that hypothesis. That too is unconvincing. The 1870s was a period when the drive for a market society was creating stress and insecurity; not only were new psychological illnesses being identified but new adjustment occupations were emerging.

The Economist's preferred explanation was that people are now more prepared to say they are stressed. Certainly, in the UK the number reporting job-related stress had increased sharply to over 400 000 per year. Philip Hodson of the British Association for Counselling and Psychotherapy said this was due to people having a greater expectation of entitlement to happiness, lowering their threshold to worry. Predictably, *The Economist* deduced that firms should spend more money and time in making employees happy.

Stress may be a threat to recommodification due to the human toll and rising cost. In Japan there has been a sharp growth of *karoshi* – death from over-labour. In Europe health insurers are worried about 'presenteeism', workers refusing to take time off to recuperate from minor illnesses due to fear of losing income or their job. By not staying at home to recover, their illness or weakened condition can degenerate into something worse. In the USA, healthcare costs for prime age adults aged 30–50 rose by more than 75 per cent between 1987 and 2000, even faster than for the elderly. The main causes were depression, angioplasty for heart patients and chronic disease and disability. Diabetes increased by 70 per cent among those in their 30s, and by 40 per cent among those in their 40s. Hypertension and musculoskeletal injuries have risen sharply among the young and middle-aged.

A concept recently thrown into public debate is 'extreme jobs', concocted by the delightfully named Hidden Brain Drain Task Force of the US Center for Work-Life Policy (Hewlett et al., 2007). It defined an extreme job as arising if a person worked more than 60 hours a week and met at least five of ten job characteristics, including doing fast-paced work under tight deadlines, having direct responsibility for profit and loss, being obliged to undertake a lot of travel, having an unpredictable flow of labour and being involved in work-related events outside working hours.

According to the Task Force, about 20 per cent of the top 6 per cent of earners in the USA met the definition of extreme worker. They were seen as working at an unsustainable level, bringing stress and a high risk of 'burnout'. Some 62 per cent of high-income earners worked more than 50 hours a week in their job, 35 per cent more than 60 hours and 10 per cent more than 80 hours, which did not include time spent in commuting to and from their main workplace (Hewlett and Luce, 2006). Two-thirds of those doing extreme jobs reported that it was undermining or had undermined their health, nearly half admitted that it disrupted their relationship with their partner or spouse, and 58 per cent said it weakened their relationship with their children.

Stress and instrumentality lead not just to lower productivity and creativity, but to a messy atmosphere of sabotage and what Polanyi called 'boondoggling', labour slacking. Modern state paternalists know they have a problem in eliciting an optimum supply of emotional labour and knowledge labour, which are easy to withhold. This leads to concern about how to motivate. But while the modern therapist may be called upon to devise ways of motivating that wonderfully post-modernist creature, the 'knowledge worker', the sabotage that takes place in the mind is hard to detect or punish.

Fret not. Therapeutic techniques are evolving to teach service workers how to provide appropriate emotions and deportment. The ability to manipulate emotions has been increased by the corrosion of communities such as the family and professions. Their weakness allows intermediary controllers of labour to construct workplaces with 'feeling rules' and 'emotion-displaying rules'. What 'human resource managers' want is for workers to internalize emotional soundness and to acquiesce in behaviour that is functional, if false. The commercialization of emotion is a sphere of struggle yet to be articulated in a way that could induce opposition to its power.

The Japanese 'salaryman' epitomizes the stressful aspect of the salariat, with *karoshi* and burnout the result of overzealous labour. Deaths from over-labour have prompted a rising number of legal cases in a revolt against the 'salaryman' model (Fackler, 2008). Lawsuits filed against employers rose by 45 per cent between 1997 and 2005 and jumped by 21 per cent in 2006 following the establishment of an arbitration court, a reflection of the relentless pressure to extract more labour in the face of stiffer competition from China and South Korea. The loyalty of 'company man' has cracked. Many of the legal cases have involved challenges to the practice of 'service overtime', the obligation to labour long hours and do unpaid overtime to demonstrate loyalty.

If professionals lose control of their work, and firms and the state gain control, or if the commercial mentality subsumes the professional or craft ethic, consumers of their services and citizens in general lose. The problem of asymmetrical information becomes more threatening, because the profit motive means the seller of a service will try to take advantage of the consumer's ignorance, especially if the purchase of the service is rare. Neo-liberal critics of regulation neglect this unmeasurable value of the professional ethic.

The existence of unlimited options leads to irrational behaviour, because people try to keep options open. They create more uncertainty for themselves, and for those with whom they deal. Individuals need constrained freedom of choice, constrained not by coercion or paternalistic pressure, but by an institutional structure in which they are informed of the range of sensible options. A well-functioning family, a neighbourhood community or an occupational community could all play that role.

One form of stress is associated with self-exploitation. It has been shown that, if a person has numerous options from which to choose, the normal reaction is to try to keep as many of them open as possible. But the desire to maintain options leads to prevarication and stress. Closing an option is experienced as a loss, and people are prepared to pay a price for avoiding the emotion of loss (Ariely, 2008). This can feed into working on too many activities for fear of missing out. It can also result in an endless process of seeking more information so as to make better judgments. The internet search engines are always running.

TIME IN DISARRAY

A mind too active is no mind at all.

('Infirmity', Roethke, 1996)

We need to think afresh about time. The global market society is snatching time and has turned it into a scarce resource. The 24-hour-7-days-a-week labour schedule, or 24/7, has been spreading. Even in 1999 Eurostat data indicated that across the EU more than 18 million people sometimes worked on Sundays, and 12 million usually did; that is, about a third of the workforce were working on what used to be the official day of rest. About 40 per cent said they sometimes or usually worked in the evening. Images of the working day and regulated working time are outdated.

Nevertheless, the clock and calendar are still there. As E.P. Thompson (1967) showed in a wonderful historical essay, the clock was a key to the development of industrial capitalism, the disciplining agent of a proletariat. As capitalism advanced, so did employers' capacity to use time to extract more labour. This induced a struggle, by employees, social democrats, trades unions and labour parties, to obtain more 'free time' and the 'eight-hour day'. That battle largely won, the next phase became more subtle. It could be portrayed as an attempt by employers to convert workers' free time into unpaid labour time and consumption time, so as to intensify the perceived need to labour.

Several analyses have railed against the loss of control over time. One called the dual-earner household an experiment in controlled chaos (Gini, 2000), although it might more accurately be called uncontrolled and stressful. The demands of labour are inducing a pathological compulsive disorder. Working life is project driven; there is more pressure in a flexible labour system to 'get ahead', be identified as a 'fast track careerist', out-perform colleagues and be a dedicated company employee, even if with only tenuous employment security. The symptoms are well known, although they may affect those in the salariat differently from those in the core or the precariat.

Some observers of this time frenzy, including Gini, believe in the thesis that jobs are disappearing. They are not. But labour is invasive, crowding out the work we might wish to do if we had control over time. Freedom is having that control, so that we can choose how to allocate it in the few decades we each have to do so.

Reversing an historical trend, recommodification involves more labour time. In the USA hours of labour have risen, holidays have been restricted and more people are reluctant or unable to take even those they have. According a global study by Expedia, the online travel agency, Americans have been taking fewer and shorter holidays. They have an average holiday entitlement of 16 days a year, and take only 14; one-third of those with entitlement to paid holiday do not take it all. Although Western Europeans have longer holiday entitlements – a month is still regarded as normal, with Italians taking 42 days, the French 37, Germans 35 and the British 28 – pressures to take less have been mounting. There is resistance, but protections are being whittled away, so that the Good Worker learns to forgo his or her 'rights' so as to ingratiate or to out-compete those who do take them. About one-quarter of employees in the UK do not take all their entitlement. Europeans are intensifying labour to match their global counterparts.

Some 137 countries have mandatory paid vacation, but the USA is the only industrialized country without it, according to Take Back Your Time, an NGO that studies overwork. One-quarter of all private sector employees in the USA do not receive any paid vacation. This is the fate of the precariat in particular; many have to give up jobs if they wish to take a holiday or use intervals between jobs, or do without it altogether. This is a form of inequality that goes unmeasured, but which is important in assessing lifestyle and well-being.

According to Expedia's survey, the number of Americans reporting that they intended to take a vacation in 2008 was the lowest since 1978, and there had been a downward trend for years. Holidays have several useful functions, including the replenishment of energies for work and help to recover distance from labour and give a broader social perspective. They also help to strengthen family and community relationships and to restore personal health. Shrinking vacations have been accompanied by a rise in ill-health (Tugend, 2008). A tracer survey of women over a period of 20 years, the Framingham Heart Study, found that those who rarely took holidays (once every six years or less) were eight times more likely to develop coronary heart disease or have a heart attack than those who had taken at least two vacations a year. A study of 12 000 men deemed to have high risk of coronary heart disease found that, over a period of nine years, those who did not take annual vacations had a 21 per cent higher risk of death from all causes and a 32 per cent higher risk of dying of a heart attack than those who did. Other research has shown that vacations induce more relaxation and better sleep afterwards, which help people work more efficiently and creatively. Reaction speed is improved by having a holiday, which gives what specialists have dubbed 'respite effects', relief from job stress – unless they remain connected to their labour while on holiday.

The erosion of holidays is only one sign and not the one to worry most of the world, where paid holidays are rare. But a more pervasive part of the market society is the personal loss of control over time and the hidden ways by which people are drawn into contributing more time to their labour and to their unpaid work-for-labour. Let us consider some of the ways that has been happening.

The old salariat and core working class were employees with full-time jobs that gave them something in common. The salariat had status, with control over the intensity and duration of labour. This was part of the ideology of professionalism. One did what one was expected to do, and it was indelicate or reprehensible to question one's working habits. It was 'bad form'. The tempo was a matter of conscience and culture, but was norm-driven by the profession. It was as much a matter of opprobrium to be seen to be labouring more than the norm as it was to be labouring less. To be responsible, it was enough to be collegial, committed to one's firm and respectful of one's peers.

This cosy world may never have existed in quite this form, but most agree that this was roughly how it was in the industrial citizenship era. No longer. The salariat has lost control of its time and professionalism. Instead, the professional is expected, and expects, to be guided by commercial self-interest – to get ahead. Not to do so is failure. Some will spend time combating such 'get-aheadism', experiencing an all-round increase in stress and alienation. Anybody who has worked in a modern office, university or other bureaucracy will have instances to recall. The Transformation has extended and deepened pressures in favour of self-interest to groups that in the past held it at bay. As Polanyi emphasized, it is self-interest that is the heart of the problem of market society.

Bureaucratic employees face a modern dilemma. Although they have their time 'structured' by routines, supervision and meetings, they are expected to be able to indulge in ad hoc flexible scheduling, meaning that they cannot retain control of their time.

The drift to multiple workplaces is also contributing to long working hours. The clocking-in system is an inaccurate indicator of the total labour time put in by service workers. They usually do a lot of off-the-workplace and off-the-clock labour, in order to be able to labour more effectively. The pressure to be competitive, to be better, creates an insatiable need to undertake unpaid work-for-labour. But it is alienated work, because work done outside paid labour should be for human flourishing and leisure, rather than to make oneself a more efficient labourer. In bizarre ways, in leading service corporations 'play' is being incorporated into labour (as at Google itself), while work-for-labour is being pushed into employees' free time. We, citizens, are out of control. No wonder stress and anxiety are modern horrors.

What is happening is the dissolution of the industrial model of time, with 'connectivity' driven by electronic communication being the defining variable of work and personal relationships. By 2008, over 3.3 billion people, more than half the world's population, subscribed to a mobile phone service, according to the International Telecommunication Union. The pressure to connect is constant and disrupts the biological rhythms established in both agricultural and industrial labour and work. This adjustment is stressful and raises the need for mechanisms to rescue individuals from a loss of control over time. Perversely, there is a constant shortage of it, linked to the reality that connectivity means there are always other 'profitable' uses to which any moment of time could be put. The image of nomad is only partially satisfactory, because it suggests – as does 'techno-Bedouin' – a leisurely rhythmical existence, with reproductive work inbuilt in the pace of living. This is not to romanticize that existence either. But the essence of connectivity is permanent motion and pressure.

It is essential to distinguish between working time and labour time. In the service-oriented market economy, there is pervasive time insecurity because much work has to be done that is linked to labour but which does not count as labour. A person contracted to provide service labour or who is employed part-time in a bureaucracy will end up working many more hours than are paid contractually.

Part of the unpaid work is due to the uncertainty that goes with service labour. This may arise from not knowing when the labour has to be performed, which disrupts planning of other activities and results in wasted time. Or it may arise from not knowing in advance about the duration of spells of paid work, which may require people to put aside more time as insurance. These are stressful aspects of being 'on call'. In some cases, clients, potential clients, colleagues or supervisors may want the person to be available at the various times when they are available. Thus, if the worker is not 'physically present' when they are, he or she may be perceived as not working, as far as they are concerned. So, the worker 'hangs around'. The phenomenon is rather well-known.

Part-time workers are particularly prone to time insecurity. They opt, or are obliged by circumstances, to sacrifice income for 'free time' or 'flexi-time'. But this does not mean they gain control over their time. More often it is others – managers, bosses, colleagues, clients – who expect them to be flexible on their terms and to work more hours than they are paid. This affects complex professional service occupations as well as clerical workers. A part-time academic, for instance, will be paid part-time but will be required to know just as much about his or her discipline as the full-timer, and will have to devote the same amount of time to reading and research. There are many other spheres where part-timers are expected to do at least the pro rata equivalent of the visible activities of their colleagues without account being taken of the fact that all have to do the same amount of work on the unseen activities. Labour unseen is too easily labour denied.

Part of the unpaid labour is connected to hazards (unpredictable but not unexpected events), as when there is a break in the supply chain or in the availability of complementary colleagues. A pervasive example relates to meetings. Meetings use up a lot of time, which may be regarded as a normal part of the employment or service contract, but they also require preparation and follow-up work, often outside contracted labour time. Peter Drucker, in his 1966 book *The Effective Executive*, made the famous quip, 'One either meets or one works. One cannot do both at the same time'. The trouble is that the service worker is under pressure to do both.

Shocks – a new piece of software requiring retraining, a new law requiring additional form filling, a new form of therapy to be considered – impose sudden extra demands on the time of the worker that are rarely compensated in labour contracts. The impact of such changes on labour, paid or unpaid, is rarely taken into account. The regulatory state is keen on auditing and establishing new 'targets' for performance or grading. Few professions can escape this incessant desire to modify rules under which they are required to operate, report or self-regulate. And the cost of not expending time on learning to cope with the shock can be high. If one does not take one's free time to learn about that new law or this new form to complete, one may lose one's position.

In a society where eyes and ears and recording devices are everywhere, insecurity is fanned by the fear of not conforming to expectations. The classic case of loss of time control emerged in the era of late labourism but set a model that contributed to globalization. In Japan, 'salarymen' have been obliged to labour for many unpaid overtime hours, which has led to a social problem of sleep deprivation and sleeping in public. The 'salaryman' model – with company housing, subsidized rent and paid holidays in company-owned resorts – created an unwieldy panopticon existence of prisoner-employees. The 'salarymen' acted out their labour role, working those unpaid hours and rarely taking their full holiday entitlement; after all, the consequence of taking all their leave would be loss of promotion and salary increments (*Economist*, 2008a). Switching jobs would penalize them even more. This has been real commodification, trapping them in dependent benefits while their labour went largely unrewarded, since whether they laboured productively or not made little difference to their income.

The 'salaryman' model has become more dualistic as Japan has adapted to globalization, with the growth of the precariat. In general, it is those in the precariat and below them who are most affected by time insecurity. They have to be flexible in being on call. This has four costs – opportunity cost, time cost, financial cost and the health cost, at least psychologically. One of the difficulties is that the need to be on standby may induce less-than-adequate commitment to activities undertaken while 'waiting'. Those who wax lyrical about 'flexicurity' ignore the loss of control over time that comes from being flexible on other people's terms.

A growing form of work that is not labour that eats up the time of the precariat and those below them is the process of applying for state benefits and services, which involves form filling, information collating, travel, interviews, filing, and so on. In the USA, a Home Services Director pointed out that some disadvantaged families had to deal with 800 pages of forms and instructions, due to convoluted targeting and multiplicity of programmes. This prompted a group to form a 'community of practice' (CP) to organize welfare applicants (Wenger et al., 2002, p. 224). The need is universal.

Leisure is the greatest casualty of labour recommodification. This reflects the time squeeze and the desire of market institutions to induce all to labour, to work-for-labour and to buy commodities. The old image of the 'harried leisure class' was that the means of enjoying play were multiplying, leaving individuals with too many options. But public and deliberative activities are suffering more.

Consider one form of leisure. In a globalizing market, people are expected to have the capacity to adapt and cope with the demands of the market. Almost inevitably, schooling is restructured so that new subjects that promise improved capacity to adapt and cope displace those that do not. The ability to enjoy a rich cultural life – music, theatre, dance, fine arts and so on – is enhanced by learning. But, with the pressure to be a competent market participant, this looks a regrettably inefficient use of time. In reality, the choice of culture and history will only be made if collective mechanisms are constructed to allow it.

Among the effects of a long-hours culture is a proliferation of sexual relationships in jobs, because that is where people spend most of their time. In response, more firms are demanding that workers declare relationships; some are demanding they sign 'love contracts', a device common in the USA whereby office couples undertake not to sue the employer for sexual harassment should their relationship end in bitterness. This may seem a bizarre example of limited relevance. But it points to emerging dilemmas and to what might contribute to their resolution. If companies were made responsible for labour and the activities surrounding labour, including illness, accidents and mishaps in performing work-for-labour, the drive to intensify labour might go into reverse.

Loss of control over time produces several psychological behaviours, one being job addiction due to crushed esteem, or jobs done to hide from personal loneliness, unhappiness or emptiness, or as the means of exercising power over others, or (according to Gini, 2000 and others) to avoid thoughts of personal mortality.

Consistent with the growing precariat, companies are emerging to cater to the 24/7 labour culture. An example is Urbanfetch.com, which began in New York in 1999 and opened in London in 2000 (Maher, 2000). This company guaranteed free delivery of more than 50 000 consumer items within one hour of an order being placed on the website. It employed dozens of couriers on a piece-rate basis. Major retailers in the UK and elsewhere have since developed similar services.

The loss of control of time is partly the outcome of inequality, since the elite, proficians and the upper part of the salariat all have adequate control of it, and enjoy the prospect of ample quality time. It is those being commodified who lack control over their time. And they are the majority.

For the moment, the horror is this. A growing number of people are performing labour 60 hours and 70 hours a week, facing incredibly intense schedules, taking their work home and their home to work, 'bowling alone' – with all the images that go with it. The frenzied pursuit of labour, and the consumerism that drives it, are psychologically threatening. The challenge is to find ways of escaping from the treadmill.

THE TERTIARY WORKPLACE

A feature of modern labour is an increasing fuzziness around the notion of 'the work-place', where there are only arbitrary boundaries between home and work. We commented earlier how labour law and regulations were set for fixed workplaces. But the ramifications do not stop there.

Modern architecture is designing buildings to reshape and facilitate modern forms of working and playing. In many ways, this is exciting, in opening up space as an urban commons. But a danger is that they could become open panopticons, with justifications for secret cameras everywhere. The challenge is to ensure the spaces are controlled for the citizenry while allowing a balance of labour, work, leisure and play.

Architects and town planners are changing designs to fit emerging working practices, turning from the fixed-place model (home, labour, entertainment) to one where people can combine activities in what are being called 'third places', a model advanced by such chains as Starbucks and the US bookshops of Barnes & Noble. But some are being turned into surveillance institutions, perhaps with innocent intentions. The Nomad Café in Oakland, California, obliges browsers to fill out a short profile, as on Facebook, which is then shown to others in the café.

Proficians and part of the precariat intermingle in what has been called a modern urban nomadism (*Economist*, 2008f). This emerging lifestyle is dissolving the notion of 'workplace', since not only are the means of production becoming mobile and priva-tized, but the infrastructure is also accessible to potential proficians at nominal cost, with maximal connectivity. This is enabling 'virtual firms', in which most employees or part-ners do not have an office or fixed workplace. The 'death of distance' has opened up new relationships to time, space and other people. Moving from internet café to café, people link up with their BlackBerries, iPhones or other smart gadgets. All of this gives people a sort of autonomy, but at a cost. Anecdotal research suggests this connected nomadism reduces the depth or intensity of relationships and accelerates contacts at the expense of deliberation and reflection. In the process, connectivity tends to strengthen 'strong ties' and weaken 'weak ties' (Granovetter, 1973). The contact through the mobile phone takes precedence over physical contact; the one interrupts, the other is put on hold and is secondary.

A difference between profician and precariat nomads is that the latter do not have control over their nomadic existence; the mobility of the precariat is considerable but is controlled by others, usually agencies or employers. Telecommuting is a sphere of the precariat. Proficians spread their time between different types of workplace. An estimate early in the twenty-first century suggested that 'creative knowledge workers' would be spending about 40 per cent of their time in corporate offices, 30 per cent in home 'offices' and the rest in public spaces, such as cafés, public libraries and the new architectural crea-tions for public work and living (Grantham and Ware, 2005).

The autonomy of unbounded rationality makes nomadic working stressful. As one Silicon Valley observer told *The Economist*, 'Anybody who works for himself has a tyrant as a boss'. The insecurity induces extra labour as a form of insurance. The observer added, 'The danger is that the anytime anyplace office will lure us into a tiger cage that is the everytime, everyplace office'. The reintegration of labour and social activity is not returning people to some pre-industrial living pattern, because then the social dominated the economic, and the solidaristic and reciprocal relations were paramount. The pressure was mainly on people to limit their labour and work, so as not to intensify differentiation. Someone seen as wanting to distance himself economically from his kin, neighbours or community would alienate the group whose support might be needed in future. Social institutions controlled the acquisitive tendency. But in the modern scenario, the economic drive dominates the social.

People are under pressure to achieve more because the technology at their disposal is so dazzlingly powerful. Yet very few are able to exploit that technology to the full extent of its capabilities, inducing a sense of constant underachievement and inadequacy. More information is the recipe on offer, reflected in the populist view that 'information is education', 'information is power', 'information is the road to greater human capital' and higher income. But as most who use the internet would wryly admit, seeking more information can become deflating and stressful, while time slips by without closure. The 'autonomy' to search for information to guide behaviour is unbounded, and the determination to make a definitive decision is made harder. What if we do not have enough information? Is that option better than another, or better than one I might identify if I spent more time looking?

Finally, the café culture is strengthening relationships between people with different work styles and lifestyles, relative to relationships that exist within workplaces between those with similar work needs and aspirations. The latter are needed for developing bargaining capacity. To achieve real decommodification, real agency is vital.

FROM CAREER TO CAREERISM

The traditional idea of a career may have been largely reserved for the crafts and professions, but was expected to become the norm. Globalization has threatened that. The globalizing of the salariat, with more middle managers being shifted around, is helping in the dismantling of occupational barriers and recommodification. Before globalization, middle management had been a cementing part of the salariat, deriving its sense of community and solidarity from its position in the corporate hierarchy. But this has been weakened as income and status gaps between executives and lower echelons of the salariat have widened (Denham et al., 1997; Peltonen, 2007). Middle managers have been obliged to accept flexibility of employment, since many of their functions are being outsourced or transferred to electronic surveillance devices, eroding their position. They have become agents of their own commodification and have lost their status as a backbone of society. Higher-ranking executives can look down on their lower-ranked colleagues with detachment, but differentiation is bound to grow. The top of the salariat may blur into the elite, while a minority will try to move into the narrow circle of super-rich who live a transnational life. The rest will adapt.

The old industrial and bureaucratic model of employment set parameters and the procedures for a safe career. Climbing the ladder was a matter of time on the job, satisfying the norms and showing loyalty. With these ladders no longer secure, competition between colleagues and Machiavellian scheming have become pivotal skills needed for those who wish to climb or even remain within the salariat. Malice work becomes as crucial as productive work.

Alongside the fading ethos of professionalism among middle management and much of the salariat, which goes once the illusion of a corporate career is removed, is the disappearance of the sense of community based on a corporate culture. This leads to administrative attempts to create an artificial culture, including a simulation of familial and intimate relations to disguise the reality of institutional uncertainty and personalized competition (Kunda [1991] 2006). It is not just the home that is being turned into a workplace; the workplace is being turned into a surrogate home. Witness the annual competitions for best workplaces in which high-scoring companies are those that provide patronizing gestures such as 'ministries of fun', six-monthly 'welfare interviews' and the appointment of a 'senior director of diversity'.

Another trend is to create a personalized standardized project of self-management, which Grey (1994) has illustrated through case studies of accountants. In this way, panopticon techniques of disciplinary power can become adjuncts of people's personal career projects. But many have claimed that, with the labour market emphasis on mobility and uncertainty, the very idea of career is dying. Thus, Demos (2008), the New Labour think-tank, claimed that the career is in 'unavoidable decline'; knowledge-based economies are destroying work practices, and careers no longer shape working lives due to the spread of part-time jobs, self-employment and information technology that has generated 'wired work' – fast, project-based and globally networked. Demos saw a future dominated by what are here called proficians, those able to master wired living and to take bold, risky decisions in building an identity through running with several talents.

Yet it all sounds too frenetic, narcissistic and hyper-competitive. It certainly contrasts with the traditional view. For instance, Harold Perkin (1989) described modern society as comprising 'career hierarchies of specialised occupations, selected by merit and based on trained expertise'. If so, how matters changed in a few years.

The idea of career has become more connected to social aspects of life, and career success is less easily defined (Arthur et al., 2005). In richer countries (and in rich parts of others), youth is showing signs of detachment from the labourist model. Some observers claim they are not interested in the 'treadmill' of a life based on secure jobs (Asthana, 2004). They see the act of conforming to the expectations of secure employment as the reverse of achievement, a denial of personality. The Renaissance spirits would have concurred with this sentiment and exalted in its revival. Of course, there is the negative side of the desire for excitement, for variety rather than steadiness. Loss of self-discipline can have disastrous consequences, not just in drifting into social illnesses but in a loss of human direction. This is the sphere of social psychologists. But it is at least a rejection of the core of the labourist model.

Career has been linked to the apparently precious principle of equal opportunity. But freedom is not just about more choice. In the old story of 'Buridan's ass', the medieval French philosopher Jean Buridan placed two equally delectable bales of hay in front of his donkey; unable to choose, the donkey nibbled neither and starved to death (Fletcher, 2006). Excessive choice can induce existential stress. Profusion brings confusion. This feeds into careers. In former times, sons followed fathers and stayed in what they started. Now, most do neither. We suffer from stress in choosing and stress in wondering whether we made the right choice. This leads to indecision and depression.

Anecdotal and statistical assessments suggest that more people are not enjoying their working lives and are not doing what they would like to do or are capable of doing.

Using psychometric tests, one UK career management company (a modern occupation in itself), Proteus Consultancy, concluded in 2008 that fewer than one in ten people were in careers or workplaces suited to their personalities. This scarcely suggests that the labour market is working for the benefit of its participants. The findings must be seen in a context in which policymakers and social policy analysts have enthusiastically wanted to alter people by making them more 'employable'. They have given nothing like as much attention to reviving the career as a means of capability development and satisfaction.

THE DECLINE OF ALTRUISM AND CIVIC RESPONSIBILITY

> Irresponsibility is the organizing principle of the neo-liberal vision.
> (Gunter Grass in discussion with Pierre Bourdieu, Grass and Bourdieu, 2002, p. 71)

A market-oriented culture has many consequences. Altruism is essential for civil society and for civic friendship. It is encouraged by the existence of institutions of social solidarity and community. The market society encourages the pursuit of self-interest, but this erodes altruistic norms. Faced with an outcome of social irresponsibility, vandalism and anomic violence and social illnesses, paternalistic libertarians are left with little else other than to demand penalties and to provide patronizing incentives to coerce the losers in society to be 'socially responsible'. ASBOs and workfare are outcomes of a pro-market society system in crisis. It is no coincidence that by 2008 the USA and UK were the countries with the highest percentage of their populations in prison, higher than at any time in their history.

Altruism has declined. For over two decades, the UK's Henley Centre, a consultancy, asked people in a survey whether they felt the quality of life was improved more by caring for community interests before their own or by looking after their own interests primarily. For years the former view gained more support. But after 2000 the gap closed and by 2006 a majority opted for self-interest. There had been what commentators called a cultural shift towards selfishness. This was reflected in many social activities, as in the case of voluntary community work, particularly by parents with young children, as they focused more on their own needs and those of their children.

The neo-liberal model encourages consumption, rapidity and flexibility, rather than reflection, creative development and political engagement. The economic system encourages impulsiveness. One analysis has suggested that this is creating a 'civility crisis'. People in labour relationships have insufficient time to be civil and may even be worried that familiarity may lead to politically incorrect behaviour. The obsession with filling every available hour with 'productive' activity creates a labour-and-consume-and-rehabilitate culture. Equating success with money-making empowers people with money to be uncivil.

The trend towards thinking in terms of market behaviour is coupled with relentless pursuit of personal autonomy. We choose personal consumption over investment and private consumption over public services. This liberal 'freedom' invites loss of civility, public manners and courtesy. There is an erosion of family and friendship relations relative to functional, peer-group relations, producing what Martin Jacques (2002) called 'the peer group society' in which friendships are more transient and contractual in nature.

In performing labour in an individualistic world, one way to 'get ahead' is by cheating, a point brought out in *Freakonomics* (Levitt and Dubner, 2005). Although this is a modern failing, one must not misplace the criticism. The lament over corrosion of character in modern capitalism, attributed to a breakdown of long-term labour relations (Sennett, 1998; Uchitelle, 2006), suggests that all was well before. To stretch the point: it is easier for people to do something wrong if their chains are removed; that should not be used to argue they should be kept in chains. The era of fictitious decommodification was as character-distorting as the era of recommodification. And the argument is circular. Many people have short-term relations *because* they have no trust, or reason for it, rather than have no trust because their relations are short-term.

Some have attributed the 'breakdown' of trust to the political emphasis given to meritocracy (Aitkenhead, 2006). Although there is much in this, it again implies that matters were fine before globalization. Meritocracy does make people who are successful think that is because of their excellence and cleverness. And this belief is likely to reduce actions of social solidarity and altruism. Modern information technology and the new occupations of achievement and adjustment, including all those compiling self-help manuals, emphasize the responsibility of the individual for success or failure. This causes stress and hubris in equal measure (Ehrenreich, 2005). As psychologically-minded observers have reported, meritocracy breeds attitudes and behaviour based on autonomy and self-belief, and rejects solidaristic associations and mechanisms. However, according to another popular book by a psychologist, *Affluenza* (James, 2007; also see De Graaf et al., 2005), the costs are psychic disorder and depression, leading to social illnesses and 'corrosion' of civil responsibility.

This leads us back to a theme of the Great Transformation. Altruism and trust go together and neither is helped by disrupting occupational communities, which are, however imperfectly, repositories of both. Dismantling occupations has consequences. A 2007 survey of doctors in the USA found that nearly half (45 per cent) did not report instances of incompetence by their colleagues. The survey's coordinator stated, 'There is a measurable disconnect between what physicians say they think is the right thing to do and what they actually do. This raises serious questions about the ability of the medical profession to regulate itself'.[3] Doctors admitted to ordering unnecessary back scans (magnetic resonance imaging), not because they were needed but simply because patients requested them. Almost all doctors said they believed they should provide care regardless of the patient's ability to pay, but only two-thirds said they accepted uninsured patients. They had lost their ethical anchor.

ADJUSTMENT PROFESSIONS AND RELIGIFICATION

As a crisis in a transformation disrupts systems of reciprocity and solidarity, the problems of stress and anxiety spawn occupations to deal with them. At the end of the nineteenth century, as the 'first period of globalization' entered its crisis, millions found it hard to adjust to the upheavals created by large factories, corporations, activist governments and growing geographical and social mobility. Although they involved some emancipation from restrictive traditions and kinship obligation systems, there was more risk and uncertainty, causing anxiety and reliance on personal survivorship skills. Many found adjusting to new places and roles intolerable.

One reaction within working-class communities was the formation of social clubs, fraternal societies and support associations, most of which offered working-class men (not women) some stability. However, to enter or remain in these required a certain status of 'decency'. The precariat of the time and the *lumpenproletariat* below them were the 'walking wounded'. Social behaviour became anomic. They took to drink and fell prone to social illnesses. These losers from a market society were not 'happy' and many drifted into 'disability'. The predictable response of the authorities was to turn to paternalism. The state set out to control social behaviour, criminalizing public drunkenness and making illness and disability social matters to be reduced. Images of the panopticon were not far away, with the workhouse and 'lunatic asylums'.

There was also a widely held middle-class perception that a generation, particularly women, was suffering a problem of 'nerves' (Abbott, 1988, p. 284). That this hit women harder may have had something to do with their lack of institutions of support. Awareness of distress led to a conflict between religious efforts to deal with it and new occupations offering unfamiliar remedies. As in other crisis periods, there was a religious revival. Religion offered a vision of compensation for a bewildered material existence and tried to placate and pacify the discontented. The new occupations offered cures for now.

For both men and women, there was loss of occupational control and disappearance of institutions that had buttressed an old way of life. Proletarianization and labour intensification led to loss of control and generated disorders, such as 'occupational neuroses', attributed to the new patterns and pace of labour, and 'functional neuroses', such as hysteria. The stress induced by changes in economic, social and family life legitimized neurology, which prescribed sedatives, hypnotics and stimulants for the nervous symptoms of elation, insomnia, sleep disturbances, headaches, anxiety and depression. These were all symptoms of insecurity.

Neurologists beat the clergy in diagnosis and treatment and fostered a psychiatric revolution, psychiatry emerging as an invasive occupation and a means of societal control. The approach assumed that individuals should be induced to adjust to social, labour and economic change, not the other way round, that violations of social norms signified mental problems and that the treatment required was individualistic, not social. Psychotherapy redefined the problems but still started from a perception of dislocation characterized by a mixture of frightening freedoms with intensifying controls.

We are at a similar stage in the Global Transformation. Is resort to social control of personal adjustment likely to be the dominant approach in response to the pressures of globalization, on time use, work–family balance and so on? Will we be encouraged to accept the emerging structures and technologies as imperatives?

Abbott argued that whereas by the 1930s the psychiatric paradigm was hegemonic, in the late 1970s a 'new re-biologizing of personal problems' emerged. The future for two occupational groups looks busy. Psychiatrists deal with recuperative or remedial adjustment; psychologists deal with preventative adjustment. Both are part of the paternalistic apparatus of control. Social work, police and prisons also deal with those who fall through the emotional problem net. All provide personal connection where little exists in the absence of occupational community.

Perhaps the most powerful adjustment mechanism is cognitive behavioural therapy (CBT), developed in the USA (Leader, 2008). In 2008, the UK government launched a national scheme for Improving Access to Psychological Therapies to train a 'workforce' of cognitive therapists to help anxious citizens. Lord Layard, its main designer, estimated that depression and anxiety was costing the economy £12 billion a year (1 per cent of GDP), whereas the therapy would cost only £750 per person treated. The launch of the scheme coincided with an announcement that the government was going to regulate mediums and spiritualists, a classic act of occupational suppression. Rather than allowing the citizenry to make up its own mind, the CBT therapists were demonstrating professional hegemony.

There is a paradox here. The panopticon utilitarians, dressed as libertarian paternalists, postulate a model of unprecedented choice for individuals in a market system. But the ignorant should be nudged by an architecture of choice while the socially damaged must be protected and steered by having choices restricted for their long-term good. Adjustment is unbounded. The model extends to our physical appearance and our personality. The adjustment occupations include those keen to take flesh off or put flesh on, the cosmetic surgeons and the auxiliaries. They should be called the personal transformation professions. They have a market interest in creating an image of perfection and perfectibility that will induce consumers to purchase a product or service they think will help make them more perfect. Meanwhile, life coaches can teach people how to change their ways of thinking and behaving as they move through life.

Behavioural approaches identify the person as a type of client and market services are created to treat each type. As some psychologists have argued, the market paternalists depict the human being as one-dimensional, pursuing autonomy and happiness. Our faults lie in ourselves and can be cured. The cognitive behaviouralists are ideal salespeople for the commodities and services that can deal with the faults. And this is extended to 'belief modification'. Holding some beliefs can be discomforting, especially if they are deviant in some way, thus causing social difficulties. Buying some drugs or buying therapy may help.

Adjusting behaviour and attitudes goes with preventing people going in undesired directions. Among the guards of the modern panopticon are the knowledge inspectors. Nothing counts as knowledge unless it has been sanctioned by experts. Researchers are required to specify in advance what practical outcome their proposed research would produce. If the outcome is unknown, or not valued by the inspectorate, it will not be funded, and the person proposing it might be denigrated.

In sum, new adjustment occupations will continue to emerge to deal with tensions associated with a globalizing market system and the labour-related symptoms of distress and insecurity – alcoholism, suicide, *karoshi*, premature ageing, sexual dysfunction, drug addiction, environmental decay and financial mismanagement or mishaps. These may be designated as the occupations of 'moral entrepreneurship' and 'immoral hazards'.

As in the early twentieth century, there will be a continuing tension between religious treatments and new occupations. They are all offering products and services in a competitive market. One set is competing for your soul and your money, the other for your body, your wounded mind and your money.

Faith-based organizations are a revived occupational sphere, subsidized by government, churches, super-rich philanthropists and the poor themselves. They are seen as better than government at changing people's behaviour, by moralizing. About 80 per cent of US churches, synagogues and mosques are doing social work. And they use money and moral pressure to induce others to adapt services to their moralistic code. The churches have used the space created by the state's withdrawal of benefits and services to market their own commodities for their own benefit. Taking advantage of the vacuum, and encouraging it in the first place, they offer a new version of an old commodity, alms. Evangelical charity requires the poor to be born again in return for subsistence.

Religion has always been used to engineer transformations. In the sixteenth century in Britain, the organized Church was given a welfare role in dealing with local suffering at parish level. That went on into Bentham's time. Its role was to ease the pain while national markets were being shaped. In the modern idiom, 'faith-based organizations' have been embraced by leading politicians and parties, including Tony Blair, George W. Bush and Barack Obama. Religious bodies have been welcomed as acceptable social institutions because they are seen as facilitating the market rather than being countervailing institutions. But at best they are merely charitable; they do not strengthen rights or freedom.

Bentham and his followers, including an admiring Alexander de Tocqueville, linked his panopticon to religion, wishing to use enforced isolation to bring transgressors through remorse to redemption and rehabilitation as hard-labouring citizens. Not a lot has changed. It is surely no coincidence that most prominent libertarian paternalists are religious.

Two other types of adjustment occupation should be noted. One consists of those working for civil society bodies or NGOs. They can act as constraints on the market society, but one danger is that the interests of finance and market efficiency will play off non-market communities against each other – the labour movement, women's movements, human rights, environment and so on. Globalization and the market society are confronted by diverse interests that individually reject the outcome of markets. Separately they can enfeeble and offset each other. An example has been the clash between environmental and development groups. In the market society, interests are in constant tension and competition for democratic support.

Politicians constitute the second type of special adjustment occupation. Their role in a global market society has become fuzzier. They have been professionalized, building up credentials and learning technical and emotional skills to deal with commercial and countervailing pressures. Unlike the days of class politics, when the interests of labour and capital clashed, now if concerns over human rights are prominent, politicians will try to appeal to that lobby; if gender inequity is highlighted by noisy campaigning, they will do something about that; if ecological problems are foremost, they will give something to that lobby. This is the nature of market society. Politicians are selling an image and a capacity; their success in retaining current income, as politicians, will depend on their appeal to donors and on conveying to enough clients (voters) images of representation and delivery. Success will also depend on securing future income through the job or network of IOUs (promises to pay) that will make corporations or interest groups regard them as an asset to employ after they leave politics.

Being a politician has become a stepping-stone occupation and part of a multiple career pattern, unlike the time when it was a lifetime career and commitment. This is not a cynical way of interpreting the modern norm; no doubt some go into politics out of altruism or class ideology. It is merely to say that we should treat 'politician' in the same way as we treat other occupations. Then we could think about how politicians could be regulated by reference to the same principles as doctors, lawyers and stonemasons.

THE PRECARIAT'S DILEMMA

The class restructuring of the global market economy is generating a political threat, as was the case in previous transformations. The political consequences of a globalizing labour market based on insecurity and inequality are frightening. Much of the remnants of the industrial working class in rich countries have drifted into the precariat; some have fallen into the detached lumpenized stratum. As they have done so, they have turned politically to the right, supporting Bush in the USA, Berlusconi in Italy and extreme nationalists in Austria, for example.

If proficians are closest to a model of free workers, the precariat is the new class in the making. It has the potential for radical revolt against market society. But the precariat is anomic, living precariously not only in short-term jobs but in its connection to work as occupation and vocation. Its members have a dilettante existence, presenting an easy target for consumerism and 'watching culture'.

The precariat has deserted traditional parties of the left. This should not be regarded as 'deranged', as some claim (Frank, 2004). The losers in the unravelling of industrial citizenship have not been offered a new vision, and it would be sensible for progressives to accept that they should not offer a vision that appeals to a dying labourism.

In every socioeconomic transformation, there is a period of danger when the insecurities and inequalities breed vicious forms of political extremism. This era is no different. There is a prospect of populist politicians using fear to secure support from the precariat and from those who fear falling into its ranks. The response to the new migrations of the globalizing labour market will be crucial. If curbs are retained, illegal and 'black labour' migration will continue, and so will the threat to the living standards and socioeconomic security of the precariat, since migrants will offer cheap labour with minimal access to enterprise or state benefits. If migrants are legalized, they may qualify for state benefits. But if these are means-tested and provided only for the poor, migrants may reach the front of the queue before local claimants. This will tend to demonize migrants, the core of the precariat, in the eyes of the old 'white' working class brought up to believe that state benefits were for them, for those who had paid their dues.

The danger is that the indigenous part of the precariat will feed populist political extremism and induce the remnants of the core working class to follow suit. The alternative is to imagine a policy future based on an alliance of interests and aspirations between the precariat and the proficians. At the moment, this has not been addressed.

THE MIND'S EYE

> In a dark time, the eye begins to see.
>
> ('In a dark time', Roethke, 1966)

It is impossible to divorce the neo-liberal model of globalization from the ecological crisis of the twenty-first century. With industrial citizenship, the main mechanisms of labour coordination were direct, visible and disciplinary in character, at the workplace through the prism of the clock and calendar. The factory was the epitome of the *workplace*, the *school* the place of learning, the *home* the place of reproduction, regeneration and play, the *commons* the place of leisure. One of the first acts by the Hayek-inspired government of Margaret Thatcher was the mass sale of playgrounds and common space of state schools, a decision that was to have a negative effect on the competitiveness of British sport over the next two decades. Rather worse was the message it conveyed that the commons could be sacrificed in the interest of increasing efficiency. This and unbridled personal consumption, and hedonic happiness, were the goals of globalization. Society paid a heavy price.

At the end of the first disembedded phase of the Global Transformation, labour and work are out of control. While the rogues of the financial markets have been exposed, social and economic insecurity has become chronic and the precariat lacks career direction or meaning. People are frenzied and stressed as they reach for new commodities, unable to forge deliberative working and productive lives. The market society replaces trust and exchange with contract, litigation and surveillance.

One of the worst features of this panopticonic neo-liberal world, whether in Shenzhen or in shopping malls anywhere, is that the means of combating the inspectors and the salespeople have been undeveloped, crushed or co-opted. The resulting vacuum is unlikely to last for long. Why so many of the phenomena traced in this chapter occur is because we lack effective agency to protect ourselves against market pressures and alienated reactions and to guide us into a work-centred existence rather than anomic labourism. It cannot make human sense to sell off our privacy, our feelings or the commons, or lose control of our time or react to material pressures by zealous over-labour to the point of self-destruction. But that is what is happening. In the face of panopticonic utilitarians using the levers of the state and the moralistic apparatus they have favoured, it is unrealistic to claim we have freedom. We need to understand the challenge and act to build an alternative architecture, institutions of collective agency that could revive freedom.

NOTES

1. The notion of 'multi-tasking' is used to criticize men, who are apparently less good at it than women. Men's capacity must be 'improved'. Courses will be provided, therapists invited to assist. One predicts that those who do not do so will be subject to childish name-calling.
2. Revelations about personal behaviour, conditions or views used to be socially reprehensible because they were regarded as betrayals of trust and a duty of care. For this to prevail, behaviour must be guided by sincerity and trust rather than self-interest. These values are preserved and interpreted by social institutions in which people live and work. Once those institutions are stripped away or dismantled, the capacity of individuals to interpret what is morally acceptable in society is weakened. In a system that not only rejects collective institutions but also advances self-interest as the only legitimate motivator, there are no countervailing pressures to respect the needs of others.
3. Eric Campbell, cited in Massachusetts General Hospital (2007), reporting Campbell et al. (2007).

9.   Reviving occupation in full freedom

> Every child is an artist. The problem is how to remain an artist once he grows up.
>
> (Pablo Picasso)

INTRODUCTION

The Global Transformation is in crisis, not because of the meltdown in the financial markets, although this may be a harbinger of radical change, but because the model is profoundly inegalitarian. Competition combined with insatiable consumption breeds opportunistic villains and resentful victims, which the modern panopticon is set to deal with through restrictive laws, surveillance by sophisticated gadgetry and paternalistic reintegration schemes.

A crisis in a transformation is when the economic system is out of control, from which there develops a realization that it must be re-embedded in society if social stability is to be restored. In the Great Transformation, the response was construction of 'industrial citizenship' around the values of labour. By analogy, in the Global Transformation, in which the building of international markets is paramount, several forms of citizenship are vying for supremacy. The argument of this chapter is that the desirable form is what we may call 'occupational citizenship'.

The primary challenge, globally, is to overcome the yawning inequality and the stress, insecurity and loss of control reviewed in the last chapter. Nobody has demonstrated that all this is necessary for economic growth or desirable for a healthy society. Those who call themselves progressive should wish to see a change in direction. Yet too many have been quiet, timid and atavistic, seemingly bereft of rational responses.

Progressives have suffered from a failure of imagination on the great issues of equality and freedom. For too long, they have been fearful of freedom, seeing it as an entry point to ideas of 'free markets' and individualism associated with inequality. They have had an image of Isaiah Berlin's negative liberty, the absence of constraints (Berlin [1958] 1969).

A result was that they lost the space of 'freedom' to the political right. It was the limitations of social democracy, not state socialism, that led to the triumph of Hayek and the Chicago School of law and economics. Ironically, the notions of equality to which progressives were drawn floundered not only on the rocks of unfreedom but on their unsustainability as globalization took off. The outcome was that progressives lost any idea of what constituted desirable equality and had nothing to say on freedom. All that was left was the paternalistic ethos of Third Wayism, leading to the latest incarnation in the form of libertarian paternalism.

The need is to create a progressive agenda that is egalitarian and freedom enhancing. In doing so, we must confront the peculiar combination of fear of freedom *and* fear of equality. Both were eroded in the disembedded phase of the Global Transformation. Both must be revived.

A new paradigm is needed. It must involve a reconstruction of work, escaping from a preoccupation with labour, a reconstruction of our image of time, away from the industrial model to one suitable for a globalizing tertiary society, and a reconstruction of ideas of career and occupation.

THE MANY FORMS OF FREEDOM

> Socialism is, essentially, the tendency inherent in an industrial civilization to transcend the self-regulating market by consciously subordinating it to a democratic society.
>
> (GT, p. 242)

A standard interpretation of freedom is Berlin's negative liberty, as absence of constraints to individual action, and positive liberty, as opportunity to pursue the good life. This is only a starting point. Two currents of thinking have been in tension, the liberal and republican. While this is not the place to go into the intricacies, there is a need to revive the republican tradition if we are to forge a desirable emancipatory egalitarianism.

The liberal and republican streams agree that coercion to be free is a contradiction. This was not accepted by Hayek, with his rationalization for coercion in favour of building a market society, or Bentham, with his panopticon to control the unhappy few. The nineteenth-century liberal philosopher, T.H. Green, pointed out that people cannot be forced to be free because freedom consists of doing as one ought, and morality depends on the motive behind actions (Roberts, 1984).

The liberal concept relates to public liberty (non-interference) and private liberty (right of conscience), the freedom to choose. The republican view is that freedom is political and social. The liberal conception is insufficient for what we may call 'full freedom'. It risks being an excuse for self-interest only. Marx, for instance, depicted 'freedom of the individual' as the freedom to be isolated, based on private property, a recipe for 'a law of egoism' – which 'lets every man find in other men not the *realization* but rather the *limitation* of his own freedom' (Marx [1844] 1967, p. 236).

If only autonomy matters, then communities will be presented as barriers to freedom, since they necessarily impose constraints on individual action. A danger of the liberal conception of liberty as freedom from political interference is that the state will be drawn to dismantle mechanisms and communities that promote social solidarity. An individualistic view removes ideas of freedom from a social context, and promotes 'bourgeois' values and consumerism. The liberal tradition owes much to Christianity, which arose in opposition to the state, and to the concern for security as freedom from government control.

The liberal credo is 'the less politics, the more freedom'. Freedom is about individual consumption and possession, not the freedom of citizens, which is political, about such matters as dignity, solidarity, creativity and natality (the capacity to bring something new into the world). To a liberal, we are clients, judging governments by their efficiency in delivering goods and services. This stands against the republican tradition, associated with Aristotle, Cicero, the Florentine Renaissance, Montesquieu, Rousseau, de

Tocqueville and Arendt, which sees freedom in terms of civic involvement, deliberation, equality, solidarity and dignity.

The republican tradition stems from ancient Greek ideas of citizenship. Freedom began with the capacity to participate in politics, outside the household. A citizen had to be exempted from 'slavish occupations', so as to be able to devote energies to action for the common good. Only in others' company could freedom be enhanced, through deliberation. This view has been refined over the centuries. As Polanyi recognized, freedom depends on social relationships. To be free is to be free to be ethical, which requires involvement in real communities of responsibility.

Hegel too believed that only within an ethical community could freedom emerge. His conception of the 'ethical life' was defined as the structure of rules, obligations and principles that people learn and internalize by living in an ethical community (Hegel [1820] 1952). He regarded the ability to choose an occupation in life as a vital freedom, and it would be consistent with this to imagine occupational communities as the space for ethical thinking and practice to take shape over a prolonged period. The social memory matters. I act this way because this is the way we do things, as a society.

Marxian accounts of liberty also differ from the liberal one by recognizing that an agent's unfreedom need not be the outcome of somebody's deliberate actions, but reflects social forces, leading to familiar themes of alienation, reification, fetishism, ideology and rationalization. As a person only has realizable rights through having political freedom, Marx favoured 'the rights of the citizen' – freedom of the political person.

Hannah Arendt best described the building blocks for a modern view of full freedom. She saw the liberal conception as preoccupied with a notion of security in which individuals have more freedom as government recedes. For Arendt, freedom requires community and government. It means citizens having the capacity for collective action. Her attitude is related to the Greek distinction between hedonic and eudaemonic happiness. Whereas the liberal sees happiness in the private realm of the individual, public happiness is about the joy of sharing a public space and participating in a social community.

For Arendt (1958), freedom is *disclosed* in the togetherness of people deliberating and acting in concert. This disclosure concept depends on the dignity of involvement. She also perceived a modern sense of homelessness in the world that required communities to harness human capabilities. Writing in the 1950s, she was one of the consciences lurking in the wings of Polanyi's Transformation. She dreaded the jobholder society and what Habermas (1976) was to depict as civic privatism.

Freedom cannot exist without vigorous exercise of citizenship. The social democrats who forged the Great Transformation may have wanted this but their institutions and policies actually precluded it. The neo-liberal version of freedom is worse. Neither encourages civic engagement, and both elevate domestic (consumer) concerns over civic participation. For Arendt, freedom consists of power embodied in *collective* action. Unless the state promotes public participation and interest representation, freedom is devalued.

If civic identity is suppressed, freedom becomes thin and easily denied. Citizens will wither into consumers, passive devourers of soap operas, computer games and trivial pursuits to eat up the time between labour and consumption, a society without community. We will be left defenceless against the architecture of the panopticon and the 'architecture of choice' kindly built by the libertarian paternalists.

For full freedom, and at its core occupational freedom, a set of communities and policies that create social engagement are needed. In contrast with republicanism, liberal freedom sees politics as instrumental, a matter of bargaining over who receives what and which share. The bargaining paradigm goes unchallenged. Thus 'domestic freedom' (liberty of the consumer) diverges from 'republican freedom' (liberty of the citizen). The free person in the former says, 'I am free because I am left to think/act/consume as I choose'. In the latter he or she says, 'I am free because *we* are able to act in concert' (Beiner, 1984, p. 369).

This leads us to ask what forms of community could advance republican freedom. Civil society is one range of community, and many NGOs have occupational implications. However, it is the occupational community that offers the possibility of an ethical space for full freedom constructed around the way people work and the leisure needed for public participation.

Looking back on industrial citizenship, none of the defining institutions – industrial unions, sectoral collective bargaining, labour law, labour-based social insurance and labour-based pensions – offered universal occupational freedom. They gave no respect to work that was not labour or to leisure that was not play. The same could be said for the mechanisms of the globalization era, social assistance, 'workfare', employment subsidies and the like. They tried to reinforce labourism, not universalism or freedom.

With the republican vision as a guide, this chapter will deal with the construction of the institutional part of associational freedom, the parameters of occupational citizenship. The final chapter will deal with the restructuring of social income to facilitate occupational freedom. First, let us reflect on two perspectives that stand in the way.

FIGHTING PATERNALISM AND MEDDLING MORALITY

> The real function of government being to maintain conditions of life in which morality shall be possible, and morality consisting in the disinterested performance of self-imposed duties, paternal government does its best to make it impossible by narrowing the room for the self-imposition of duties and for the play of disinterested motives.
>
> (T.H. Green [1879] 1999, p. 14)

If decommodification is about forging freedom and equality, transformations are about the repositioning of these great claims. The trouble with industrial citizenship was that it offered only partial egalitarianism based on a redistribution from 'capital' to 'labour', while remaining sceptical or hostile to popular ideas of freedom, seeing them as little more than a route to more inequality, exploitation and oppression.

The weakest link in the industrial citizenship model was its clinging to paternalism in its many guises – family, state, political party, union, religion and community.[1] People had to be confronted not just by constraints on their actions but by guidance, for their own good and the good of their family, class, religion, party, race or whatever. Among the more disgraceful forms of state paternalism in the 'embedded' era was the German *Jugendamt*, set up in 1917 and expanded under Nazism, by which the state could intervene in child support and remove children from parents deemed unsuitable. The *Jugendamt* still exists.

In the mid-twentieth century, totalitarian systems spawned fearful scenarios etched into the literary landscape by George Orwell, Aldous Huxley and others. But almost as a consequence of those visions, the reality has been paternalism by stealth. The current 'libertarian paternalism' takes the view that political and corporate bodies should guide less well-informed citizens and steer their attitudes and behaviour in ways that contribute to their own long-term well-being.

Paternalism has evolved to create a strange consensus. Traditionally, social democrats legislated for compassion, Christian democrats legislated for morality. After the collapse of labourism, social democrats moved to legislate for morality as well. And after their setbacks in the 1990s, Christian democrats moved to legislate for compassion as well. Both mainstream political strands became more openly paternalistic, and both have welcomed corporate paternalism, considered in the next section.

In an influential refinement of libertarian paternalism, Thaler and Sunstein in *Nudge* (2008) argue that 'choice architecture' can be used to guide people in desirable directions at little cost to their sense of autonomy. Drawing on behavioural economics, they note that people suffer from information overload and often misjudge their best interests. So they need to be 'nudged' to change their behaviour for 'the better'. This view has permeated welfare reform, corporate human resources strategy and fiscal policy.

With modern surveillance techniques and fiscal engineering to play with, the paternalists will not go away. The standard libertarian answer of more knowledge is inadequate. The answer must be to find ways of counteracting the paternalists themselves. Freedom requires us to overcome paternalistic controls just as much as the direct exploitative controls on which attention is usually placed. The choice architects need to be kept in check and confronted by countervailing power in the form of Voice.

Tolerating state paternalism is a feature of middle-class political democracy. Most voters can easily believe they will not be affected and that it is socially necessary to induce the less fortunate to behave in ways that would improve their well-being and make them more socially and economically functional. The class inequality that globalization has thrown into sharper relief contributes to this political arithmetic, making it harder to envisage countervailing mechanisms, or to persuade enough groups to support them.

The transformation of civil services is a contributing factor. The traditional attitude towards professionals and civil servants has been that they are motivated by morality, altruism and a professional ethic, capable of regulating themselves. An opposite view is that they are not knights but knaves, as Le Grand (2003) put it, being motivated by self-interest.[2] The argument that civil servants and professionals treat citizens as passive clients and are careless of resource use has led to more monitoring and direction of these groups, proletarianizing many. Governments have subjected them to league tables, targets, multiple inspections, multiple forms of regulation and other methods of reining in professional freedom. The intrusions chip away at the professional work ethic. The regulatory apparatus actually weakens the 'knightly' tendency. There are immoral hazards, such as a tendency to neglect activities for which there are no targets and to 'massage' figures or reporting criteria.

The reassessment of regulations has induced paternalists to give more power to consumer-clients, promoting competition and directing public money to where consumer choice leads, apparently believing that competitive services will induce knightly behaviour. One could reach a different conclusion; competition in services could lead to winner-takes-all situations and 'star markets' that funnel high incomes to an elite. That may promote rapacious self-interest and competitive practices, further eroding the professional ethic and stratifying occupations into elites and mass precariats. The egalitarian would wish to promote the craft ethic and to revive social solidarity and structured reciprocities, or civic friendship. Closing the income gap between winners and others would strengthen the solidarity that would preserve or induce ethical attitudes and behaviour, and pressure of peers on fellow professionals.

The thesis of behavioural economics is that unbounded choice creates cognitive difficulties, requiring government intervention to improve individual well-being. One tactic is to stigmatize behaviour deemed abnormal so as to discourage people from harming themselves and reduce anxiety arising from too many options. But the use of stigma encourages dubious behaviour and leads to harder paternalism. A common belief – more prevalent in the USA than in Europe – is that the poor are poor because they are lazy. Being poor makes people 'unhappy'. So, the poor must be penalized for their laziness, and the cost of laziness must be raised to discourage it. How do we know they are lazy? Because they are poor. The poor must be penalized, since it is administratively easier to identify poverty than laziness. Such circular reasoning is scarcely an exaggeration of mainstream thinking.

This should not lead to the libertarian response that policies favouring private decision-making are the only desirable way of avoiding the paternalistic twitch. That is too naive in a world comprising elites, corporations and state agencies with vast resources at their disposal. In the era of industrial citizenship, class-based political parties, unions, local neighbourhood associations and extended family networks provided some countervailing pressure. In this phase of the Global Transformation, the collective bodies able to protect and emancipate are weak. New forms of occupational community, networks and associations could offer a structure that would guard against the paternalists. But we are still a long way from realizing that.

Freedom and security are compromised by the increasingly sophisticated nature of paternalistic policies. With libertarian paternalism, the essence of Third Wayism, the twist is to make abnormal choices costly. Thus, advocates propose 'sin' taxes rather than restrictive regulations, procedures to require people to opt out of schemes deemed good for them rather than to opt in, and time-consuming and costly procedures that people must satisfy to indulge in behaviour deemed bad for them. Thaler and Sunstein claim 'nudge' paternalism functions best when the decisions concern complex issues with poor feedback and few opportunities for learning (pension investment, for example). But if the policy of limiting options and manipulating incentives succeeds in steering people's choices, there will be little incentive to improve feedback and learning. This could lead to a cycle of distortions, exposing people to more uncertainty rather than less.

Mechanisms must be found to combat such social engineering. The alternative to it is for policy to be behaviourally neutral, and for resources to be devoted to informing citizens of the costs and benefits of alternative options.

Moralists would legislate on the basis of morality in the absence of individual harm; paternalists would legislate on the basis of individual welfare in the absence of individual consent. Thus, paternalists claim that regulation or prohibition of a citizen's conduct may be justified without showing that the conduct harms others. As Gutmann and Thompson (1996, p. 261) noted, 'The paternalist claim is not that the conduct is morally wrong but that it is harmful to the citizen herself'. The paternalists substitute their judgment of what constitutes harmful behaviour for the individual's own. This is not to argue that there should be no restrictions of individual freedom in the absence of harm to others. Regulations are justifiable if they counter market failure, reduce risks or uncertainty, increase access to information for making rational decisions or equalize bargaining powers. But they should not be paternalistic.

Behavioural economics is a child of the global market society. Amid a blur of products, advertising and pressure to consume, psychologists have been brought in to fashion a new rationality. In the first flush, its practitioners indulged in point scoring against a straw-man version of *homo economicus*.[3] But this 'science' offers new tools to marketing people and to a generation of earnest policymakers. As individuals are observed to behave in ways that could do harm to themselves, as when they 'over-borrow', behavioural econo-mists propose curbing freedom in what they claim is the interest of those whose freedom is being curbed. As one enthusiast, Dan Ariely (cited in Chakrabortty, 2008), put it, 'What's the big deal? Let's limit people's ability to hurt themselves in borrowing, like we do with seatbelts in driving'. We may guess that it is unlikely to end with seatbelts.

An egalitarian riposte to the over-borrowing would be to deal with those who took advantage of the borrowers' weakness of will by lending when their professional training should have told them the risk was too high. The lender, the expert, should have had to bear the risk. This is the answer to the second question set out in Chapter 8.

Libertarian paternalists further claim that a person who chooses a 'nudged' option is exercising free choice if the option is perceived by policymakers and the person as in his 'best interest'. An example is revealing. In Missouri, gambling addicts are given an option of signing a statement banning themselves from gambling in riverboat casinos (the only gambling facilities allowed), which are legally obliged to refuse their bets. Even leaving aside the probability that they enter such contracts under duress, would the libertarian paternalist state offer a desirable alternative to the nanny state by rescuing individuals from their demons? If a person becomes addicted because circumstances propel him to such behaviour, then banning him from one addiction may merely propel him to another. The availability of a paternalistic answer may deter the state from considering policies to tackle the cause of the behaviour. Treat the symptoms and the problem may become merely one of managing the victims. One round of paternalism would lead to a need for more. We could all end up having spells of the equivalent of the riverboat treatment – being blocked from going on the boat, for our own good as a result of our own decision. But once self-convicted the sentence in Missouri is permanent. You are never allowed back, even if you could demonstrate that you had overcome your addiction. Where would the paternalism stop? One doubts it would.

An egalitarian riposte in this case would be to look at the educational system and the market signals, and perhaps the pattern of inequality in which the only realistic hope of escaping from poverty might lie in winning the lottery. To make the point even more clearly, the libertarian paternalist would try to raise the cost of jumping off the bridge whereas the non-paternalist would want to look at why the person climbed onto the bridge.

Paternalistic governments have shifted spending in the direction of bribing citizens to behave in ways regarded as normal or in ways experts regard as socially desirable. There are policies to give parents subsidies or vouchers to care for their children and send them to school, to lose weight, to eat well, to stop smoking, to travel by bicycle, to read to their children, to take jobs or go to training. Each of these subsidies has a cost, and chips away at freedom, however benevolently. There is no evidence that fiscal paternalism achieves its ostensible objective, and there are few proper evaluations, which would have to take account of deadweight effects (a subsidy being provided to someone who would have done that anyway), substitution effects (reduced spending on one 'bad' habit being offset by increased spending on another) and the impact on inequality.

Above all, the modern paternalists are utilitarians, who should keep copies of Bentham's *Panopticon* ([1787] 1995) by their bedsides. They want to make us happy, and believe that being in a job is the main way to achieve this. Those not in jobs must be persuaded, or coerced, into jobs in their own best interest, long-term happiness. Labourists and all shades of paternalist here fall into a trap.

For the ancient Greeks, *eudemia* ('happiness') came from escape from labour, from being able to indulge in other activities, including *schole*, leisure. Early Christianity saw labour as the consequence of original sin, man being condemned to toil because of Adam's moment of weakness. Labour was not miserable by accident. In the Renaissance, work became equated with creative endeavour. But the souls who struggled with their hands and eyes, the likes of Michelangelo, Leonardo da Vinci, Dürer and the stream of geniuses, did not have jobs and were rarely happy in the hedonic sense. Artistic work was unalienated because it was done as an expression of creativity and pursuit of something authentic and glorious. Had these Renaissance figures been happy in the hedonistic sense, one suspects they would have dabbled, and their names would be unknown to us.

Only in management manuals, among certain academics and in a few self-satisfied bureaucrats, do we find the expectation that jobs engender happiness. To tell a servant she should be happy in her job is patronizing. Most people in most jobs would be unimpressed. But much sophistry is dedicated to sustaining the false consciousness that jobs are the source of happiness and well-being. They are not, if only for one reason, that they are not created for that purpose. Only in bourgeois society did jobs and happiness become linked, largely because of the convenient view that in a market society economic outcomes are predicated on merit. The founders of the USA, including Thomas Jefferson and Benjamin Franklin, shared this view of the society they were setting up.

It was a short step from the bourgeois equation of merit-worthiness and income success to the linking of occupational titles with merit and place in society. All social science students know of the role of the 'Protestant ethic', whether or not they subscribe to the thesis of Weber and Tawney. Job titles became social classifiers, and those without a worthy title became objects of pity if not contempt. It was a short step to saying that someone without a worthy job title could not be happy, or if they were, there must be something wrong with them. From that it is an even shorter step to saying that something has to be done about them.

The jobs most people are obliged to do are boring, restrictive, stressful and rarely 'freely chosen'. Put that proposition to most people in most streets of the world and you would probably receive a puzzled look for saying something obvious. This is why labour should be regarded as a real commodity. Labour may be necessary but the glorification of jobs is not. As Alain De Botton (2004) noted, if we stop thinking our jobs should be the primary source of our happiness, we will give other spheres more sensible attention.

Usually, we cannot obtain satisfaction from jobs because they are determined for us. To claim that we should be happy in jobs is to demand something beyond our control. At best, we may find peace of mind. But it is not in the control of the person being paid to labour. Moreover, a rational person should not wish somebody else to be deciding on his or her happiness. And some people do not wish to be happy, thank you very much.

Indeed, one may achieve greater satisfaction, and so be inclined to apply more effort, by accepting that one's labour is largely a means to an end and applying an instrumental ethic to the job. One will not suffer from as much frustration as someone who expects a job to provide 'meaning to life'.

Contrary to what some management writers and human resource managers claim, it may be inadvisable to try to overcome the phenomenon of 'psychological withdrawal' from jobs. Efforts to induce more job commitment are almost exercises in deception. Fear those bonding retreats, those urns of petrol-stewed coffee! Fear HRM manuals and the bevy of consultants with their buzzwords and scientific euphemisms. These are exercises in sophistry that belittle speakers and listeners.

It would be better if labour *were* done on an instrumental basis. This is the adult way. It is not my soul you are buying, but my time. Do not offer me happiness; that is my responsibility. Just let us treat each other with mutual respect. You pay me X and I will give you a fair effort as a bargain. Save the 'value statements', 'mission statements' and schemes for work–life balance. Of course, I exaggerate. But you understand the drift.

In general, paternalists assume that people need to be induced to be rational; they lack self-control, take a short-sighted view against their longer-term interests and so must be protected from themselves. Of course, the state will always be paternalistic, and one must accept that some degree of paternalism is justifiable, as in the case of children and the mentally incapacitated. However, freedom and occupational citizenship along the lines outlined in the following depend on resisting anything but the bare minimum. This should be our starting position. As Kant argued:

> For [a political community] to coerce its citizens to enter an ethical community with each other would be a contradiction in terms, for the latter involves in its very concept freedom from coercion. . . But woe to the legislator who would wish to bring about through coercion a constitution directed to ethical ends. For he would not only bring about the exact opposite of his ethical goals, but also undermine his political goals and render them insecure.
>
> (Cited in Taylor, 1984, p. 109)

Coercion by altering incentives and penalties, and by creating uncertainty via surveillance and the discretionary behaviour-testing of the modern welfare state, is a recipe for a resentful citizenry. Kant's view amounts to a criticism of state paternalism and implicit support for occupational citizenship.

CORPORATE CITIZENSHIP

A form of paternalism that has crept up is 'corporate citizenship', a revived form of welfare capitalism prevalent in the early twentieth century. It is nurtured by multinational corporations, management specialists and many politicians and international bureaucrats.

An influential approach has been called 'communities of practice' (CPs) (Wenger et al., 2002). This veers between analysis of what is happening and what organization theorists want to happen. It is part of fictive decommodification, dressed up as non-hierarchical and collaborative, in which enterprise benefits are part of an implicit labour contract based on employee commitment. Much is just old-fashioned corporate paternalism.

Take Google as a quintessential example. Applicant employees are judged by their perceived 'Googliness', possessing a set of characteristics indicating a predisposition to labour hard in a collaborative way. In Googleplex, its Californian headquarters, and its various outposts around the world, employees are provided with free breakfast, lunch, dinner and transport, as well as an on-site laundry service, hairdressing and even massage. Offices are decorated with 'fun objects' in primary colours and giant bean-bags lend a sense of informality. In return, employees are expected to work long hours, although engineers are allowed 20 per cent of their time on the job to pursue 'projects' (Palmer, 2007).

For corporations, the construction of communities covering members from their various units promises efficiency gains as well as improvement in corporate ethos and self-disciplining loyalty of employees, who might otherwise not see the company as their vehicle for self-realization. Companies have come up with numerous names for these forms of incorporation – 'knowledge communities', 'interest groups', 'competency networks', 'communities of practitioners', 'epistemic communities' and so on (Porac et al., 1989; Wenger et al., 2002). Preserving independence from full incorporation will be a challenge to those wishing to construct occupational citizenship, because the primary interests of companies, understandably, relate to markets and profits.

Corporate citizenship initiatives include 'participation schemes' and 'social dialogue', on terms acceptable to managements. But labour is a matter of alienating one's time for somebody else, and not on one's own terms. The employer may be a splendid person, or may be solely concerned with obtaining the most out of the worker. In either case, the employer must be primarily concerned with making a profit. In that regard, employee involvement schemes often have strategic objectives such as marginalization of unions, higher productivity or a desire to obtain the knowledge inherent in the workforce (Beale, 1994; Kelly, 1998; Black and Lynch, 2001; Belfield and Heywood, 2004). This may be legitimate, but it is not freedom.

Corporate citizenship initiatives create closed circuits of knowledge sharing and development. But they are intended to serve the firm's commercial needs. The members of the community are not in control, and there is a high probability that the primary objectives are to improve profitability and to make 'community members' supply more time to corporate objectives, rather than to their own. The labour supplied is seamless and disguised, even from community members, so that it is often much more than the time actually compensated.

The corporate citizenship model has been strengthened by a belief among management specialists that a corporation's success depends on retaining the loyalty of a core of employees, even when it externalizes much of its labour. Multinationals find their most productive employees are those belonging to strong networks (Kelley and Caplan, 1993). So, to bind them to the corporation, the salariat is encouraged to participate in peer-group CPs (Cappelli, 2000; Cohen and Prusak, 2001).

Moreover, outsourcing is seen as more successful if accompanied by the development of CPs by which the firm can maintain control over expertise and outsourcing partners. Inter-organizational CPs are also part of the flexibilization process, building a network system that raises transactional efficiency. Nominally independent service contractors are linked to the coordinating firm, making their independence more formal than real.

> Toyota, for instance, has invested a great deal of effort in creating a knowledge-sharing network among its suppliers. . . It expects companies that it helps improve quality and efficiency to share their lessons with other selected suppliers. As one Toyota manager explained, 'That's one of our requirements, because if we take the time and effort to transfer the know-how, we need to be able to use the supplier's operation as a vehicle to help other suppliers'.
>
> (Wenger et al., 2002, p. 221)

Apparently, this has boosted productivity (Dyer and Nobeoka, 2000). Other corporations are using such 'trust-based' mechanisms to increase innovations (Adler, 2001). They are managing without being employers or managers, highlighting the increasingly blurred distinction between employees and independent contractors.

Many observers highlight the positive aspects of 'distributional' communities where groups come from several firms. However, corporate-driven CPs are scarcely ideal structures for learning. They may involve a shared domain of knowledge and create bonds of trust. But the learning is shaped by the needs and beliefs of the corporation. It may create a restrictive comfort zone. But it will give little attention to the public sphere or caring roles outside the corporate sphere. Nor should it.

There are downsides. Corporate CPs are easily driven by plain competitiveness, with members aiming to boost earnings and lower costs while taking a larger share of corporate revenue, in income, perks or access to corporate security, status and upward mobility. To avoid this they will be subject to surveillance by management, which may place loyalists in their midst to report on activities and to encourage them to undertake some activities and to avoid others. Even their most enthusiastic proponents see them as advancing organizational interests and leveraging internal expertise (Wenger et al., 2002, p. 217).

They may also become vehicles of frustration, with members dissipating energy in coalescing around a grievance agenda, becoming 'gripe communities', without the constitutional setup to be representation-and-bargaining agents. And as even their most enthusiastic proponents admit, they are prone to the bureaucratic failings of documentism (excessive collection of minutes, records and such like), amnesia (forgetting what was decided and thus repeating procedures), dogmatism (from repeated expressions of perceived success) and mediocrity (due to the most earnest being able to dominate).

The CP perspective paints a rosy picture of collaboration, without considering the need for safeguards against opportunism and free riding. It also opens up the prospect of new forms of managerial control. Consider the following description of McKinsey's approach:

> Much of the 'measurement and management' of practice activity is actually handled at the level of individual community members. This happens via the mental calculations of McKinsey's achievement-oriented consultants, who constantly ask themselves: 'What can I do today that will contribute most to getting results or building capacity?' This performance ethic pervades the firm and provides a crucial foundation for the firm's practice-management efforts. Every consultant goes through an extremely rigorous biannual, 360-degree appraisal that determines bonuses and promotions. Members who lead specific practice-building initiatives include this work in their performance review.
>
> (Wenger et al., 2002, p. 163)

Wenger and his colleagues advised corporations to train 'coordinators' in the art of 'corporate community organizing'. Selected employees are expected to be a means by which communities are integrated in the firm's commercial objectives. But such communities are compromised as vehicles for liberating personal development and rights.

Companies also influence the way people consume by fostering consumer communities, through e-commerce and web-driven networks. Thus, they can commodify do-it-yourself work by inducing employees to purchase their products and do the work of construction or maintenance, outsourcing time-intensive activities that provide little profit if retained as labour (Hagel and Armstrong, 1997; Figallo, 1998; McWilliam, 2000).

Clearly, much ingenuity has gone into building corporate citizenship. While some of those involved are mainly interested in consultancy work they hope to obtain, others surely do believe in its capacity to improve the working environment and raise productivity. There are sceptics who dismiss it all as bogus and 'bluewash'. We will not review that debate here, let alone the wider corporate social responsibility (CSR) movement (for reviews, see Hopkins, 2006; Standing, 2007b). But even *The Economist* (2008b) concluded, 'Much good corporate citizenship is a smug form of public relations'. CSR has become risk-cutting expenditure. A firm pilloried for pollution or possible use of child workers could fail to attract talented workers or a high credit rating. *The Economist* was surely correct to express scepticism about 'multi-stakeholder initiatives' by which companies link up to operate social policy. This is the responsibility of government, not firms that exist by their ability to make profits. A company's interests should properly differ from an individual's development interests. That said, corporate citizenship is unlikely to fade. It is not necessarily in conflict with occupational citizenship, but it may strengthen commodification rather than liberate us from it.

OCCUPATIONAL CITIZENSHIP

At the outset, the idea of occupation was linked to vocation and to civic friendship, partly captured in the modern idiom of the occupational community. As far as vocation is concerned, we may be experiencing an intellectual equivalent of the Renaissance, a realization that our work should not be set by some *deus ex machina*, be it a boss, an awesome technology embodied in massive buildings or machines, or some monolithic agent of the state. In the future, individual men and women will be able to shape their own careers, a vocational mix of work statuses, competencies and forms of remuneration.

The type of work we do, and how we combine work and leisure, is what gives us our identity. We see ourselves in occupational terms, as we sign visa applications or register at hotels or tell a stranger at a bar. As industrial citizenship has declined, so occupational identities have spread. Only secondarily are these provided by the institution where we currently work. More people in modern society, as in pre-industrial society, see themselves as belonging to an occupational community. Part of this derives from the shift from an industrial society based on manufacturing to one based on services; part is related to rising levels of schooling, however distorted that may be, and to qualifications; and part is due to the desire to combine different types of work, including reproductive work.

The general idea of occupational citizenship recalls Durkheim's thesis that 'professional groups' might become 'the chief source of social solidarity' and 'the foundation of the moral order' (Durkheim [1893] 1964, p. 333). This route was envisaged at a time of crisis in Polanyi's Transformation, and was a road not taken because the labourist route was too dominant. Its time may come.

Traditionally, occupations involved productive and reproductive aspects, binding practitioners together through civic friendship. But in the late eighteenth century, a productivist bias created a breach between productive and reproductive forms of work. The later error of labourism was giving a bias to labour that produced goods or that facilitated the production of goods, while systematically neglecting reproductive work. Recall how Adam Smith in *The Wealth of Nations* ([1776] 1979, p. 430) classified service occupations as unproductive. Now, reproductive work in occupations must be rescued, as both nurturing and caring, and involving civic friendship.

Thinking of occupation builds in consideration of inter-worker and 'horizontal' relationships, between peers and between networks who share common interests. The labourist model focused on hierarchical or 'vertical' relationships, between capital and labour, bosses and workers, employers and employees, managers and the 'shop floor'. Sociologists looked at occupational communities, while historians recalled the guilds. But industrial relations, labour law and bodies such as the ILO concentrated on the hierarchical elements, distorting regulations and elevating the values of labour over those of work and occupation.

Let us define the nucleus of a Good Occupation. It would be a range of activities that allowed for self-development, facilitating steadily improving competence, should the person want or have the capacity to achieve that. It would require individuals doing the range of tasks to sustain a sense of identity and status. A Good Occupation cannot be defined in terms of competitiveness or efficiency. We need 'inefficiencies', as defined by conventional economic criteria of production. Observe a true craftsman or artist and marvel at the inefficiencies.

We may approach occupation from complementary angles, the need for self-governance and the need to facilitate a capability-enhancing combination of types of activity. A Good Occupation would enable people to sustain a career, to combine reproductive and productive activities, and to have control over time, over skill development and use, over the necessary raw materials and means of production, over the use to which the output or service is put and over the income derived from the work (allowing choice about how the earnings are spent). It would also allow for civic friendship and would give access to affordable, desirable social protection. And it would provide avenues for individual and collective agency, for dealing with employers, with libertarian paternalists, with fellow workers and those with competing or complementary interests. With those points in mind, a few normative issues should be borne in mind in devising desirable institutions for advancing occupational citizenship.

Identity

Citizenship is partly about the right to possess an identity, a sense of knowing who one is and with whom one has shared values. Identity sits uneasily with liberalism, since that presumes a common personhood, as was implicit in the US Constitution. As Fukuyama (2007, p. 28) has argued, 'Modern liberal societies in Europe and North America tend to have weak identities; many celebrate their own pluralism and multiculturalism, arguing in effect that their identity is to have no identity'. Amartya Sen (2006) has called the outcome 'plural monoculturalism'. Both of these claims miss something.

Having multiple identities is not the same as having weak identity. Multiple identities seem quite healthy, limiting obsessiveness. Among the identities that people hold is their occupational identity. In Europe the schism of Christianity in the Reformation could be said to have influenced how occupational identity evolved. Luther attacked the Catholic emphasis on works – conformity to rules – and the Reformation identified religiosity as a personal state. This led to a disjuncture between people's inner and outer selves, and a breakdown of rigid barriers to social mobility. Henceforth, status could be achieved in careers 'open to the talents' rather than being ascribed. Identity has always hinged on occupation in some way. Modern identity is also inherently political, because it demands legalized recognition, including for group identities.

Occupations are part of multiculturalism. For instance, in Muslim society, the focus of Fukuyama's essay just cited, individual identity is given by parents and the local environment. Moving to another society causes problems of authenticity because of the gap between a person's inner identity as a Muslim and the behaviour required by a market society. Analogous concerns afflict the world of work in the globalizing labour market. If a person acquires an occupational identity – plumber, mason, economist, dentist – he or she can move with a sense of authenticity, even if the surrounding culture is alien. But if the person possesses no occupational identity or has to function outside it, attitudes, behaviour and psychological health may be impaired.

The challenge is further complicated because service occupations are more likely to involve multiple identities than manufacturing or agrarian occupations. Most involve several distinct functions, some of which are in other occupations. For instance, a person may be an economist and a writer. The desirable response to this should be to create mechanisms by which anyone can become part of several communities, each of which represents perceived interests or identity. There should be no need to abandon identity, or to think that it is not being recreated because it does not correspond to old stereotypes. The challenge is to enable those identities to coalesce in progressive ways, to advance personal freedom and satisfying capabilities.

Education for Occupation

An occupation encourages learning through work and within a community, to the extent that it exists. A society in which there are thriving occupational communities is likely to favour an education system that emphasizes character, civic friendship, discursive reasoning and an appreciation of cultural and technical history.

There is what should be called 'occupational education' alongside other forms of schooling and education. The notion of vocational education has been captured to mean technical training, to be an engineer or plumber. That strips the idea of occupation of its mystery and social cloak. The traditions and culture of a particular occupation are reproduced through the semi-autonomous community of the occupation. Such education does not just exist alongside other forms; it stands against the domination of a standardizing norm-driven system.

In the early twentieth century, school systems had three streams – one for the elite, oriented to the ruling class and their socially approved professionals, one for manual skilled workers who needed secondary schooling to ply their trade and one for the proletariat.

One might say that the first group received education, the second a little education and a lot of schooling, and the third merely elementary schooling to inculcate discipline.

While education is for occupation, schooling is for labour. In the twentieth century, as argued in Chapter 5, schooling gained ground over education. Neo-liberals give a high value to schooling, which produces the 'human capital' they regard as necessary for integrating economies and individuals into the globalized system. But schooling and human capital are not education. A society committed to occupational citizenship would give a high value to education, a lower value to schooling.

In a gem of intellectual insight, Hegel described education as 'the art of making men ethical'. He argued, 'The final purpose of education . . . is liberation and the struggle for higher liberation still' (Hegel [1820] 1952, §187). Schooling tends to teach people to be competitive, opportunistic and – for those expected to labour – disciplined. By contrast, education teaches beauty, in the mind and in the hand. We all suffer from an education deficit; most of us suffer from a surfeit of schooling.

A Good Occupation is one in which the values of education, ethics and reflection are inculcated in its members. Awareness of and curiosity about abstract concepts and knowledge are given precedence over specific procedures. The insight of Hegel was to see education as facilitating the ethical life, which is the structure of rules, obligations and normative principles that we internalize through participating in an ethical community. The working community is a vital construct; if one is outside an occupational community one is, almost definitionally, unable to develop the ethical parameters of freedom. Hegel emphasized that in civil society an important freedom was that of being able to choose an occupation (Pelczynski, 1984, p. 156).

As they emerge, occupations initially are based on traditions of general learning, but once established this informal legitimation tends to be replaced by technical legitimacy. And in the process there is a shift from legitimacy of character to legitimacy of technique (Abbott, 1988, p. 190).

State schools have been a way of advancing occupational citizenship, setting standards of competence, of criteria for inclusion and exclusion, of identity. However, they always had a dialectical character, being a means of discipline as well as a means of liberation, and their capacity to induce a craft ethic has been weakened by the commodification discussed in Chapter 5. Privatization and liberalization, allowing commercial multinational services to enter national educational and training markets, threaten the appreciation of local history and culture so essential for occupational citizenship. They threaten the liberating capacities of education and strengthen the commodifying functions of schooling. If liberalization is to continue, the state must counteract that tendency. To do that requires policymakers to recognize the problem.

Much of the knowledge embodied in an occupational practitioner is tacit rather than codifiable and may be little understood even by the practitioner until or unless required in response to specific circumstances (Schon, 1983). The answer to the conundrum of reviving liberating education is outside the scope of this book. However, a modern occupation requires a sense of self-discipline, and a well-disciplined mind is one that masters one discipline in order not to be at the mercy of others (Gardner, 2007). Education should prepare people for specialization, but also for synthesizing information in unanticipated ways. A good education should enable people to do many forms of work that are not labour, but which are essential for an occupational existence in a market society.

Time for Occupation

A crucial aspect of occupation is the ability to allocate time to complementary activities. In a service-oriented society, a person's occupation cannot be neatly determined by how much time is devoted to paid activity. This we may call labour-for-labour, that done for income. But there is also a great deal of work-for-labour, done so as to perform labour satisfactorily, which may be an unwritten obligation or may be essential to maintain contact with occupational work. There is also the time needed for work-for-reproduction, or care. Then there is work-for-leisure, the work needed to enable a person to participate in social activities around employment, including work needed to participate as a citizen. The Greeks saw this as the most vital work of a citizen. We should be just as respectful of it. Finally, there is play, the allocation of time to repose, some of which helps people to function in labour.

We deal with liberating time in the next chapter. Here we are concerned with aspects linked to occupation. There are numerous forms of work-for-labour in a modern tertiary society. Consider just a few. One is financial management work, the handling of personal finances. This is generating new or enlarged occupations of financial advisers. However, ordinary citizens must develop basic capabilities if they are not to be disadvantaged. Acquiring and using these skills takes time. The elite, proficians and salariat have more access to financial knowledge, which is a source of inequality, while the precariat is hurt by lack of knowledge and advice. In 2008, in reaction to the sub-prime crisis in the USA, a President's Council on Financial Literacy was set up when it became obvious that many mortgage borrowers had not understood the risks. It established a Financial Literacy Corps, echoing the US Peace Corps, to mobilize volunteers to advise those in financial difficulties. These gestures came out of a globalization shock. The structural challenge is to find ways of enabling people to have the time and capability to integrate such work into their occupational life.

In the UK, a 2004 survey found that 9 million people were 'financially phobic', meaning they did all they could to avoid anything to do with financial information. Since governments and businesses have pushed more responsibility for financial well-being onto individuals, not only is there more primary insecurity (due, for instance, to the shift to personally managed retirement accounts) but there is also more secondary insecurity (greater likelihood that the less well-educated and less 'lucky' will make financial mistakes). This responsibility is stressful and imposes time-consuming work on the citizen. It breeds a hidden source of inequality, since the person with a full-time job that leaves little free time will be disadvantaged compared with someone with a more leisurely livelihood. Quality free time means time when a person has the energy, capacity to concentrate and the means of consulting those with expertise. Thus, there are reasons for saying that financial management learning and work should be integral parts of a person's occupation. It is a basic need of modern society.

Other forms of work that are unequally distributed but which could become less so if incentive structures were refined include 'free' work allowed by firms. It has been found that companies can improve performance by *reducing* controls on time use in the workplace. The company 3M, for instance, operates a '15 per cent rule' under which employees can spend 15 per cent of their labour time on 'pet projects'. This might appear to deprive shareholders of profits, but apparently leads to innovations and dynamic efficiency. But it is also a source of inequality because those who benefit tend to be in the salariat.

Similarly, 'corporate volunteering' allows employees of large corporations, particularly in their early restless stages, to absent themselves to work for a 'non-profit' NGO for a few months. This is attractive for the employee and for the company, which can advance its image through 'company philanthropy' while being a draw when it goes to college campuses to recruit. Corporate volunteering helps the employee's career, broadens CVs and enhances social skills. But it increases inequality, since the perk goes to higher-earning employees. It is a way of extending corporate reach while colonizing civil society, eroding its subversive and anti-bureaucratic ethos. 'Experteeism' may displace a creative chaotic egalitarianism. In an egalitarian society, the state would ensure that volunteering became a citizenship right or option, rather than a privilege for the salariat.

The citizen is also being required to undertake work that used to be available as commercial services, with self-checkouts at grocery stores, automated check-in services at airports and 'ordering screens' in restaurant chains. Private hospitals in the Heritage Valley Health System in Pennsylvania operate check-in kiosks for emergency units, where the person (or accompanying person) touches an image of the part of the body where there is pain. In these and other cases, people are performing what was part of the production and service economy. The work is still done, but productivity and profits are enhanced for the benefit of the company.

Ethics represent another type of work important in a tertiary society. It is a 'skill' that takes time and effort to acquire. Medical professionals have been required to undergo ethical training since the 1970s, and such training has been creeping into accountancy. The study of ethics should be part of work in other occupations as well. If teaching is necessary, time must be freed to enable all citizens to learn a growing part of work. A carpenter needs to develop ethical appreciation just as much as a doctor.

Knowledge acquisition is also work that is not labour. The standardization and packaging of knowledge, in do-it-yourself manuals and websites, are breeding more time investment in self-service work. The Open Source movement – epitomized by the 'inventor' of the World Wide Web, who wonderfully did not turn it into a profit-making venture – has made it possible for enthusiasts to share ideas with little financial cost. But the sharing and search for knowledge does cost time, sometimes a lot.

The major form of work that is not labour is care work. An occupational profile should allow for reproductive work, including the care of relatives and the imparting of knowledge and support to fellow practitioners. These are undervalued in a market society because they do not boost conventional measures of economic growth. However, care for sick relatives or children is welfare enhancing and 'productive'. Without it, children would be neglected, people would suffer and claims on social services would be increased. The market society leaves such work out of account. A civilized society would recognize it as work and wish to reduce the pressure to labour that reduces the time people would otherwise choose to spend on it.

For people to be able flexibly to combine forms of work and labour, there must be more appreciation of occupational citizenship, in which those practising tasks that comprise an occupation can follow rules they regard as fair. In a Good Occupation, there should be equal opportunity for all practitioners to gain 'upward' mobility. Status mobility should be based on demonstrated capabilities rather than contacts. There must be equal opportunity for locational mobility, should practitioners wish to move, and equal checks on opportunism. And governance of the occupation should be based firmly on deliberative democracy (Bohman and Rehg, 1997). It should aim to achieve a shared sense of meaning and common will.

The 'price' of labour should be determined as much as possible by common criteria, and incomes should not reflect a winner-takes-all model. That will be among the hardest challenges. Ultimately, mechanisms of redistribution are needed within occupations so that solidarity is strengthened, based on mutual help and structured reciprocities. At this point, we will not suggest how these could arise; they are addressed in the final chapter.

As for life-cycle flexibility, most occupational trajectories involve paths that allow for capability development, with points along the way when the person can choose from several options. Consider any modern occupation, such as 'editor'. Someone who edits the writing of others can be described as a professional, being 'skilled', having credentials and being experienced. An editor is also something of an artist, particularly when required to rescue turgid texts. This engenders differentiation within the occupation. There are editors who do little more than 'copy-edit' and there are editors who rewrite manuscripts to make them presentable. In effect, when a person enters an occupation, he or she should be enabled to follow a career path of choice.

These options allow people the scope to develop aspects of their working lives in flexible ways. They constitute just one aspect of the huge variety of time uses that open up if we think of occupation as a career of combining types of work, labour, leisure and play. An egalitarian should wish that all have the opportunity to pursue their own sense of occupation as best they can.

Career, Not Careerism

Building a lifetime career and careerism do not fit well together. Careerism implies a stressful desire to climb the ladder inside an enterprise or organization, and is a form of alienated labour. It involves interpersonal competition, when one person's gain is another's loss. It is disingenuous to present jobs and the labour process as enabling everyone 'to get ahead' if they would only invest more in human capital. And yet we can imagine forms of advance that are non-conflictual. A liberal typically makes no distinction. An egalitarian should try to do so.

How could mechanisms for collective improvement emerge? Consider a familiar scenario. Suppose there were to be a prize for the person who comes top of the class. This will give an incentive to the contenders to conceal information from competitors, resulting in a lower achievement all round, especially as time and effort would have to be devoted to concealment. If the prize were offered to the whole class if the average achievement passed a threshold level, the concealment would decline but an opposite problem would emerge. The leading lights would be less motivated, because the prize would be shared and they would be obliged to drag laggards with them. And the time they could devote to their own work would be cut. Neither solution would be optimum; a mix of incentives is required. Some incentive to collective development is desirable.

Professionalism tried to confront this dilemma. A professional career crystallized as a strategy to permit a coherent individual life within a fluctuating market economy. But professionalism is only one form of career. Organizational and bureaucratic careers are others. None provide a strong prospect of coherent life in the context of globalization. We will have to look to another form that avoids their shortcomings.

In the old professions a career was prolonged and generally an older, more experienced person was more 'expert'; much professional knowledge reflected 'character' and the ingrained politics of an occupation. But in the late twentieth century, the rapidity of technological advance and the domination of 'science' and 'technique' over 'character' meant that age and experience became perceived as unreliable guides to expertise. In the twenty-first century, in many spheres of work, younger cohorts will have more technical skill than older 'senior' cohorts. The gulf in expertise between the generations may make occupational rupture in mid-life more likely, with people switching to other ways of working and living rather than remaining in their original career path. This may not occur if the pace of the scientific revolution were to slow. But it is the likely scenario.

Traditionally, labour markets have adhered to a vacancy model or a career model. With the former, entry to upper levels is based on waiting for departures and filling them from the internal labour market; it has no pre-determined chronology or history. With the career model, progression depends primarily on experience and acquisition of additional qualifications. While most labour markets have operated with a mix of both, a question is whether the emerging model will be 'career-less'.

There is evidence that relatively educated youth do not aspire to the old notion of a career consisting of long-term attachment to a firm, or a predetermined career. Desire to be a model employee is not high on the list of priorities. In 2008, a UK survey found that 40 per cent of workers aged under 35 who were in private sector employment wanted to move into public service or charity work, and one-third were considering such a move (CHA, 2008). More than 60 per cent of those aged 18–25 claimed to want 'more worthwhile work'. Generation-Y (aged 20-something) is light on its feet. It is not looking for 'decent employment'. This is not an elitist reaction. It is a clash between capability development and a productivist system. Dissonance can lead to an anomic reaction, passive and even self-destructive, or a frustrated reaction shown by anger. No doubt, in many cases anomie and alienation will coexist.

Some claim that all this reflects a failure of employers to engage with employees. In 2008, Gallup Poll surveys on employee satisfaction found that large numbers responded negatively to the statement, 'I know what is expected of me at work'. The conventional response would be to make the firm an engine of CSR, to induce employee commitment. The alternative would be to strip firms of these pretensions and make employment more commercial, not less. Although workers might still wish to move on, they should receive the full value of their labour, and not have part of the income used for fancy engagement schemes, enterprise perks and glossy brochures.

At present, careerism and career building are aspects of inequality in a society in which the salariat is granted cumulative advantages. Only a minority are privileged. For instance, an aspect of corporate paternalism is the tactic used by some companies to develop flexible careers for their salaried employees, designed to retain loyalty. Deloitte devised a scheme its executives called 'mass career customization', intended to tailor the firm's labour to individual needs. Employees are provided with a menu of options in four areas – pace of career progress, workload, location and intended role, from 'leader' to 'individual contributor' (Benko and Weisberg, 2007).

Such selective privileges could be generalized as part of an egalitarian occupational strategy. There is no reason to believe that career building for proficians and for those in the precariat could not be equally developed, perhaps through the involvement of career development agents, part of the armoury of service adjustment occupations. But rather than having split loyalties, as must be the case inside firms, such agents should be working solely in the interests of their clients, the citizens.

De-professionalization: Respect for Proficians

In the twentieth century, professionalism and casualization were seen as opposites. Professionalism exists because a common body of knowledge is perceived to exist for a group that is in more or less continual demand. In the twenty-first century, there may be de-professionalization, since increasingly there will not be enough individuals with similar distinctive bodies of knowledge, or people will be operating partly as commodified workers depending on commodified (packaged) knowledge. Part of our knowledge will be commodifiable. Part of it will not be in continual demand. And the abstract knowledge required will pass more quickly from a monopoly stage (possessed by a group with specialized knowledge) to a non-abstract stage (known to non-professionals).

Abbott argued that professionalism exists because competing forms of institutionalization have not yet overwhelmed it. This may change as alternative forms of structuring expertise evolve, through the internet, courses, NGOs and commodified packages of knowledge and processes. Although commodification 'democratizes expertise' it does so in a structured environment, leaving commodity users helpless when systems go wrong.

Some believe the twenty-first century will be the century of 'amateurs' and that the 'reign' of professionals has passed (Leadbeater, 2002a, 2002b). The idea is that amateurs will thrive via the internet, which allows endless access to information and the means of coordination of activities and networks. But some work requires 'hardware' that amateurs cannot hope to possess. Moreover, amateurism may be synonymous with dilettantism, resulting in superficiality and lack of direction. Need for hardware points to the desirability of a 'pro-am' model, in which corporations link to networks of proficians. This may lead to concern over the means by which firms manipulate the loyalty of proficians, to ensure they obtain the value added by their labour. But the point is that new forms of work are proliferating, outside the realm of labour.

If professionalism is to mean combining specialist and flexible knowledge, rather than dilettantism or extreme specialization, we need to rethink the status of 'casual' within occupational work. There is no doubt that the notion of 'casual labour' throws up negative images. One thinks of the docklands (and scenes from *On the Waterfront*), of workers waiting forlornly on corners for a day job, jostling for position with fellow supplicants. One thinks of seamstresses waiting for a middleman to come round with work, requiring a payment of some kind in return. One thinks of workers without contracts, employment security or the assurance of a reasonable income.

Yet we must not be one-sided. The word 'casual' is usually regarded as synonymous with 'informal'. Think of casual wear as opposed to formal attire. The image is 'you decide', a lack of standardization or imposed discipline by an authority figure. The downside is unpredictability, being at someone's beck-and-call, insecure, dependent and patronized. This two-sided character means that an increase in casual employment may not be an indicator of deteriorating labour markets. When the ILO's Socio-Economic Security Programme (ILO, 2004) asked about work satisfaction in worker security surveys, many in casual jobs expressed more satisfaction than many in non-casual employment.

Occupational citizenship must be about being in control. In rethinking casualization we should ask: 'Casual on whose terms?' If the casualness is at the whim of an employer the worker will be insecure. If the choice is the worker's, the employer may suffer the insecurity. Labour contractualization should be reconsidered. The challenge is to make contracts balanced, providing mutual advantages. Although existing casualization does have huge disadvantages, the upsides include the effect on autonomy. Too many people admit late in life that they were trapped by clinging to long-term jobs that had rarely given them satisfaction or joy. Contracts and labour market mechanisms should seek to equalize the advantages of casual and 'permanent', and not make the costs of non-permanent status so high. Workers and firms should be able to negotiate more flexible schedules that suit both sides without huge costs and insecurity.

It is claimed that casual labour offers a route from unemployment into regular employment, acting as a stepping stone in a process of assimilation. But it may result in a person building up a profile of instability via a series of short-term contracts. An occupational citizenship perspective should break down such stereotypes. If you leave five lousy jobs in the hope of finding one that suits your personality and needs, you should not be typecast by profilers as a social misfit. You may be, but there should be no presumption that you are.

Casual labour may also respond to a person's needs. With more youth at university or college, more in that age group want only casual jobs to help pay for their studies. Similarly, young women contemplating having children may prefer casual jobs (although there should be no presumption that they should take them). More significant is the vast number of older workers who have left a career job and would welcome casual work to boost an inadequate pension or stay active and socially involved.

Recognizing the positive aspects leads back to the proficians. Casual work, if intense, is their life. In most respects, their life is to be envied. In 2005, the UK government's bill for consultants was over £2.2 billion. Consultants typically earned three times as much as regular employees doing similar work alongside them, and in several government departments the bill for consultants exceeded the wage bill for all salaried staff. One section of the Department of Health had almost as many consultants as full-time officials. Meanwhile, UK private firms have been spending more on consultancies, including 4 per cent of their annual expenditure just on management consultants, according to the Management Consultants Association.

Casual work is good in this realm of the labour market. It makes sense for companies and proficians. Productivity may be higher, overhead costs lower, labour relations smoother. As the number of proficians grows in tertiary society, a challenge for policymakers and civil society bodies will be to enable more of the precariat to become something closer to proficians.

For that to happen, people must have basic economic security to enable them to develop their capabilities into bundles of portable skills, which means the educational system and employment services will have to adapt. It also means establishing a floor of universal socioeconomic rights, which we consider in the next chapter. But reflect on the fact that the main collective bargaining regime of the twentieth century entailed commitment to minimum standards for employees. It was sexist, and increased gaps between those outside the labour market and those in the standard employment relationship. But it had advantages over the current 'employment rights' regime, with its plethora of judicial rules coupled with 'HRM' techniques, which has sharpened divisions between those in different work statuses. Labour law has become more of an instrument of division, protecting some and not others. In conceptualizing occupational citizenship, one should presume that the same protection should be given to everybody.

The Right to Practise

To conclude the conceptualization of occupational citizenship, one must confront issues raised by a fundamental libertarian claim. Is there a right to practise whatever occupation one wishes? If so, what, if any, legal obligations should be imposed? What moral obligations should be expected? What sanctions would be appropriate if obligations or morality were breached?

We have seen how occupational licensing is under attack. The claim that it is a restraint of trade and a denial of the right to work cannot be dismissed easily. The Lochner era in the USA between 1905 and 1937 (see Chapter 2) has been described by libertarians as 'the Golden Age of the right to work'. The Lochner ruling stemmed from the Magna Carta of 1215, which affirmed a right to buy and sell unhindered. But the libertarian glee was a response to its blocking of collective interventions in defence of workers.

Now, as pro-market reforms have weakened professions and their guilds, there is a need to build occupational associations. The precariat, and to some extent the proficians, are trapped by labour law and anti-trust regulations. Individuals seen as independent workers may be classified as independent contractors, supplying a service to clients, rather than employees supplying labour. As such, they will be blocked from taking collective action against an employer or anybody else. Their associational freedom is denied. This impasse can only be broken by constructing institutions and policies that enable them to sustain careers, allowing productive, reproductive and leisure work around civic friendship and solidarity, rather than pitching life as one of constant competition. In a tertiarized society, a new tyranny of the clock and calendar that was at the heart of industrial labour must be overcome.

Citizenship is about rights. Do I have a right to do what I am doing? If you have a right to be a lawyer, it must mean there should not be any arbitrary or non-technical impediment to you becoming a lawyer and that you must have as good an opportunity to practise as a lawyer as anybody else. A difficulty arises in determining what would be a legitimate barrier to you becoming a lawyer and practising law for an income. If you have occupational freedom, it should mean there are no constraints to doing the work you choose, other than that you satisfy rules that prevent you from doing harm to others. That raises the familiar problem of knowing what harm you could do, cited as the justification for licensing. Libertarians would argue that licensing interferes with the freedom of both the practitioner and consumer. They are essentially correct, as long as potential externalities can be settled, given that unqualified practitioners have a relatively high probability of incurring them.

Ideally, members of an occupation pursue two freedoms – freedom from the power of others, and freedom to retain the capacity for choice itself. But they may also seek freedom to dominate surrounding occupations, to dominate clients, to negotiate with the state, and to negotiate with civil society. The first two comprise the essence of occupational citizenship – developmental freedom. What we have elsewhere called subordinated flexibility is its opposite. The other freedoms are less easy to justify, requiring regulation and associational responses.

As occupational citizenship should imply that individuals have reasonable control over their working lives, policies and institutions should be judged by whether or not they advance occupational rights. But they should also honour the justice and freedom principles presented in the final chapter.

BEYOND THE ILO?

A global strategy to promote work rights and occupational citizenship requires a regulatory system, which means an institution responsible for setting standards, guidelines and procedures. Is the ILO capable of playing that role?

The ILO was set up to take wages and labour out of international competition, as Polanyi put it. It cannot do so in a globalized open economy. It was geared to national labour markets and industrial citizenship based on labour law, collective bargaining and tripartism, with employer organizations confronting trades unions, mediated by the state. It promoted the standard employment relationship, rephrasing that at the end of the century as 'decent work', which soon reverted to 'decent jobs'. Faced with the erosion of its labourist model, it advocated an agenda of 'extension' of social security and regulations to the 'informal sector', coupled with 'active labour market policy'. It could not escape from the mindset that jobs were desired by everybody. It adhered to labour force statistics designed in the 1930s, and a governance structure stuck in the industrial era, with trades unions called Workers and employers' bureaucratic organizations called Employers, as if unions and employer bodies were the only representatives in the globalizing work process.

Could an organization steeped in a century of labourism adjust to an agenda of occupational citizenship? There is a need for an international body, but it must be one that can escape tripartism, that acknowledges that labour *is* a commodity and that is able to foster occupational standards, collaborative bargaining and occupational citizenship rights. For the ILO to fulfil that role, it would have to be radically overhauled. It is doubtful whether it has the will or capacity to do so, being trapped in its governance structure, where bureaucratic employers and labour unions have a gridlock on voting procedures. It is relevant that none of the international bodies representing occupations participate in the ILO's annual conferences and are nowhere near its governing body.

The Global Transformation requires appropriate global institutions of governance. A world financial organization may emerge from the financial debacle of 2008, ideally with a mandate to curb tax competition and beggar-my-neighbour fiscal policies. The global labour process similarly requires a new kind of organization. If the ILO cannot be restructured, a new body should be established to regulate global work arrangements.

Such an organization should focus on occupational regulation – taking over responsibility for setting global standards, occupational accreditation procedures and right-to-practise guidelines, converting MRAs into global arrangements, making Mode 4 (movement of natural persons) of the GATS a reality, and so on. It is historically significant that the ILO was left out of the GATS process concerned with regulating occupational work and determining what forms of regulation should be deemed acceptable. By contrast, the World Bank and its International Finance Corporation established a framework ('toolkit') for occupational licensing, as part of a more general approach to regulation. Neither of those financial institutions should be dealing with work rights. Neither has a mandate or expertise to do so.

The global work body should shift from building labour entitlements to work rights, making them genuinely universal for all types of work. It should also help labour law become part of common law, and convert labourist conciliation, mediation and arbitration councils into work commissions that can deal with inter-occupation, intra-occupation and other work issues rather than just employer–employee complaints. And it should escape from the vapidity of 'social dialogue', adopted by the ILO when it abandoned its industrial relations department in 1999, by promoting what we will call collaborative bargaining, helping to legitimize associations that represent all interests in all forms of work. In forging occupational citizenship rights, there is much that it could do.

REGULATING LABOUR MIGRATION

We cannot contemplate occupational citizenship without considering how migration is to be regulated. Unless something terrible were to happen, plunging the international system back into closed societies and brutal confrontation, as occurred in the disembedded phase of the Great Transformation, the global system will involve continuing growth of human mobility. One can realistically imagine a world in which a majority spend at least part of their lives working outside the country of their birth.

Much of the growing migration is linked to the transient nature of labour relations. Economists are unsure how types of mobility affect patterns of poverty and inequality. There is evidence that migrants follow particular occupational streams, with networks of earlier migrants being the means of assimilation, and that those who do follow their compatriots into the same occupation do better than others (Patel and Vella, 2007). The mobility of the privileged and educated is extraordinary, with growing numbers circulating around the globe, many attached to multinationals or supra-national agencies. They have been shaping the design of social and labour market policy.

Then there is the growth of international household chains, whereby millions migrate from low-income countries to perform menial labour in richer countries, leaving behind structurally vulnerable households dependent on remittances. The remittances bolster living standards for those fortunate enough to receive them, while accentuating class differentiation in sending areas and in the urban areas to which many migrants go.

While migration may reduce poverty, and while we should favour liberalizing the movement of people, the challenge is to devise policies that address the adverse effects of movement. Inevitably, the migration has been associated with a growing number of people who are short-term residents wherever they are, often illegal or undocumented. They feed the precariat. The treatment of migrants is a source of impoverishment around the world. One of the most glaring instances is the situation in China. Many enterprises there do not enrol migrant workers in social insurance – avoiding a sizable part of the wage bill (over 30 per cent) – and this is tacitly allowed by local governments (Liu, 2003). Half the working population of Shenzhen, that industrial workshop so eerily close to a panopticon society, consists of migrants, most of whom lack the basic rights supposed to hold for all Chinese workers.

The globalizing labour market requires more sophisticated interventions to regulate migration, not to restrict it. The knee-jerk reaction of some Third Worldists is that there should be unlimited migration from developing to developed countries. This would accord with a liberalized market system. Some economists have estimated that if migration was liberalized the world economy would grow hugely. But this would be politically explosive and lead to the opposite of what liberals wish. Demagogues would exploit the perceived threat to living standards of the working class and precariat. Coercive social policy would soon follow. Migrants would be subject to discrimination, abuse and expulsion, and the remittances so crucial in the fight against economic insecurity in developing countries would shrink.

Far better would be a gradual, regulated process by which investment would shift to countries in which real wages are lower because living standards and living costs are lower, while migration to the rich countries increases at a pace that can be absorbed without being seen to lower living standards of workers there.

Policies to facilitate circulation could also help. In that regard, the proposal made in 2007 by the EU's Commissioner for Justice and Home Affairs for a 'Blue Card' (like the USA's Green Card) is sensible. It would ease temporary in-migration for specific jobs, with contracts drawn up before departure. It could limit the super-exploitation of poorer vulnerable migrants, spread a form of *Gastarbeiter* (guest worker), and might even lead to countries operating import quotas for foreign workers.

There would be drawbacks. But any political solution would be a compromise. The fact remains that, just as unlimited capital mobility is conducive to economic instability, so unlimited labour mobility would be conducive to social instability and could easily foment xenophobia and unsavoury political extremism.

Starting in Mali, the EU has been setting up job centres in Africa to offer a legal avenue for labour circulation into EU jobs. This is a pioneering policy, an experiment that deserves careful monitoring before being replicated. Many questions arise. Should such agencies be required to operate on an efficiency or social equity basis? Should the costs be borne by governments, migrant workers or employers of migrants? Where should migrants' income be taxed? Under which country's labour laws should they be protected? Should the agencies provide advisory services and social protection to the migrants? Where would legal liability lie, in case of injury or illness, or even false information as to qualifications or working conditions? Should the job centre operate an affirmative action function, giving priority to women, the poorest or members of disadvantaged groups? There are no easy answers. But some should be given and made transparent. There is a wider point too. The globalizing labour process is changing the concept of citizenship and patterns of earning and income distribution. Innovative labour policy should be part of that process. There is no longer social policy in one country; it is being globalized.

REPOSITIONING REGULATIONS FOR OCCUPATIONAL CITIZENSHIP

For occupational citizenship, what sorts of regulation are needed and what should they seek to achieve? The standard answer is that regulations should protect the vulnerable, to which the Chicago School added that they should promote growth and efficiency.

Libertarians have added that they should not interfere with the 'right to practise' and should not interfere with market forces.

From an occupational perspective, regulations should create a space for equal Voice, equalizing the bargaining strength of all those involved in labour and work relationships. They should increase equity in labour relations and set parameters for governance structures so as to facilitate deliberative democracy within occupations. They are needed to monitor accreditation practices. They should create conciliation, mediation and arbitration services for all types of work–labour relations, not just those between employers and employees. And they should oversee moral and immoral hazards, preventing punitive actions against practitioners by their peers.

If we start from the view that pursuit of occupation should be self-determined, subject to meeting principles that enhance freedom, then there should be a prima facie presumption that laws and regulations setting work parameters should not be overly prescriptive. The more prescriptive a law, the more likely people will abuse it. As Rob McCallum, one of Australia's foremost labour lawyers, noted in predicting the unsustainability of his country's controversial Work Choices legislation, 'When laws are overly prescriptive, people usually bypass them in one form or another' (McCallum, 2007, p. 442).

For instance, if legislation tried to give substance to a 'right to dignity', employers would reduce the risk of being accused of causing indignity by distancing themselves from workers and depersonalizing work relations to the detriment of informal 'friendly' relationships of mutuality, weakening the sense of fraternity.

As methods of regulating occupations have evolved, there has been a tendency to dismiss defence of occupational communities. Under liberalization, governments and international agencies have sought to open them up to outsiders, while regulators have sought to make regulations supportive of competition and consumers rather than community insiders. The imbalance has gone too far.

Associational regulation must be redefined. One under-appreciated objective of licensing, and occupational regulation generally, is the promotion (or defence) of a *culture* of occupational community. Few analysts criticize institutions of 'identity community' (religious institutions, and so on) or neighbourhoods, because these are presumed to have social or cultural rather than economic functions, whereas occupations are presumed to have just commercial objectives. This is simplistic. Many local community associations or identity bodies support discriminatory practices. And occupations have many social functions.

If policymakers were to legislate consistently for a market society, citizens would be banned from operating buy-local campaigns or 'buy-from-our-community' rules, which distort prices and earning opportunities. Governments do not interfere because these communities have a social function. Occupational bodies share with other bodies a desire to sustain their community and to give protection and security to their members. They may set prices for their services higher than would otherwise be the case, so as to pool resources for distribution to colleagues in distress, to invest in research on new practices, or for other purposes oriented to the improvement of the occupation, its community and the services it provides.

Presuming some licensing will remain, what sort of body should operate it? One view is that licensing and accreditation schemes should be run purely by experts, meaning representatives of the occupation. Most licensing boards in the USA still consist entirely of practitioners (Summers, 2007, p. 18). Critics are justifiably sceptical about the moral hazards of such arrangements.

The trend is towards having boards with some public lay membership. This seems to result in more disciplinary actions being taken against practitioners (Graddy and Nichol, 1989, 1990), though a problem has been a tendency for the non-experts to defer to practitioners (Hood, 1992). A better option might be a 'multipartite' board system, with representatives not only of practitioners and consumers, but also of employers, other workers and civil society. An obvious concern is that this would produce a complex and confusing procedure, with excessive cost and inefficiency.

Occupational regulation should strengthen a culture of work as occupation, as well as serve consumer interests. Yet the trend is to make it more supportive of market principles. The main objective has been to compensate for perceived informational asymmetry between practitioners and consumers. An alternative would be to use regulation to reduce the asymmetry by making information more transparent and readily available. If this were achieved, the strictness of protective regulation could be relaxed. Measures might include dissemination of information on the reputation of the provider for quality and price. However, in the case of healthcare the requisite information might be hard to identify and might set up peculiar moral hazards. For instance, if reputation were based on indicators of successful operations, a surgeon might forego taking difficult or risky cases. The same could apply to lawyers and other professions.

Service quality has several perspectives, that of customer, practitioner and evaluator/ policymaker. Some analysts of medical services, for instance, have divided quality into technical aspects, inter-personal aspects and amenities of care. Others have assessed them by reference to qualifications, application of procedures and outcomes. It is unclear what weight should be given to each of these. In other occupations, similar difficulties would arise.

The traditional rationale for regulation is a presumption that one party, being less well-informed and more vulnerable, needs 'protection'. An alternative would be to try to reduce ignorance and vulnerability. The UK's Office of Fair Trading (2001, p. 34) proposed different regulations for transactions between companies, between firms and private consumers, and between standardized services and complex services. While superficially attractive, this would open up the prospect of arbitrary distinctions, to the delight of lawyers.

In the globalizing labour market, occupational practice must be regulated in ways that respect practitioners, their communities and those who interact with them, as clients or fellow workers. Among the unresolved issues are determining whose interests should be protected, the threats against which protection should be provided, and how to prevent emerging regulating and adjustment occupations from eroding civil liberties.

It is surely desirable that consumers should be involved in regulating occupations to ensure a balance of benefits for consumers and occupational communities. But the balance has been lost. There is a need to preserve and enhance the craft ethic and the ethos of solidarity within occupations. Consumer activism helped legitimize socially oriented professional services for disadvantaged groups, including low-income neighbourhoods, racial minorities and the disabled. Legal clinics for the poor emerged, and students were given a role in evaluating teaching, weakening the autonomy and self-evaluation of academics. These are surely desirable. However, the capacity of occupations to preserve their values and identity must not be lost in the process.

INTERNATIONAL REGULATION OF OCCUPATIONS

Developing countries have been urged, by UNCTAD (2005, p. 18) among others, to develop frameworks for occupational regulation and to support professional bodies. A danger is that they will adopt standard models from affluent countries with long experience of regulatory systems. It cannot be presumed that a 'participatory multi-stakeholder approach', involving the interests of trade negotiators, regulators, legislators, professional bodies and civil society groups, would ensure an equitable outcome, although that should help. Better would be an international independent body to assist in this process, which could also help overcome difficulties faced by small low-income countries in the GATS negotiations. Poorer countries should also receive help to raise standards to internationally prescribed levels, as part of aid-for-trade programmes.

Another danger is that globalization will distort occupational citizenship by generating a geopolitical division of labour *within* professions and divisive patterns of occupational hierarchy. For instance, research on the frontiers of a discipline may take place only in large corporations or well-endowed universities in affluent countries, and in a few cities of large industrializing countries, while professionals elsewhere have no opportunity to compete, change or deviate from a norm. This is not a nice prospect; emerging international regulations and institutions must devise methods to fight it.

RESTRUCTURING LABOUR LAW

As we have seen, labour law and social security systems were built for those in the standard employment relationship (SER). Unless workers could prove they were employees, doing labour in specific jobs, their so-called rights under the law and international conventions were limited. With the growth of the precariat and proficians, tensions in the regulatory system have become acute.

Whether in China, India, Europe or the USA, labour law is still geared to the SER and is changing from being a means of labour protection to one of enhancing competitiveness. As such, it is strengthening forms of inequality and insecurity. There are two possible routes to reform.

One is to extend protection to those deemed to be in near-standard employment. Thus, agency workers and temps could be given the same entitlements as full-time workers, with part-timers entitled to pro-rata benefits. This might cut exploitation and oppression of migrants and agency workers, and curb use of illegal migrants. To give it teeth, governments should expand labour inspectorates. This could limit exploitation in outsourced arrangements. But it would still leave the standard employment model intact. It would still mean the most insecure would be unprotected. This route would merely prop up the labourist conception of activity deemed to be legitimate and accentuate a dualism of precariousness and labour recommodification.

An alternative would be to create a floor of rights for everybody doing *all* types of work. There is nothing sacrosanct about the SER, which represents a form of dependency and a way of dividing workers into breadwinners and caregivers. Reform should not stretch the standard dualism but replace the premises on which it was based. Labour law must be phased out, not further refined; it should become part of common law, covered by contract and tort law. Labour law exists to protect *labourers*, which means accepting the 'right to be managed', in a position of subordination. In the globalization era, not even the quid pro quo of decent protection in return for the supply of effort was accepted. Labour markets deny more people even that much. And with the growing legitimacy of forms of work that are not labour, a separate labour law does not make sense. All people doing all forms of work should have an equal right to freedom of association and freedom to bargain collectively. This is not the case at the moment.

Many types of worker affected by outsourcing do not have those freedoms. Domestic workers usually do not. In many countries, managers or those in administrative positions are denied the freedom to bargain collectively, on the grounds of conflict of interest since they are deemed to owe their employers loyalty. In many countries, some occupations – all prominent in offshoring – are excluded from labour law protection on the grounds that practitioners are 'entrepreneurs', not 'employees'. Some systems exclude some people on the grounds they do not have a specific workplace. In sum, the fact that labour law is becoming more dualistic and more an instrument of labour control makes the development of independent Voice even more important.

At present, labour law mainly exists to protect *employees* in their dealings with *employers*. In the global labour process, that leaves out an enormous number who work, even by conventional definitions of worker. Attempts to extend the definition of employee, as recommended recently in Australia, for instance (Bromberg and Irving, 2007), are arbitrary, convoluted and ineffective. Extension still leaves a dichotomy.

The trouble is compounded because common law blocks people in occupations from coalescing to represent and to bargain; as independent contractors they run up against anti-trust rules. And even if they are allowed to set up as collective bodies, they are not able to bargain, because there is no legalized counterpart. There is always a difficulty to identify the party with which occupations can bargain. This should be rectified under the law.

As we saw in Chapter 7, many occupations have established legal 'rights' through licensing schemes. Although these are supposed to protect consumers, and professional standards and ethics, critics claim that licensing interferes with the citizen's right to practise. In the USA, this has been depicted as contrary to the Fourteenth Amendment of the Constitution. This problem is resolvable through the use of certification systems instead of simple licensing systems. But that should be accompanied by stronger mechanisms to build and legitimize occupational associations governed by principles of deliberative democracy. Then one could envisage laws being used to protect occupational rights and deal with issues arising from what we will describe as collaborative bargaining.

RESTRUCTURING ADJUDICATION MECHANISMS

To shift to a model of occupational rights, legislators must reform institutions of labour regulation, notably conciliation, mediation and arbitration boards or councils. They should encompass disputes between occupational bodies and individual practitioners, and between regulatory bodies and individual workers, whether actual or potential practitioners. One could envisage occupational conciliation, mediation and arbitration councils charged with dealing with all disputes relating to occupational life, including complaints over refusals of licences, suspensions from the right to practise, and simple blockages on the right to practise. In other words, they should deal not only with 'unfair labour practices' between employees and employers but with inter-occupational, intra-occupational and occupational-regulator complaints.

Regulations involve disciplines, which require proper procedures and mechanisms for appeals. Again, these must be based on the informational asymmetry presumptions that have motivated licensing, and recognition of the high probability that the individual worker will have fewer resources than the regulatory body.

Complaints procedures should be easily accessible, flexible, transparent and accountable, with Voice involvement. The cost issue is familiar. It is easy to recommend that it should be free of charge for the appellant/complainant. But this is potentially unfair on the plaintiff and defendant, especially if charges are frivolous. A danger is that extending the process to occupational relations, to deal with disputes within occupations and between practitioners of different occupations, for instance, will merely result in further litigation.

Such an outcome cannot be avoided altogether. But there are ways of limiting it. Each occupation should allow for an ombudsman function, a facility for consumers (clients) and practitioners to bring complaints about practices, barriers to the right to practise and other matters. Such a facility should be independent of any interest and yet be well-informed by all of them. Challenges include making sure that all interests are given equal weight, determining what constitutes ethical practice and avoiding the risk of an excessively legalistic process that imposes high costs on practitioners and customers. The first goal should be educational and informational, ensuring that practitioners learn about ethical or professional codes, how to adhere to them, ensure that fellow workers adhere to them and how to take action should the need arise.

Among the rules that should be respected, and which is currently ignored, is that no occupational association or licensing or accreditation scheme should be permitted to exclude qualified practitioners on grounds unrelated to the performance of the work.

Conciliation, mediation and arbitration councils should be a public social service, with a multipartite governance system in which representatives of occupational bodies should figure along with those of employers in general and workers in general. Contrary to what has been happening in labour markets, everybody should have the right to go to public arbitration, subject to some cost to avoid frivolous claims. Problems with old-style councils include under-budgeting, costs for workers bringing complaints and long delays. They have been mainly a mechanism for individual Voice, mainly over dismissals, although they have also dealt with collective labour disputes. Moving to make them deal with occupational matters would require a reorientation. For that reason, it might be better to set up separate, complementary bodies.

FROM 'LABOUR RIGHTS' TO 'WORK RIGHTS'

In recent years, several charters of employment rights have been drawn up by groups of social democratic social scientists, mostly labour lawyers (Ewing and Hendy, 2002 in the UK; Bromberg and Irving, 2007 in Australia). They were intended to sit alongside such revered declamations as the UN's Universal Declaration of Human Rights, the 1966

International Covenant on Economic, Social and Cultural Rights and the ILO's 1998 Declaration on Fundamental Principles and Rights at Work. They could have been set alongside a more up-to-date document, the Charter of Emerging Human Rights agreed at the Barcelona Forum in September 2004 (IDHC, 2004).

A historical perspective would involve asking, what is included in, and what excluded from, such charters that would have been excluded from or included in one put together 50 years earlier? In this regard, it is remarkable that in the Australian charter there is repeated reference to 'the rights of employers' and the 'worker's duty to obey', to show 'fidelity' and 'loyalty to the employer'. The ethos of labourism had been internalized and accepted. It is essential to escape from that perspective.

Another feature is the systematic exclusion of occupational rights and consideration of relations *between* groups of workers; the sole focus is on the relationship between employers and employees. Work rights cannot evolve from such a framework.

The vision presented here links rights to occupation. A critic might contend that this would penalize those who have no occupation. But occupation is defined in terms broader than can be captured by labour. Occupation embraces all forms of work and labour, so that somebody doing independent work or unpaid care should be covered by any charter of work rights. Basic security should be provided to all. For instance, the extensive amount of community work in civil society and inter-organizational initiatives implies a model in which much labour of firms and public service providers will be transferred to citizens who are unpaid for their work.

Part of the double movement in the Global Transformation must be to shift from labour law and labour legislation to work rights legislation. It should not be necessary to prove that one is an 'employee' in order to be able to form a 'combination' for representation and bargaining purposes without fear of prosecution for being a 'conspiracy in restraint of trade'.

In this regard, consider the case of freelance editors in Canada. This is a modern profession, with identifiable skills, credentials and a semblance of a career. They are independent, in that they work on a project basis for multiple clients. They experience vulnerabilities, most working with an ethic of invisibility (Vosko, 2005). They negotiate incomplete contracts in that quality and intensity of work can vary according to inclination. Work arrangements can be highly variable. Editors usually have to reach a dual bargain, with a publisher and with an author, and may have a third bargain with an agent who subcontracts work to them. To add to the complexity of their situation in Canada, there are jurisdictional tensions in allowing workers to form unions if one exists that is deemed to cover that sphere of work.

As freelance editors were deemed to be independent contractors, they were excluded from labour and social protection. So a group formed an association. As with any new profession, they set out to establish standards and criteria for membership, and soon created an internal hierarchy, with 'associate membership' for inexperienced editors and 'voting membership' for editors who had done at least 500 hours of editing in the year preceding the application to join. They also set up a mechanism for matching editors with clients, that is, an 'employment agency' function although better described as a 'work agency' function. And they developed standard contract forms and gave information on appropriate fee scales to members.

All this makes these freelancers look like an occupational community. But they faced the problems of any group trying to forge an identity outside the standard employment relationship. They were not employees under the definition in the Canada Labour Code. Nor were they deemed to be dependent contractors, which would have given them some labour 'rights'. There was also a problem with calling themselves professionals, given that many professional employees could be excluded from collective bargaining law. And if they were deemed to be independent contractors, their right to form a union would have been denied, since it would have been deemed to be a mechanism to interfere with competition.

The impasse was partially broken in 1992, when Canada became the first country to enact legislation granting collective bargaining rights to freelance or self-employed professional artists, regarded as independent contractors (albeit undefined) in the Status of the Artist Act. This unleashed a decade of legal wrangling as challenges were made to their new right, a struggle epitomizing the state of the global debate on non-standard employment.

The Act made a mockery of a century of conceptual distinctions by defining self-employed artists belonging to artists' associations as combinations of employees. It thereby exempted them from liability under the country's Competition Act for acting in concert. The Competition Act bars independent entrepreneurs from limiting the supply of products or holding up prices. But the Artist Act relieved certified artists' associations from the threat of prosecution as conspiracy in restraint of trade (MacPherson, 1999).

It also constructed a bargaining regime based on minimum terms, known as scale agreements. The idea is that artists' associations negotiate scale agreements with producers, on the basis of which artists can negotiate individual contracts, which must not pay below the minima. Here is a model for setting a floor of security for precarious working. It is flawed because it depends on the existence of a producers' association to bargain with. The artists' associations have been trying to overcome that by developing model agreements that all its members could use. There should be no need for a collective body to legitimize such principles.

Two-tier contracts and bargaining instruments nevertheless offer a promising route forward as part of the future work pattern, in which statutory law and negotiated agreements set floors of basic conditions that do not depend on employer–employee relationships. They could apply to all regarded as independent contractors – a difficulty in the Canadian case, which extends solely to those selected by the state as independent. Any 'extension' is also an act of exclusion. The Act thus did not overhaul the old labour system, but merely supplemented it by use of the language of extension.

An intriguing aspect of the Canadian Act was the distinction drawn between professional artists and hobbyists. A professional editor is defined as someone who is paid for work described as artistic, is recognized by other artists as an artist, or is in the process of becoming an artist according to the practices of the artistic community, and is a member of an artists' association that adheres to by-laws pertaining to membership. This is a remarkably restrictive definition and highlights the state's determination to regulate occupational communities. It might be interpreted as self-regulation in that it legitimizes a body to control the work of those in the occupation. But it represents a modern way of state regulation in which members of an occupational community are expected to perform regulatory functions themselves. A libertarian would object that it infringes the right to practise. An egalitarian should wish to see safeguards against arbitrary oppression and suppression along with transparent democratic governance.

Another aspect of the Artist Act that relates to the repositioning of work is its treatment of copyright. Under the Canadian Copyright Act, there is a presumption that copyright in works created by employees belongs to the employer, whereas copyright of works created by self-employed artists can be determined by negotiation and contract. The mechanism set up by the Artist Act – the Canadian Artists and Producers Professional Relations Tribunal (CAPPRT) – suggested that scale agreements should contain provisions relating to copyright in works commissioned by producers. But this does not fully resolve the difficulty in treatment of intellectual property rights in working relationships where notions of employee and employer are unclear. This will be a part of the economics of control as occupations and working patterns evolve.

The Canadian law marks a promising attempt to come to terms with aspects of the right to practise and the right to representation outside labour relationships. More generally, if there is such a right, the right to practise should be strengthened by phasing out licensing. There is also a need for Voice in auditing applications for a right to practise. Applicants should be provided with reasons in writing for licences being granted or not. The reasons should be risk-based, for example, that the person would cause an unacceptable risk to the public or to the client, or possibly the profession. Regulatory bodies should be required to show that they are trying to refine risk-based assessment techniques and are monitoring the applicability of existing techniques. Voice means not only having the right to obtain information but also the capacity to do something with it.

THE TWENTY-FIRST-CENTURY WORKPLACE

Complicating the construction of a work rights regime suitable for occupational citizenship is the simple fact that the workplace is becoming more nebulous. For over a century it has been the fulcrum of labour law, labour relations and collective bargaining. But the concept is crumbling, particularly with so much more work-for-labour.

From time to time in the twentieth century, particularly in Scandinavia, there was pressure for industrial democracy and a demand for workplace democracy, reiterated in the above-mentioned Charters of Workers' and Employment Rights (Ewing and Hendy, 2002; Bromberg and Irving, 2007). In the Global Transformation, it is unclear how this would help.

For a start, with labour externalization and telecommuting, what *is* the workplace? In considering workplace democracy, we should unpackage the term since a growing number of people work in several places. At the heart of labour law is the physical workplace, the factory, farm, mine or office. These days, this may be the least fixed, contrary to the image still conveyed by industrial relations theory. A second notion of workplace is the home, to where a growing number take their work. The dwindling of fixed workplaces, and the growth of 'location-neutral' businesses, is transforming working arrangements. For instance, in the USA and elsewhere, costs and opportunities have led to 'virtual suburbanization' as people move to live and work in rural areas so as to enjoy a more congenial lifestyle. Because of a fear of isolation, many of them are joining local communities and participating in local community work. This is an exciting aspect of occupational development. It offers a route into public work, or what we might call leisure work.

A third workplace, perhaps the most fixed psychologically or aspirationally, is our craft or profession. This may have several layers, from a local community, responsible for overseeing local performance, to an international association with powerful regulatory functions. One can see this occupational workplace as a mini-society, since it may embrace functions that have been the sphere of the state such as the establishment and monitoring of qualification standards or determination of entitlement to social protection. As with states, occupations vary in the comprehensiveness of their policies. But they have a growing role in shaping and managing work.

In short, the notion of physical workplace is too restrictive. If workers have a say in their workplace about the toilet lights, one would not be too impressed by claims about workplace democracy if they had to work for a given fee for a given number of hours, and only if they had a given level of qualifications and experience, and if they did not have any right to determine any of those. There would be a representation gap.

What happens in the physical workplace may be the least important part of a person's work, one scarcely worth making into the cornerstone of a charter. For a growing number of people, the occupational workplace is more important than the office or shop-floor where they happen to be working now. There is a need for occupational democracy as part of occupational rights.

Separation of workplace from home had a liberating effect by weakening the suffocating controls of patriarchy and familial reciprocities, allowing experimentation and pursuit of skill. Now, separation of work from the workplace could have a similar liberating effect. More distanced controls limit the power of supervision, and workers can join alternative networks, forcing employers to think harder about incentives to obtain a high and consistent effort bargain. The threat is that people lose control over time; the workplace is everywhere and the labour process is invasive of space, time and relationships. In the background are the panopticon and surveillance state. Liberation is possible, but far from assured.

OCCUPATIONAL ASSOCIATIONS

Thinking of 'workplace democracy' should lead us to reflect anew on guilds, cooperatives and community unionism. Romantics are drawn to historical cases such as Robert Owen's early cooperative endeavours and William Morris's late nineteenth-century craft community. For their time and place, like the guilds, these were locations of human flourishing.

Whatever their limitations, the guilds comprised one of the great institutions of history. Recall that there were two main types – merchant guilds and occupational guilds. The modern equivalents of merchant guilds are chambers of commerce; they have not been attacked by neo-liberals opposed to occupational guilds. Merchant guilds offered insurance for their members and enforced contracts and codes of behaviour. In their way, they created an ethical community. They could also impose a boycott if action were taken against one of their members. One could imagine a modern equivalent in which an occupational association would act on behalf of a member against an employer or purchaser, where going through a lengthy legal process would be prohibitively expensive or risky, a common enough occurrence.

However, occupational guilds are more relevant for our purposes. As we saw in

Chapter 1, they were self-governing and relatively democratic in allowing votes by master craftsmen. A modern case could be made for this form of occupational democracy, in that master craftsmen had shown they possessed the capabilities required for a sustainable community. They raised work standards by controlling quality, fostered transparent exchange and raised the price of their output by reputation, at the cost of managing labour relations. They fostered good citizenship, and played a fictive kinship role in helping at times of crisis. Similar bodies could emerge as globalization erodes family solidarity and forms of social security that prevailed under industrial citizenship.

What type of occupational association could operate best in the future? The challenge is to identify forms that minimize the prospect of regulatory capture, optimize development of occupational pride, and promote deliberative democracy and reciprocity as part of a system of rights. Seeking this delicate combination is a matter of statecraft, requiring a mix of statutory regulation and incentives, including fiscal.

A point learned from the guilds is that if occupational bodies are left as vehicles of self-regulation, they do reveal symptoms of regulatory capture and distributional failure. So laws and institutional mechanisms should oblige occupational associations to adhere to a rights-based framework. Among the safeguards required are mechanisms to limit occupational invasion. But this must be done in a way that does not block the advance of the technical division of labour.

The attack on modern variants of occupational guilds, in the name of competition, has been successful. But communities are still required to give space for craftsmanship, professionalism, work ethics and forms of learning and sharing. In rebuilding barriers to commodification and strengthening occupational citizenship, political action will be required to build a structure of occupational associations, networks and occupational communities. These should be seen as distinct layers of Voice and representation.

The state could play a role in ensuring that occupational associations practise deliberative democracy, which puts emphasis on obtaining a shared sense of meaning and common will (Bohman and Rehg, 1997). Critical decisions on work standards require procedures of participation and democratic assessment, recognizing that in an information-saturated market society there is a danger of thinning democracy.

Occupational associations should be seen as formal structures that set boundaries of professional and craft rationality, and create what some call 'occupational cultures' (Schein, 1996). Occupational citizenship must be based on the careful construction of international and national associations, which set the sphere of the occupation, standards of practice, entry and mobility procedures, and so on. This is related to Durkheim's vision. He saw the French *ordres* – professional associations – as regulating the moral behaviour of professionals, which would overcome the anomie of his era (Durkheim [1900] 1957). However, market forces have penetrated most professions since the 1970s. For a while, it was possible to claim they were resisting state intervention as an agent of market forces (Freidson, 1970). But, as Krause (1996) concluded, and as evidence since has shown, that view has become untenable.

Consider what a structure of occupational associations might look like as the Global Transformation proceeds. At the top are a growing number of international bodies. Gradually, European federations of professions have emerged, so far with monitoring and advisory powers, such as the FEANI (European Federation of National Engineering Associations) and the CCBE (Council of Bars and Law Societies of Europe). Global professional organizations are also taking shape, such as the International Council of Nurses, the WFEO (World Federation of Engineering Organizations) and the FIP (International Pharmaceutical Federation). There is also a national inter-professional association, the Inter-Professional Group Forum on European and International Affairs (UK IPG). Revealingly, none of these has been enabled to play any role in the ILO.

The trend towards occupational citizenship can be illustrated by efforts being made by federations of medical professionals. They have a long tradition of national and international federations, in the case of nurses starting in the nineteenth century. Now they have formed the World Health Professions Alliance (WHPA), a confederation of related professionals, as if one occupation would be insufficient to fight the institutions building the market society. In May 2008, about 500 representatives of medical professions, including surgeons, dentists, physiotherapists, auxiliary nurses, pharmacists and psychiatrists, drew up a plan of action. They will not be the last to do so.

The World Medical Association, which groups national doctors' associations, was so alarmed by the global slippage in the ability of the profession to control its services that, in the immediate aftermath of the financial debacle of 2008, its president issued a statement expressing fear that the crisis would accelerate government efforts to shift work from doctors to lower-cost professionals. This tension will be played out at international level to an increasing extent.

At national level, occupational associations are in a state of flux due to the onslaught by the market builders. But they are still needed. They should be the primary mechanism for establishing and refining standards of practice, and for disseminating knowledge and 'best practices' to practitioners as well as discouraging ineffectual practices. They will need to overcome the inefficiencies that bedevil all associations in these respects. Even within corporations, dissemination of ideas can be remarkably slow. One study of the transfer of 'best practices' in large corporations found that on average they took about three years (Szulanski, 1996).

To be fully effective, occupational associations must be coupled with informal networks of practitioners and communities of colleagues. Associations can be instruments of civic friendship. But more informal communities are needed as well to prevent the community becoming closed, resulting in a 'toxic cosiness' that feeds on prejudice (Wenger et al., 2002, p. 144). Closed communities may also produce what psychologists have called 'groupthink', resulting in myopia and a failure to perceive alternative points of view.

While informal networks are not binding in a regulatory sense, they may establish moral codes and knowledge-sharing practices. Some networks have persisted for generations, as in the case of the tiny craft of violin-making. Without such networks, craftsmen and professionals easily lose touch not only with innovations in their own sphere but also with their own knowledge. The spread of the virtual workplace makes capability depletion more likely and requires compensating network activity. That cannot occur if the person has lost control over time and skill development. Alienation and exploitation go together. Gaining control of time is a necessary step to an occupational career. The fact is that most services require considerable non-labour work, much of it uncompensated. Policymakers need to help liberate people's time so that they can, if they wish, indulge in this productivity-raising work (Drucker, 1999).

Because the pace of change is so fast, collective mechanisms are essential to disseminate knowledge equitably and efficiently. Without them, inequalities will intensify because individuals who miss a change or a piece of knowledge in their sphere may be cut off from a train of developments. A global competitive economy requires mechanisms to ensure knowledge sharing, so as to ensure fair outcomes and markets that are sustainable without winner-takes-all, loser-loses-all outcomes.

Associations must exist at several levels, and this is one reason for believing that occupational regulation must be crafted by policymakers, not left to the market. Thus, small local occupational networks are needed because personal interaction is essential. Psychological surveys have shown that people respond to 'eyes' more than to images and factual information. From this, one may conclude that groups in which people meet and can expect to meet will be more effective in inducing social solidarity and altruism. And size of group is important, as argued in the popular book *Freakonomics* (Levitt and Dubner, 2005). Selfish and opportunistic behaviour is more likely in environments in which there are few institutional or emotional deterrents. Self-interest and selfishness are accentuated in a secular society where most of us do not think a God is judging sternly from somewhere. One does not need to recreate a God, but one does need institutions to curb such behaviour morally, especially in a market society that idealizes self-interest and autonomous self-fulfilment. In short, there is a need to curb immoral hazards.

Occupational associations generate constructive social relationships, a sense of belonging, a spirit of enquiry and professional confidence (Higgins and Kram, 2001). Communities of practice offer a layer of stability and a 'home for identity' (Wenger et al., 2002, p. 20). They can also help practitioners to avoid, or at least deal with, knowledge overload (Davenport and Beck, 2001). Dynamic societies also need occupational networks in order to foster a knowledge-generating environment.

Proficians and those who remain in the salariat with employment security but without job security, as is typical of civil services and international agencies, have no 'organizational home' (Malone and Laubacher, 1998). They need anchoring networks or associations that can strengthen socialization and occupational development, and pool resources for social protection and insurance purposes (Laubacher and Malone, 2000). Put differently, occupational citizenship requires a combination of regulatory associations – setting the sphere of activities regarded as the domain, standards of acceptable practice, entry and mobility procedures and so on – coupled with informal networks of communication, knowledge sharing and personalized reciprocities.

Occupational networks relate to what some call 'distributed communities', a term that is preferable to 'virtual' or 'online', since there may also be actual meetings of practitioners. As in the case of distance learning, these involve several dimensions of distance, not just geographical (Figallo, 1998; Preece, 2000).

A community suggests the image of a family, in which the gift relationship dominates a market mentality. Anthropologists (and common sense) have taught us that we cannot have close relationships of trust and personalized reciprocity with more than a small circle of people, perhaps as few as 20. Whereas occupational associations promote 'generalized reciprocation', smaller communities promote individualized reciprocity. Just as with collective bargaining, communities require a 'shadow of the future' in order to limit opportunism and assertions of power that turn cooperation into compliance.

So, networks and communities must be more informal, allowing civic friendship, or fraternity, to flourish. That should provide the means of helping individuals avoid burnout and marginalization (Berry et al., 1990). Networks allow practitioners to have 'conversation' with their professional domain, enabling reflection and recall of knowledge (Schon, 1983). Without regular informal contact, even practising doctors lose touch with their field, and may become unreliable (Cohen and Prusak, 2001). Personal interaction helps in the generation and preservation of knowledge, and thus raises competence and productivity. This is crucial in academic life, for instance, which is why the proletarianization and pursuit of targets have corroded professional competence (Gersick et al., 2000).

In sum, occupational citizenship will require a combination of international associations, national associations and informal networks.

COLLABORATIVE BARGAINING

If we think in terms of occupational collaborations, or associations, we must ask about the scope or purpose of representation. This leads us to consider new forms of bargaining. As a collective, an occupation may bargain with employers. It may also bargain with clients or consumers, as represented by a commercial interest or a body set up by the state to negotiate on behalf of some notion of the public. There could also be negotiations between components of an occupation, which may be nominal or considerable, due to dissimilar statuses in the occupation. There are also inter-occupational negotiations, as between barristers and solicitors, doctors and nurses, and physiotherapists and chiropractors.

We could also entertain the idea of bargaining between types of work that make up a composite occupational career in which all types of work are respected. For instance, if rules and contractual arrangements were only about remuneration and working conditions in the labour of the occupation, those wishing to combine their labour with, say, care work, volunteering and ethical learning would be neglected.

We may describe this multi-dimensional process as the sphere of collaborative bargaining. The term collective bargaining was co-opted to mean one type of bargaining, that between capital, as employers, and 'labour', as unions representing employees deemed vulnerable. Other forms of bargaining were left aside.

One form of collaborative bargaining is between members of an occupational community to help reproduce their collective labour power. A study of newly qualified podiatrists found burnout to be more common than had been recognized, due primarily to a lack of professional status and to geographical and professional isolation (Mandy and Tinley, 2004). Here was a profession in need of an association that could self-regulate for the benefit of its practitioners and ultimately for the benefit of other citizens as well. It was an instance of market failure. The requirement was a bargaining process to limit self-destructive competition.

Consider a generic issue. A worker, A, can relate to another as a complement, B, or as a potential substitute, C, or as a citizen with common interests, claims or rights, D. As a complement, B may be someone on whom A depends to achieve a specific type of work, or someone whose productive activity helps A's work. In those cases, A and B could form an alliance to try to obtain a better outcome from employers and the state. But in other cases, A may see the other person as a substitute competing for a larger share of the income. Many occupations have elements of complements and substitutes, as in the case of the medical professions. Doctors see nurses as complements but also to some extent as substitutes. Not only can nurses do many of the tasks done by doctors; doctors are also in a struggle with nurses for their share of the total income spent on medical services. The same applies to other groups in the medical sphere. This type of situation shows the need for institutions to conduct collaborative bargaining.

Collaborative bargaining has to be constructed. Practitioners bargain mainly with fellow practitioners and those who complement them, in order to limit destructive competitiveness and obtain control over key limited resources and assets. For example, left to themselves as individuals, fishers compete against each other and deplete fish stocks, since short-term profits dictate what they do. If they remained in competition with each other in the neo-liberal way, attempts to impose external regulation would be resented, and they would attempt to circumvent the rules. Collaborative bargaining would tend towards the preservation and reproduction of fish stocks and would promote professional standards that would act to constrain individualistic competition.

Another example comes from India where a growing number of young professionals report working 14–16 hours almost every day because of a perceived need to be more competitive than others in their field. Some said they feared losing out to others more prepared to keep up the networking and website checks. Some acknowledged they did not have time for 'family' or socializing that did not involve a 'work agenda'. Survival of the fittest was literally true because the non-physical labour was requiring physical stamina. In a labour surplus society, in which the stock of self-exploiting practitioners can be turned over repeatedly, as the walking wounded absent themselves or fade into lower-level jobs, the gainers are those who can sustain the intensive labour. But the lesson of Darwinism is that human survival has been achieved through collaboration, through regulating potentially destructive competitive behaviour. The only way for the proficians, salariat and precariat to recover a balance and control over the key assets that confront them – notably time, space and security – is for them to collaborate around those issues. Only through associations and a process of collaborative bargaining can control be wrested back.

The full range of collaborative bargaining should be legitimized. In sketching the direction of thinking, we may merely consider a few of the emerging issues. An obvious one is that of an occupational association bargaining with a body representing purchasers of their services or outputs. Most practitioners would be at a disadvantage if they had to negotiate individually, and in practice that does not happen. The problem is that the association could be presented as a monopoly acting as a restraint of trade. This needs to be reformed and clarified.

Take a case that excites passions. Collaboration can be defended on the grounds that it is the service itself that is on offer. This is an argument used to justify the English Premier League selling TV rights as a collective, since it is the contest that is on offer. But why should sport be treated differently from other services, as allowed under the EU's Nice Treaty of 2000? *The Economist* (2007c) argued that 'joint selling' was acceptable in this case because it ensured that revenue was shared and because individual bargaining would leave weak teams without bargaining power. This is no truer of sport than medicine, law or masonry. Many services could benefit from some joint selling and income sharing. But when would it lurch from collaboration to collusion, from socially beneficial solidarity to monopolistic practice? In the case of football, *The Economist* rationalized its defence of collaborative bargaining (although it does not use the term) on the grounds that 'poorly supported teams' would lose revenue 'which over time could destroy the competitive balance of leagues' to the detriment of consumers and the teams. That argument could be made in favour of collaborative bargaining by most occupations. Presumably, neo-liberals would claim that it would drive up the price and give the occupation/service monopolistic profits. Since this would depend on the price elasticity of demand, neo-liberals would probably add that if demand is inelastic then anti-trust law should block collaborative bargaining. Yet this is precisely the situation with a sport such as football.

Numerous spheres are becoming like professional sport, with winner-takes-all situations. In each case, an elite emerges partly by talent, partly by luck, timing and locational advantage. Their individual excellence cannot sensibly be divorced from their community. Great players owe their greatness to playing with and against good players. If they did not do so, their skills would remain dormant or be only partially developed. If this holds for prominent professions, it surely holds for most occupations. It is not just competition or latent merit that produces excellence or individual prowess.

To continue the footballing case, consider the implications of the 'Bosman ruling' of 1995. This granted footballers in the EU freedom at the end of their contracts to move clubs, without any transfer fee; it also stipulated that quotas for foreign players were incompatible with freedom of contract and mobility within the EU. Predictably, the Bosman ruling accentuated a two-tier structure of clubs, with the best players gravitating to the few clubs likely to qualify for the Champions League. Back came proposals to require clubs to have 6 of the 11 players on the pitch coming from the home country. These were rejected by the EU competition authorities.

A compromise could be a revenue-sharing mechanism. If all players (practitioners) were paid transfer fees and if all clubs received transfer fees, part of the income could go into a practitioner fund for sharing among all clubs (firms) and the professional players' association (occupational association). This would spread the benefits across all clubs, thereby offering dignifying incentives to those with talent.

The Economist concluded its review of the arguments by claiming that exemptions from anti-trust rules covering joint selling should depend solely on whether that would help consumers. But surely the interests of practitioners and their successors must also be considered. All occupations need mechanisms for their reproduction and refinement. Any rule limiting competition will be a compromise, and it will rarely be clear whether the interests of today's consumers are being given too much or too little weight relative to tomorrow's. There is a democratic vacuum in this market-led regulation of occupations and no evidence that the citizens subject to it benefit. A balance should be sought, respecting the interests of consumers and practitioners equally, while not ignoring the interests of potential and future consumers and practitioners.

Another form of collaborative bargaining occurs within occupations. It is needed to deal with the dangers of hierarchy, elite capture of rental income, occupational splintering into elites and precarious majorities, and the twin tendencies of suppression and oppression. So far, no model exists to deal with all these tendencies. They are matters of governance, require systems of deliberative democracy and should respect the egalitarian principles laid out in the next chapter.

ETHICS

Occupational communities are mechanisms for instilling ethical codes. If competition or anti-trust legislation prevents practitioners from forming associations capable of doing that, the consequences could be serious. This happened in the smug community of chartered accountants, which led to the collapse of Arthur Andersen in 2002 and the frauds at Enron, WorldCom and Parmalat. The accountancy profession needed an association to set standards for practitioners. Its elite were not held in check, and were content to earn huge short-term incomes, knowing these were sufficient to give them a lifetime of affluence. An associational strategy should require all occupational associations to formulate ethical codes.

One outcome of the onslaught on the professions has been weaker association power over practitioners, sapping the professional ethos. State regulators have started to regulate for moral standards, setting formal rules in place of time-honoured moral codes set by the community itself. This is reregulation, not deregulation. And it is part of commodification because it is restricting *agency*. Practitioners, not the state, understand what ethics comprise in their sphere of work.

In the case of accountancy, regulators and corporate bodies have been tightening ethical codes and instigating mandatory ethical training courses (Fraser, 2008). This is being led by the profession, fearful of more interventionist state regulation that would take away other privileges, including its monopoly of auditing. But it is moot whether such a monopoly is justifiable on grounds of freedom to practise, or the right to work.

Morality does not lend itself to formal regulation. But associations can shape the ethics of their occupation. They can decide what morality should be used to determine whether a practitioner is ethical. In accountancy, for instance, there is tension between a business perspective and a philosophical one, between a utilitarian approach based on expected outcomes and a Kantian rules-based approach, and a difficulty in deciding whether the ethics should rely on virtue based on competence of the moral agent. In the absence of a civic friendship community, can motives be presumed or judged?

It is worth recalling that Tawney, appealing for better education in the crisis before the Great Transformation, advocated 'a discipline in professional ethics'. As he explained:

> It would aim at driving home, as a fixed habit, a certain standard of professional conduct. It would emphasize that there were certain things – like advertising, or accepting secret commissions, or taking advantage of a client's ignorance, or rigging the market, or other analogous practices of the present commercial world – which 'the service can't do'. It would cultivate the *esprit de corps* which is natural to young men, and would make them feel that to snatch special advantages for oneself, like any common business man, is, apart from other considerations, an odious offence against good manners. And since the disposition of all occupations – the 'trades' quite as much as the 'professions' – is to relapse into well-worn ruts and to make an idol of good average mediocrity, it would impress upon them – what is one of the main truths of all education whatsoever – 'that, if the young are rarely as right as they suppose, the old for different reasons are too often wrong', and that the first duty of youth is, not to avoid mistakes, but to show initiative and take responsibility, to make a tradition not to perpetuate one.
>
> (Tawney, 1921, pp. 155–6)

In the 1920s, it was too early to turn those adages in the direction of occupational citizenship. The industrial model was just becoming hegemonic. It was not so much a road not taken as a road that was not yet there to take.

THE ROLE OF GOVERNMENT

What should be the government's role in the generation of occupational citizenship? Some studies suggest that the strength of occupational communities is determined by government, others that it is the occupations themselves that shape state policy on occupational regulation (Johnson, 1972; Freidson, 1973; Larson, 1977; Van Maanen and Barley, 1984). More likely is a struggle between interests. In a period of disembeddedness, when those pushing for a market society are in ascendancy, occupational communities will be picked off for proletarianization or splintering into elites and proletarianized employees. The problem for occupations is that there is no inherent social solidarity across occupational communities. Some anticipate gains from the weakening of others and cannot anticipate reciprocity later from supporting an occupational community that is being dismantled.

Of course, the state's political makeup always reflects a mix of interests. One would not expect a government made up largely of lawyers to operate against the interests of the legal professions, any more than one would expect one made up largely of employer or trade union interests to go against their own. But this well-known view can be over-stretched. As important in determining state policy is the balance of conflicting interests between financial and productive capital and between large-scale corporations and occupational communities.

In a period of embeddedness, controls exercised by dominant interests can be expected to stabilize the occupational structure. In a period of disembeddedness, the state will be an arena in which some communities are dismantled while others are strengthened. The symbols of occupational success are the granting of privileges of accreditation, the issue of licences, special tax breaks and the formal legitimation of a monopoly to sell the service. In some cases, the state may require that certain citizens must purchase the service or suffer a penalty for not doing so. But occupational citizenship means far more than that.

CONCLUDING REFLECTIONS

> I can imagine a bank manager being on his death bed and saying he wished he had been a poet, but I doubt that it would be the other way round.
>
> (David Hockney, 1997)

A vision for the twenty-first century is that occupation – working life – will be chosen in freedom, allowing individuals to realize vocation as their capabilities develop. People will define themselves through having a combination of competencies, a variable combination of work statuses and an ability to give more time to reproductive work and education, so allowing space for leisure alongside 'work'.

A Good Occupation is nothing less than full freedom, which requires positive and negative liberty coupled with good opportunity to develop one's competences, and associational freedom to provide for bounded rationality. It must entail control over time and an appreciation of the need to incorporate the reproductive activities of life and the activities of citizenship.

Occupational citizenship will be strengthened if social policy and institutions favour personal development rather than the market. A danger of the competing paradigm of corporate citizenship is that under the rubric of 'corporate social responsibility' social policy will be turned into 'a productive factor', as the EU puts it. This reorientation is profoundly alienating. At the moment, governments are restructuring policies – fiscal, educational, training and social protection – to fit the dictate of competitiveness. They implicitly reject the appeal of occupational citizenship in favour of corporate citizenship and individualization. It starts early, in schools, in the banalities of children's consumerist and passively entertained lifestyles. It continues into college and training. It reaches its apogee in 'welfare-to-work' schemes, tailored for the designated 'socially excluded'.

Citizenship is about rights, about belonging to linked communities. 'The market' eschews communities. A market is where everything can be bought and sold; it is about commodification. Citizenship is about community that resists laws of commodification. This is the primary function of occupational communities of the future.

Occupational citizenship represents a form of community between the market and the state. Historically, pre-industrial society consisted of a set of complementary crafts, embedded in guilds that jockeyed for position in the affairs of state. These had benign and malign tendencies – 'mischiefs of faction', in the words of James Madison (1787) – in terms of any secondary association in a political democracy. It is important to emphasize the two sides of the idea of occupational community, since a market society rejects occupational citizenship and thereby the positive side, as well as the negative. We need occupational representation, and we need occupations to be 'mischiefs'. Otherwise, the jobholder society is the future.

There is one well-known danger in the proposals of this chapter. The multicultural model that predated liberal society was based on group recognition and group rights. Such a model can cede too much to cultural communities to define rules for their members that diverge from those of other communities. The legacy of that form of multiculturalism persists. European countries still respect corporatism, that is, communal rights for groups, usually religious, and fail to separate church from state. They are still corporatist in having policies and institutions based on collective identities such as 'workers' and 'shareholders'. This is a source of inequality and social divisiveness. Although we need to belong to communities, it is essential that mechanisms are built to ensure that they coexist in an egalitarian way and that those who choose to remain outside any association-defended community are not denied freedom or basic equality.

We must rescue 'reproductive' work that contributes to occupations, seeing it not just as nurturing and caring, but also as involving acts of civic friendship that reproduce community (sharing). An occupation values Aristotelian *philia* – wishing well for the other. In a labour market there is no intrinsic place for friendship; individuals are encouraged to see themselves in competition with others. In a true occupation, by contrast, there is a place for civic friendship; one can admire another's workmanship, share the craft ethic and value a shared sense of identity. There is an intrinsic psychic value for the work and the social relations in which the work is embedded.

In a market society, the public sphere is under threat, as economic self-interest crowds out – or 'colonizes', as Arendt put it – political and leisure activity. This has a corrosive effect on human capability. The re-embedding of the economy in society requires a revival of the public sphere; occupational associations offer the most promising route to gain control over work and help create a universal sphere of leisure, as defined in Chapter 1. The notion of private implies privacy and 'autonomy', a simple notion of freedom. Although valuable, we should recall Arendt's recognition that the private sphere is one of 'deprivation' (Arendt, 1958, p. 58). It is needed to sustain life, but insufficient to enable us to achieve a life, which requires a non-private existence. As Heidegger ([1927] 2000) put it, if there is only a private sphere one perishes, slowly. But if the public sphere is reduced to consumption and labour, we will lose sight of the need to achieve a humanizing existence, qua political being. We need a means through which to develop the capacity to work and 'to leisure'. This is surely the sphere of occupational citizenship.

Occupation is about pursuing, in however modest a way, a sense of glory and honour. Citizens should be able to pursue glory, to be in the collective memory. The drabness of industrial citizenship was a denial of individual glory in craft. Occupational citizenship would allow for creative achievement and the honour that goes with that. As Francis Bacon ([1625] 2007, p. 156) wrote, 'Vaine Glory helpeth to Perpetuate a Man's Memory'. Love of honour is respect for one's independence and could be called the proper face of pride, an unyielding dignity. This could be achieved in an occupational community, properly constructed.

In the Greek tradition, occupational citizenship could be construed as the creation of a public space where the politics of everyday life is practised, the equivalent of the *polis*, where citizens organize themselves among equals, defined as those who understand each other's needs and aspirations. This understanding also helps to define class membership.

By way of conclusion, recall the memorable words of John Ruskin, written as he observed proletarianization in the nineteenth century:

> Men were not intended to work with the accuracy of tools, to be precise and perfect in all their actions. If you will have that precision out of them, and make their fingers measure degrees like cog-wheels, and their arms strike curves like compasses, you must unhumanize them. All the energy of their spirits must be given to make cogs and compasses of themselves. . . On the other hand, if you will make a man of the working creature, you cannot make a tool. Let him but begin to imagine, to think, to try to do anything worth doing; and the engine-turned precision is lost at once. Out come all his roughness, all his dulness, all his incapability; shame upon shame, failure upon failure, pause after pause; but out comes the whole majesty of him also.
>
> (Ruskin, 1853, pp. 161–2)

He went on to stress the vital need to overcome the artificial division of labour in which some are allowed 'to think', some are made to labour. Sadly, being a man of his time and class, he was unable to appreciate the need to incorporate a place for reproductive work as well. It is the combination of all three, coupled with that control over time that can allow for contemplation that is vital to an occupational life.

NOTES

1. One could cite numerous examples. Just consider the following comment by a prominent early thinker in the British Labour Party, Douglas Jay, writing in 1937: 'In the case of nutrition and health, just as in the case of education, the gentleman in Whitehall really does know better what is good for people than the people know themselves' (Jay, 1937, p. 317).
2. After that book was published, Le Grand was appointed a policy adviser in No. 10 Downing Street, reporting to Tony Blair.
3. As one behaviouralist put it, 'Economists treat all people as selfish; as independent; as rational. These are the assumptions that underpin economics' (cited in Chakrabortty, 2008).

10. Economic rights: the progressive agenda

> I refuse to renounce the great classical discourse of emancipation.
>
> (Derrida, 1996, p. 82)

INTRODUCTION

No transformation can occur unless there is a progressive redistribution of some sort and an agenda of equality. What is it that should be equalized in the Good Society of the twenty-first century? Put differently, each transformation is resolved through a struggle over the strategic assets of the economic system. In feudalism, the struggle was mainly over land and water; in national industrial capitalism it was mainly over ownership of the means of production. The key assets in a tertiary economy are less tangible and include time, ecological space, information and financial capital.

The progressive challenge is complicated by three fundamentalisms – the moralistic 'religification' of social policy based on invisible hands from above, the neo-liberal faith in invisible hands in markets and the paternalistic faith in guiding hands, which come together in the constructivism of the surveillance society. This chapter has nothing to say about the moralistic challenge, other than to state that it is a form of paternalism and that the separation of church and state should be restored. It is implicit that paternalism should be checked. As for markets, while essential, they must be embedded in society, used for allocative purposes and subject to social control. They must not be a rationalization for rejecting egalitarianism.

Before considering how the strategic assets can be redistributed, recall that the objective is to enable people to pursue their own sense of occupation, combining work, labour, play and leisure in ways they think are advantageous to the development of their capabilities and their civic friendship. There should be equal opportunity to pursue occupational aspirations. For that, reproductive work and other work-that-is-not-labour must be raised to the same plateau as labour. What stands in the way is the combination of neo-liberalism and libertarian paternalism. Looming in the foreground is the panopticon society offered by the utilitarians.

To escape, it is essential to advance associational freedom and deliberative democracy, a right to participate as well as a right to vote, a right to leisure as well as a right to work. But it is also well to ponder the possibility that, whereas a market society will crash through the hubris of financiers, the paternalists once entrenched will be harder to roll back.

WHO WILL FIGHT FOR A POLITICS OF PARADISE?

A redistributive agenda will only be realized if there are groups not only wanting the changes but prepared to demand them and impose costs on those who resist. Where is the agency to lead a struggle for redistribution? The globalization era produced a remarkable passivity, which must have delighted and surprised the winners as they stashed away their millions and billions. The failure of progressives was that no politics of paradise was offered. All the protests were against events, rather than for a vision.

A progressive agenda must build on the energies, anger and aspirations of those most likely to become active. Historically, that has meant mainly youth, particularly those in the growing class. In today's tertiary society, that is the precariat. The danger is that many in it will be seduced by a demagogic populism that is utilitarian in the worst possible way. That should be a spur to those wishing for a new politics of paradise.

If a progressive strategy must be one that appeals to youth and the precariat, it should also appeal to other advancing groups across the globe, the elderly, migrants and women. One puts women there as a 'reality check'. Previous transformations have been flawed by defining egalitarianism mainly in terms of male interests. Industrial citizenship brought labour security for male employees. In building occupational citizenship, all forms of work and leisure should be given equal respect. Lifestyles and work styles that have been largely frozen along gender lines should be unfrozen, for the benefit of men as well as women.

The growing number of migrants means that any strategy must also offer a viable vision for people who want or need to move. It must give them avenues for citizenship, for effective rights and identity. And the agenda must appeal to those above what was considered the 'retirement' age. The notion of retirement may fade. In many places, it is already a source of amused euphemism rather than deferential status.

Given identification of groups most likely to support a new progressive agenda, what will motivate them? Think back. All utopian visions have had characteristics of gentleness, conviviality, fraternity and social solidarity. Those characteristics cannot be developed unless the economic system gives them a chance. During globalization, they were disregarded. A utopian vision goes against current realities.

While much has been said about loss of 'identity', no systemic way of developing and defending identities has been proposed. Instead, paternalists have concocted an agenda of 'happiness', facilitating consumption and strengthening civic privatism.

THE ECOLOGICAL IMPERATIVE

In developing a progressive agenda, there is one overriding requirement. Globalization has created an awesome existential threat. No progressive vision could be of practical interest unless it addressed the ecological crisis. This embraces the environment but should be interpreted more broadly. It is about altering the way we live and work. Global warming and the eradication of species are not issues to be relegated to footnotes. They are everything. There is no prospect of occupational freedom when nature is shrivelling around us.

Yet the economic system is geared to production and depletion of resources, and militates against values of reproduction. The neo-liberal model and utilitarianism give no weight to preservation. When environmental issues are recognized through public alarm they are confronted through the prism of market mechanisms, epitomized by carbon trading arrangements, green taxes and investment in energy-saving technology. These are stop-gap measures, not societal rebalancing actions. It is the way we live that is the problem.

The idea of checking consumption is anathema, since profits, jobs and growth are seen as essential. Depressingly, the libertarian paternalists have proposed 'nudges' to make people conform to the market economy and its norms, rather than to an ethical system in which behaviour is geared more to reproduction, civic friendship and preservation of the commons. The 'lukewarm left' social democrats who entered government in the 1990s failed to alter the trend. They pandered to the weakness of will.

One deficiency of the global market society is that all its levers have favoured short-term considerations. Society needs levers to induce longer-term thinking and a reflective imagination about the future. It is crucial to prevent emergence of a new dualism, with environmentalism being separated from the economy. It is an ecological crisis; it is about the way people work, labour, leisure and play.

REAL DECOMMODIFICATION

> In an established society, the right to non-conformity must be institutionally protected.
>
> (Polanyi, GT, p. 263)

The objective of an egalitarian should be to decommodify everyone, equally. We may define decommodification of people as full freedom, or associational freedom. In reflecting on how to achieve that, one can begin by asking how Polanyi's right to non-conformity could be realized. This has become a bigger question than when the advance of 'civil rights' seemed unstoppable. Although his argument was undeveloped, Polanyi's view is clear:

> The individual must be free to follow his conscience without fear of the powers that happen to be entrusted with administrative tasks in some of the fields of social life. Science and the arts should always be under the guardianship of the republic of letters. Compulsion should never be absolute; the 'objector' should be offered a niche to which he can retire, the choice of a 'second-best' that leaves him a life to live. Thus will be secured the right to non-conformity as the hall-mark of a free society (GT, p. 255).

No tosh here about no rights without responsibilities, as used by modern moralists to take away freedom from the precariat. Now, as then, the keys to decommodification are the same as for full freedom – self-control and a context in which social solidarity is feasible and intelligible. Polanyi realized that freedom to live a second-best lifestyle had to be 'institutionally protected'.

We will not see the end of a market economy and, unless there were some nightmare of machines taking over production, labour will persist as central to economic growth. But labour should be a commodity to be bought and sold. For that to take place in decency, the bargaining strengths of sellers and buyers must be equalized. In the era of fictitious decommodification the state acted paternalistically. The needs of employees and their families were norms. As long as workers conformed to the norms of wage labour, they were protected. But to be obliged to be a norm, or penalized for not being one, is not freedom.

In terms of social income, people should be able to do what they want with the income they receive from selling labour, and this is more likely if they are paid in money, not in predetermined forms of non-wage benefit. A money wage is the least paternalistic form of remuneration; it allows buyer and seller to appreciate what is being bought and its price. The transparency represents proper alienation. As far as reasonable, labour *should* be commodified; the money wage should be a large proportion of social income. Let the individual decide what to do with the income. On this a progressive should accept an axiom of the right – 'freedom to choose'. It is a mistake for progressives to allow themselves to be depicted as against individual freedom or in favour of state paternalism, epitomized by social democracy and New Labour.

Enterprise benefits (EB) should be transferred out of the sphere of labour. People need assured sickness benefits and care. But there is no reason for employers to provide them to people who happen to be working for them for wages. Depending on the wishes of workers, EB could be transferred to unions, occupational associations or insurance funds. The objection to private insurance is the danger of cherry-picking, with insurance companies refusing to accept high-risk individuals, or imposing higher premiums on them. Those who believe they are low risk will tend to take options that do not respect social solidarity criteria. There are ways of dealing with these hazards. But the erosion of EB should be welcomed, not resisted. EB for all groups should be transferred, and since they are a source of so much inequality they should be taxed more.

If labour were fully commodified, freedom would be strengthened. If one believes in freedom, one should give people the freedom to make choices on the type of benefit they want, subject to principles of solidarity. EB are paternalistic. They are a form of social insurance, in which higher-risk groups are subsidized by lower-risk groups. Not only does this increase inequality, it also does not work well in a flexible labour process.

A Gallup survey in 2001 found that 80 per cent of employees in the UK lacked commitment to their jobs. One commentator attributed this to poor management because many thought managers did not care about their needs (Scase, 2001). Why should they? Managers should not be nannies whose job is to make employees happy. An alternative would be to align the monetary compensation better to the expected or desired effort bargain, offering higher wages (W) and less 'feel-good' EB, so that people as employees do not look to their employers as providers of happiness. That is not their job and they are unlikely to do it very well.

If firms tied W to profitability and operated profit-sharing schemes, the incentive to labour would be stronger than if 'job-enriching' schemes were used. Rather than trying to manufacture trust between managers and employees, it would be more honest and adult if the labour arrangement started from a presumption that their interests are not the same. Make the commodity character of labour real. If there is disengagement, there will be space for real trust, rather than suspicion that the paternalistic scheme is to induce more labour. Neither external performance measures nor paternalistic management offers a recipe for a democratic work process. Organizational specialists may wish to restructure paternalism to induce a committed 'psychological contract' from employees. It would be better to reject such trickery.

There is also a particular problem of tertiary labour. In the Taylorist-Fordist model of capitalism, the worker sold his labour en bloc, since he was locked into a standard employment relationship consisting of a set number of hours every week, unless the employer changed that at whim. The employee supplied 48 hours, and was expected to have the remainder of the week for reproductive work, recuperation and play. In the global flexibility regime, a worker's time is not so easily divided into blocks of paid labour and reproductive time.

Increasingly, workers are paid for fewer hours – the working week having been cut – but are expected to provide more unpaid labour. Their labour is insufficiently alienated. The modal service worker rents out labour but it is not properly commodified, because time is added that is uncompensated financially. If a service worker contracts to supply 40 hours a week, being properly commodified would mean total labour time would be 40 hours. But in a growing number of service jobs, workers are expected to supply more. Free time is rarely free. They are expected to spend part of their free time keeping up with tasks connected with labour. Some could be construed as investment work, yielding higher earnings, promotion or a lower probability of losing the job. But part involves necessary tasks connected with the current job.

Some unpaid labour is administrative, some networking, some keeping up to date with essential or potentially important information, techniques, clients, competitors and so on. Many people obliged to do such tasks may resent it, or their families will. But in a flexible labour system, few workers will be in a strong enough position to avoid them. In terms of labour relations and 'employability', the risk is simply too great. This applies to some in the salariat, some clinging to their status in the core stratum, and almost all the precariat.

Thus, employees are required to do labour off-the-job, outside the standard working week. Much involves electronic communications and the laptop, the new sweatshop. The salariat and proficians have made a Faustian bargain to receive high incomes in return for the obligation to labour at all times of the day and night (Waldmeir, 2007). The protective regulations on working time, overtime, holidays and meal breaks, achieved by a century of working-class struggle, simply do not apply.

Labour law and regulations were conceived when it was reasonable to presume the workplace was a single location where employees were under direct supervision. When workers started to take labour home, employers still had responsibility to monitor working time but did not do so. However, in the USA, courts have ruled that if an employee is injured while doing labour away from the workplace, the firm may be liable. In one case, a company was ordered to pay someone US$500 000 because an employee had been encouraged to do business from his car and had been involved in an accident while using a mobile phone.

If all employers were made liable for accidents and illnesses associated with labour away from the workplace, they would be less inclined to require employees to do such extra labour and would have an incentive to discourage it. This would increase proper labour alienation and help in the struggle for control over time. It would also increase the sense of freedom because workers would understand that they have a right to 'free time'. The libertarian should not complain about the liability since choice by both parties would remain. It would be better than exhorting managements to lessen their employees' stressful labour in the interest of their long-term health. In sum, non-wage remuneration should be monetized and work-for-labour should be legitimized and recompensed.

An egalitarian strategy means that labour should be commodified more, while 'labour power' should be decommodified. The former has been happening; it should go further. The latter has yet to be tried. Fortuitously, the financial crisis of 2008 gave impetus to both. One phenomenon that came to public attention was the degree of corporate welfare (EB) built up under globalization. Politicians could suddenly strike a populist chord by demanding that perks and non-wage payments should be curbed. As it happens, cutting them would have beneficial effects for efficiency and income distribution. To encourage proper labour commodification, non-wage benefits and bonuses should be taxed more than wages, and tax breaks (fiscal subsidies) that have encouraged them should be removed.

Labour commodification should involve contracts identifying expectations on both sides. One way to help would be to delink benefit entitlements from employment. A person doing labour should be paid in money, the proper medium of exchange in a market economy. It distorts the labour market if employees acquire rights to future income that have little to do with the labour performed. This may seem obvious, except that is not what happens. Going largely to the upper groups in the global class structure – the salariat and core employees – benefits such as state pensions and sickness benefits are often worth more than the money wage. Linking them to labour status distorts the arrangement and creates a dependency that is contrary to full freedom. It is also inconsistent with occupational citizenship and ecological balance. To promote occupation in the sense defined earlier, all forms of work should be treated equally. For instance, there should be no presumption that pouring the tea for a boss should be given more income protection than doing so for a sick relative. If the boss wants to pay someone to pour her tea and the person wants to do that, then the payment should reflect what each wishes to pay and accept. Giving the tea pourer extra benefits instead of a proper payment would be unfair on those not doing that labour. If the employer had to pay the full price she might pour the tea herself. Suppose the employee is paid US\$1 and the boss pays US\$1 in contributions for sickness or pension benefits, and the state matches her contribution with US\$1, which is roughly what happens, then the state is subsidizing the labour of tea pouring for a boss, when it is not doing so for someone doing the same work for a sick relative.

The state is also subsidizing labour that most citizens would not wish to be done, let alone paid for in their name. This is why fictitious decommodification is relevant for those concerned with ecological externalities. Taxpayers are subsidizing someone doing polluting labour just as much as the tea pourer.

The principle of treating labour like any other contract requires several conditions to be egalitarian. Recall that the traditional justification for labour law is that it is needed to protect the vulnerable party. This might be reasonable in an industrial society with mass production and fixed workplaces. But in a flexible labour market, where many people have a bundle of capacities that they could withhold in providing a service, there is no reason to suppose the employer is always the one with power. Egalitarians may not like to read that. Then they should think if they have ever been an employer themselves, or when they last hired someone to come to their home to do 'a job'.

A second premise is dependency, the rule being that an employee has a duty of loyalty to the employer. This is enshrined in labour law everywhere. It is unrealistic and demeaning. Yet social democrats have always subscribed to it. Here the libertarians are mostly right but should be consistent. A person providing labour should not have any such 'duty'. Labour is a matter of contract, not a generic duty of loyalty or deference. Worse, labour law not only presumes vulnerability and loyalty but seeks to reinforce those conditions. And it sets up a system that seeks to privilege one group, those in stable employment.

To help achieve labour commodification, civil liberties advanced through decades of labour law should be provided for every citizen. In effect, 'labour rights' should be converted into 'work rights'. We consider what this implies for care work and some marginalized services later.

Labour contracts should be treated as commercial contracts, in which a presumption of neutrality prevails; there is no presumption that one party should be favoured. That is not being heartless. It forces the egalitarian to look at the source of the problem and avoid the vulnerability. Rather than institutionalizing vulnerability, the progressive strategy should be to overcome it so that parties to labour contracts are as equal as possible. The main reason for labour law is that employers have more resources than workers. As anybody who has employed a lawyer will know, that is often far from the truth. If workers had access to proper information and were secure enough to be able to say 'No!' in extremis, neutrality could be fairly presumed.

A defender of labour law would retort that this is why a distinction is made between a supplier of services and a service worker. This distinction is hard to sustain in a globalizing market characterized by short-term contracts, triangulation and informalization. And it is not worth preserving. Some employed on a short-term basis will be more vulnerable than others, but the status of the labour relationship is surely not a reliable guide to the relative vulnerability of the parties to what should be a binding contract.

This leads back to agency. A goal should be to ensure equality in bargaining capacity. Having a big labour union exerting pressure over a small firm with a huge overdraft because of investments in innovative products should be no more acceptable to an egalitarian than having a corporation exerting pressure on a woman outworker desperate to earn enough to buy food for her children. But to make legal distinctions between 'small' and 'big' employers is arbitrary and conducive to moral and immoral hazards. Instead of building a multi-layered legal labyrinth, it would be better to enable parties to a labour agreement to have more equal and transparent bargaining capacities.

This means Voice must be promoted for all interests, including the precariat. We considered collaborative bargaining earlier, and why labour unions did not offer a promising vehicle for occupational citizenship. It was easy to be critical of unions as they battled against globalization. They tried to impede change and restore labourist benefits they had been instrumental in gaining. Ineffectual, they have tended to become instruments of management in a desire to be relevant and tolerated. But criticism should be muted, since everybody needs organizations to represent their interests. The challenge is to identify the type that could best represent the precariat. It must help those outside occupational communities to develop realistic occupational avenues, which means assisting them in having access to various services and collaborative as well as collective bargaining, dealing with other groups of workers, agencies, occupational bodies and local authorities as well as with employers.

Two innovative models, one in India, one in the USA, may be harbingers of the sort of organization needed for flexible labour markets in which more people work at a distance from formal worksites. In India, the Self-Employed Women's Association (SEWA) has mushroomed into an organization of over a million outworkers, giving street vendors, *beedi* (hand-rolled cigarette) workers, tobacco workers, garment workers, construction workers, wastepaper pickers and others an organizational base, awareness of their rights and social entitlements, and access to a range of services. The SEWA model is being emulated. It offers work-related services for women doing informal labour, trying to provide basic security while organizing them to put pressure on employers, intermediaries, local authorities and the consuming public.

For several decades, labour unions in India and globally refused to recognize SEWA, claiming it was not a union because it did not represent workers in the standard definition of that term and its members were not covered by labour law. Without employment contracts they are deemed to be providing services. And SEWA is a social movement, with objectives not encompassed by collective bargaining or workplace representation. It provides members with literacy courses, microcredit, banking facilities, social protection schemes and, until recently, access to cooperative childcare. It was not until 2006, after years of costly lobbying, that the international union confederation, then the ICFTU, allowed SEWA to join. Meanwhile, in India a Commission was set up to devise a scheme to give outworkers social protection. After seven drafts, a bill was prepared, but it was not promising, since all attempts to 'extend' traditional social security and labour law protection were flawed. Nevertheless, the SEWA model is spreading, giving Voice to the precariat, those in indirect labour – 'providing services' – who are at the end of the labour chain in which outsourcing and offshoring fit. It is a part of the associational revolution taking place in response to globalization and the withering of the labourist model.

A second example comes from the USA, where several organizations for the precariat have emerged. The Freelancers' Union, based in New York State, was set up to provide services to those doing precarious labour. Its founder, Sara Horowitz, recognized that 'self-employed' contractors, as home workers or on short-term contracts, lacked benefits essential for a decent life. So, the Union negotiated a collective health insurance for members. Initially, it called itself the Portable Benefits Network, since it offered members benefits such as assistance in education and healthcare. It went on to provide a 401(k) defined-contribution retirement-savings account as part of a menu of services its members could purchase. In effect, the Union became a means of filling gaps left by the erosion of enterprise and state-based social protection.

In both cases, associational freedom is being advanced. Instead of a dubious paternalism, with nudges to individuals to make the 'right' choice, associations are emerging to articulate mechanisms for security and occupational freedom. A progressive agenda would wish to legitimize this, and strengthen occupational and other collaborative bargaining rights.

Part of the needed reorganization concerns institutional governance, so as to give work-that-is-not-labour higher priority. Among feasible institutions are national councils for work and negotiated compacts between workers' bodies, employers and governments. Here too, old models will not suffice. Fortunately, we are seeing new forms of civil society group trying to come to terms with the insecurity. Many may be flawed, but they reflect a continuing desire for Voice.

While community unions or civic associations may be the means by which the precariat can be represented, there are dangers, including the threat of such bodies being co-opted by interests not grounded in work. To give a topical example, organizations run by a religion are usually run *for* a religion, operating discriminatory practices. It is for this sort of reason that one should want associations adhering more to principles of occupational guilds. The best option would be to draw the precariat into self-chosen occupational associations.

As shown by the refusal of the international trade unions to recognize SEWA, labourism is resistant to legitimizing non-standard work. Those who fear jobs being offshored should reflect on the adage that a chain is only as strong as its weakest link. Labour battalions in rich countries long made pronouncements in support of 'the international labour movement', but acted in their nationalistic interest. There were exceptions. But the legacy of the AFL-CIO of George Meany and Lane Kirkland included fragmented workers' movements where outsourcing is now booming. The challenge is to assist the weakest in the global labour chain. If their income security and their Voice were strengthened, all would stand to gain. Global markets and corporations require global association.

Besides agency vis-à-vis employers, the precariat needs agency for dealing with the state. Anything that uses up time and resources is a sphere of work. One of the most time-consuming and costly activities is dealing with the bureaucratic state apparatus. Someone in the precariat has to spend more time in such work than someone in the salariat. It is a regressive 'time tax'. There is usually no Voice acting on behalf of the precariat in this work. There is an egalitarian argument for saying that if the surveillance state expands at the cost of some groups more than others, then those most inconvenienced through no fault of their own, other than ill-luck or natural infirmities, should be compensated. This is an argument for universalizing basic security.

In sum, real decommodification requires agency and collective associations. Only independent representation can overcome vulnerability. It is not sufficient for the purpose, but it is essential.

REDEFINING SECURITY AS ECONOMIC RIGHTS

Insecurity is the defining feature of globalization. The labour security built up in the Great Transformation was flawed. But its demise ushered in a period when insecurity affected all groups almost everywhere. Even the financial elite eventually experienced the nemesis of a hubristic yet emotionally insecure existence. Others had experienced more prosaic insecurity, epitomized by the nomadic existence of the world's precariat. The insecurity was not accidental. Many people celebrated 'the risk society'. The neo-liberal strategy sought to dismantle institutions that gave some security.

Economic insecurity reflects exposure to several forms of risk and uncertainty and a limited capacity to cope with adverse outcomes and to recover from them. Insecurity should be considered in terms of risk taking, shocks, hazards and uncertainty. Any individual is exposed to idiosyncratic risk reflecting life-cycle contingencies, such as a spell of unemployment or an illness. This is the sphere of classic social security. But there are also shocks, involving covariant risk – where one adverse event tends to trigger others – and systemic risk, where whole communities are exposed.

There has been a secular rise in the incidence of shocks, and it has been harder to cope with and recover from them. This has reflected the global market society, the dismantling of institutions of social protection and the vagaries of global warming.

Idiosyncratic risk is more insurable than systemic risk, but it is the latter that has grown. If risks are uninsurable or if they affect whole families, groups and communities rather than individuals, they are more threatening. A risk taken by a financier on the other side of the world can send your life plunging into utter misery.

Natural disasters hit communities in an instant of shock and awe, as nature sweeps away their material base. Governments and international agencies rush to provide emergency aid. But there is not much difference between such shocks and the slow-fuse shocks of decaying structures and epidemics. And the globalizing economic system means there is little chance that any community can be shielded from the effects of decisions taken elsewhere, over which the victims have no democratic control.

Not only are more people exposed to risks and uncertainty from shocks but adverse effects are more likely to be serious and persistent. It is harder to cope and to recover, since community relationships of support are dislocated. In terms of social income, this reflects the weakening of community benefits and family support as well as state benefits and enterprise benefits. For instance, if all members of a family or neighbourhood have their livelihoods destroyed, then if one member obtains an income there will be demands from the others, creating a poverty trap and several moral hazards.

Situations of shock differ from hazards. Hazards arise from predictable life events that have a high probability of an adverse economic effect. They include births or deaths in the family, a migration event and retirement. These involve necessary expenses, or strong moralistic pressure to incur them to preserve status, respect and hope of reciprocity.

The resultant costs can erode a household's capacity to sustain its livelihood base, by pushing it into debt, mortgaging property or preventing it from investing in capability development. Given the high probability of such events, an insurance policy would entail high premiums or would not be feasible. Insurance may also involve a moral hazard; the prospect of compensation would make it more likely for the event to occur, which means an insurer would wish to monitor people's behaviour and link compensation to proof of costs incurred or to a predetermined level of costs. The panopticon state likes dealing with hazards. The monitoring and threat of reprisals induce fear. More timorous citizens will think many times about claiming, even if they feel 'deserving'.

Insecurity also arises from uncertainty. With uncertainty, one is unsure about one's interests or how to realize them. The outcome of decisions cannot be predicted with confidence, and one does not know what to do if an adverse outcome materializes. Uncertainty pushes people into risk-averse behaviour, especially if consequences could be catastrophic. For instance, those doing activity dependent on climate conditions face chronic uncertainty. Anything that lessened it would prompt higher-yielding investment, innovation and purposive decision-making.

So, basic economic security requires limited exposure to unwanted risks, uncertainty, hazards and shocks; it requires an ability to cope if they materialize; and it requires an ability to recover from adverse outcomes.

So far, one may have a picture of insecurity linked to labour and capital markets and to ecological shocks. Three other forms of insecurity have grown as the global market society has taken shape. First, there is identity risk, a feeling that it is harder to maintain an identity in a fluid social and economic structure. Yet it is hard to insure one's identity; everybody is urged to accept that they may need to change and adapt.

Second, there is occupational risk. With the dismantling of occupational communities, people are more likely to have to change their occupation. They take more risk when they enter a profession or craft that they will at some point have to move out of it or accept changes that alter the nature of the work and the intrinsic and extrinsic rewards. This too is uninsurable, and is likely to stay so. An egalitarian should not wish that risk to deter people from pursuing an occupational career.

A third uninsurable form of insecurity could be called freedom insecurity. The nudges are out there, many unknown. We may not know what we should not be doing; that may be the intention of those doing the oversight. Or the range of demands for correctness may be so broad that it surpasses our capacities. We cannot check the small print all the time or remember all the rules.

If economic insecurity is more pervasive and less insurable, it is inappropriate to concentrate on ex-post compensation mechanisms, since attributing responsibility for adverse outcomes would be largely arbitrary. Who should be insured for identity loss? The argument should lead to a search for ex-ante security, limiting the threat and ensuring individuals and communities have basic security in which to cope and recover from shocks for which they could not realistically prepare.

Security is also instrumentally good, because only secure people can be expected to make non-opportunistic and rational decisions, and because only secure people can resist the unwanted nudge of others. Insecure people are easily dominated by the needs of survival. A moderate degree of security is also needed for leisure and participation in public life. Thus, a scheme for citizenship income security could be expected to promote public participation and make the political process more altruistic and civilized.

If we accept that security is the base of full freedom, we should accept that 'dependent security' or paternalism is incompatible with it. If someone is dependent on the good will of a benefactor, be it a relative such as a husband, a landlord, a moneylender or the state, that person cannot have full freedom. There should be a presumption that paternalism is incompatible with security, unless there is proof that specific behaviour would be harmful to others, or that particular groups need protection because they cannot provide it themselves, as in the case of children, the mentally incapacitated and the frail elderly. Even in those cases, the burden of proof should be placed on the paternalists.

Security requires and builds on a sense of social solidarity, necessitating mechanisms and institutions of reciprocity and mechanisms to strengthen civic friendship. This was glossed over in the labourist model, with the presumption that unions, industrial enterprises and collective bodies representing employers were sufficient. Now new forms of association are needed to forge security and develop collaborative bargaining.

Solidarity requires compassion, not pity. An association to assert work rights, rather than labour entitlements, would be oriented to compassion. A civil society organization set up to alleviate poverty or to help the sick is a body of charity motivated primarily by pity. This is valuable. However, charity does not establish rights; it may even alleviate pressure for rights. Only if an association is embedded as part of the economic system can it become a rights-based mechanism. Arendt said sagely that 'solidarity is a principle that can inspire and guide action, compassion is one of the passions, and pity is a sentiment' (Arendt, 1990, p. 89).

If universal security is about freedom, identity and social solidarity, one should acknowledge a caveat. What is proposed is a claim right to universal *basic* security, not total security. One can have too much as well as too little. Excessive security may lead to indolence, irresponsibility and opportunism. This is a reason for favouring a cap on incomes and wealth, because a rich individual is capable of inflicting far more damage on others than a poor one. What we should argue for is universal basic economic security.

If one is an egalitarian believing in basic security, are there criteria by which to evaluate policy proposals and institutional changes? Let us propose five Decision Principles, drawing from several philosophical traditions.

The Security Difference Principle

A policy or institutional change is socially just only if it improves the security and work prospects of the least secure groups in society.

This is a starting point, even if it invites Paretian-type concerns about inter-personal comparisons. An egalitarian can assert that if equal basic security is desirable, then reducing the insecurity of the most insecure should have priority, and action that intensifies their insecurity should be unacceptable. So, if a policy boosted the job opportunities of middle-income groups while worsening the prospects of more disadvantaged groups, that could not be justifiable unless the losers were compensated in ways they found acceptable. The Security Difference Principle stems from Rawls (1973), who from a liberal perspective argued that inequalities are socially just only if they allow for the betterment of the worst-off groups in society.

This principle can stand as a moral precept. A policy should be judged by whether it helps the least secure. If it does not, one should be uneasy, unless some other principle is recognized as demonstrably superior. If so, it would be up to the policy proponent to state that alternative and show that the policy being proposed would yield superior outcomes. A point is that there should be a right to a minimal amount of resources so as to enhance the capacity to develop and to exercise effective freedom.

Consider an occupational association in terms of the Security Difference Principle. To function effectively, group solidarity may have to be the operating principle rather than strict egalitarianism. So, there may be a need to make concessions to administrative hierarchy in order to preserve reasonable egalitarianism based on the security of the least advantaged in terms of ability, education, training, earning power and physical or mental handicaps.

The Paternalism Test Principle

A policy or institutional change is socially just only if it does not impose controls on some groups that are not imposed on the most free groups in society.

As we have seen, paternalism is rife, repackaged as libertarian paternalism. It is the biggest intellectual challenge for egalitarians. Underlying this principle is the Millian liberal view that there is a prima facie case against paternalism (except in the case of children and the medically frail), particularly against those forms that constrain the freedoms of the disadvantaged.

This principle requires that all who could be subject to paternalistic direction have an effective independent Voice (collective and individual) to represent their interests.

Only with Voice can people have some control over their work and lives, and only by having control can there be real meaning in the ideas of universalism and occupational citizenship.

Relevant to the paternalism principle, research on happiness has reiterated that people who have control over their work are happier, even taking account of the influence of access to benefits (Haidt, 2006). Control means having the capacity and opportunity to make decisions for oneself, without that being determined by the state, or by patriarchal figures or religious or other institutions that seek to dictate how people must behave.

This principle is relevant to considering how governments have pursued 'social integration' through welfare reform. It also relates to identity, since paternalism typically has little time for the person's own character. At its mildest, it wants to nudge people to change. It rarely stops there. While a libertarian paternalist would rely on nudges, an egalitarian would rely on strengthening Voice in collaborative bargaining rather than better direction and default options from the state.

There is one twist in the tail. Libertarians claim to believe in trusting people to make their own decisions. But the poor have not been trusted. In fact, it is where the potentially adverse consequences of trust failure are greatest that there is some justification for guidance and surveillance. The affluent elite should be subject to more paternalism, since they can unleash systemic insecurity affecting others besides themselves.

The Rights-Not-Charity Principle

A policy or institutional change is socially just if it enhances the rights of the recipient of benefits or services and limits the discretionary power of the providers.

A right is possessed as a mark of a person's humanity or citizenship, and ceases to be a right if entitlement is made dependent on some prior behavioural conditionality. People should not be expected to have to plead for assistance, or to rely on the selective benevolence of civil servants. Entitlements should be *rights*, not matters for the discretionary decisions of bureaucrats, philanthropists or aid donors, however well meaning they may be. A universalistic approach is one that emphasizes compassion and strengthens protection through social solidarity and reciprocity.

Some have identity thrust upon them, in seeking a dependent situation that is scarcely enviable. Consider 'the supplicant beggar'. No sensible observer could regard such a person as secure. Even if she were able to occupy the same corner every day where benefactors placed coins in a hat, there would be no moral bond associated with the charitable act, only humiliation. A beggar must be careful not to dress too well, beg too aggressively or show insufficient gratitude. The identity and agency being shown are those of dependent insecurity.

Similarly, a migrant may rely on a network of patrons, intermediaries and brokers, who provide the means of acquiring a job. Again, this is dependent insecurity, since what is given can be taken away. *Mafioso* patrons play on individual insecurities and manipulate those enticed into their net. Gangster social protection flourishes in all market societies that tolerate chronic inequality. Public works are a benevolent form of the supplicant beggar situation, as is philanthropy by the super-rich, the elite of the global order.

The Ecological Constraint Principle

A policy or institutional change is socially just only if it does not involve an ecological cost borne by the community or by those directly affected.

Ecological security is something most of us can understand. Smell the air, taste the water, look for the disappearing species. This rule is a quintessential twenty-first century principle. Potential ecological consequences should be built into policies, not added as an afterthought. For instance, there may be a trade-off between more jobs and the ecological sustainability and revival of a local area. The commercial drive to pursue growth and profits without taking account of externalities is a recipe for ecological disaster.

The ecological constraint principle means that all policies, such as job creation schemes, should be subject to the constraint that they should not deliberately or wilfully (carelessly) jeopardize the environment. In this context, one could argue that subsidies intended to boost skills, employment or job-creating investment should promote only ecologically beneficial work.

The principle raises emotional reactions, with claims that such a condition is a protectionist device penalizing poor countries, forcing them to slow growth and incurring costs that hinder development. Regrettably, global warming and other pollution – including that emanating from poor working conditions in the specious interest of job promotion – will hurt more people in developing countries and do so more devastatingly than elsewhere. The principle must be respected everywhere.

The Occupational Work Principle

A policy or institutional change is just only if it does not block people from pursuing their sense of occupation in a dignified way and if it does not disadvantage the most insecure groups in that respect.

This involves the judgments that occupational work is worth promoting and that policies should enhance the range and quality of work options of the most insecure. While this may seem complicated, the point is to determine whether a scheme favours development of freely chosen opportunities and work. Policies should not block off a person's pursuit of an occupational career, as activities to develop personal capabilities. A policy that prevented or penalized someone undertaking work that was not labour would offend this principle.

* * *

In sum, in building a new egalitarianism these five principles offer a framework in which occupational citizenship could be constructed. Identifying trade-offs and setting priorities are inevitable. But these should be transparent and subject to democratic processes. Policies that satisfied all the principles would be ideal.

BUILDING INCOME SECURITY

The bedrock of a new egalitarianism, one committed to emancipatory freedom, is a strategy to delink basic security from labour. If we accept the egalitarian rationale and the policy decision principles, then consider this chapter's central proposal. It is that the Global Transformation's double movement hinges on a right to basic income security. No progressive strategy will make sense otherwise.

Before explaining why, it is worth making a plea to those hostile to the idea to reconsider what may have been rejected in different times. Too often, progressives who want to see improvements in the lives of their fellow humans express what Albert Hirschman (1991) saw as the reactions to every progressive idea – claims of futility (it will not work), jeopardy (it will endanger other goals) and perversity (it will have unintended consequences).

The proposal is that every citizen, or legal resident, should have a right to receive a monthly basic income, either as a tax credit or a cash payment. It would be given to each person individually, regardless of age, marital status or work or labour status, and would be fully portable, being paid wherever the person was living in the country.

The proposal has a long pedigree and has drawn support from many distinguished people.[1] What is new is the Global Transformation, which has created the conditions for incorporating it into the mainstream. While neo-liberals may oppose the idea for ideological reasons, the paternalists have most reason to scowl.

Let us start by clarifying the key words. To say there should be a 'right' to a basic income is to assert a claim or republican right, implying that policies and institutional changes should move progressively towards realizing it. One could envisage it being incorporated into a country's constitution, which is close to what happened in post-apartheid South Africa. A right – and this is important given how social policy debates have evolved – is *unconditional* in behavioural terms. You do not have a right if you must do x or y to have an entitlement.

Whereas paternalists instinctively argue that people are entitled to something only if they behave in a certain way, egalitarians place faith in their fellow citizens and affirm that people's attitudes and behaviour stem from having dignity. A person mired in poverty cannot be expected to behave in an exemplary way, and it is unfair for a moralist to require 'socially responsible behaviour' from those denied conditions of civility and security.

The next word is 'basic'. To speak of a basic right is to imply that it must be met if other basic rights are to be realized (Shue, 1996). It must also be meaningful, in being adequate to provide agency or freedom. A basic income must make a difference to economic security, enabling people to survive in dignity if they choose or are obliged to rely on it. It must be meaningful, not a gesture, enough to give dignity but not so much that it leads to indolence. It must be enough to impart the security needed to make rational choices and to enable someone to say 'No!' if treated badly. It would, for the first time, give dignified meaning to the right to work.

A right to basic income security does not imply a right to have basic needs satisfied, should someone choose to squander the means of satisfying them. A right to an adequate standard of living implies that people should be *enabled* to meet their basic needs (Copp, 1992). Another way of putting this is that everybody should have rights of agency. This is linked to Kant's dictum that we should act towards others in ways we would wish them to act towards us. This requires each person to be able to exercise human agency, which is only possible on the basis of freedom and adequate security.

The other word is 'income'. Peculiarly, some progressives are suspicious about people having money. We are not arguing that money is a panacea. But income must come in a non-paternalistic form. It should not be given as a discretionary gesture, out of the goodness of somebody's heart; it is not charity. It must be in a form that allows the recipient to decide how to use it, unlike vouchers or food stamps that presume the 'poverty' is of a certain type. This is unfair to those who do not need or value the items singled out by the state or donor. The income must be individual and equal, with supplements for those with special needs such as the disabled and frail elderly. It must be in a form that enables people to make rational choices, which is vital for promoting gender equality, for instance.

To avoid misunderstanding (and misrepresentation), note that a basic income should be regarded as the base of a social protection system that could be supplemented by insurance benefits and collaboratively bargained occupational benefits. And a basic income should be seen as a form of continuity. It is not as radical as some enthusiasts convey and critics seem to believe. In many countries, the elements exist already. Essentially, it means giving every citizen, as a right of citizenship, a modest amount of non-taxed income. All income beyond that would be subject to tax. There would be no poverty trap, since only income above that would be taxed. For those earning wages or with other income it would amount to tax relief. Implementation would be made easier by integration of tax and benefit systems, which is coming.

One criticism should be dismissed with derision. It is that a basic income would amount to a 'hand-out', a reward for sloth and a tax on those who labour. Those making this claim are usually those who have been given plenty of something for nothing. It would be just to think of it as a social dividend. Every moderately affluent person in every society owes their good fortune largely to the labour, work, energy and inventiveness of their forebears and the forebears of their lower-income fellow citizens. Today's wealth, including the capacity to buy fancy consumer goods, is largely a reflection not of our labour but of that of generations before us. If everyone were provided with a basic income with which to develop their capabilities, that would amount to a small dividend from the effort, investment and good luck of those who came before. This was essentially the rationale advanced by Tom Paine in *Agrarian Justice* written in 1795.

Many who believe a basic income should underpin a redistributive strategy advocate a step-by-step approach, weaving the patchwork of existing schemes into a universal base, while phasing out behavioural testing of existing schemes. Some see it coming 'through the back door' (Atkinson, 2004). Several transition routes have been proposed. Some believe the amount should be low initially, building up to a decent level as it became accepted. Others believe it should be paid initially to groups deemed most vulnerable to poverty and be gradually extended to others. The latter route has been taken in Brazil, with its *renda minima* (minimum income) and *bolsa escola* (school stipend) schemes that evolved into the *bolsa familia* (family stipend).

Others, including Tony Atkinson, have advocated a 'participation income' as a step towards a full basic income, in which some community work would be a condition for entitlement. The intention is to legitimize the concept with the middle class. This has the virtue that it would make it politically easier to phase in the grant. It would be better than most forms of conditionality. But it would impose labour on those who may not wish to perform it or be unable to do it without discomfort or cost. And it might have substitution effects, reducing opportunities for people who might otherwise be employed to do such work and lowering their wages. We will come back to a variant of this proposal at the end.

Finally, the name itself should not distract from the essentials of the idea. The point is that we are talking about a fundamental economic right. Other names include citizenship income grant and social dividend. A name that would capture the spirit of the idea is a work grant. Whatever the name, the objective is to help promote egalitarian or emancipatory freedom.

An agenda for basic income security aims to move the contours of labourist welfare states towards an 'architecture' of egalitarian freedom, to use a conventional word. Thus, subsidies to capital are unjustifiable by any worthy principle. Means testing offends freedom by setting up stigmatizing oversight mechanisms along with poverty traps and moral and immoral hazards. These are inherently divisive, dividing the population into deserving, undeserving and transgressing 'poor'. Above all, welfare state policies did not entail a strategy for redistributing the crucial assets of the tertiary society.

As Pateman (2008) and others have argued, a basic income can also be justified as an instrument of democratization, since all citizens need material resources to make rights meaningful. A basic income would help establish individual self-government *and* equal self-respect. Late eighteenth-century radicals, such as Paine and Mary Wollstonecraft, conceived democratization as the universalization of freedom, equality and independence, the last based on the Lockean 'natural freedom' principle that someone should be able to act without having to ask for consent. Independence is central to emancipatory rights. It could be said to depend on having a right to subsistence. One of the founders of the US Constitution, Alexander Hamilton (1788), put it nicely, 'A power over a man's subsistence amounts to a power over his will'.

The idea of emancipatory rights entails recognizing that democracy is not solely concerned with collective self-government in the sense of voting, but also emancipation from dependence and unwanted control by others (Shapiro, 1999; Goodhart, 2005). Democracy is about the creation of mechanisms and institutions that block arbitrary use of power.

As Michael Goodhart (2007, p. 107) noted, 'Calling basic income a *democratic* program emphasizes that its primary justification is its role in achieving and securing emancipation for all members of society'. If welfare comes with stigma, it scarcely advances freedom or independence, or equal public standing. Human rights are rights of agency.

The idea of basic security as a right has been espoused by liberals as well as republican theorists. John Stuart Mill ([1861] 1972, p. 275) stated: 'The rights and interests of every and any person are only secure from being disregarded when the person is himself able, and habitually disposed, to stand up for them'. Surely, only people with basic income security and access to associations able to represent their social and economic interests could develop that habitual disposition.

A basic income would also boost social work and forms of work that are not labour. We will come back to this, but it should be noted that there is no evidence that granting people basic income security results in less work.

Having universal basic security would also help to revive altruism, a desirable public good that is diminished by its non-marketability. Altruism derives from deep biological and social forces. But it is a fragile human trait. If people do not feel they are treated fairly, they are less likely to help others or feel well disposed towards them. It is unsurprising that a society based ostentatiously on reward for merit and moneymaking skills, denying economic security to its losers, experiences an erosion of altruism. Basic security for all would revive altruism for the same reason. People who feel less threatened by the spectre of destitution are more altruistic.

People who feel secure are also more likely to be tolerant of strangers. The precariat is chronically insecure, and it should be no surprise that it is susceptible to politically intolerant agendas. A basic income would help improve tolerance of minorities. In these times of global capitalism, measures to strengthen social solidarity and weaken the fear that leads to support for vengeful politics are essential.

A basic income is not a panacea but must be part of an egalitarian strategy. In terms of income security, it should be combined with occupational social protection schemes and with a democratic sharing of capital income.

CAPITAL SHARING

Globalization has generated more inequality and insecurity. But the economic and financial crisis that began in 2008 has opened up an opportunity to address both these ills, in the process improving economic development in an ecologically sustainable way.

Capitalism based on sovereign wealth funds, hedge funds, pension funds and investment funds may have become less impressive since the debacle of 2008, but it will continue to be central to global capitalism. Sovereign wealth funds are essentially vehicles for depositing capital gains, which can be used for investment, fiscal purposes or distribution to citizens as social dividends. The Norwegian fund started as a vehicle to prevent 'Dutch disease', where booming oil revenues drive up the exchange rate and cause deindustrialization. But by depositing part of the revenues in a fund, the state created a means of paying for public expenditure as the oilfields were depleted. Other countries had governments that were less prudent or egalitarian when they had the opportunity. But there is no reason why all governments could not establish sovereign wealth funds, which could be guided by ecological and ethical investment principles and by a commitment to use profits to help fund a basic income. The Alaska Permanent Fund provides a model, paying out an annual dividend to every legal resident of Alaska. Since it was launched in 1986, it has worked successfully.

Fund capitalism strengthens the financial base for a basic income. The moral and economic case was strengthened by the events of 2008 and the political reaction to it. Governments intervened to reduce systemic risk, a defining feature of global capitalism, by providing ex-ante security to the financial community. Though inegalitarian, this acknowledged that state intervention is essential to provide stability. And if citizens are insuring rich financiers from systemic risk, they too should be given similar ex-ante security. This is a matter of morality and economics.

When governments recapitalized banks and other financial firms in late 2008, they missed an opportunity to go to the next step. It would not be nationalization if governments took a *permanent* 10 per cent stake in each of them, in the form of ordinary shares held on behalf of the citizenry. The state would nominate a board member with a mandate to encourage the bank to direct its activities towards long-term profits rather than short-term gains. As banks return to profitability, the returns to the public stake would be deposited in a citizens' security fund, akin to the Alaska Permanent Fund or a sovereign wealth fund. This could invest on behalf of the citizenry, and help pay for citizenship dividends.

Meanwhile, all corporate subsidies should be reviewed and rolled back. They have become a vast drag on public finances and have induced corporate irresponsibility and inefficiency while increasing inequality. Crises produce moments of opportunity. This could put the global market economy on a healthier footing.

END SUBSIDIES AS WE KNOW THEM!

Advocates of basic income security as the bedrock for occupational citizenship and a new egalitarianism must show that a basic income can be funded. Most critics add up the population, cost a basic income and then compute the tax requirement. There are reasons for dismissing that way of proceeding (Standing, 2002). One is the failure to take into account the huge amount now paid out in subsidies and tax breaks to favoured groups.[2]

The global economy is awash with subsidies. They account for a rising share of national income, yet most are indefensible on efficiency or equity grounds. A large proportion goes to profitable corporations and the elite. In developing countries over 6 per cent of GDP is provided to corporations in subsidies. Those who claim a basic income is unaffordable or that it would go to people who had not contributed to society or who had not shown social responsibility should just consider the pattern of subsidies.

If workers lose a job, they are less likely these days to receive an unemployment benefit. If they fall sick, they are less likely to receive sickness benefit, or to have earnings maintained or to have all expenses paid. Meanwhile, if a financial company makes mistakes or indulges in recklessness, there is a higher probability that the government will give, lend or guarantee support to prevent bankruptcy. The rescue of Bear Stearns in early 2008 and the systemic bailout in late 2008 represented subsidies to capital and insurance against risk taking. Risk taking is the essence of capitalism. If a risk is lessened by an implicit promise of support in the event of a crisis, capital's effective share of the economy is raised, since it is guaranteed support from taxpayers, most of whom earn their income from labour. This is global capitalism in the early twenty-first century. Morally, it is hard to defend.

In countries such as the USA where tax subsidies are given to firms offering employees healthcare insurance, the subsidy goes to the salariat and core employees. It could be redirected to a national fund for financing a basic income, which everybody could use to invest in supplementary healthcare insurance if they wished. The subsidy to firms is unjustified by economic or philosophical criteria.

Some subsidies are concealed. For instance, subsidized employee stock ownership has spread, to the extent that many workers could earn more from share investment in their own companies than from wages. In principle, a situation could arise when they would be prepared to labour for a sub-subsistence wage, because they would stay as employees while gaining a higher income from their company's success. As competitiveness is driven partly by relative labour costs, real wages could fall as employees earn more from shares, becoming part of the *rentier* economy. An emerging practice is for firms to divert part of the wage to the purchase of company stock, which is held in a fund, perhaps administered by union officials, as in Austria. In one scheme, when they quit or retire, workers receive what they put in, plus the change in value if that is positive.

The European Federation of Employee Share Ownership argues that this encourages workers to think more strategically about their firms and deters hostile takeovers. But such workers will be politically compromised. Governments in Austria and Germany, for example, subsidize worker ownership of company stock through tax breaks (Dougherty, 2008). In 2008 6–7 per cent of employees in those countries owned shares in their own companies, compared with 20–30 per cent in the UK, Ireland and the USA. But the subsidies increase inequality, since the beneficiaries are the salariat and core employees, not the precariat. They offend the Security Difference Principle.

Another set of subsidies breach the Ecological Constraint Principle. To combat global warming, higher taxes on energy use are needed. These hit the poor more than the rich because fuel accounts for a higher share of their living costs and income, and because the rich can more easily afford energy-saving measures such as insulation and hybrid cars. And if land is diverted from food crops to biofuel, food costs rise. This hits the poor because they devote more of their budget to food. In the UK, the reaction so far has been to look at differential pricing options and subsidies (Joseph Rowntree Foundation, 2004). A better solution would be to provide security through a basic income, while taxing energy use to provide the right incentives. As with labour, the approach should be to commodify fully, avoiding subsidies that are inefficient, inequitable and wasteful.

In many countries, including India, some 3 per cent of GDP goes in fuel subsidies. This pleases firms that rely on fuel and consumers whose living costs are held down. But subsidies are not environmentally or economically sensible. They encourage waste and excessive use of the resource in production and excessive and inefficient use in consumption. Egalitarians should be appalled. There are high Type A and Type B errors, with subsidies going to many who have no need and not reaching many in need. Again, it would be more efficient *and* equitable to give the money directly to citizens to cover the extra fuel costs that would come from charging a market price. That would also have the virtue of leaving the choice to the individual.

Some transfers act as if they were subsidies. Bear in mind that subsidies distort opportunities, so if one group is subsidized it gains an advantage. Consider older workers. In market economies, the 50–70 age group already accounts for a quarter of all those aged 20 to 70. If someone aged 55 can retire from employment, receiving a full company pension and a partial state pension while taking a job elsewhere, that person will have an advantage over younger workers.

In the past, this was rare. Income was taxed at a higher rate, and taking a pension usually precluded labour force participation. Fewer were in that age group, fewer had access to early pensions, fewer were healthily active and there were fewer jobs available or suitable for older workers. In a tertiary society, in which flexible arrangements are common, and when 'active ageing' is encouraged by governments, the scope for substitution is greater. Younger workers will find that those with what is in effect a guaranteed basic income are competing for jobs.

The effect of the subsidized labour supply on relative employment may be hard to detect, because younger workers may take jobs by accepting lower wages. Unfortunately for them, the problem does not stop there. Older workers will be more prepared to forego non-wage enterprise benefits, because they already have those needs covered (for example, health insurance and pension) or because they anticipate having no need for them (for example, parental or maternity leave). This will be taken into account by employers in selecting the workers to employ and the type of contract to offer. If all received a basic income, and labour was fully paid by wages rather than enterprise benefits, the disadvantage of younger workers would be reduced.

There is another form of selective subsidy that should be reconsidered. At present, some groups are subsidized by virtue of their social status, including children, students, pregnant women, the elderly, the disabled and those deemed legally married. Most of us have no difficulty in accepting that such groups may need protection. But we should acknowledge that selection is based on moralistic, political and historical factors. In every case, the subsidy involves an arbitrary element. And usually unfairness is involved.

Consider two examples least favourable to the argument. Why should men and women who are legally married be given benefits that are not available to those who fail or choose not to marry? Marrying is a free action in a market society. It is regarded by many as a 'private good'. Why penalize those who do not have it? The second example is even more sensitive. Why should a woman, whose 'right to choose' should be a fundamental right, be given money when she chooses to have a baby and acquire something most of us regard as precious? Another woman may want a baby but not have one. The person with one advantage is then given a subsidy. The counter-argument, that society needs to foster its next generation, would not be relevant under a basic income system. Once a child came into the world he or she would be granted basic income security personally, presumably given to the primary caregiver until legally an adult. One is not proposing here abolition of maternity benefit, merely pointing to its non-egalitarian basis.

In sum, the system of selective subsidies should be reviewed. The biggest subsidies go to those who are among the most secure groups and interests. Almost all encourage inefficient use of resources, many have adverse ecological implications, and most offend all five of the policy principles laid out earlier.

END PATERNALISTIC WELFARE POLICY!

The major trend in social policy has been paternalistic, attaching behavioural conditions and using fiscal policy to boost labour. This is contrary to full freedom, distorts labour markets and is costly. An agenda for occupational citizenship and emancipatory egalitarianism should roll back such paternalism.

Welfare based on social insurance, social assistance or labour conditionality offends the egalitarian principles laid out earlier. Increasingly, welfare is a matter of pity, coupled with a narrow utilitarian interpretation of social solidarity, based on fear, for oneself, one's friends or for those like us in our society. This is why it was not defended very well as new forms of inequality sharpened. The paternalists who support welfare usually fall back on a notion of the 'deserving poor', seeing welfare as ex-post compensation for some mishap, from a shock or hazard. By contrast, ex-ante security would establish a right, based not on charity or fear, but on compassion and a broad concept of social solidarity.

As governments turned to paternalistic conditionality, they whittled away at freedom and made it clearer that they do not trust people. If policies are constructed on the basis that people should receive a benefit only if they do what is deemed good for them, policy-makers obviously think their fellow citizens are ignorant or foolish. Such a presumption is presumptuous.

Take one incarnation of paternalism, a scheme called Opportunity NYC, launched in 2007 in New York City on a pilot basis, and funded by charities and the mayor's own fortune. It has had a favourable press (for example, Grimes, 2008). Based on Mexico's *Opportunidades* scheme, 2500 families were paid conditional cash transfers dependent on performance of tasks supposed to help them escape poverty, such as healthcare checks and passing school exams. The formula was detailed and directive. If a parent attended a parent-teacher conference she received US$25; if a child obtained a library card the family received US$50; if a student attended school on 95 per cent of school days the family received US$100; if the student passed a high school exam the family received US$600; if a parent worked over 30 hours a week in a job she was paid a bonus of US$300; if she worked over ten hours a week while attending an approved training course she received between US$300 and US$600. The list goes on.

Leaving aside the motives behind the scheme, is it wise or liberating? In effect, people are being bribed to do what is in their interest. This cannot satisfy the Rights-not-Charity Principle or the Paternalism Test Principle. Defenders of the scheme may contend that penalties work less well than incentives, that the challenge is to overcome barriers to socially correct behaviour and that the conditions spur parents to recalculate their self-interest, favouring their longer-term welfare. Without the cash incentive, for example, mothers would go to jobs rather than take their child to a clinic. If so, a more cost-effective policy would be to require employers to give mothers sufficient flexibility to take their children to the clinic. In other words, liberate time, just a little.

A libertarian should criticize such conditional transfers for eroding individual responsibility. If people do something primarily for extrinsic reasons, it will be valued less and done with less commitment than if they wished to do it. If the scheme is only for those in poverty, it could pay some of the near-poor to become poor in order to qualify for the bonuses. There are also problems of equity. Those who have made an effort to do those laudable actions themselves, perhaps sacrificing other welfare-enhancing activities, will be penalized relative to those covered by the scheme. Is that fair?

The evidence of beneficial effects of cash transfers is overwhelming. In Mexico, they have been linked to improvements in child height, reduced obesity and improved motor-cognitive development and linguistic skill. But is the conditionality needed or desirable? It is stigmatizing, and may set up perverse signals. A doctor may think that a patient forced to come can be treated less seriously than one who chooses to come. A teacher may be inclined to pass a student improperly because she knows the family needs money. So, the subsidy to good behaviour may induce bad behaviour as well.

A final problem is the selectivity. No doubt, conditional grants for the elderly, the disabled, migrants or even prime-age adults would have beneficial effects as well. The schemes favour one group and leave out many of the most insecure. Meanwhile, there would be no end to the nudging and steering. In all respects, a basic income would be better.

Now consider incapacity benefits, which have become a sphere for paternalistic direction, as discussed in Chapter 5. An egalitarian non-labourist view would be that someone with a disability should be given a share of the community's product to equalize their life chances, regardless of what they do. None of us has the endowments we would like the gods to have bestowed on us. But we exist as citizens and should want equal endowments. A disabled person deserves as much as anybody else. If you have the energy and talent to do well for yourself you should gain. But would you deny the other a decent existence?

Disability benefits put people into a double trap. The moral hazard is that it pays to stay incapacitated; a minor improvement might risk losing the only income available, whereas becoming incapacitated would yield an income. Traditionally, disability grants did not require claimants to look for jobs. The amount tended to rise with duration of receipt and was not means tested, except for those with large pensions. The paternalist trend has altered all that. The benefit is a source of security, giving recipients predictability about how to live and what to consume. To take a precarious job and give up that security would be irrational, perhaps traumatizing. For those bumped from core jobs with status, or from the salariat, a job that put them in the precariat would be demeaning, more so than having to say they were on incapacity benefit. Work may be good for them but jobs may not be.

Although governments have banned discrimination against the disabled, the labour market dynamics are increasing their disadvantage. Policymakers, wanting to push them into jobs, have tightened up tests of disability. And as mental problems are a rising cause of disability, psychological and medical specialists are being used to make sufferers more employable. This panopticonic paternalism offends the Security Difference, Paternalism Test and Rights-not-Charity Principles, highlighting the need for countervailing associational freedom.

The latest twist of utilitarian policy is to promote philanthropy, faith-based organizations and self-appointed NGOs as the means of increasing income security. This is leaving it to pity organizations, emphasizing charity rather than rights. However noble the motives, these are not democratic or universal initiatives. Sometimes the motives are not noble. One evolutionary biologist has even argued that philanthropic generosity by the rich is a demonstration of potency to potential mates. Others have depicted much of it as commercially motivated. It is not too cynical to see some of it as a commodification of philanthropy, the economic return being enhanced status and lasting fame. And philanthropy often deters state initiatives and undermines measures of social solidarity. It is part of the problem, contrary to what admirers of super-rich philanthropists claim (Bishop and Green, 2008). It strengthens a regime of pity and weakens one of rights. Philanthropy and civil society are desirable, but they must be supplementary, not primary.

The alternative to paternalism and pity is to provide basic income security as a right and facilitate growth of associations that can assist people to be ethical and capable human beings. If people are denied assets needed to function in a market society, paternalism is an unattractive answer.

The initial results of a pilot for an unconditional, individual basic income being conducted in an impoverished African community suggest that, given the chance, even in the most difficult circumstances, people act in their own best interest without being bribed or forced to do so (Basic Income Grant Coalition, 2008). There is no reason to think this is not a universal human trait.

LIBERATING TIME

Time is an asset; it has value and is scarce. In a market society, access to quality time is very unequally distributed. An egalitarian agenda that set out to equalize access to quality free time would be one that enabled and encouraged everybody equally to allocate their time freely to the four types of use – labour, work, play and leisure.

This does not mean that someone in the precariat would allocate time in the same way as someone in the salariat. An egalitarian strategy would mean that there should be no institutional barrier preventing someone in the precariat from allocating time in the same way as anybody else. If a lower-income person is forced to use time on activities that others do not have to do, that would be inconsistent with egalitarian freedom.

It would be inconsistent with occupational citizenship if policies gave emphasis and incentives only to labour and play, or consumption, which is currently the case. In both neo-liberal and social democratic models, it has been costly and risky for the citizen to reallocate time from labour to work or from labour or play to leisure. A consequence has been that people do too much labour relative to work and too little leisure relative to everything else.

There are ways of readjusting nudges so as to make it easier, less costly and more rewarding to switch to work that is not labour and to leisure that is not play. The point is not to steer but to neutralize the nudges. To some extent, the state has started to experiment with methods of increasing work that is not labour, even if it has done so to save public expenditure and facilitate labour. It has also given subsidies to the 'leisure community', but this often means a subsidy to wealthier sophisticates, for museums or art galleries. A bigger problem is that modest efforts to promote work that is not labour have been overwhelmed by efforts to promote labourism, with subsidies such as tax credits and behaviour tests for allocating benefits. These dwarf the tentative measures to promote certain types of work that are not labour, such as tax credits for approved types of care.

The pattern of subsidies and behavioural nudges has put pressure on uses of time that the state has not approved or noticed. A casualty is political and community participation, the essence of citizenship since ancient Greece. Being an active citizen is expensive in the modern market society. One could even think the state does not want people to be active citizens. As a result, such participation is underperformed and left increasingly to those who can afford it, the salariat and the elite. The precariat is disinclined to participate as it is scrambling to survive, cannot afford the costs and has least sense of a future to protect.

A basic income could promote work and leisure because it would tilt the balance of costs and benefits in uses of time. Suppose it enabled those in the precariat and unemployed to turn down low-paying degrading jobs because they were able to be more 'choosy'. Neo-liberals and paternalists might condemn them for laziness. But what would be the dynamics? The wages for such unappealing jobs would rise, drawing more people to take them. Some jobs would be automated out of existence; some would cease to be done because their cost would exceed the perceived value (the boss would start pouring her own tea, local authorities would provide more litter bins, and so on). All these reactions would remind people that driving wages to sub-subsistence level is not the best way to foster civilized behaviour.

Similarly, moralistic politicians who regard as reprehensible the idea that a few may sit in bed 'living off the dole' should own up to having a pessimistic view of their fellow humans. They should ask whether there is something else that is leading to such self-destructive behaviour. They could also reason that the fiscal cost of policing 'scroungers' exceeds the economic loss from having a few squandering their lives in slothful inactivity.

Those prone to moralizing about others' behaviour should also reflect on the evidence that basically secure people are more likely to be active, energetic, confident and directed than those who are insecure and subject to surveillance and coercion as they live a life on the edge. Those who do not use their time to take risks by developing their competences are mostly those who see no future in the mirror or who are left to look around at other failures.

Market society imposes more demands on the time of the precariat and other low-income groups. This inequality has grown. It extends to the acquisition of insurance products necessitated by the market society. The less educated and the precariat have to spend more time around labour – in seeking or waiting for labour, for instance – and have to do more work in their non-labour time, including finding, understanding and filling in application forms for benefits. And because they tend to be less competent, they spend more time dealing with bureaucratic requirements, eating up time that could be allocated to work or leisure. They are more prone to mistakes, because they cannot find the time to do those procedures carefully and because the decisions they have to make are more complex and potentially disastrous. Then they face the humiliation of paying more for their needs, because they are less insurable or because salespeople take advantage of their relative ignorance.

The libertarian paternalist's answer would be to simplify procedures, increase information and introduce nudges to good decisions. Certainly, the state should stimulate the flow of information. But if constraints to rational decision-making are not addressed, the paternalist answer would still turn citizens into clients, protected by benevolent bureaucrats, perhaps more careless as they will think things have been done for them. Nudges push towards conformism, not freedom. That must come from having the capacity to make real decisions, which requires control over time and the capacity to comprehend and the capacity to draw on the expertise of one's fellow citizens.

Basic economic security would also curb ecologically unhealthy forms of labour. Put crudely, people who feel secure are less likely to waste in haste or to rely on prepackaged food, and are more likely to slow down, rather than rush around because time is so 'scarce'. They are more likely to deliberate with friends rather than conspire to make more money with colleagues. Basically secure people are more inclined to wish to reproduce and improve what they see around them rather than indulge in resource-depleting competitive 'scrambling'. In their labour, they are less likely to do malice work (or malice-for-labour work). So characteristic of bureaucratic organizations, this uses up a high share of time in labour. And malice work – backstabbing, conspiring for careerist positions, and so on – induces countervailing malice work. Would anybody be surprised if such activity accounted for 20 per cent of labour time in bureaucracies?

People in a hurry, insecure and driven by market-induced ambition, are ecologically damaging, to their organizations, communities and themselves. Providing citizens with basic security would not eradicate work-for-labour. But it would help to reduce the pressure that leads to it, and should be taken into account when considering the alleged cost of providing universal basic security.

A citizenship income would facilitate forms of work that are not labour. For instance, although there should be scepticism about how much can be done to reduce secondary (financial) insecurity due to financial ignorance, most people in a market society need to devote time to management of their finances. According to Richard Thaler, 'The depressing truth is that financial literacy is impossible, at least for many of the big financial decisions all of us have to take' (*Economist*, 2008e). Is the answer to make the world easier by steering, as Thaler argued? Making decisions easier is desirable, in putting lower boundaries on potential error. But the requirements should include reduced pressure on time, so that we can try to come to grips with such work.

The libertarian paternalists' prescription is that 'Humans' (the term they use to oppose the straw-man, 'Econs') must be nudged by an architecture of choice (Thaler and Sunstein, 2008). They are surely correct in saying that the global market society is too complex to induce optimum decisions from most people, who have neither the time nor the skills to sift through the information to make economically correct decisions. Under pressure and uneducated, many go by behavioural rules that do not conform to those postulated by conventional economics. This leads them to opt for simple rule-of-thumb decisions. Nothing in this diagnosis is surprising. It is the libertarian paternalists' answer that is incomplete.

The sub-optimum decision-making would not be solved by nudges, restricting choice or building a choice architecture. These would still leave citizens as bewildered objects of the market society, led by better invisible and visible hands. Part of an egalitarian response to the complex demands that disadvantage the disadvantaged should be to free up time so that citizens can have the means to make better decisions. The libertarian paternalists did not consider this option. And, while education is being sharpened, people should have access to citizenship associations that could act as their representatives in dealing with such matters.

Making decisions simpler is not the answer to the commodification of life. Imagine an insane idea. If you felt emotionally illiterate, felt you had no time to spare and wished to find a partner to share your uncertain life, you might pay a matchmaking service to fit you up with a partner. Commodifying such a decision would be absurd, the ultimate in nudging . . . except, of course, it is happening in the global market society. Speed dating and electronic profile matching offer simplicity and efficiency. Pay your money and take your pick. The libertarian paternalists should approve, since there is no obligation to accept the proffered choices. They would add that prospective partners would have to wait for six months before they can marry, so they do not do something in the heat of the moment. But the process corrodes the human capacity to use time to develop the human skill of making choices about life partners. The nudging celebrates commodification; it does not put a humanizing brake on it.

The libertarian paternalists' framework is close to 'dumbing down'. The fact is that most of us need to make mistakes as a way of learning to make good decisions. And making decisions without being nudged will make us feel more responsible for our actions, in that we took them without being led there by some commercial or time-saving device.[3]

Activities are commodified in a market society as soon as the price of time goes up. So, occupations emerge whenever a social activity becomes time consuming, as with matchmaking. If we liberate time, we will undertake those activities ourselves. Decommodify matchmaking, before it is too late! It goes with the rescue of privacy. A basic income would help, in that it would reduce the cost of doing activities that are central to civilized living.

Now reflect on statements from two historical voices. The nineteenth-century American, Henry Thoreau, endearingly described as an eccentric, commented: 'My greatest skill has been to want but little' (Thoreau [1851] 1962, p. 1). And rather earlier, Epicurus sent an aphorism through the ages: 'Nothing satisfies the man who is not satisfied with a little'.

If one empathizes with those sentiments, the challenge is to reduce the costs of adhering to behaviour implied by them. It is part of the ecological challenge. If someone is penalized for 'wanting but little', for being satisfied with little, or for slowing down, something is wrong. Polanyi's own take on the idea was to assert a right for a second-best option. So, policy should minimize the costs associated with self-chosen limited wants. But it does not. The neo-liberal state penalizes behaviour geared to slowing down. For example, suppose a person on a disability benefit wishes to take a part-time job; he or she may lose more in benefits than a slow-time job would provide. The system is designed to encourage full-time jobs. Mainstream politicians subscribe to the cliché that they want to 'reward hard-working families'. The flip side is 'penalize non-hard-working families'. The posturing might not matter if work were liberally interpreted. But what is meant is 'hard-labouring families', those earning money.

How are the less frenetic penalized? For a start, work that is not labour is uncompensated. Those not earning enough are then penalized by not being covered for life-cycle risks for which money is needed. Then they might not receive tax credits, and a cycle of deprivation builds from there.

In rich market economies, millions say they wish to 'downshift' from a conventional career, so as to live a less complex driven existence, while continuing to work in various ways. One report found the number opting for a slower lifestyle in Europe was rising rapidly (Datamonitor, 2003). There is nothing novel about the desire, but the growing number seeking it is impressive. It harks back to Rousseau, Wordsworth, Thoreau, Ruskin and Morris, and to the German *Werkbund* of 1907 and the US Shaker movement, among others.

Unfortunately, the complexity of gaining livelihood simplicity is depressingly underestimated. Anybody who has had the good fortune to be able to seek a simpler livelihood, or who stumbles on a need for it, could testify to the time-consuming skills required to succeed, including the ability to network electronically and socially to avoid a drift to aimlessness. Decommodifying oneself does not mean reducing the pressure on oneself to work or to forge an occupational existence. It is an attempt to take control of one's time, which is far from easy to achieve.

The need to shift time from labour to work is integral to an occupational existence in which all forms of work are respected equally. Why, for example, should we always want to maximize the efficiency with which we work? One can think of numerous instances when we should not wish to do so. To buy, prepare, cook and eat food involves a lot of work. Most of us could do that in a fraction of the time we actually take. But instead of the satisfaction that comes from lingering over a set of activities, as well as the time for contemplation that may accompany it, we would end up more stressed. If we did everything as efficiently as we could, almost every activity would be a source of stress. But that is the logic of a market society in which the demands of labour permeate a high proportion of all time. In sum, to give people greater control, there is a need for a Slow Time Movement.

Another way of looking at the challenge is to recall the encroachment of labour. If time use is indistinguishable because work-for-labour, labour-outside-labour, and even play-for-labour, crowd into time outside labour, the citizen is in danger of being commodified in all time. The asset worth struggling for is quality time, that which people can use to develop or revive their capabilities. A fear is that only privileged groups – the elite, upper echelons of the salariat and proficians – will have control over their time. This is why collective associations are essential that represent those groups vulnerable to loss of time control.

The future norm will be the tertiary worker. Skills derived from schooling and training will be constantly under threat, not just because of obsolescence but because non-tangible competencies and emotional skills will figure in any individual's capability profile. The modes of exploitation and oppression that characterize tertiarization will be the focus of politics and policy, and the biggest threat is loss of control over non-labour time. This leads to the need to redistribute time over the life-cycle to facilitate an occupational lifestyle. A priority will be to combat ageism. According to a poll conducted by Harris Interactive in 2008, people in six rich countries on average desired to retire from employment between the age of 58 in the UK and 60 in the USA. Most thought they would have to retire much later; in the UK the expectation was 66 and in the USA over 67. The politically easy solution would be to raise the age at which pensions are paid. A more interesting response would be to move away from the industrial citizenship model altogether. Reject the calendar.

In all countries (France, Germany, Italy, Spain, the UK and the USA) people rejected a mandatory retirement age, even though the ECJ had just ruled that EU countries could enforce retirement at age 65. Under industrial citizenship, older workers were regarded as secondary workers expected to withdraw to make way for prime-age male employees. Now, the elderly are seen as a burden on public finances and on younger workers, forcing up taxes and contributions and draining pension funds. This will change.

There should be neither barriers to work by the elderly nor policies that give them a labour market advantage. Rights should be equal and universal. Women should have the same as men, minorities the same as the majority, legal migrants the same as others. People of all ages should be enabled to choose how they allocate their time without interventions that penalize some uses, restrict others or give some groups subsidies that make it harder for others to do some types of work and labour.

THE RIGHT TO WORK

The 'right to work' is relevant here. Usually interpreted as the right to a job, it makes no sense. If there is a right, there must be an obligation on someone to provide the work, enforce the right and penalize those who fail to meet their obligations. Who would have that obligation and how could they be held to it? One cannot sensibly say there is a right for every person to be given a job of their unrestrained choice. Not everybody can be president. But should someone who is employing others be *obliged* to provide them with jobs? In a market economy, saying that everybody has a right to a job means that private firms must guarantee everybody a job. This is absurd.

If it means that the government must act as employer of last resort, would citizens have a right to sue if they were unemployed? A government might argue that in order to raise growth and contain inflation it must allow a level of 'frictional' unemployment, to raise employment in the longer term. How could judges enforce the right to a job in such circumstances?

The only way to rescue the right to work is to interpret it in terms of work, not labour. This means, in part, returning to the contentious issue of the right to practise tentatively laid out in the Magna Carta of 1215 and brought to its extreme in the Lochner era in the USA (see Chapter 2). Licensing has restricted the right to practise and should be rolled back, in moving to an accreditation system. Where there is no danger to consumer citizens, there should be freedom to practise, and that should apply equally to all citizens and all forms of work. Privileges or barriers to practising in some favoured occupations cannot be justified.

A problem arises in dealing with intellectual property rights. If someone invents a steam engine that enables him to work on producing something, others' opportunity to do that work will be blocked by James Watt's hastily registered patent. Thus, the right to practise is denied. Private property trumps the right to work. What is the answer?

Occupation has been depicted by some as a right of private property, where the property is the bundle of skills needed to practise. John Locke asserted that every man had a right to work and that 'every man has a property in his own person. This nobody has any right to but himself. The "labour" of his body and the "work" of his hands, we may say, are properly his' (Locke, 1690, Sec. 27).

The right to work must be a right to practise. But to say that everybody has a right to the 'fruits of his industry', as Thomas Jefferson interpreted Locke to mean, implies that they could have a right to a permanent patent on any innovation, unless one interprets ideas as part of the commons, the 'general intellect' of society. That would undermine the case for patents. In reality, to encourage research and inventiveness, governments do grant time-limited patents and, like occupational licensing, these restrict the right to practise. The impact on the right to practise is a neglected issue in the debate over the extent to which intellectual property protection strikes a balance between the interests of inventors and those of citizens.

Similarly, licensing and accreditation schemes should be assessed in terms of contravening the right to practise. Suppose someone was disbarred from practising the work of their choice because they had not done it for five years. How could they recover the right to practise? At least, work rights should balance the need to ensure respect for standards with the right to work. That might require those wishing to renew work to undergo refresher courses. A rights-based charter should propose ways of resolving such conflicting objectives – reassurance for consumers of a service and the right to practise for those wishing to work.

The right to work cannot mean an unlimited right to practise. It should mean the removal of barriers to work of any type that does not contravene the rights of others. The right should include enabling everybody to refuse intolerable jobs and to do work that is not labour without being penalized. This returns us to the constitutional commitment to basic income security, which would enable people to undertake work that is not labour.

What one could defend is the principle that all should have a claim right to an equal good opportunity to pursue and develop their competencies. Guaranteeing people jobs they do not want is scarcely an affirmation of any right. But creating the security for them to pursue a dignifying working life surely is.

In this regard, there is merit in Article 1 of Title 1 of the Charter of Emerging Human Rights adopted at the Barcelona Forum in 2004, drawn up by an international group including representatives of all relevant UN bodies. This asserted a right to existence under conditions of dignity, comprising rights to security of life, to personal integrity, to a basic income, to healthcare, to education, to a worthy death and to work, defined as:

> The right to work, in any of its forms, remunerated or not, which covers the right to exercise a worthy activity guaranteeing quality of life. All persons have the right to the fruits of their activity and to intellectual property, under the condition of respect for the general interests of the community.

In sum, policies and schemes should be evaluated by whether they strengthen or weaken movement towards the realization of those rights.

REACHING THE PRECARIAT

If citizenship were defined in terms of occupational rights, then the precariat, particularly migrants in it, lacks citizenship, in the same way that the *metics* (resident aliens) in ancient Greece lacked it. The precariat may have *play* but it does not have the material basis, or the occupational space, to develop leisure and participate politically. It is easily swayed by the theatrics of political salespeople, because it does not have a firm sense of identity to defend. The Italian precariat would have voted for Berlusconi, and may have seen his venality and banalities as inconsequential, identifying instead with his battle against the bureaucracy. The precariat does not have freedom because it lacks security.

The elite are richer in terms of public participation as well as in other terms. They have the means of shaping the public sphere. The egalitarian challenge is partly to enable the precariat to have the same forms of freedom – associational and security – as any other group, particularly proficians.

If we wish to enable people to pursue their sense of occupation, let us consider an unpromising case, the 'oldest profession'. Sex service workers are numerous everywhere. The occupation is riddled with status differentiation – courtesans, trophy wives, call girls, escort agency workers, masseuses, housewives earning pin money, brothel workers, bonded labourers, street workers and exotic dancers. Each of these has some control over what they sell and how they sell their commodity, sex services. Others rent out physical and mental labour; they rent out their body. Like other occupations, they experience exploitation, self-exploitation and oppression, and may be lured into gift relationships. Their labour is instrumental, and they have a need for income security, Voice security and work security.

There is also a trend to winner-takes-all markets; a few earn very high income. A minority use their skills to escape from the precariat into proficians. All need financial advice, protection and insurance against sickness, loss of employment and loss of skills (for example, good looks), and liability insurance (AIDS, and so on). If a client or sex worker knowingly passes on a disease, there should be consequences. But if the service is illegal, neither party can be held responsible. Legalizing sex services could reduce oppression and increase the elasticity of supply, driving down wages, which would act as a disincentive to supply sex services. Legalization would also weaken the bargaining position of pimps, increasing the net income of sex workers.

One may not like sex services, but if people voluntarily choose to practise such activity, legalizing the work and providing social and economic rights would do more to protect and enhance the quality of life of practitioners. Thus, Vancouver sex workers formed a cooperative, extending their activities to 'craft products'; they set up social protection funds, for emergencies and for scholarships for children of dead or sick workers; they developed a group medical plan, drew up occupational safety guidelines, provided an information service for potential entrants to the profession, and developed courses to teach 'life skills'. They could do all this because they were legalized.

By contrast, in 2007, the UK government announced a plan to ban people paying for sex. This was a typically paternalistic regulation. It identified what it considered an anti-social activity, took a moralistic position and proposed to penalize it by criminalizing users and service providers. Brothel keeping, kerb crawling and soliciting were already illegal. The Women's Minister depicted the ban as a way of tackling the 'sex trade' and 'sex trafficking'. Sweden has also made paying for sex illegal. Prostitutes argue that by criminalizing brothels, women are pushed into the streets. And once someone has a record for prostitution or soliciting, it becomes hard to obtain a legal job. Perversely, they are restricted to sex services.

Globally, the sex services industry is growing, and efforts to ban it are doomed, with horrid consequences. To some extent, it reflects the fragile nature of families. With more divorces, more family members migrating and looser ties of reciprocity, the supply and demand for sex services have expanded. The commercialization of sex has added to the market.

An egalitarian response would be to legalize the profession, giving it the same rights as any other occupation, and afford its practitioners normal labour protection, such as liability insurance, while banning unfair labour practices by pimps, agents and brothel owners. Instead of penalizing sex service workers, such a response would look for ways to give them economic rights, by which they could, if they wished, move up the spectrum of their profession, or preferably out of it altogether.

This is the hardest example one could find. There are many other occupations needing effective association and rights. The principle is that people should be decommodified while their rights should be strengthened. If members of the precariat had basic security, they would be able to make choices about what type of work and occupational profile they wished to develop. That security would be derived from having basic income security and rights of association with which to protect and enhance their status and freedom.

RESCUING CARE WORK

Now consider the work of care, bearing in mind that this covers forms of ecological work, concerned with preservation and reproduction of humanity, the commons and the environment. Care is work that cannot be professionalized but depends on a professional ethos. What symbolizes a profession is trust. No occupational community could survive without trust within and between it and those with whom it interacts. Yet so far there has been no care workers' community. It is a sphere of work that is chronically insecure. Who is the more insecure, the giver or receiver of care? The answer most would give is the recipient. But it is not obvious.

Care work is becoming more important, because of the demographics, the deconstruction of families, the improving status of women, and the overhaul of welfare states. Care will be part of our *identity* and, unlike the past, performing care work will be part of our freedom and sense of occupation. The images that still shape attitudes are of harassed mothers scurrying between crying infants, the kitchen and shops, or of a middle-aged woman trying to cope in caring for an elderly relative. It is the image of the *gift relationship*, distinct from the market with its social attractions and financial rewards. But this is changing. In particular, the world's middle classes are seeing a need to perform care themselves, for their children (to give them a competitive edge) and for elderly relatives. And they foresee a need to receive care in old age, wondering whether relatives will be around to help. The opportunistic pressure of the median voter may do more to legitimize care work than all the economic and sociological reasons for doing so.

As we have seen, the twentieth century was the first to make the performance of labour the locus of social rights. Care work not only vanished statistically. It became an impediment to norm-based entitlements, a 'barrier to work', something to be minimized so that we could do more labour. The negative aspects were emphasized – squalor, social isolation, burden, drudgery and oppression. It was as if none of these were characteristic of most labour. To be doing care work became a source not just of low status but of pity. And as David Hume ([1751] 1975, p. 248) rightly noted, pity is akin to contempt.

Care has more dimensions than many other forms of work, and is distinctive in that the time allocated to it exceeds the amount used. Often a person must be available, just in case of need. The effort is variable and, relative to many forms of labour, unpredictable. The time and skill put into it are matters of discretion. Care also combines several types of skill, with emphasis on emotional work. This entails a high stress cost, a set of fears greater than in most labour, such as the fear of failing the recipient, failing observers and regulators in the background, and oneself. So, there are reasons for suggesting that care work should be compensated more than many forms of labour.

Should there be a *right* to receive care? We may argue that everybody needing care has a right to be cared for, however foul or undeserving. However, 'need' can vary from a wish to be cared for and cherished to dire necessity. In practice, we fall back on societal norms. A frail elderly person may have lost the capacity to look after herself. We say that her right to dignity requires care by others. But should that be based on some administrative test of capacity to look after herself? Saying yes opens the door to moral hazards, giving her an interest in behaving in ways that demonstrate to adjudicators that care is needed.

The other side is even more problematical. Should there be a right to provide care? Provision of care might seem a matter of morality. But a society faced by family dissolution might wish to give incentives to potential carers, beyond assisting those needing care. This way of looking at care is unusual. As there are so many incentives and pressures on people to do other work, one could say caring is discouraged. Yet it has potential value to the carer as well as the receiver, and for others not directly involved. The positive externalities mean there is a case for subsidizing care. To some extent, this is recognized by the spread of parental leave, a rationale for which is the strengthening of family bonds, paternal responsibility and a culture of caring. But giving a subsidy just to those in regular employment is hard to justify from an egalitarian viewpoint.

In the twenty-first century, the right to care will advance first as a right to receive care. The notion of need will be broadened to include more contingencies until there is a perception of universal need. Quietly growing will be a debate on the right perceived as a right to provide care. Properly embedded in an enriched idea of occupation, care work need not be regarded as a matter of pity. Doing it could and should be a source of joy and balance. Few people die wishing they had spent more time in the office and less time looking after their children or mothers.

Types of carer have become more sharply defined. Relatives and neighbours have been supplemented by public and private health services, social workers paid and regulated by the state, community organizations and NGOs, including faith-based organizations. All have mixed motives. Some can perform functions for some groups that others cannot, but there is considerable substitutability.

Some types of carer have more qualifications than others. As market society gives great weight to human capital, thinking of care should be a useful antidote. Paid care can be a marvellous social service, and those providing it are among society's most decent citizens. But most of us would not want to rely on paid carers if we could avoid it, for financial and status reasons. Care is a social relationship, involving sentiments such as affection, altruism, mutual respect, dignity and meaningful reciprocities. This is one reason for wishing it to be a sphere of freedom, integrated in our working lives rather than treated as something outside it.

In thinking how that could occur, it is important to recognize the depth of insecurities to be addressed. For the recipient, paying for care entails several sources of anxiety – fear of the carer's incompetence, phoney expertise (misleading qualifications), unreliable delivery (contract failure), non-provision of anticipated care (compact failure), regulatory failure, cost escalation or unknown long-term costs, and unanticipated reciprocities introduced by the carer. For the carer, the insecurities will depend on the type of relationship and include fear of performance failure (incompetence) with consequences for both parties, fear of criticism for inadequacy or status denigration, fear of displacement, particularly if long-term commitments are made, fear of income insecurity due to non-payment, and self-exploitation.

At the centre of the process is the recipient. But besides the carer other people and organizations are often involved, with the state establishing a regulatory framework, consisting of laws setting standards of acceptable behaviour by providers and recipients, and standards for institutions with roles to play. It may decide what transfers and services should be provided, and establish a monitoring, evaluation and penalization system. And it may create institutions for supplementary care. For instance, in a rural economy the state might encourage village elders to use moral suasion or provide communal facilities. In state socialism, it encouraged enterprises to develop facilities on or near the premises. In welfare states, public agencies were set up and subsidies provided to private agencies. More recently, the state has subsidized faith-based organizations and civil society groups to do care work, to fill a perceived care deficit. Each of these state functions raises familiar governance issues, involving trade-offs between efficiency and equity, different forms of efficiency, and accountability, transparency, legitimacy and democracy.

The process of care also involves a support system. Recipients need an assurance of 'last resort' assistance, that if there is market or governance failure, somebody else will be available, albeit at a cost to the support system or recipient, possibly offering a lower-quality substitute. Less recognized, they need representation security, somebody to represent their interests vis-à-vis carers, intermediaries such as care agencies, and the state. The need for collective and individual Voice for recipients has been neglected; sometimes, the vacuum has been filled by a well-meaning or opportunistic body subject to governance failure.

There is also a need for associational Voice for carers, particularly those doing care outside a commercial relationship. The long-time carer is often an oppressed person, weighed down by a sense of duty, shuffling through life dependent on the person to whom she is giving care. This form of dependency is embedded in religious, class, gender and cultural structures. Whatever the causes, the high probability that carers will be led to self-exploitation means they need Voice to guard themselves from themselves as well as from others who take advantage of their devotion or gentle character.

A collective body capable of providing care-work security must have bargaining capacities as well as lobbying functions, and should be protected as much as any union or occupational association. Such bodies are needed to give representation security for those providing and receiving care. Without them, all those involved, including intermediaries, will be insecure. An egalitarian should wish to foster this form of collaborative bargaining, reinterpreting freedom of association to encompass organizations of care work as well as labour organizations and occupational associations.

The other side of occupational freedom is the need for basic security. Care recipients should have a right to income security, as should those providing care. Admittedly, there are some who believe that care should not be treated as equivalent to paid work because it reflects a gift relationship or a reciprocity relationship, as described in Chapter 5. This is unconvincing for reasons given there. It is unreliable since gifts and reciprocities cannot be enforced; it is also inequitable. Much the same could be said about delegating care to civil society organizations, including faith-based organizations, where questions of quality, accountability, transparency and representativeness arise.

If it is accepted that care should be compensated, there are several methods by which the state could enhance the income security of carers and recipients. We should assess them by whether security is extended to all forms of care work, not just to those doing labour. As it is, most workers could not survive without the unpaid work of carers; the economic value of such work is enormous.[4]

The state may enhance the income security of carers and care recipients through social insurance, social assistance or citizenship rights. Traditional social insurance left out care and, for reasons stated earlier, because contributions are tied to paid employment, a social insurance-based care income would be inegalitarian. Most governments have relied on means-tested measures, provided recipients satisfy tests of eligibility. Tests of need for care can be arbitrary and humiliating, and means testing produces poverty traps that can be devastating when applied to elderly people through savings or assets tests. They can only obtain help if they have little or no savings, obliging them to run down that source of income security. The tests stigmatize and result in low take-up of benefits. For carers, means testing prevents them taking even a part-time job, condemning them to dependent insecurity and denying them the chance of an occupational career. In the UK, carers unable to earn because they were providing unpaid care may have 'lost' £5 billion of potential income in 2007 (Moullin, 2008).

The third way of paying is the extension of universal rights. Recall that as more women became regular labour force participants, loss of citizenship status while caring and being out of the labour force became more transparently unjust. To overcome gender bias in social protection, care had to become a dimension of citizenship with rights equal to those received from employment (Knijn and Kremer, 1997).

If commodifying care strengthened the sexual division of labour, with women doing most of the care, it would be a form of inequality. However, if carers were properly remunerated, and if there were care-work associations, there would be two mechanisms tending to reduce such segmentation. A third would be to provide men and women with equal rights to provide care. Over time, proper commodification will lead to technological improvements in the quality of care and conditions of care work, making it intrinsically more rewarding for carers as well as recipients.

Another fear is that commodification could lead to a Taylorization of care, obliging people to obtain licences to perform types of care, with restrictions based on demarcation and procedural rules. This would prevent occupational security, induce moral hazards and intensify self-exploitation, with the carer giving more time than justified by the allowance because the gift relationship dominated the market one. Or it could intensify exploitation through the recipient taking advantage of the carer's labour. These suggest that the care market would remain sexually segregating.

This scenario could be avoided through a mix of citizenship rights and Voice regulation. Unless there are associations for carers *and* care recipients, balanced reciprocity cannot be obtained. Intermediary associations have been springing up to fill these representation spaces. They should be enabled to conduct collaborative bargaining, and to develop ways of protecting carers from themselves.

How care is integrated into a broader conception of occupation will shape the character of society. For instance, vouchers have been mooted as a low-cost paternalist device. One could imagine a future in which each citizen had a voucher card, with so many points for care, so many for education, so many for health, so many for training, and so on. This would be the paternalists' dream.

If payment were through tax credits or family-based benefits, it would be gender-segregating and would not grant citizenship rights, since it would be a family-unit entitlement. If care were provided by the state, paternalism and bureaucratic control of access and cost would come into play. If payment went to nominated carers that would strengthen individual rights, but would produce moral hazards and monitoring problems. The carer could make the recipient dependent on the need for care, or not provide care for which payment is made. The recipient would rarely have agency. If payment were made to the recipient, similar problems would arise. Often a recipient would not know what is required or provided, being young, elderly or frail. So, all options raise problems. But proper commodification should be the guide. Those needing care should have the means of purchasing or paying for it.

The trend to cash promises less bureaucratic control and stronger citizenship, by giving contractual rather than just procedural rights. Payment for care, although commodification, represents legitimation of work that is not labour. The payment allows more self-control and reduces the paternalism of social workers. It also erodes the distinction between the gift and market economy. But individuals are not equal in their bargaining position, or with respect to the information needed to make optimal decisions. This is why Voice associations are needed for all interests in care work, carers, recipients and intermediaries.

In Europe there are experiments giving disabled and elderly people care budgets, enabling them to choose from types of care. In the Flanders region of Belgium, half the government budget for the disabled and elderly is used by care recipients to pay family members, mostly women. The problem is that if the carer is a relative, moral and immoral hazards abound, involving exploitation, oppression and self-exploitation. One suggestion is that family members should be paid by the state, to avoid commodifying a personal relationship. But then a disabled person choosing a relative as carer would have more budget money left than someone who opted to pay a non-relative. If the budget were reduced to take account of the lower payment to the relative, a wage relation would be merely disguised. Another proposal is that a carer should be provided with a carer's budget with which to obtain help (Moullin, 2008). If used as a wage, this would run into problems of equity and efficiency. A more effective solution would be to cut through the maze with a basic income, using a supplementary carer's budget to pay for actual expenses. An expense-account approach, coupled with a basic income, would give a sense of greater control by all parties and make caring less concealed and less 'heroic'.

The UK government is planning to give care budgets to those with a long-term medical condition, which they can use to choose from a designated range of services. This libertarian paternalism may be superficially attractive. But the moral hazard is that if people receive a budget only if they have a medical condition, they will have an interest in allowing the condition to persist, at least while seeking to retain the budget.

Over 10 million people in Britain have long-term ailments or disabilities, more than one in six of the population. One can imagine the difficulty of determining who should receive budgets, the range of services, who should decide and to whom such decisions would be accountable. The chief executive of the National Health Service said there should be a brokerage system that would bring together groups with particular conditions to commission care in bulk. Rather than an exercise in freedom, this is guided choice. Debate has concentrated on showing how budgets would contradict a founding principle of the NHS, that care should be free at the point of delivery. That is not the problem. It is time for progressives to review this. Labour that is free will vary in quality inversely to the extent it is provided as a gift. Whether the commodity is water or care, both sides will treat it with more respect if it is paid for in some way. The practitioner of a service should not be treated as a free good or expected to provide a gift. If available for free, skills and time will tend to be taken for granted.

Policies should commodify the labour provided in the care of citizens in a proper way. They should do so while rolling back the paternalism. If citizens are to have an individual budget with which to obtain the care they believe they need, they should have it as a right, not as an act of benevolence from a Commissioner armed with a smile and discretionary power over what happens. The onus of proof should be placed on demonstrating that the citizen could not reasonably make a choice for herself. At every point, there must be a means of challenging decisions that affect the individual. Medicine is an imperfect science and art. On many issues, doctors may disagree on diagnoses and prescriptions. This is no criticism of the profession, but a reflection of the imperfection of all occupations. Citizens should be encouraged to take responsibility for decisions on their well-being. This is only possible if they can take several opinions and test the form of care of their own choosing.

Giving doctors the right to allocate budgets to patients places discretionary power in their hands. This could put a doctor in a moral bind, required to be social policy practitioner as well as medical expert. To have to decide who is deserving or undeserving, an exercise in selective pity, is scarcely a rights-based policy in a society respecting occupational citizenship. Decisions on the range of care services should be independent of diagnosis of condition and independent of the decision to provide a budget.

We have given care special emphasis because it is work that takes up more time than any other, most still done by women. Proper commodification must come with proper security and rights. A basic income would help to legitimize care work, strengthening the position of carers and recipients. It will help best if there are associations to advance collaborative bargaining. There are many other forms of work that are not labour that should be seen through the same lens. Civil society organizations are the most dynamic part of social participation. Recognizing that much of their activity is work subverts labourism. We need to measure it, ensure that those involved have basic security and that the vulnerable drawn to a cause can retain self-control while pursuing a sense of occupation along with everybody else. The forward march of labour may have ended; the forward march of work and occupation has just begun.

GIVE LEISURE A CHANCE

Adequate leisure has always been regarded as central to citizenship. Without it, one cannot think and act rationally. The ancient Greeks understood that better than we do. Their rationale for excluding from citizenship those who performed labour as hired workers (*banausoi*) was that they did not have the time to participate properly in the *polis*, the sphere of public deliberation. We do not need to interpret that as a claim against deliberative democracy. It should be seen as a claim that full citizenship requires the freedom to escape from labour (and the regenerative activities around it) to be able to work and 'to leisure' in an active, self-determined sense. Leisure is not play. The latter is a necessary correlate of labour. People forced to do onerous or tedious labour for a large part of the day are unlikely to have the energy or concentration to want to leisure at the end of it. Rather, they will be in need of play, be it passive or physical. We all need play, but we need to create and guard a space and capacity for leisure.

A form of work the ancient Greeks also understood better than we do is participation in political life. Any society should value that. Yet in modern market society, for all the rhetorical commitment to democracy, there is a growing deficit in this type of work. That stems partly from the fact that it does not compete well with labour and consumption. If progressives wish to sustain political deliberation, they should advocate ways to free time for it. That should not be done by force or instructive regulation. There should be incentives.

Why make benefits conditional on labour rather than other work? If the paternalists' reciprocity principle is to be given any moral substance it should relate to public citizenship rather than labouring. If policymakers wish to continue with conditionality, then make receipt of a citizenship income conditional on participation in public life. There is a precedent, as something like it was a feature of ancient democracies, including Athens in 403 BCE; the idea was to free sufficient leisure to participate in public life.

Today's squeeze on leisure, rather than play, suggests that if there is one type of participation that could be attached to a basic income, to help legitimize it, it would be the obligation to participate in socio-political life. One could even imagine enlightened governments replacing means tests by stipulating that this condition should apply to all claimants.

One rationalization for making political participation the condition and not labour is that there would be no substitution effects, while at present there are no market incentives for leisure. The condition could be justified as the least likely to distort the labour market, compared with other work or labour conditions, although insofar as it encouraged redistribution from labour it might have a tiny effect. A government could provide a basic income grant with the condition that the person participates in the political process (subject to capacity to do so), perhaps by attending policy debates in town halls twice a year, or participating in jury duty, as well as voting in elections. Such a condition could help counter the overwhelming pressure to use time in labour and consumption. It is something that should even meet the approval of libertarian paternalists, if they are concerned with society rather than just nudging behaviour in a market-optimizing way.

A basic income would also be a means of redistributing leisure as well as inducing a shift to better forms of non-labour time. This is because at present it is the elite, salariat and proficians who have most capacity to be efficient in uses of time for work and labour. A basic income would strengthen that slow-time movement, and allow more time for leisure by those with the least access to it.

An outcome of human commodification has produced civic privatism, involving political abstinence and a frenzy of consumption and careerism. Building occupations could help combat this if they were built on basic security and collective-interest communities. Without such structures, citizens are merely clients. Civic privatism renders people apolitical, without the capacity to act. We need to combat that; a basic income linked to political participation would help, at least as an interim measure of legitimation. In the longer run there should be a right, without any condition at all.

IN SEARCH OF THE ARTISAN

Occupational citizenship should be about raising the status of work and leisure over labour and play. It does not mean denigrating labour or play. Occupational citizenship is about achieving a balance and emphasizing aspects of life neglected by industrial citizenship and neo-liberal globalization. There is a care deficit, a civic friendship deficit and a deficit in the time we can devote to forms of work that are not labour that are essential for citizenship. Above all, there is a leisure deficit. The nudges have been towards labour and more efficient decision-making in the market economy. The counter-nudges should be towards work and leisure, and the need to equalize control over time.

Leisure is an essential part of our occupational future, including the capability to develop and use our imagination, to reflect on what we are and what we can be. Leisure helps us to be ethical, and thus it is essential for freedom. However, it is only one part of an occupational future opening up. Most of us are not craftsmen or artists; we cannot excel in one area of life. Yet we can aspire to be artisans, being good and better at a variety of activities, helping to reproduce our communities and the environment around us.

I need to free up time to help my elderly neighbour. We need to find time to clear the stream in the woods that is drying up because of pollution and neglect. We need to learn the laws they are trying to introduce that a newspaper critic has said threaten our liberty. We need time to find out how the surveillance society is closing in on our space. The drive to labour, insatiable consumption and mentally exhausted play are not liberating; they are enervating.

A progressive vision must build on 'faith', the faith that human beings belong to a species that thrives on social solidarity and civic friendship and that wants to work to develop and sustain our humanity. Markets and paternalists insult us with their posturing. We can do better and we will.

Occupations are zones in which there is a tension between atavism, looking back to how things were done and how people behaved, and utopianism, of how life ideally could be. Does an occupation experience nostalgia, a word derived from Greek, a longing (*algia*) to return home (*nostos*)? Globalization offered no utopianism other than endless consumerism. Yet we are swamped by nostalgia, recalling a lifestyle when time was not a precious commodity, and where 'the slow rhythm of reflective time made possible the dream of freedom' (Boym, 2001). In a globalized society, we are nostalgic for a time when we were not nostalgic. Perhaps we should distinguish between restorative and reflective nostalgia, the former referring to a reconstruction of a lost home, which is reactionary (nationalistic, fundamentalistic), the latter being concerned to dissolve the underlying anxiety, involving appreciation of social not national memories.

This was where Hannah Arendt was led. At risk of seeming pretentious, it is where occupational citizenship can go too, for an ontological existence of being is an exciting prospect. We are what we are aspiring to be. And achieving a healthy balance of work, labour, leisure and play, where values of reproduction and civic friendship put the market in its proper place, is a lifestyle worthy of a human being and a society worth constructing.

NOTES

1. See www.basicincome.org, the website of BIEN (Basic Income Earth Network). For alternative and complementary rationales, see, inter alia, Van Parijs (1995) and Standing (2002, ch. 9).
2. In 2008, the Washington-based Institute for Policy Studies estimated the tax subsidy for executive pay in the USA at more than US$20 billion a year.
3. Arranged marriages apparently have a reasonable 'success' rate, which should please libertarian paternalists. However, the cultural context may induce acceptance of lower-level compromises; staying together may reflect a high cost of marital breakups.
4. The UK's Office for National Statistics estimated that in 2006 the economic value of unpaid domestic work was nearly £900 billion, the majority of it done by women.

Bibliography

Abbott, A. (1988), *The System of Professions: An Essay on the Division of Expert Labor*, Chicago and London: University of Chicago Press.

Abel, Richard (1989), *American Lawyers*, New York and Oxford: Oxford University Press.

Ackerman, B., A. Alstott, P. van Parijs et al. (2005), *Redesigning Distribution: Basic Income and Stakeholder Grants as Cornerstones of a More Egalitarian Capitalism*, London: Verso.

Adams, A.F., R.B. Ekelund and J.D. Jackson (2003), 'Occupational licensing of a credence good: The regulation of midwifery', *Southern Economic Journal*, **69**(3), 659–75.

Adler, Paul (2001), 'Market, hierarchy and trust: The knowledge economy and the future of capitalism', *Organization Science*, **12**(2), 215–34.

Agamben, Giorgio (1998), *Homo Sacer: Sovereign Power and Bare Life*, Stanford: Stanford University Press.

Aitkenhead, D. (2006), 'It's all about me', *The Guardian*, 3 July, pp. 17–18.

Aitkenhead, D. (2007), 'Class rules', *The Guardian*, 20 October, pp. 21–22.

Akerlof, G. (1970), 'The market for lemons: Qualitative uncertainty and the market mechanism', *Quarterly Journal of Economics*, **84**(3), 488–500.

Alford, Robert (1975), *Health Care Politics: Ideological and Interest Group Barriers to Reform*, Chicago: Chicago University Press.

Allen Consulting Group (2007), *A Framework for Considering the Use of Occupational Licensing*, Report to Consumer Affairs Victoria, Melbourne: Allen Consulting Group.

Alston, P. and J. Heenan (2004), 'Shrinking the international labor code', *International Law and Politics*, **36**(2/3), 221–64.

Amiti, M. and S.-J. Wei (2005), 'Fear of service outsourcing: Is it justified?', *Economic Policy*, **20**(42), 308–47.

Anderson, G.M., D. Halcoussis, L. Johnston and A.D. Lowenberg (2000), 'Regulatory barriers to entry in the healthcare industry: The case of alternative medicine', *Quarterly Review of Economics and Finance*, **40**(4), 485–502.

Araki, Takashi (2002), 'The impact of fundamental social rights on Japanese law', in Bob Hepple (ed.), *Social and Labour Rights in a Global Context*, Cambridge: Cambridge University Press, pp. 215–37.

Arendt, Hannah (1951), *The Origins of Totalitarianism*, New York: Harcourt.

Arendt, Hannah (1958), *The Human Condition*, Chicago: University of Chicago Press.

Arendt, Hannah (1990), *On Revolution*, London: Penguin.

Ariely, Dan (2008), *Predictably Irrational: The Hidden Forces That Shape Our Decisions*, New York: HarperCollins.

Aristotle ([350BCE] 1999), *Nicomachean Ethics*, Kitchener, Canada: Batoche Books, available at: http://socserv.mcmaster.ca/econ/ugcm/3ll3/aristotle/Ethics.pdf (accessed 12 March 2009).

Arrow, K.J. (1963), 'Uncertainty and the welfare economics of medical care', *American Economic Review*, **53**(5), 941–73.

Arrow, K.J. (1971), *Essays in the Theory of Risk Bearing*, Amsterdam: North-Holland.

Arthur, M.B., S.N. Khapova and C.P.M. Wilderom (2005), 'Career success in a boundaryless career world', *Journal of Organizational Behavior*, **26**(2), 177–202.

Asthana, Anushka (2004), 'We are a generation not just afraid of commitment but opposed to it', *The Observer*, 12 September, p. 27.

Atkinson, A.B. (2004), 'How basic income is moving up the policy agenda: News from the future', in Guy Standing (ed.), *Promoting Income Security as a Right: Europe and North America*, London: Anthem Press, pp. 41–52.

Atkinson, A.B. (2007), 'The distribution of earnings in OECD countries', *International Labour Review*, **146**(1–2), 41–60.

Attali, Jacques (2008), *Rapport de la Commission pour la Libération de la Croissance Française*, Paris: XO Editions, La Documentation Française, available at: http://lesrapports.ladocumentation francaise.fr/BRP/084000041/0000.pdf (accessed 15 March 2009).

Bacon, Francis ([1625] 2007), *Essays of Francis Bacon*, Charleston, SC: BiblioBazaar.

Banfield, G. (2000), 'Schooling and the spirit of enterprise: Producing the power to labour', *Education and Social Justice*, **3**(2), 23–8.

Barber, Benjamin (2007), *Consumed: How Markets Corrupt Children, Infantilize Adults and Swallow Citizens Whole*, New York: W.W. Norton.

Barley, S. and G. Kunda (2004), *Gurus, Hired Guns and Warm Bodies: Itinerant Experts in a Knowledge Economy*, Princeton and Oxford: Princeton University Press.

Barley, S. and G. Kunda (2006), 'Contracting: A new form of professional practice', *Academy of Management Perspectives*, **20**(1), 45–66.

Basic Income Grant Coalition (2008), *BIG Pilot Project*, Windhoek, Namibia: Basic Income Grant Coalition, available at http://www.bignam.org/page5.html (accessed 20 October 2008).

Batson, A. (2008), 'What growth is right for China?', *Wall Street Journal*, 17 April.

Beale, D. (1994), *Driven by Nissan? A Critical Guide to New Management Techniques*, London: Lawrence & Wishart.

Beiner, Ronald (1984), 'Action, natality and citizenship: Hannah Arendt's concept of freedom', in Z. Pelczynski and J. Gray (eds), *Conceptions of Liberty in Political Philosophy*, London: Athlone Press, pp. 349–75.

Belfield, C.R. and J.S. Heywood (2004), 'Do HRM practices influence the desire for unionization? Evidence across workers, workplaces and co-workers for Great Britain', *Journal of Labor Research*, **25**(2), 279–300.

Bellman, E. (2005), 'Legal services enter new world of outsourcing', *Wall Street Journal*, 28 September.

Benko, C. and A. Weisberg (2007), *Mass Career Customization: Aligning the Workplace with Today's Nontraditional Workforce*, Cambridge, MA: Harvard Business School Press.

Ben-Shahar, Tal (2007), 'Cheer up. Here's how. . .', *The Guardian*, 29 December.

Bentham, Jeremy ([1787] 1995), *Panopticon; or The Inspection-House*, reprinted in Miran Bozovic (ed.), *The Panopticon Writings*, London: Verso, pp. 29–95.

Berlin, Isaiah ([1958] 1969), 'Two concepts of liberty', *Four Essays on Liberty*, London: Oxford University Press, pp. 118–72.

Berry, L., V. Zeithaml and A. Parasuraman (1990), 'Five imperatives for improving service quality', *Sloan Management Review*, **31**(4), 29–38.

Bezat, Jean-Michel (1987), *Les Toubibs*, Paris: J.C. Lattès.

Bishop, Matthew and Michael Green (2008), *Philanthrocapitalism: How the Rich can Save the World*, London: Bloomsbury.

Biswas, Shreya (2008), 'Business of education catches on with India Inc.', *Economic Times*, 6 January.

Bivins, R. (2007), *Alternative Medicine? A History*, Oxford: Oxford University Press.

Black, A. (1984), *Guilds and Civil Society in European Political Thought from the Twelfth Century to the Present*, Ithaca: Cornell University Press.

Black, J. (2003), 'Mapping the contours of contemporary financial services regulation', Discussion Paper No. 17, ESRC Centre for Analysis of Risk and Regulation, London: London School of Economics.

Black, S.E. and L.M. Lynch (2001), 'How to compete: The impact of workplace practices and information technology on productivity', *Review of Economics and Statistics*, **83**(3), 434–45.

Blackhurst, R. (2008), 'Homes from home', *Financial Times Magazine*, 5/6 April, pp. 14–17.

Blankenberg, E. and U. Schultz (1988), 'German advocates: A highly regulated profession', in R. Abel and P.S.C. Lewis (eds), *Lawyers in Society, Vol.2*, Berkeley: University of California Press, pp. 124–59.

Bledstein, B.J. (1976), *The Culture of Professionalism*, New York: Norton.

Blinder, Alan (2005), 'Fear of offshoring', CEPS Working Paper No. 119, Princeton, NJ: Center for Economic Policy Studies, Princeton University.

Blinder, Alan (2007), 'How many US jobs might be offshorable?', CEPS Working Paper No. 142, Princeton, NJ: Center

for Economic Policy Studies, Princeton University.

Bohman, James and William Rehg (eds) (1997), *Deliberative Democracy: Essays on Reason and Politics*, Cambridge, MA: MIT Press.

Bok, D. and J.T. Dunlop (1970), *Labor and the American Community*, New York: Simon and Schuster.

Bond, R.S., J.E. Kwoka, J.J. Phelan and I.T. Whitten (1980), *Effects of Restrictions on Advertising and Commercial Practice in the Professions: The Case of Optometry*, Bureau of Economics, Federal Trade Commission, Washington, DC: US Government Printing Office.

Botero, J., S. Djankov, R. La Porta and F. López de Silanes (2004), 'The regulation of labor', *Quarterly Journal of Economics*, **119**(4), 1339–82.

Boulier, B.L. (1980), 'An empirical examination of the influence of licensure and licensure reform on the geographical distribution of dentists', in S. Rottenberg (ed.), *Occupational Licensure and Regulation*, Washington, DC: American Enterprise Institute, pp. 73–97.

Bouwen, P. (2006), 'National business associations and European integration: The case of the financial sector', in W. Streeck, J.R. Grote, V. Schneider and J. Visser (eds), *Governing Interests: Business Associations Facing Internationalization*, New York: Routledge, pp. 178–96.

Bowen, H.R. and J.H. Schuster (1986), *American Professors*, New York: Oxford University Press.

Boym, Svetlana (2001), *The Future of Nostalgia*, New York: Basic Books.

Braverman, Harry (1974), *Labor and Monopoly Capital: The Degradation of Work in the Twentieth Century*, New York: Monthly Review Press.

Bridges, William (1994), *Jobshift: How to Prosper in a Workplace Without Jobs*, New York: Perseus Books.

Bromberg, Mordy and Mark Irving (eds) (2007), *Australian Charter of Employment Rights*, Prahan, Victoria: Hardie Grant.

Brooks, A. (2008), *Gross National Happiness: Why Happiness Matters for America – and How We Can Get More of It*, New York: Basic Books.

Brown, J.S. and P. Duguid (2001), 'Knowledge and organization: A social practice perspective', *Organization Science*, **12**(2), 198–213.

Brown, L.R. (2006), *Santa Claus is Chinese, or Why China Is Rising and the United States Is Declining*, Washington, DC: Earth Policy Institute, 14 December, available at: http://www.earth-policy.org/Updates/2006/Update62.htm (accessed 3 July 2008).

Bryant, C.D. (1972), 'Sawdust in their shoes: The carnival as a neglected complex organization and work culture', in C.D. Bryant (ed.), *The Social Dimensions of Work*, Englewood Cliffs, NJ: Prentice-Hall.

Burchell, B. (2006), 'Anglais, encore un effort! L'intensité du travail au Royaume-Uni', *Actes de la Recherche en Sciences Sociales*, No. 163, 2006/3, 90–100.

Burniaux, J.M. and F. Padrini (2006), 'Labour market performance, income inequality and poverty in OECD countries', Economic Development Working Paper, Paris: Organisation for Economic Co-operation and Development.

Butler, Samuel (2008), 'A new place for some old ways of thinking: Arendt and Aristotle on leisure, work and freedom', paper presented at USBIG Section, Eastern Economics Association Conference, Boston, 7–9 March.

Butter, I.H. and B.J. Kay (1988), 'State laws and the practice of lay midwifery', *American Journal of Public Health*, **78**(9), 1161–9.

Caldwell, C. (2007), 'Virtue and virtual reality', *Financial Times*, 1–2 September, p. 9.

Caldwell, C. (2008a), 'The lazy, crazy middle class', *Financial Times*, 12 April.

Caldwell, C. (2008b), 'More mortal than some', *Financial Times*, 26 April.

Cameron, Sue (2002), *The Cheating Classes*, London: Simon and Schuster.

Campbell, D. (2007), 'Beauty surgery's ugly secret', *The Observer* (London), 25 November.

Campbell, E.G, S. Regan, R.L. Gruen, T.G. Ferris, S.R. Rao, P.D. Cleary and D. Blumenthal (2007), 'Professionalism in medicine: Results of a national survey of physicians', *Annals of Internal Medicine*, **147**(11), 795–802.

Campbell, Ian and P. Brosnan (2005), 'Relative advantages: Casual employment and casualisation in Australia and New Zealand', paper presented at workshop on Globalization and Industrial Relations Reform in Australia and New Zealand, Sydney, February.

Caplow, Theodore (1954), *The Sociology of Work*, Minneapolis: University of Minnesota Press.

Cappelli, Peter (2000), 'A market-driven approach to retaining talent', *Harvard Business Review*, **78**(1), 103–11.

Carroll, S.L. and R.J. Gaston (1981), 'Occupational restrictions and the quality of service received: Some evidence', *Southern Economic Journal*, **47**(4), 959–76.

Carr-Saunders, A.M. and P.A. Wilson (1933), *The Professions*, Oxford: Oxford University Press.

Casey, C. (1995), *Work, Self and Society after Industrialism*, London and New York: Routledge.

Cave, Stephen (2008), 'Time in our hands', *Financial Times*, 24 May.

CHA (2008), *Worthwhile Work*, London: CHA, available at: http://zookri.com/

Portals/6/reports/worthwhile%20work. pdf (accessed 20 October 2008).

Chakrabortty, A. (2008), 'Why we buy what we buy', *The Guardian*, 20 May, p. 12.

Chantrell, Glynnis (ed.) (2004), *Oxford Dictionary of Word Histories*, Oxford: Oxford University Press.

Chaunu, Pierre and Georges Suffert (1976), *La Peste Blanche: Comment Éviter le Suicide de l'Occident*, Paris: Gallimard.

Chura, Hillary (2007), 'Independence, but at what cost?', *International Herald Tribune*, 10 March, pp. 3,19.

Clifton, J., D. Diaz-Fuentes and C. Marichal (2007), 'Taking control: Telecommunications in Mexico', in J. Clifton, F. Comin and D. Diaz-Fuentes (eds), *Transforming Public Enterprise: Networks, Integration and Transnationalisation*, Harmondsworth: Palgrave-Macmillan.

Cohen, D. and L. Prusak (2001), *In Good Company: How Social Capital Makes Organizations Work*, Boston, MA: Harvard Business School Press.

Cole, M. (1998), 'Globalisation, modernisation and competitiveness: A critique of the New Labour Project in Education', *International Studies in Sociology of Education*, **8**(3), 315–32.

Commission on Vulnerable Employment (2008), *Hard Work, Hidden Lives*, London: Trades Union Congress.

Contreras, P. (2003), 'Extending the disciplines on domestic regulation for accounting to other professional services', paper presented to Focus Workshop on Trade, 15th General Meeting of the Pacific Economic Cooperation Council, Brunei Darussalam, 1 September.

Copp, D. (1992), 'The right to an adequate standard of living: Justice, autonomy and basic needs', in E.F. Paul, F.D. Miller and J. Paul (eds), *Economic Rights*, Cambridge: Cambridge University Press, pp. 231–61.

Cottrell, Stephen (2007), *Do Nothing to Change Your Life: Discovering What Happens When You Stop*, London: Church House Publishing.

Council of Australian Governments (2005), *Mutual Recognition Agreement Legislation Review*, Canberra: Council of Australian Governments.

Cox, C. and S. Foster (1990), *The Costs and Benefits of Occupational Regulation*, Washington, DC: Bureau of Economics, Federal Trade Commission.

Cox, W.M. and R. Alm (2008), 'You are what you spend', *International Herald Tribune*, 14 February.

Croft, J. (2005), 'Financial services sector "could move up to 20% of jobs offshore by 2010"', *Financial Times*, 16 November.

Darby, M.R. and E. Karni (1973), 'Free competition and the optimal amount of fraud', *Journal of Law and Economics*, **16**(1), 67–88.

Datamonitor (2003), *Simplicity*, London: Datamonitor.

Davenport, T.H. and J.C. Beck (2001), *The Attention Economy: Understanding the New Currency of Business*, Boston, MA: Harvard Business School Press.

Deakin, S. and B. Ahlering (2006), 'Labour regulation, corporate governance and legal origin: A case of institutional complementarity?', ECGI Working Paper Series in Law No. 72, Brussels: European Corporate Governance Institute.

De Angelis, Massimo (2002), 'Hayek, Bentham and the global work machine: The emergence of the fractal-panopticon', in Ana C. Dinerstein and Michael Neary (eds), *The Labour Debate: An Investigation into the Theory and Reality of Capitalist Work*, Aldershot: Ashgate, pp. 108–33.

De Botton, Alain (2004), *Status Anxiety*, London: Penguin Books.

De Graaf, J., D. Wann and T.H. Naylor

(2005), *Affluenza: The All-Consuming Epidemic*, San Francisco: Berrett-Koehler.

Deighton-Smith, R., B. Harris and K. Pearson (2001), 'Reforming the regulation of the professions', National Competition Council Staff Discussion Paper, Canberra: AusInfo.

Deloitte Touche Tohmatsu (2007), *Global Financial Services Offshoring Report 2007: Optimizing Offshore Operations*, available at: http://www.deloitte.com/dtt/research/0,1015,cid%253D161519,00.html (accessed 27 September 2008).

Demos (2008), *Entrepreneurship and the Wired Life – Work in the Wake of Careers*, London: Demos.

Dench, G., K. Gavron and M. Young (2006), *The New East End*, London: Profile Books.

Denham, N., P. Ackers and C. Travers (1997), 'Doing yourself out of a job? How middle managers cope with empowerment', *Employee Relations*, **19**(2), 147–59.

Derber, C. (ed.) (1982a), *Professionals as Workers: Mental Labor in Advanced Capitalism*, Boston, MA: G.K. Hall.

Derber, C. (1982b), 'Professionals as new workers', in C. Derber (ed.), *Professionals as Workers: Mental Labor in Advanced Capitalism*, Boston, MA: G.K. Hall, pp. 3–10.

Derber, C., W.A. Schwartz and Y. Magrass (1990), *Power in the Highest Degree*, New York: Oxford University Press.

Derrida, Jacques (1996), 'Remarks on deconstruction and pragmatism', in S. Critchley, J. Derrida, E. Laclau and R. Rorty (eds), *Deconstruction and Pragmatism*, London: Routledge.

Deutsch, C. (2008), 'A harsher spotlight, yet pay rises at top', *International Herald Tribune*, 7 April.

Dew-Becker, I. and R.J. Gordon (2005), 'Where did the productivity growth go? Inflation dynamics and the distribution of income', NBER Working Papers No. 11842, Cambridge, MA: National Bureau of Economic Research.

DiMatteo, L.A., K. Dosanjh, P.L. Frantz, P. Bowal and C. Stoltenberg (2003), 'The Doha Declaration and beyond: Giving a voice to non-trade concerns within the WTO trade regime', *Vanderbilt Journal of Transnational Law*, **36**(1), 95–160.

Dinerstein, Ana C. and Michael Neary (eds) (2002), *The Labour Debate: An Investigation into the Theory and Reality of Capitalist Work*, Aldershot: Ashgate.

Dingwall, R. (1999), 'Professionals and social order in a global society', *International Review of Sociology*, **9**(1), 131–40.

Dingwall, R. and M.D. King (1995), 'Herbert Spencer and the professions: Occupational ecology reconsidered', *Sociological Theory*, **13**(1), 14–24.

Dingwall, R. and P. Lewis (eds) (1983), *The Sociology of the Professions: Lawyers, Doctors and Others*, Harmondsworth: Macmillan.

Dixon, J. (1992), 'China', in J. Dixon and D. Macarov (eds), *Social Welfare in Socialist Countries*, New York and London: Routledge, pp. 10–46.

Djankov, S., E. Glaeser, R. La Porta, F. López de Silanes and A. Shleifer (2003), 'The new comparative economics', *Journal of Comparative Economics*, **31**(4), 595–619.

Dobbin, Frank and John Sutton (1998), 'The strength of a weak state: The rights revolution and the rise of human resources management divisions', *American Journal of Sociology*, **104**(2), 441–76.

Dore, Ronald (1973), *British Factory–Japanese Factory: The Origins of National Diversity in Industrial Relations*, London: George Allen & Unwin.

Dougherty, C. (2008), 'Encouraging

workers in Europe to own stock', *International Herald Tribune*, 1 April, p. 11.

Drucker, Peter (1966), *The Effective Executive: The Definitive Guide to Getting Things Done*, New York: Harper & Row.

Drucker, Peter (1999), 'Knowledge-worker productivity: The biggest challenge', *California Management Review*, **41**(2), 79–94.

Dumont, M. (2006), 'Foreign outsourcing, labour demand and the choice of functional form', *Journal of Applied Economics*, **IX**(2), 255–73.

Durkheim, Emile ([1893] 1964), *Division of Labor in Society*, New York: Free Press.

Durkheim, Emile ([1900] 1957), *Professional Ethics and Civic Morals*, London: Routledge & Kegan Paul.

Dyer, J.H. and K. Nobeoka (2000), 'Creating and managing a high-performance knowledge-sharing network: The Toyota case', *Strategic Management Journal*, **21**(3), 345–67.

Eaglesham, J. (2008), 'Brown pledges corporation tax cut to stem exodus', *Financial Times*, 1 May.

Earl, M.J. and I.A. Scott (1999), 'What is a Chief Knowledge Officer?', *Sloan Management Review*, **40**(2), 29–38.

Easterbrook, S. (ed.) (1993), *CSCW: Cooperation or Conflict*, New York: Springer-Verlag.

Eckholm, Erik (2008), 'Way of life vanishes in blue-collar midwest', *International Herald Tribune*, 17 January, p. 6.

Eckstein, Zvi and Eva Nagypál (2004), 'US earnings and employment dynamics 1961–2002: Facts and interpretation', 2004 Meeting Papers No. 182, New York: Society for Economic Dynamics.

Economist (2004), 'Never a dull moment', *The Economist*, 28 August, p. 29.

Economist (2005), 'A survey of higher education', *The Economist*, 10 September, pp. 14–15.

Economist (2006), 'The search for talent', *The Economist*, 7 October, p. 11.

Economist (2007a), 'Shifting sands', *The Economist*, 6 January, p. 61.

Economist (2007b), 'The business of making money', *The Economist*, 7 July, pp. 68–70.

Economist (2007c), 'Sporting chance', *The Economist*, 14 July, p. 73.

Economist (2007d), 'Changing how Japan works', *The Economist*, 29 September, p. 70.

Economist (2007e), 'Of horses' teeth and liberty', *The Economist*, 27 October, p. 60.

Economist (2007f), 'In God's name', *The Economist*, 3 November.

Economist (2007g), 'Doing well by being rather nice', *The Economist*, 1 December, p. 74.

Economist (2007h), 'The race is not always to the richest', *The Economist*, 8 December, pp. 68–9.

Economist (2007i), 'The new (improved) Gilded Age', *The Economist*, 22 December, p. 114.

Economist (2008a), 'Employment in Japan', *The Economist*, 5 January, p. 58.

Economist (2008b), 'A stitch in time', *The Economist*, 19 January.

Economist (2008c), 'More unequal than others', *The Economist*, 15 March, p. 48.

Economist (2008d), 'The joys of parenthood', *The Economist*, 29 March, p. 53.

Economist (2008e), 'Financial literacy', *The Economist*, 5 April, p. 72.

Economist (2008f), 'A special report on mobility: Nomads at last', *The Economist*, 12 April.

Economist (2008g), 'Help not wanted', *The Economist*, 12 April, p. 54.

Economist (2008h), 'Feet, dollars and inches', *The Economist*, 19 April, p. 82.

Economist (2008i), 'Legally barred', *The Economist*, 24 April.

Economist (2008j), 'The rise of the Gulf', *The Economist*, 26 April, p. 15.

Economist (2008k), 'Let them heat coke: How green taxes hurt the poor', *The Economist*, 14 June, p. 76.

Economist (2008l), 'The Swedish model', *The Economist*, 14 June, p. 69.

Economist (2008m), 'Divorce and economic growth: Negatively correlated', *The Economist*, 26 July, p. 42.

Economist (2008n), 'When fortune frowned: A special report on the world economy', *The Economist*, 11 October, p. 10.

Economist (2009), *Economics A–Z*, London: Economist.com, available at: http://www.economist.com/research/Economics/alphabetic.cfm?letter = L # lumpoflabourfallacy (accessed 11 March 2009).

Edin, Kathryn and Maria Kefalas (2005), *Promises I Can Keep: Why Poor Women Put Motherhood Before Marriage*, Berkeley and Los Angeles: University of California Press.

Ehrenreich, B. (2005), *Bait and Switch: The Futile Pursuit of the American Dream*, New York: Metropolitan Books.

Ehrenreich, B. and J. Ehrenreich (1979), 'The professional-managerial class', in P. Walker (ed.), *Between Labor and Capital*, Boston, MA: South End, pp. 5–48.

Einhorn, Bruce and Catherine Arnst (2008), 'Outsourcing the patients', *Business Week*, 24 March, p. 36.

Elliott, Larry and Dan Atkinson (2008), *The Gods that Failed: How Blind Faith in Markets has Cost Us Our Future*, London: Bodley Head.

Elliott, Margaret and Walt Scacchi (2003), *Conflict Management in an Occupational Community for Free Software Development*, Irvine, CA: Institute for Software Research, University of California, available at: http://www.ics.uci.edu/~wscacchi/Papers/New/Elliott-Scacchi-GNUe-Case-Study.pdf (accessed 26 July 2008).

Emanuel, Ezekiel and Victor Fuchs (2008), *Healthcare, Guaranteed: A Simple, Secure Solution for America*, New York: PublicAffairs.

Esping-Andersen, Gøsta (1990), *The Three Worlds of Welfare State Capitalism*, Cambridge: Cambridge University Press.

Estlund, C.L. (2002), 'An American perspective on fundamental labour rights', in Bob Hepple (ed.), *Social and Labour Rights in a Global Context*, Cambridge: Cambridge University Press, pp. 192–214.

Etzioni, A. (1988), *The Moral Dimension: Towards a New Economics*, New York and London: Free Press.

European Industrial Relations Observatory (1998), 'Major restructuring plan at Telefónica in Spain', Dublin: European Foundation for the Improvement of Living and Working Conditions, 28 June, available at: http://www.eurofound.europa.eu / eiro / 1998 / 06 / inbrief/es9806266n.htm (accessed 3 July 2008).

European Union (2006), 'Directive 2006/123/EC of the European Parliament and of the Council of 12 December 2006 on services in the internal market', *Official Journal of the European Union*, 27 December.

Evetts, Julia (2003), 'The sociological analysis of professionalism: Occupational change in the modern world', *International Sociology*, **18**(2), 395–415.

Evetts, Julia (2005), 'The Management of professionalism: A contemporary paradox', paper presented at conference on Changing Teacher Roles, Identities and Professionalism, King's College, London, 19 October.

Ewing, Keith and John Hendy (eds) (2002), *A Charter of Workers' Rights*, London: Institute of Employment Rights.

Fackler, Martin (2008), 'Japanese are starting to stand up to their employers', *International Herald Tribune*, 11 June.

Feldman, R. and J.W. Begun (1985), 'The welfare costs of quality changes due to professional regulation', *Journal of Industrial Economics*, **34**(1), 17–32.

Ferris, Joshua (2007), *Then We Came to the End*, London: Viking.

Fifield, Anna (2008), 'Samsung sows for the future with its garden of delights', *Financial Times*, 4 January.

Figallo, Cliff (1998), *Hosting Web Communities: Building Relationships, Increasing Customer Loyalty and Maintaining a Competitive Edge*, New York: Wiley.

Financial Express (2007), 'Create a level playing field', *Financial Express* (New Delhi), 14 October.

Financial Services Authority (2000), *Better Informed Consumers' Report, April 2000*, cited in London Economics, *Polarisation and Financial Services Intermediary Regulation*, Report to the Financial Services Authority, London: FSA.

Financial Times (2007), 'The new Luddites: Technology not globalisation is causing inequality to rise', leader article, *Financial Times*, 8 February.

Financial Times (2008), 'Paying by the hour: Lawyers could reap rewards from a fixed fee revolution', leader article, *Financial Times*, 26 February.

Fletcher, Winston (2006), 'Like Buridan's ass, humanity is suffering from too much choice', *The Guardian*, 18 February, p. 22.

Floris, Giovanni (2007), *Mal di Merito: L'Epidemia di Raccomandazioni che Paralizza l'Italia*, Milan: Edizioni Rizzoli.

Foote, N.W., E. Matson and N. Rudd (2001), 'Managing the knowledge manager', *McKinsey Quarterly*, No. 3, 120–29.

Forbath, W.E. (1985), 'The ambiguities of free labor: Labor and the law in the gilded age', *Wisconsin Law Review*, **4**(1985) 767–817.

Fossum, J. (2002), *Labor Relations: Development, Structure and Process*, New York: McGraw.

Foucault, Michel ([1976] 1998), *The History of Sexuality, Vol. 1: The Will to Knowledge*, London: Penguin.

Foucault, Michel (1977), *Discipline and Punish: The Birth of the Prison*, A. Sheridan (trans.), London: Penguin Books.

Fourcade, M. (2006), 'The construction of a global profession: The transnationalization of economics', *American Journal of Sociology*, **112**(1), 145–95.

Fournier, V. (1999), 'The appeal to "professionalism" as a disciplinary mechanism', *Social Review*, **47**(2), 280–307.

Frank, Robert (2007a), *Richistan: A Journey through the American Wealth Boom and the Lives of the New Rich*, New York: Crown Books.

Frank, Robert (2007b), 'Mr Gates probes hearts, minds of peers', *Wall Street Journal*, 15 November, p. 35.

Frank, Thomas (2004), *What's the Matter with Kansas? How Conservatives Won the Heart of America*, New York: Metropolitan Books, Henry Holt.

Fraser, Ian (2008), 'Accountants face up to the moral maze', *Financial Times*, 3 January.

Freeman, Richard (1995), 'Are your wages set in Beijing?', *Journal of Economic Perspectives*, **9**(3), 15–32.

Freeman, Richard (2005), 'What really ails Europe (and America): The doubling of the global workforce', *The Globalist*, 3 June, available at: http://www.theglobalist.com/StoryId.aspx?StoryId = 4542 (accessed 3 July 2008).

Freidson, Eliot (1970), *Professional Dominance: The Social Structure of Medical Care*, New York: Atherton Press.

Freidson, Eliot (1973), 'Professions and the occupational principle', in Eliot Freidson (ed.), *The Professions and*

Their Prospects, Beverly Hills: Sage, pp. 19–38.

Freidson, Eliot (1986), *Professional Powers: A Study of the Institutionalization of Formal Knowledge*, Chicago: University of Chicago Press.

Freidson, Eliot (1994), *Professionalism Reborn: Theory, Prophecy and Policy*, Chicago: University of Chicago Press.

Freidson, Eliot (2001), *Professionalism: The Third Logic: On the Practice of Knowledge*, London: Polity Press.

Friedman, M. and S. Kuznets (1945), *Income from Independent Professional Practice*, New York: National Bureau of Economic Research.

Froomkin, M. (2000), 'The death of privacy?', *Stanford Law Review*, **52**(5), 1461–543.

Fudge, J. and L.Vosko (2001), 'By whose standards? Re-regulating the Canadian labour market', *Economic and Industrial Democracy*, **22**(3), 327–56.

Fukuyama, F. (2007), 'Identity and migration', *Prospect*, Issue **131** (February), 26–31.

Fung, A., D. O'Rourke and C. Sabel (eds) (2001), *Can We Put an End to Sweatshops?*, Boston: Beacon Press.

Furedi, Frank (2004), *Where Have All the Intellectuals Gone?*, London: Continuum.

Gallie, D. (2002), 'The quality of working life in welfare strategy', in G. Esping-Andersen, D. Gallie, A. Hemerijck and J. Myles, *Why We Need a New Welfare State*, Oxford: Oxford University Press, pp. 96–129.

Gapper, J. (2005), 'The danger of rewriting Chapter 11', *Financial Times*, 13 October, p. 13.

Gardner, Howard (2007), *Five Minds for the Future*, Cambridge, MA: Harvard Business School Press.

George, S. (1997), 'How to win the war of ideas: Learn from the Gramscian right', *Dissent*, **44**(3), 47–53.

Gersick, C.J.G., J.M. Bartunek and J.E. Dutton (2000), 'Learning from academia: The importance of relationships in professional life', *Academy of Management Journal*, **43**(6), 1026–44.

Gibson, Mary Jo and Ari Houser (2007), *In Brief: Valuing the Invaluable: A New Look at the Economic Value of Family Caregiving*, Washington, DC: AARP Public Policy Institute, available at: http://www.aarp.org/research/housing-mobility/caregiving/inb142_caregiving.html#SECOND (accessed 14 March 2009).

Giddens, Anthony (1990), *The Consequences of Modernity*, Cambridge: Polity Press.

Giddens, Anthony (1991), *Modernity and Self-Identity*, Cambridge: Polity Press.

Gini, A. (2000), *My Job, Myself: Work and Creation of the Modern Individual*, New York: Routledge.

Giridharadas, A. (2007), 'India outsources its own outsourcing', *International Herald Tribune*, 25 September.

Gladstone, J.A (2006), 'A call from the panopticon to the judicial chamber "Expect privacy!"', *Journal of International Commercial Law and Technology*, **1**(2), available at http://www.jiclt.com/index.php/JICLT/article/view/22/10 (accessed 20 October 2008).

Glaeser, E.L. (2006), 'Paternalism and psychology', *Regulation*, **29**(2), 32–8.

Glasman, Maurice (1994), 'The great deformation: Polanyi, Poland and the terrors of planned spontaneity', *New Left Review*, **205**, 59–86.

Global Commission on International Migration (2005), *Migration in an Interconnected World: New Directions for Action*, Geneva: Global Commission on International Migration.

Gold, M., P. Cressey and E. Leonard (2007), 'Whatever happened to social dialogue? From partnership to managerialism in the EU Employment Agenda', *European Journal of Industrial Relations*, **13**(7), 7–25.

Goodhart, Michael (2005), *Democracy as Human Rights: Freedom and Equality in the Age of Globalization*, New York: Routledge.

Goodhart, Michael (2007), '"None so poor that he is compelled to sell himself"': Democracy, subsistence and basic income', in S. Hertel and L. Minkler (eds), *Economic Rights: Conceptual, Measurement and Policy Issues*, Cambridge: Cambridge University Press, pp. 94–114.

Goodin, Robert, James Rice, Antti Parpo and Lina Eriksson (2008), *Discretionary Time: A New Measure of Freedom*, Cambridge: Cambridge University Press.

Goodwin, R.E. and J. Le Grand (1987), *Not Only the Poor: The Middle Classes and the Welfare State*, London: George Allen & Unwin.

Gospel, H. and A. Pendleton (eds) (2004), *Corporate Governance and Labour Management*, Oxford: Oxford University Press.

Graddy, E. and M.B. Nichol (1989), 'Public members on occupational licensing boards: Effects on legislative regulation reforms', *Southern Economic Journal*, **55**(3), 610–25.

Graddy, E. and M.B. Nichol (1990), 'Structural reforms and licensing board performance', *American Politics Research*, **18**(3), 376–400.

Granovetter, Mark (1973), 'The strength of weak ties', *American Journal of Sociology*, **78**(6), 1360–80.

Granovetter, M. (1985), 'Economic action and social structure: The problem of embeddedness', *American Journal of Sociology*, **91**(3), 481–510.

Grantham, C. and J. Ware (2005), *Business Community Centers as Third Places*, Prescott, AZ, and Berkely, CA: Work Design Collaborative, available at: http://www.thefutureofwork.net/assets/Business_Community_Centers.pdf (accessed 20 October 2008).

Grass, Günter and Pierre Bourdieu (2002), 'The "progressive" restoration: A Franco-German dialogue', *New Left Review*, **14** (March/April), 63–77.

Gray, John (1998), *False Dawn: The Delusions of Global Capitalism*, London: Granta Books.

Grayling, A.C. (2007), *The Choice of Hercules: Pleasure, Duty and the Goodlife in the 21st Century*, London: Weidenfeld & Nicolson.

Green, F. (2006), *Demanding Work: The Paradox of Work Quality in the Affluent Economy*, Princeton, NJ: Princeton University Press.

Green, F. and S. McIntosh (2001), 'The intensification of work in Europe', *Labour Economics*, **8**(2), 291–308.

Green, Thomas Hill ([1879] 1999), *Lectures on the Principles of Political Obligation*, Kitchener, Ontario: Batoche Books. available at: http://cupid.ecom.unimelb.edu.au/het/green/obligation.pdf (accessed 20 October 2008).

Grey, Christopher (1994), 'Career as a project of the self and the labour process discipline', *Sociology*, **28**(2), 479–97.

Grey, Christopher (1999), '"We are all managers now"; "We always were": On the development and demise of management', *Journal of Management Studies*, **36**(5), 561–85.

Grimes, Christopher (2008), 'Do the right things', *Financial Times, FT Weekend*, 24–25 May, pp. 16–21.

Guthrie, J. (2008), 'Britain's "coping classes" feel financial pinch', *Financial Times*, 28 February.

Gutmann, Amy and Dennis Thompson (1996), *Democracy and Disagreement*,

Cambridge, MA: Harvard University Press.

Haagh, Louise (2002), *Citizenship, Labour Markets and Democratization: Chile and the Modern Sequence*, Basingstoke: Palgrave.

Haas-Wilson, D. (1986), 'The effect of commercial practice restrictions: The case of optometry', *Journal of Law and Economics*, **29**(1), 165–86.

Haas-Wilson, D. (1992), 'The regulation of health care professionals other than physicians', *Regulation (Cato Review of Business and Government)*, **15**(4), 40–46.

Habermas, Jürgen (1976), *Legitimation Crisis*, London: Heinemann.

Habermas, Jürgen (1984), *The Theory of Communicative Action, Vol.1: Reason and the Rationalization of Society*, Boston, MA: Beacon Press.

Hacker, J.S. (2006), *The Great Risk Shift: The Assault on American Jobs, Families, Health Care and Retirement And How You Can Fight Back*, New York: Oxford University Press.

Hagel, J. and A.G. Armstrong (1997), *Net Gain: Expanding Markets Through Virtual Communities*, Boston, MA: Harvard Business School Press.

Haidt, Jonathan (2006), *The Happiness Hypothesis: Putting Ancient Wisdom to the Test of Modern Science*, New York: Basic Books.

Hall, P. and D. Soskice (eds) (2001), *Varieties of Capitalism*, Oxford: Oxford University Press.

Halperin, Sandra (2004), 'Dynamics of conflict and system change: The Great Transformation revisited', *European Journal of International Relations*, **10**(2), 263–306.

Halsey, A.H. (1992), *Decline of Donnish Dominion*, Oxford: Oxford University Press.

Hamilton, Alexander (1788), 'The judiciary continued', *The Federalist*, No.79,

18 June, available at http://www.constitution.org/fed/federa79.htm.

Handler, Joel (2005), 'Social citizenship and workfare in the United States and Western Europe: From status to contract', in Guy Standing (ed.), *Promoting Income Security as a Right: Europe and North America*, London: Anthem, pp. 567–608.

Handy, Charles (1994), *The Empty Raincoat: Making Sense of the Future*, London: Hutchinson.

Handy, Charles (1995), *The Age of Unreason*, Cambridge, MA: Harvard Business School Press.

Handy, Charles (2001), *The Elephant and the Flea: Reflections of a Reluctant Capitalist*, Cambridge, MA: Harvard Business School Press.

Hardt, Michael and Antonio Negri (2000), *Empire*, Cambridge, MA: Harvard University Press.

Hardt, Michael and Antonio Negri (2004), *Multitude: War and Democracy in the Age of Empire*, New York: Penguin Press.

Hare, Ivan (2002), 'Social rights as fundamental human rights', in Bob Hepple (ed.) (2002), *Social and Labour Rights in a Global Context*, Cambridge: Cambridge University Press, pp. 153–81.

Harkins, James (2007), 'Show me the money', *The Guardian*, 24 February.

Hartmann, E., S. Haslinger and C. Scherrer (2006), 'Liberalization of higher education and training: Implications for workers' security', in Ellen Rosskam (ed.), *Winners or Losers? Liberalizing Public Services*, Geneva: International Labour Organization, pp. 55–119.

Hassard, J., L. McCann and J. Morris (2007), 'At the sharp end of new organizational ideologies: Ethnography and the study of multinationals', *Ethnography*, **8**(3), 324–44.

Hawes, W.R. (2000), 'Setting the pace

or running alongside? ACAS and the changing employment relationship', in B. Towers and W. Brown (eds), *Employment Relations in Britain: 25 years of the Advisory, Conciliation and Arbitration Service*, London: Blackwell, pp. 1–30.

Hayashi, Yuka (2008), 'In Japan, temporary workers leave lasting mark on economy', *Wall Street Journal*, 4–6 January, pp. 14–15.

Hayek, Friedrich (1944), *The Road to Serfdom*, Chicago: University of Chicago Press.

Hazlett, T.W. and J.L. Fearing (1998), 'Occupational licensing and the transition from welfare to work', *Journal of Labor Research*, **19**(2), 277–94.

Healey, D. (1973), 'The effect of licensure on clinical laboratory effectiveness', PhD dissertation, Los Angeles: University of California.

Hecksher, Charles (1995), *White Collar Blues: Management Loyalties in an Age of Corporate Restructuring*, New York: Basic Books.

Heeter, C.P. (1995), 'Key findings of the IFAC survey on issues related to international trade in accountancy services', paper presented on behalf of Arthur Andersen and Co. to Seminar on Issues and Measures affecting Accounting Services, Geneva: World Trade Organization, October.

Hegel, G.W.F. ([1820] 1952), *The Philosophy of Right*, Oxford: Clarendon Press, available at: http://www.marxists.org/reference/archive/hegel/works/pr/ (accessed 15 March 2009).

Heidegger, Martin ([1927] 2000), *Being and Time*, Oxford: Blackwell.

Heidenheimer, A.J. (1989), 'Professional knowledge and state policy in comparative historical perspective: Law and medicine in Britain, Germany and the United States', *International Social Science Journal*, **41**(4), 529–53.

Helleiner, Eric (2000), 'Globalization and *haute finance – déjà vu?*', in K. McRobbie and K.P. Levitt (eds), *Karl Polanyi in Vienna: The Contemporary Significance of 'The Great Transformation'*, Montreal: Black Rose Books, pp. 12–31.

Heller, P. (2003), *Who Will Pay? Coping with Ageing Societies, Climate Change and Other Long-Term Fiscal Challenges*, Washington, DC: International Monetary Fund.

Henkin, L. (1994), 'Economic rights under the United States Constitution', *Columbia Journal of Transnational Law*, **32**, 97–128.

Hepple, Bob (ed.) (1986), *The Making of Labour Law in Europe*, London: Mansell.

Hepple, Bob (1999), 'Labour regulation in internationalized markets', in S. Picciotto and R. Mayne (eds), *Regulating International Business: Beyond Liberalization*, Basingstoke and London: Macmillan, pp. 183–202.

Hepple, Bob (ed.) (2002), *Social and Labour Rights in a Global Context*, Cambridge: Cambridge University Press.

Herbert, Douglas (2001), 'Europe tests waters of e-politics', *Time.com*, available at: http://www.time.com/time/interactive / stories / society / e _ politics.html (accessed 15 March 2009).

Hewlett, S.A. and C.B. Luce (2006), 'Extreme jobs: The dangerous allure of the 70-hour workweek', *Harvard Business Review*, **84**(12), 49–59.

Hewlett, Sylvia Ann, Carolyn Buck Luce, Sandra Southwell and Linda Bernstein (2007), *Seduction and Risk: The Emergence of Extreme Jobs*, New York: Center for Work-Life Policy.

Hibbert, C. (1974), *The Rise and Fall of the House of Medici*, London: Penguin Books.

Higgins, M.C. and K.E. Kram (2001), 'Reconceptualising mentoring at work:

A developmental network perspective', *Academy of Management Review*, **26**(2), 264–88.

Hijzen, A., H. Gorg and R.C. Hine (2004), 'International outsourcing and the skill structure of labour demand in the United Kingdom', Discussion Paper No. 1249, Bonn: IZA (Institute for the Study of Labour).

Hill, Dave (2007), 'School's out, for ever', *The Guardian*, 14 April.

Himmelfarb, Gertrude (1965), 'The haunted house of Jeremy Bentham', in Richard Herr and Harold T. Parker (eds), *Ideas in History: Essays Presented to Louis Gottschalk by his Former Students*, Durham, NC: Duke University Press, pp. 199–238.

Hirschleifer, Jack (2001), 'Anarchy and its breakdown', in J. Hirschleifer, *The Dark Side of the Force: Economic Foundations of Conflict Theory*, Cambridge: Cambridge University Press, pp. 102–30.

Hirschman, A. (1991), *The Rhetoric of Reaction: Perversity, Futility, Jeopardy*, Cambridge, MA: Harvard University Press.

Hirshon, Robert (2002), 'Law and the billable hour', *ABA Journal*, February.

Hobsbawm, Eric (2005), 'Retreat of the male', *London Review of Books*, 4 August, available at: http://www.lrb.co.uk/v27/n15/hobs01_.html (accessed 13 October 2008).

Holbeche, L. and N. Springett (2004), *In Search of Meaning in the Workplace*, London: Roffey Park Institute and Management Today, available at: www.roffeypark.com/whatweoffer/Research/reports/Pages/InSearchofMeaningintheWorkplace.aspx (accessed 3 February 2009).

Hood, J. (1992), 'Does occupational licensing protect consumers?', *The Freeman: Ideas on Liberty*, **42**(11), November, available at: http://www.fee.org/PUBLICATIONS/THE-FREEMAN/article.asp?aid=2356 (accessed 2 August 2008).

Hopkins, Michael (2003), *The Planetary Bargain: Corporate Social Responsibility Matters*, London: Earthscan.

Hopkins, Michael (2006), *CSR and International Development*, London: Earthscan.

Houlder, Vanessa (2007), 'Europe's tax rivalry keeps multinationals on the move', *Financial Times*, 19 January.

Houlder, Vanessa (2008), 'Out of the door: Tax treatment tempts businesses to relocate', *Financial Times*, 6 May.

Houseman, Susan, Arne Kalleberg and George Erickcek (2003), 'The role of temporary help employment in tight labor markets', *Industrial and Labor Relations Review*, **57**(1), 105–27.

Howard, R.M. (1998), 'Wealth, power, and attorney regulation in the US states: Licensing entry and maintenance requirements', *Publius*, **28**(4), 21–33.

Hume, David ([1751] 1975), 'An enquiry concerning the principles of morals', *Enquiries Concerning Human Understanding and Concerning the Principles of Morals*, Oxford: Oxford University Press.

Huselid, M.A. (1995), 'The impact of human resource management practices on turnover, productivity and corporate financial performance', *Academy of Management Journal*, **38**(3), 635–72.

Huws, Ursula (2003), *The Making of a Cybertariat: Virtual Work in a Real World*, New York: Monthly Review Press.

IDHC (2004), *Charter of Emerging Human Rights*, Barcelona: Institut de Drets Humans de Catalunya.

Ikiara, G.K. (2000), *Professional Services in Kenya: Constraints and Opportunities for Trade*, Geneva: United Nations

Conference on Trade and Development (UNCTAD).

ILO (1999), *Decent Work*, Geneva: International Labour Organization.

ILO (2004), *Economic Security for a Better World*, Geneva: International Labour Organization.

ILO (2008), *Income Inequalities in the Age of Financial Globalization*, Geneva: International Labour Organization.

IMF (2007), *World Economic Outlook: Spillovers and Cycles in the Global Economy*, Washington, DC: International Monetary Fund.

Ip, G. (2007), 'U.S. wealth gap expands', *Wall Street Journal*, 15 October.

Jackall, R. (1988), *Moral Mazes: The World of Corporate Managers*, New York and Oxford: Oxford University Press.

Jackson, D.L., J.M. Lang, W.H. Swart et al. (2003), 'Outcomes, safety, and resource utilization in a collaborative care birth center program compared with traditional physician-based perinatal care', *American Journal of Public Health*, **93**, 999–1006.

Jacques, Martin (2002), 'The age of selfishness', *The Guardian*, 5 October.

James, Oliver (2007), *Affluenza*, London: Vermilion.

Jameson, Fredric (2007), *Archeologies of the Future*, London: Verso.

Jamieson, Annie (ed.) (1991), *Home Care for Older People in Europe: A Comparison of Policies and Practices*, Oxford: Oxford University Press.

Jay, Douglas (1937), *The Socialist Case*, London: Faber & Faber.

Jensen, M. (1989), 'Eclipse of the public corporation', *Harvard Business Review*, **67**(5), 61–74.

Johns, H. and P. Ormerod (2007), 'Do not rely on the state to make you happy', *Financial Times*, 17 July.

Johnson, Jo and Khozem Merchant (2005), 'India skills shortage threatens offshore IT', *Financial Times*, 12 December, p. 7.

Johnson, K. (2006), 'With illegal immigrants fighting wildfires, West faces a dilemma', *New York Times*, 28 May.

Johnson, Samuel ([1751] 2003), 'The Rambler', No. 145, reprinted in David Womersley (ed.), *Selected Essays*, Harmondsworth: Penguin.

Johnson, T.J. (1972), *Professions and Power*, Basingstoke: Macmillan.

Johnson, T.J. (1982), 'The state and the professions: Peculiarities of the British', in A. Giddens and G. Mackenzie (eds), *Social Class and the Division of Labour: Essays in Honour of Ilya Neustadt*, Cambridge: Cambridge University Press.

Johnson, T.J. (1990), 'Thatcher's professions: The state and the professions in Britain', paper presented at the World Congress of Sociology, Madrid, 9–13 July.

Johnstone, D.B., A. Arora and W. Experton (1998), 'The financing and management of higher education: A status report on worldwide reforms', Working Paper No. 19129, Washington, DC: World Bank.

Joseph Rowntree Foundation (2004), 'Reducing the impact of "green" taxes and charges on low-income households', available at: www.jrf.org.uk/knowledge/findings/housing/074.asp (accessed 16 October 2008).

Juvin, Hervé (2005), *L'Avènement du Corps*, Paris: Gallimard.

Kahn, J. and D. Barboza (2007), 'Chinese workers gain new protections under labor law', *International Herald Tribune*, 2 July.

Kahn-Freund, Otto (1968), *Labour Law: Old Traditions and New Developments*, Toronto: Clarke, Irwin & Co.

Karasek, R.A. and T. Theorell (1990), *Healthy Work: Stress, Productivity and the Reconstruction of Working Life*, New York: Basic Books.

Keller, B. and H.-W. Platzer (eds) (2003), *Industrial Relations and European Integration: Trans- and Supranational Developments and Prospects*, Aldershot: Ashgate.

Kelley, R. and J. Caplan (1993), 'How Bell Labs creates star performers', *Harvard Business Review*, **71**(4), 128–39.

Kelly, J.E. (1998), *Rethinking Industrial Relations: Mobilization, Collectivism and Long Waves*, London: Routledge.

Kirk, D. (1989), 'German universities: bursting at the seams', *Science*, **2431**(4897), 1427–28.

Kissam, P.C. (1983), 'Antitrust law and professional behavior', *Texas Law Review*, **62**(1), 1–66.

Klein, Naomi (2008), 'Police state 2.0', *The Guardian: Media Section*, 3 June, pp. 4–9.

Kleiner, M.M. (2006), *Licensing Occupations: Enhancing Quality or Restricting Competition?*, Kalamazoo, MI: Upjohn Institute.

Knijn, T. and M. Kremer (1997), 'Gender and the caring dimension of welfare states: Towards inclusive citizenship', *Social Politics: International Studies in Gender, State and Society*, **4**(3), pp. 328–61.

Kohn, M.L and C. Schooler (1983), *Work and Personality: An Inquiry into the Impact of Social Stratification*, Norwood, NJ: Ablex Publishing.

Korpi, Walter (1983), *The Democratic Class Struggle*, London: Routledge & Kegan Paul.

Krause, E. (1996), *Death of the Guilds: Professions, States and the Advance of Capitalism, 1930 to the Present*, New Haven: Yale University Press.

Krueger, D. and F. Perri (2006), 'Does income inequality lead to consumption inequality? Evidence and theory', *Review of Economic Studies*, **73**(1), 163–93.

Kuckes, Niki (2007), 'The hours: The short unhappy history of how lawyers bill their clients', *Legal Affairs*, November 2007, available at: http://www.legalaffairs.org/printerfriendly.msp?id=240 (accessed 2 August 2008).

Kuhn, Thomas ([1970] 1996), *The Structure of Scientific Revolutions*, (3rd edition) Chicago: University of Chicago Press.

Kunda, Gideon ([1991] 2006), *Engineering Culture: Control and Commitment in a High-Tech Corporation*, (revised edition), Philadelphia: Temple University Press.

Kunda, Gideon, Stephen Barley and James Evans (2002), 'Why do contractors contract? The experience of highly skilled technical professionals in a contingent labor market', *Industrial and Labor Relations Review*, **55**(2), 234–61.

Langenfeld, J.A. and L. Silvia (1993), 'The Federal Trade Commission's horizontal restraint cases: An economic perspective', *Antitrust Law Journal*, **61**(3), 653–97.

La Porta, R., F. López de Silanes, A. Shleifer and R.W. Vishny (1998), 'Law and finance', *Journal of Political Economy*, **106**(6), 1113–55.

Larkin, G. (1983), *Occupational Monopoly and Modern Medicine*, London: Tavistock.

Larson, M.S. (1977), *The Rise of Professionalism*, California: University of California Press.

Larson, M.S. (1980), 'Proletarianization and educated labor', *Theory and Society*, **9**(1), 131–75.

Laslett, Peter with Richard Wall (eds) (1972), *Household and Family in Past Time*, Cambridge: Cambridge University Press.

Laubacher, R. and T. Malone (2000), 'Retreat of the firm and the rise of guilds: The employment relationship in an age of virtual business', Twenty-First Century Initiative Working Paper No.33,

Cambridge, MA: MIT Sloan School of Management.

Lawrence, T.B. (1998), 'Examining resources in an occupational community: Reputation in Canadian forensic accounting', *Human Relations*, **51**(9), 1103–31.

Layard, Richard (2005), *Happiness: Lessons from a New Science*, London: Penguin.

Lazzarato, Maurizio (2006), 'La construction du marché du travail culturel', Vienna: European Institute for Progressive Cultural Policies, available at: http://eipcp.net/policies/cci/lazzarato/fr (accessed 12 October 2008).

Leadbeater, Charles (2002a), *Up the Down Escalator: Why the Global Pessimists are Wrong*, London: Viking.

Leadbeater, Charles (2002b), 'Welcome to the amateur century', *Financial Times*, 23 December.

Leader, Darian (2008), 'A quick fix for the soul', *The Guardian*, 9 September.

Le Bianic, Thomas (2003), 'Bringing the state back in the study of professions: Some peculiarities of the French model of professionalisation', paper presented at 6th European Sociological Association Conference, Research Network Sociology of Professions, University of Murcia, Spain, 24–26 September.

Le Bianic, Thomas (2007), 'Pratiques et identités professionnelle des psychologues du travail en France de l'entre-deux-guerres à nos jours: Une perspective socio-historique', *Bulletin de psychologie*, **60**(1), pp.71–81.

Leffler, K.B. (1978), 'Physician licensure: Competition and monopoly in American medicine', *Journal of Law and Economics*, **21**(1), 165–86.

Le Grand, Julian (2003), *Motivation, Agency and Public Policy: Of Knights and Knaves, Pawns and Queens*, Oxford: Oxford University Press.

Leland, H.E. (1979), 'Quacks, lemons and licensing: A theory of minimum quality standards', *Journal of Political Economy*, **87**(6), 1328–46.

Levitt, Steven D. and Stephen J. Dubner (2005), *Freakonomics: A Rogue Economist Explores the Hidden Side of Everything*, New York: HarperCollins.

Levy, Frank and Richard Murnane (2004), *The New Division of Labor: How Computers Are Creating the Next Job Market*, Princeton: Princeton University Press.

Lewis, R. and J. Clark (1993), *Employment Rights, Industrial Tribunals and Arbitration: The Case for Alternative Dispute Resolution*, London: Institute for Employment Rights.

Lichtenstein, N. (1989), 'From corporatism to collective bargaining: Organized labor and the eclipse of social democracy in the postwar era', in S. Fraser and G. Gerstle (eds), *The Rise and Fall of the New Deal Order, 1930–1980*, Princeton: Princeton University Press, pp. 122–52.

Lindsay, C.M. (1973), 'Real returns to medical education', *Journal of Human Resources*, **8**(3), 331–48

Lister, Ruth (1994), 'Dilemmas in engendering citizenship', paper presented at Crossing Borders Conference, University of Stockholm, May.

Littler, C.R. (1982), *The Development of the Labour Process in Capitalist Societies*, London: Heinemann.

Liu, K.M. (2003), *Migrant Labour in South China*, Beijing: Xinhua Publishing House.

Locke, John (1690), 'Second treatise of civil government: Chapter 5 – Of Property', available at: http://www.constitution.org/jl/2ndtr05.htm (accessed 20 October 2008).

Lyon-Caen, Antoine (2002), 'The legal efficacy and significance of fundamental social rights: Lessons from the European experience', in Bob Hepple (ed.), *Social and Labour Rights in a Global Context*, Cambridge: Cambridge University Press, pp. 182–91.

MacPherson, Elizabeth (1999), 'Collective bargaining for independent contractors: Is the Status of the Artist Act a model for other industrial sectors?', *Canadian Journal of Labour and Employment Law*, 7(3), 355–89.

Madison, James (1787), 'The Federalist No.10: The utility of the Union as a safeguard against domestic faction and insurrection', available at: http://www.constitution.org/fed/federa10.htm (accessed 20 October 2008).

Maher, Kris (2008), 'More in US are working part-time out of necessity', *Wall Street Journal*, 10 March.

Maher, R. (2000), 'The new economy work cycle', *Wall Street Journal*, 21 September.

Makimoto, Tsugio and David Manners (1997), *Digital Nomad*, Chichester: Wiley.

Maks, J.A.H. and N.J. Philipsen (2005), 'An economic analysis of the regulation of professions', in E. Crals and L. Vereeck (eds), *Regulation of Architects in Belgium and the Netherlands*, Leuven: Lannoo Campus, pp. 11–45.

Malone, Thomas (2004), *The Future of Work: How the New Order will Shape Your Organization, Your Management Style and Your Life*, Cambridge, MA: Harvard Business School Press.

Malone, Thomas and Robert Laubacher (1998), 'The dawn of the e-lance economy', *Harvard Business Review*, 76(5), 144–52.

Mandy, A. and P. Tinley (2004), 'Burnout and occupational stress: Comparison between UK and Australian podiatrists', *Journal of the American Podiatric Medical Association*, 94(3), 282–91.

Maremont, Mark (2008), 'Companies promise CEOs lavish posthumous paydays', *Wall Street Journal*, 11 June.

Marlowe, Christopher ([1604] 2001), 'Doctor Faustus', in Sylvan Barnet (ed.), *Doctor Faustus*, New York: Signet Classics.

Marmot, M.G. et al. (1991), 'Health inequalities among British civil servants: The Whitehall II study', *The Lancet*, 337(8754), 1387–93.

Marshall, T.H. (1950), *Citizenship and Social Class and Other Essays*, Cambridge: Cambridge University Press.

Marx, Karl ([1844] 1967), 'On the Jewish Question', *Writings of the Young Marx on Philosophy and Society*, New York: Doubleday Anchor, pp. 216–64.

Marx, Karl ([1844], 1976) *The Economic and Philosophic Manuscripts of 1844*, in *Marx-Engels Collected Works, Vol.3*, New York: International Publishers.

Marx, Karl ([1863] 1969), *Theories of Surplus Value, Part 1*, London: Lawrence & Wishart.

Marx, Karl ([1867] 1967), *Capital: Vol.1: A Critical Analysis of Capitalist Production*, New York: International Publishers.

Massachusetts General Hospital (2007), 'Nearly one-half of the nation's doctors fail to report incompetence or medical errors, journal study reports', press release, Boston, MA: Massachusetts General Hospital, 3 December.

Maxey, M. ([1938] 1975), *Occupations of the Lower Classes in Roman Society*, Chicago: University of Chicago Press.

Mayerhofer, H., L.C. Hartmann, G. Michelitsch-Riedl and I. Kollinger (2004), 'Flexpatriate assignments: A neglected issue in global staffing', *International Journal of Human Resource Management*, 15(8), 1371–89.

Mazumdar, Dipak and S. Sarkar (2006), 'Growth of employment and earnings in the tertiary sector 1983–2000', in Institute for Human Development, *India:*

Meeting the Employment Challenge, Conference on Labour and Employment Issues in India, July 27–29, 2006, New Delhi: Printech, pp. 294–305.

McCallum, R. (2007), 'Australian labour law after the Work Choices avalanche: Developing an employment law for our children', *Journal of Industrial Relations*, **49**(3), 436–54.

McClelland, C.E. (1990), 'Escape from freedom? Reflections on German professionalization 1870–1933', in R. Torstendahl and M. Burrage (eds), *The Formation of Professions: Knowledge, State and Strategy*, London: Sage, pp. 97–113.

McCracken, Jeffrey and John Stoll (2008), 'Bankruptcy fears rise as GM and Chrysler seek US aid', *Wall Street Journal*, 28 October, p. 14.

McDonald, C. and G. Marston (2005), 'Workfare as welfare: Governing unemployment in the advanced liberal state', *Critical Social Theory*, **25**(3), 374–401.

McKinlay, J. (1982), 'Toward the proletarianization of physicians', in C. Derber (ed.), *Professionals as Workers: Mental Labor in Advanced Capitalism*, Boston, MA: G.K. Hall, pp. 37–62.

McKinlay, J. and J. Stoekle (1988), 'Corporatization and the social transformation of doctoring', *International Journal of Health Services*, **18**(2), 191–205.

McKinsey Global Institute (2005), 'The emerging global labor market', June, available at: http://www.mckinsey.com/mgi/publications/emerginggloballabormarket/index.asp (accessed 5 July 2008).

McNeil, Donald (2008), 'Gates Foundation's influence criticized', *New York Times*, 16 February.

McWilliam, G. (2000), 'Building stronger brands through online communities', *Sloan Management Review*, **41**(3), 43–54.

McWilliams, Gary (2007), 'Fired ad executive blasts Walmart', *Wall Street Journal*, 29 March.

Meireis, T. (2004), 'Calling: A Christian argument for a basic income', in G. Standing (ed.), *Promoting Income Security as a Right*, London: Anthem Press, pp. 147–64.

Mill, John Stuart ([1861] 1972), 'Considerations on representative government', in J.S. Mill, *Utilitarianism, On Liberty and Considerations On Representative Government*, Cambridge: Cambridge University Press.

Mill, John Stuart (1867), *Inaugural Address Delivered to the University of St Andrews, Feb. 1st 1867*, London: Longmans, Green, Reader, and Dyer, available at: http://www.archive.org/stream/inauguraladdress00milliala/inauguraladdress00milliala_djvu.txt (accessed 16 March 2009).

Mommsen, W.J. (1987), 'The academic profession in the Federal Republic of Germany', in B. Clark (ed.), *The Academic Profession*, Berkeley: University of California Press, pp. 60–92.

Monbiot, George (2006), 'Willy Loman syndrome', *The Guardian*, 27 June.

Moore, A.P. and A.A. Tarr (1989), 'General principles and issues of occupational regulation', *Bond Law Review*, **1**(1), 119–34.

Morris, J. (1993), *Independent Lives? Community Care and Disabled People*, Basingstoke: Macmillan.

Morris, N. and B. Russell (2008), 'More than 1,000 children jailed for breaching Asbos', *The Independent*, 25 August.

Moullin, Sophie (2008), *Just Care? A Fresh Approach to Adult Services*, London: Institute for Public Policy Research, available at: http://www.ippr.org/publicationsandreports/publication.asp?id=605 (accessed 20 October 2008).

Moynagh, M. and R. Worsley (2005), *Working in the Twenty-First Century*, London: Economic and Social Research Council and The Tomorrow Project.

Muzondo, T.R. and B. Pazderka (1980), 'Occupational licensing and professional incomes in Canada', *Canadian Journal of Economics*, **XIII**(4), 659–67.

Naim, M. (2005), *Illicit: How Smugglers, Traffickers and Copycats are Hijacking the Global Economy*, New York: Doubleday.

National Science Foundation (2006), *US Doctorates in the 20th Century*, Arlington, Virginia: National Science Foundation.

Neary, Michael (2002), 'Labour moves: A critique of the concept of social movement unionism', in Ana Dinerstein and Michael Neary (eds), *The Labour Debate: An Investigation into the Theory and Reality of Capitalist Work*, Aldershot: Ashgate, pp. 149–78.

Neily, C. (2005), 'Six feet under: It's time to kill the special-interest funeral industry', *National Review Online*, 19 January, available at: http://www.nationalreview.com/comment/neily200501190848.asp (accessed 5 July 2008).

Nelson, P. (1974), 'Advertising as information', *Journal of Political Economy*, **82**(4), 729–54.

Nelson, R. and S. Winter (1982), *An Evolutionary Theory of Economic Change*, Cambridge, MA: Harvard University Press.

Nguyen, A.N., J. Taylor and S. Bradley (2003), 'Job autonomy and job satisfaction: New evidence', Department of Economics Working Paper No. 2003/050, Lancaster: Lancaster University Management School.

Noether, M. (1986), 'The effect of government policy changes on the supply of physicians: Expansion of a competitive fringe', *Journal of Law and Economics*, **29**(2), 231–62.

OECD (2006), *The Share of Employment Potentially Affected by Offshoring – An Empirical Investigation*, Working Party Report on the Information Economy (DSTI/ICCP/IE(2005)8/FINAL), Paris: Organisation for Economic Co-operation and Development, available at: http://www.oecd.org/dataoecd/37/26/36187829.pdf (accessed 5 July 2008).

OECD (2007a), *Pensions at a Glance: Public Policies across OECD Countries*, Paris: Organisation for Economic Co-operation and Development.

OECD (2007b), *Employment Outlook 2007*, Paris: Organisation for Economic Co-operation and Development.

Offe, Claus (1985), *Disorganized Capitalism: Contemporary Transformations of Work and Politics*, Cambridge: Polity Press.

Office of Fair Trading (2001), *Competition in Professions*, London: Office of Fair Trading, available at: http://www.oft.gov.uk / advice _ and _ resources / publications / reports / professional_bodies/oft328 (accessed 5 July 2008).

Office of the Legislative Auditor, State of Minnesota (1999), *Occupational Regulation*, St Paul, MN: Office of the Legislative Auditor.

Olin-Wright, Eric (1978), *Class, Crisis and the State*, London: New Left Books.

Olofsson, Gunnar (1995), 'Embeddedness and integration: An essay on Karl Polanyi's "The Great Transformation"', in Nils Mortensen (ed.), *Social Integration and Marginalization*, Frederiksberg: Samfundslitteratur, pp. 72–113.

Olson, M. (1965), *The Logic of Collective Action: Public Groups and the Theory of Groups*, Cambridge, MA: Harvard University Press.

Olson, M. (1982), *The Rise and Decline of Nations: Economic Growth, Stagflation and Social Rigidities*, New Haven: Yale University Press.

O'Neill, Jim (2008), 'Boom time for the

global bourgeoisie', *Financial Times*, 16 July.

Orwell, George ([1937] 1962), *The Road to Wigan Pier*, Harmondsworth, Middlesex: Penguin.

Osborne, Roger (2007), *Civilization: A New History of the Western World*, London: Pimlico.

Paine, Tom ([1776] 2005), 'Common sense', in *Common Sense and Other Writings*, New York: Barnes & Noble, pp. 11–69.

Paine, Tom ([1795] 2005), 'Agrarian justice', in *Common Sense and Other Writings*, New York: Barnes & Noble, pp. 321–45.

Palmer, Maija (2007), 'Google advances on Europe', *Financial Times*, 27 September.

Parker, D., B. Cornley and V. Beri (1997), 'The reform of occupational regulation in Australia', paper presented at an APEC Workshop on Competition Policy and Deregulation, Quebec, Canada, May.

Parsons, Talcott (1951), *The Social System*, New York: Free Press.

Pashigian, B.P. (1980), 'Has occupational licensing reduced geographical mobility and raised earnings?', in S. Rottenberg (ed.), *Occupational Licensure and Regulation*, Washington, DC: American Enterprise Institute, pp. 299–333.

Patel, K. and F. Vella (2007), 'Immigrant networks and their implications for occupational choice and wages', mimeographed job market paper, Washington, DC: Georgetown University.

Pateman, Carole (2008), 'Democracy, human rights and a basic income in a global era', paper presented to 12th Congress of the Basic Income Earth Network (BIEN), Dublin, 20–21 June, available at: http://www.cori.ie/Justice/Basic_Income/62-Basic_Income/541-bien-world-congress-on-basic-income (accessed 20 October 2008).

Peel, M. (2007), 'Indian and UK lawyers reach pioneering deal', *Financial Times*, 15 January.

Peel, Q. (2008), 'Nordic states stay hot on globalization', *Financial Times*, 11 April.

Pelczynski, Z. (1984), 'Freedom in Hegel', in Z. Pelczynski and J. Gray (eds), *Conceptions of Liberty in Political Philosophy*, London: Athlone Press, pp. 150–81.

Pelczynski, Z. and J. Gray (eds) (1984), *Conceptions of Liberty in Political Philosophy*, London: Athlone Press.

Peltonen, Tuomo (2006), 'Frequent flyer: Speed and mobility as effects of organizing', in P. Case, S. Lilley and T. Owens (eds), *The Speed of Organization*, Copenhagen: Liber Press, pp. 70–87.

Peltonen, Tuomo (2007), 'In the middle of managers: Occupational communities, global ethnography and the multinationals', *Ethnography*, **8**(3), 346–60.

Perkin, Harold (1989), *The Rise of Professional Society: England Since 1880*, London and New York: Routledge.

Perot, Ross (1992), 'Debating our destiny: The third 1992 presidential debate', *Newshour*, US Public Broadcasting Service, 19 October, available at: http://www.pbs.org/newshour/debatingourdestiny/92debates/3prez2.html (accessed 12 March 2009).

Perucci, R. and J.E. Gerstl (1969), *Profession without Community: Engineers in American Society*, New York: Random House.

Pfeffer, J. (1974), 'Administrative regulation and licensing: Social problem or solution?', *Social Problems*, **21**(4), 468–79.

Pimlott, Ben (2008), 'Tax cuts and world trade widen US gap between rich and poor', *Financial Times*, 9 April, p. 9.

Pinker, S. (2008), *The Sexual Paradox: Men, Women and the Real Gender Gap*, London: Scribner.

Piore, Michael and Sean Safford (2006), 'Changing regimes of workplace governance, shifting axes of social mobilization, and the challenge to industrial relations theory', *Industrial Relations*, **45**(3), 299–325.

Piore, Michael and Andrew Schrank (2006), 'Trading up: An embryonic model for easing the human costs of free markets', *Boston Review*, **31**(5), 1–22.

Pistor, K. (2005), 'Legal ground rules in coordinated and liberal market economies', ECGI Working Paper Series in Law No. 30, Brussels: European Corporate Governance Institute.

Polanyi, Karl ([1944] 2001), *The Great Transformation: The Political and Economic Origins of Our Time*, Boston, MA: Beacon Press.

Polanyi, Karl (1945), 'Universal capitalism or regional planning?', *London Quarterly of World Affairs*, **10**(3), 86–91.

Polanyi, Karl (1957), 'The economy as instituted process', in M. Granovetter and R. Swedberg (eds) (1992), *The Sociology of Economic Life*, Boulder: Westview, pp. 29–52.

Porac, J.F., H. Thomas and C. Baden-Fuller (1989), 'Competitive groups as cognitive communities: The case of the Scottish knitwear manufacturers', *Journal of Management Studies*, **26**(4), 397–416.

Posner, R. (1978), 'The right of privacy', *Georgia Law Review*, **12**, 393–422.

Prasad, Raeka (2007), 'India's shrinking families', *The Guardian*, 14 April.

Preece, J. (2000), *Online Communities: Designing Usability, Supporting Sociability*, New York: Wiley.

Preston, J. (2006), 'Rules collide with reality in the immigration debate', *New York Times*, 29 May.

Pugh, D.S. and D.J. Hickson (1993), 'Elliott Jaques and the glacier investigations', in D.S. Pugh and D.J. Hickson, *Great Writers on Organizations*, Aldershot, UK, and Brookfield, VT: Dartmouth, pp. 25–30.

Quine, S. (1986), 'Comparisons of Australian occupational prestige scales 1', *Journal of Sociology*, **22**(3), 399–410.

Rajan, Raghuram (2006), 'Foreword' to IMF, *World Economic Outlook: Globalization and Inflation*, Washington, DC: International Monetary Fund, pp. xi–xiii.

Ratha, D. and W. Shaw (2005), 'South–South remittances and migration', World Bank Working Paper No.102, Washington, DC: World Bank.

Rawls, John (1973), *A Theory of Justice*, Cambridge: Cambridge University Press.

Reich, Robert (2007), *Supercapitalism: The Transformation of Business, Democracy and Everyday Life*, New York: Knopf.

Revill, J. (2007), 'Blair's adviser on the NHS. . .', *The Observer*, 11 November, p. 23.

Rifkin, Jeremy (1995), *The End of Work: The Decline of the Global Labor Force and the Dawn of the Post-Market Era*, New York: Putnam.

Rikowski, G. (2001), *The Battle in Seattle: Its Significance for Education*, London: Tufnell Press.

Roberts, Dan (2004), 'Services on the assembly line: New technology brings the methods of Henry Ford to offices around the globe', *Financial Times*, 15 April, p. 11.

Roberts, J. (1984), 'T.H. Green', in Z. Pelczynski and J. Gray (eds), *Conceptions of Liberty in Political Philosophy*, London: Athlone Press, pp. 243–62.

Robinson, Tony (2004), *The Worst Jobs in History: Two Thousand Years of Miserable Employment*, London: Pan Books.

Roethke, Theodore (1966), *Collected Poems of Theodore Roethke*, New York: Doubleday.

Rose, N. (1999), *Powers of Freedom: Reframing Political Thought*, Cambridge: Cambridge University Press.

Rosskam, Ellen (ed.) (2006), *Winners or Losers? Liberalizing Public Services*, Geneva: International Labour Organization.

Rothblat, S. (1968), *The Revolution of the Dons*, New York: Basic Books.

Rothkopf, David (2008a), *Superclass: The Global Power Elite and the World They are Making*, New York: Farrar, Straus and Giroux.

Rothkopf, David (2008b), 'Change is in the air for the financial superclass', *Financial Times*, 16 May.

Rothman, R.A. (1984), 'Deprofessionalization: The case of law in America', *Work and Occupations*, **11**(2), 183–206.

Rottenberg, S. (1980), 'Introduction', in S. Rottenberg, *Occupational Licensure and Regulation*, Washington, DC: American Enterprise Institute, pp. 1–13.

Ruskin, John (1853), *The Stones of Venice, Vol. 2: The Sea-Stories*, London: Smith, Elder & Co. Digitized by Google, August 2007.

Saks, M. (1995), *Professions and the Public Interest: Medical Power, Altruism and Alternative Medicine*, London: Routledge.

Sandiford, P. and D. Seymour (2007), 'The concept of occupational community revisited: Analytical and managerial implications in face-to-face service occupations', *Work, Employment and Society*, **21**(2), 209–26.

Sandman, P. (1997), *Responding to Community Outrage: Strategies for Effective Risk Communication*, Virginia: American Industrial Hygiene Association.

Sapelli, Giulio (1981), 'Gli "organizzatori della produzione": Tra struttura d'impresa e modelli culturali', *Storia d'Italia 4 'Intellectuale e potere'*, pp. 590–696.

Sayers, R.S. (1965), *The Vicissitudes of an Export Economy: Britain since 1880*, Sydney: University of Sydney Press.

Scase, Richard (2000), *Britain in 2010:*

The New Business Landscape, Oxford: Capstone.

Scase, Richard (2001), 'Why we're so clockwise', *The Observer*, 26 August.

Schein, E.H. (1996), 'Three cultures of management: The key to organizational learning', *Sloan Management Review*, **38**(1), 9–20.

Schmidt, Vivien (2000), 'Values and discourse in the politics of adjustment', in F.W. Scharpf and V.A. Schmidt (eds), *Welfare and Work in the Open Economy, Vol.1: From Vulnerability to Competitiveness*, Oxford: Oxford University Press, pp. 229–310.

Schon, D.A. (1983), *The Reflective Practitioner: How Professionals Think in Action*, New York: Basic Books.

Schwarzenbach, Sibyl (1996), 'On civic friendship', *Ethics*, **107**(1), 97–128.

Schwarzenbach, Sibyl (2004), 'The limits of production: Justifying guaranteed basic income', in Guy Standing (ed.), *Promoting Income Security as a Right*, London: Anthem Press, pp. 107–14.

Scott, C. (2002), 'Private regulation of the public sector: A neglected facet of contemporary governance', *Journal of Law and Society*, **29**(1), 56–76.

Sen, Amartya (1999), *Development as Freedom*, Oxford: Oxford University Press.

Sen, Amartya (2006), *Identity and Violence: The Illusion of Destiny*, London: Allen Lane.

Sennett, Richard (1998), *The Corrosion of Character: The Personal Consequences of Work in the New Capitalism*, New York: Norton.

Sennett, Richard (2008), *The Craftsman*, London: Allen Lane.

Sewell, Graham and Barry Wilkinson (1992), 'Someone to watch over me: Surveillance, discipline and the just-in-time labour process', *Sociology*, **26**(2), 271–89.

Shaked, A. and J. Sutton (1981), 'The self-regulating profession', *Review of Economic Studies,* **48**(2), 217–34.

Shapiro, C. (1986), 'Investment, moral hazard and occupational licensing', *Review of Economic Studies*, **53**(5), 843–62.

Shapiro, I. (1999), *Democratic Justice*, New Haven: Yale University Press.

Shellenbarger, S. (2007), 'Inspiring them to soar', *Wall Street Journal*, 1 October.

Shepard, L. (1978), 'Licensing restrictions and the cost of dental care', *Journal of Law and Economics*, **21**(1), 187–201.

Shepherd, G.B. (2000), 'Cartels and controls in legal training', *Antitrust Bulletin*, **45**(2), 437–66.

Shue, H. (1996), *Basic Rights: Subsistence, Affluence and US Foreign Policy*, Princeton, NJ: Princeton University Press.

Simitis, S. (1987a), 'Reviewing privacy in an information society', *University of Penn–sylvania Law Review*, **135**(3), 707–46.

Simitis, S. (1987b), 'Juridification of labour relations', in G. Teubner (ed.), *Juridification of Social Spheres*, Berlin: Walter de Gruyter, pp. 113–62.

Simpson, R.L. (1985), 'Social control of occupations and work', *Annual Review of Sociology*, **11** (1985), 415–36.

Singh, Ajit (1977), 'UK industry and the world economy: A case of de-industrialisation', *Cambridge Journal of Economics*, **1**(2), 113–36.

Singh, S. and E. Ernst (2008), *Trick or Treatment? Alternative Medicine on Trial*, London: Bantam Press.

Skapinker, Michael (2007), 'How to run a school–business partnership', *Financial Times*, 4 December.

Smith, A.D. (1999), 'Problems of conflict management in virtual communities', in M.A. Smith and P. Kollock (eds), *Communities in Cyberspace*, New York: Routledge, pp. 134–63.

Smith, Adam ([1776] 1979), *The Wealth of Nations*, Harmondsworth: Penguin.

Smith, M. and P. Ewer (1999), *Choice and Coercion: Women's Experiences of Casual Work*, Sydney: Evatt Foundation.

Sol, E. and M. Westerveld (eds) (2005), *Contractualism in Employment Services: A New Form of Welfare State Governance*, The Hague: Kluwer Law International.

Spangler, E. (1986), *Lawyers for Hire*, New Haven: Yale University Press.

Spidla, Vladimir (2005), 'To reform the "social" model does not mean to abandon it', *Financial Times*, 7 October.

Standing, Guy (1999), *Global Labour Flexibility: Seeking Distributive Justice*, Basingstoke: Macmillan.

Standing, Guy (2000), 'Modes of control: a labour-status approach to decent work', Socio-Economic Security Paper No.4, Geneva: International Labour Organization.

Standing, Guy (2002), *Beyond the New Paternalism: Basic Security as Equality*, London: Verso.

Standing, Guy (ed.) (2003), *Minimum Income Schemes in Europe*, Geneva: International Labour Organization.

Standing, Guy (2004), 'Globalization: Eight crises of social protection', in L. Beneria and S. Bisnath (eds), *Global Tensions: Challenges and Opportunities in the World Economy*, New York: Routledge, pp. 111–33.

Standing, Guy (ed.) (2005), *Promoting Income Security as a Right*, London: Anthem Press.

Standing, Guy (2007a), 'Building a progressive flexibility in South Africa: Labour and social policy for the 21st century', Pretoria: Department of Labour, mimeo.

Standing, Guy (2007b), 'Decent workplaces, self-regulation and CSR: From puff to stuff?', DESA Working Paper No. 62, New York: United Nations

Department of Economic and Social Affairs.

Standing, Guy (2008), 'The ILO: An agency for globalization?', *Development and Change*, **39**(3), 355–84.

Steiger, T.L. and W. Form (1991), 'The labor process in construction: Control without bureaucratic and technological means?', *Work and Occupations*, **18**(3), 251–70.

Stephens, J.D. (1979), *The Transition from Capitalism to Socialism*, London: Macmillan.

Stone, Katherine (1981), 'The post-war paradigm in American labor law', *Yale Law Journal*, **90**(7), 1509–80.

Stone, Katherine (1996), 'Mandatory arbitration of individual employment rights: The Yellow Dog Contract of the 1990s', *Denver University Law Review*, **73**(4), 1017–49.

Summers, A.B. (2007), *Occupational Licensing: Ranking the States and Exploring Alternatives*, Los Angeles: Reason Foundation.

Sunder, Shyam (2005), 'Political economy of the accounting collapse in US', mimeo, New Haven: Yale University, available at: http://www.wiwi.uni-muen ster.de/26/downloads//icg/ws0708/Liter ature/ICG06c-Lit.pdf (accessed 17 October 2008).

Sweeney, John (2006), 'Why workers count', *OECD Observer*, No. 255, pp. 20–21.

Szreter, S.R.S. (1993), 'The official representation of social classes in Britain, the United States and France: The professional model and "les cadres"', *Comparative Studies in Society and History*, **35**(2), 285–317.

Szulanski, G. (1996), 'Exploring internal stickiness: Impediments in the transfer of best practices within the firm', *Strategic Management Journal*, **17**, Special Issue: Knowledge and the Firm, 27–43.

Tawney, R.H. (1921), *The Acquisitive Society*, London: Bell and Sons.

Tawney, R.H. (1926), *Religion and the Rise of Capitalism*, London: John Murray.

Taylor, C. (1984), 'Kant's theory of freedom', in Z. Pelczynski and J. Gray (eds), *Conceptions of Liberty in Political Philosophy*, London: Athlone Press.

Taylor, Paul (1999), 'The United Nations in the 1990s: Proactive cosmopolitanism and the issue of sovereignty', *Political Studies*, **47**(3), 538–65.

Teather, David and Jill Treanor (2007), 'Corporate buccaneers caught in a political storm', *The Guardian*, 24 February, p. 10.

Thaler, R. and C. Sunstein (2008), *Nudge: Improving Decisions About Health, Wealth and Happiness*, New Haven: Yale University Press.

Therborn, Göran (2004), *Sex and Power: Family in the World 1900–2000*, London: Verso.

Thomas, Albert (1931), 'Preface' to ILO, *The International Labour Organization: The First Decade*, London: George Allen & Unwin for the ILO, pp. 5–12.

Thomas, D. (2008), 'World's rich shrug off credit crunch and swell to 8m', *Financial Times*, 21 April.

Thompson, E.P. (1967), 'Time, work-discipline and industrial capitalism', *Past and Present*, **38**(1), 58–97.

Thompson, E.P. (1968), *The Making of the English Working Class*, Harmondsworth: Penguin.

Thoreau, H.D. ([1851] 1962), 'Thoughts, July 19, 1851', cited in E.W. Theale (ed.), *The Thoughts of Thoreau*, New York: Dodd Mead.

Thornhill, John (2005), 'France fails to "reap benefits" of offshoring', *Financial Times*, 24 July.

Thornhill, John (2008), 'Income inequality seen as the great divide', *Financial Times*, 19 May, p. 3.

Thornhill, John, Richard Milne and

Michael Steen (2008), 'Accent on *égalité*', *Financial Times*, 9 June.

Titmuss, Richard ([1970] 1997), *The Gift Relationship: From Human Blood to Social Policy*, London: New Press.

Tough, P. (2002), 'Dad's performance review', *New York Times Magazine*, 15 December, p. 65.

Travis, Alan (2006), 'Competitive instinct', *The Guardian*, 8 November, p. 3.

Treggiari, S.M. (1980), 'Urban labour in Rome: *Mercenarii* and *Tabernarii*', in P. Garnsey (ed.), *Non-Slave Labour in the Greco-Roman World*, Cambridge: Cambridge Philological Society, pp. 48–64.

Trice, H.M. (1993), *Occupational Subcultures in the Workplace*, Ithaca, NY: ILR Press.

Tugend, Alina (2008), 'As vacations shrink, health risk may rise', *International Herald Tribune*, 10 June, pp. 4,12.

Turner, D. (2008a), 'Parents place premium on English lessons', *Financial Times*, 27 February.

Turner, D. (2008b), 'New Zealand's state system reaps rewards', *Financial Times*, 27 February.

Uchitelle, Louis (2006), *The Disposable American: Layoffs and their Consequences* New York: Alfred Knopf.

Uchitelle, Louis (2007), 'A return to the Gilded Age for US executives', *International Herald Tribune*, 16 July, p. 2.

Uglow, Jenny (2002), *The Lunar Men: The Friends who made the Future*, London: Faber & Faber.

Ullman, W. (1966), *Individual and Society in the Middle Ages*, Baltimore: Johns Hopkins University Press.

UNCTAD (2005), *Trade and Development Aspects of Professional Services and Regulatory Frameworks*, TD/B/COM.1/EM.25/2, Geneva: United Nations Conference on Trade and Development.

UNCTAD (2008), *World Investment Report 2008: Transnational Corporations and the Infrastructure Challenge*, New York and Geneva: United Nations Conference on Trade and Development.

UN Population Division (2006), *International Migration and Development: Report of the Secretary-General to the 60th session of the UN General Assembly*, A/60/871, New York: United Nations.

Van Maanen, J. and S. Barley (1984), 'Occupational communities: Culture and control in organizations', in B.M. Staw and L.L. Cummings (eds), *Research in Organizational Behavior, Vol.6*, Greenwich, CT: JAI Press, pp. 287–365.

Van Parijs, Philippe (1995), *Real Freedom for All: What (if Anything) Can Justify Capitalism*, Oxford: Clarendon Press.

Van Welsum, Desirée and Graham Vickery (2005), 'Potential offshoring of ICT-intensive using occupations', Directorate for Science, Technology and Industry Information Economy Working Paper DSTI/ICCP/IE(2004)19/FINAL, Paris: Organisation for Economic Co-operation and Development.

Vara, V. (2008), 'Divine intervention? Indians seek the blessings of the "Visa God"', *Wall Street Journal*, 4 January.

Veblen, Thorstein ([1899] 1967), *The Theory of the Leisure Class*, New York: Viking.

Vosko, Leah (2005), 'The precarious status of the artist: Freelance editors' struggle for collective bargaining rights', in C. Cranford, J. Fudge, E.C. Tucker and L. Vosko (eds), *Self-Employed Workers Organize: Law, Policy and Unions*, Montreal and Kingston: McGill-Queen's University Press, pp. 136–70.

Wachtel, P. (2003), 'Full pockets, empty lives: A psychoanalytic explanation of the contemporary culture of greed', *American Journal of Psychoanalysis*, **63**(2), 103–22.

Waldmeir, Patti (2007), 'The high cost of

working on holiday', *Financial Times*, 11 September.

Walsh, M.R. (1977), *Doctors Wanted: No Women Need Apply*, New Haven: Yale University Press.

Weber, Max ([1922] 1978), *Economy and Society: An Outline of Interpretive Sociology*, Berkeley and Los Angeles: University of California Press.

Wedderburn, K.W. (1965), *The Worker and the Law*, Harmondsworth: Macmillan.

Wedderburn, K.W. (2002), 'Common law, labour law, global law', in Bob Hepple (ed.), *Social and Labour Rights in a Global Context*, Cambridge: Cambridge University Press, pp. 19–54.

Wcise, K. (2007), 'Corporate tax warning', *OECD Observer*, No. 261, May, p. 23.

Wenger, E. (1998), *Communities of Practice: Learning, Meaning and Identity*, Cambridge: Cambridge University Press.

Wenger, E., R. McDermott and W.M. Snyder (2002), *Cultivating Communities of Practice*, Boston, MA: Harvard University Press.

Whalley, P. (1985), *The Social Production of Technical Work*, New York: Macmillan.

Whatman, R., O. Harvey and R. Hill (1999), 'The effects of employment regulation: Case study research in the accommodation, winemaking and brewing industries', Occasional Paper, Wellington, New Zealand: Department of Labour.

White, W.D. (1983), 'Labor market organization and professional regulation: A historical analysis of nursing licensure', *Law and Human Behavior*, 7(2/3), 157–70.

Wighton, David (2006), 'Movement of tasks overseas jumps up skills chain relentlessly', *Financial Times Report: The World 2006*, 25 January, p. 4.

Wilcock, Ann (2000), 'Development of a personal, professional and educational occupational philosophy: An Australian perspective', *Occupational · Therapy International*, 7(2), 79–86.

Wilensky, Harold (1964), 'The professionalization of everyone?', *American Journal of Sociology*, 70(2), 137–58.

Wilkinson, Richard (2005), *The Impact of Inequality: How to Make Sick Societies Healthier*, London: Routledge.

Williams, Raymond (1961), *Culture and Society*, Harmondsworth: Macmillan.

Wilson, E.O (1975), *Sociobiology: The New Synthesis*, Cambridge, MA: Belknap, Harvard University Press.

Winroth, K. (2003), *Professionals in Investment Banks: Sharing an Epistemic Practice or an Occupational Community*, GRI report 2003:1, Göteborg: School of Economics and Commercial Law, Gothenburg Research Institute.

Wolf, Martin (2007a), 'The new capitalism', *Financial Times*, 19 June, p. 9.

Wolf, Martin (2007b), 'Why immigration is hard to tackle', *Financial Times*, 2 November.

Wolff, Jonathan (2008), 'What's wrong with wanting to know your students' names?', *The Guardian, Higher Education Guardian*, 3 June, p. 10.

Wright Mills, C. (1956), *White Collar: The American Middle Classes*, New York: Oxford University Press.

WTO (2005), *World Trade Report 2005: Exploring the Linkages Between Trade, Standards and the WTO*, Geneva: World Trade Organization.

WTO (2008), *World Trade Report 2008: Trade in a Globalizing World*, Geneva: World Trade Organization.

Young, S.D. (1993), 'Occupational licensing', in *The Concise Encyclopedia of Economics*, Washington, DC: Library of Economics and Liberty, available at: http://www.econlib.org/library/Enc1/Occu pationalLicensing.html (accessed 5 July 2008).

Index